First Canadian Edition

Electrical Wiring Industrial

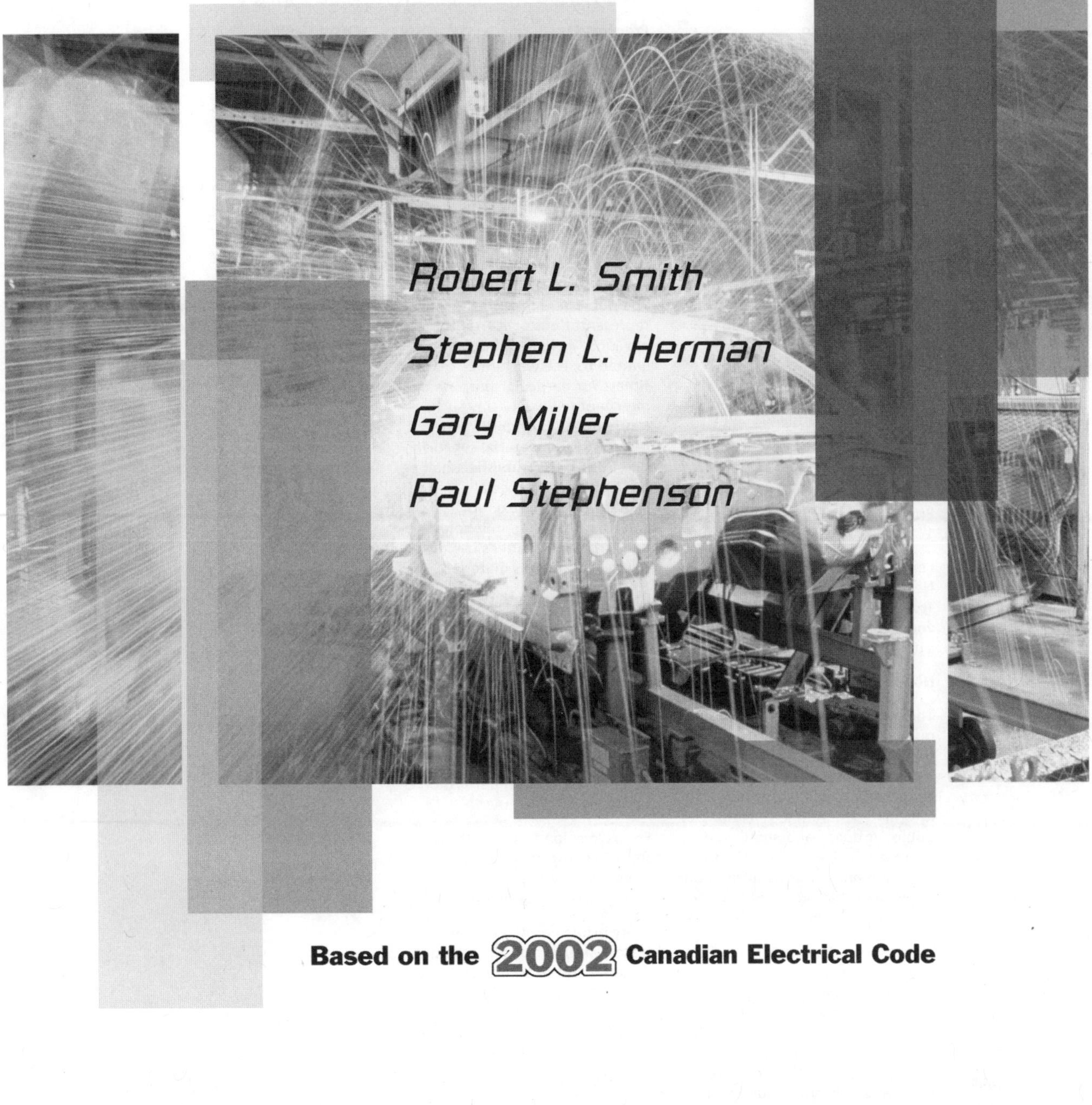

Robert L. Smith

Stephen L. Herman

Gary Miller

Paul Stephenson

Based on the 2002 Canadian Electrical Code

THOMSON NELSON

Australia Canada Mexico Singapore Spain United Kingdom United States

THOMSON
NELSON

Electrical Wiring: Industrial
First Canadian Edition

Robert L. Smith, Stephen L. Herman,
Gary Miller, and Paul Stephenson

Editorial Director and Publisher:
Evelyn Veitch

Acquisitions Editor:
Anthony Rezek

Executive Marketing Manager:
Kevin Smulan

Senior Developmental Editor:
Elke Price

Production Editor:
Tammy Scherer

Copy Editor:
Laurel Sparrow

Proofreader:
Dawn Hunter

Indexer:
Jim Leahy

Production Manager:
Renate McCloy

Creative Director:
Angela Cluer

Interior Design Modifications:
Erich Falkenberg

Cover Design:
Erich Falkenberg

Cover Image:
Paul A. Souders/Corbis/Magma

Compositor:
Janet Zanette

Printer:
Webcom

Adapted from *Electrical Wiring: Industrial,* Eleventh Edition, by Robert L. Smith and Stephen L. Herman, published by Delmar Learning. Copyright 2002 by Delmar.

Printed and bound in Canada
1 2 3 4 07 06 05 04

For more information contact Nelson, 1120 Birchmount Road, Toronto, Ontario, M1K 5G4. Or you can visit our Internet site at http://www.nelson.com

Notice to the Reader

The publisher does not warrant or guarantee any of the products described herein, or perform any independent analysis in connection with any product information contained herein. The publisher does not assume, and expressly disclaims, any obligation to obtain and include information other than that provided to it by the manufacturer.

The reader is expressly warned to consider and adopt all safety precautions that might be indicated by the activities described herein and to avoid all potential hazards. By following the instructions contained herein, the reader willingly assumes all risks in connection with such instructions.

The publisher makes no representations or warranties of any kind, including, but not limited to, the warranties of fitness for particular purpose or merchantability, nor any such representations implied with respect to the material set forth herein, and the publisher shall not be liable for any special, consequential, or exemplary damages resulting, in whole or in part, from the reader's use of, or reliance upon, this material.

National Library of Canada Cataloguing in Publication

Electrical wiring : industrial / Robert L. Smith ... [et al.]. — 1st Canadian ed.

Includes index.

ISBN 0-17-641597-1

1. Factories—Electric equipment—Installation. 2. Electric wiring, Interior. I. Smith, Robert L., 1926-

TK3283.E24 2004 621.319'24
C2004-901154-5

CONTENTS

PREFACE

The First Canadian edition of *Electrical Wiring—Industrial* is based on the 2002 *Canadian Electrical Code* (*CEC*). The *CEC* is used as the standard for the layout and construction of electrical systems. To gain the greatest benefit from this text, the learner must use the *Canadian Electrical Code* on a continual basis. In addition to the *CEC,* the instructor should provide the learner with applicable provincial and local wiring regulations, as they may affect the industrial installation.

In addition to the accurate interpretation of the requirements of the *CEC*, the successful completion of any wiring installation requires the electrician to have a thorough understanding of basic electrical principles, a knowledge of the tools and materials used in installations, familiarity with commonly installed equipment and its specific wiring requirements, the ability to interpret electrical construction drawings, and a constant awareness of safe wiring practices.

Electrical Wiring—Industrial builds on the knowledge and experience gained from working with the other texts in the Nelson electrical wiring series and related titles. The basic skills developed in previous applications are now directed to industrial installations. The industrial electrician is responsible for the installation of electrical service, power, lighting, and special systems in new construction; for the changeover from old to new systems in established industrial buildings; for the provision of additional electrical capacity to meet the growth requirements of an industrial building; and for periodic maintenance and repair of the various systems and components in the building.

HIGHLIGHTS OF THE FIRST CANADIAN EDITION

The following content and features have been incorporated into this Canadian edition:

- Up-to-date coverage based on the 2002 *Canadian Electrical Code*
- Metrication in keeping with the 2002 *CEC*
- Expanded information on plans, site work, and electrical distribution systems
- Photographs of the most current equipment in use
- Current information on fire alarm systems
- Coverage of available fault currents in Unit 14, "Short-Circuit Calculations"
- All lighting systems grouped into a single unit
- Coverage of installation and wiring requirements in Unit 10, "Programmable Logic Controllers"
- Data infrastructure coverage, including copper wiring systems
- A complete set of working drawings, including architectural, electrical, mechanical, and structural plans
- A specifications format that more accurately reflects industry standards

ACKNOWLEDGMENTS

The authors and publisher want to thank the following reviewers for their contributions:

Robert J. Jones, *Cambrian College*
Fred Lawton, *New Brunswick Community College*
Bill Maxwell, *Southern Alberta Institute of Technology*
Frank McLaren, *St. Lawrence College*
A. David Murray, *Northern Alberta Institute of Technology*
Tony Poirier, *Durham College*
Don Zaklan, *British Columbia Institute of Technology*

The authors also want to thank Jason Allair and Craig Wonch for their assistance in preparing the blueprints for this book. They are also indebted to the following companies for their contributions of data, illustrations, and technical information:

Allen-Bradley Co., Drives Division
Allen-Bradley Co., Systems Division
Allis Chalmers
American Standard Co.
ARCO Electrical Products Corp.
Audisone Inc.
Biddle Instruments
Bulldog Electrical Products Co.
Burndy Co.
Chrysler Corporation, Air-Temp Division
Clarage Fan Co.
Crouse-Hinds ECM
Eaton Corp. Cutler-Hammer Products
Edwards Co., Inc
ESE
G&W Electrical Specialty Co.
General Electric Co.
Harvey Hubble, Inc., Kellems Division
Ideal Industries (Canada), Inc.
Jensen Electric Company
Wm. J. O'Connell and Stipes Publishing Company
Square D Company
Uticor Technology
Westinghouse Electric Corporation

Applicable tables and section references are reprinted with the permission of the Canadian Standards Association. Material is reproduced from CSA Standard, **C22.1-02,** which is copyrighted by Canadian Standards Association, 178 Rexdale Blvd., Toronto, Ontario, M9W 1R3, www.csa.ca. Although use of this material has been authorized, CSA shall not be responsible for the manner in which the information is presented, nor for any interpretations thereof.

ABOUT THE AUTHORS

Robert L. Smith, P.E., is an Emeritus Professor of Architecture at the University of Illinois, Urbana-Champaign. He worked in electrical construction for more than 20 years. He taught electrical apprentice classes for the IBEW and industrial electricity at Parkland Community College and Environmental Technology for the School of Architecture. Mr. Smith has frequently lectured on the application of the *National Electrical Code.*® He was an active member of the Illuminating Engineering Society, of the Illinois Society of Professional Engineers, and of the International Association of Electrical Inspectors.

Stephen L. Herman has been both a teacher of industrial electricity and an industrial electrician for many years. Mr. Herman received his formal education at Stephen F. Austin University in Nacogdoches, Texas, and at Catawaba Valley Technical College in Hickory, North Carolina. During his years as an industrial electrician, he gained a practical and theoretical knowledge of electricity as applied to industrial applications. He has taught electrical maintenance at Randolph Technical College in Asheboro, North Carolina, and presently teaches electrical technology at Lee College in Baytown, Texas.

Gary M. Miller has been a professor of Electrical Apprenticeship in Ontario since 1989. He holds licences as a construction and maintenance electrician, an industrial electrician, and a master electrician. He has also been trained as a data network designer and installer. His wide range of field experiences in construction and electrical service has been a great asset in his position as a professor and an author. He is presently employed as a professor at Fanshawe College of Applied Arts and Technology in London, Ontario, where he has also held the position of staff developer/trainer.

Paul Stephenson is a professor in the Building Technology Division at Fanshawe College, where he has taught courses in electrical apprenticeship and electrical technology for more than 25 years.

UNIT 1

Contract Documents and Drawings

OBJECTIVES

After studying this unit, the student should be able to:

- identify contract documents
- identify the layout of specifications
- identify the drawings in a typical construction drawing set
- perform conversions between metric and U.S. customary units
- read site plans to determine the locations of specific items
- identify the forms used for preparing an electrical estimate

CONTRACTS

A contract is an agreement, enforceable in law, to supply goods or perform work at a stated price. A construction contract differs from most contracts in that the owner has the right to make changes to the contract as the project progresses. A construction contract is made up of the working drawings and the specifications. A bound volume of specifications and a set of working drawings are provided to all contractors that undertake to bid a job. The drawings and specifications are often referred to as the contract documents.

SPECIFICATIONS

Specifications are written descriptions of materials, construction systems, and quality of work. Specifications are generally laid out in the following manner:

- Notice to bidders
- Instructions to bidders
- Proposal (bid) form
- Owner–contractor agreement form
- Schedule of drawings
- General conditions
- Supplemental general conditions
- Alternates
- Technical sections

Notice to Bidders

This is the advertisement of the project. Electrical contractors may be subcontractors (they sign a contract with the general contractor) or they may be the prime contractor (they sign a contract with the owner or owner's representative—the architect or engineer).

The notice to bidders identifies the project, the project location, the closing date for bids, where the bidding documents may be obtained, and the amount of the deposit required for the bidding documents.

Instructions to Bidders

The instructions to bidders provide a brief description of the project and its location. They also include information on the type of payment, with the most common types being lump sum, unit price, or cost plus fee. A lump sum agreement stipulates that the contractor will satisfactorily complete the job for a fixed sum, regardless of any difficulties the contractor may encounter. If the unit price agreement is used, all bidders base their bids on a unit price basis (per outlet, per pole, per fixture). When the unit price method of payment is used, the actual quantities and classifications are determined by an engineer or quantity surveyor. Cost plus fee agreements are used where the job is extremely complex or construction must begin before complete drawings and specifications have been prepared.

The instructions to bidders normally require the bidder to visit the site and stipulate the time and date of site visits.

The instructions to bidders may require the bidder to provide the owner with information showing that the contractor has the ability to complete the contract. The information requested may include evidence that the bidder is licensed to do business in the jurisdiction where the project will be constructed, a list of work to be subcontracted, the names of the subcontractors, and the work the contractor currently has in progress.

Bonds Four types of bonds are commonly used in the construction industry. They are surety, bid, performance, and material and labour bonds.

A surety bond is a guarantee made by the bonding company to meet the obligations of the contractor. If the contractor is unable to fulfill the terms of the contract, the bonding company must complete the contract (up to the amount of the bond) and then try to recover the money from the contractor. Owners require contractors to be bonded to ensure that they will complete the project and pay their bills.

Bid bonds ensure that if a contractor is awarded a contract, the contractor will proceed with the contract within a stipulated time period. If the contractor does not accept the contract, the bond is forfeit to the owner. Bid bonds are normally 10% of the bidding price.

Performance bonds guarantee an owner that the contractor will complete the contract. Performance bonds are normally 100% of the contract price. The premiums charged by the bonding company will vary according to the contractor's experience and financial stability.

Material and labour bonds guarantee the payment of the contractor's bills to third parties who supply material or labour to the project.

Addenda An addendum is a written addition to the contract documents issued before the bidding is closed. An addendum is used to:

- Clarify questions raised by bidders regarding conflicts, errors, omissions, and ambiguities
- Add to or reduce the scope of the work
- Provide additional information to bidders in the way of explanations
- Change the provisions of the contract

Proposal (Bid) Form

A proposal (bid) form is included in a set of specifications. This allows the owner to evaluate all the bids on the same basis. A typical proposal form would include the following:

- Name of tendering company
- Name of owner
- Lump sum tender price
- Breakdown of lump sum price
- Schedule of unit prices
- Alternates
- Statutory declaration

- Agreement to bond
- Statement of experience
- Statement of senior supervisory staff

See Figure 1-1 for a simplified form of tender.

Figure 1-1 Simplified form of tender.

Tender by: ____

A company duly incorporated under the laws of ______________________, hereinafter called "the Tenderer."

To: Your Corporation

1234 The Great Northern Road

Your Town, Your Province

Your Postal Code

hereinafter called "the Owner."

1. **The Tenderer, having carefully examined the site of the proposed works and all contract documents relating thereto, hereby tenders and offers to enter into a contract to construct the proposed addition in accordance with the contract documents including all taxes, patent fees, import duties, foreign exchange, and all other charges for the lump sum tender price of: ______________________________ Canadian dollars, subject to additions and deductions as may be ascertained in accordance with the contract.**
2. **The aforesaid lump sum tender is based on the assumption that the engineers' written order to commence work will be issued within 60 days of the opening date of the tenders.**
3. **The Tenderer declares the tender is made without any comparison or arrangement with any other firm or person making a tender for this work.**
4. **The Tenderer agrees to execute additional work or make deletions as ordered by the engineer. Payment for such additions and deletions shall be made in conformance with the provisions of the contract documents.**
5. **The Tenderer agrees that this tender is subject to a formal contract being prepared and executed.**
6. **A tender deposit consisting of a certified cheque or bid bond in the amount of 20 000 dollars shall be made payable to the Owner. The Tenderer agrees that the tender deposit may be used at the discretion of the Owner if the Tenderer fails to enter into a contract when notified by the Owner. The Tenderer is to provide as part of the tender an "Agreement To Bond" in the amount of 100% of the tender price.**
7. **The Tenderer agrees to complete the work within a period of ________ weeks from the date of the engineers' written order to commence the work.**
8. **Tenderers wishing to use alternative equipment or materials must submit details of the equipment and price savings at the time of tendering. However, equipment and materials specified must be used in the tender price.**

Continued

9. The Tenderer declares that he or she has completed the attached statements covering the names and experience of supervisory personnel, work of a similar nature, and construction plant used.

Dated at ______________________ this ______ day of ______ in the year of ____________.

____

Signature of authorized person signing for the Tenderer

____

Figure 1-1 Simplified form of tender. ***(Continued)***

Alternates

An alternate is a request by the owner for a price on alternate materials or methods of construction. Alternates are listed on the proposal form. The alternates may be "add price" or "subtract price," meaning that the alternate will add to the base bid or subtract from it.

Technical Sections

Specifications are divided into a number of divisions. Each division covers some portion of the work. Technical sections contain descriptions of materials and instructions on methods of construction. Table 1-1 describes divisions commonly found in specifications.

THE DRAWING SET

A set of drawings is made up of numbered sheets. If there is a large number of sheets in a set, the set will be broken down into subsets of architectural, electrical, mechanical, and so on. The electrical drawings will be numbered E1, E2, E3, and so on.

A typical set of construction drawings will include a site (plot) plan, floor plans, elevations, details and sections, a legend of symbols, schedules, diagrams, and shop drawings.

A Site (Plot) Plan

The site plan will show:

- The dimensions of the lot
- A north-facing arrow
- The location of utilities and their connection points
- Any outdoor lighting
- Easements (rights to the property by someone other than the owner)
- Contour lines to show changes in elevation
- Accessory buildings
- Trees to be saved

Floor Plans

Depending on the complexity of the building, a set of drawings may have only a single floor plan for each storey of the building. As the complexity of the building increases, there will be a number of floor plans for each storey, one for each trade. A logical breakdown would be:

- Architectural
- Electrical
- Mechanical

Division	Title	Information Relating to the Electrical Trade
1	General Requirements	
2	Site Construction	Site Preparation, Utility Services
3	Concrete	
4	Masonry	
5	Metals	
6	Wood and Plastics	
7	Thermal and Moisture Protection	Thermal Protection Fire and Smoke Protection Type of Construction
8	Doors and Windows	
9	Finishes	
10	Specialties	Pedestrian Control Devices Scales Access Flooring Telephone Enclosures
11	Equipment	Laundry Equipment Loading Dock Equipment Medical Equipment Parking Equipment
12	Furnishings	
13	Special Construction	Incinerators Instrumentation Nuclear Reactors Vaults Swimming Pools
14	Conveying Systems	Powered Scaffolding Hoists and Cranes
15	Mechanical	Controls and Instrumentation Refrigeration Equipment Heat Generation Equipment
16	Electrical	Division 16 is broken down into subdivisions, each of which covers a portion of the work. Examples include 16010—General Requirements 16050—Basic Material and Methods 16105—Concrete Encased Duct Banks 16106—Installation of Cables in Trenches 16107—Direct Buried Cables 16111—Raceways 16122—Wires and Cables 16123—Voice/Data Cable 16141—Wiring Devices 16400—Service and Distribution 16402—Underground Service 16421—Service Board 16428—Digital Metering 16440—Disconnect Switches 16461—Dry-Type Transformers (600 V) 16471—Panelboards 16477—Moulded Case Circuit Breakers 16478—Fuses 16500—Lighting 16505—Lighting Equipment 16519—Exit Lights 16600—Special Systems 16700—Communications 16800—Heating and Cooling 16900—Controls and Instrumentation

Table 1-1 Specification divisions.

- Plumbing
- Structural

On very complex installations, different electrical systems—such as power, lighting, voice/data, fire alarm, and security/access control—may each have their own plan for each storey.

Elevations

Elevations show the vertical faces of buildings, structures, and equipment. Elevations are used to show both interior and exterior vertical faces.

Details and Sections

Details are large scale drawings that are used when sufficient detail cannot be provided on floor plans and elevations. Sheet S3 shows details of structural elements of the building.

A Legend of Symbols

A legend of symbols provides the contractor with the information to interpret the symbols shown on the drawing.

Schedules

Schedules are lists of equipment. Electrical schedules are made for equipment such as lighting fixtures (luminaires), panelboards, raceways and cables, motors, and mechanical equipment connections.

Diagrams

One-line and riser diagrams are provided to quickly show the flow of power throughout the building. Riser diagrams may be used to show power, telephone, or fire alarm systems.

Shop Drawings

Shop drawings are used by equipment manufacturers to show details of custom-made equipment for a specific job. Manufacturers' drawings of switchgear and motor control centres (MCCs) are examples of shop drawings.

UNITS

Construction drawings may be drawn in metric units (metric scale) or U.S. customary units (architects' scale), which use feet (′), inches (″) and fractions of an inch as units of measure. A standard tape measure that uses U.S. customary units is divided into feet, inches, and fractions of an inch. The first 12 in of the tape normally have divisions of 1/32 of an inch. The remainder of the tape has divisions of 1/16 of an inch. Figure 1-2 shows how to read a tape measure using U.S. customary units. Figure 1-3 gives useful conversions from metric to U.S. units.

Scale

A drawing of an object that is the same size as the object is said to be drawn full scale or at a scale of 1:1.

Construction drawings reduce the size of a building to fit on a piece of paper by drawing everything proportionally smaller than it actually is. This is called reduced scale. A drawing that

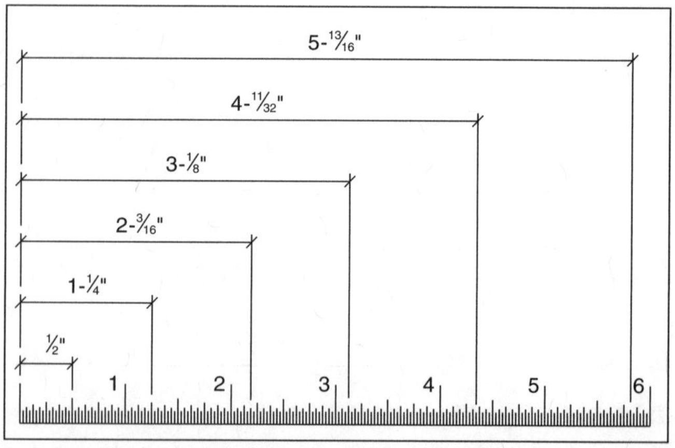

Figure 1-2 Reading tape measure divisions.

To convert:	
mm to in	multiply by 25.4
mm to ft	multiply by 304.8
mm to yd	multiply by 914.4
m to in	multiply by 0.0254
m to ft	multiply by 0.328
m to yd	multiply by 0.984
mm^2 to sq in	multiply by 0.0016
m^2 to sq ft	multiply by 10.764
m^2 to sq yd	multiply by 1.196

Figure 1-3 Useful conversions.

uses a scale of 1:50 indicates that the building is 50 times larger than the drawing. A drawing with a scale of 1/4 in = 1 ft has a scale of 1:48.

Types of Scales (Measuring Instruments)

Three types of scales are commonly used on construction drawings. For metric drawings, a metric scale is used. Figure 1-4 shows a metric scale.

When working with measurements that use feet and inches, an architectural scale is used. Figure 1-5 on page 8 shows a portion of an architect's triangular scale showing the 1/8″ and 1/4″ scales.

When working with civil drawings that are measured in feet and tenths of a foot (roads, dams, bridges, etc.) an engineering scale is used, as shown in Figure 1-6 on page 8. Table 1-2 on page 9 lists common construction drawing scales.

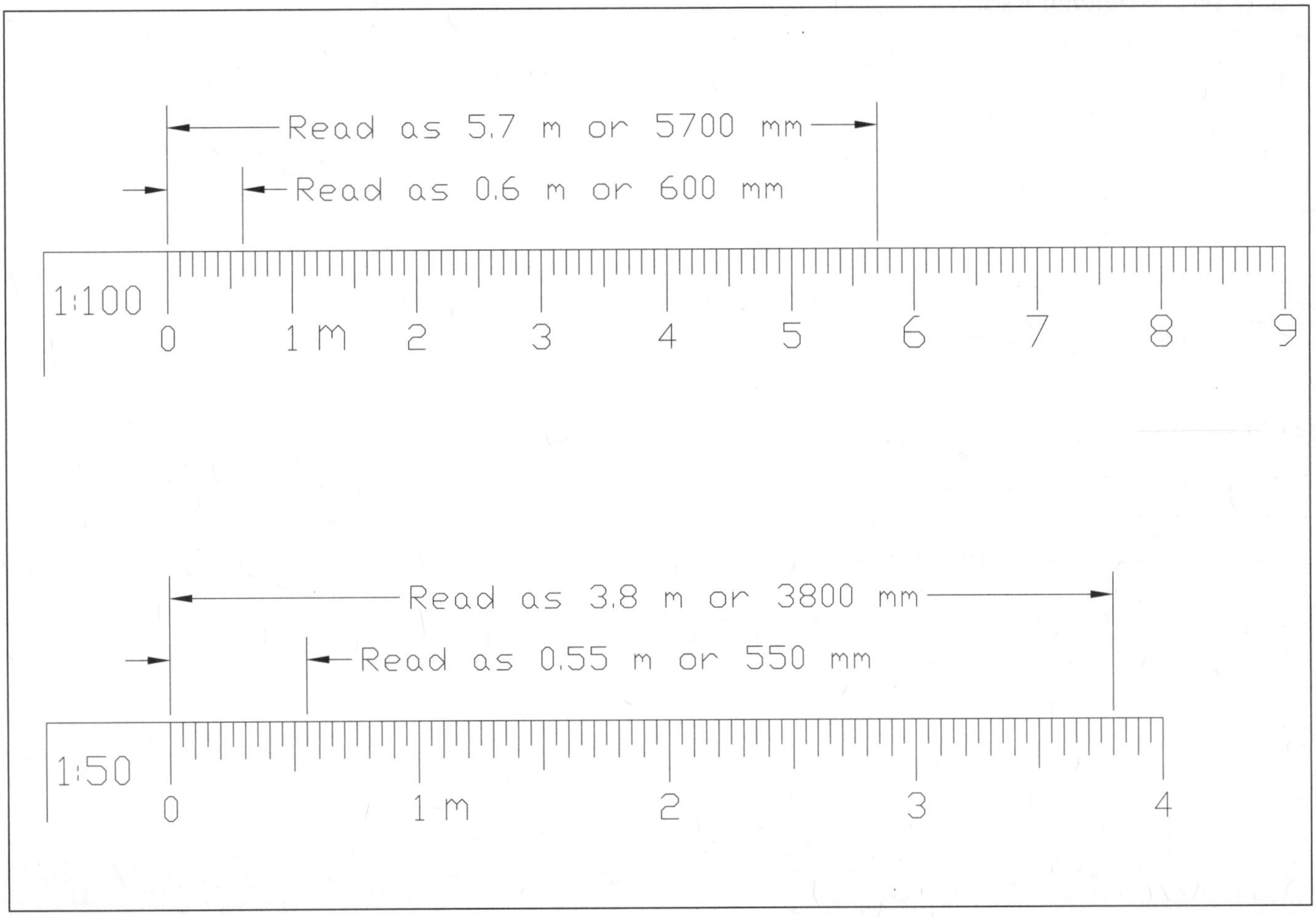

Figure 1-4 Metric scale.

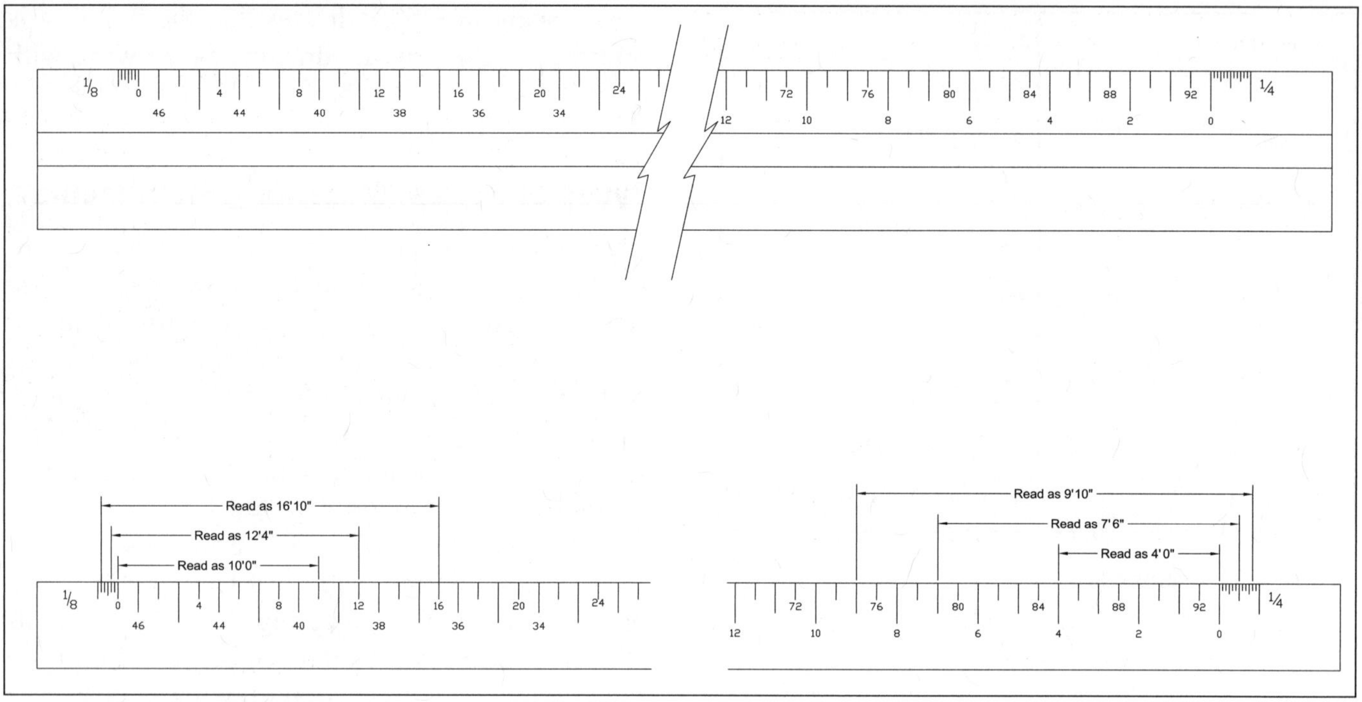

Figure 1-5 Architectural scale.

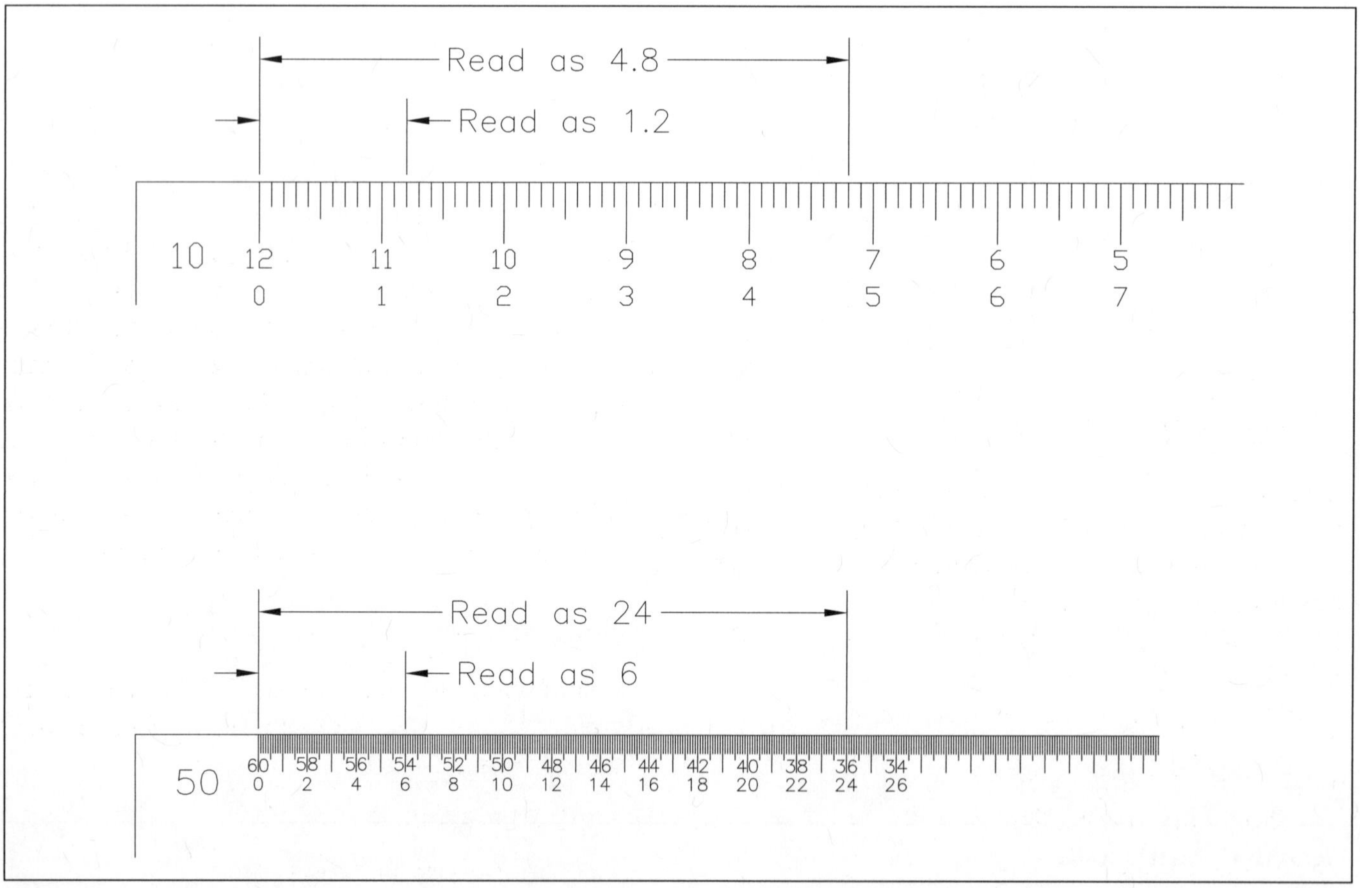

Figure 1-6 Engineering scale.

Metric	Architectural	Engineering
1:20	1/2″ = 1′0″	20
1:50	1/4″ = 1′0″	40
1:100	1/8″ = 1′0″	100

Table 1–2 Common drawing scales.

Working with the Drawings

- Check that the drawing set is complete.
- Review the floor plans and elevations to get a mental picture of the size and shape of the building.
- Orient the building to the site using the plot plan. Be sure you know which sides are north, south, east, and west. Add this information to your floor plans.
- Check the scale of all drawings.
- Identify the type (combustible or non-combustible) of construction materials and components shown in the drawings. Nonstandard items should be shown in a legend of symbols.
- Read all notes on the drawings carefully.
- Relate details to larger views.
- Note multiple or identical drawings. *Typical* means uniform throughout the building.

ESTIMATING

Estimating is the process of determining the cost of a project by counting, measuring, and listing items of material, assigning labour units to the material based on the conditions of the installation, and determining direct job expenses, overhead, and return on investment.

The main steps in estimating are:

- Preparing a material take-off
- Tabulating and pricing
- Summarizing

Material Take-Off

A material take-off involves counting, measuring, and listing the quantities of materials and equipment necessary to complete the installation. Material is normally taken off by systems and listed on the take-off sheets in a manner that will permit labour units to be assigned easily.

The exact method and forms used by a contractor will be determined by personal preference or the computerized estimating system used by the contractor. One breakdown of systems in the order they would be taken off might be:

- Lighting fixtures (luminaires)
- Outlets
- Branch circuits
- Service, metering, and grounding
- Distribution equipment
- Feeders and busways
- Telephone
- Special systems

Pricing

Pricing is the process of assigning labour and prices to items of material that have been tabulated and listed on pricing sheets. Labour is assigned using standard labour units and adjusted to account for the conditions of the installation.

A standard labour unit is defined as the time required to handle and install an item under specified working conditions. Labour units are found in estimating manuals developed by such organizations as the Canadian Electrical Contractors Association and its provincial counterparts.

Summarizing

A summary bid sheet lists all of the projected costs of the project. The summary sheet includes such information as:

- Material costs
- Labour hours and costs

- Job factors (working height, multiple identical buildings, etc.)
- Direct job expenses (equipment, travel, warehousing)
- Overhead
- Profit

JOB MANAGEMENT

It is the responsibility of the job manager (whoever is running the job) to ensure that:

- Tools and materials arrive at the job at the time they are required
- There are adequate facilities for storage and protection of materials, tools, and equipment
- There is adequate labour to complete the work as scheduled
- Information is provided to the work force to allow the work to proceed
- The paperwork associated with the job is handled properly
- Company policies are followed with respect to safety, employment regulations, and job requirements

The following steps will be helpful during the initial preparation for a project.

- Familiarize yourself with the project by studying the drawings and specifications.
- Prepare a list of materials required for the job. The estimator may provide you with the estimate sheets or you may decide to do your own materials take-off and prepare a bill of materials yourself. Materials should arrive on the site according to the activity that is being undertaken at the time. You will know how well you are doing by keeping track of all the materials that you have ordered, what had to be returned, and any delays in work assignments that were caused by lack of materials. Materials arriving on-site should be inspected, inventoried, and stored in a clean, dry, and secure location. Packing slips should be carefully checked and back-ordered items recorded.
- Using electrical estimate sheets and the general contractor's construction schedule, determine when electrical activities should occur. Table 1-3 lists the main construction events and corresponding electrical activities.
- Prepare a schedule of electrical construction activities that corresponds to the general contractor's construction schedule. The activity schedule will be the basis for determining labour force requirements, when materials should be delivered to the site, and what tooling will be required. Figure 1-7 is an example of a construction activity schedule.

Construction Event	Electrical Activity
Site preparation	Trenching and underground work
Footings and foundations	Embedded work
Superstructure and floors	Embedded work and hangers
Building enclosure	Feeders, equipment, and branch circuits
Interior walls, partitions, and ceilings	Panelboards, branch circuits, and pulling wire
Trimming and decorating	Lighting
Floor finishing	Finishing

Table 1–3 Construction events.

CHANGE ORDERS

A change order is a change in the drawings or specifications that is made after the contract has been awarded. Change orders result from such things as:

- Requests for additional work from the owner
- Errors or omissions in the drawings and specifications
- Delays in construction

When an owner requests a change in the contract that will affect the contract price, an estimate of the costs involved in making the changes is prepared and a Request for Change Order is submitted to the owner. (This is a document that outlines the changes to be made and authorizes the contractor to make the changes. It must be signed

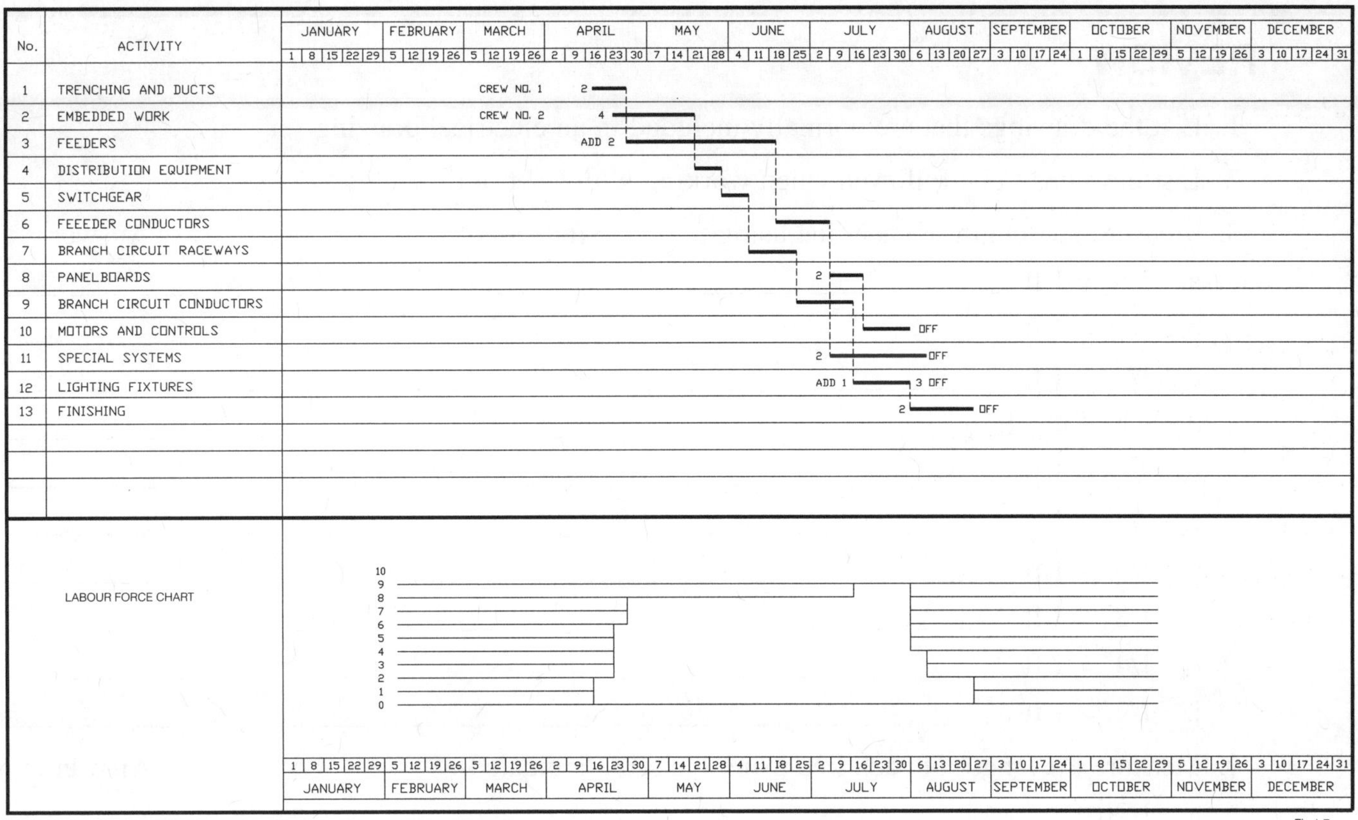

Figure 1-7 **Construction activity schedule.**

by the owner or owner's representative.) The most important thing about change orders is that they should be handled promptly and fairly.

APPROVAL OF EQUIPMENT

All electrical equipment sold or installed in Canada is required to be approved for its intended use. Approved equipment has met specified safety standards of federal and provincial governments. Currently several companies are accredited by the Standards Council of Canada to approve electrical equipment. Equipment that has been approved by an approval agency will have an identifying label such as the Canadian Standards Association (CSA) or the Underwriters' Laboratories of Canada (ULC). For equipment that has not been approved, arrangements may be made for field approval by contacting the inspection authority in your province. It should be able to provide you with a complete list of companies that can approve electrical equipment in your province.

Electrical Inspection

The *Canadian Electrical Code (CEC)* requires that a permit be obtained for the inspection of all work with respect to the installation, alteration, or repair of electrical equipment. It is the responsibility of the electrical contractor or person doing the work to obtain the permit. When the installation has passed inspection, the inspection authority will issue a connection permit (sometimes referred to as authorization for connection or current permit) to the supply authority. The supply authority will then make connection to the installation.

REVIEW

1. List the drawings that are normally included in an electrical drawing set.
2. List the steps to be followed when working with a set of drawings.
3. Measure the length of each line using the scale indicated. Answer
   a. 1/8″ = 1 ft ____________________ ________
   b. 1/4″ = 1 ft ____________________ ________
   c. 1/2″ = 1 ft ____________________ ________
   d. 1-1/2″ = 1 ft ____________________ ________
   e. 3/8″ = 1 ft ____________________ ________
   f. 3/4″ = 1 ft ____________________ ________
   g. 1/4″ = 1 ft ____________________ ________
   h. 1/8″ = 1 ft ____________________ ________
   i. 1/4″ = 1 ft ____________________ ________
   j. 1/2″ = 1 ft ____________________ ________
4. Measure the length of each line using the scale indicated. Answer
   a. 1:20 ____________________ ________
   b. 1:50 ____________________ ________
   c. 1:100 ____________________ ________
   d. 1:75 ____________________ ________
   e. 1:25 ____________________ ________
   f. 1:125 ____________________ ________
   g. 1:100 ____________________ ________
   h. 1:20 ____________________ ________
   i. 1:50 ____________________ ________
   j. 1: 100 ____________________ ________
5. Identify which section of Division 16 covers the following work. Answer
   a. Raceways ____________________ ________
   b. Dry-type transformers (600 V) ____________________ ________
   c. Light fixtures ____________________ ________
   d. Basic material and methods ____________________ ________
   e. Panelboards ____________________ ________
   f. Direct buried cables ____________________ ________
   g. Wires and cables ____________________ ________
   h. Voice/data cable ____________________ ________

6. Identify the construction event during which the following electrical activities should take place.
   a. Trenching and underground work
   b. Feeders
   c. Finishing
   d. Panelboards
   e. Branch circuits and pulling wire
   f. Embedded work
7. Draw the symbol for the following items found on a site plan.
   a. Existing contour lines
   b. Finished contour lines
   c. Benchmark
   d. Gas line
   e. Fence line
   f. Property line
8. Give the measurement indicated by each dimension in the diagram below.

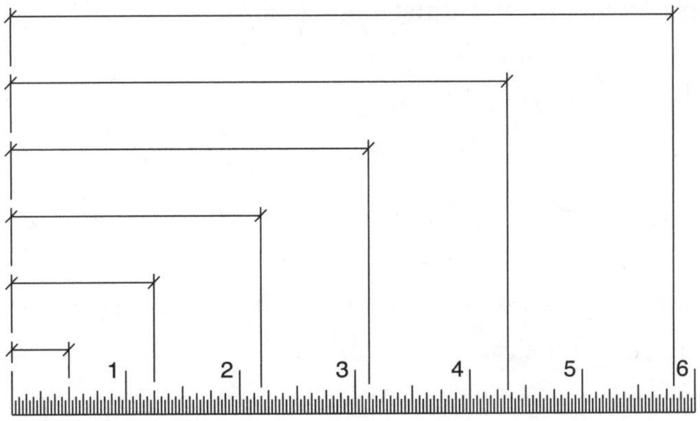

9. Determine the following using the blueprints supplied with this textbook.
   a. What is the distance from the south lot line to the southeast corner of the building?
   b. What is the benchmark elevation?
   c. Where is the new electrical room located?
   d. What size and voltage transformers are used to supply this building?
   e. Where is the chiller located?
   f. Where is lighting panel "D" located?
   g. What is the voltage and current rating of power panel 102?
10. Perform the following conversions.
   a. 12.5 mm to in
   b. 25.4 mm to in
   c. 500 mm to in
   e. 3412 mm to ft
   f. 0.025 mm to ft
   g. 1/8″ to mm
   i. 1/2″ to mm
   j. 9/64″ to mm

UNIT 2

Industrial Distribution Systems and Service Equipment

OBJECTIVES

After studying this unit, the student should be able to:

- identify industrial distribution systems
- identify the components of an industrial service
- select the proper size of high-voltage fuse
- explain how to set transformer taps
- describe how a ground detector operates
- describe substation grounding
- describe installation procedures for underground ducts
- describe installation procedures for underground conductors
- calculate cable pulling tension

INDUSTRIAL DISTRIBUTION SYSTEMS

There are several types of industrial power distribution systems, including the radial system, the modified radial (load centre) system, the primary selective system, the loop system, and the secondary selective system.

The Radial System

The type of distribution system used to supply power to an industrial building depends on the requirements of the industrial process, and the cost of the installation.

The simplest distribution system is the radial system, which looks like an inverted tree. The radial system receives power from the utility at a single outdoor substation, unit substation, or pad-mount transformer, and reduces the voltage down to the utilization level. Low-voltage feeders run from the substation transformer to building switchgear. Larger substations may have a secondary bus with more than one feeder. In this case, each feeder will be supplied through a circuit breaker. Figure 2-1 shows some variations of the radial system.

The advantages of the radial system are:

- The entire load of the building is supplied from a single source. The diversity of loads within the building permits the smallest possible transformer to be used.
- It is the least costly distribution system as there is no duplication of equipment.

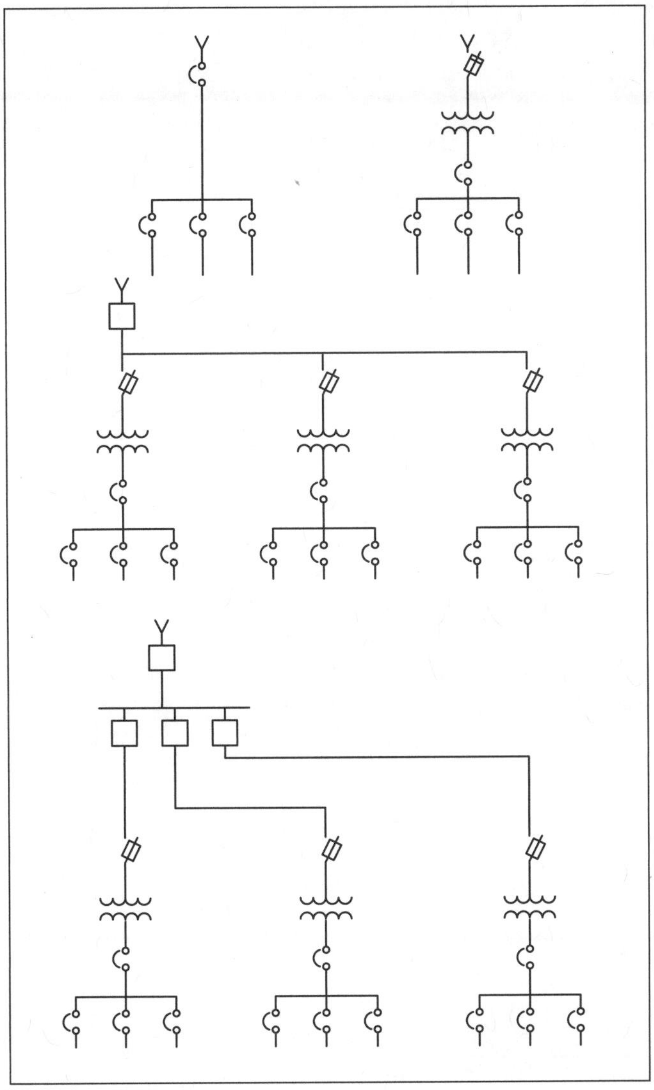

Figure 2-1 Variations of the radial system.

- It is the easiest and safest to operate.

The disadvantages of the system are:

- The system does not offer any redundancy. A fault on the substation or supply feeder will interrupt power to the building until the necessary repairs have been made.
- Efficiency and voltage regulation can be problems.
- It can be cost prohibitive if the system is large

The Modified Radial (Load Centre) System

The modified radial distribution system distributes power at the primary voltage. The voltage is stepped down to utilization level by unit substations located at each load area. The advantages of this system are lower losses, better voltage regulation, and reduced feeder costs. The main disadvantage is that the transformer located in each area must be capable of carrying the peak load in the area.

Figure 2-2 shows a 2500 kVA transformer on the right and outdoor medium voltage switchgear on the left. The 27 kV switches are used to supply unit substations at each load area.

The Primary Selective System

The primary selective system (Figure 2-3 on page 16) employs two primary feeder circuits. Each transformer can be supplied from the two sources. Normally, half of the load is supplied by each of the primary feeders. If one of the primary feeders is lost, all of the transformers are connected to the good primary feeder.

The Loop System

The loop-primary has a high-voltage loop around the plan. It provides for quick restoration of power should a fault occur on a primary feeder or transformer. A primary voltage loop is supplied from a

Figure 2-2 A 2500 kVA transformer and outdoor

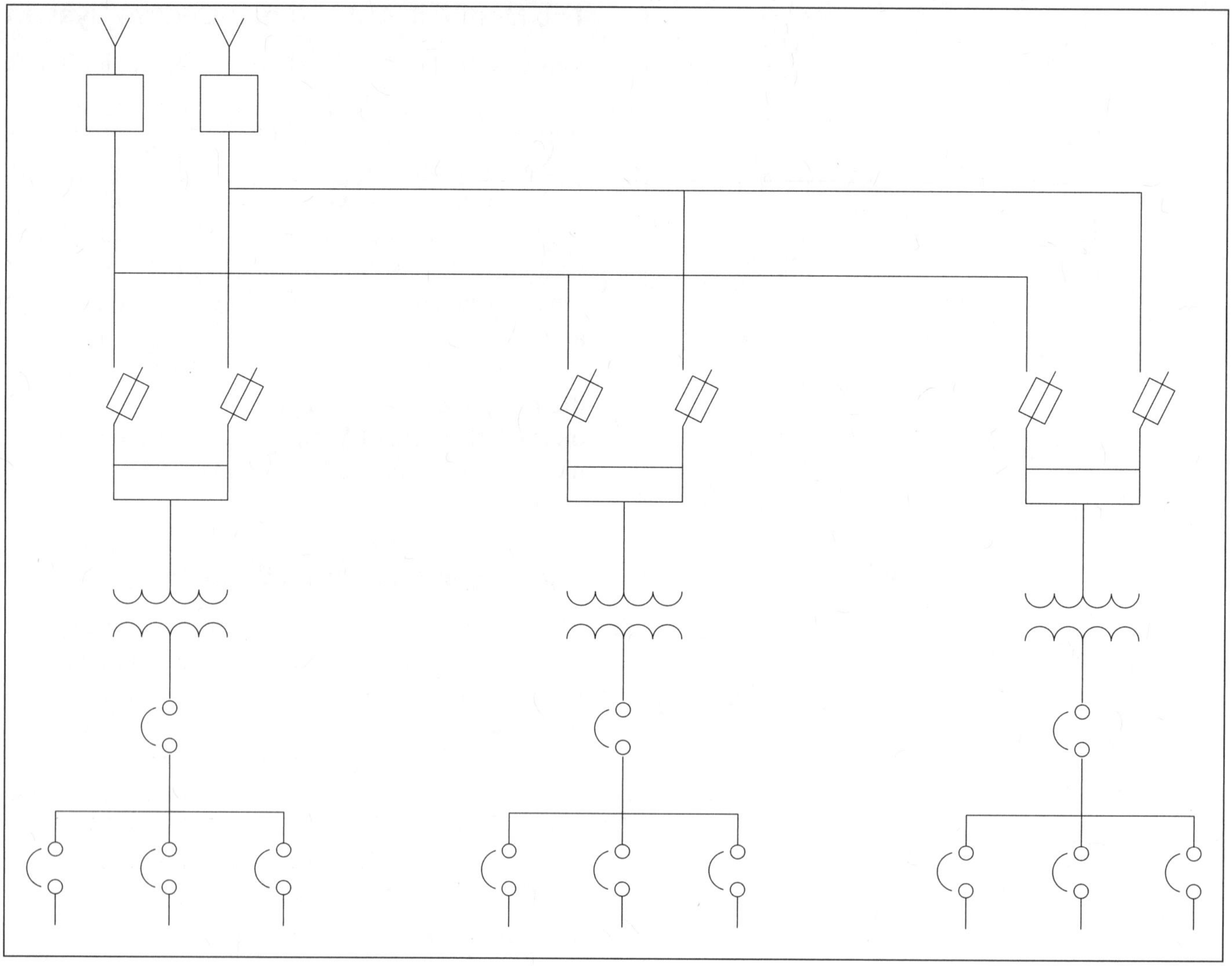

Figure 2-3 Primary selective system.

single primary feeder breaker. Load break switches are installed in the feeder at each transformer. This makes it possible to isolate a faulted transformer or section of primary feeder. The loop may be operated open or closed; however, most customers will have the loop open at one point. See Figure 2-4 for a diagram of a loop system.

The Secondary Selective System

The secondary selective radial system (Figure 2-5) is widely used for industrial, commercial, and institutional applications. This arrangement allows for quick restoration of service if a primary feeder or transformer fails.

Each load is supplied by two primary feeders and two transformers. A secondary-bus tie breaker is used to connect each load centre. The tie breaker is normally in the open position and the system operates as two independent parallel systems. If a fault occurs on a primary feeder or transformer, the transformer or feeder is isolated from the system and the total system load is fed from the remaining transformer. The tie breaker is interlocked with the transformer breakers so that it cannot be closed unless one of the transformer breakers is in the open position.

Service Equipment

Small industrial buildings generally will be supplied by either a pad-mounted transformer or a unit substation. When pad-mounted transformers are used, the high-voltage connections are made in

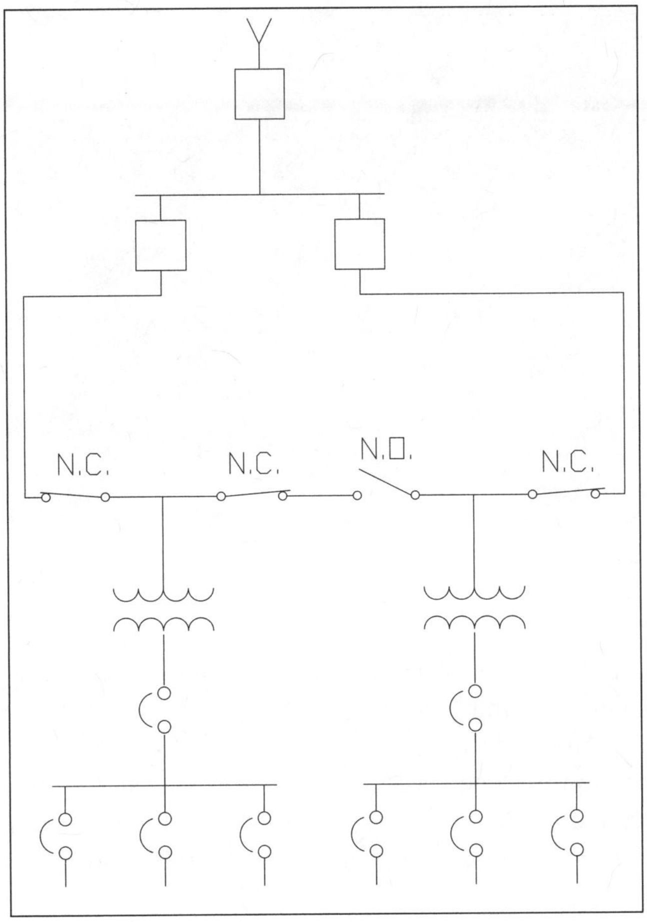

Figure 2-4 **Loop system.**

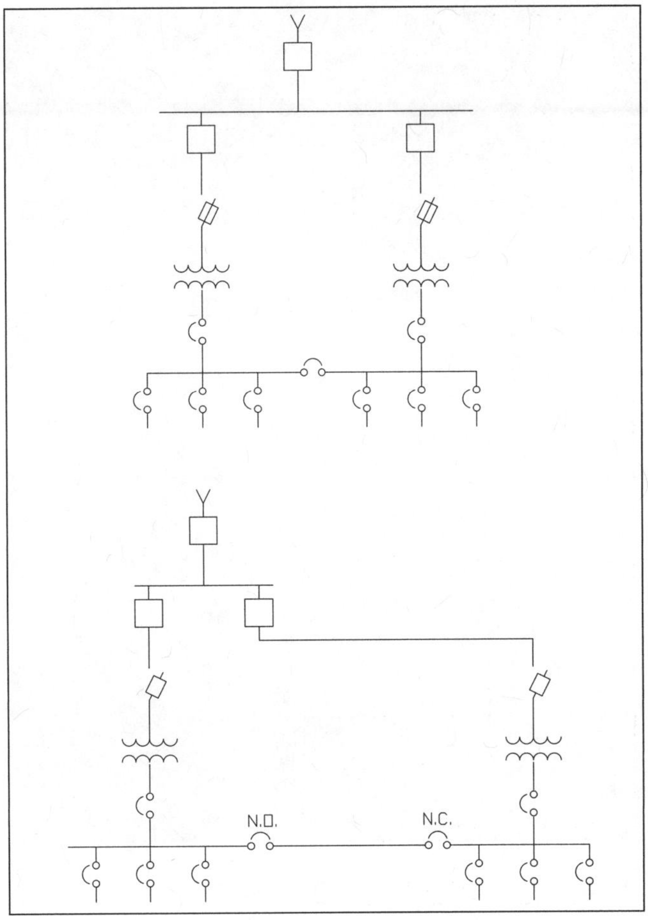

Figure 2-5 **Secondary selective radial system.**

the pad-mounted transformers and low (utilization) voltage feeders are run into the building.

For the industrial building, a secondary selective system having two 1000 kVA pad-mounted transformers will be used.

The system starts at an overhead 27 kV line, as in Figure 2-6 on page 18. The 27 kV shielded cable runs down the pole and underground through Manhole 1 to the two pad-mounted transformers (Figure 2-7 on page 18).

Unit Substations

A unit substation consists of a high-voltage section, transformer section, and low-voltage distribution section. (See Figure 2-8 on page 18.) The high-voltage section contains a primary switch

voltage section contains metering equipment, a main circuit breaker, and distribution breakers. When used indoors, unit substations will generally use dry-type transformers.

The High-Voltage Section The high-voltage section includes a switch and fuse assembly.

Lightning Arresters Lightning arresters (Figure 2-9 on page 19) are installed on buildings in areas where lightning storms are common. These devices are designed to provide a low-impedance path to ground for any surge currents such as those resulting from a lightning strike. Surge arresters are installed on each ungrounded overhead service conductor. The internal components of the arrester vary according to the type

Figure 2-6 Connection to 27 kV line.

Figure 2-7 A 1000-kVA pad-mounted transformer.

electrician must ensure that a good ground connection is made to the arrester.

Note: If the transformer section of the unit substation is to be given a megohmmeter test, the line connection to the arrester must be disconnected during the test to prevent a false ground reading.

Figure 2-8 The unit substation.

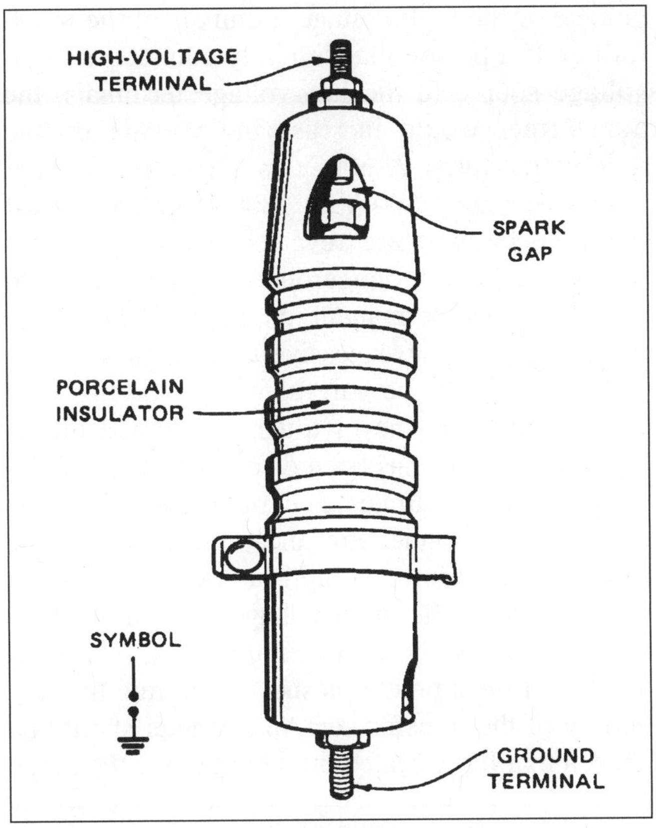

Figure 2-9 Lightning arrester.

HIGH-VOLTAGE, CURRENT-LIMITING FUSES

High-voltage, current-limiting fuses are installed as protective devices in power distribution systems such as the one installed in the industrial building. The selection of the proper fuse is based on several factors, including the continuous current rating, voltage rating, frequency rating, interrupt rating, and coordination. The fuse selected for a particular installation must meet the predetermined voltage and frequency requirements listed. Fuses are available for both 25-Hz and 60-Hz systems and for voltage ratings of 2400 V and up (Figure 2-10).

Continuous Current Rating

High-voltage fuses are available with either an N or an E rating. These ratings indicate that certain standards established by the Institute of Electrical and Electronic Engineers, Inc. (IEEE) and

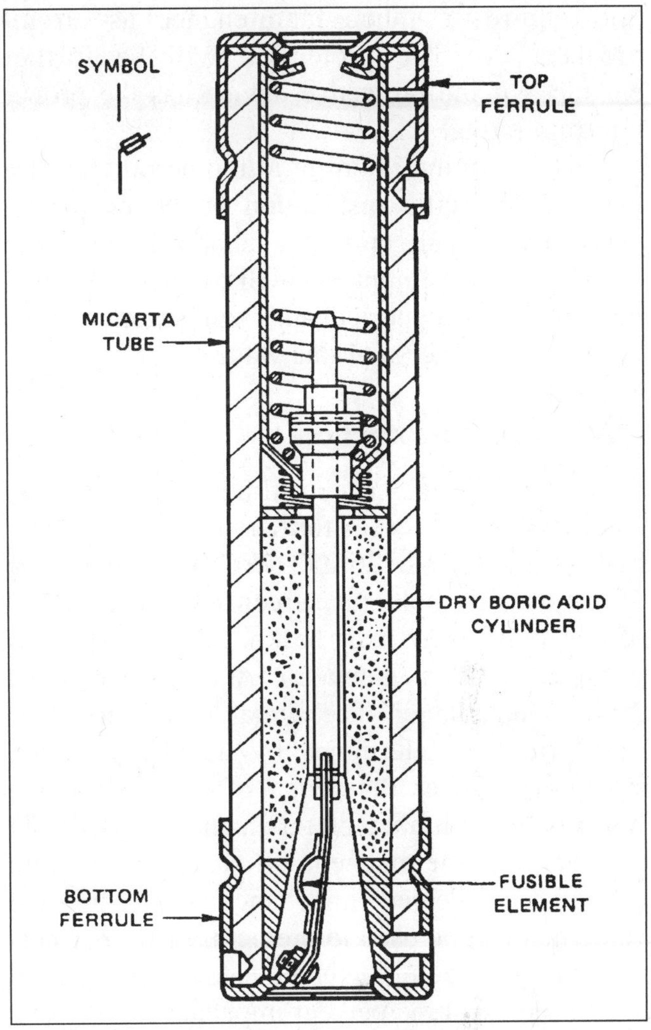

Figure 2-10 Cutaway view of high-voltage fuse.

(NEMA) have been met. The N rating represents an older set of standards and indicates that a cable-type fuse link will open in less than 300 seconds at a load of 220% of its rated current.

An E-type fuse rated at 100 A or less will open in 300 seconds at a current of 200% to 240% of its rating. Above 100 A, an E-rated fuse will open in 600 seconds at a current of 220% to 264% of its rated current. The electrician should note, however, that an E-rated fuse does not provide protection in the range of one to two times the continuous load current rating.

TRANSFORMER PROTECTION

In general, fuses are selected for high-voltage protection because they are less expensive than other not require as much maintenance as circuit breakers do. The protection will be further enhanced if the protective device has the proper interrupt rating.

The minimum interrupt rating permitted for a fuse in a specific installation is the maximum symmetrical fault current available at the fuse location. Power companies will provide the information when requested and will recommend a fuse rating in excess of this value.

Overcurrent Protection

Interrupt Rating The maximum rating of overcurrent devices for transformers rated at 750 V or higher is set forth in 26-252 *CEC Part 1* and Table 51. To use this table, the percent impedance (*%Z*) of the transformer must be known. This value is stamped on the nameplate of transformers rated 25 kVA and larger. The actual impedance of a transformer is determined by its physical construction, such as the gauge of the wire in the winding, the number of turns, the type of core material, and the magnetic efficiency of the core construction. Percent impedance is an empirical value that can be used to predict transformer performance. It is common practice to use the symbol *%Z* to represent the percent impedance.

%Z is required to determine the maximum available fault current on the load side of a transformer. Percentages must be converted to decimal form before they can be used in a mathematical formula.

When this conversion has been made, the symbol (.Z) will be used to represent the decimal impedance, that is, the percent impedance in decimal form. The percent value is converted to a numerical value by moving the decimal point two places to the left; thus, for example, 5.75% becomes 0.0575. This value has no units, as it represents a ratio.

Determining Transformer Impedance When working with any transformer, it is important to keep in mind the full meaning of the terms *primary* and *secondary* and *high voltage* and *low voltage*. The primary is the winding that is connected to a voltage source; the secondary is the winding that is connected to an electrical load. The source may be connected to either the low-voltage or the high-voltage terminals of the transformer. If a person inadvertently connects a high-voltage source to the low-voltage terminals, the transformer would increase the voltage by the ratio of the turns. A 600-V to 200-V transformer would become a 600-V to 1800-V transformer if the connections were reversed. This would not only create a very dangerous situation, but could also result in permanent damage to the transformer because of excessive current flow in the winding. Always be careful when working with transformers, and never touch a terminal unless the power source has been disconnected.

The percent impedance of a transformer is measured by connecting an ammeter across the low-voltage terminals and a variable voltage source across the high-voltage terminals. This arrangement is shown in Figure 2-11. The connection of the ammeter is short-circuiting the secondary of the transformer. An ammeter should be chosen that has a scale with about twice the range

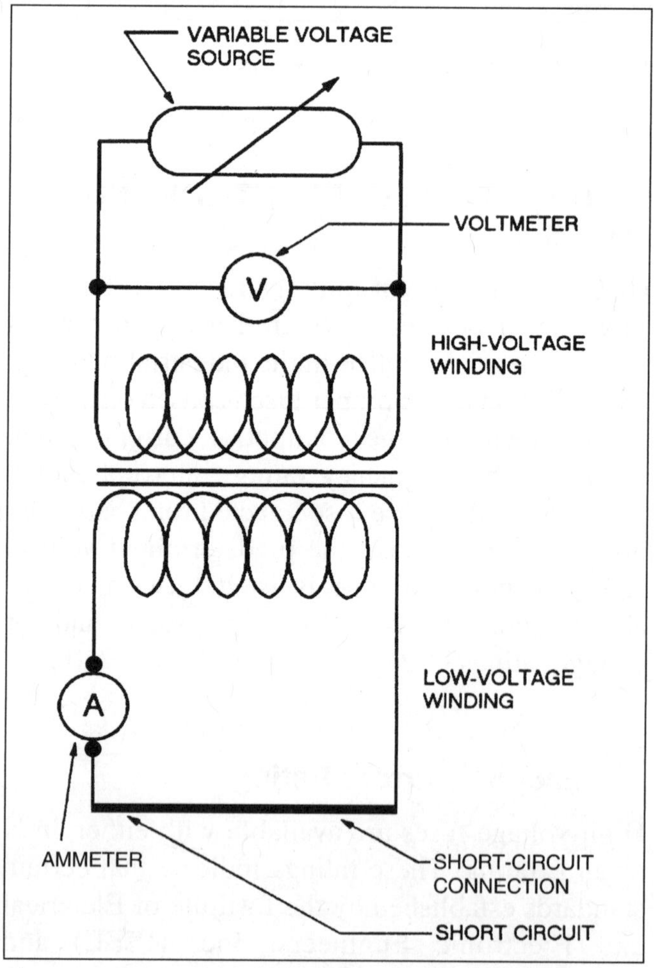

Figure 2-11 Determining transformer impedance.

of the value to be measured so that the reading will be taken in the middle of the range. If the current to be measured is expected to be about 30 amperes, a meter with a 0-A to 60-A range would be ideal. Using a meter with a range under 40 A or over 100 A may not permit an accurate reading.

After the connections have been made, the voltage is increased until the ammeter indicates the rated full-load current of the secondary (low-voltage winding). The value of the source voltage is then used to calculate the decimal impedance (.*Z*). The .*Z* is found by determining the ratio of the source voltage as compared to the rated voltage of the high-voltage winding.

Example Assume that the transformer shown in Figure 2-11 is a 2400/600-V, 15-kVA transformer. To determine the impedance of the transformer, first compute the full-load current rating of the secondary winding. Given the transformer rating in VA, and the secondary voltage, E, the secondary current *I* can be computed:

$I = VA / E = 15\,000 / 600 = 25.0\text{ A}$

Next, increase the source voltage connected to the high-voltage winding until there is a current of 25.0 A in the low-voltage winding. For the purpose of this example, assume that voltage value to be 138 V. Finally, determine the ratio of applied voltage as compared to the rated voltage.

$.Z = \text{Source voltage / Rated voltage}$

$.Z = 138 / 2400 = 0.0575$

To change the decimal value to %Z, move the decimal point two places to the right and add a % sign. This is the same as multiplying the decimal value by 100.

$\%Z = 5.75\%$

Transformer impedance is a major factor in determining the amount of voltage drop a transformer will exhibit between no load and full load and in determining the current in a short-circuit condition. When the transformer impedance is known, it is possible to calculate the maximum possible short-circuit current. This would be a current would decrease as the length of the connecting wires increased the impedance. The following formulas can be used to calculate the short-circuit current value when the transformer impedance is known:

$$\text{(Single-phase) } I_{SC} = \frac{VA}{E \times .Z}$$

$$\text{(Three-phase) } I_{SC} = \frac{VA}{E \times \sqrt{3} \times .Z}$$

The equation $I = VA\ /\ .Z$ is read "amperes equals volt-amperes divided by the decimal impedance." This equation is not an application of Ohm's law because decimal impedance is not measured in ohms. The purpose of the equation is to determine the current in a circuit when the transformer capacity (volt-amperes) and the percent impedance are given.

The equation for computing the rated current for a single-phase transformer is:

$$I = \frac{VA}{E}$$

The equation for computing the rated current for a three-phase transformer is:

$$I = \frac{VA}{E \times \sqrt{3}}$$

The short-circuit current can be determined by dividing the rated secondary current by the decimal impedance of the transformer:

$$I_{SC} = \frac{I_{SECONDARY}}{.Z}$$

The short-circuit current for the transformer in the previous example would be:

$$I_{SC} = \frac{25.0}{0.0575}$$

$$I_{SC} = 434.78\text{ A}$$

Determining Transformer Fuse Size

It will be assumed that the transformer shown in Figure 2-11 is a step-down transformer and the

480-V winding is used as the secondary. The *CEC Part 1* indicates that for transformers rated at 750 V or more, a fuse rated at 150% of the rated primary current (or next higher standard size if the rated primary current does not correspond to a standard size) may be used.

Example

$I = 15\ 000 / 2400$

$I = 6.25$ A

The fuse size will be:

$6.25 \times 1.5 = 9.375$ A

Transformers Rated 600 V or Less

Protection for transformers rated 600 V or less is stipulated by *CEC Part 1* Rules 26-254 and 26-256, depending on whether it is a dry-type transformer or oil-filled transformer. When protecting a dry-type transformer on the primary side, the protection must consist of an individual overcurrent device rated at 125% of the rated primary current. If 125% of the primary current does not correspond to a standard fuse or circuit breaker, the next higher standard fuse or breaker may be used.

When selecting overcurrent protection for a dry-type transformer, Appendix B of the *CEC Part 1* contains the following recommendation to prevent nuisance tripping of the overcurrent devices:

> Select an overcurrent device that can carry 12 times the rated primary current of the transformer for a minimum of 0.1 seconds and 25 times the rated primary current for a minimum of 0.01 seconds.

When protecting a dry-type transformer using protective devices in both the primary and secondary circuits, Rule 26-256(2) applies.

Coordination

Coordination is the process of selecting protective devices so that there is a minimum of power interruption in case of a fault or overload. In other words, for a particular situation, a value of high-voltage fuse should be selected that ensures that other protective devices between it and the loads can react to a given condition in less time.

Coordination studies require that the time–current characteristic charts of the different protective devices be compared and that the selection of the proper devices be made accordingly. Problems in the coordination of high-voltage fusing occur most frequently when:

1. Circuit breakers are used as secondary protective devices, and
2. A single main protective device is installed on the secondary side of the transformer. This subject will be covered in detail in Unit 12.

THE TRANSFORMER SECTION

There is little difference between the transformer in a unit substation and any other power transformer (see the connection diagram in Figure 2-12). However, the topic of transformer taps should be explained in some detail.

Taps

Although voltage systems are generally classified by a voltage value, such as a 2300-V or a 4160-V system, this exact value is rarely the voltage provided at the transformer. To compensate for this

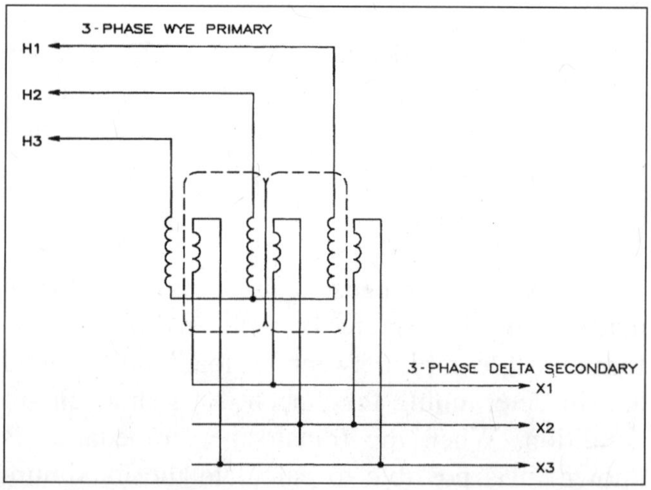

Figure 2-12 Three-phase power transformer delta connection diagram.

probable voltage difference, taps are built into the transformer (Figure 2-13). These taps are usually provided at 2.5% increments above and below the standard rated voltage. For example, taps on a 4160/480-V transformer may provide for voltages of 3952 V, 4056 V, 4160 V, 4264 V, and 4368 V. Connections at the proper voltage levels will provide the desired 480 V on the secondary.

The Low-Voltage Section

After the incoming voltage is reduced to the desired value, it is taken by busbars into the low-voltage section. Here, protective devices are installed to distribute the voltage throughout the area to be served. Numerous variations in the arrangements of these devices are possible depending upon the needs of the installation. A main device can be installed to interrupt the total power or any combination of main and feeder devices can be used.

GROUNDING

The majority of the connections to ground are made in the low-voltage section. However, the electrician should be aware that a grounding bus usually runs the entire length of the unit substation. This bus provides the means for a positive ground connection between the compartments, as well as a convenient place to make other ground

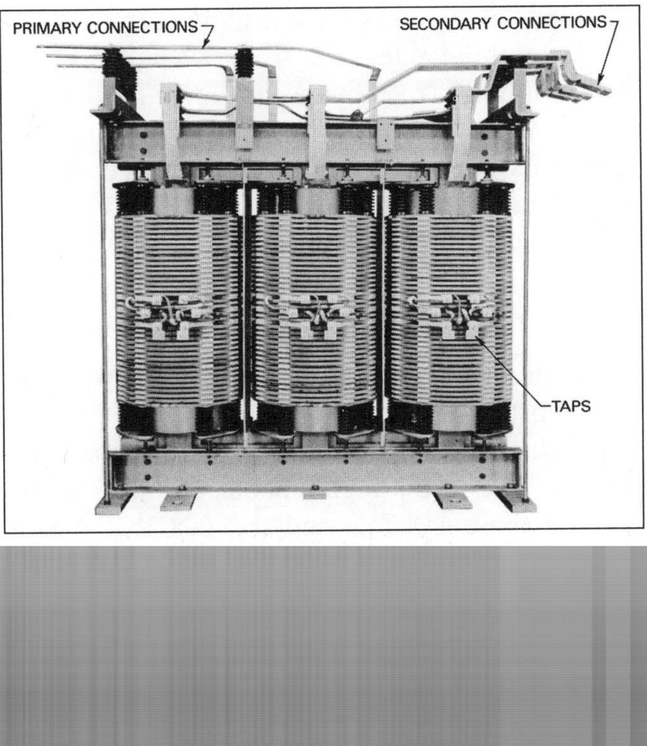

connections. Two types of grounding connections are of special interest. The system grounding connection is used to connect a phase or the neutral of the transformer secondary to ground. This system grounding conductor is sized according to *CEC Part 1* Rule 10-812 and Table 17.

The second grounding connection of special interest is the connection of all the incoming metal raceways to the grounding system. There are no problems in grounding when the raceways enter the substation through the metal structure. However, when a raceway enters through the base of the unit, a grounding connection must be installed between the conduit and the grounding system. This conductor is sized according to *CEC Part 1* Rule 10-814 and Table 16.

Ground Detectors

If the distribution system in an industrial building is a three-phase, three-wire delta system, the system will incorporate ground detectors (Figure 2-14) to detect any unintentional system grounding. It should be noted that if a conductor makes contact with ground at any point, the entire system is grounded. Such a ground may not be an effective ground connection but will result in unusual voltage readings. However, if a second ground occurs on a different phase, this effectively short-circuits the two phases and serious equipment damage can result.

The ground detector system in Figure 2-14 consists of three lamps connected as shown. The lamps used have the same voltage ratings as the

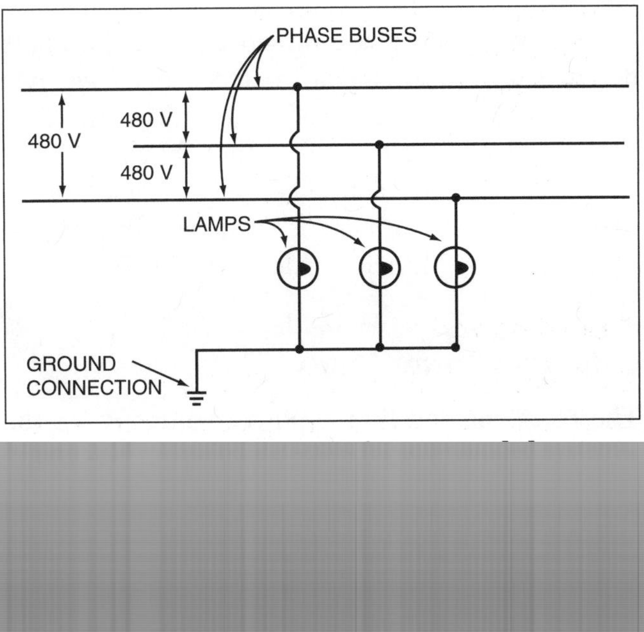

line-to-line voltage. The lamps light dimly when there are no grounded conductors. If any phase becomes grounded, however, the lamp connected to that phase dims even more or goes out entirely while the other two lamps become brighter. Thus, a quick visual check by maintenance personnel can determine whether a ground has developed.

Metering Equipment

The specifications for the industrial building indicate that to provide for energy use measurements, two 35-mm conduits must be run from the metering sections of the switchboard to a cabinet located in the main electrical room (Figure 2-15).

The meters are mounted on a backplate and installed by the utility. The meters and metering equipment are owned by the utility. This installation also includes power monitoring equipment mounted in the main switchboard so the owner can follow consumption patterns and provide corrective action if peak demand is too high or the plant power factor is too low.

Figure 2-16 shows metering connections from a 4160-V system. The autotransformer is designed to provide voltage components of the proper magnitude and at the correct phase angles to the potential coils of the reactive meter (to be described shortly). These voltage components are 90° out of phase with the line voltage. The left-hand meter socket is wired to receive a standard socket-type watthour meter that measures active kilowatt hours. The right-hand meter socket will receive a reactive varhour (volt-amperes-reactive) meter. This second meter measures reactive kilovarhours.

The two meters are provided with 15-minute demand attachments. The meters each have two elements and maximum ratings of 150 V and 5 A. The two demand attachments (not shown) register the demand in kilowatts and kilovars for the respective meters if the demand is sustained for a period of more than 15 minutes at any one time.

Industrial Power Rates

The rates charged by the power company for the energy used are based on the readings of the meter

Figure 2-15 Meter cabinet.

registers and the maximum demand indicators. Some power companies charge a penalty if the power factor falls below a certain level, as indicated in the example shown in Figure 2-16, Note 3. Assume that the reactive meter reading is one-half the kilowatt-hour reading. Thus, the tangent of the phase angle is 5/10 or 0.5, and the cosine of the phase angle is 0.9. As a result, no penalty is imposed by the power company because the power factor is 90%.

If the power factor is unity (1.00), it is evident that the reactive meter (varhour meter) indicating disc is stationary. However, if the power factor falls below unity, then the varhour meter disc will rotate in one direction for a lagging current and in the opposite direction for a leading current.

Preferential rates are given when the power transformer is owned by the customer. Further rate reductions may be made when the metering measurements are taken on the high-voltage side of the transformer.

Outdoor Substations

For medium and large industrial applications, outdoor substations are used (Figure 2-17).

High-voltage installations require special precautions due to the high amount of energy available on these systems and the fact that merely being in proximity to an uninsulated live high-

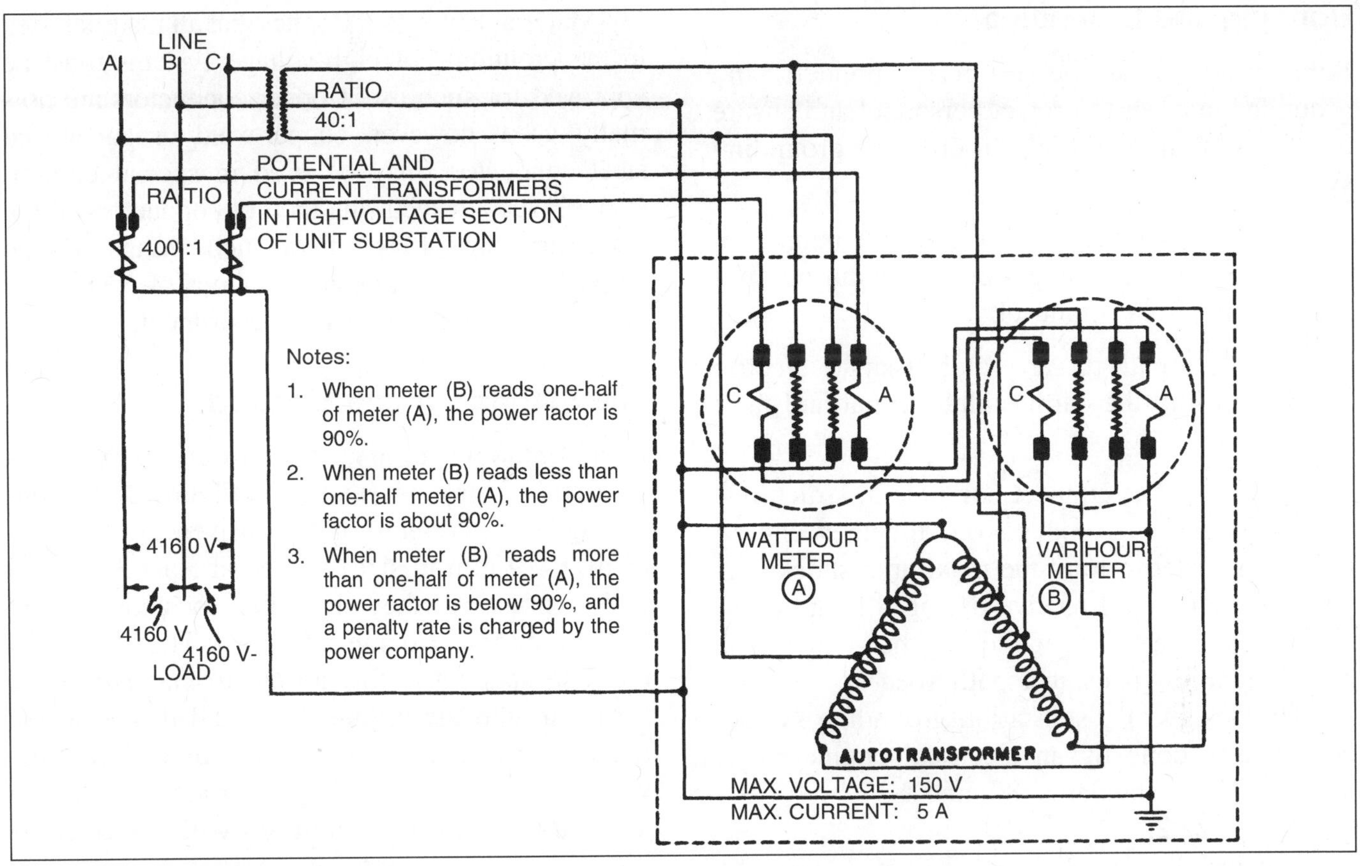

Figure 2-16 Connections for high-voltage metering of watthours and varhours.

voltage conductor can be a threat to life. Some of the special precautions include fences and barriers to keep unauthorized persons away from the equipment, and special signs (Danger, High voltage, Do not open under load, etc.), installation, bonding, and grounding requirements to protect personnel working around or inside the station.

Section 36 of the *CEC Part 1* applies to all installations operating at 750 V or more and describes wiring methods, bonding and grounding procedures, and control and protective equipment that apply to systems operating at 750 V or more.

Special terminology as defined by the *CEC Part 1* that applies to high-voltage installations:

- Step voltage—The potential difference between two points on the earth's surface separated by a distance of one metre, in the direction of maximum voltage gradient.
- Touch voltage—The potential difference between a grounded metal structure and a point on the earth's surface separated by a distance equal to normal maximum horizontal reach.
- Ground grid conductor—A horizontally buried conductor used for interconnecting ground rods or similar equipment that forms the station ground electrode.

Bonding and Grounding

Substations must be properly bonded and grounded in order to protect personnel and ensure reliable station operation. An effective grounding system will:

- Protect personnel by limiting the maximum step and touch voltages produced during fault condition to a safe level.
- Provide a path to carry and dissipate electric current into the earth under normal and fault conditions.

The idea is to connect equipment, structures, operating handles, and so on, together and to ground in order to limit the maximum shock current a person could receive during a fault condition to a safe level while at the same time providing a low-resistance path to earth.

The design of a substation grounding system is normally done by an electrical engineer following IEEE Standards 80 and 837 and CSA Standard C22.2.

The installation of a high-voltage grounding system must meet the job specifications and the requirements of Sections 10 and 36 of the *CEC Part 1*. The procedure required by Rule 36-304 may be found in CEA Report 249 D541—*Simplified Rules For Grounding Customer-Owned High Voltage Substations*.

A substation grounding system consists of a network of bare copper conductors buried horizontally and a number of driven ground rods. Ground rods are used because the resistivity of lower-layer soil is more constant than that of upper-layer soil, which can change because of freezing or dryness. The network must encompass the entire substation and extend one metre beyond the perimeter of the station. Connections to the ground rods must be accessible for inspection and testing purposes.

CEC Requirements

The following outlines the general requirements for substation grounding. It does not cover all applications or special circumstances. For complete information, see Section 36 and Appendix B of the *CEC Part 1*.

Material Rule 36-300 states that all material used in the grounding of high-voltage systems must be approved for such use. Copper conductors are normally used; however, copper-weld or galvanized steel conductors may be used in special circumstances (such as recurring theft of conductors) if the necessary data to confirm such things as the ampacity of conductors and methods of connection are supplied to the inspection department.

The Station Ground Electrode

Every outdoor station must be grounded by means of a station ground electrode (Figure 2-18) consisting of a *minimum* of four driven ground rods (3 m × 19 mm in size) spaced at least 3 m apart and, if practical, they should be located adjacent to the equipment being grounded. The reason for the 3 m spacing is that an electromagnetic shell forms around the ground rods, and if the ground rods are too close together, the shells will interfere with one another. Four ground rods spaced 6 m apart in uniform soil conditions will reduce resistivity 80% over a single ground rod.

The rods must be connected together with 2/0 bare copper wire located a minimum of 150 mm below the finished station grade and not more than 600 mm below the rough station grade. Outdoor stations have a ground surface covering layer of materials such as crushed stone, concrete, or asphalt. Rough station grade occurs where the natural soil stops and the ground surface covering layer starts.

The ground grid must be connected to all non-current-carrying metal parts of equipment and structures and must form a loop around the equipment to be grounded if possible.

Indoor substations are required to be grounded in a manner similar to outdoor substations.

Station Ground Resistance (36-304) The maximum permitted resistance of the station ground electrode is determined by the maximum available fault current of the station. The electrode resistance must limit the voltage rise of all parts of the station (under fault conditions) to 5000 V or less and step and touch voltages to those found in Table 52 of the *CEC*. At the completion of the

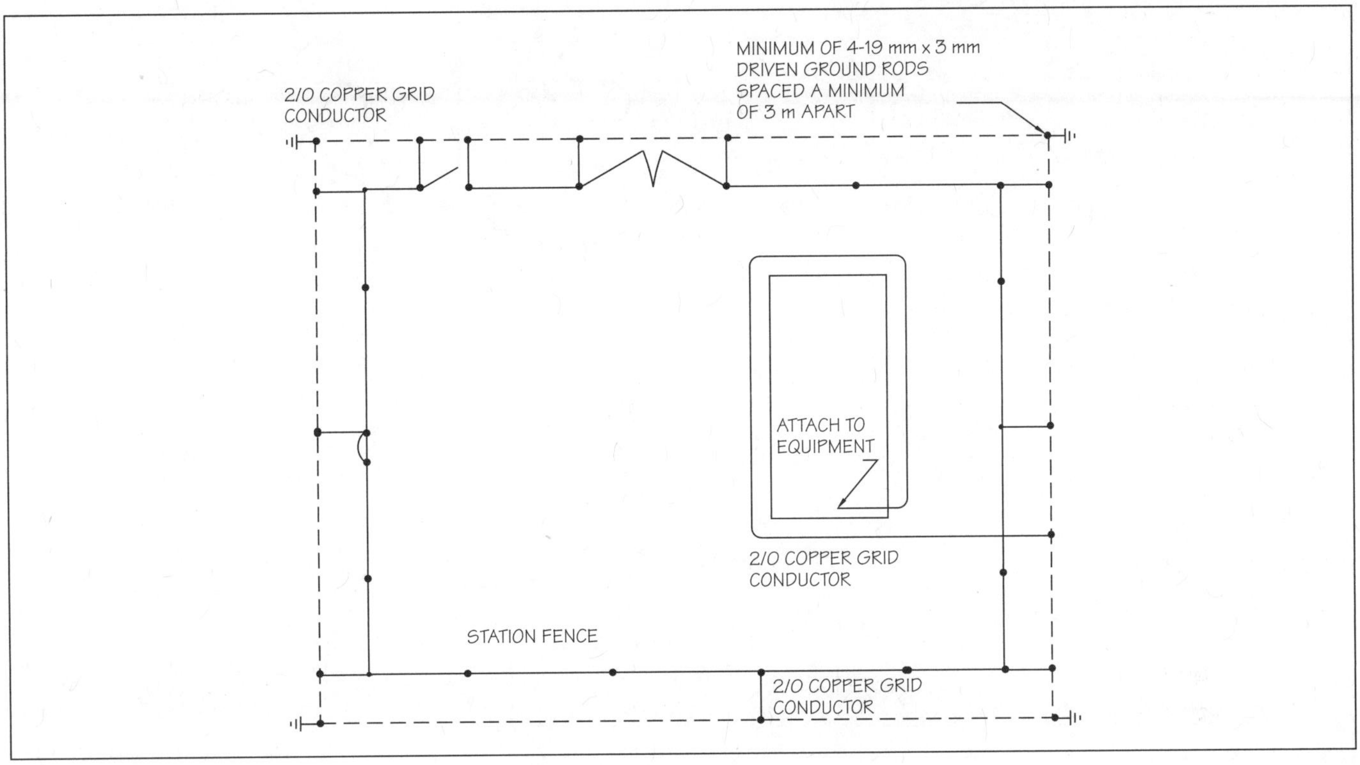

Figure 2-18 Station ground electrode.

installation, the resistance of the station ground must be verified.

Grounding Structures and Equipment (36-308) All non-current-carrying metal equipment and structures must be grounded to the station ground electrode.

Metal structures require a minimum 2/0 copper conductor from each column.

Metal equipment such as tanks, transformer frames, reclosers, and so on, requires a minimum 2/0 copper conductor.

Grounding Gang-Operated Switches (36-308, 310) The metal bases of gang-operated switches—and the operating handles of gang-operated switches not enclosed in metal—must be connected to the station electrode with a minimum 2/0 copper conductor.

A gradient control mat, placed where the operator will stand while operating the switch, must be connected to the operating handle with a minimum of two 2/0 copper conductors.

The gradient control mat is required to be 1.8 m × 1.2 m, must be placed on 150 mm of crushed stone, and may be covered by 150 mm of crushed stone, concrete, or asphalt.

Grounding the Fence (36-312) A minimum 2/0 copper conductor tap conductor must run from the station ground electrode to each corner post, end post, and gate post. Intermediate posts must be grounded at intervals that do not exceed 12 m.

The gate post must be connected to the gate by means of a flexible copper conductor not less than 2/0 in size.

The fence is grounded by connecting a minimum 2/0 copper conductor to the fence post and bottom tension wire, weaving the conductor through the fence at a minimum of two places, then connecting the conductor to the top fence rail and the barbed wire strands. The fence rails must be bonded together with a minimum 2/0 copper conductor. (See Figure 2-19 on page 28.)

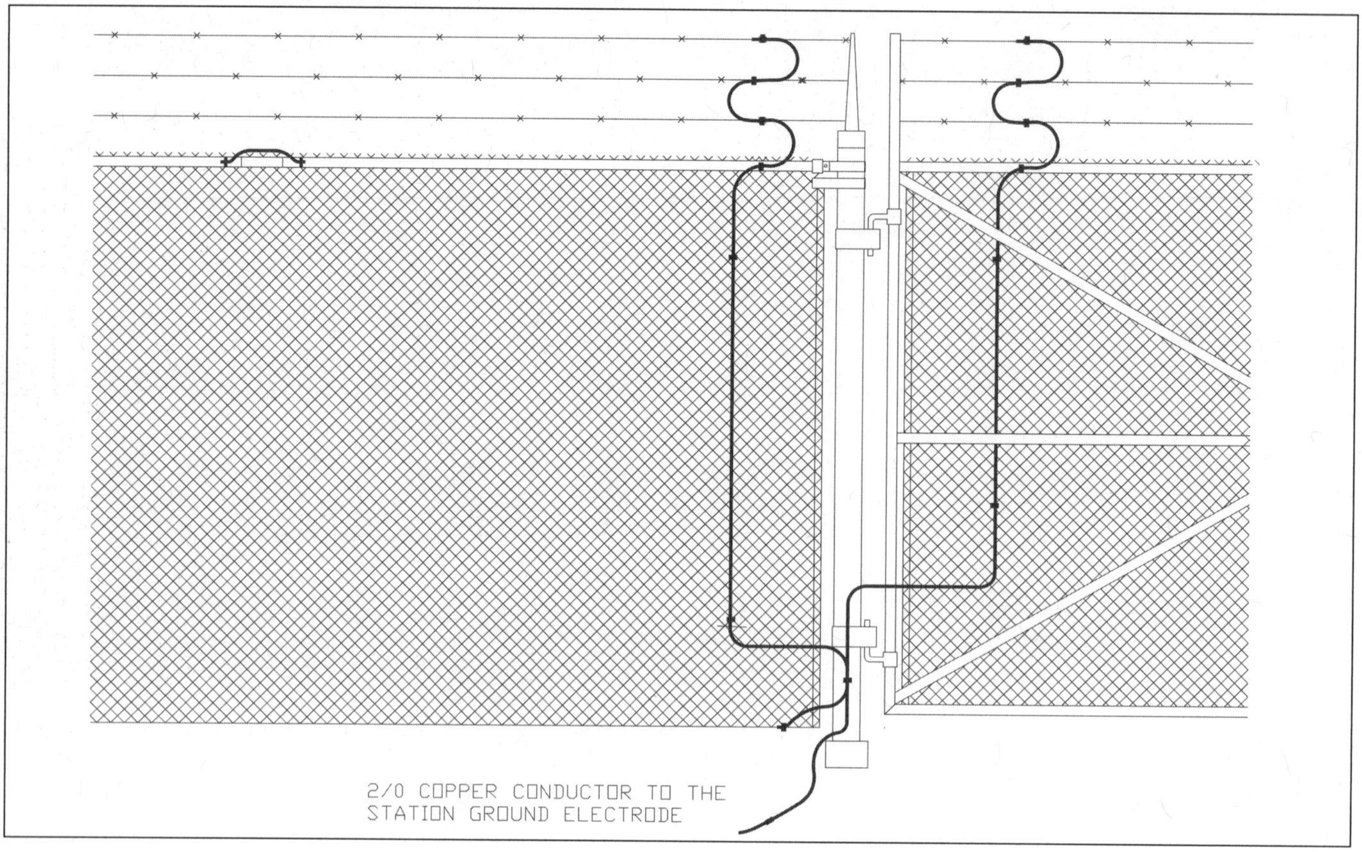

Figure 2-19 Grounding of substation fence.

Grounding Surge Arresters Surge arresters are required to be connected to the station ground electrode with a minimum 2/0 copper conductor.

The grounding conductor must be as short, straight, and direct as possible.

Other Connections Other connections to the station ground electrode include such things as transmission line overhead ground wires, non-current carrying parts of metal equipment such as cable tray, raceways, and exposed metal work on buildings, grounded neutral conductors, and transformer neutrals. See Figure 2-20 for typical switch handle grounding.

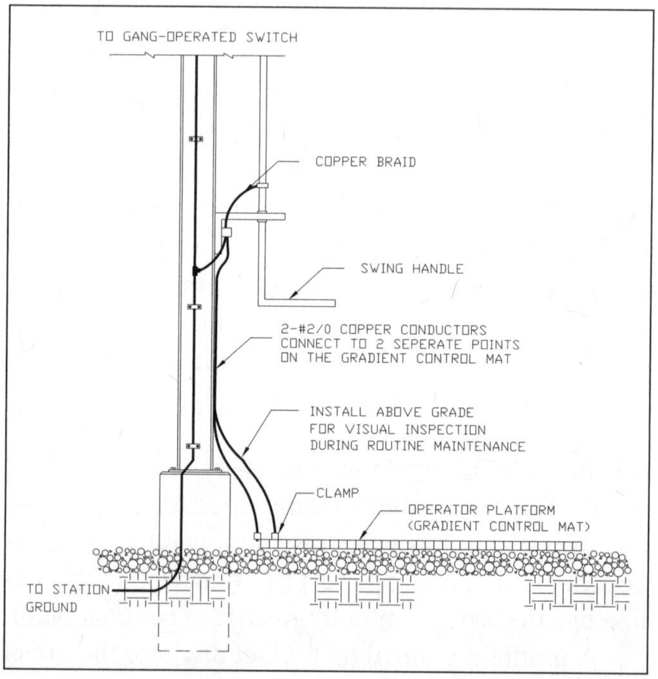

Figure 2-20 Typical switch handle grounding.

UNDERGROUND DUCTS

The installation of underground ducts must meet the requirements of Section 12 of the *CEC Part 1*. See Figures 2-21 and 2-22 for rough-ins of duct banks. When installing duct banks, the following points should be considered.

Figure 2-21 Rough-in of duct bank at low-voltage switchgear.

Figure 2-22 Rough-in of duct banks at pad-mounted transformers.

- Use only CSA-approved conduits and supports.
- Ensure that ducts are laid as straight as possible. Dips in ducts can cause them to hold water, and trapped water can freeze and damage cables. Runs should also be sloped to drain away any water that seeps into them.
- Use as few bends as possible. The more bends used, the higher the pulling force required. Long runs with many bends may exceed the maximum pulling tension that may be applied to the cable.
- Ducts entering handholes or manholes should line up both vertically and horizontally.

Manholes

Manholes (Figure 2-23 on page 30) and handholes are used in underground installations to install, splice, and rearrange cables. Manholes come in various shapes and sizes. They must be large enough to permit the installation of cables and provide proper support for the cables. They are normally made of precast concrete. The distance

When working in a manhole, remember that it is a confined space. Entry into confined spaces without proper precautions can result in injury or death. Before entering a confined space you should:

- Obtain a confined space entry permit.
- Read and observe the entry permit requirements.
- Obtain and use protective equipment required by the permit.
- Test the atmosphere.
- Monitor the atmosphere during the entry.
- Have an attendant stationed outside the workspace.
- Stay alert to hazards that may be found in a confined space.

Immediately exit the confined space if ordered to do so by the attendant; an automatic alarm sounds; you notice signs of dizziness, blurred vision, or shortness of breath in you or others; or

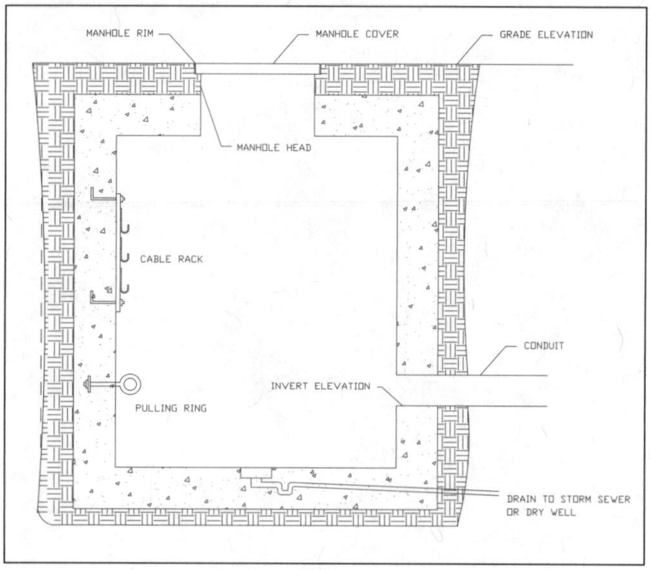

Figure 2-23 Manhole.

INSTALLING UNDERGROUND CABLES

The installation of underground cables is covered by Rules 6-300, 12-012, and 12-112, and Table 53.

When installing cables in underground raceways, the following items should be observed.

- Determine the direction of the pull based on safe pulling tensions.
- Select the correct size pulling eyes or grips.
- Select a pulling rope that has low stretch characteristics and adequate breaking strength.
- Install a dynamometer to measure pulling tension.
- Prior to pulling the cable, swab out the conduit to ensure that it is clean and free of debris.
- For long, heavy pulls, pre-lubricate the conduit.
- Locate the cable reels in such a manner as to minimize pulling tension.
- Provide radios or cell phones for communication on long runs.
- Apply a pulling lubricant according to the manufacturer's directions.
- Try to avoid stopping the pull partway through the run.
- As soon as the cables are installed, seal the ends of the cable to prevent the entrance of moisture.
- Check the cables with a megger after the installation. See discussion in Unit 6.

Medium-Voltage Cables

Unshielded cable is normally used for voltages up to 2000 V. Above 2000 V, a conductor shield is required. At voltages above 5 kV, an insulation shield is required. When power cable is referred to as *shielded*, it means it has an insulation shield. A shielded cable is defined as an insulated conductor enclosed in a non-magnetic conducting envelope, which is constructed in such a manner as to maintain every point on the cable at ground potential or some predetermined point with respect to ground.

Medium-voltage cables may have copper or aluminum conductors (Figure 2-24). Stranded conductors may be compressed, compacted, or segmented. This will affect the overall diameter of the conductor as well as its flexibility and load current density.

The conductor shield is a semi-conductor material that helps to provide a uniform dielectric field around the conductor by preventing the field from being distorted by the shape of the outer strands of the conductor.

Common insulations in medium-voltage cables are ethylene propylene rubber and cross-linked polyethylene.

The insulation shield is a two-part system consisting of a semi-conducting tape and a metallic shield of wire or tape. The insulation shield:

- Equalizes voltage stresses on the insulation
- Confines the electric field within the cable
- Limits electrostatic and electromagnetic interference
- Conducts leakage currents to ground

The metallic shield carries the insulation's leakage current, any short current, and, in the case of concentric neutral cables, the system neutral current.

Copper tape metal shields are used mainly for industrial cables, while concentric neutral metal shields are used on underground utility distribution cables.

The cable jacket will normally be an extruded synthetic material such as linear low-density poly-

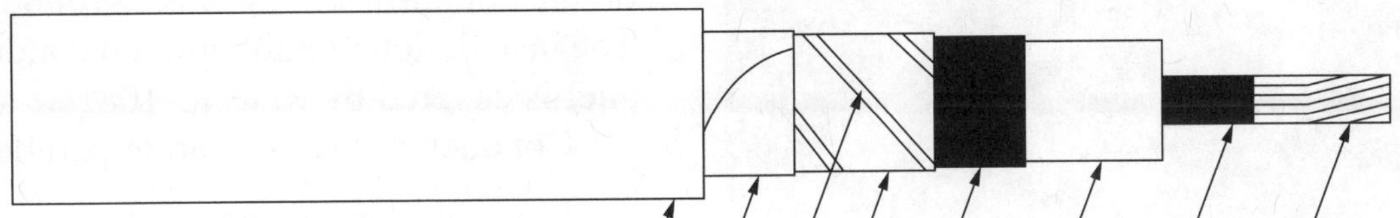

Figure 2-24 Medium-voltage cable.

ethylene and may have additional metal sheath wires or armouring.

The voltage rating of a cable is based on the thickness of the insulation and the type of system to which the cable is connected.

- 100% voltage level—grounded neutral system, ground faults are cleared within one minute
- 133% voltage level—formerly designated as an ungrounded system, cables in this category are applied when ground faults are cleared within one hour
- 173% voltage level—these cables should be applied to systems where faults exist for an unlimited time.

Cable manufacturers have agreed to standard voltage classifications of 5 kV, 15 kV, 25 kV, 35 kV, 46 kV, and 69 kV.

Terminating Medium-Voltage Cables

When medium-voltage cables are terminated, the insulation shield is removed. (See Figure 2-25 on page 32.) At the point where the insulation shield ends, there is a sudden change in the dielectric field that results in a concentration of electrical stresses on the insulation at that point. This can cause the insulation to break down and the cable to fail.

To prevent this, shielded cable terminations must be made using a stress cone or device with a high dielectric constant. Stress cones provide stress control by expanding the diameter of the cable at the point where the insulation shield ends, resulting in a reduction of the stress at that spot. If a device with a high dielectric constant is placed over the point at which the insulation shield ends, it will reduce the stress on the insulation by bending the electrical flux lines at that point on the cable. This is due to the difference in the K-values of the two neighbouring dielectric layers. High-K termination kits are more commonly used today than stress cones because of savings on labour costs and reductions in the chance of error. The exact procedure to follow is determined by each manufacturer. General procedures to be followed for a silicone rubber termination kit include the following:

- Follow personal safety procedures strictly.
- Ensure the cable is not energized before proceeding.

Figure 2-25 Terminated medium-voltage cables in pad-mounted transformer.

- Prepare the cable, by removing the outer jacket, semi-conductor, and insulation to the length specified by the termination assembly manufacturer.
- Bundle together the concentric neutrals and twist until tight when preparing the neutrals. Remove tape or corrugated shields by following the manufacturer's instructions.
- Apply bottom mastic seal and ground braid.
- Install cable lug using an approved crimping tool and die.
- Install termination onto the cable and remove core, allowing termination to shrink into place.
- Connect ground braids to system ground.

Low-Voltage Feeders

Low-voltage parallel feeders run from the pad-mounted transformers to the low-voltage switchgear located in the electrical room. Refer to Drawing E9 for details of the duct bank and conductor sizes. Figures 2-21 and 2-22 show details of the rough-in of the underground duct banks. The installation of underground conductors in parallel is covered by Rule 12-108.

Conductors that are run in parallel must:

- Have similar conductivity
- Be free of splices throughout their length
- Have the same circular mil area
- Have the same type of insulation
- Be terminated in the same manner

Allowable Conductor Ampacities

The allowable ampacity of conductors in an underground run is covered by Rule 4-004, 1(d) and 2(d), and Appendices B and D of the *CEC Part 1*.

When determining conductor ampacity, the following guidelines should be used:

- To use the tables in Appendix D, the installation configuration of the conduits and cables should conform to those in Appendix B (Diagrams B4-1 to B4-4).
- When using copper conductors, refer to Tables D8, 9, 13, and 15. If aluminum conductors are used, use Tables D10, 11, 14, and 16.
- Determine whether the load is continuous or non-continuous. If the load is continuous and either end of the cable terminates at a service box, circuit breaker, fusible switch, or panelboard, use the "B" tables. For all other applications, use the "A" tables.

EXAMPLE What is the ampacity of each conductor in an underground installation consisting of four runs of four #500 kcmil copper conductors in PVC ducts that are supplied from a 347/600 V system? The cables run from a pad-mounted transformer to a switchboard located in the building and terminate in a circuit breaker.

Using Diagram B4-4 and Table D14B, the allowable ampacity of the conductors is 319 amps.

The allowable ampacity of the run is 319 × 4 = 1276 A.

CABLE PULLING TENSION

Pulling tension should be calculated prior to the installation of cables. Cable manufacturers provide guidelines for calculating pulling tensions on cables and there are a number of computer programs that can be used to calculate cable pulling tensions.

Some of the parameters that are taken into consideration when calculating pulling forces with computer programs are:

- Weight of the cable
- Coefficient of friction
- Number of bends
- Raceway size
- Cable configuration
- Jamming potential
- Sidewall bearing pressure

Cable manufacturers or electrical wholesalers can provide data on:

- The maximum pulling force permitted on the cable
- The weight of the cable per foot or per metre
- The expected pulling friction of the cable

Maximum Pulling Tension

The maximum allowable pulling tension exerted on a cable with a pulling eye may be found from the formula:

$$T_m = \text{K} \times n \times CMA$$

where

T_m = Maximum pulling tension expressed in kilograms

K = A constant: 0.003 64 for copper, and 0.0027 for aluminum

n = number of conductors

CMA = Circular mil area for one conductor

Example What is the maximum allowable pulling tension that may be exerted on (a) a single 1/0 copper conductor, (b) three 1/0 copper conductors?

(a) For one 1/0 copper conductor.

$$T_m = \text{K} \times n \times CMA$$
$$= 0.003\,64 \times 1 \times 105\,500 = 383 \text{ kg}$$

(b) For three 1/0 copper conductors

$$T_m = \text{K} \times n \times CMA$$
$$= 0.003\,64 \times 3 \times 105\,500 = 1152 \text{ kg}$$

If a cable grip is used to pull non-lead jacketed cable, the pulling tension should not exceed 454 kg (1000 lb) per grip or the manufacturer's recommendations. When cable grips are used, use the lower value of 454 kg per cable grip or the calculated tension from the equation above. For this example, the maximum pulling tension on the three 1/0 conductors would be limited to 454 kg if a single cable grip is used with the three wires. If a pulling eye or three cable grips are used, the maximum pulling tension would be 1152 kg.

Calculating Pulling Tension

For a straight section of conduit, the pulling tension (T_s) is found from:

$$T_s = L \times W \times f$$

where

L = Length in metres

W = Weight of cable per metre

f = Coefficient of friction (when unknown use 0.5)

For a bent section of conduit, the pulling tension after the bend is equal to the pulling tension at the beginning of the bend times the bending coefficient.

$$T_b = T_s \times C_b$$

T_b = Tension after bend

T_s = Tension at start of bend

C_b = Bending coefficient

See Table 2-1 on page 34 for a summary of some common bending coefficients.

Angle of Bend	Bending Coefficient
15°	1.15
22.5°	1.2
30°	1.3
45°	1.5
60°	1.7
75°	1.9
90°	2.2

Table 2-1 Bending coefficients.

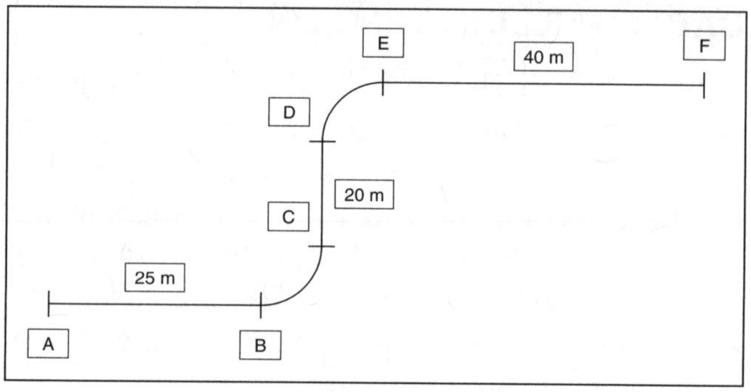

Figure 2-26 Pulling tension example layout.

EXAMPLE Three 1/0 AWG, RW90XLPE copper conductors with weights of 0.55 kg/m each are to be pulled into the layout in Figure 2-26. What is the pulling tension applied to the cable?

Maximum pulling tension on cable:

For three 1/0 copper conductors:

$$T_m = K \times n \times CMA$$
$$= 0.00364 \times 3 \times 105\,500 = 1152 \text{ kg}$$

Pulling from point F (feeding in at A)

Cable weight = 0.55 × 3 = 1.65 kg/m

Pulling tension:

at point A $\quad T_s = 0$

at point B $\quad T_{S1} = L \times W \times f$
$= 25 \times 1.65 \times 0.5$
$= 20.625$ kg

at point C $\quad T_{B1} = T_{S1} \times$ bending coefficient
$= 20.625 \text{ kg} \times 2.2$
$= 45.375$ kg

at point D $\quad T_{S2} = T_{B1} + (L \times W \times f)$
$= 45.375 + (20 \times 1.65 \times 0.5)$
$= 61.875$ kg

at point E $\quad T_{B2} = T_{S2} \times$ bending coefficient
$= 61.875 \text{ kg} \times 2.2$
$= 136.125$ kg

at point F $\quad T_{S3} = T_{B2} + (L \times W \times f)$
$= 136.125 + (40 \times 1.65 \times 0.5)$
$= 169.125$ kg

Pulling from point A (feeding in at F)

Pulling tension:

at point F $\quad Ts = 0$

at point E $\quad T_{S1} = L \times W \times f$
$= 40 \times 01.65 \times 0.5 = 33$ kg

at point D $\quad T_{B1} = T_{S1} \times$ bending coefficient
$= 33 \text{ kg} \times 2.2$
$= 72.6$ kg

at point C $\quad T_{S2} = T_{B1} + (L \times W \times f)$
$= 72.6 + (20 \times 1.65 \times 0.5)$
$= 89.1$ kg

at point B $\quad T_{B2} = T_{S2} \times$ bending coefficient
$= 89.1 \times 2.2$
$= 196.02$ kg

at point A $\quad T_{S3} = T_{B2} + (L \times W \times f)$
$= 196.02 + (20 \times 1.65 \times 0.5)$
$= 212.52$ kg

Pulling in either direction will not exceed the maximum pulling tension of the cable. However, it requires considerably less pulling tension if the cable is fed in at point A and pulled from point F.

REVIEW QUESTIONS

All answers should be written in complete sentences, and calculations should be shown in detail.

1. Draw the diagram of a simple radial system.
2. What are the main advantages and disadvantages of a secondary selective system over a simple radial system?
3. The three main components of a unit substation follow. For each component, name the principal parts and identify their function(s). The parts are listed in Figure 2-8.
   a. High-voltage section
   b. Transformer section
   c. Low-voltage section
4. Explain the operation of ground detectors and identify the situation that would require their use.
5. Describe a station ground electrode.
6. List the procedures to be followed when entering a confined space.
7. Calculate the pulling tension on a run of conduit containing three conductors that weigh 3 kg per metre each. The run consists of a straight section 40 m long, a 90° bend, and a second straight section 25 m long.
8. Why is a stress cone or high-K termination required on medium-voltage shielded cables?

UNIT 3

Busways

OBJECTIVES

After studying this unit, the student should be able to:

- set forth the benefits of using busways
- identify common applications of busways
- list the components of busways
- describe various support systems

BUSWAYS

Modern industrial electrical systems use several methods to transport electrical energy from the source of supply to the points within the plant where panelboards or switchboards are located. These methods may include the use of heavy feeder conductors in raceways, single- or multiconductor cables run in troughs or trays, and busways. A busway is an assembly of copper or aluminum busbars mounted on insulators and enclosed in a ventilated or non-ventilated (enclosed) metal trough. A plug-in busway system is specified and shown on the plans.

Two types of busways are commonly used in industrial buildings: feeder busways and plug-in busways. Feeder busways are used for service entrances and feeder ties between pieces of equipment such as switchboards and MCCs. Feeder busway is available in sizes up to 5000 A. Plug-in busways are used to supply power to multiple loads and provide a flexible distribution system for industrial buildings that frequently change the layout of equipment. (See Figure 3-1.)

Feeder Busway

Feeder busway sections are available in standard 10 ft (3 m) lengths and in other lengths on special order. Numerous fittings can be used to make branches, turn corners (in both the edgewise or flat type of installation), and, in general, follow the contours of a building. See Figure 3-2 on page 38.

The enclosure containing the buses is constructed of two identical ventilated steel halves. When these halves are bolted together, they form a complete housing for the busbars. The busbars are supported on insulators inside the enclosure (Figure 3-3 on page 38).

Feeder busway is constructed of flat, closely spaced, completely insulated, paired-phase busbars enclosed in a ventilated steel casing. Straight sections, elbows, tees, and crosses are standard components available for use so that the duct can be installed horizontally or vertically, edgewise or flat, and can meet any turn or elevation requirements. See Figure 3-4 on page 39. The casing ends of adjacent sections overlap and are bolted together to form a rigid scarf-lap joint.

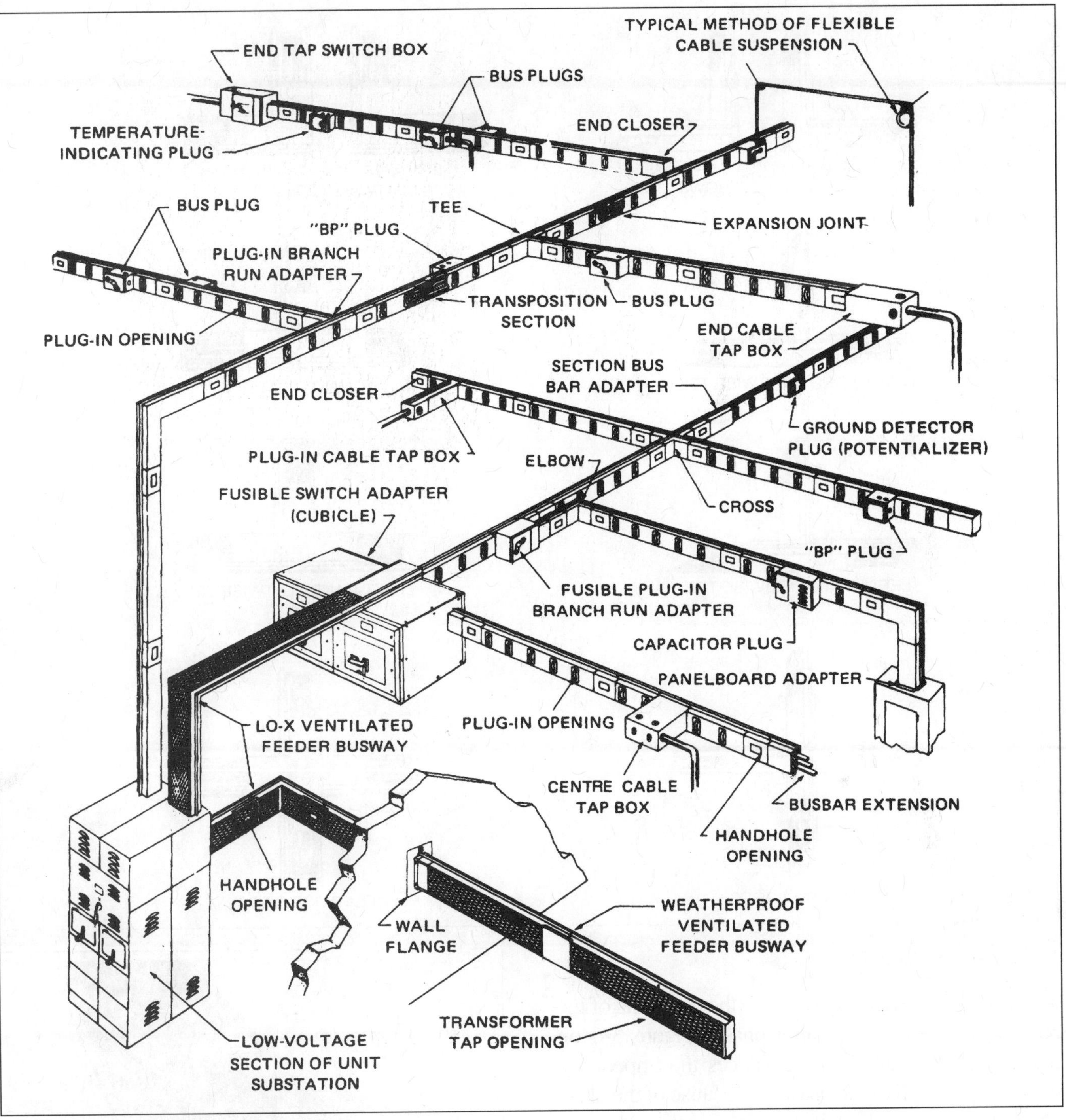

Figure 3-1 Power distribution system.

The flat busbars overlap in the same manner as the casing. The busbars are bolted together with spring washers, cap screws, and splined nuts furnished with the sections. Vinyl plastic snap-on covers insulate the bolted busbar sections (see Figure 3-5 on page 39). There are two busbars per phase for a total of six bars. Each bar measures 1/4 in by 27/16 in (6 mm by 58 mm). The enclosure contains six busbars that are connected together in pairs to form a three-conductor system (Figure 3-6 on page 40).

The connection of the busway to enclosures such as unit substations or switchboards is accomplished with flanged end connections. In addition, these

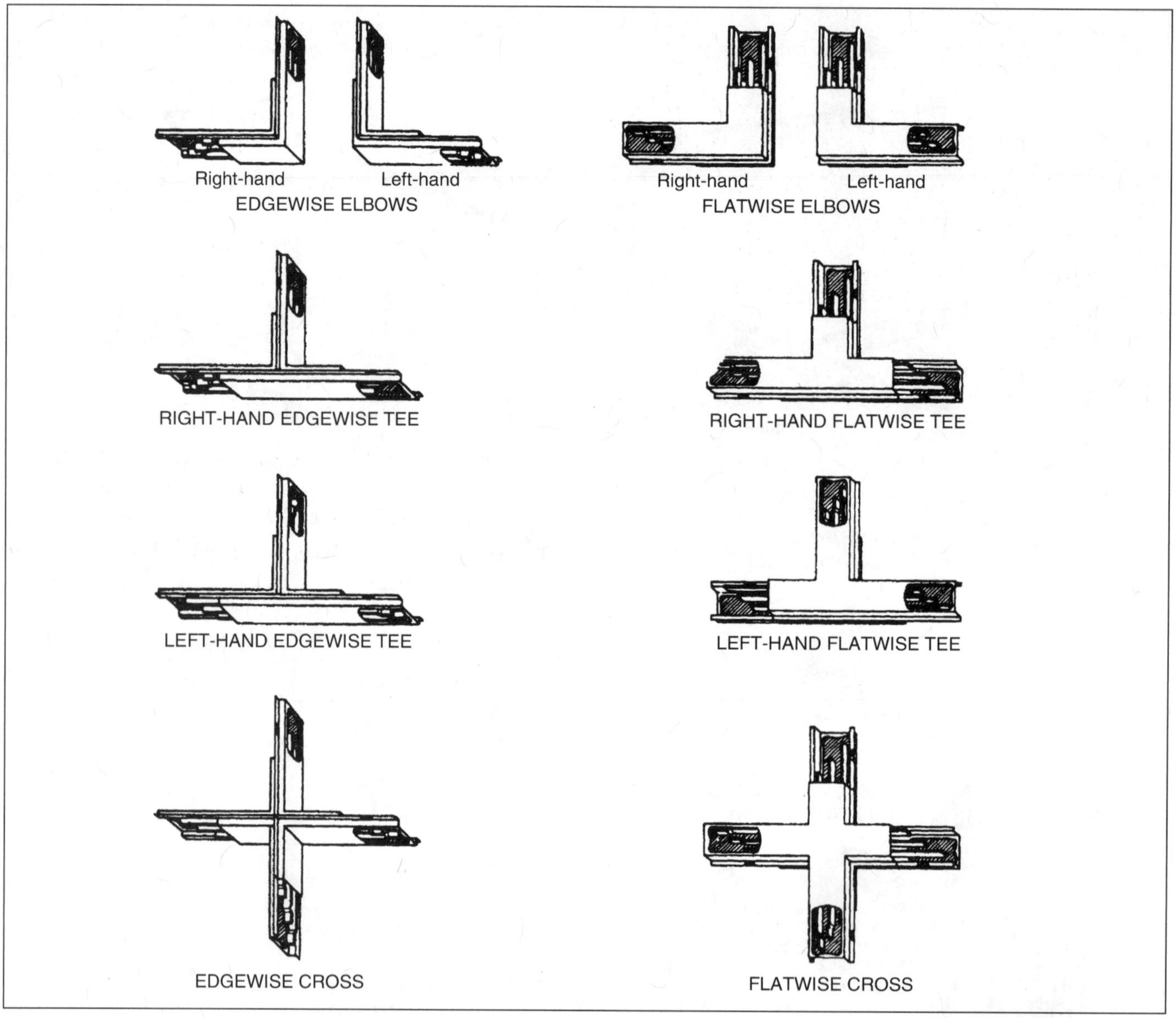

Figure 3-2 Busway fittings.

connections are used to transpose the positions of the buses connected to the same phase (Figure 3-6 on page 40). This transposition reduces the impedance of the total length of the busway. Because of the close phase-to-phase spacing of the busbars, the effects of the magnetic field are reduced and the opposition to the current flow (impedance) is also reduced.

Each busbar has a cross-sectional area of 0.61 sq in (394 sq mm); thus, the total area per phase is 1.22 sq in (788 sq mm). Since the assembly is rated for 1600 A, the current density in the busbars is:

1600 A / 1.22 sq in = 1311 A/sq in (of cross-sectional area)

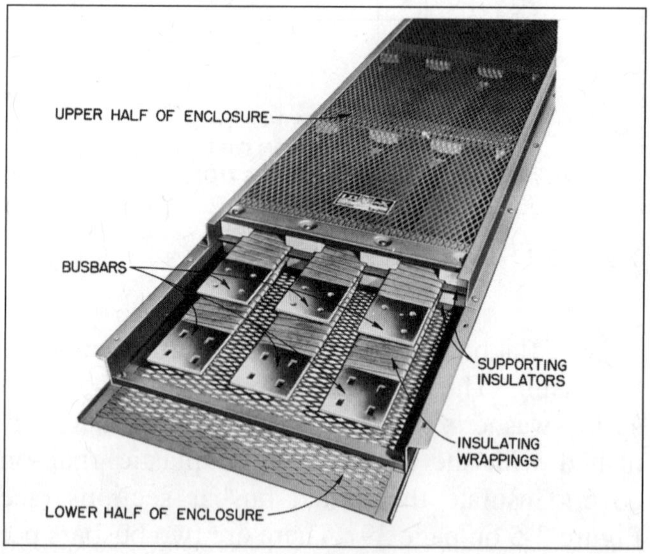

Figure 3-3 Feeder busway section.

Figure 3-4 Outdoor feeder busway.

1600 A / 788 sq mm = 2 A/sq mm

When compared with a standard density value of 1000 A per square inch (1.55 A per square millimetre), the value of transposing the buses to reduce the impedance is evident.

Power can be tapped from the feeder busway at any *handhole opening*. The handhole openings are located at every joint in the enclosure. For standard lengths, the joints and the handhole openings are 10 ft (3 m) apart. Cable tap boxes are used for cable or conduit tapoff or feed-ins at any handhole opening (Figure 3-8 on page 40). Tap box cable lugs and straps (Figure 3-9 on page 40) are provided with each tap box. Fusible switch adapters (cubicles) and circuit-breaker cubicles are available for use when it is necessary to connect loads to the feeder busway.

The Circuit-Breaker Cubicles

Circuit-breaker cubicles are used to connect feeder busways to plug-in busway runs (Figure 3-10 on page 40). The circuit-breaker cubicle consists of a cube-shaped steel housing. This housing can be attached to the lower side of a ventilated feeder duct. Openings in the sides of the cubicle permit the attachment of a plug-in busway. The circuit breakers protect the plug-in duct from overloads as required by the *CEC Part 1*.

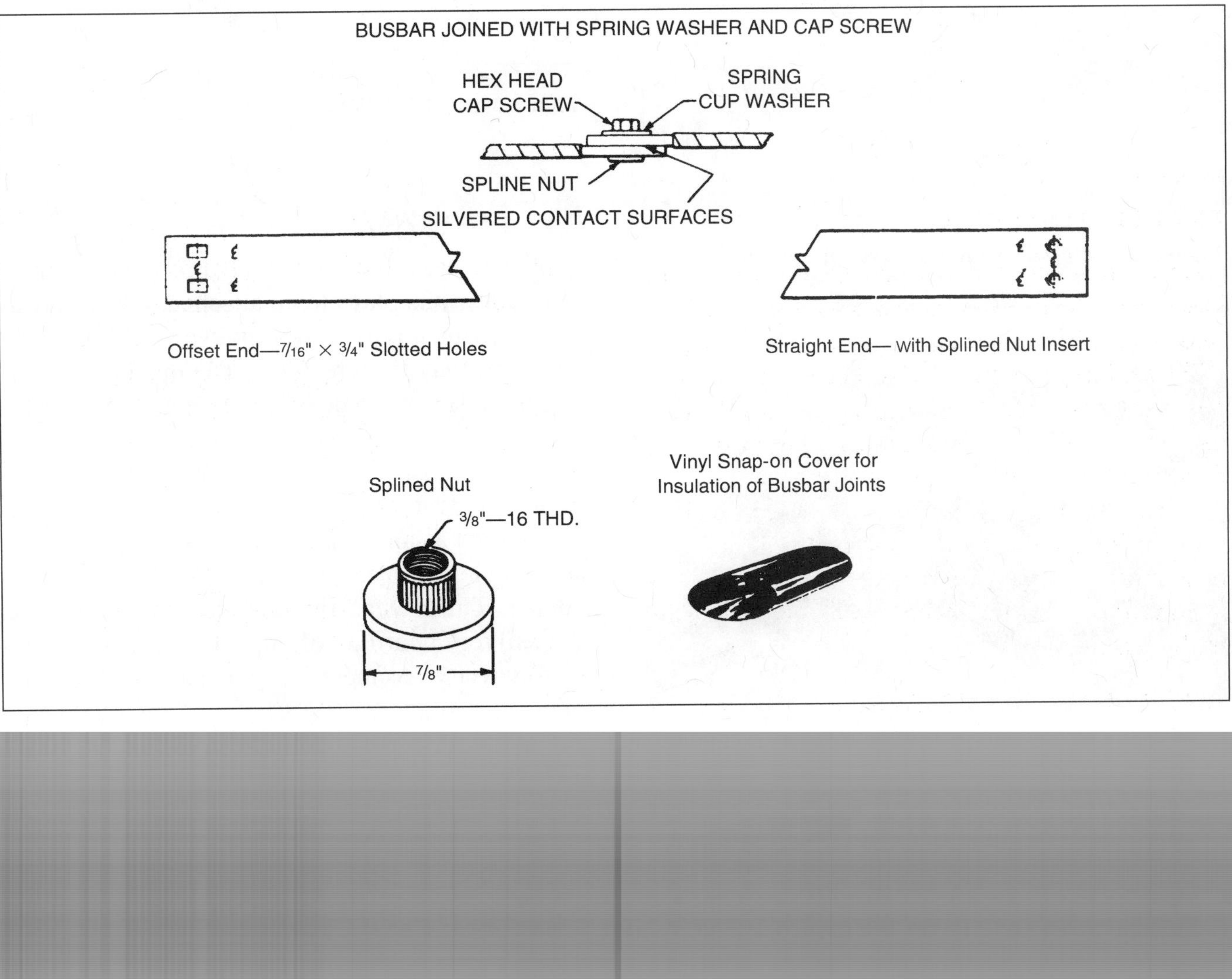

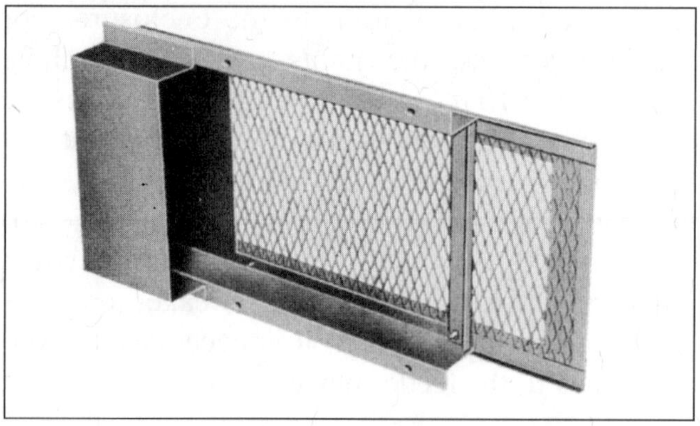

Figure 3-6 End closure of ventilated busway.

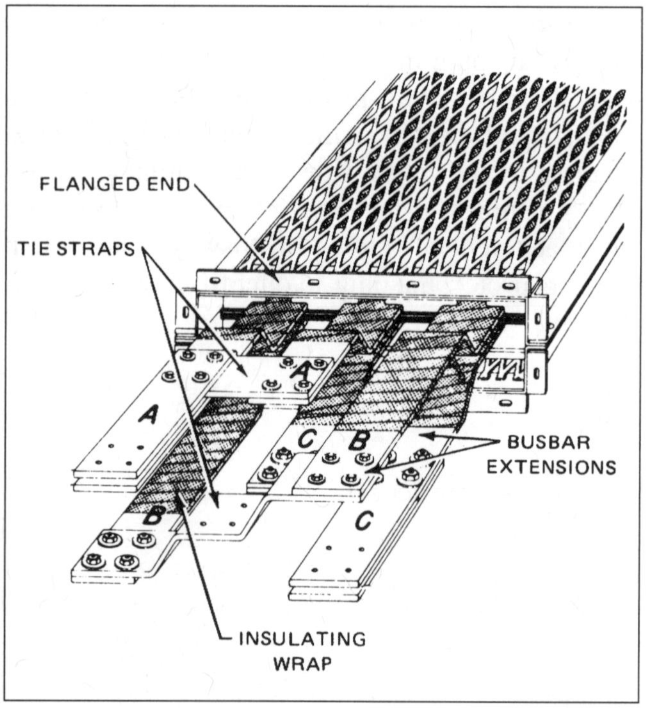

Figure 3-7 Busway showing cross connections of phases.

Figure 3-8 Busway with cable tap box.

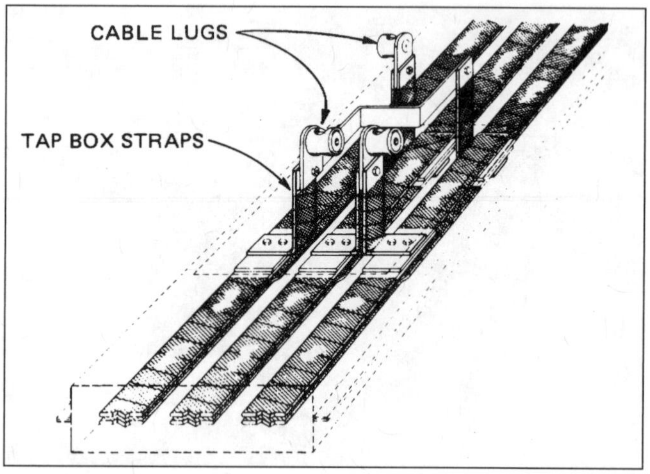

Figure 3-9 Bus extension to facilitate cable connections.

Figure 3-10 Circuit-breaker cubicle.

Plug-in Busway

A plug-in busway is constructed in such a manner as to allow bus plugs to be attached to the busway at approximately 600 mm intervals on both sides of the busway (Figure 3-11). The openings generally include some type of hinged cover to close the opening should the bus plug be removed.

Some busways will have the busbars coated with silver at each connection point. Silver is unequalled as an electrical conductor. In addition, silver is less subject to pitting (corrosion) than is copper. Thus, when the bus plug fingers contact the silver coating of the busbars, a high-conductivity connection is assured. Standard plug-in sections are 10 ft (3 m) in length and consist of two identical formed steel halves that are

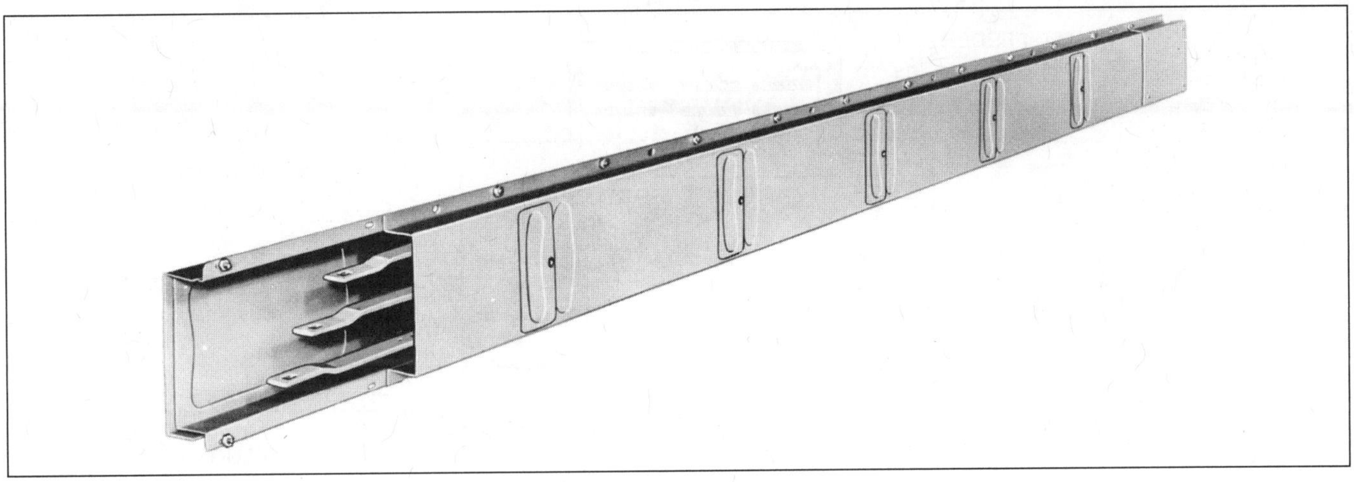

Figure 3-11 Plug-in busway.

bolted together to form the complete outside housing (Figure 3-11). This housing also provides the scarf-lap feature, which permits two adjacent duct sections to overlap each other by 12 in (300 mm). The resulting lap simulates an interlocked joint and provides high rigidity and strength to the assembly (Figure 3-12).

The busway specified for the addition to the industrial building is three-phase duct and is rated at 400 A and 600 V. Ells, tees, and cross sections (or fittings) are available for use when specified by the design or layout. Some of these fittings are shown in Figure 3-2.

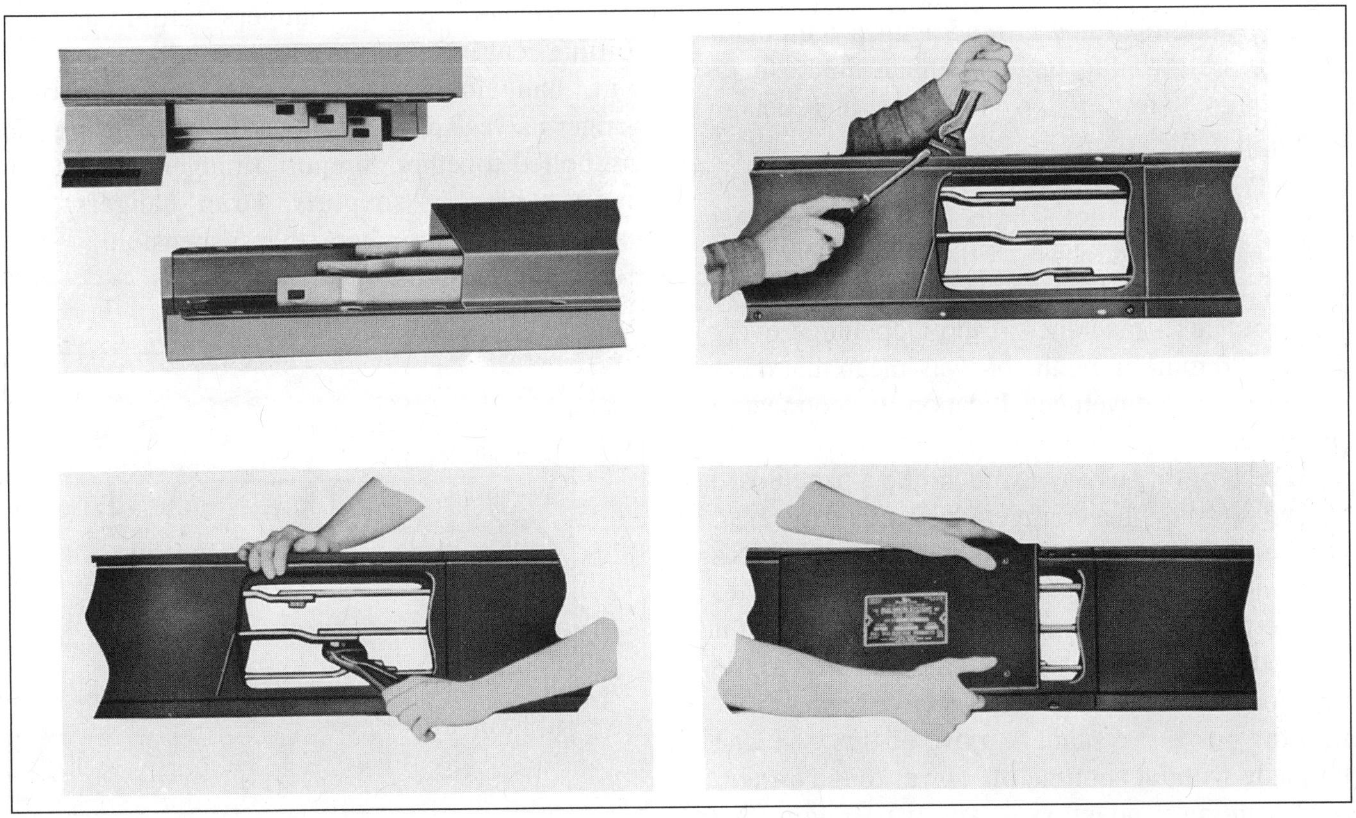

Figure 3-12 Joining plug-in bus duct sections.

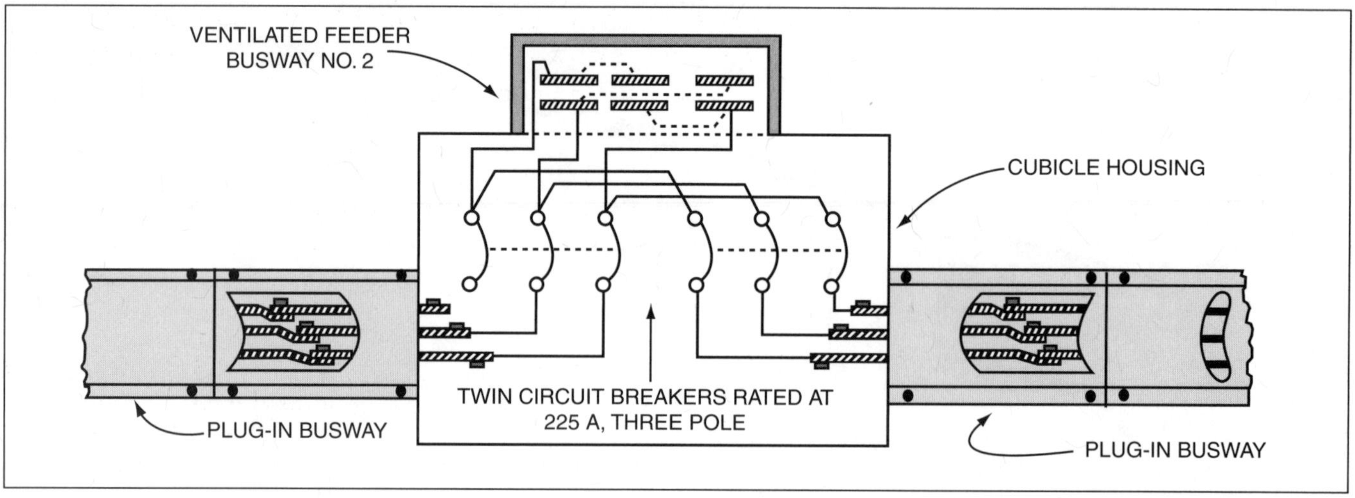

Figure 3-13 Plug-in busway.

Power take-off plug-in openings are spaced at convenient intervals on alternate sides of the enclosure. (Each side has the same number of openings.) Bus plugs can be inserted into any one of these openings. In this manner, branch circuits can be dropped to any item of equipment requiring electric power. The design of the bus plugs is such that they ground against the enclosure before the plug fingers contact the busbars. Additional safety is provided by this design during plug insertion (Figure 3-13).

A plug-in busway is used to provide a flexible tapoff means for motor branch circuits. In other words, the plug-in busway transports electrical energy from the switchboard to the locations of the production machines. Tapoff openings every 12 in (300 mm) along the busway mean that there is always a convenient location to connect a machine.

The plug-in busway is much like a panelboard extending through a complete load area. However, the busway system is much more flexible. If a machine is to be moved from one location to another, it is a simple matter to unplug the circuit protective device, move it and the machine to the new location, and plug the protective device back into the busway system. A move of this type can be made without shutting off power to the system or disrupting production in any way. Figure 3-1 shows a typical power distribution system.

METHODS OF SUSPENSION

There is an almost unlimited number of methods for hanging or supporting the plug-in busway. Support arrangements are shown in Figure 3-14, which illustrates some of the more common methods of hanging sections using clamp hangers. Prefabricated clamp hangers eliminate the drilling, cutting, or bending generally associated with hangers constructed on the job. Clamp hanger halves are slipped over the duct casing and are bolted together. Support arrangements shown include bracket supports, strap hangers, rod hangers, and messenger cable suspension.

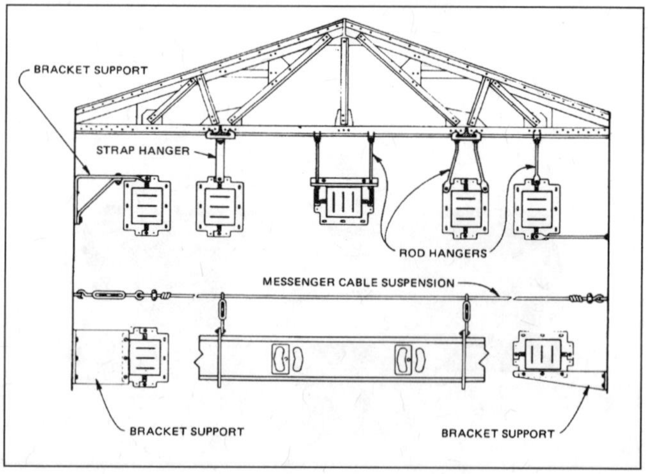

Figure 3-14 Support methods for busway.

The busway used in the industrial building is supported by rods and messenger cables. These cables, in turn, are supported from the overhead structure. The busways are all supported at intervals of 5 ft (1.5 m) or less in accordance with *CEC Part 1*.

Bus Plugs

One bus plug (Figure 3-15) must be furnished for each machine in the manufacturing area of the plant. According to the plans and specifications for the industrial building, there are 111 machines to be supplied with power from the plug-in system. The numbers and sizes of the bus plugs required are summarized in Table 3-1.

The bus plugs provide branch-circuit protection for each of the machines and must be selected according to the specific requirements of the individual machines. The plug-in devices are identified on Sheet E4 of the plans with regard to the type of machine tool to be supplied. More detailed information is given in the specifications. One advantage of the fusible plug-in unit is that a minimum number of sizes is needed. The plug-in unit size is based on the switch ampere rating. In addition, the protective device rating can be easily changed. Where such devices are located out of reach of the machine operators, suitable means must be provided for operating the disconnect.

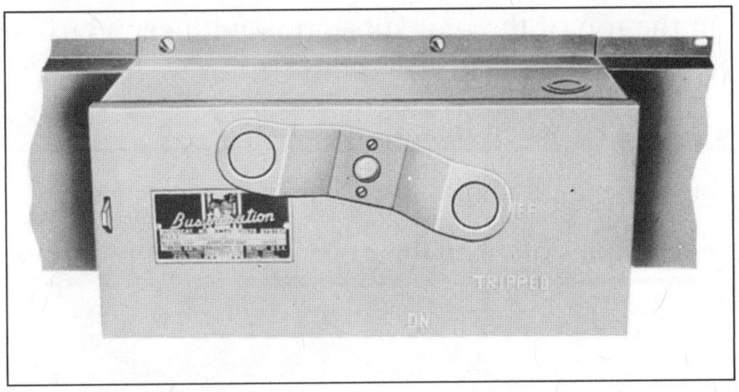

Figure 3-15 Bus plug.

Number of Bus Plugs Required	Switch Rating, Amperes
13	30
1	60

Table 3-1 Number and size of required bus plugs.

Layout and Measurement of Busway Installations

1. From the drawings, specifications, and manufacturer's data sheets, determine:

- Rating of the busway (e.g., 1000 A 600 V 3PH 4 W 50%GND Aluminum Feeder Busway)
- Points of termination

Example Switchboard 1

- Height 92″ (2337 mm), width 36″ (914.4 mm), depth 36″ (914.4 mm)
- Busway connection top centre

Switchboard 2

- Height 92″ (2337 mm), width 36″ (914.4 mm), depth 36″ (914.4 mm)
- Busway connection top centre
- Mounting height of busway—The busway should be routed above the bottom cord of the building steel to protect the busway from damage by forklifts and cranes.
- Dimensions of the busway—for example, H 5.88″(149 mm) W 5.34″ (136 mm)

2. Prepare a single line isometric drawing showing the proposed busway layout. Note the:

- Portions of the run in which the busway is mounted flatwise, edgewise, or vertically
- Locations of walls and thicknesses
- Types of hangers required
- Flanges required
- Locations and types of tees, ells, reducers, expansion joints, and tap boxes
- For risers. note floor thickness, closet dimensions, floor-to-floor height, side on which plugs are to be mounted and type and quantity per floor.

3. Review the architectural, structural, and mechanical drawings for conflicts with the run (expansion joints, steel changes, plumbing lines, HVAC equipment, or ducts).
4. Take all measurements from fixed points, such as the building steel, columns, or existing walls.

See Sheet E4—Ground Floor Power for busway routing.

Busway Installation

Busway must be installed in accordance with the job specifications and the *CEC Part 1*, Section 12-2000. Some installation practices to follow are:

- Confirm the busway route is free of conflicts. Notify other trades of your intended route as soon as possible.
- When receiving busway, inspect for damage, check the busway with a megger, and store it in a clean dry location.
- Ensure that proper lifting equipment is available for raising the busway into place.
- Properly torque all connections to the manufacturer's ratings.
- Check the completed system with a megger when the installation is complete.

REVIEW

All answers should be written in complete sentences, calculations should be shown in detail, and Code references should be cited when appropriate.

1. The current density of the 1600-A busway was calculated to be 1313 A per square inch. Compare this with the allowable current density of a 500-kcmil, type RW90-XPLE copper conductor.
2. Would it be permissible to cut six openings in the top of the unit substation with each busbar installed through an individual opening? Why or why not? (Refer to the *CEC*.)
3. List five installation practices that should be followed when installing busway.
4. Describe when it is appropriate to use feeder busways and when plug-in busways are preferred.
5. Describe at least three support methods and give examples of when their use would be appropriate.

UNIT 4

Panelboards

OBJECTIVES

After studying this unit, the student should be able to:

- identify panelboard types
- select and adjust circuit breakers
- make feeder connections to panelboards

PANELBOARDS

Circuit control and overcurrent protection must be provided for all circuits and the power-consuming devices connected to these circuits. Lighting and power panelboards located throughout the building provide this protection and control. Lighting panelboards provide energy to lighting circuits and convenience receptacles. Power panels supply motors, welders, and other high-power loads. Panel schedules for the lighting panels are found in the specifications.

All of the required panelboards are listed in the specifications and are shown on the plans or are referred to on the riser diagram. Table 4-1 shows that, in the addition, there are three lighting panelboards and three power panelboards. A panelboard for which more than 10% of its overcurrent devices are rated at 30 A or less, and for which neutral connections are provided, is defined as a lighting and appliance branch-circuit panelboard (Figure 4-1 on page 46). Throughout this text, this type of panelboard will be called a *lighting panelboard*. A typical lighting and appliance panel schedule is shown in Figure 4-2 on page 47. Panelboards not meeting these requirements are known as power or distribution panelboards (Figures 4-3 and 4-4 on page 48). Sometimes lighting and appliance panelboards are referred to as *load centres*. Strictly speaking, however, the term *load centre* refers to a panelboard rated at 225 A or less and intended for residential applications.

Panelboard No.	Location	Mains	Voltage Rating	No. of Circuits
LP-D	Shop Floor	100 A	347/600 V	24
LP-E	El. Rm.	225 A	120/208 V	42
LP-F	Second Floor	100 A	120/208 V	42
PP-101	El. Rm.	225 A	347/600 V	42
PP-102	Shop Floor	225 A	120/208 V	42
PP-103	Chiller Rm.	800 A	347/600 V	30
PP-201	Penthouse	225 A	347/600 V	30

Lighting and Appliance Panelboards

The basic requirements for panelboards are given in the *CEC Parts 1* and *2*. For these panelboards, the following applies:

- The panelboard must be protected using an overcurrent device with a trip setting not exceeding the rating of the panelboard (Rule 14-606).
- The total load shall not exceed 80% of the panelboard rating except when the panelboard is specifically rated for 100% continuous duty (Rule 8-104).

Panelboards are available with standard main ratings of 100 A, 225 A, 400 A, 600 A, 800 A, and 1200 A.

Panelboard Terminology

- Spare—An unused circuit position that includes the protective device (circuit breaker).
- Space—An unused circuit position that includes provisions for mounting a future protective device but does not include the device.
- Blank—An unused circuit position in the panelboard with no provision for mounting a future protective device. (The main buses do not extend to that point in the panel.)

Panelboard Selection Factors

When selecting panelboards, the following factors must be considered:

- Service and voltage
- Number and types of circuits
- Rating and type of main buses
- Overcurrent protection (main and branch)
- Interrupting capacity (mains and branches)
- Ambient temperature
- Environment in which the panel will be placed

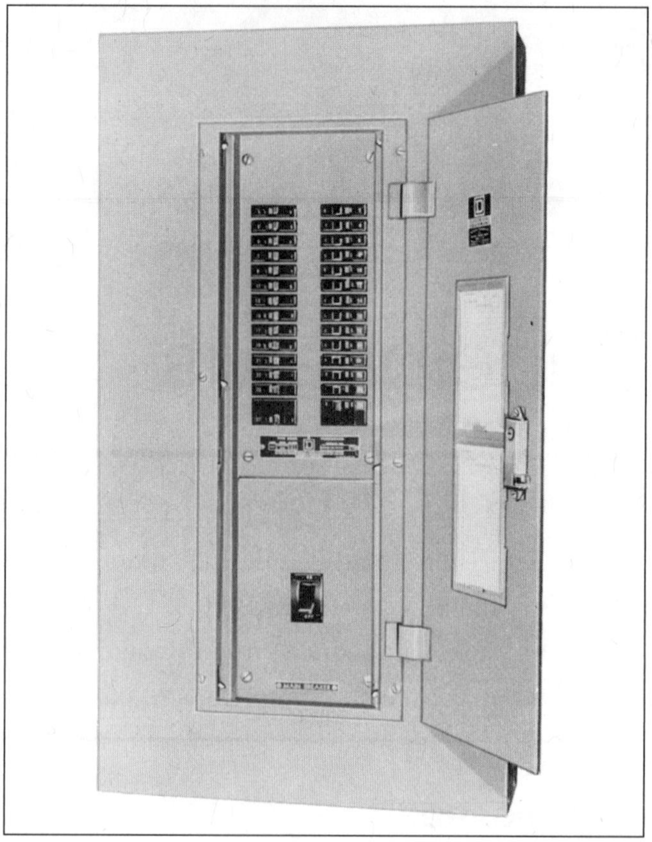

Figure 4-1 Lighting and appliance panelboard with main breaker.

BRANCH-CIRCUIT PROTECTIVE DEVICES

The schedule of panelboards for the industrial building, Table 4-1, and the panel schedules in the specifications or in the specs show that lighting panelboards have a combination of single-pole, two-pole, and three-pole breakers. A single-pole breaker takes up one circuit position in the panel, a two-pole, breaker takes up two circuit positions in the panel, and a three-pole breaker takes up three circuit positions. Half-width breakers are not used in industrial applications. Figures 4-5, 4-6, and 4-7 on page 48 show branch circuit breakers for use in lighting panelboards. When the panelboards are purchased, the interiors are specified by the total number of poles required; the circuit breakers are ordered separately.

PANEL SCHEDULE									
VA	LOAD DESCRIPTION	BREAKER POLES	BREAKER AMPS	CCT (A B C)	CCT	BREAKER AMPS	BREAKER POLES	LOAD DESCRIPTION	VA
240	RECEPTACLES EL. RM.	1	15	1	2	15	2	FAN COIL UNIT	718
240	RECEPTACLES CHILLER RM.	1	15	3	4	15			718
240	REC. COLUMN E11-12	1	15	5	6	15	2	FAN COIL UNIT	718
240	REC. COLUMN E13-14	1	15	7	8	15			718
240	REC. COLUMN D11-12	1	15	9	10	15	2	FAN COIL UNIT	718
240	REC. COLUMN D13-14	1	15	11	12	15			718
240	REC. COLUMN C11-12	1	15	13	14	15	2	FAN COIL UNIT	718
240	REC. COLUMN C13-14	1	15	15	16	15			718
120	REC. COLUMN C15	1	15	17	18	15	1	UNIT HEATER UH-001	240
240	REC. COLUMN B11-12	1	15	19	20	15	1	UNIT HEATER UH-002	240
240	REC. COLUMN B13-14	1	15	21	22	1			1
240	REC. COLUMN A11-12	1	15	23	24	1	2		1
240	REC. COLUMN A13-14	1	15	25	26	1		1	1
400	CNC-1 MILL. COMP. TABLE	1	15	27	28	1	3	GRINDER GDR-01	1
400	CNC-2 MILL. COMP. TABLE	1	15	29	30	1			1
1	1	1	1	31	32	1			1
1	1	1	1	33	34	1	3	GRINDER GDR-02	1
1	1	1	1	35	36	1			1
1	1	1	1	37	38	1			1
1	1	1	1	39	40	15	1	SPARE	1
1	1			41	42	15	1	SPARE	1

LOCATION	TYPE	MOUNTING	MAINS SIZE	MAIN BKR	NO. CCTS	VOLTAGE	PHASE	WIRE
MAIN EL. RM.	NBLP	SURFACE	225 A	200 A	42	120/208V	3	4

PANEL	REVISIONS NO.	DATE	DESCRIPTION		PHASE A	PHASE B	PHASE C	FEEDER
LP D				LOAD				
				REMARKS				

Figure 4-2 Panel schedule.

Panelboard Protective Device

The main protective device for a panelboard may be either a fuse or a circuit breaker. This text will concentrate on the use of circuit breakers. The selection of the circuit breaker should be based on the necessity to:

- Provide the proper overload protection
- Ensure a suitable voltage rating
- Provide a sufficient interrupt current rating
- Provide short-circuit protection
- Coordinate the breaker(s) with other protective devices

The choice of the overload protection is based on the rating of the panelboard. The trip rating of the circuit breaker cannot exceed the ampacity of the busbars in the panelboard. The number of branch–circuit breakers generally is not a factor in the selection of the main protective device except in a practical sense. It is a common practice to have the total amperage of the branch breakers exceed the rating of the main breaker by several times.

The voltage ratings of the breakers must be higher than that of the system. Breakers are usually rated at 250 V or 600 V.

The importance of the interrupt rating is covered in later units. The student should recall from *Electrical Wiring—Commercial* that if there is any

Figure 4-3 An 800-A distribution panelboard.

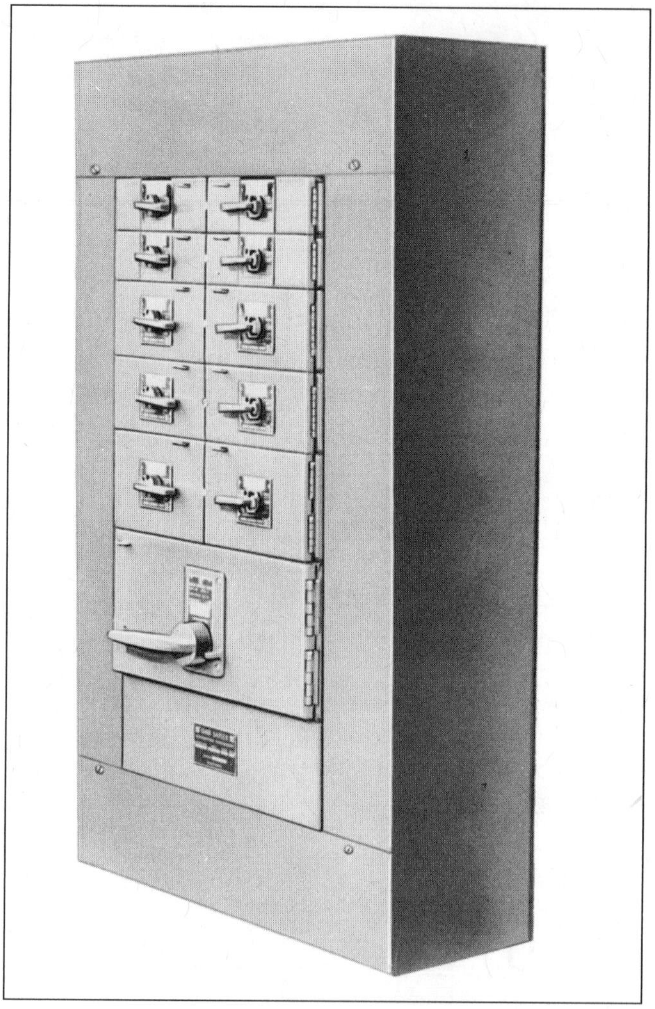

Figure 4-4 A typical fusible power panelboard.

Figure 4-5 Single-pole breaker.

Figure 4-6 Two-pole breaker.

Figure 4-7 Three-pole breaker.

question as to the exact value of the short-circuit current available at a point, a circuit breaker with a high interrupt rating is to be installed.

Many circuit breakers used as the main protective device are provided with an adjustable magnetic trip (Figure 4-8). Adjustments of this trip determine the degree of protection provided by the circuit breaker if a short-circuit occurs. The manufacturer of this device provides exact information about the adjustments to be made. In general, a low setting may be 10 or 12 times the overload trip rating. Two rules should be followed whenever the magnetic trip is set:

- A lower setting provides greater protection.
- The setting should be lower than the value of the short-circuit current available at that point.

Figure 4-8 Circuit breaker with adjustable magnetic trip.

Power Panelboards

A typical fusible power panelboard is shown in Figure 4-4, and a breaker panelboard is shown in Figure 4-3. A common interior arrangement for a three-wire fusible panelboard is shown in Figure 4-9. The panelboard is supplied from a major source such as a transformer. The panelboard then provides circuits to individual loads.

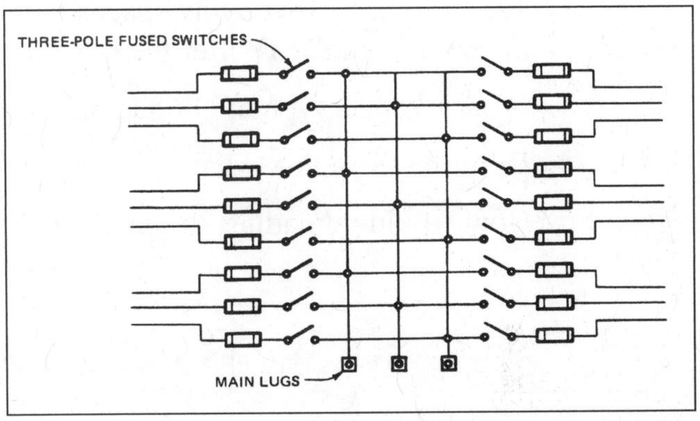

Figure 4-9 Fusible power panelboard connections.

REVIEW

All answers should be written in complete sentences, calculations should be shown in detail, and Code references should be cited when appropriate.

1. The schedule of panelboards is given in Table 4-1. How many of these are power panelboards and how are they different from the others?
2. Three-phase, four-wire panelboards are usually constructed with an even number of spaces available for each phase, thus the total number of spaces would be in increments of 6, such as 12, 18, or 24. How many spaces would be available for the later addition of circuit breakers in panelboard LP-D after the panelboard has been equipped as scheduled?
3. What size and type of conductors are used to supply LP-D?
4. Describe, in detail, what is illustrated in Figure 4-10.
5. How would you adjust the magnetic trip on a circuit breaker?

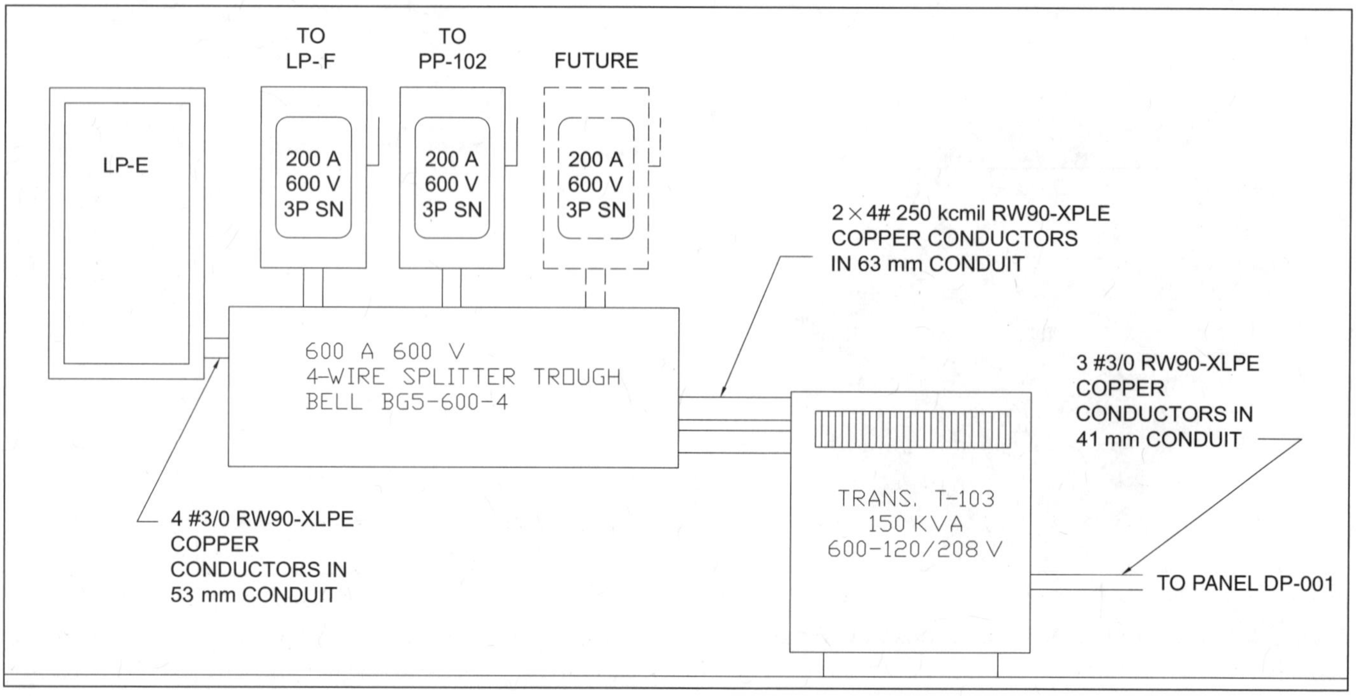

Figure 4-10 Detail of floor-mounted transformer T-103, located in the main electrical room of the industrial building (scale: 1:20).

UNIT 5

Trolley Busways

OBJECTIVES

After studying this unit, the student should be able to:

- identify features of a trolley busway installation
- select components to support cord drops

THREE-PHASE TROLLEY BUSWAY

Many modern industrial plants use systems of mobile trolley outlets that move along specially constructed busways. The industrial trolley bus is a 100-A, enclosed busbar electrical system. Such a trolley bus provides a continuous outlet system for feeding electrical energy to portable electric tools, cranes, hoists, and other electrical loads.

When the trolley system is installed over production and assembly lines, it provides current to equipment through trolleys that move along with the particular object being assembled. Because the busbars are totally enclosed in a steel casing, there are no exposed live parts to provide hazards to worker safety. This system eliminates the need for and the hazards of portable cords plugged into fixed outlets at the floor level.

THE TROLLEY BUSWAY RUNS

The industrial building plans show the layout of the four trolley busway runs to be installed. The specifications provide more detailed information about the trolley busway system. The four runs as shown on Sheet E10 are labelled *A*, *B*, *C*, and *D*. These runs are 20 m (66 ft), 13.5 m (44.5 ft), 10 m (33 ft), and 8 m (26.4 ft) long, respectively.

The trolley systems are constructed of straight sections joined end to end, as in Figure 5-1 on page 52. The standard section is 3 m (10 ft) long, but sections of less than standard length may be custom ordered so that a run can be made to exact dimensions. Curved sections and other fittings are also available.

Trolley Busway Run *A*

Trolley run *A* consists of straight busway extending for 20.7 m (68 ft). One three-phase drop-out section is installed at the approximate midpoint of the run. A drop-out section provides the means for removing or inserting the trolleys (Figure 5-2 on page 52). As shown in Figure 5-2, the drop-out section contains two hinged doors that open when a lever is raised. When the lever is in the down position, the doors are firmly closed and the trolleys move past this section smoothly. Blocking straps ensure that a trolley cannot be placed in the duct incorrectly. This feature also ensures that the polarity is always correct after the trolleys are inserted. Drop-out sections are available in lengths of 3 m (10 ft), and one drop section must be installed in each run.

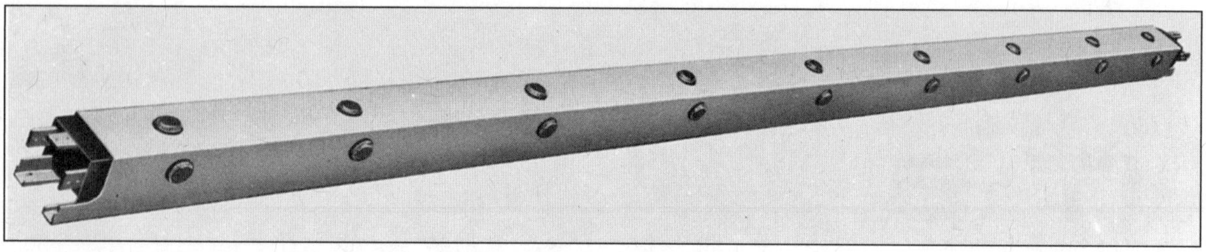

Figure 5-1 Standard 3 m (10 ft) section of trolley busway.

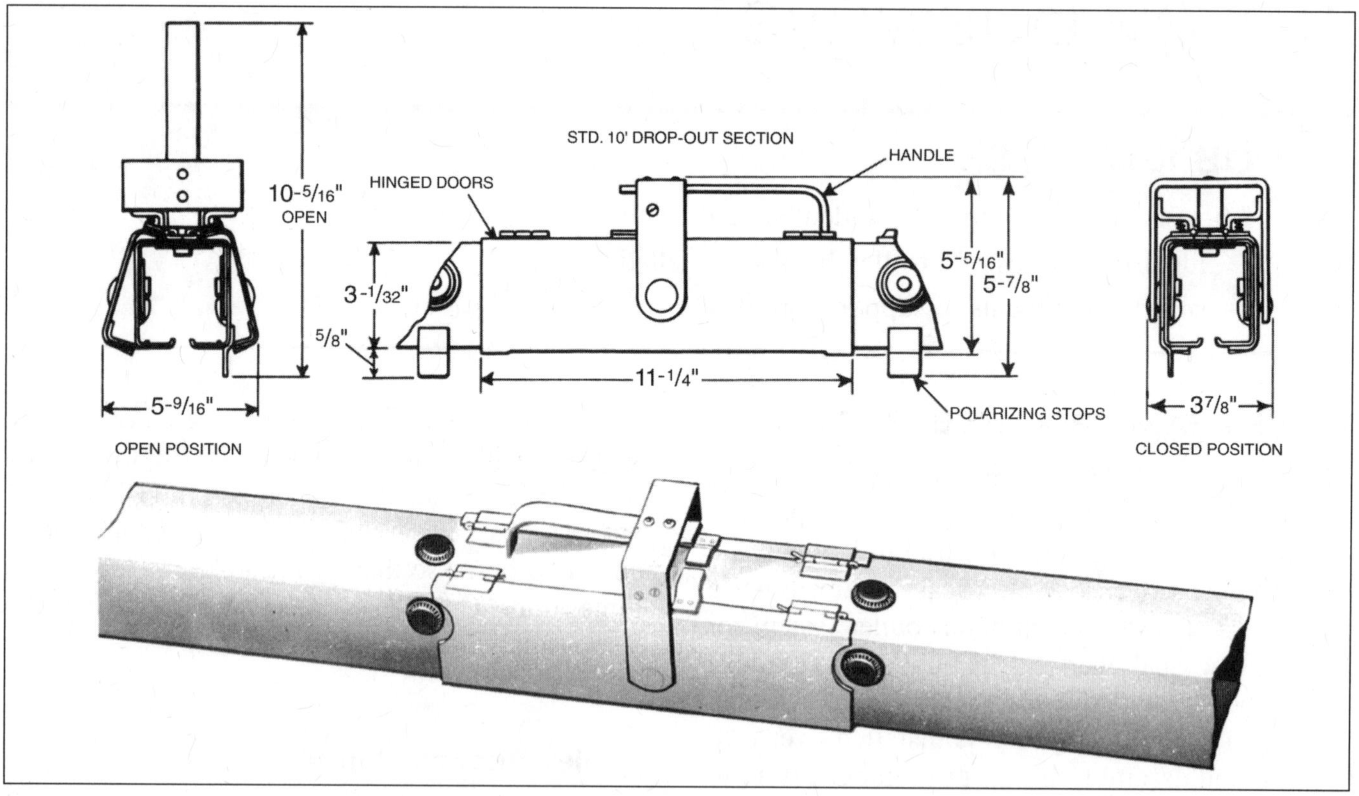

Figure 5-2 Standard drop-out section.

The trolley busway is suspended 2.5 m (8 ft) above the floor according to the specifications and is supported by standard hangers. These hangers also serve as a means for joining adjacent sections and automatically aligning the busbars. The hangers are formed from 12-gauge steel. However, the only tool needed to join the industrial-type trolley duct is a screwdriver.

Intermediate-type hangers are used at the midpoint of each standard 3 m (10 ft) section to give extra support. The intermediate hangers fit snugly around the duct sections but do not interfere with the free passage of the trolleys. The combination of the standard hangers and the intermediate hangers supports the busway at 1.5 m (5 ft) intervals, resulting in a very rigid and secure installation (Figure 5-3). The standard and intermediate hangers are attached to the overhead structure by rod or strap-type supports (Figure 5-4).

Each end of the busway is capped with an end plate and bumper assembly. This device closes the ends of the busway run and acts as a bumper for any trolley reaching the end of the busway. The bumper absorbs shock and protects the trolley from damage.

Feed-in Adapter

The power supply from the panelboard is fed into the busway run through a *feed-in adapter* (Figure 5-4).

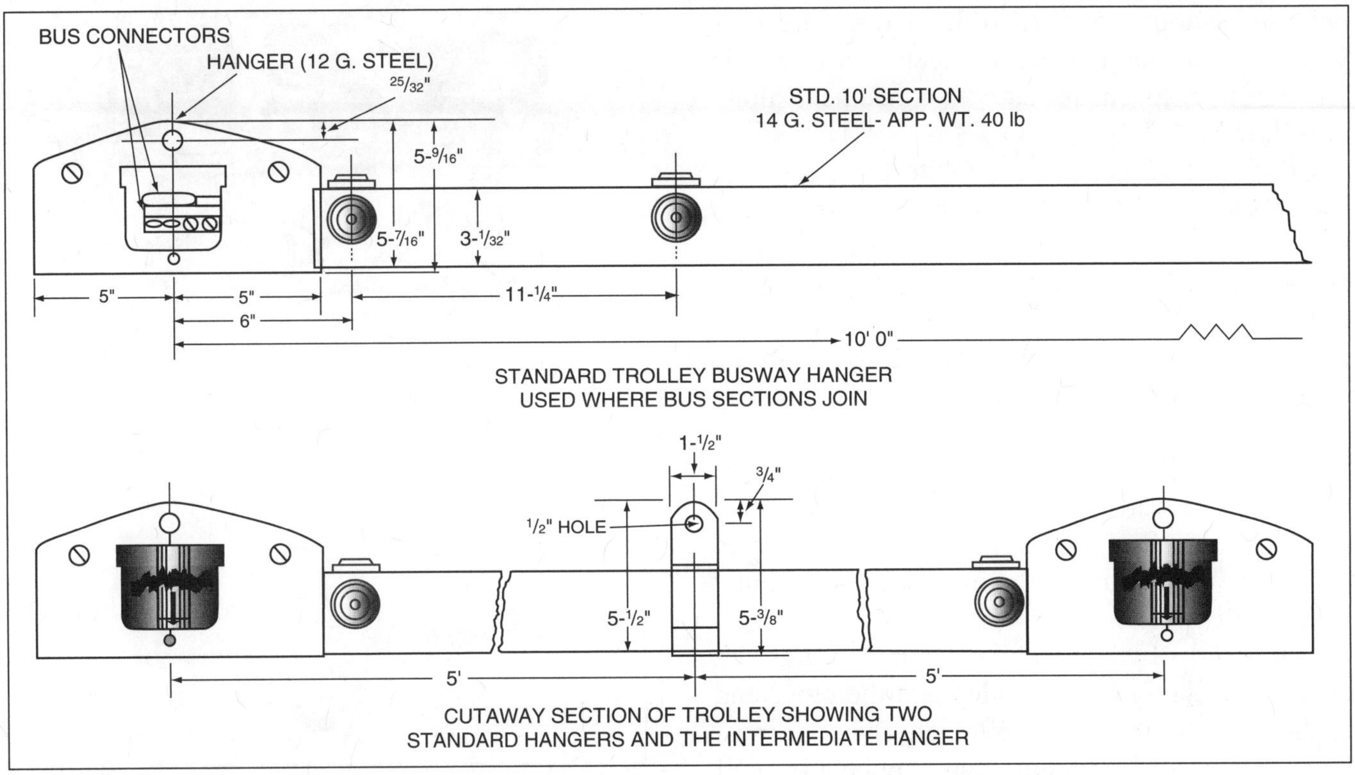

Figure 5-3 Supporting trolley busway.

The feed-in adapter has pressure-type wire terminals. This adapter can be used at the end of a run or it can be installed in the centre of the busway to provide centre feed for the connection of the conduit or cable from the panelboard. Conduit must be installed between the power panelboard and the feed-in adapter to bring power to the trolley busway. A 100-A circuit will run in this conduit from panelboard P-15.

The Trolleys

Several types of both fused and unfused trolleys are available. The trolley specified for the industrial building is a fusible, box-type tool hanger with a heavy-duty rating. The box tool hanger, Figure 5-5 on page 54, has a hinged cover and is provided with puller-type fuse cutouts, plug receptacles, and cord clamps. For the industrial

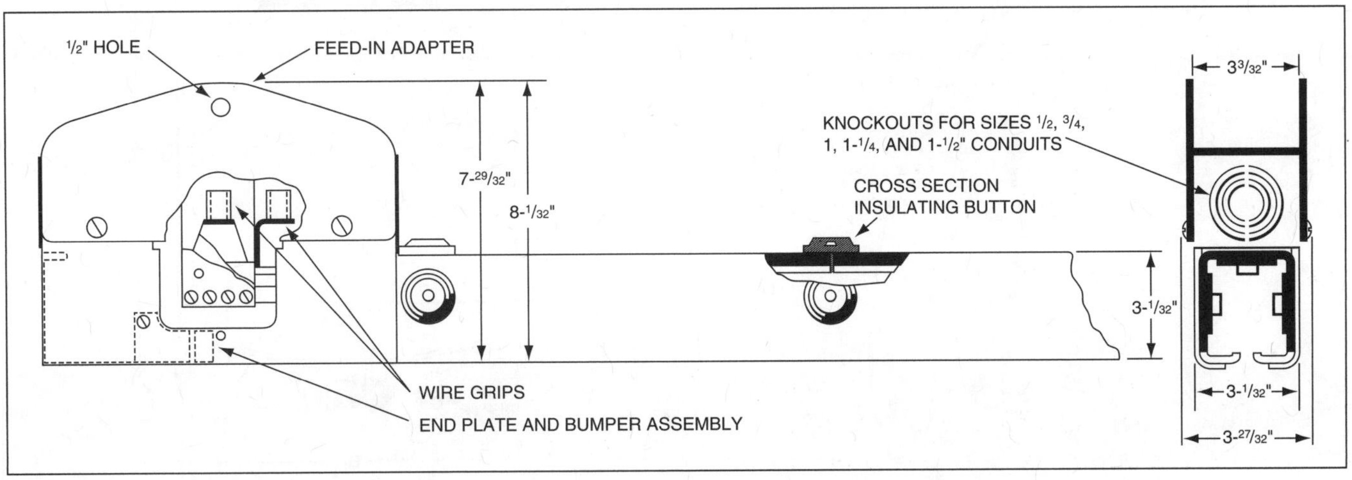

Figure 5-4 Trolley busway section with feed-in adapter and end plate with bumper.

building, cutouts for 0-A to 30-A fuses are provided. The trolley has eight wheels and four side thrust rollers to ensure smooth movement along the busway.

The trolleys have six graphite bronze shoes. These shoes make contact with the busbars and provide a path that continues through the fuse cutout and receptacle to the heavy-duty, four-wire rubber cord. This cord is used to attach the various portable tools—such as electric drills, buffers, grinders, and other equipment—to the busway system (Figure 5-6).

The four-wire rubber cord provides three conductors to operate the three-phase portable tools used on the job. The fourth conductor (green in colour) is used to bond the equipment to ground (*CEC* Rule 4-036).

One end of the bonding conductor must be attached securely to the trolley and the other end to the housing of the portable tool. The cord must be approved for heavy duty and may be a type SJ containing 12 AWG conductors. The fuses in the trolley are rated at 20 A (Figure 5-7).

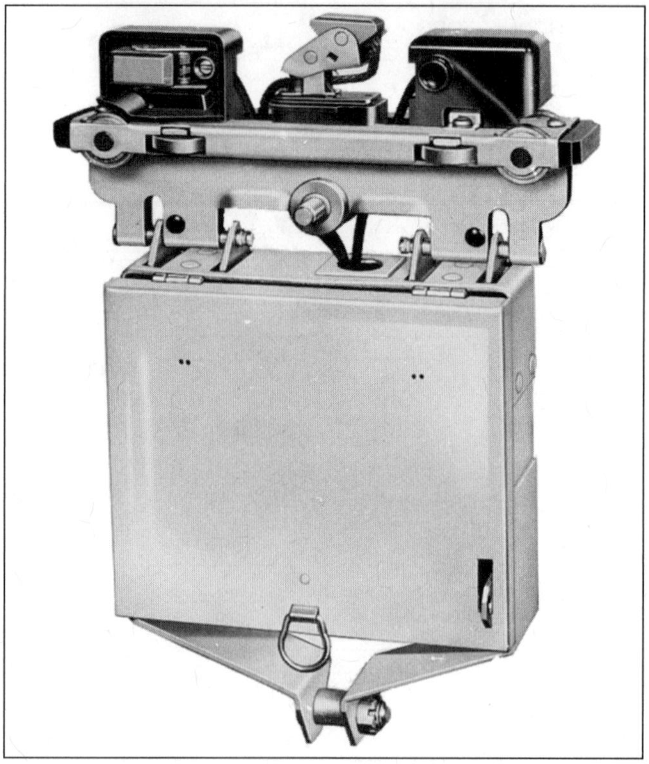

Figure 5-5 Trolley with box tool hanger.

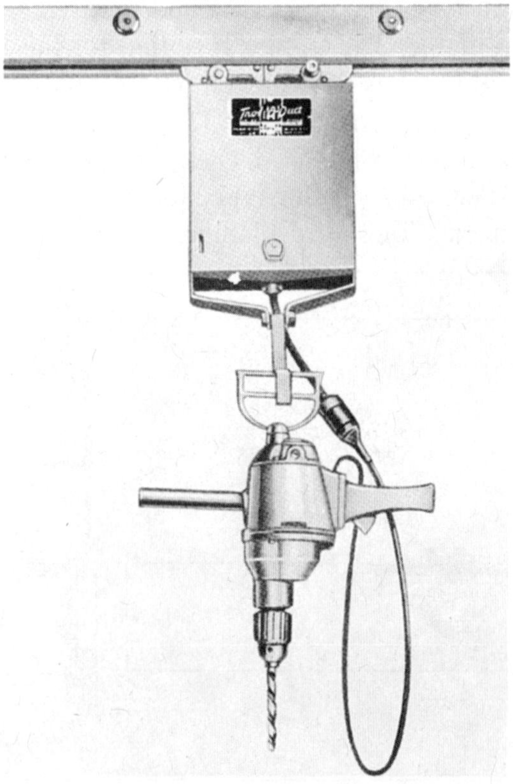

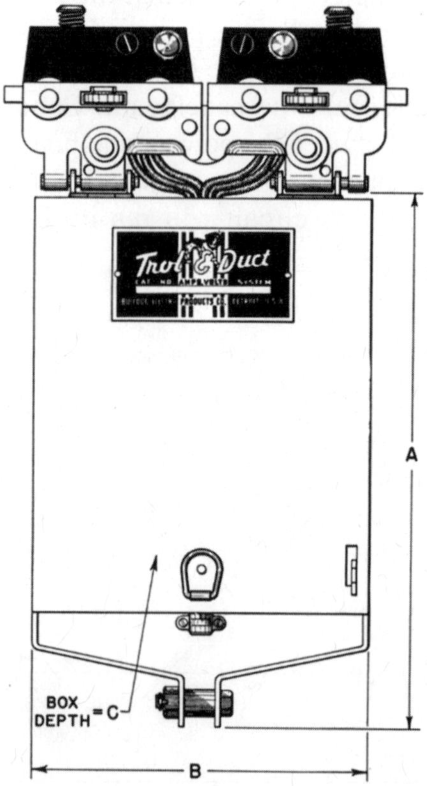

Figure 5-6 Heavy-duty trolley with box tool hanger.

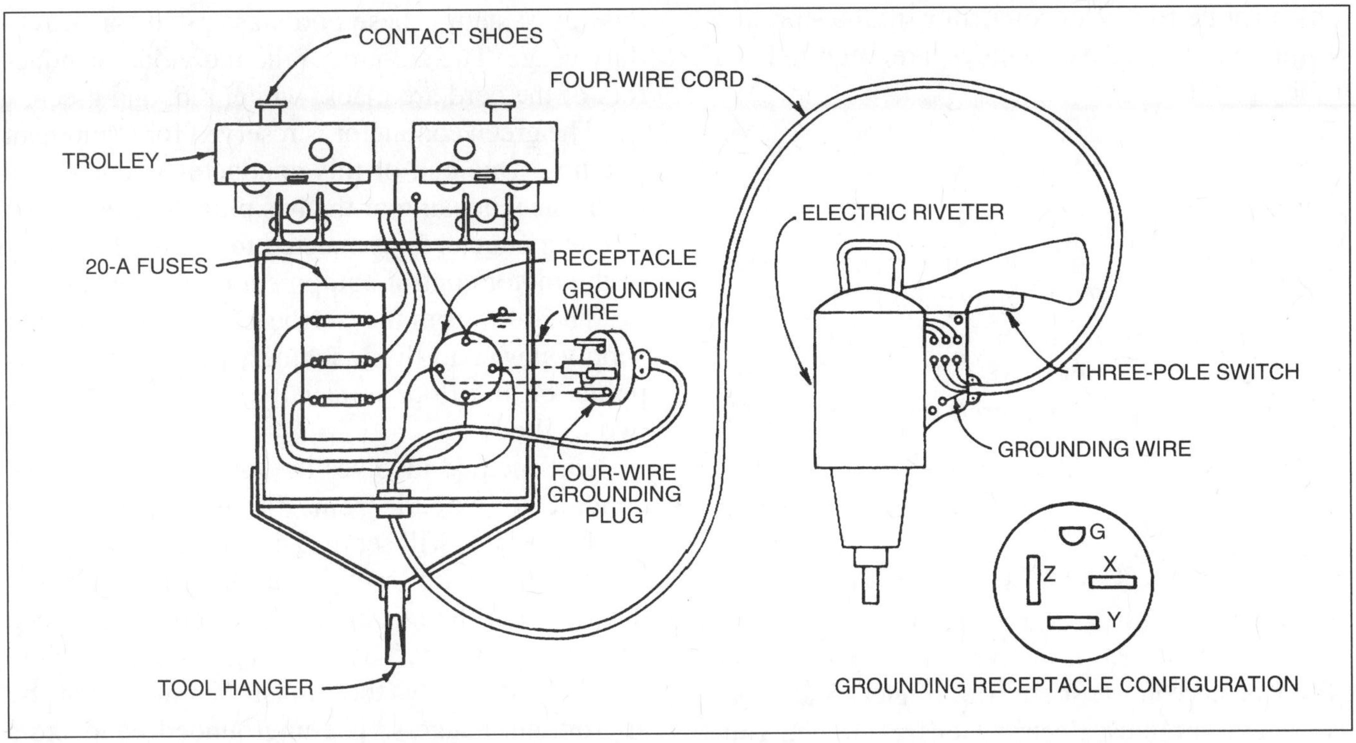

Figure 5-7 Details of trolley box-type tool hanger showing grounding connections.

Figure 5-8 Trolley busway may be used to feed

The specifications for the industrial building call for the use of one trolley for each 3 m (10 ft) or fraction thereof of trolley busway. Thus, for run *A* [20 m (66 ft) long], the contractor must furnish seven trolleys. Figure 5-8 shows a typical installation of trolley busway.

The Conduit Run

Conduit must be installed from the feed-in adapter to the power panelboard to bring electrical energy to the duct runs. A 100-A feeder circuit will run in this conduit from panelboard PP-1.

Trolley Busway Run *B*

As shown on the plans, trolley busway run *B* extends 13.5 m (44.5 ft) in length. The information supplied for busway run *A* also applies to trolley runs *B*, *C*, and *D*. The location of run *B* is shown on Sheet E10. The conduit from run *B* must runs must be routed to conform with the structure of the building. Five trolleys are required for trolley run *B*.

Trolley Run *C*

Trolley run *C* is a straight run extending 10 m (33 ft) (see Sheet E10 of the plans). This run is connected to power panelboard PP-1 by conduit from the feed-in adapter located at the end of the run. Three trolleys are required for trolley run *C*.

Trolley Run *D*

Trolley run *D* is 8 m (26.4 ft) long. The installation methods and parts used for this run are the same as those used in the other runs. Panelboard PP-1 (located on the south wall of electrical room #1) again supplies electrical energy to the run. According to the specifications, run *D* requires three trolleys including tool hangers to be installed, one for every 3 m (10 ft) or fraction thereof of busway.

Each of the four trolley systems (*A* through *D*) is a three-phase system and is rated at 208 V and 100 A. The equipment attachment plugs used with the duct system are polarized. This feature eliminates several problems when portable tools having three-phase motors are used. For example, reversed phases and the resulting reversal in the direction of rotation of the portable tools are eliminated.

These trolley systems have several advantages. The runs follow the production and assembly lines of the plant. This convenience tends to increase the amount of work that can be completed. A neater and safer production area is maintained because the tools the worker commonly uses are not scattered over the floor but rather are suspended directly over the working area.

The Cord Drops (*CEC* Rule 4-010)

The specifications call for the use of four-conductor-type SJ rubber cord to connect the various machines in the manufacturing area to the busway system. These cords are rated for heavy-duty usage. The colours of the individual conductors of the cord are black, white, red, and green.

The green conductor is reserved for equipment bonding. One end of this conductor is connected to the steel housing of the bus plug. The other end of the conductor is connected to the steel housing of the motor control equipment on the machine.

The drop from the overhead busway system to supply power to the machines located at various points on the floor is usually made by either of two methods.

One method involves the use of rigid or EMT conduit to extend from the bus plug to the machine that it will serve. The conduit may be run horizontally with or without bends to a point directly over the machine to be supplied and then dropped vertically. The resulting system is a rigid raceway assembly that must be supported by appropriate hangers. The ungrounded conductors are pulled into the conduit that serves as the equipment ground.

One disadvantage of this method is its inflexibility when the layout of the machines being served must be rearranged. In such a case, the conduit assemblies must be taken down, the wire removed, and the conduit disassembled. Then, the entire run must be rebuilt to fit the new location using new wire and new conduit for part or all of the assembly.

The second method is to use rubber cord drops from the bus plug to the machine being served (Figure 5-9). This method is flexible in terms of making changes and, thus, is commonly used. The industrial building uses the rubber cord drop method.

Strain Reliefs

Strain relief grips are used in the cord drop method of supplying equipment. The strain relief type of grip is designed for use at the terminals or ends of the rubber cord drop where it enters or leaves a knockout opening in the bus plug, in the disconnecting switch, or in a motor controller.

The bus drop grips are used at or near the ends of the rubber cord runs and also where the cord changes direction from the horizontal to the vertical, as in Figures 5-9 and 5-10.

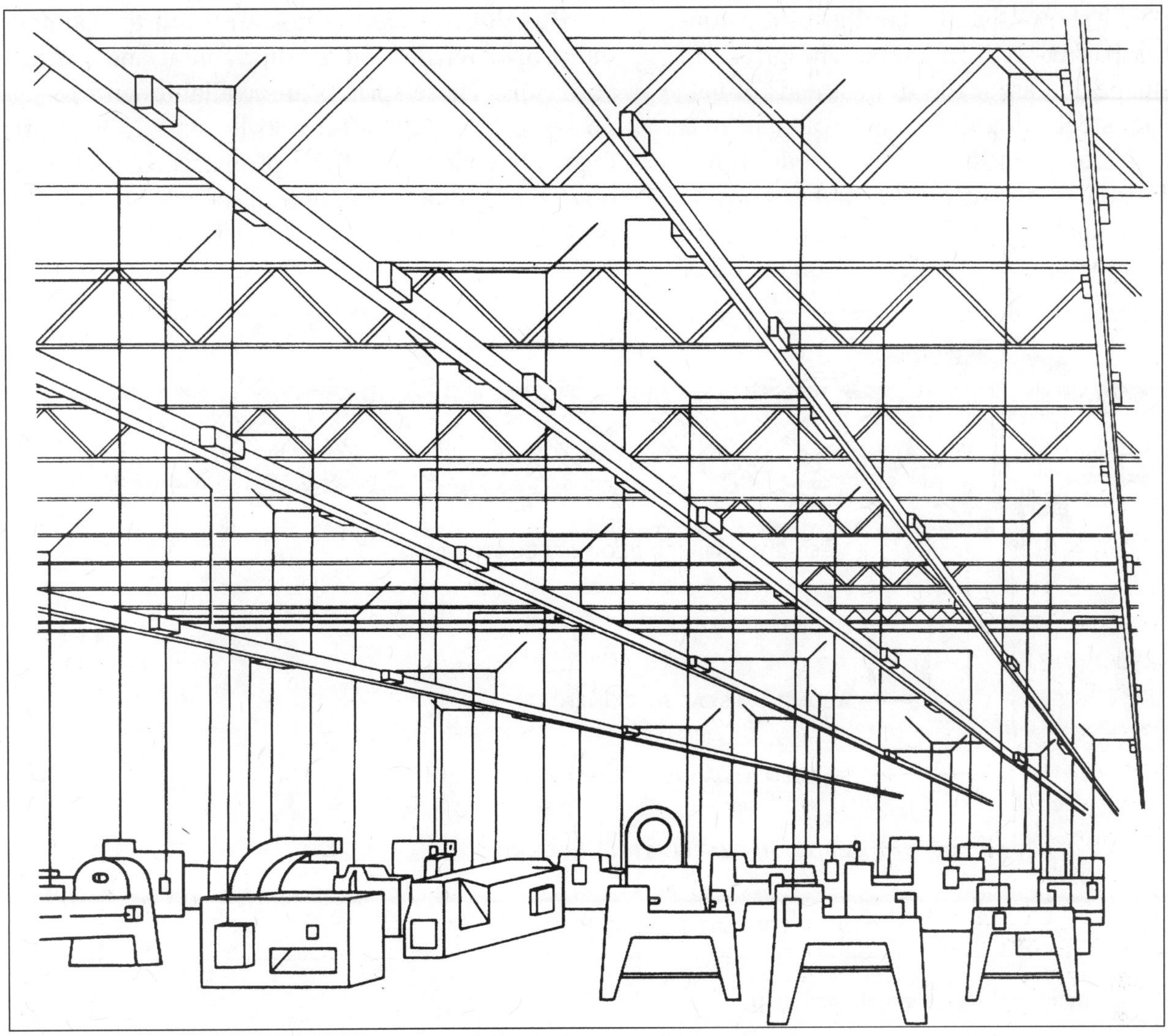

Figure 5-9 Machines supplied by rubber cords from overhead busway.

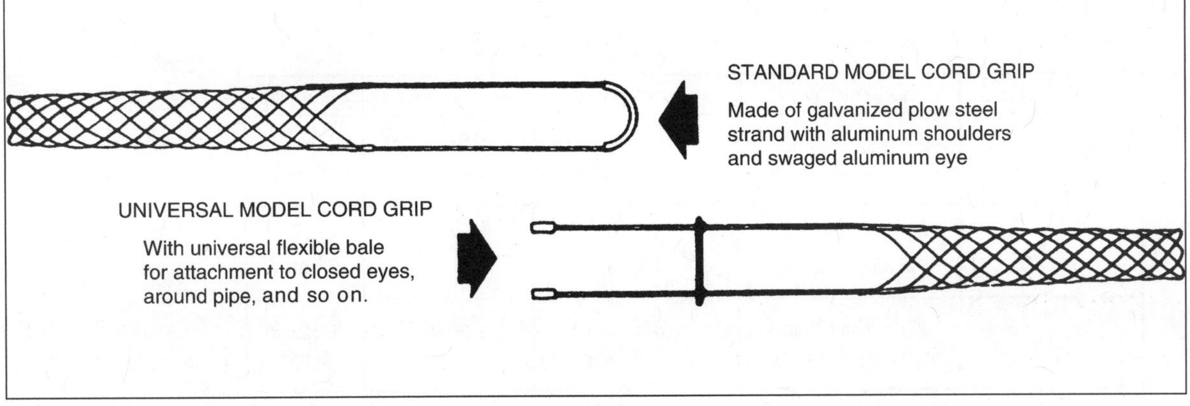

Figure 5-10 Cord grip models.

Figure 5-11 shows that the cord grips are constructed in a basket-weave pattern. The grips are tubular in shape and are made from strands of galvanized plow steel wire. Grips are available in a variety of sizes to fit most cables or cords. When strain or tension is placed on the rubber cord so that it is pulled taut, the basket structure of the cord grip contracts to apply a stronger grip on the cord.

Bus drop safety springs are used to maintain the proper tension on the horizontal and vertical cord runs. These springs are available with 18-kg, 36-kg, and 68-kg (40-lb, 80-lb, and 150-lb) ratings. The selection of the proper spring depends upon the weight and length of the cord being supported (Figure 5-12).

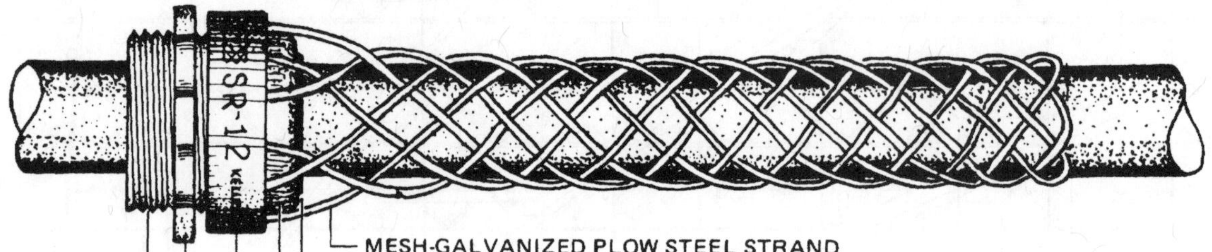

Figure 5-11 Bus drop and strain relief cord grip.

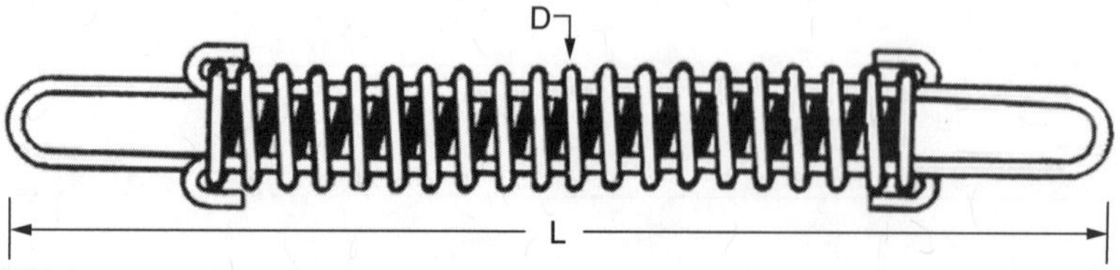

CATALOGUE NUMBER	MAXIMUM DEFLECTION	BREAKING STRENGTH	NO LOAD LENGTH	DIAMETER
40 lb	2.875 in @ 45 lb 73.0 mm @ 20.4 kg	500 lb 227 kg	7.25 in 184 mm	0.75 in 19 mm
80 lb	2.62 in @ 110 lb 66.5 mm @ 50 kg	850 lb 385 kg	8.25 in 209 mm	1 in 25 mm
150 lb	2.38 in @175 lb 60.5 mm @ 79 kg	850 lb 385 kg	8.25 in 209 mm	1.125 in 28 mm

Figure 5-12 Bus drop safety spring.

Several different ways of using cord grips are shown in Figure 5-13.

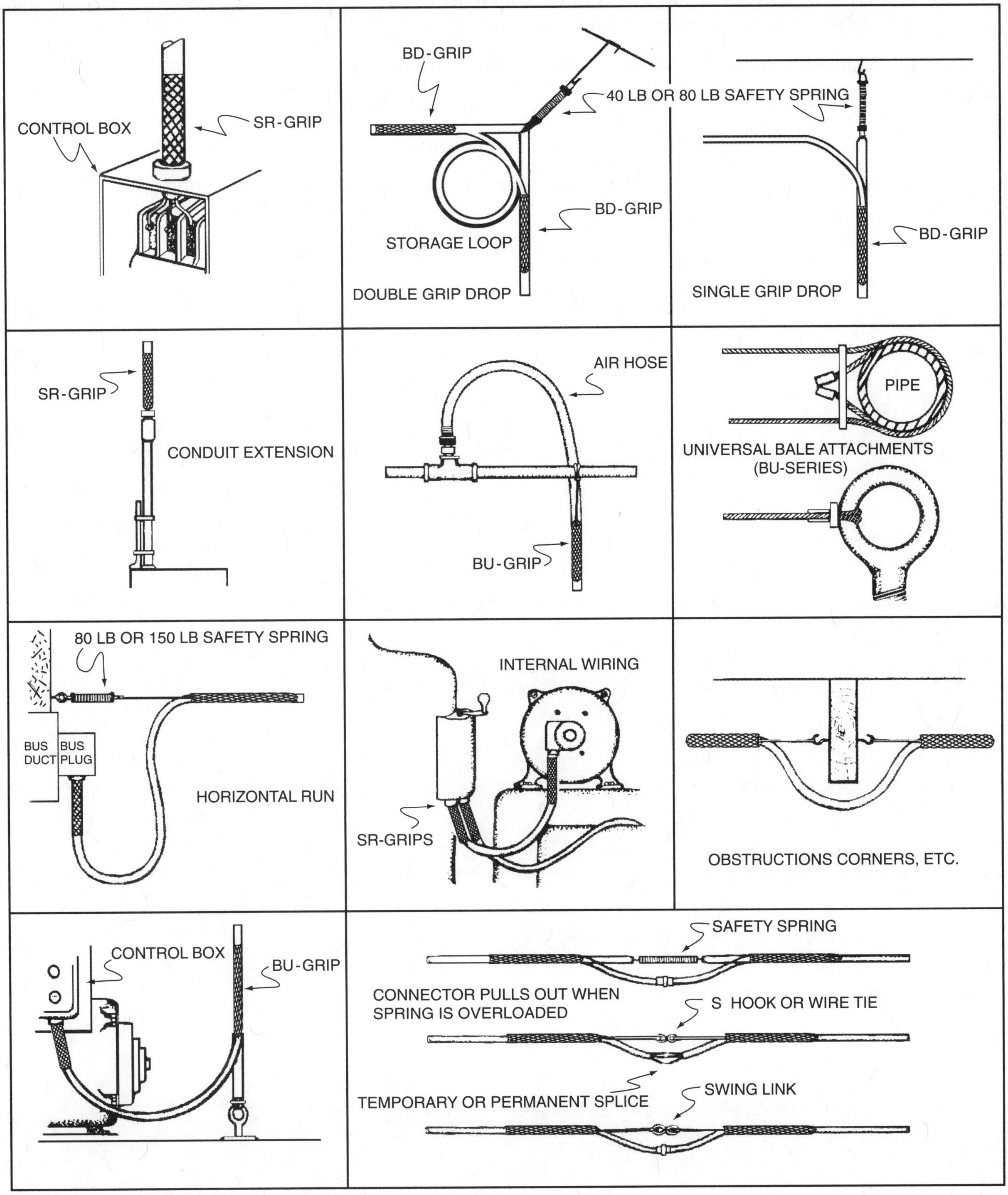

REVIEW

All answers should be written in complete sentences, calculations should be shown in detail, and Code references should be cited when appropriate.

1. What advantages are there to having a trolley busway installed?
2. Is the trolley busway considered a feeder or a branch circuit?
3. What features does a trolley box-type hanger provide?
4. Describe the operation of strain relief grips and identify their basic function.

UNIT 6

Using Wire Tables and Determining Conductor Sizes

OBJECTIVES

After studying this unit, the student should be able to:

- select a conductor from the proper wire table
- discuss the different types of wire insulation
- determine insulation characteristics
- use correction and adjustment factors to determine the ampacity of conductors
- determine the resistance of long lengths of conductors
- determine the proper wire sizes for loads located long distances from the power source
- list the requirements for using parallel conductors
- discuss the use of a megohmmeter for testing insulation

CONDUCTORS

- *CEC* Section 4 addresses conductors for general wiring.
- *CEC* Table 19 outlines conditions of use and allowable conductor temperatures for wire and cables.
- *CEC* Table D1 lists the type designations and voltage ratings for wire and cables other than flexible cord.
- *CEC* Tables 1 to 4 are used to determine a conductor size according to the ampacity of a circuit.
- *CEC* Table 2 lists allowable ampacities for not more than three insulated, copper conductors in a raceway, based on an ambient air temper-
- If the ambient temperature is above 30°C, a correction factor must be applied as outlined in *CEC* Table 5A.
- If there are four or more conductors in the raceway, a correction factor shall be applied. These factors are given in *CEC* Table 5C.

INSULATION TYPE

A factor that determines the amount of current a conductor is permitted to carry is the type of insulation used. The insulation is the nonconductive covering around the wire, as shown in Figure 6-1 on page 62. Different types of insulation can withstand more heat than other types. The voltage rating of the conductor is also determined by the characteristics of the insulation. The amount of voltage a

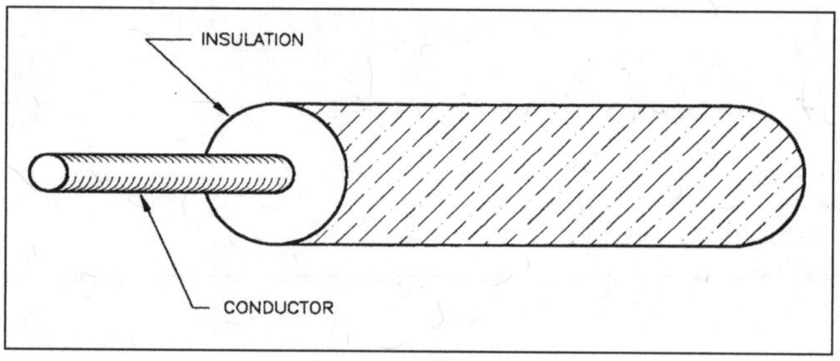

Figure 6-1 An insulated conductor.

breaking down is determined by the type of material from which it is made and its thickness. *CEC* Table 19 lists the conditions of use and maximum temperature ratings of wire and cable.

CEC Table 19 is divided into five columns. The first column lists the condition of use or the environment in which the wire or cable is to be installed; the second lists its trade designation; the third column lists the CSA type designation for the wire and cable; and the fourth shows the maximum allowable conductor temperature. The fifth column is a numerical reference to notes at the end of the table. It is very important to refer to these notes as they contain information that may affect the usage of the wire or cable.

PROBLEM 1

Find the maximum operating temperature of type RW90 insulation. Refer to *CEC* Table 19.

Using the column identified as CSA Type Designation, scan down through the table until type RW90 is located. By moving over to the temperature column, it is shown that a type RW90 conductor has a temperature rating of 90°C.

PROBLEM 2

Can a conductor with type RW90 insulation be used in wet locations?

Using the column marked Condition of Use, move down through the column, looking for references to wet location. You will note that type RW90 insulation is approved for installation in wet locations.

Conductor Metals

Another factor that determines the allowable ampacity of the conductor is the type of metal used for the wire. The *CEC* lists the current-carrying capacity of both copper and aluminum conductors in Tables 1 to 4. Upon examination of these tables, you will note that Tables 1 and 2 are for copper conductors while Tables 3 and 4 are for aluminum. The tables are further identified with Tables 1 and 3 being for conductor installations in free air and Tables 2 and 4 being for conductor installations in cable or raceway. Since installations of copper conductors in raceway or cable are the most common, *CEC* Table 2 is shown in Table 6-1. A study of *CEC* Tables 1 to 4 reveals that a copper conductor is permitted to carry more current than an aluminum conductor of the same size and insulation type when installed under the same conditions. A #8 AWG copper conductor with type RW90 insulation has an allowable ampacity of 45 A when installed in a cable or raceway. A #8 AWG aluminum conductor with type RW90 insulation has an allowable ampacity of 30 A when installed in the same manner.

CORRECTION FACTORS

One of the main conditions that determines the current a conductor is permitted to carry is the ambient, or surrounding, air temperature. *CEC* Tables 1 to 4 list the allowable ampacity of copper and aluminum conductors in free air and in cable or raceway. These allowable ampacities are based on an ambient air temperature of 30°C. If these conductors are to be used in a location with a higher ambient temperature, the ampacity of the conductor must be reduced.

CEC Table 5A and Table 6-2 on page 64 provide the necessary correction factors for ambient temperatures from 40°C to 140°C. This table is divided into the same number of columns as the wire tables (*CEC* Tables 1 to 4). The correction factors in each column are used for the conductors listed in the same column of the wire table.

- After reduction, the current-carrying capacity of a conductor is referred to as the ampacity, not the allowable ampacity.

CEC Table 2

(See Rules 4-004, 8-104, 12-012, 12-2210, 26-000, 26-742, 42-008, and 42-016 and Tables 5A, 5C, 19, and D3)

Allowable Ampacities for Not More Than 3 Copper Conductors in Raceway or Cable

*Based on Ambient Temperature of 30°C**

Size AWG, kcmil	Allowable Ampacity†‡‡					
	60°C‡	75°C‡	85–90°C‡	110°C‡	125°C‡	200°C‡
	Type TW	Types RW75, TW75	Types R90, RW90, T90 NYLON / Paper / Mineral-Insulated Cables**	See Note	See Note	See Note
14	15	15	15	30	30	30
12	20	20	20	35	40	40
10	30	30	30	45	50	55
8	40	45	45	60	65	70
6	55††	65	65	80	85	95
4	70	85	85	105	115	120
3	80	100	105	120	130	145
2	100	115	120	135	145	165
1	110	130	140	160	170	190
0	125	150	155	190	200	225
00	145	175	185††	215	230	250
000	165	200	210	245	265	285
000	195	230	235	275	310	340
250	215	255	265	315	335	—
300	240	285	295	345	380	—
350	260	310	325	390	420	—
400	280	335	345	420	450	—
500	320	380	395	470	500	—
600	355	420	455	525	545	—
700	385	460	490	560	600	—
750	400	475	500	580	620	—
800	410	490	515	600	640	—
900	435	520	555	—	—	—
1 000	455	545	585	680	730	—
1 250	495	590	645	—	—	—
1 500	520	625	700	785	—	—
1 750	545	650	735	—	—	—
2 000	560	665	775	840	—	—
Col. 1	**Col. 2**	**Col. 3**	**Col. 4**	**Col. 5**	**Col. 6**	**Col. 7**

*See Table 5A for the correction factors to be applied to the values in Columns 2 to 7 for ambient temperatures over 30°C.
†The ampacity of aluminum-sheathed cable is based on the type of insulation used on the copper conductors.
‡These are maximum allowable conductor temperatures for 1, 2, or 3 conductors run in a raceway, or 2 or 3 conductors run in a cable and may be used in determining the ampacity of other conductor types in Table 19, which are so run, as follows: From Table 19 determine the maximum allowable conductor temperature for that particular type; then from Table 2 determine the ampacity under the column of corresponding temperature rating.
**These ratings are based on the use of 90°C insulation on the emerging conductors and for sealing. Where a deviation has been allowed in accordance with Rule 2-030, mineral-insulated cable may be used at higher temperatures without decrease in allowable ampacity, provided that insulation and sealing material approved for such higher temperature is used.
††For 3-wire 120/240 and 120/208 V residential services or subservices, the allowable ampacity for sizes No. 6 and No. 2/0 AWG shall be 60 A and 200 A respectively. In this case, the 5% adjustment of Rule 8-106(1) cannot be applied.
‡‡See Table 5C for the correction factors to be applied to the values in Columns 2 to 7 where there are more than 3 conductors in a run of raceway or cable.
Note: These ampacities are only applicable under special circumstances where the use of insulated conductors having this temperature rating is acceptable.

Table 6-1 Allowable ampacities for not more than three copper conductors in raceway or cable.

CEC Table 5A

(See Rules 4-004(8) and 12-2210 and Tables 1, 2, 3, 4, 57, 58, and D3)

Correction Factors Applying to Tables 1, 2, 3, and 4

Ampacity Correction Factors for Ambient Temperatures Above 30°C

(These correction factors apply, column for column, to Tables 1, 2, 3, and 4. The correction factors in column 2 also apply to Table 57.)

Ambient Temperature °C	Correction Factor					
	60°C Type TW	75°C Types RW75, TW75	85–90°C Types R90, RW90, T90 NYLON	110°C See Note (2)	125°C See Note (2)	200°C See Note (2)
40	0.82	0.88	0.90	0.94	0.95	1.00
45	0.71	0.82	0.85	0.90	0.92	1.00
50	0.58	0.75	0.80	0.87	0.89	1.00
55	0.41	0.65	0.74	0.83	0.86	1.00
60	—	0.58	0.67	0.79	0.83	0.91
70	—	0.35	0.52	0.71	0.76	0.87
75	—	—	0.43	0.66	0.72	0.86
80	—	—	0.30	0.61	0.69	0.84
90	—	—	—	0.50	0.61	0.80
100	—	—	—	—	0.51	0.77
120	—	—	—	—	—	0.69
140	—	—	—	—	—	0.59
Col. 1	Col. 2	Col. 3	Col. 4	Col. 5	Col. 6	Col. 7

Notes:
(1) The ampacity of a given conductor type at these higher ambient temperatures is obtained by multiplying the appropriate value from Table 1, 2, 3, or 4 by the correction factor for that higher temperature.
(2) These ampacities are only applicable under special circumstances where the use of insulated conductors having this temperature rating is acceptable.

Table 6-2 Correction factors applying to Tables 1, 2, 3, and 4.

PROBLEM 3

What is the ampacity of a #4 AWG copper conductor with type RW90 insulation that will be used in an area with an ambient temperature of 43°C?

Determine the allowable ampacity of a #4 AWG copper conductor with type RW90 insulation. Type RW90 insulation is located in Column 4 of *CEC* Table 2 and Table 6-1. The table lists an allowable ampacity of 85 A. Using Table 6-2 (*CEC* Table 5A), in the left-hand column, select a temperature range that is equal to or greater than 43°C. The table lists a correction factor of 0.85. The ampacity is to be multiplied by the correction factor.

$$85 \times 0.85 = 72.25 \text{ A}$$

PROBLEM 4

What is the ampacity of a #1/0 AWG aluminum type RA90 conductor installed in free air, in an area with an ambient air temperature of 38°C?

Using *CEC* Table 3 for aluminum conductors in free air, note that type RA90 is not listed. When this occurs, the ampacity of the conductor is based on the temperature rating of the conductor insulation, in this case 90°C. Using the 90°C column of *CEC* Table 3 (Column 4) it is determined that the 1/0 aluminum conductor has an allowable ampacity of 190 A. By referring to the same column of CEC Table 5A and an ambient temperature equal to or greater than 38°C in Column 1, the correction factor is found to be 0.90. Multiply the ampacity of the conductor by this factor.

$$190 \times 0.90 = 171 \text{ A}$$

MORE THAN THREE CONDUCTORS IN RACEWAY

CEC Tables 2 and 4 list allowable ampacities for not more than three conductors in a raceway or cable assembly. If a raceway or cable is to contain more than three conductors, the allowable ampacity of the conductors must be derated. This is because the heat from each conductor combines with the heat produced by the other conductors to produce a higher temperature inside the raceway or cable. *CEC* Table 5C and Table 6-3 list the correction factors. If the raceway is used in a space with a greater ambient temperature than that listed in the appropriate wire table, the temperature correction formula shall also be applied. For installations using free air conductors in which conductors are in contact, the correction factors as outlined in *CEC* Table 5B shall be used. Before applying the correction factors of *CEC* Tables 5B or 5C, be sure to refer to *CEC* Rule 4-004 to determine the correct number of conductors to be counted. Conductors that do not need to be counted for application of these tables include grounding and bonding conductors and most neutral conductors as defined in Section 0 of the *CEC*.

- When using only two phases and the neutral of a three-phase system, the neutral conductor must be counted for the purposes of derating.
- When multiconductor cables are run in contact with each other for distances exceeding 600 mm, the factors of *CEC* Table 5C must be applied

***CEC* Table 5C**

(See Rules 4-004 and 12-2210 and Tables 2 and 4)

Ampacity Correction Factors for Tables 2 and 4

Number of Conductors	Ampacity Correction Factors
1–3	1.00
4–6	0.80
7–24	0.70
25–42	0.60
43 and up	0.50

Table 6-3 Ampacity correction factors for Tables 2

PROBLEM 5

Twelve 14 AWG copper conductors with type RW90 insulation are to be installed in conduit in an area with an ambient temperature of 38°C. What will be the ampacity of these conductors?

First, determine the allowable ampacity of a 14 AWG copper conductor with type RW90 insulation. Type RW90 insulation is located in Column 4 of *CEC* Table 2 and Table 6-1. A 14 AWG copper conductor has an allowable ampacity of 15 A. The next step is to use the correction factor for ambient temperature. Using Column 4 of *CEC* Table 5A or Table 6-2 and an ambient temperature equal to or greater than 38°C from Column 1, the correction factor is found to be 0.90.

$$15 \times 0.90 = 13.5 \text{ A}$$

Next, a correction factor from *CEC* Table 5C or Table 6-3 shall be applied based on the number of conductors in the raceway. The table indicates a factor of 70% when 7 through 24 conductors are installed in a raceway.

$$13.5 \times 0.70 = 9.45 \text{ A}$$

A 14 AWG, type RW90 conductor when installed in a raceway, with a group of twelve conductors, in a 38°C ambient has an ampacity of 9.45 A.

UNDERGROUND CONDUCTORS

When conductors are installed underground, their ampacity is to be determined by *CEC* Rule 4-004 (1d) for copper conductors and Rule 4-004 (2d) for aluminum conductors. When referring to the *CEC* Appendix B for these rules, information is found regarding the method of calculating the conductor ampacities based on the IEEE standard. However, if the conductors are installed using the configurations outlined in Diagrams B4-1 to B4-4 in the *CEC* Appendix B, the ampacities as indicated in *CEC* Tables D8 to D15 can be applied. These ampacities have been calculated using the IEEE standard. *CEC* Tables D8 to D15 have an A and a B version. Be sure to consult the notes at the bottom of each table for the correct application. In general terms, the A version is for most loads, while the B version is for service or panelboard applications.

PROBLEM 6

A three-phase, three-wire underground service is to use two parallel runs of 350 kcm copper conductors in raceway. Each set of three-phase conductors is to be installed in a separate raceway. What is the ampacity of each phase conductor?

Using the *CEC* Appendix B to determine the layout of the conduits and cables, Detail 2 of Diagram B4-4 is the only one that meets the installation needs. Referring to *CEC* Tables D8 to D15, it is found that Tables D14A and D14B refer to installations based on Diagram B4-4. Upon closer examination of the notes at the bottom of these two tables, it is decided that the ampacities of Table D14B must be applied. Based upon the third column, two conductors per phase, Detail 2, and a conductor size of 350 kcm, the ampacity is found to be 321 A per conductor.

LONG WIRE LENGTHS

When the length of the conductors is excessively long, it may become necessary to compute wire sizes instead of using the tables in the Code. The listed ampacities in the Code tables assume that the length of the conductor will not significantly increase the resistance of the circuit. When the wire length becomes extremely long, however, it is necessary to compute the size of wire needed.

All wire contains resistance. As the length of wire is increased, it has the effect of adding resistance in series with the load. This resistance will cause a voltage drop over the length of the conductor. *CEC* Rule 8-102 specifies that the maximum voltage drop on an installation from the point of supply to the point of utilization cannot exceed 5% of the nominal voltage, while the voltage drop in any feeder or branch circuit must not exceed 3%. Four factors determine the resistance of a length of wire:

1. The material from which the wire is made. Different types of material have different wire resistances. A copper conductor will have less resistance than an aluminum conductor of the same size and length. An aluminum conductor will have less resistance than a piece of iron wire the same size and length.

2. The diameter of the conductor. The larger the diameter, the less resistance it will have. In Imperial units, the diameter of a wire is measured in mils. One mil equals 0.001 in. The circular mil area of a wire is the diameter of the wire in mils squared.

EXAMPLE Assume a wire has a diameter of 0.064 in. Converting to mils:

$$0.064 \text{ in} \times 1000 \text{ mils per in} = 64 \text{ mils}$$

The area in circular mils is:

$$64^2 = (64 \times 64) = 4096 \text{ cmil}$$

In SI units, the diameter of a conductor is measured in millimetres. The area of a conductor is measured in square metres. Since the area of a conductor is considerably smaller than 1 m^2, and there are 1 million square millimetres in a square metre, area is usually expressed as:

$$= \frac{\text{mm}^2}{1\,000\,000} = \frac{\text{mm}^2}{10^6} = \text{mm}^2 \times 10^{-6}\ \text{m}^2$$

EXAMPLE A conductor has a diameter of 1.5 mm. Find the area of the conductor in square metres.

Area in square millimetres

$$= \pi r^2$$

$$= \pi\left(\frac{d}{2}\right)^2$$

$$= \pi \times \left(\frac{1.5}{2}\right)^2$$

$$= \pi \times 0.5625$$

$$= 1.767 \text{ mm}^2$$

Area in square metres = Area in $\text{mm}^2 \times 10^{-6}$

$$= 1.767 \times 10^{-6} \text{ m}^2$$

3. The length of the conductor.
The longer the conductor, the more resistance it will have. Adding length to a conductor has the same effect as connecting resistors in series.

4. The temperature of the conductor.
As a general rule, most conductive materials will increase their resistance with an increase of temperature. Some exceptions to this rule are carbon, silicon, and germanium, which are classified as semi-conductors. If the coefficient of temperature for a particular material is known, its resistance at different temperatures can be computed. Materials that increase their resistance with an increase of temperature have a *positive* coefficient of temperature. Materials that decrease their resistance with an increase of temperature have a *negative* coefficient of temperature.

In Canada, we still use a wire sizing system known as the American Wire Gauge. In this system, the standard value of resistivity is the ohm/mil foot. It is used to determine the resistance of different lengths and sizes of wire. A mil foot (Figure 6-2) is a piece of wire 1 ft long and 1 mil in diameter. However, the standard measurement of distance in Canada is the metre. When lengths and diameters of conductors are measured in metres, the resistivity of the conductors is expressed in ohm-metres. Since this value is extremely small, it is often more convenient to express the resistivity in microhm-millimetres. To convert this value to ohm-metres, we would multiply by 10^{-9}. A chart listing the resistances of different wire materials at 20°C in both Imperial and SI units is shown in Table 6-4. Notice the wide range of resistances for different materials.

	Imperial Units	SI Units
Material	**Ohms per mil foot @ 20°C**	**Microhm-millimetres @ 20°C**
Aluminum	17.1	28.3
Carbon	22 000	36 384.6
Constantan	295	487.9
Copper	10.4	17.2
Gold	14	23.2
Iron	60	99.2
Lead	126	208.4
Mercury	590	975.8
Nichrome	675	1 116.3
Nickel	52	86.0
Platinum	66	109.2
Silver	9.6	15.9
Tungsten	33.8	55.9

Table 6-4 Resistivity of materials.

COMPUTING RESISTANCE

Now that a standard measure of resistance for different types of materials is known, the resistances of different lengths and sizes of these materials can be computed. The formula for computing resistance of a certain length, size, and type of wire is:

$$R = \frac{\rho \times L}{A}$$

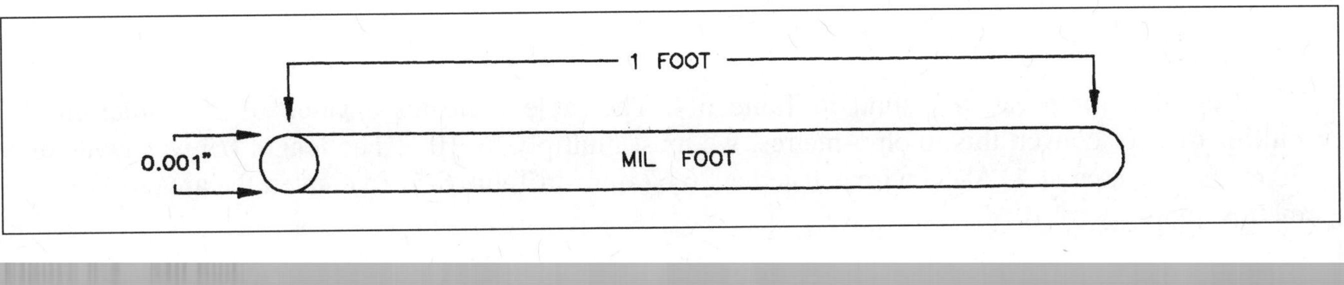

where

R = Resistance of the wire

ρ = Ohms per mil foot

L = Length of conductor in feet

A = Circular mil area of the wire

or where

R = Resistance of the wire

ρ = Ohm-metre

L = Length of conductor in metres

A = Area of conductor in square metres

This formula can be converted to compute other values in the formula such as size, length, and area of wire.

To find the size of wire, use:

$A = \rho \times L / R$

To find the length of wire use:

$L = R \times A / \rho$

To find the type of wire use:

$\rho = R \times A / L$

Table 6-5 on page 69, as found in *CEC* Table D5, Stranding of Building Wire and Cable, is specific to stranded wire and includes the conductor area in square millimetres. The only reference to solid building wire is in *CEC* Table 10 and includes both the conductor diameter in millimetres and the area in square millimetres. However, the *CEC* Table 10 values include the conductor insulation.

PROBLEM 7

Find the resistance of #6 AWG copper conductor 550 ft long. Assume a temperature of 20°C. The formula to be used is:

R (ohms) = ρ (ohms per mil ft) × L (ft) / A

The value for ρ can be found in Table 6-4, where the resistance and temperature coefficients of several types of materials are listed. The table indicates a value of 10.4 ohms per cmil foot for a copper conductor. The length (L) was given at 550 ft, and the area of #6 AWG wire is listed at 26 250 cmil as shown in Table 6-5.

$R = 10.4 \times 550 / 26\,250 = 0.218$ ohms

PROBLEM 8

Find the resistance of a #3 AWG aluminum conductor 30 m in length. Assume a temperature of 20°C. The formula to be used is:

R (ohms) = ρ (ohm-metres) × L (metres) / A

The value for ρ can be found in Table 6-4. The table indicates a value of 28.3 microhm-millimetres. To convert this to ohm-metres, we must multiply by 10^{-9}. The length (L) was given at 30 m, and the area of #3 AWG wire is listed at 26.67 mm^2 in Table 6-5. To convert the area to square metres, multiply by 10^{-6}.

***CEC* Table D5**

Standings for Building Wires and Cables

Nominal		Standard*			Flexible			Extra Flexible		
Conductor Size AWG or kcmil	Conductor Area mm²	Number of Wires†	Diameter mm	Occupied Area‡ mm²	Number of Wires	Diameter mm	Occupied Area‡ mm²	Number of Wires	Diameter mm	Occupied Area‡ mm²
14	2.08	7	1.84	2.74	19	1.87	2.74	37	1.87	2.74
12	3.31	7	2.32	4.34	19	2.35	4.34	37	2.35	4.34
10	5.26	7	2.95	6.94	19	2.97	6.94	37	2.97	6.94
8	8.37	7	3.71	11.1	19	3.76	11.1	37	3.76	11.1
6	13.3	7	4.67	17.5	19	4.72	17.5	37	4.72	17.5
4	21.2	7	5.89	28	19	5.97	28	37	5.99	28.2
3	26.7	7	6.6	35	19	6.68	35	37	6.71	35.3
2	33.6	7	7.42	44.4	19	7.52	44.4	37	7.54	44.7
1	42.4	19	8.43	56.2	37	8.46	56.2	61	8.46	56.2
1/0	53.5	19	9.47	70.9	37	9.5	70.9	61	9.53	71.3
2/0	67.4	19	10.6	89.4	37	10.7	89.4	61	10.7	89.8
3/0	85	19	11.9	112	37	12	112	61	12	113
4/0	107	19	13.4	142	37	13.4	142	61	13.5	142
250	127	37	14.6	168	61	14.6	168	91	14.7	169
300	152	37	16	202	61	16	202	91	16.1	202
350	177	37	17.3	236	61	17.3	236	91	17.3	236
400	203	37	18.5	269	61	18.5	269	91	18.5	270
450	228	37	19.6	280	61	19.6	280	91	19.7	304
500	253	37	20.7	337	61	20.7	337	91	20.7	337
550	279	61	21.7	370	91	21.7	370	127	21.7	371
600	304	61	22.7	405	91	22.7	405	127	22.7	405
650	329	61	23.6	438	91	23.6	438	127	23.6	438
700	355	61	24.5	472	91	24.5	472	127	24.5	472
750	380	61	25.3	506	91	25.4	506	127	25.4	506
800	405	61	26.2	540	91	26.2	540	127	26.2	541
900	456	61	27.8	606	91	27.8	606	127	27.8	608
1000	507	61	29.3	674	91	29.3	674	127	29.3	675
1250	633	91	32.7	843	127	32.8	843	169	32.8	843
1500	760	91	35.9	1010	127	35.9	1010	169	35.9	1010
1750	887	127	38.8	1180	169	38.8	1180	217	38.8	1180
2000	1010	127	41.5	1350	169	41.5	1350	217	41.5	1350

*Compact conductor diameters of equivalent cross-sectional area are reduced by up to 10% of the dimension indicated. Compressed conductor diameters of equivalent cross-sectional area are reduced by 2% of the dimension indicated.
†The number of wires indicated may be reduced by one in each layer.
‡Area of circumscribing circle; use for conduit space calculations.

Table 6-5 Strandings for building wires and cables, *CEC* Table D5.

PROBLEM 9

An aluminum conductor 2250 ft long cannot have a resistance greater than 0.2 ohm. What is the minimum size wire that may be used?

To find the size of wire, use:

$$A = \rho \text{ (ohms per mil ft)} \times L \text{ (ft)} / R \text{ (ohms)} = 17 \times 2250 / .2 = 191\ 250$$

The standard size conductor for this installation can be found in Table 6-5. Since the resistance cannot be greater than 0.2 ohm, the conductor cannot be smaller than 191 250 circular mils. The smallest acceptable standard conductor size is #4/0 AWG, which has an area of 211 600 circular mils.

PROBLEM 10

A copper conductor will have a length of 280 m. It is determined that the resistance of this conductor must not be greater than 2 ohm. Find the minimum size conductor for this application.

To find the size of wire, use:

$$A \text{ (square metres)} = \rho \text{ (ohm-metres)} \times L \text{ (metres)} / R \text{ (ohms)}$$

$$A = \frac{17.2 \times 10^{-9} \times 280}{2} = 2.408 \times 10^{-6}\ \text{m}^2 = 2.408\ \text{mm}^2$$

The standard size conductor for this installation can be found in Table 6-5. Since the resistance cannot be greater than 2 ohm, the conductor cannot be smaller than 2.408 mm^2. The smallest acceptable standard conductor size is 12 AWG, which has an area of 6530 circular mils.

Good examples of when it becomes necessary to compute the wire size for a particular installation can be seen in the following problems.

PROBLEM 11

A workshop is to be installed in a facility separate from the main building. The workshop is to contain a small arc welder, air compressor, various power tools, lights, and receptacles. It is determined that a 100-A, 120/240-V, single-phase panelboard will be needed for this installation. The distance between the buildings is 62 m. An extra 3 m of cable is to be added for connections, making a total length of 65 m. The maximum current will be 100 A. The voltage drop, at full load, is to be kept to a maximum of 3%, as required by *CEC* Rule 8-102. An ambient temperature of 20°C is to be assumed. What size copper conductors should be used for this installation?

The first step is to determine the maximum amount of resistance the conductors can have without producing a voltage drop greater than 3% of the applied voltage.

The maximum voltage drop can be determined by multiplying the applied voltage by the decimal equivalent of 3%.

$$240 \times 0.03 = 7.2\ \text{V}$$

Ohm's law can now be used to determine the resistance that will permit a voltage drop of 7.2 V at 100 A.

$$R = E / I = 7.2\ \text{V} / 100\ \text{A} = 0.072\ \text{ohms}$$

The length of cable between the main building and the workshop is 65 m. To determine the length of the conductor in feet, the length in metres must be multiplied by 3.28.

$$65 \times 3.28 = 213.2$$

Since current exists in two conductors at the same time, it is the same as having the conductors connected in series, which effectively doubles the length of the conductor. Therefore, the conductor length will be 213.2 ft × 2 = 426.4 ft.

cmil = ρ (ohms per mil ft) × L (ft) / R (ohms)

cmil = 10.4 × 426.4 / 0.072 = 61 591 cmil

Using Table 6-5, it is determined that a 2 AWG copper conductor with an area of 66 360 circular mils would be required.

PROBLEM 12

This problem concerns conductors used in a three-phase system. It is to be assumed that a motor is located 760 m from its power source and operates on 575 V. When the motor starts, the current will be 168 A. The equipment manufacturer has suggested that the voltage drop at the motor terminals should not be greater than 5% of the source voltage during starting. What size aluminum conductors should be used for this installation?

When we work with long distances and higher currents, as in this problem, we often determine that conductors larger than 4/0 AWG are required. The sizes of conductors larger than 4/0 AWG are listed by their circular mil area. In these instances, it is not practical to calculate conductor area in square millimetres and then convert to a wire size. It is far more convenient to convert the length from metres to feet and use the resistivity of the conductor in mil feet. The answer to the problem will be in cmils, allowing easy selection of the correct conductor size.

First, find the maximum voltage drop that can be permitted at the load by multiplying the source voltage by 5%.

$E = 575 \times 0.05 = 28.75$ V

The second step is to determine the maximum amount of resistance of the conductors. To compute this value, the maximum voltage drop will be divided by the starting current of the motor.

$R = E / I = 28.75 / 168 = 0.171$ ohms

The third step is to compute the lengths of the conductors. In the previous example, the lengths of the two conductors were added to find the total amount of wire resistance. In a single-phase system, each conductor must carry the same amount of current. During any period of time, one conductor is supplying current from the source to the load, and the other conductor completes the circuit by permitting the same amount of current to flow from the load to the source.

In a balanced three-phase circuit, there are three currents that are 120° out of phase with each other (Figure 6-3 on page 72). These three conductors share the flow of current between source and load. In Figure 6-3, two lines labelled *A* and *B* have been drawn through the three current waveforms. Notice that at position *A*, the current in Phase 1 is maximum and in a positive direction. The currents in Phases 2 and 3 are less than maximum and in a negative direction. This condition corresponds to the example shown in Figure 6-4 on page 72. Notice that the maximum current exists in only one conductor.

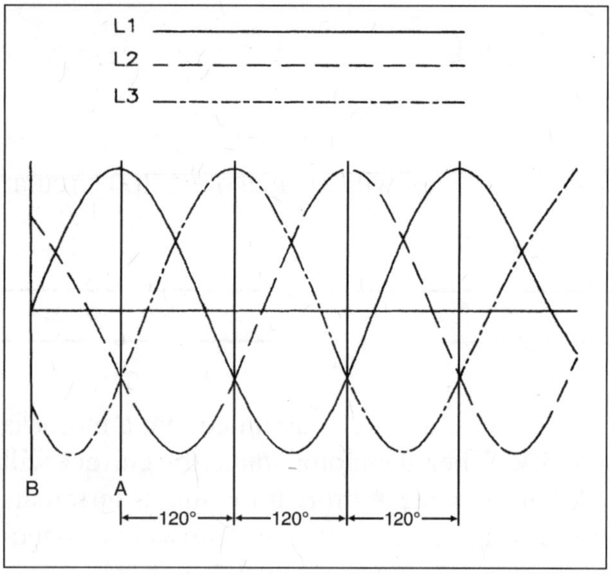

Figure 6-3 Currents of a three-phase system are 120° out of phase with each other.

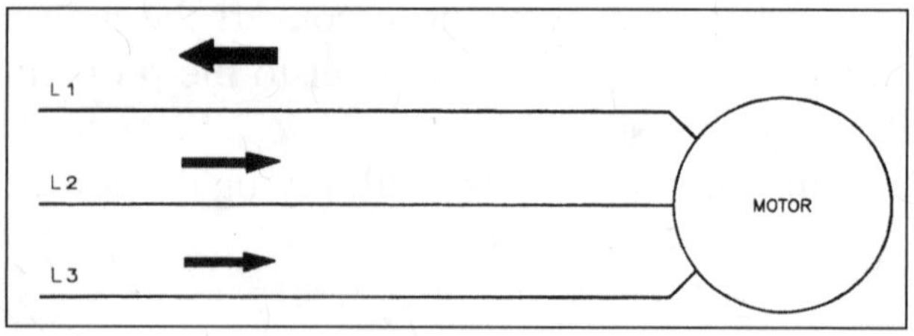

Figure 6-4 Current is maximum in one conductor and less than maximum in two conductors.

Figure 6-5 Currents in only two conductors.

Observe the line marking position *B* in Figure 6-3. The current in Phase 1 is zero, and the currents in Phases 2 and 3 are in opposite directions and less than maximum. This condition is illustrated in Figure 6-5. Notice that only two of the three phase lines are conducting current, and that the current in each line is less than maximum.

Since the phase currents in a three-phase system are never maximum at the same time, and at other times the current is divided between two phases, the total conductor resistance will not be the sum of two conductors. To compute the resistance of conductors in a three-phase system, a demand factor of 0.866 is used.

In this problem, the motor is located 760 m from the source. The effective conductor length (*Le*) will be computed by doubling the length of one conductor and then multiplying by 0.866.

$$Le = 760 \times 2 \times 0.866 = 1316.3 \text{ m}$$

To convert the length in metres to feet, multiply by 3.28.

$$Le = 1316.3 \text{ m} \times 3.28 = 4317.5 \text{ ft}$$

Now that all the factors are known, the size of the conductor can be computed.

$\rho = 17$ (ohms per mil foot for aluminum)

$$\text{cmil} = \rho \times L / R = 17 \times 4317.5 / 0.171 = 429\ 225 \text{ cmil}$$

Therefore, three 500-kcmil conductors will be required.

VOLTAGE DROP

The maximum voltage drop allowed from the point of supply to the point of utilization cannot exceed 5% of the nominal voltage (*CEC* Rule 8-102). The voltage drop in any feeder or branch circuit cannot exceed 3%. As a result, it is often necessary to oversize conductors in order to keep the percent voltage drop within the acceptable range. Before determining the minimum size conductor required for an application, the following information must be known:

- The minimum AWG of the conductor
- Current on the conductor

- Length of the conductor from the point of supply to the load
- Rated conductor temperature
- Percent of the allowable ampacity on the conductor
- Type of conductor (copper or aluminum)
- Desired percent voltage drop
- Voltage applied to the circuit

By utilizing *CEC* Table D3, shown in this text as Table 6-6 on page 74, and the following formula, the maximum length of conductor for a two-conductor circuit for a given voltage drop may be found.

L = T.D3 dist. × % VD × DCF × volts / 120

where

L = Maximum length of two-wire copper conductor run in metres

T.D3 dist. = The distance shown in *CEC* Table D3 for the size of wire and the actual load on the circuit

% VD = The maximum percent voltage drop allowed on the circuit. *Note:* this number is shown as a whole number, not as a decimal.

DCF = Distance correction factor. This is taken from the table in *CEC* Table D3, Note 3. The correction factor depends on the rated conductor temperature and the percentage of allowable ampacity (% Allowable ampacity = Actual load amperes / Allowable conductor ampacity × 100)

Volts = The voltage at which the circuit operates

EXAMPLE Find the maximum length of run for a two-wire circuit of #12 AWG RW90 conductors with a load of 16 A operating at 208 V. The maximum allowable voltage drop will be 3%.

1. Using *CEC* Table D3, the maximum length of run for a 16 A load on a #12 AWG conductor is 6.1 m.
2. Determine the distance correction factor. The percent load is determined by:

   Load amperes / Maximum conductor

   16 / 20 × 100 = 80%

   Using the 80% value of allowable load and the conductor temperature rating of 90°C, the distance correction factor is found to be 1.00 from *CEC* Table D3, Note 3.
3. Using the formula:

   L = T.D3 dist. × % VD × DCF × V / 120

   = 6.1 × 3 × 1.00 × 208 / 120

   = 31.72

If the length of conductor is to be longer than this distance, a larger conductor would have to be selected and the calculation repeated to ensure that the voltage drop does not exceed the maximum allowable by *CEC* Rule 8-102.

If the conductor is made of aluminum, refer to *CEC* Table D3, Note 5. Be sure to calculate the distance correction factor based on the connected load and the ampacity of the aluminum conductor from *CEC* Tables 3 or 4, not the ampacity of the equivalent copper conductor.

PARALLEL CONDUCTORS

Under certain conditions, it may become necessary or advantageous to connect conductors in parallel. One example of this condition occurs when conductor size is very large, as is the case in Problem 12. In Problem 12, it was computed that the conductors supplying a motor 760 m from its source would have to be 500 kcmil. A 500-kcmil conductor is very large and difficult to handle. For this reason, it may be preferable to use parallel conductors for this installation. The *CEC* lists several conditions that must be met when conductors are connected in parallel (*CEC* Rule 12-108):

1. The conductors must be 1/0 AWG or larger
2. The conductors must be the same length
3. The conductors must be made of the same material
4. The conductors must have the same circular mil area
5. The conductors must have the same type of

CEC Table D3

(See Rule 8-102 and Appendix B Note to Rule 4-004)

Distance to Centre of Distribution for a 1% Drop in Voltage on Nominal 120 V, 2-Conductor Copper Circuits

Current Amperes	Copper Conductor Size in AWG														
	18	16	14	12	10	8	6	4	3	2	1	1/0	2/0	3/0	4/0
	Distance in Metres to Centre of Distribution Measured Along the Conductor Run, Calculated for Conductor Temperature of 60°C														
1	24.2	38.5	61.4												
1.25	19.4	30.8	49.1												
1.6	15.1	24.1	38.4	61.0											
2	12.1	19.3	30.7	48.8											
2.5	9.7	15.4	24.6	39.0	62.0										
3.2	7.6	12.0	19.2	30.5	48.5										
4	6.1	9.6	15.3	24.4	38.8	61.7									
5	4.8	7.7	12.3	19.5	31.0	49.3									
6.3	3.8	6.1	9.7	15.5	24.6	39.1	62.2								
8	3.0	4.8	7.7	12.2	19.4	30.8	49.0								
10	2.4	3.9	6.1	9.8	15.5	24.7	39.2	62.4							
12.5		3.1	4.9	7.8	12.4	19.7	31.4	49.9	62.9						
16		2.4	3.8	6.1	9.7	15.4	24.5	39.0	49.1	62.0					
20			3.1	4.9	7.8	12.3	19.6	31.2	39.3	49.6	62.5				
25				3.9	6.2	9.9	15.7	24.9	31.4	39.7	50.0	63.1			
32					4.8	7.7	12.2	19.6	24.6	31.0	39.1	49.3	62.1		
40					3.9	6.2	9.8	15.6	19.7	24.8	31.3	39.4	49.7	62.7	
50						4.9	7.8	12.5	15.7	19.8	25.0	31.5	39.8	50.1	63.2
63						3.9	6.2	9.9	12.5	15.7	19.8	25.0	31.6	39.8	50.2
80						3.1	4.9	7.8	9.8	12.4	15.6	19.7	24.8	31.3	39.5
100							3.9	6.2	7.9	9.9	12.5	15.8	19.9	25.1	31.6
125								5.0	6.3	7.9	10.0	12.6	15.9	20.1	25.3
160									4.9	6.2	7.8	9.9	12.4	15.7	19.8
200										5.0	6.3	7.9	9.9	12.5	15.8
250												6.3	8.0	10.0	12.6
320													6.2	7.8	9.9

Notes:

(1) Table D3 is calculated for copper wire sizes No. 18 AWG to No. 4/0 AWG and gives, for each size specified, the approximate distance in metres to the centre of distribution measured along the conductor run for a 1% drop in voltage at a given current, with the conductor at a temperature of 60°C. Inductive reactance has not been included since it is a function of conductor size and spacing.

(2) The distances for a 3% or 5% voltage drop are 3 or 5 times those for a 1% voltage drop.

(3) Since the distances in Table D3 are based on conductor resistances at 60°C, these distances must be multiplied by the correction factors below according to the temperature rating of the conductor used and the percentage load with respect to the allowable ampacity.

Table 6-6 ***CEC*** **Table D3.**

6. The conductors must be terminated in the same manner
7. The conductors must be free of splices

In the previous example, the actual conductor size needed was computed to be 429 225 circular mils. This circular mil area could be obtained by connecting two 250-kcmil conductors in parallel for each phase, or three 3/0 AWG conductors in parallel for each phase.

Note: Each 3/0 AWG conductor has an area of 167 800 circular mils. This is a total of 503 400 circular mils.

Another example of when it may be necessary to connect wires in parallel is when conductors of a large size must be run in conduit. The conductor of a single phase from a multiphase system is not permitted to be run in metallic conduit, as shown in Figure 6-6. The reason for this is that when current exists in a conductor, a magnetic field is produced

Rated Conductor Temperature	Distance Correction Factor Per Cent of Allowable Ampacity						
	100	90	80	70	60	50	40
60°C	1.00	1.02	1.04	1.06	1.07	1.09	1.10
75°C	0.96	1.00	1.00	1.03	1.06	1.07	1.09
85–90°C	0.91	0.95	1.00	1.00	1.04	1.06	1.08
110°C	0.85	0.90	0.95	1.00	1.02	1.05	1.07
125°C	0.82	0.87	0.92	0.97	1.00	1.04	1.07
200°C	0.68	0.76	0.83	0.90	0.96	1.00	1.04

(4) For other nominal voltages, multiply the distances in metres by the other nominal voltage (in volts) and divide by 120.

(5) Aluminum conductors have equivalent resistance per unit length to copper conductors which are smaller in area by two AWG sizes. Table D3 may be used for aluminum conductors because of this relationship, ie, for No. 6 AWG aluminum use the distances listed for No. 8 AWG copper in Table D3. Similarly, for No. 2/0 AWG aluminum use the distances for No. 1 AWG copper.

(6) The distances and currents listed in Table D3 follow a pattern. When the current, for any conductor size, is increased by a factor of 10, the corresponding distance decreases by a factor of 10. This relationship can be used when no value is shown in the Table. In that case, look at a 10 times larger current. The distance to the centre of distribution is then 10 times larger than the listed value.

(7) For multi-conductor cables, ensure wire size obtained from this Table is suitable for ampacity from Table 2 or 4, and Rule 4-004.

(8) For currents intermediate to listed values use the next higher current value.

(9) Example on use of Table: Consider a 2-conductor circuit of No. 12 AWG copper NMD90 carrying **16 A** at nominal **240 V** under maximum ambient of 30°C. The maximum run distance from the centre of distribution to the load without exceeding a 3% voltage drop is: Maximum run length for No. 12 AWG, **16 A**, 1% voltage drop at nominal **120 V** from Table is: **6.1 m** Distance Correction Factor to be used is: From Table 2, allowable ampacity for 2-conductor No. 12 AWG NMD90 (**90°C** rating per Table 19) is **20 A**. The given current is 16 A or 80% (16/20) of the allowable ampacity. The Distance Correction Factor to be used, from Note (3), **90°C** row, 80% column, is 1.00. The maximum run length is:

$$6.1\text{ m} \times (3\%) \times 1.00 \times \frac{240\text{ V}}{120\text{ V}} = 37\text{ m}$$

Beyond this distance a larger size of conductor is required, ie, No. 10 AWG (**30 A** allowable ampacity) beyond 37 m up to and including 62 m.

$$9.7\text{ m} \times (3\%) \times 1.06 \times \frac{240\text{ V}}{120\text{ V}} = 62\text{ m}$$

Table 6-6 ***CEC* Table D3. (continued)**

around the conductor. In an alternating-current circuit, the current continuously changes direction and magnitude, which causes the magnetic field to cut through the wall of the metal conduit. This cutting action of the magnetic field induces a current, called an eddy current, into the metal of the conduit. Eddy currents can produce enough heat in high-current circuits to melt the insulation surrounding the conductors. All metal conduits can have eddy current induction, but conduits made of magnetic materials such as steel have an added problem with hysteresis loss. Hysteresis loss is caused by molecular friction. As the direction of the magnetic field reverses, the molecules of the metal are magnetized with the opposite polarity and swing to realign themselves. This continuous aligning and realigning of the molecules produces heat due to friction. Hysteresis losses become greater with an increase in frequency.

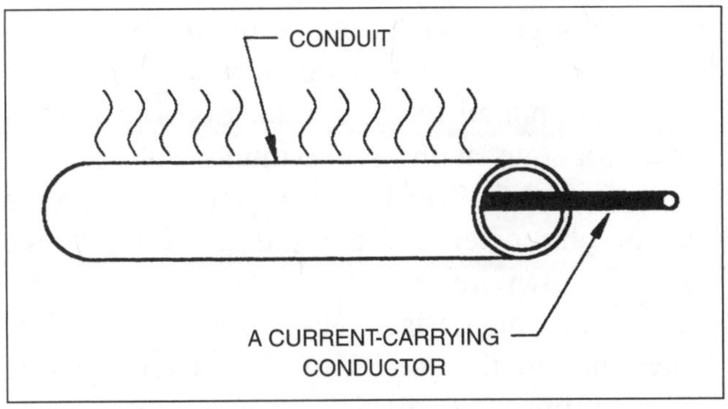

Figure 6-6 The current in the conductor causes heat to be produced in the conduit.

To correct this problem, a conductor of each phase must be run in each conduit (Figure 6-7 on page 76). When all three phases are contained in a single conduit, the magnetic fields of the separate conductors cancel each other, resulting in no current being induced in the walls of the conduit.

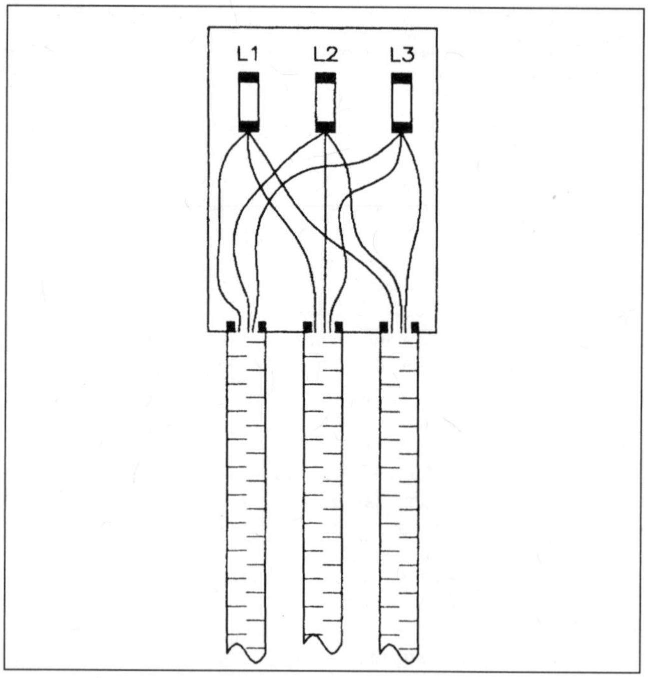

Figure 6-7 Each conduit contains a conductor from each phase.

TESTING WIRE INSTALLATIONS

After the conductors have been installed in conduits or raceways, it is accepted practice to test the installation for grounds and shorts. This test requires an ohmmeter, which not only can measure resistance in millions of ohms but also can provide a high enough voltage to ensure that the insulation will not break down when rated line voltage is applied to the conductors. Most ohmmeters operate with a maximum voltage that ranges from 1.5 V to about 9 V, depending on the type of ohmmeter and the setting of the range scale. To test wire insulation, a megohmmeter is used with a voltage from about 250 V to 5000 V, depending on the model of the meter and the range setting. One model of megohmmeter is shown in Figure 6-8. This instrument contains a hand crank that is connected to the rotor of a brushless AC generator. The advantage of this particular instrument is that it does not require the use of batteries. A range selector switch permits the meter to be used as a standard ohmmeter or as a megohmmeter. When it is used as a megohmmeter, the selector switch permits the test voltage to be selected. Test voltages of 100 V, 250 V,

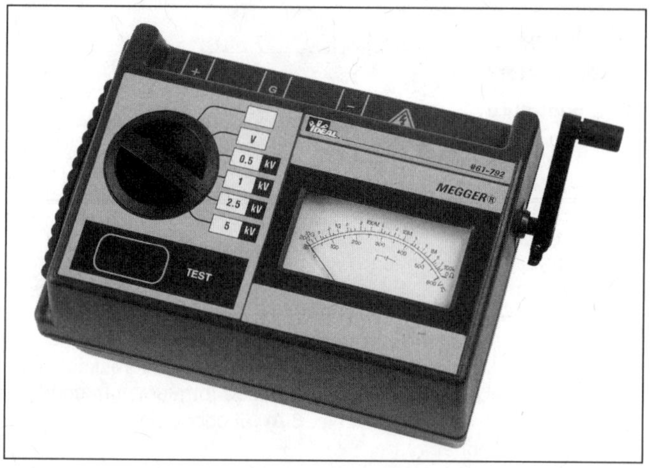

Figure 6-8 Hand-cranked megohmmeter. (Courtesy of Ideal Industries (Canada), Inc.)

500 V, and 1000 V can be obtained. Many hand-cranked megohmmeters do not have a voltage selector switch. The voltage is determined by the rate at which the crank is turned.

A megohmmeter can also be obtained in battery-operated models, as shown in Figure 6-9. These models are small, lightweight, and particularly useful when it becomes necessary to test the dielectric of a capacitor.

Wire installations are generally tested for two conditions: shorts and grounds. Shorts are unintended low-impedance current paths that exist between conductors. To test an installation for shorts, the megohmmeter is connected across two conductors at a time, as shown in Figure 6-10. The circuit is tested at rated voltage or slightly higher.

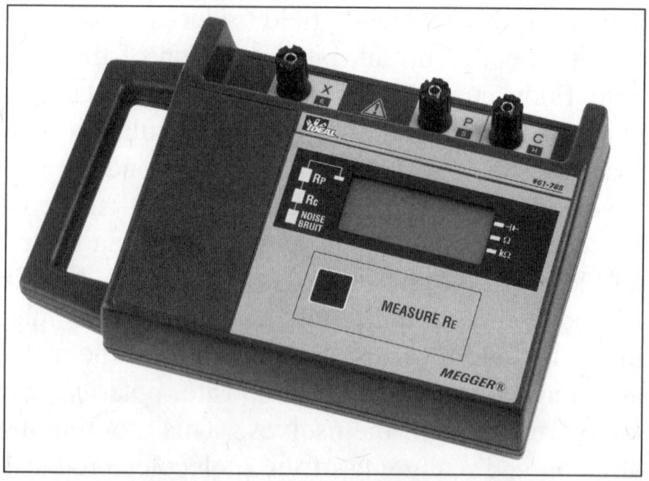

Figure 6-9 Battery-operated megohmmeter. (Courtesy of Ideal Industries (Canada), Inc.)

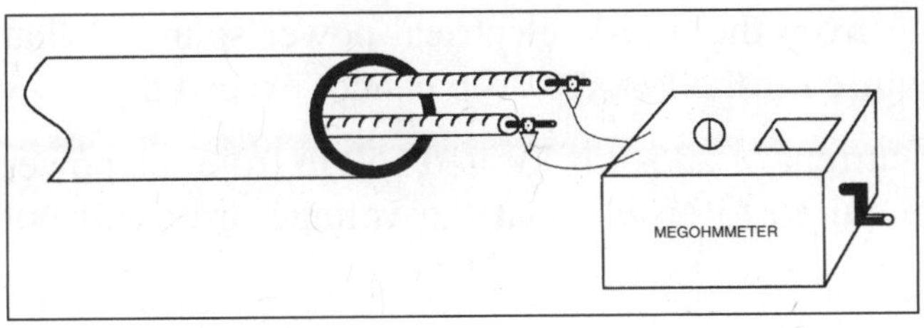

Figure 6-10 Testing for shorts with a megohmmeter.

The megohmmeter indicates the resistance between the two conductors. Since both conductors are insulated, the resistance between them should be extremely high. Each conductor should be tested against every other conductor in the installation.

To test the installation for grounds, one lead of the megohmmeter is connected to the metallic raceway, as shown in Figure 6-11. The other meter lead is connected to one of the conductors. The conductor should be tested at rated voltage or slightly higher. Each conductor should be tested.

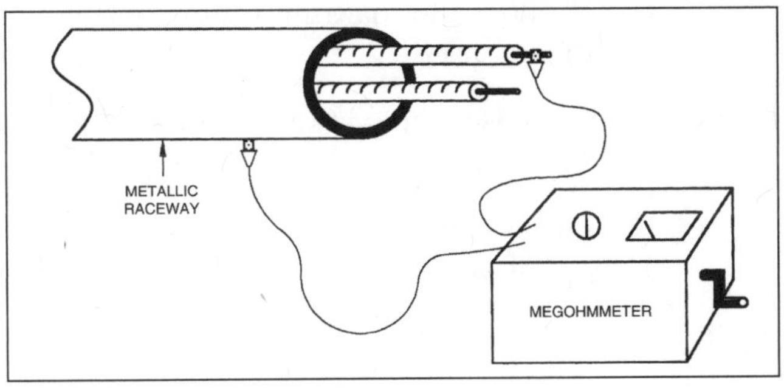

Figure 6-11 Testing for grounds with a megohmmeter.

REVIEW

All answers should be written in complete sentences, calculations should be shown in detail, and Code references should be cited when appropriate.

Unless specified otherwise, the ambient temperature is 30°C, the location is dry, the termination has a temperature rating equal to or greater than the conductor, and the wire is copper. Where the phrase *allowable ampacity* is used, it refers to a value taken from one of the tables. When the phrase *ampacity* is used, it refers to the allowable ampacity as corrected and adjusted and in compliance with *CEC* Rule 4-004.

1. What is the temperature rating of a type NMWU conductor when used in a wet location?
2. What types of conductors are approved for direct burial?
3. What types of conductors are approved for underground use?
4. Three #6 AWG, type TW conductors are to be installed overhead between poles on individual insulators. What will the conductor ampacity be?
5. Motor feeders consisting of six #1/0 AWG type RW90 aluminum conductors are to be installed in a rigid metal conduit in an ambient temperature of 40°C. What will be the conductor ampacity? What will be the circuit ampacity?
6. Explain what it means to install "conductors in parallel," and state seven conditions that must be satisfied if this is done.
7. What is the size of the largest solid (not stranded) conductor approved for installation in raceways?
8. How is a #4 AWG grounded circuit conductor in a raceway identified?
9. What insulation colours are used for three-phase installations?

10. A single-phase, 86-A load is located 850 m from the 480-V electrical power source. What minimum size aluminum conductors are required if the voltage drop cannot exceed 3%?

11. A three-phase, 600-V motor with a starting current of 235 A is located 550 m from the power source. What size copper conductors are required to ensure that the voltage drop will not exceed 6% during starting?

12. What is the maximum noncontinuous load that can be connected to a #2 AWG, type RW90 conductor?

13. What is the maximum continuous load that can be connected to a #2 AWG, type RW90 conductor?

14. An installation has 110 A of continuous load and 40 A of noncontinuous load on a single-phase, 240/120-V feeder. What is the minimum copper conductor size if installed in raceway or cable?

UNIT 7

Signalling Systems

OBJECTIVES

After studying this unit, the student should be able to:

- describe and install the master clock
- describe and install the program system
- describe and install the paging system
- describe and install the fire alarm system

A signalling circuit is defined in *CEC* Section 0 as any electric circuit that energizes signalling equipment such as bells, buzzers, or signal lights. A signalling system may include one or more signalling circuits. For example, in the industrial building, there are several electrical systems that give recognizable visual and audible signals and are classified as signalling systems:

- a master clock
- a program system
- a paging or locating system
- a fire alarm system

THE MASTER CLOCK

The master clock is a clock designed to drive some number of units that display the time. The display units are not actually clocks themselves but depend for their operation on signals received from the master clock. The display unit may use light-emitting diodes (LEDs) to indicate the time or an analog display using numbers and hands. Digital displays are generally designed to accommodate large LEDs that can be seen from a long distance. If a display with a number larger than about 0.55 in (14 mm) is desired, it will generally use a planar gas discharge display rather than an LED display.

Several methods can be used to sense time in the master clock unit. One of the most common methods for many years was to use a single-phase synchronous motor. The speed of the synchronous motor is proportional to its number of poles and the line frequency. This method uses the 60-Hz line frequency to measure time. This is the same method often used to operate electric clocks in the home. Sensing the line frequency is relatively accurate. Clocks using this method to sense time are generally accurate to within a couple of minutes per month.

Another method that has become popular is the sensing of vibrations produced by a piece of quartz crystal. When an AC voltage is impressed across two faces of the crystal, it will resonate at some specific frequency. This resonant frequency is extremely constant and, therefore, can be used to measure time accurately. The frequency at which the quartz will resonate is inversely proportional to the size of the crystal. The smaller the crystal, the higher the resonant frequency will be. The shape of the crystal also plays a part in determining the resonant frequency. Quartz clocks are generally accurate to within one second per month. Some quartz clocks will even compensate for fluctuations in temperature and aging of the quartz crystal, increasing the accuracy to within approximately one second per year.

Some installations sense time by receiving a radio signal from WWV, a radio station that broadcasts time pulses. WWV is operated by the National Bureau of Standards and is used as a time standard throughout the United States. A cesium beam atomic clock is used to produce the pulses that are transmitted. WWV can be received on frequencies of 18 kHz, 20 kHz, and 60 kHz, and on frequencies of 2.5 MHz, 5 MHz, 10 MHz, 15 MHz, 20 MHz, and 25 MHz. At the beginning of each minute, a 1000-Hz signal is transmitted, except at the beginning of each hour, when a 1500-Hz signal is transmitted. The master clock would contain a radio receiver capable of receiving WWV pulses. The timing of the clock depends on the pulses received, and, in this way, the time clock is continually updated each minute.

Modern master clock systems will generally receive their time from the Internet or a Global Positioning System (GPS) satellite. In many installations, a personal computer (PC) is used as the master clock rather than a separate unit. By using a PC, time synchronization can be picked up from government websites via the Internet. An alternative method is to use a separate master clock fitted with a GPS receiver. The master clock would then receive the time synchronization directly from the GPS satellite.

The clock also requires a backup power source. In the event of a power failure, it will be necessary to keep the correct time. Most quartz clock systems and personal computer-based systems only require a small button cell to keep the accuracy of the time. If it is necessary to display the time during an interruption of power, a small, off the shelf, uninterruptable power supply (UPS) would be required.

Master Clock Communication

Older master clock systems required three or more conductors. They would operate by supplying a continuous power source to the clocks and updating the clocks on the hour by sending a series of pulses on additional conductors. Lengths of runs had to be considered when sizing conductors due to voltage drop. Modern master clock systems use several different methods of communicating.

Serial Bus By using a digital serial bus consisting of only two conductors, up to 200 analog or 1000 digital slave clocks may be connected to a single master clock. If more clocks are needed, a signal booster can be installed. The clocks are powered directly from the serial bus, so no additional power supply is required. By using the signal boosters, any number of slave clocks can be installed.

Ethernet Standard ethernet communication—as used for computer networking—may also be utilized. By using the data infrastructure already existing in many offices and industry, it is possible to install a master clock system with minimal modifications to the wiring structure. By connecting the clock ethernet network to the office computer network, the master clock can be used to synchronize all of the building clocks and the office computers.

Power Line A master clock with a power line interface module is used for this type of system. Both single-phase and three-phase models are available. Simply plug the master clock and the slave clocks into any power source. The pulses required to keep the clocks in sync are sent by the master clock over the existing power wiring and received by the slave clocks located throughout the building. The maximum distance from the master clock to the slave unit is approximately 500 m, depending on the line current and any “noise” on the lines. The slave unit can be set to rebroadcast the pulse, effectively doubling this distance.

Many master clock systems allow for combinations of the basic communication methods. For example, let’s assume that a master clock system has been installed throughout the office using the spare ethernet network drops originally intended for the office computers. To extend the system onto the plant floor, an interface module is installed to convert from ethernet to serial bus. The plant can be wired with two-conductor twisted-pair cable rather than more expensive Category 5 or better cable. Considerable money may also be saved by the elimination of the more costly ethernet terminations. This entire system will sync to a single master clock. Now consider that there is a storage building located 100 m away from the main building. To get a clock into this building using the serial bus or ethernet method will involve the expensive and often impractical installation of overhead or underground conductors. If the outbuilding already has power in it, and it most likely will, an interface module can be installed on the serial bus or the ethernet network, converting to power line synchronization. A power line slave clock is then installed in the outbuilding and plugged into any power source.

THE PROGRAM SYSTEM

The program system is used to provide automatic signals for the operation of horns, bells, and buzzers. These devices are used in industry to signal the beginning and ending of shifts, lunch periods, and breaks. Different parts of the plant operate on different time schedules. Office workers, for example, begin and end work at different times than do employees who work in the manufacturing area of the plant. Lunch and coffee break times also vary. For this reason, the program control system must be capable of providing different signals to different parts of the plant at the proper times.

The program controller used in this installation is shown in Figure 7-1. This controller is a microprocessor-based programmable timer. This unit has 32 separate output channels and can be programmed for up to 1000 events. Each channel contains a normally open reed relay. Each relay can be operated by momentary contact or latching, or the unit can be set so that there can be 16 of each. A simple modification will permit 16 double-pole relays to be used instead of 32 single-pole relays. The 1000 events can be entered into the unit randomly, as opposed to entering them in chronological order. Cyclic events can be programmed to occur every minute, hour, day, or week, or in any combination desired. Any of the 32 output channels can be turned on at the same time.

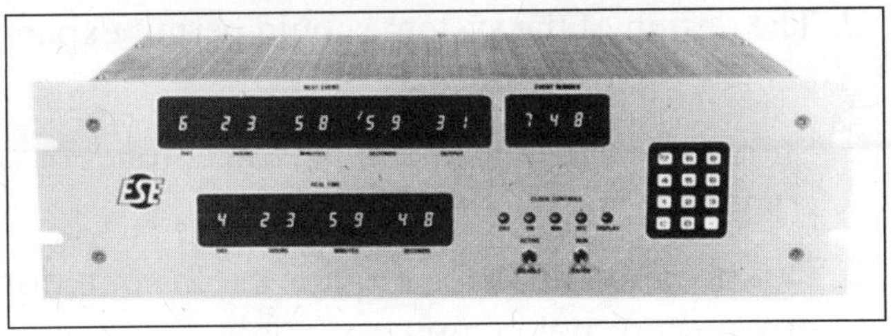

Figure 7-1 Programmable timer.

Programming is done with a 12-button keyboard located on the front of the unit. The keyboard contains numbers 0 through 9, and CLEAR and ENTER buttons. Two toggle switches, also located on the front of the panelboard, are used to provide active/disable and run/enter functions. These switches permit programmed events to be viewed without interrupting the program. Once the timer has been programmed, it is possible to save the program on a cassette tape. This is done by connecting a cassette tape recorder to a jack provided on the rear of the timer. If for some reason the timer should have to be replaced, the same program can be loaded into the new unit from the cassette tape, saving the time and effort involved in having to reprogram the unit.

The program timer also contains a digital clock operated by an internal crystal oscillator. A battery and battery charger are provided with the unit in case of power failure. With the addition of a serial time code generator, the program timer also can be used as a master clock. The time code generator gives the unit the capability of driving up to 100 display units.

THE PAGING SYSTEM

In many industrial installations, it is important to convey messages to all areas of the plant. When selecting a paging system, several factors should be taken into consideration, such as:

1. What is the amount of area to be covered and the number of paging units needed?

2. The design of the system should permit expansion as the plant increases in size.
3. Should the paging system be voice, tone, or a combination of both?
4. Do areas of the plant require explosionproof or weatherproof equipment?
5. What is the ambient noise level of the plant?

A very important consideration when choosing the type of equipment to be used is the ambient or surrounding noise level. The chart shown in Figure 7-2 illustrates different levels of noise measured in decibels (dB). For a signal or voice to be heard, it should be at least 5 dB louder than the surrounding noise level at the workstation. Another important consideration is the distance of the speaker from the workstation; as a general rule, sound decreases by 6 dB each time the distance from the speaker is doubled.

Reaction	dB	Source Comparison
Uncomfortably loud (possible ear pain)	140 120 195	Jackhammer at 2 ft (600 mm) Thunder (near) Circular saw at 2 ft (600 mm)
Very loud	90 to 100	Industrial plant Wire mill boiler factory
Loud	80 to 90	Foundry factory, press room
Moderate	70 to 75	Normal conversation in office at 3 ft (900 mm)
Quiet	40 to 55	Hospital room
Very quiet	30 to 35	Whisper at 2 ft (600 mm)

Figure 7-2 Comparable sounds.

The paging system chosen for this plant is manufactured by Audiosone Inc. and has the capability of producing both voice and tone signals. Two types of paging units will be used. The first

PROBLEM 1

A speaker is rated to produce 110 dB at a distance of 10 ft (3 m). The ambient noise level at the workstation is measured at 80 dB. If the speaker is mounted 160 ft (49 m) away from the workstation, will the worker be able to hear the messages clearly?

Figure 7-3 illustrates the amount of sound decrease with distance. Notice that the chart starts with a value of 110 dB at a distance of 10 ft (3 m), and decreases 6 dB each time the distance is doubled. At a distance of 160 ft (49 m), the sound level should be 86 dB. This is loud enough to permit the worker to hear the voice or tone.

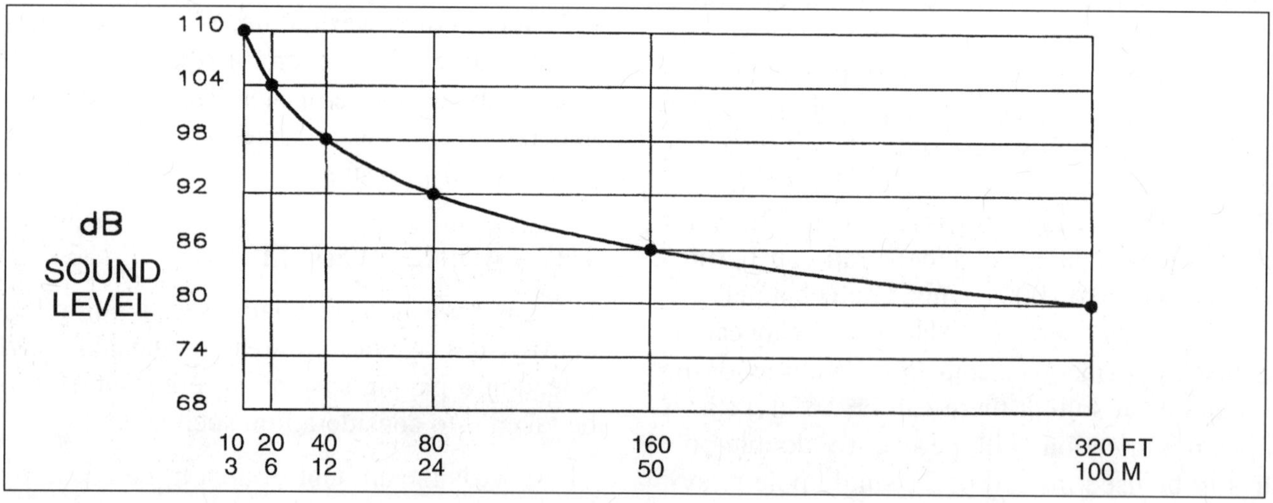

Figure 7-3 Effects of sound relating to distance.

type can be used to send voice messages only. The second type, shown in Figure 7-4, can send both voice and tone messages. Each paging unit contains its own amplifier, Figure 7-5. This permits an almost unlimited number to be used when they are connected in parallel to a four-conductor circuit.

The system also can be expanded to use a voice evacuation alarm, shown in Figure 7-6. This unit permits taped messages to be used, which can instruct employees as to the nature of the emergency. Four separate tones can be generated:

1. WAIL: (conventional siren)
2. HI-LO: alternating high and low (European siren)
3. WHOOP: ascending low to high, repeated
4. HORN: steady tone

The tones are to be used to announce different conditions. One is to be used as a fire signal and will be connected to the fire alarm system. The other three tones can be used to announce such conditions as plant evacuation, shift change, and so on. Two types of speakers will be used, as in Figure 7-7. These speakers will be located at strategic points throughout the plant.

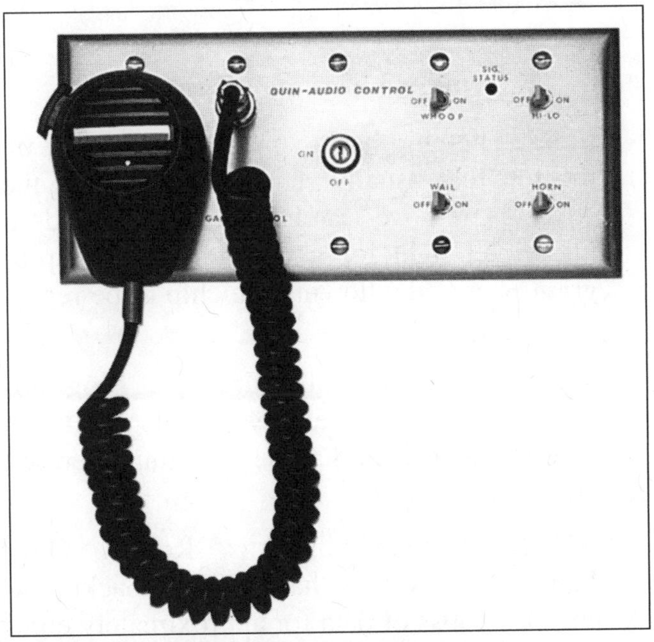

Figure 7-4 Unit used to send voice and tone messages.

THE FIRE ALARM SYSTEM

Microprocessors are in almost every type of equipment that we use today, from coffeemakers to computers, and fire alarm systems are no exception. With microprocessors becoming faster,

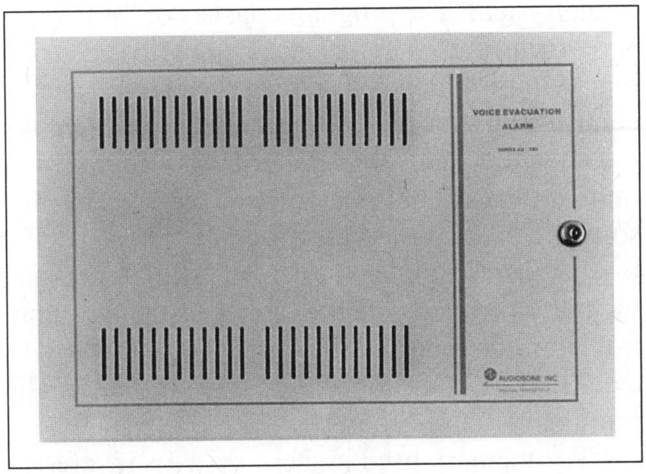

Figure 7-6 Voice evacuation alarm.

more powerful, and more affordable, they have even been integrated to some degree into conventional fire alarm systems.

Microprocessor systems, as in Figure 7-8, have many benefits. Each device has a specific identification so that it can be determined which device initiated the alarm rather than just which general area within the building. Field wiring is less expensive and with the programmable abilities of the system, operational sequences are easily altered or suspended. However, errors in programming may cause unintended system operations that could be dangerous or fatal.

Figure 7-8 A microprocessor fire alarm unit.

System Architecture

As in a computer, the central processing unit (CPU) is the heart of the system. As defined by the program, it accepts inputs from the field devices, analyzes that input, and carries out instructions. The program is a set of procedures that is stored in memory and controls the functions and operation of the system. The program consists of "software" and "firmware." The firmware is the basic structure within which the software operates and is controlled by the system manufacturer. Often, the manufacturer may provide firmware upgrades to improve the overall operation of the system. The software is the part of the program that is specific to the installation and the building. This may include operations such as fan and damper control, elevator control, different alarm tones to indicate the location of the alarm, or automatic printing of status reports.

The memory used in these systems is referred to as non-volatile memory, that is, memory that does not lose its contents upon power failure. There are several different types of non-volatile memory chips:

- ROM—Read Only Memory. The data or instructions are permanently stored in the chip.
- PROM—Programmable Read Only Memory. This is programmed by the system manufacturer. If the firmware or program changes, a new PROM would need to be installed.
- EPROM—Erasable Programmable Read Only Memory. This type can be programmed many times. The chip has a small clear window on the top that usually remains covered. If the cover is removed and the chip exposed to ultraviolet light for a few minutes, the program is erased, allowing the chip to be reprogrammed.
- EEPROM—Electrically Erasable Programmable Read Only Memory. This is similar to an EPROM except that the chip can be erased electrically.
- NOVRAM—Non-Volatile Read Only Memory. This type has built in backup to ensure no loss of data for approximately eight years.

Advantages of a Programmable Microprocessor System

Because of the large number of components integrated into a microprocessor, these systems generally contain fewer electronic components, resulting in reduced cost, weight, size, and power consumption. Because data is sent to the controller from the field devices on a serial trunk, more devices can be installed on a single circuit, thereby requiring less field wiring. With the use of addressable devices, an alarm condition can be identified to a specific device rather than just a zone or area. The microprocessor's ability to perform logic functions allows the system to perform functions that would be impossible with a conventional fire alarm system. The processor also provides integration of timers, counters, system reports, and event logs, and various levels of password protection for access to system functions.

Microprocessor-based systems do have some disadvantages. These systems are much more sensitive to static electricity, power surges, and lightning, often requiring an uninterruptible power supply to provide clean, stable power. Electromagnetic interference can cause noise on the field wiring that may be misinterpreted as an alarm condition. When installing or altering a microprocessor system, all the field devices must be approved by the manufacturer for use on the system. Alterations to the physical wiring will most likely require reprogramming of the system, which could result in improper operation.

System Communication

In a conventional fire alarm system, the current that flows in an initiating circuit is affected by the length and size of the conductors and the position of the device on the circuit. A microprocessor system operates with only two voltages: one representing an "off" or false condition and one representing an "on" or true condition. The off condition is said to be "logic 0" and the on as "logic 1." Each logic 0 or logic 1 represents a binary digit referred to as a "bit." These bits are usually grouped in an eight-bit group called a byte. Since the microprocessor receives eight bits at a time, it is capable of processing data more quickly.

Serial data transfer allows for reduced wiring by sending large amounts of data over only two conductors. Data is transferred as a series of pulses sent along the conductor one after another in groups of eight bits. Depending on the system and the type of microprocessor, data can be sent in one direction only (simplex), in either direction but only one direction at a time (half duplex), or in both directions at the same time (full duplex).

The two-conductor serial circuit is called a data communication link (DCL). This link is used

communication link may be configured in one of three formats:

- DCLA—similar to a class "A" conventional system in which both ends of the circuit are connected to the CPU in the form of a loop.
- DCLB—similar to a class "B" conventional system in which only one end of the circuit is connected to the CPU.
- DCLR—provides a redundant wiring circuit. Similar to two DCLB circuits to each device.

Field Devices

Field devices (Figure 7-9 on page 86) used on a microprocessor fire alarm system—such as heat detectors, smoke detectors, and pull stations—can be individually identified by the control unit to determine their presence in the circuit and their status in the system. These devices are referred to as *active devices*.

Approximately 200 of these devices can be wired on a single circuit while still being able to provide unique device identification. With a conventional system, the annunciator indicates the general area of the alarm or trouble indication. However, addressable systems will provide an alphanumeric indication as to the exact location and status of the device creating the alarm or trouble indication.

Device Addressing

Each device in an addressable system has a unique address assigned to it, allowing the control unit to send out "requests" to the field device. One at a time, the address of each device is sent out over the DCL. When the device recognizes its own address, it sends a response to the controller. The responses will be "normal" or "alarm." No response to the request indicates trouble. After all of the devices have been polled, the cycle starts over again.

Two methods of addressing are used, with the most common being automatic addressing. When the system is powered up, addresses are assigned to the automatic devices. Some devices require the address

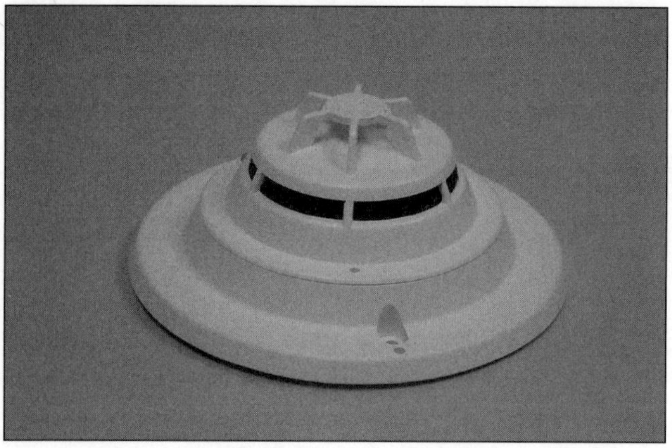

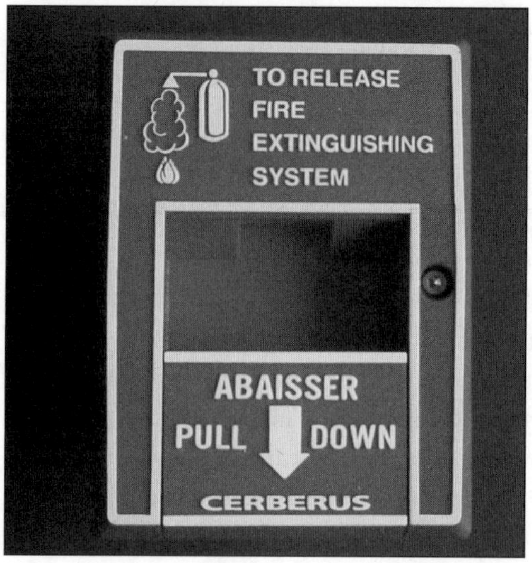

Figure 7-9 Field devices.

The operation of addressable devices falls into two categories: standard and analog. Standard devices will only have one of two responses to a request by the control unit—"normal" or "alarm." Analog devices will respond to the control unit with a full range of responses. For example, an analog smoke detector may be able to report the actual level of smoke obscuring the sensor. This will allow the microprocessor to respond differently depending on the levels of smoke. These analog devices often have additional features that will assist in maintaining the system. An analog smoke detector may automatically adjust and compensate for dust buildup while the control unit sends a message identifying the device and that sensor cleaning is required.

Zoning

The physical size of a "zone" in a conventional fire alarm system is generally small, with few devices connected. If this zone should have trouble, only a small portion of the building will be unprotected. Zones in an addressable system are very large, often containing up to 200 devices. If a zone of this size should develop trouble, the results could be disastrous, leaving large parts of the building unprotected and potentially putting lives at risk. The ULC standard stipulates that the largest amount of a system that can be affected by a fault be not more than one floor or 2000 m^2, whichever is less. In order to adhere to the ULC standard, fault isolators are connected into the circuit between floors and between 2000-m^2 sections. Fault isolators will disconnect a faulty section of a zone, while keeping the rest of the system functional. At the same time, trouble is announced by the control unit.

Distributed Systems

Distributed systems utilize data-gathering panels, called transponders, which act as a remote fire alarm panel. The status of the devices connected to the transponder is reported to the main control panel, which controls the output devices connected to the transponder. Transponders are polled by the main control unit, just like any other addressable device. Based on that response, the main control unit may operate the transponders' output devices.

If, for any reason, the communication between the transponder and the main control unit is lost, the transponder will revert back to the programmed firmware. It will then function as its own freestanding fire alarm system. An alarm condition on any device connected to the transponder will cause the alarm devices connected to that transponder to be operated. Therefore, the ULC standard requires that the signal devices in the area served by the transponder be connected to that transponder.

Integration with Existing Systems

As a building expands, it may outgrow the existing fire alarm system. If a new microprocessor system is installed, a decision must be made as to how the existing circuits will be handled. Often, it is cost prohibitive or impractical simply to replace the existing circuits with new addressable devices. For this reason, manufacturers of microprocessor systems make zone interface modules that will link the older, conventional fire alarm zones to the new panel (Figure 7-10).

Monitoring of Contacts

In all fire alarm systems, it is often required that the status of contacts be monitored. Items such as sprinkler valve switches, fan control, and elevator control are just a few examples. To monitor the status of these contacts, an addressable interface module is used (Figure 7-11).

Figure 7-10 Zone interface module.

Additional Devices

Microprocessor systems allow for greater flexibility than conventional systems. Many peripheral devices may be connected, including computer terminals with text messaging or a graphical building layout, touch screens, and printers. Some systems have modules that may be added to allow voice communication throughout the protected building.

Electrical Code Requirements

The installation of fire alarm systems and equipment is outlined in Section 32 of the *CEC*. Be sure that all installations conform to rules of Section 32. If the device circuit consists of two individual conductors pulled into a raceway, a minimum of #16 AWG conductors is required. If a two-conductor cable is used, the conductors must be of a minimum #19 AWG. When using a cable assembly, be sure to check the fire rating of the cable jacket. Industrial buildings are usually classed as non-combustible, requiring the use of cable with an FT6 fire rating.

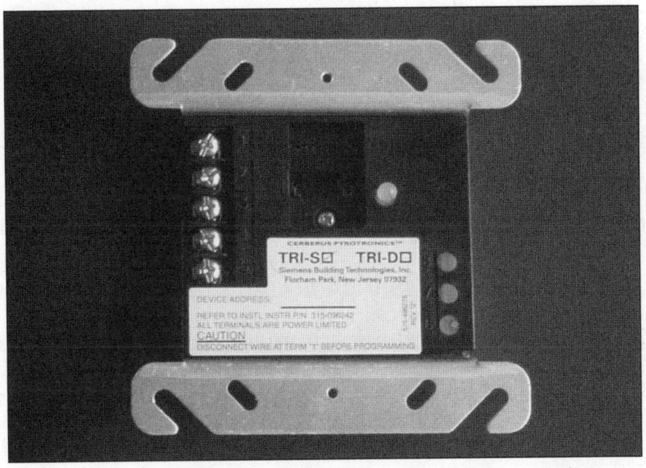

Figure 7-11 Contact interface module.

REVIEW

All answers should be written in complete sentences, calculations should be shown in detail, and Code references should be cited when appropriate.

1. What is a signal circuit?
2. Where is the definition of a signal circuit found in the *Canadian Electrical Code*?
3. Are the display units used in this installation actually clocks?
4. What is WWV?
5. What type of clock is used to provide the pulses broadcast by WWV?
6. What type of clock is used to operate the program timer?
7. How many separate events can be programmed in the program timer?
8. How many output channels are provided with the program timer?
9. What is the primary purpose of the paging system?
10. Name five factors that should be taken into consideration when selecting a paging system.
11. Assume the surrounding noise level in a certain area of the plant is 80 dB. If a message is to be clearly heard, what should be the minimum sound level of the message?
12. How many tones can be generated by the paging system?
13. What is the purpose of the CPU in a microprocessor fire alarm system?
14. Explain the difference between firmware and software.
15. What is non-volatile memory?
16. What is a data communication link?
17. How many field devices may be connected on a single circuit?
18. Describe the difference between a standard addressable device and an analog addressable device.
19. What is the maximum area that may be affected by a fault on a DCL?
20. What device is installed in the circuit to meet the requirement of Question 19?
21. Describe the function of a data-gathering panel.
22. What failsafe is built into a data-gathering panel in the event that communication with the CPU is lost?
23. Can conventional fire alarm zones be connected to a microprocessor fire alarm system? If so, what device is used?
24. What device would be used to monitor the status of the switch on a sprinkler valve?
25. What section of the *Canadian Electrical Code* governs the installation of fire alarm systems?

UNIT 8

Motors and Controllers

OBJECTIVES

After studying this unit, the student should be able to:

- describe the machine layout in the industrial building
- describe the various types of motors used in the industrial building
- explain the operation of the types of motor controllers used
- describe how the motor branch circuits are installed

Units 3 and 5 of this text detailed the method of distributing power to the various machines in the manufacturing area of the industrial building. Recall that plug-in busway is installed throughout the plant and bus plugs are installed at selected points. With the use of rubber cord drops to each machine, power is supplied to the motor branch circuit that operates each machine.

THE MACHINES AND THEIR MOTORS

Sheet E2 of the industrial building plans shows the layout of the 111 machines in the manufacturing area. The various types of machines are identified by a code number, as noted in the drawings.

Each of these machines has a three-phase motor rated at either 208 V or 575 V. The current required by each motor is based on the horse-power rating of the motor. The current can be determined by the equation:

$$\text{Amperes} = \frac{\text{hp} \times 746}{\text{volts} \times 1.73 \times \text{eff} \times \text{PF}}$$

where

hp = Horsepower

1.73 = The square root of 3

eff = The assumed efficiency

PF = The power factor (estimated)

746 = Watts per horsepower

Applying this equation to a 5-hp, 575-V motor, the current required can be determined.

$$\text{Amperes} = \frac{5 \times 746}{575 \times 1.73 \times 0.82 \times 0.86} = 5.32$$

The efficiency of 82 percent and the power factor of 86 percent were taken from Table 8-1 on page 90. Note that larger motors may have slightly higher efficiencies, while smaller motors usually have lower power factors and lower efficiencies. The values used in the equation are the assumed values at full load. When the motor is less than fully loaded, the values are much lower. If the motor power factor and efficiency are not known, *CEC* Table 44 may be used. Be sure to refer to the

Average Efficiencies and Power Factors for Polyphase Squirrel-Cage Induction Motors						
	Efficiencies			Power Factor		
Hp	One-half Load	Three-fourths Load	Full Load	One-half Load	Three-fourths Load	Full Load
¼	60.0	67.0	69.0	45	56	65
½	64.0	68.0	69.0	48	58	65
1	75.0	77.0	76.0	57	69	76
1-½	75.0	77.0	78.0	64	76	81
2	77.0	80.0	81.0	68	79	84
3	80.0	82.0	81.0	70	80	84
5	80.0	82.0	82.0	76	83	86
7-½	83.0	85.0	85.0	77	84	87
10	83.0	85.0	85.0	77	86	88
15	84.0	86.0	88.0	81	85	87
20	87.0	88.0	87.0	82	86	87
25	87.0	88.0	87.5	82	86	87
30	87.5	88.5	88.0	83	86.5	87
40	87.5	89.0	89.5	84	87	88
50	87.5	89.0	89.5	84	87	88
60	88.0	89.5	89.0	84	87	88
75	88.5	89.5	89.5	84	87	88
100	89.0	90.0	90.5	84	88	88
125	90.0	90.5	91.0	84	88	89
150	90.0	91.5	92.0	84	88	89
200	90.0	91.5	92.0	85	89	90
250	91.0	92.5	93.0	84	89	90
300	92.0	93.5	94.0	84	89	90

Table 8-1 Motor efficiencies and power factors.

Although either of these methods may be used to determine the calculated full load current of a motor, they may be used as a guide only. Whenever conductor, overcurrent, and overload device ampacities are calculated, the rated full load current of the motor—as found on the motor nameplate—must be used.

MOTOR TYPES

Several different types of motors having entirely different characteristics or patterns of performance are required for the various machine tools. One of the most commonly used motors is the squirrel-cage type. Refer to Figure 8-1 for a listing of motor control symbols.

SINGLE-SPEED SQUIRREL-CAGE INDUCTION MOTOR

The squirrel-cage type of induction motor does not have a conventional rotor winding. Instead, the laminated steel rotor has copper or aluminum bars that run axially around the periphery of the rotor. These bars are short-circuited by copper or aluminum end rings. When aluminum is used for the assembly, the bars and end rings are usually cast in one piece.

Three-phase squirrel-cage motors have a good starting torque, and their performance characteristics make them an ideal motor for general use. Figure 8-2 on page 92 is a cutaway view of a three-phase squirrel-cage motor.

An induction motor is much like a transformer, except that the secondary winding and core are mounted on a shaft set in bearings. This arrangement permits the secondary winding to rotate (hence the name "rotor"). An induction motor consists of two electrical circuits (the stator and the rotor) linked by a common magnetic circuit. Electric current applied to the stator winding induces a secondary current in the rotor winding. This winding is a closed circuit, either a short circuit or nearly so. The induced current in the secondary always flows in a direction opposite to that of the applied current. In addition, the induced

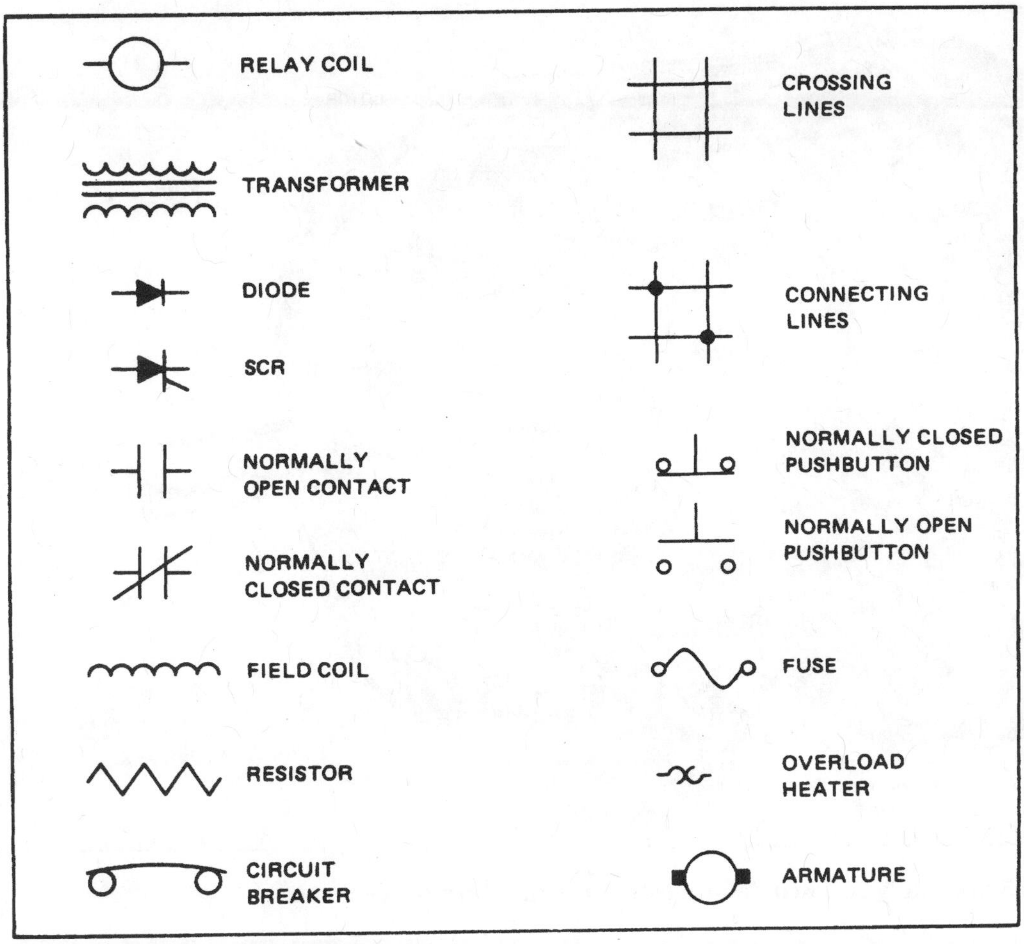

Figure 8-1 Electrical symbols.

current lags 90° or one-quarter cycle behind the applied current. Magnetic fields are set up in the stator and rotor in a manner that gives rise to attracting and repelling forces. Since these forces are in the same direction (either clockwise or counterclockwise), a torque is produced and rotation results.

For example, Figure 8-3 on page 92 shows that the north and south poles of the induction motor stator rotate at synchronous speed. That is, the poles of the stator and rotor are always in the position shown, with respect to each other. Since unlike poles attract and like poles repel, forces are set up that produce rotation. The force acting at the rim of the rotor multiplied by the radius from the centre of the rotor is called the torque. Torque can be determined by the following equation:

$$\text{Torque} = \frac{\text{Horsepower} \times 5250}{\text{rpm}} \text{ (lbft)}$$

Figure 8-3 also shows that the magnetic poles of the rotor are always midway between the magnetic poles of the stator so that the attracting and repelling forces work together. The frequency of the current in this case is 60 Hz (supplied by the power company). Current of 60 Hz is applied to the stator winding, but the frequency in the rotor is very low at operating speed and varies with the slip. The slip is the difference between the synchronous speed of the motor and its actual speed under full load. If the rotor were to turn at the same number of revolutions per minute (rpm) as the stator, induction in the rotor would cease. Since the magnetic field in the rotor is created by the current flow caused by the induced voltage, the rotor must always turn at a speed less than synchronous speed. As the motor is loaded, the amount of slip will increase. As the slip increases, the induced voltage will increase, thereby causing

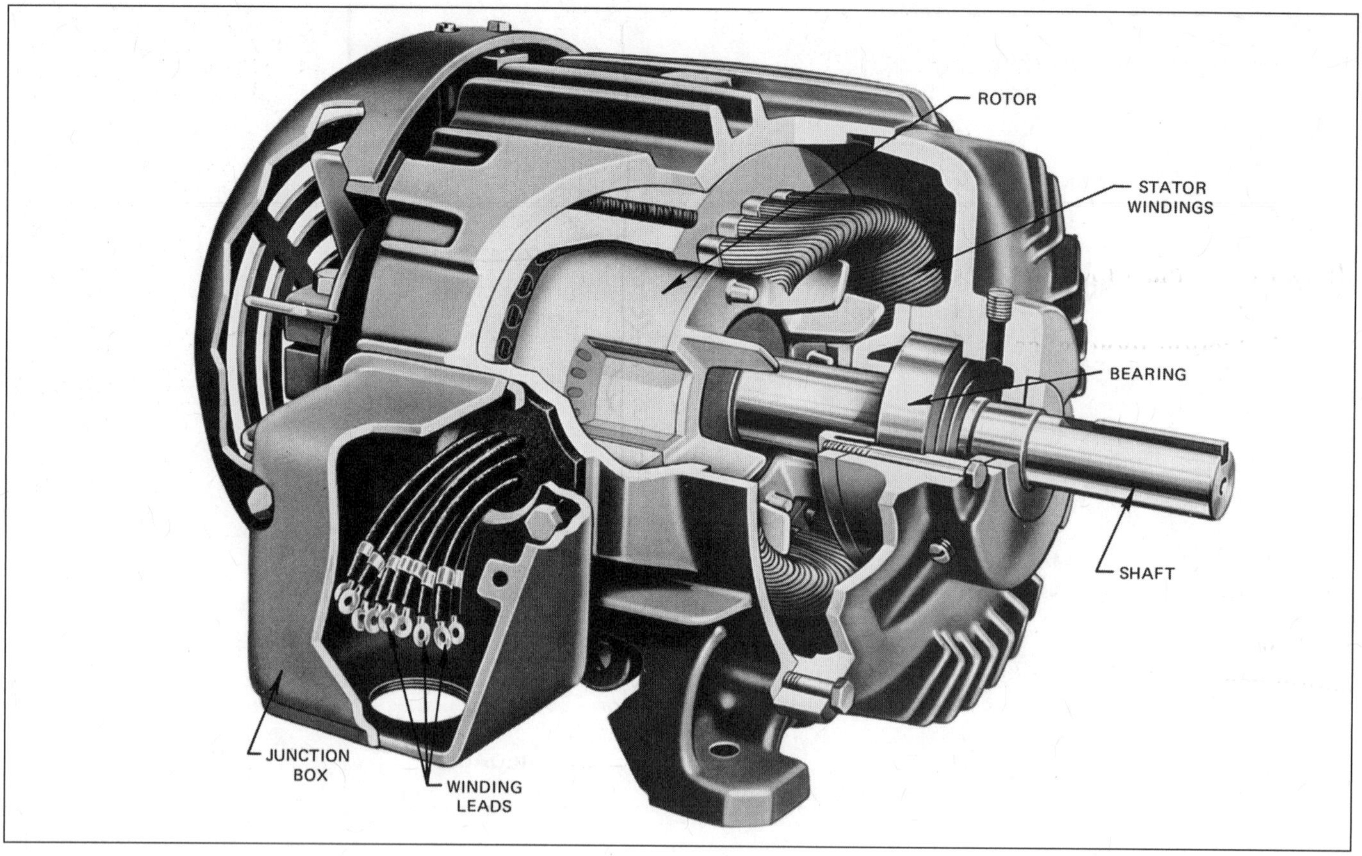

Figure 8-2 Cutaway view of 5-hp, totally enclosed, fan-cooled, standard squirrel-cage motor.

an increase in current flow and a strengthening of the magnetic field in the rotor. As the strength of the magnetic field increases, so does the torque.

The synchronous speed of an AC motor is obtained from the formula given as follows:

$$N = \frac{120N}{P}$$

where

N = Synchronous speed in rpm

F = Frequency in hertz

P = Number of poles per phase

Thus, for a four-pole, 60-Hz motor, the synchronous speed is:

$$\text{Synchronous speed} = \frac{120 \times 60}{4} = 1800 \text{ rpm}$$

If the load causes the rotor to slip 75 rpm below the value of the synchronous speed, then the actual speed under full load is 1800 minus 75, or 1725 revolutions per minute.

Similarly, the synchronous speed of a six-pole, 60-Hz motor is:

$$\text{Synchronous speed} = \frac{120 \times 60}{4} = 1200 \text{ rpm}$$

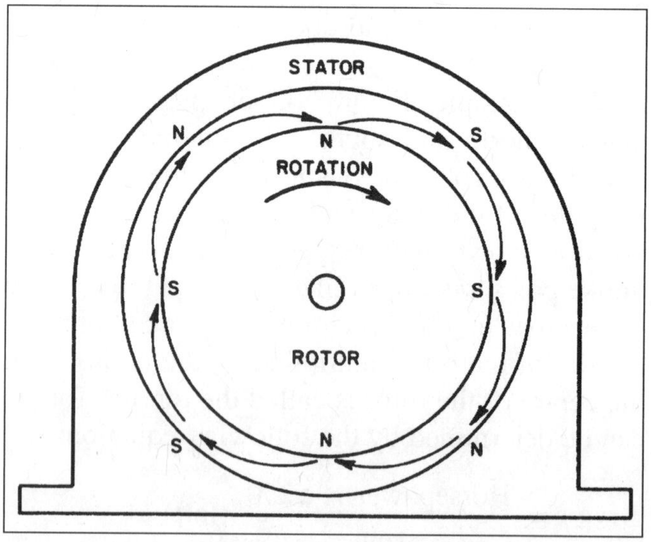

Figure 8-3 Diagram of four-pole induction motor.

Thus, with a full-load slip of 60 rpm, the actual full-load speed of the motor is 1200 minus 60, or 1140 rpm.

Induction Motors in the Industrial Plant

Many of the machines in the industrial building are driven by three-phase, squirrel-cage, single-speed induction motors, as listed in Table 8-2. In addition to the motors in Table 8-2, other single-speed squirrel-cage motors are used as listed in Table 8-3.

The smaller sizes of squirrel-cage motors use controllers known as across-the-line starters (Figure 8-4). The controller is a magnetic switch or contactor including overload relays that provide running protection for the motor. A pushbutton station can provide a means for starting, stopping, reversing, or jogging the motor (Figure 8-5 and Figure 8-6).

Code Number	Kinds of Machines	Horsepowers of Motors
MA	Engine Lathes	5
MB	Turret Lathes	7.5
MC	Vertical Drills	1
ME	Milling Machines	10, 1, 1
MF	Shapers	7.5
MG	Boring Mills	3, 3, 3
MI	Power Hacksaws	3
MJ	Band Saws	5
MK	Surface Grinders	10
ML	Cylindrical Grinders	7.5
MO	Special Machines	5

Table 8-2 Single-speed squirrel-cage induction motors.

Number of Motors	Description of Motors
3	exhaust fans, chiller, penthouse, and electrical room
2	liquid chiller motors used in conjunction with the air-conditioning equipment
6	3/4-hp motors for the fan coil units
6	1/12-hp motors for the unit heaters
3	1⁄4-hp motors used at the three machines equipped with oil fog precipitation units (Unit 11)

Figure 8-4 Full voltage non-reversing motor starter.

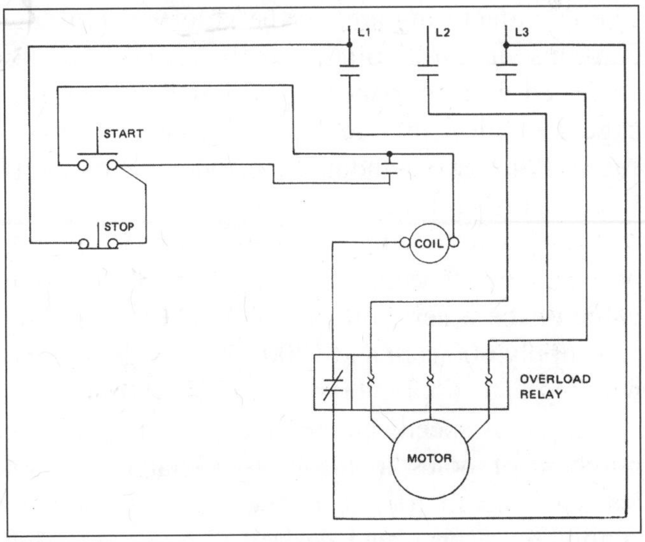

Figure 8-5 Wiring diagram of an across-the-line starter.

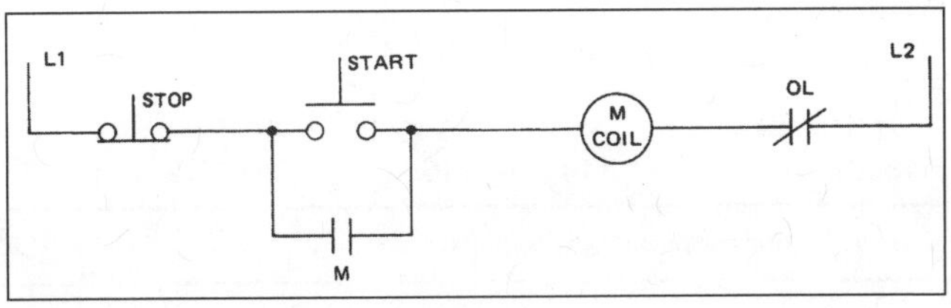

Figure 8-6 Schematic diagram of an across-the-line

MOTOR CONTROL IN INDUSTRY

In industry, it may be necessary to do more than just start a motor. Often, factors such as speed, starting torque, or starting current must be controlled. For many years, the most effective method of speed control was to use DC machines. Starting torque and starting current were controlled by using complex starters utilizing resistors, transformers, or multiwinding motors. Many industries still utilize these methods, and therefore they deserve mention in this text. However, most modern installations will use AC variable frequency drives to accomplish speed control, and "soft start" electronic starters for control of starting torque and current. Both of these methods are discussed later in this chapter.

Four-Speed Squirrel-Cage Motors

The manufacturing area of the industrial building contains a multispindle drill (MD) that is equipped with four-speed, two-winding, squirrel-cage induction motors. For this type of motor, each of the two windings can produce two different speeds for a total of four speeds. The windings are not used at the same time as each winding provides two speeds, one of which is half the value of the other. For example, the first winding can supply 600 rpm and 1200 rpm and the second winding can supply 900 rpm and 1800 rpm.

The four speeds are obtained by changing the numbers of poles in the motor. That is, certain leads of the motor are connected to the power supply for each speed desired (Table 8-4). This type of motor has 14 terminal leads. The controller is usually arranged so that the sequence of speeds is Reverse–Off–600 rpm–900 rpm– 1200 rpm–1800 rpm (Figure 8-7).

Speed	L1	L2	L3	Together
R 600	T2	T1	T3, T7	—
F 600	T1	T2	T3, T7	—
F 900	T11	T12	T13–T17	—
F 1200	T6	T4	T5	T1, T2, T3, T7
F 1800	T16	T14	T15	T11, T12, T13, T17

Note: All other terminals are left open.

Table 8-4 Connection of leads for various desired speeds.

This multispeed squirrel-cage induction motor is shown partially wired. The motor has 14 terminal leads. Controllers are made in various forms such as a drum type, a cam type, and an automatic pushbutton type. Numbered terminals on the motor are connected to the corresponding numbers on the controller.

REDUCED-VOLTAGE STARTERS

Primary Resistance Starters

The milling machines are equipped with primary resistance starters. For this type of starter or controller, the heavy starting current results in a voltage drop while it passes through the primary resistors; thus, there is a lower voltage value at the motor terminals. The motor accelerates gently with less torque than is the case when line starters are used. When the motor has almost reached its normal speed, a time-delay relay (set for about five seconds) closes a second contactor to short out the primary resistors. At this point, the motor receives the full line voltage and accelerates to its normal speed (Figure 8-8 on page 96).

Autotransformer Starter

The motors used on the surface grinders have another type of controller called an autotransformer starter (Figure 8-9 on page 96), which uses an autotransformer to obtain a reduced voltage. When the starting pushbutton is depressed, a magnetic five-pole switch connects the autotransformer to the line. Taps are made from the autotransformer at a value of about 70 percent of the line voltage at the start portion of the cycle. Several seconds after the motor begins to rotate, a timing relay opens the first contactor and closes a second three-pole contactor. This action disconnects the autotransformer from the line and connects the motor directly across the line. As a result, the motor is accelerated to its normal speed (Figure 8-10 on page 97).

The controllers covered in the unit to this point are used with squirrel-cage motors. Several other types of controllers are used on other motors of various types in the industrial building.

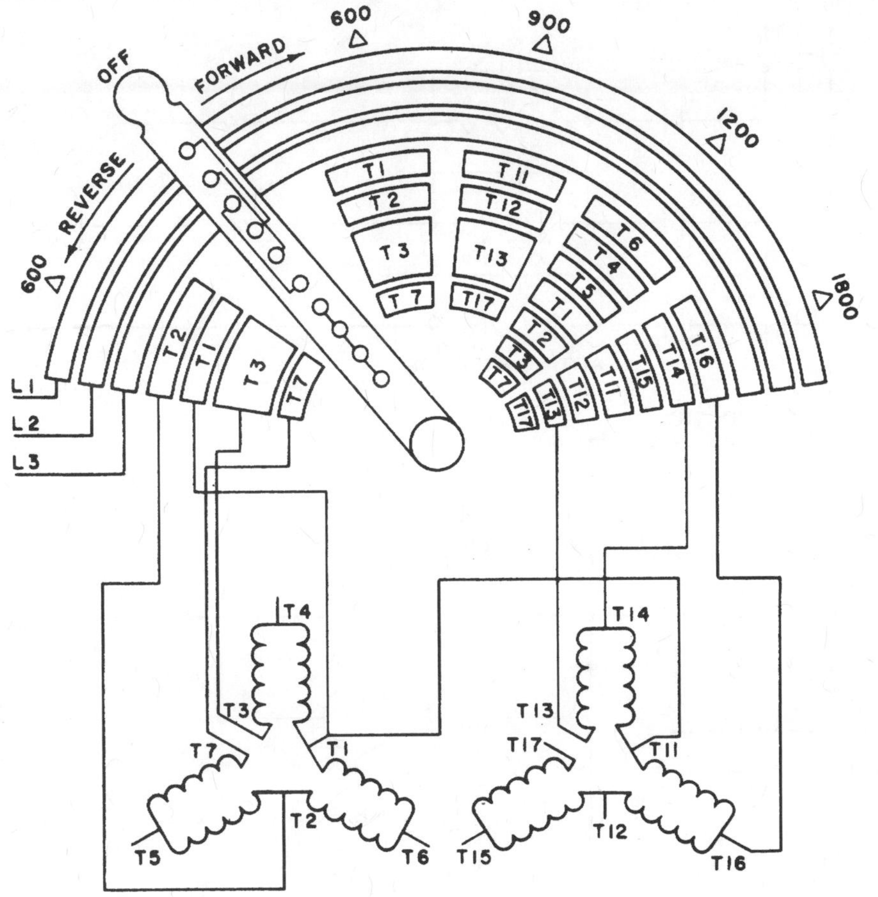

This multispeed squirrel-cage induction motor is shown partially wired. The motor has 14 terminal leads. Controllers are made in various forms such as a drum type, a cam type, and an automatic pushbutton type. Numbered terminals on the motor are connected to the corresponding numbers on the controller.

Figure 8-7 Four-speed, two-winding induction motor and controller.

The Wound Rotor Induction Motor

The punch presses (MN) are equipped with wound rotor induction motors that operate on the same principles as an ordinary squirrel-cage induction motor. However, there are many differences in the construction and performance of the two types of motors (Figure 8-11 on page 97).

For example, the rotor does not have the solid bar and end ring construction of the squirrel-cage rotor. Rather, the wound rotor has a three-phase winding that is very similar to the bronze collector rings mounted concentrically with the shaft of the motor. Three sets of low-resistance carbon-graphite brushes set in brush holders make contact with and collect current from these collector rings (Figure 8-12 on page 97).

Secondary Resistance Controller

The three brush holders are connected to three external resistors having a common connection. These resistors can be shorted out in steps. When all of the resistors are connected into the circuit, the total resistance of the rotor is increased. This increased resistance has the effect of greatly increasing the torque or rotational force of the

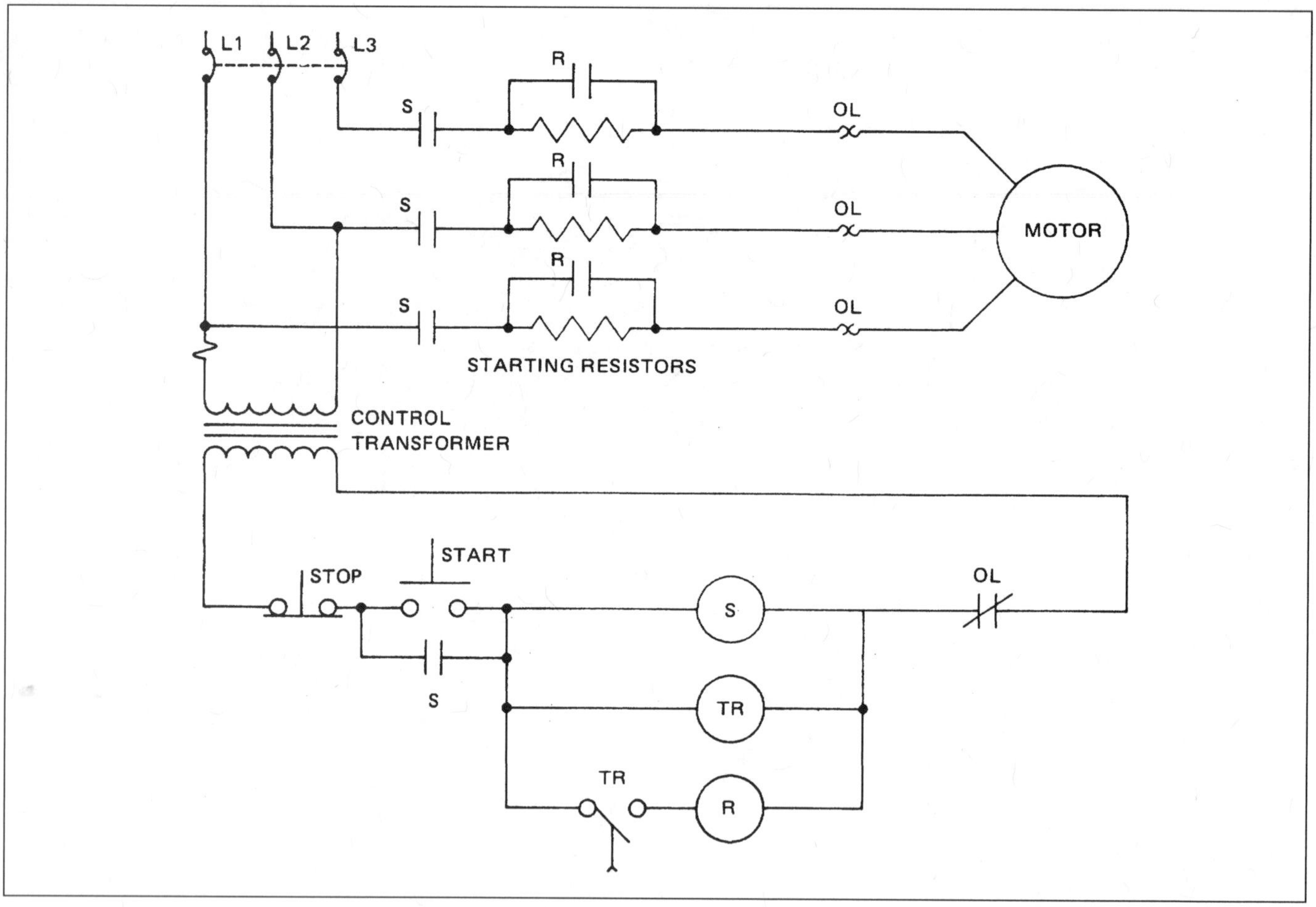

Figure 8-8 Typical primary resistance starter.

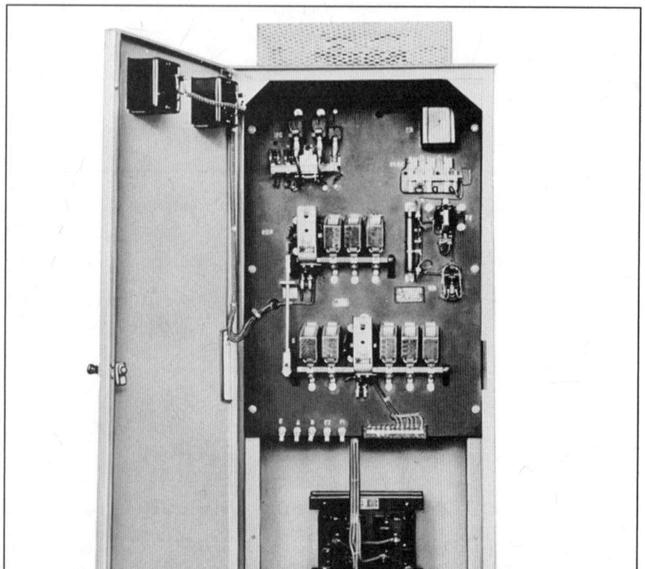

Figure 8-9 Reduced voltage starter.

motor while it is operating. As the torque increases, the speed decreases by a proportional amount. As resistance is shorted out, the motor speed increases and the torque decreases. When all of the resistance is removed from the circuit and the brush holders themselves are short-circuited, the motor is running at full speed (Figure 8-13 on page 98).

The wound rotor induction motor has a shaft with a larger-than-normal-diameter. This increased size is required to handle the torque, which may reach a value as high as 300% of the normal torque. This high value is reached when all of the resistance is connected into the rotor circuit. The shaft at this point is subjected to severe strain.

The wound rotor motor is used for extra heavy-duty starting. Typical applications include the use of this type of motor with pumps having an extremely high back pressure, or with machines having a very high static inertia. The secondary resistance controller is used to bring the motor up

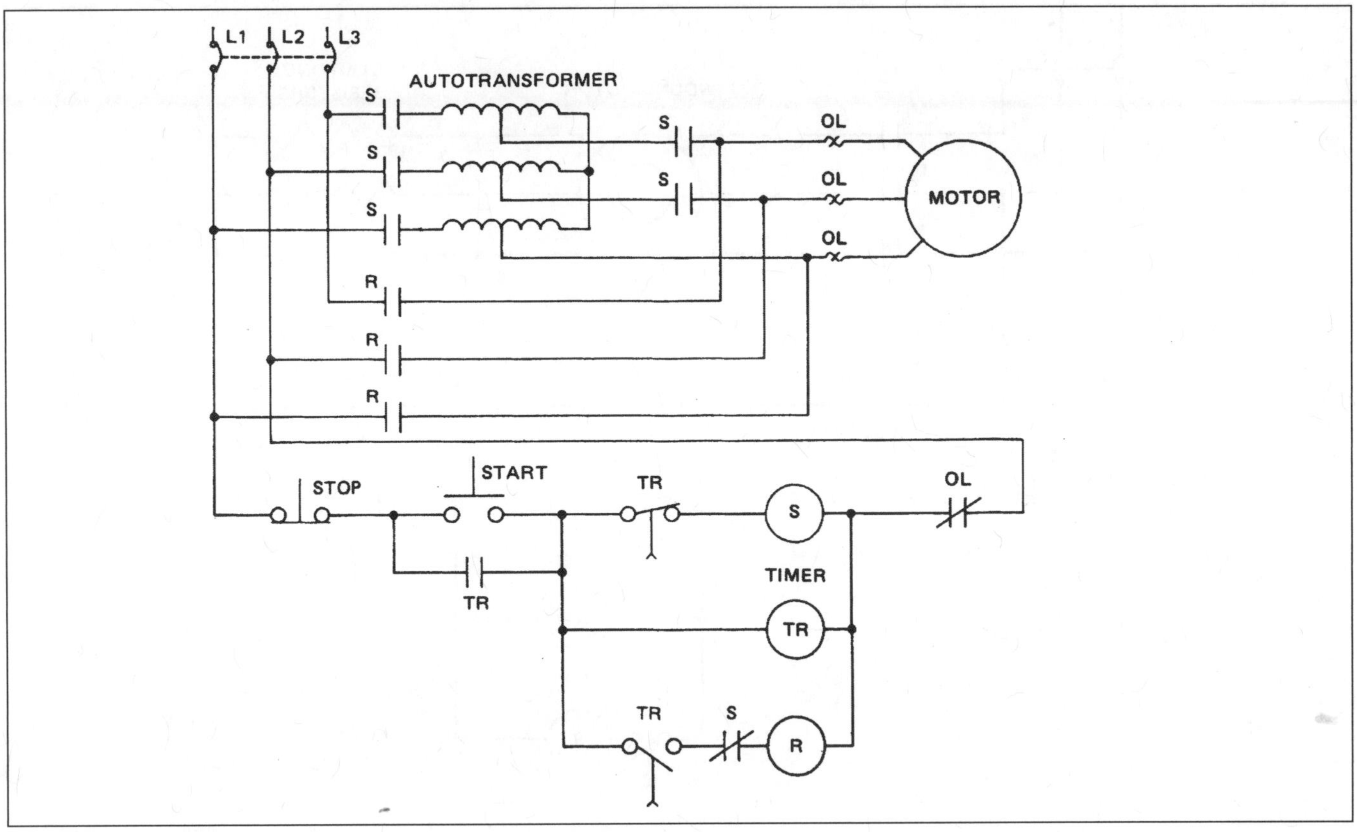

Figure 8-10 Schematic of an autotransformer-type reduced voltage starter.

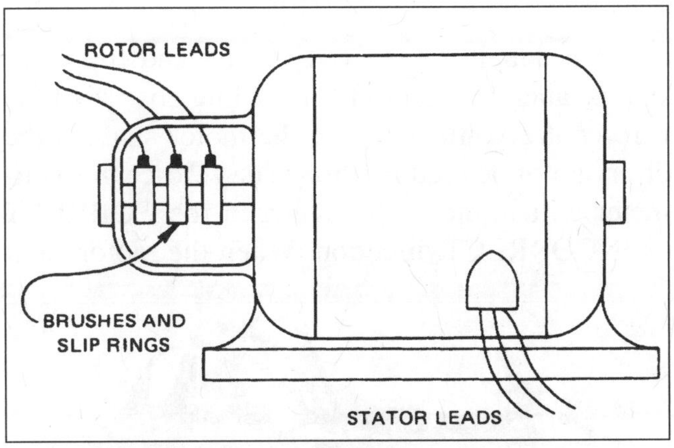

Figure 8-11 Wound rotor induction motor.

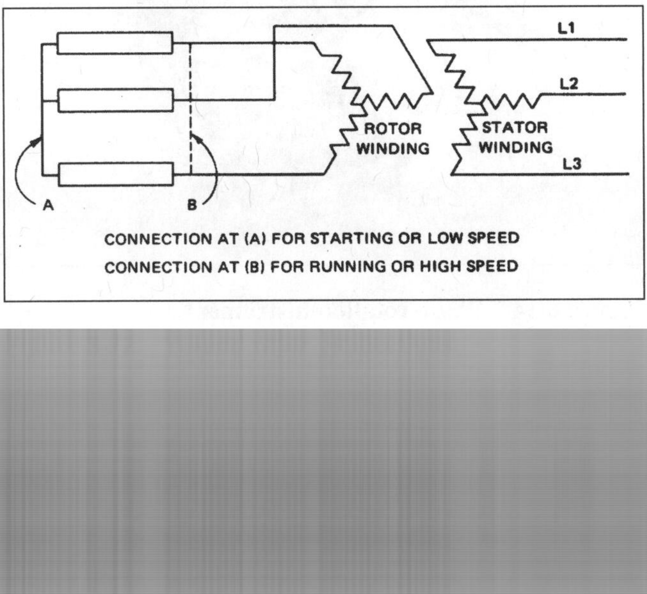

to speed smoothly. In addition, this controller is used in normal running operations to adjust the torque and speed to any desired values.

DETERMINING DIRECTION OF ROTATION FOR THREE-PHASE MOTORS

On many types of machinery, the direction of rotation of the motor is critical. The direction of rotation of any three-phase motor can be changed by reversing two of its stator leads. This causes the direction of the rotating magnetic field to reverse. When a motor is connected to a machine that will not be damaged when its direction of rotation is reversed, power can be momentarily applied to the motor to observe its direction of rotation. If the rotation is incorrect, any two line leads can be interchanged to reverse the motor's rotation.

When a motor is to be connected to a machine that can be damaged by incorrect rotation, however, the direction of rotation must be determined before the motor is connected to its load. This can

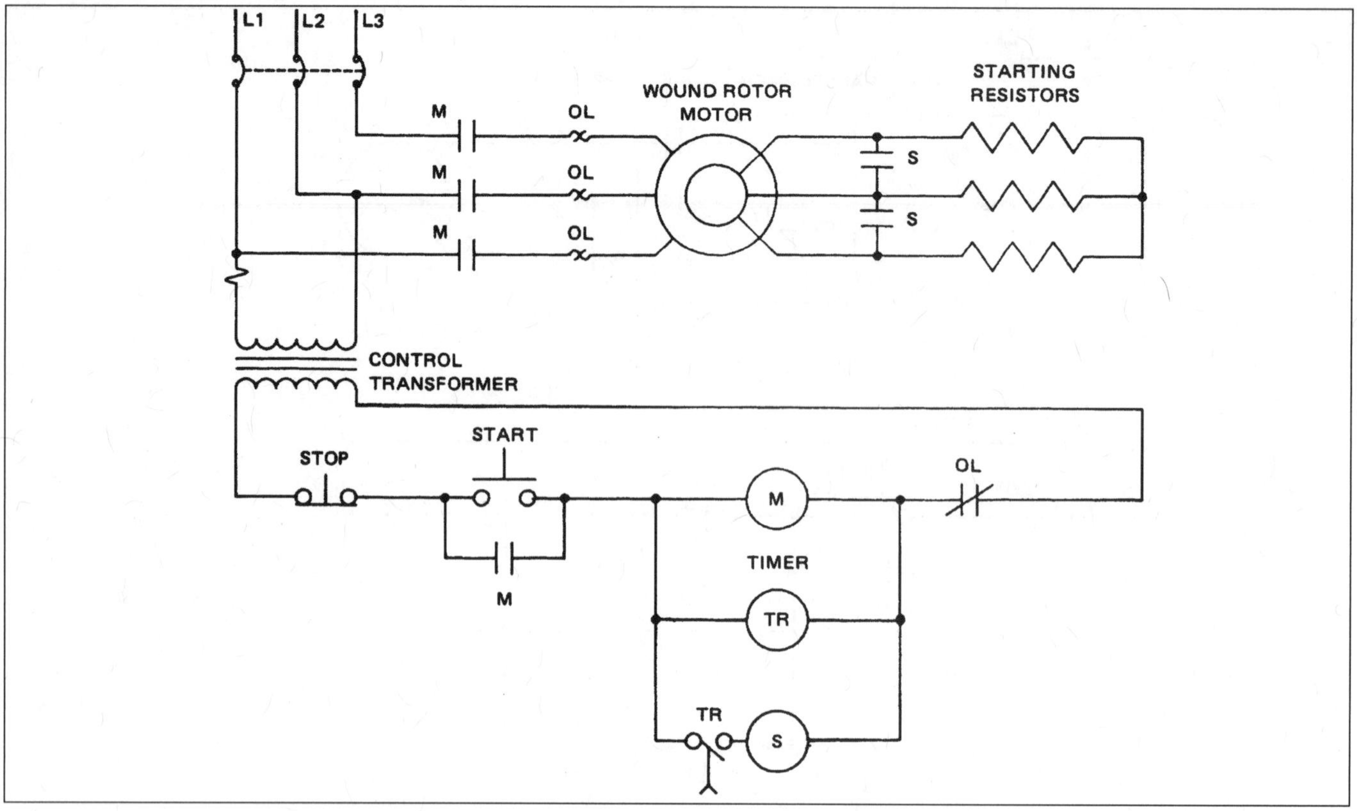

Figure 8-13 Two-step automatic starter for a wound rotor motor.

make electrical connection to the motor before it is mechanically connected to the load. The direction of rotation can then be tested by momentarily applying power to the motor before it is coupled to the load.

There may be occasions when this is not practical or convenient. It is possible to determine the direction of rotation of a motor before power is connected to it with the use of a phase rotation instrument, as shown in Figure 8-14. The phase rotation instrument is used to compare the phase rotation of two different three-phase connections. The meter contains six terminals or leads. Three of the terminals or leads are labelled "Motor" and are further identified as *A*, *B*, or *C*. The *line* terminals or leads are labelled *A*, *B*, or *C*.

To determine the direction of rotation of the motor, first calibrate the instrument, if necessary, by following the instructions provided by the manufacturer. Connect the three *motor* leads of the meter to the "T" leads of the motor, as shown in Figure 8-15. The phase rotation instrument contains a zero-centre voltmeter. One side of the voltmeter is labelled "INCORRECT," and the other side is labelled "CORRECT." While observing the zero-centre voltmeter, turn the motor shaft in the direction of desired rotation. The zero-centre voltmeter will immediately swing in the CORRECT or INCORRECT direction. When the motor shaft

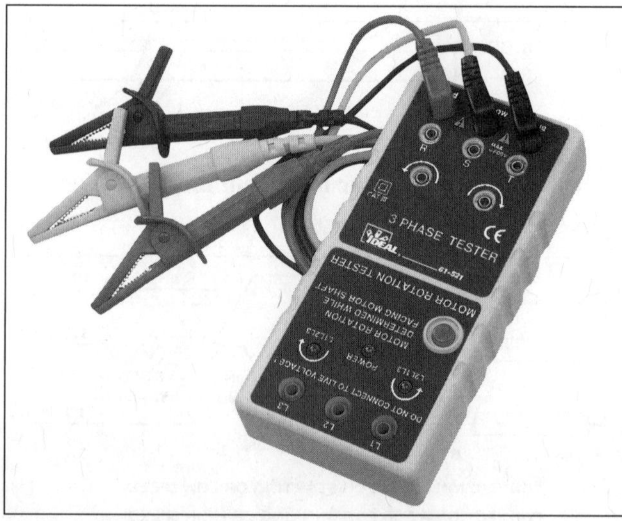

Figure 8-14 Phase rotation instrument. (Courtesy of Ideal Industries (Canada), Inc.)

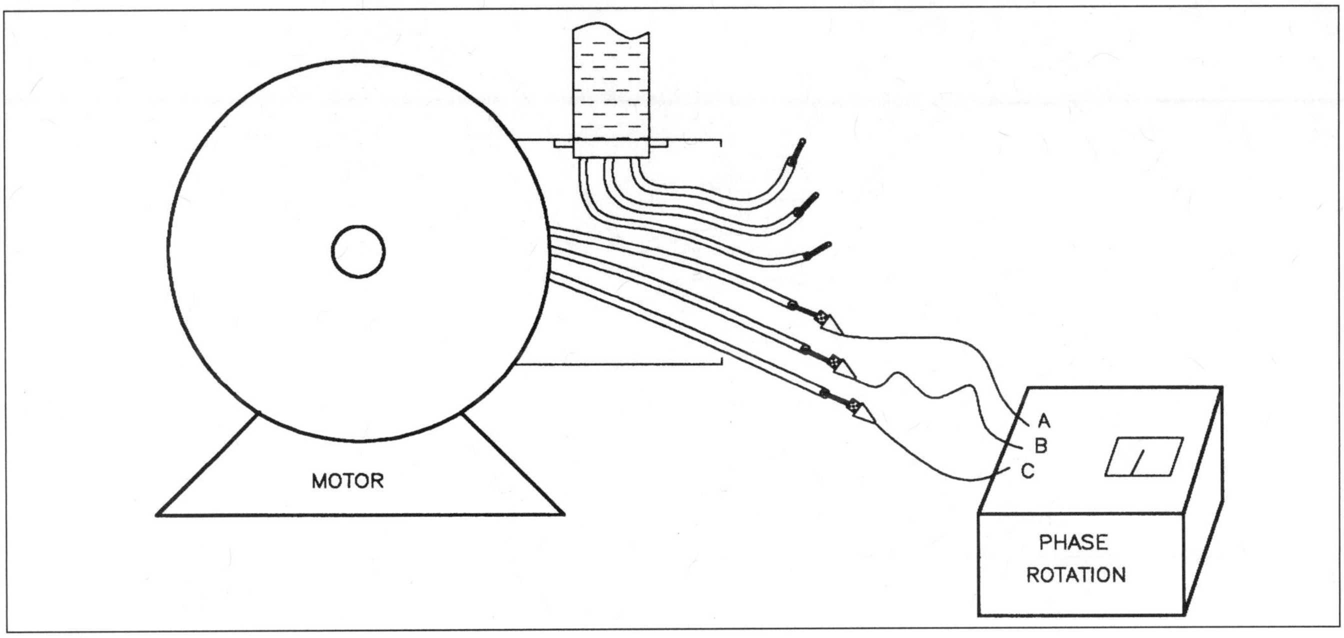

Figure 8-15 Connecting the phase rotation instrument to the motor.

stops turning, the needle may swing in the opposite direction. It is the *first* indication of the voltmeter that is to be used.

If the voltmeter needle indicated CORRECT, label the motor "T" leads *A*, *B*, or *C* to correspond with the *motor* leads from the phase rotation instrument. If the voltmeter needle indicated INCORRECT, change any two of the *motor* leads from the phase rotation instrument and again turn the motor shaft. The voltmeter needle should now indicate CORRECT. The motor "T" leads can now be labelled to correspond with the *motor* leads from the phase rotation instrument.

After the motor "T" leads have been labelled *A*, *B*, or *C* to correspond with the leads of the phase rotation instrument, the rotation of the line supplying power to the motor must be determined. Set the selector switch on the phase rotation instrument to the *line* position. After making certain that the power has been turned off, connect the three *line* leads of the phase rotation instrument to the motor supply line (Figure 8-16 on page 100). Turn on the power and observe the zero-centre voltmeter. If the meter is pointing in the CORRECT direction, turn off the power and label the line leads *A*, *B*, or *C* to correspond with

If the voltmeter is pointing in the INCORRECT direction, turn off the power and change any two of the leads from the phase rotation instrument. When the power is turned on, the voltmeter should point in the CORRECT direction. Turn off the power and label the line leads *A*, *B*, or *C* to correspond with the leads from the phase rotation instrument.

Not all phase rotation instruments will use a centre-reading voltmeter. Indicating lights are often used in place of the meter movement as shown in the instrument in Figure 8-14.

Now that the motor "T" leads and the incoming power leads have been labelled, connect the line lead labelled *A* to the "T" lead labelled *A*; the line lead labelled *B* to the "T" lead labelled *B*; and the line lead labelled *C* to the "T" lead labelled *C*. When power is connected to the motor, it will operate in the proper direction.

Notice that the phase rotation instrument can be used to determine the *phase rotation* of two different connections. It cannot determine which of the three phase lines is *A*, *B*, or *C*, or which line lead is L1, L2, or L3. The phase rotation instrument can be used to determine the rotation of two separate three-phase systems. For example, assume all the

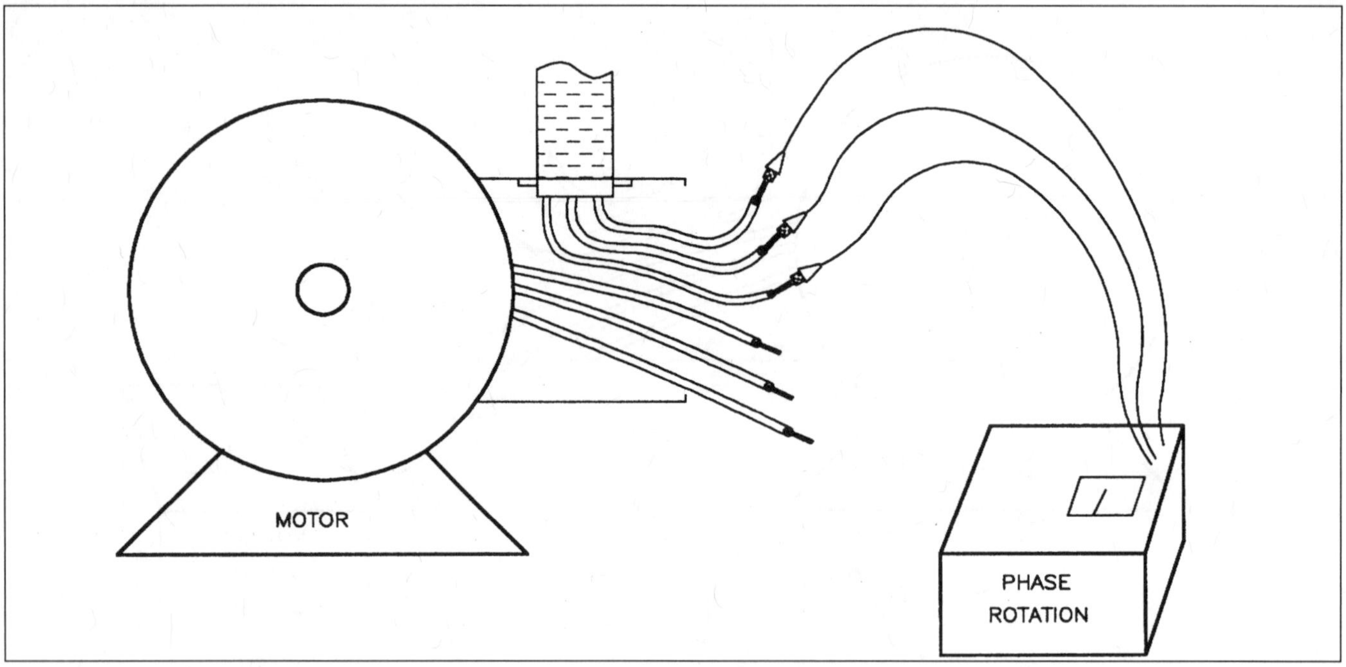

Figure 8-16 Connecting the phase rotation instrument to the line.

an existing three-phase system must be replaced. To minimize downtime, a temporary three-phase service will be connected to supply power while the existing switchgear is being replaced. It is critical that the phase rotation of the temporary service be the same as the existing service when power is applied. The phase rotation instrument can be used to ensure that the connection is correct.

The first step is to connect the *line* leads of the phase rotation instrument to the existing power (Figure 8-17). If the zero-centre voltmeter indicates CORRECT, label the load side of the service *A*, *B*, and *C* to correspond with the leads of the phase rotation instrument. If the voltmeter indicates INCORRECT, change two of the meter leads. This should cause the phase rotation instrument to indicate CORRECT. Label the load side of the service to correspond with *A*, *B*, or *C* of the phase rotation instrument leads.

Before connecting the temporary service to the load side of the circuit, connect the phase rotation instrument to the line side of the temporary service (Figure 8-18). Obtain a CORRECT reading on the phase rotation instrument by changing two of the meter leads if necessary. After the correct reading has been obtained, label the service leads *A*, *B*, or *C* to correspond with the leads of the phase rotation instrument. If the marked temporary service leads are connected to their like-marked load leads, the phase rotation of the temporary service will be the same as the existing service.

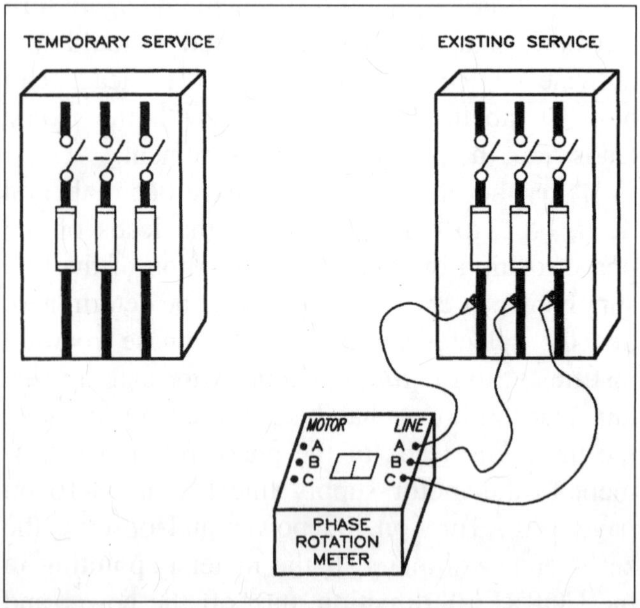

Figure 8-17 Testing phase rotation of the existing service.

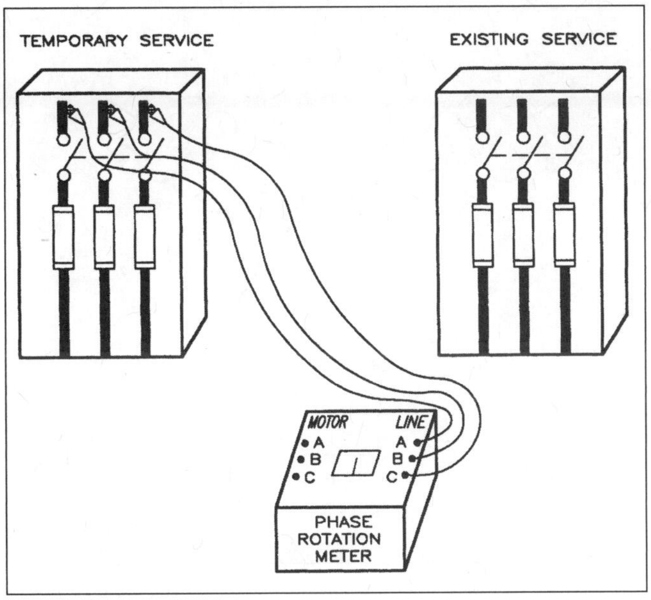

Figure 8-18 Testing the phase rotation of the temporary service.

CONNECTING DUAL-VOLTAGE THREE-PHASE MOTORS

Many of the three-phase motors used in industry are designed to be operated on two voltages, such as 240 V to 480 V. Motors of this type contain two sets of windings per phase. Most dual-voltage motors bring out nine "T" leads at the terminal box. There is a standard method used to number these leads, as shown in Figure 8-19. Starting with terminal 1, the leads are numbered in a decreasing spiral as shown. Another method of determining the proper lead numbers is to add three to each terminal. For example, starting with lead 1, add 3 to 1. Three plus one equals four. The phase winding that begins with 1 ends with 4. Now add 3 to 4. Three plus four equals seven. The beginning of the second winding for phase 1 is 7. This method will work for the windings of all phases. If in doubt, draw a diagram of the phase windings and number them in a spiral.

Three-phase motors can be constructed to operate in either wye or delta. If a motor is to be connected to high voltage, the phase windings will be connected in series. In Figure 8-20 on page 102, a schematic diagram and terminal connection chart for high voltage are shown for a wye-connected motor. In Figure 8-21 on page 102, a schematic diagram and terminal connection chart for high voltage are shown for a delta-connected motor.

When a motor is to be connected for low-voltage operation, the phase windings must be connected in parallel. Figure 8-22 on page 103 shows the basic schematic diagram for a wye-connected motor with parallel phase windings. In actual practice, however, it is not possible to make this exact connection with a nine-lead motor. The schematic shows that terminal 4 connects to the other end of the phase winding that starts with terminal 7. Terminal 5 connects to the other end of winding 8, and terminal 6 connects to the other end of winding 9.

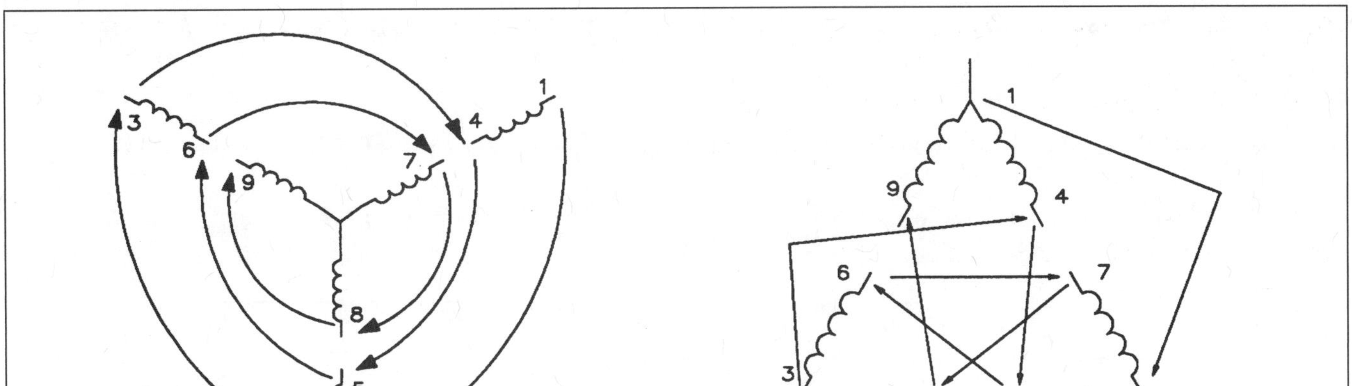

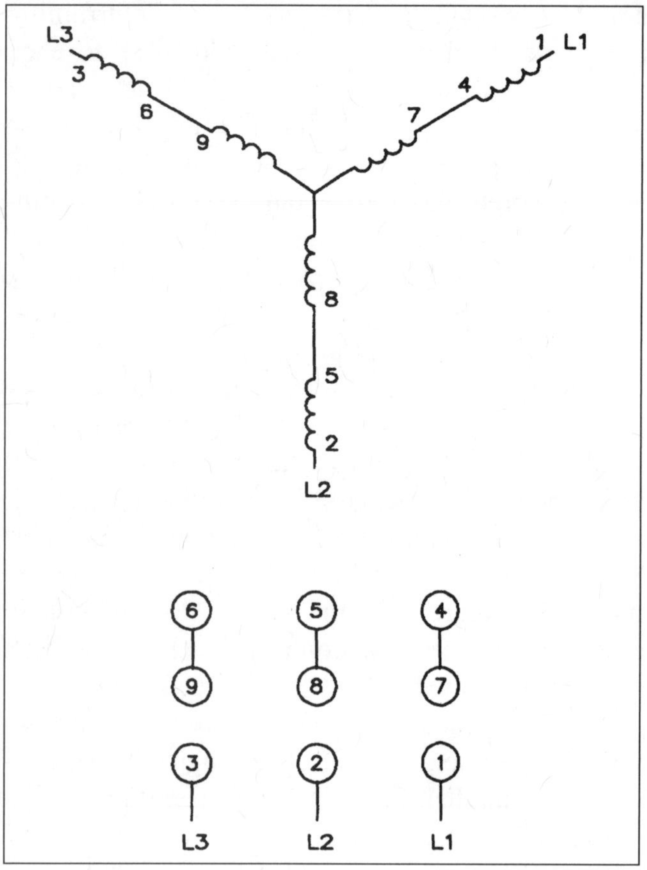

Figure 8-20 High-voltage wye connection.

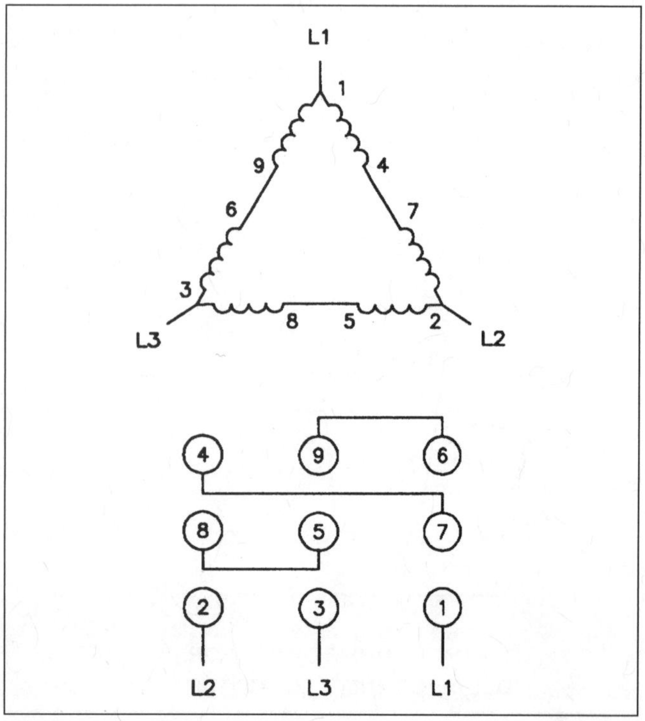

Figure 8-21 High-voltage delta connection.

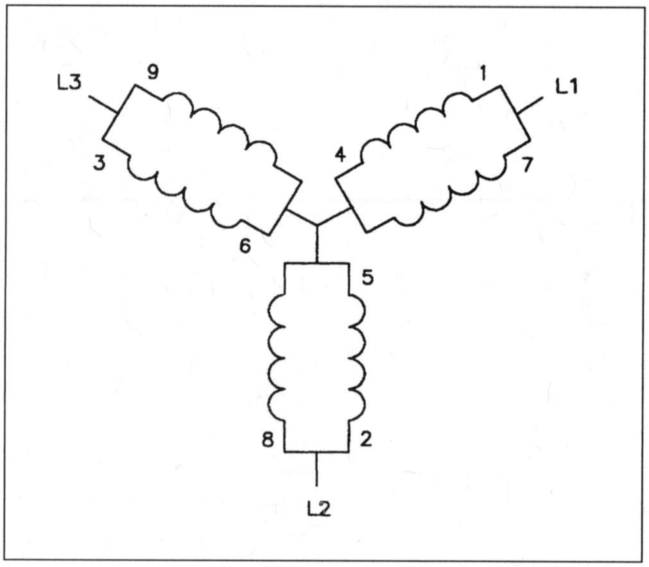

Figure 8-22 Stator windings connected in parallel.

In actual motor construction, the opposite ends of windings 7, 8, and 9 are connected together inside the motor and are not brought outside the motor case. The problem is solved, however, by forming a second wye connection by connecting terminals 4, 5, and 6, as shown in Figure 8-23.

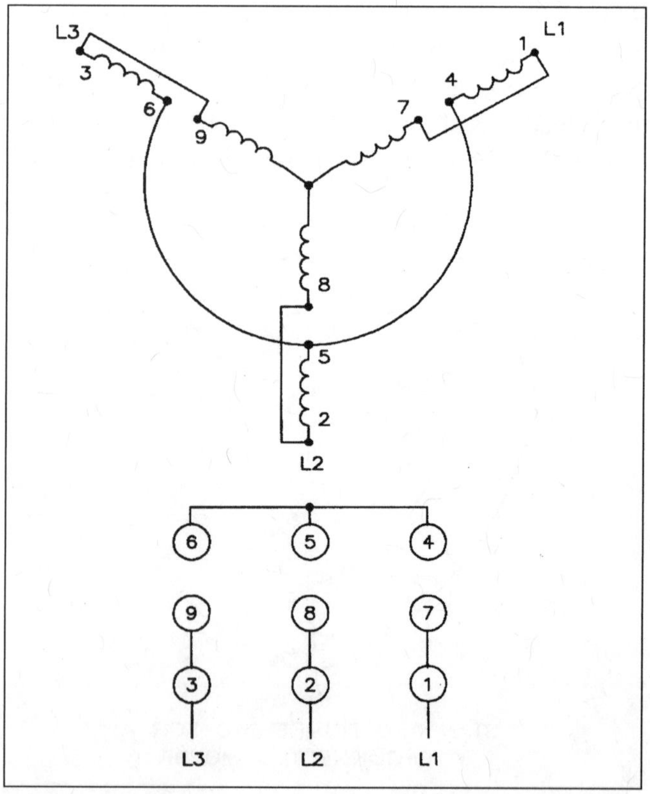

Figure 8-23 Low-voltage wye connection.

The phase winding of a delta-connected motor must also be connected in parallel for use on low voltage. A schematic for this connection is shown in Figure 8-24. A connection diagram and terminal connection chart for this hookup are shown in Figure 8-25.

Some dual-voltage motors will contain twelve "T" leads instead of nine. In this instance, the opposite ends of terminals 7, 8, and 9 are brought out for connection. Figure 8-26 on page 104 shows the standard numbering for both delta- and wye-connected motors. Twelve leads are brought out if the motor is intended to be used for wye–delta starting. When this is the case, the motor must be designed for normal operation with its windings connected in delta. If the windings are connected in wye during starting, the starting current of the motor is greatly reduced.

Dual-Voltage Single-Phase Motors

Many single-phase motors are designed to be connected to either 120 V or 240 V. Most dual-voltage single-phase motors will be of the split-phase type, which contains both run and starting windings. Figure 8-27 on page 104 shows the schematic diagram of a split-phase motor designed for dual-voltage operation. This particular motor contains two run windings and two start windings. The lead numbers for single-phase motors are also numbered in a standard manner. One of the run windings has lead numbers of T1 and T2. The other run winding has its leads numbered T3 and T4. This particular motor uses two different sets of start winding leads. One set is labelled T5 and T6, and the other set is labelled T7 and T8.

If the motor is to be connected for high-voltage operation, the run windings and start windings will be connected in series, as shown in Figure 8-28 on page 104. The start windings are then connected in parallel with the run windings. It should be noted that if the opposite direction of rotation is desired, T5 and T8 will be changed.

For low-voltage operation, the windings must be connected in parallel, as shown in Figure 8-29 on page 104. This connection is made by first connecting the run windings in parallel by hooking

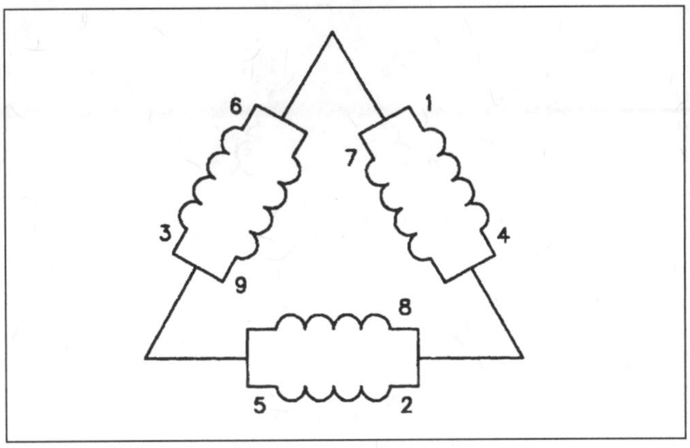

Figure 8-24 Parallel delta connection.

start windings are paralleled by connecting T5 and T7 together and T6 and T8 together. The start windings are then connected in parallel with the run windings. If the opposite direction of rotation is desired, T5 and T6 should be reversed.

Not all dual-voltage single-phase motors contain two sets of start windings. Figure 8-30 on page 105 shows the schematic diagram of a motor that contains two sets of run windings and only one start winding. In this illustration, the start winding is labelled T5 and T6. It should be noted,

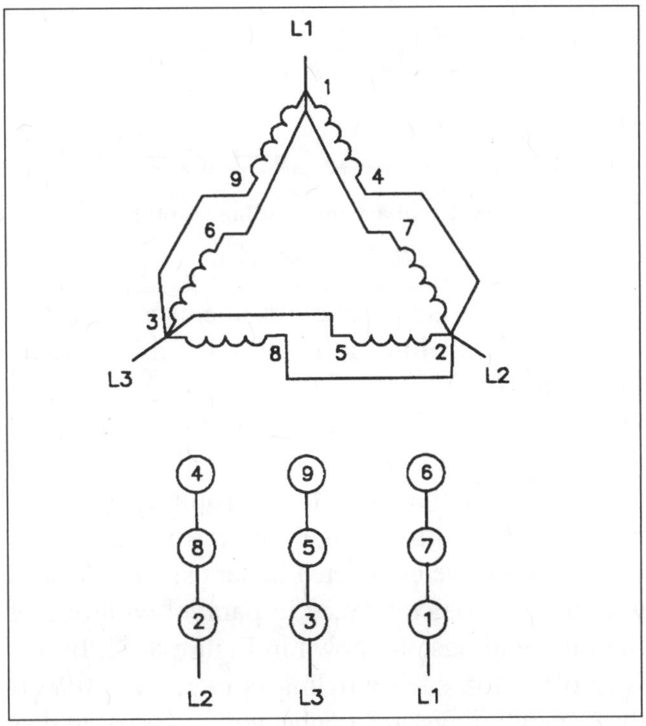

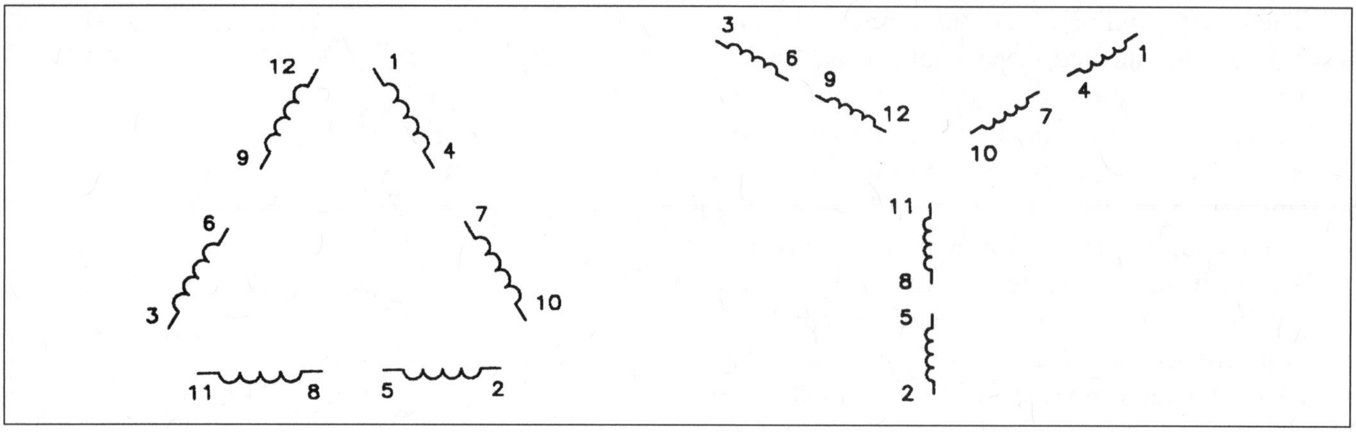

Figure 8-26 Twelve-lead motor.

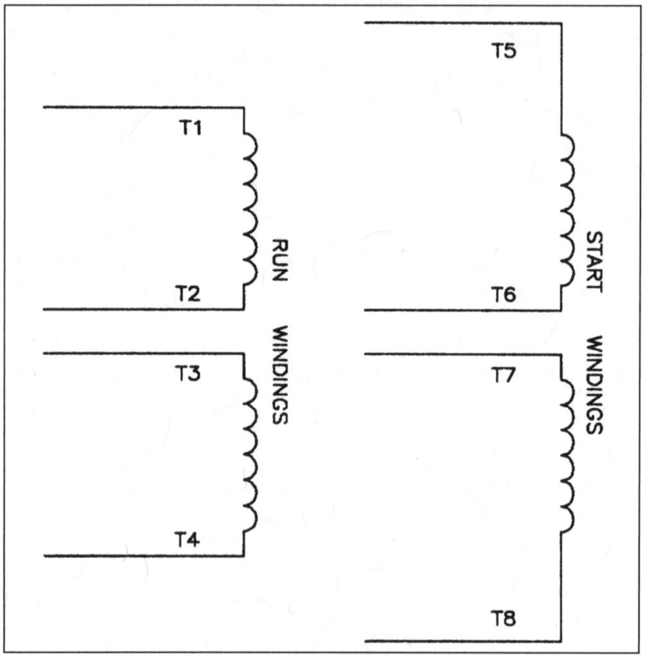

Figure 8-27 Single-phase dual-voltage motor.

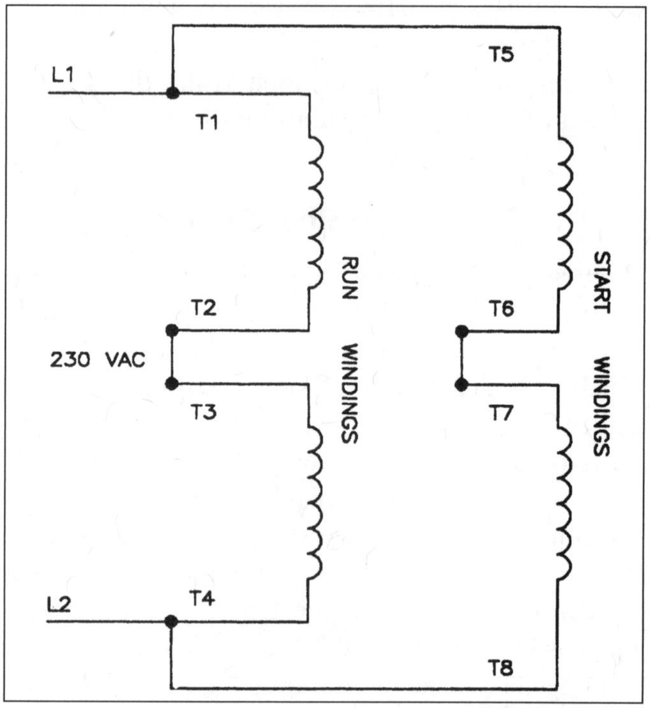

Figure 8-28 High-voltage connection for single-phase motor with two run windings and two start windings.

however, that some motors identify the start winding by labelling it T5 and T8, as shown in Figure 8-31.

Regardless of which method is used to label the terminal leads of the start winding, the connection will be the same. If the motor is to be connected for high-voltage operation, the run windings will be connected in series, and the start winding will be connected in parallel with one of the run windings, as shown in Figure 8-32. In this type of motor, each winding is rated at 120 V. If the run windings are connected in series across 240 V, each winding will have a voltage drop of

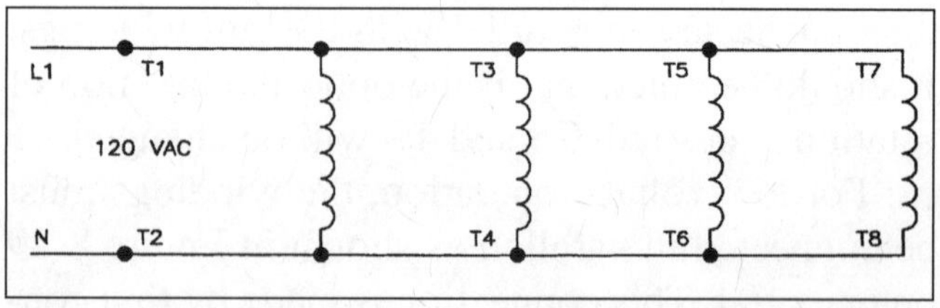

Figure 8-29 Low-voltage connection for single-phase motor with two start windings.

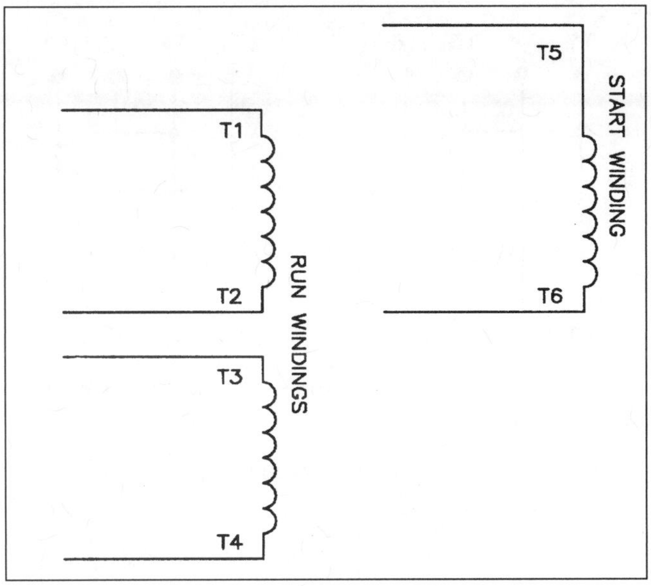

Figure 8-30 Dual-voltage motor with one start winding labelled T5 and T6.

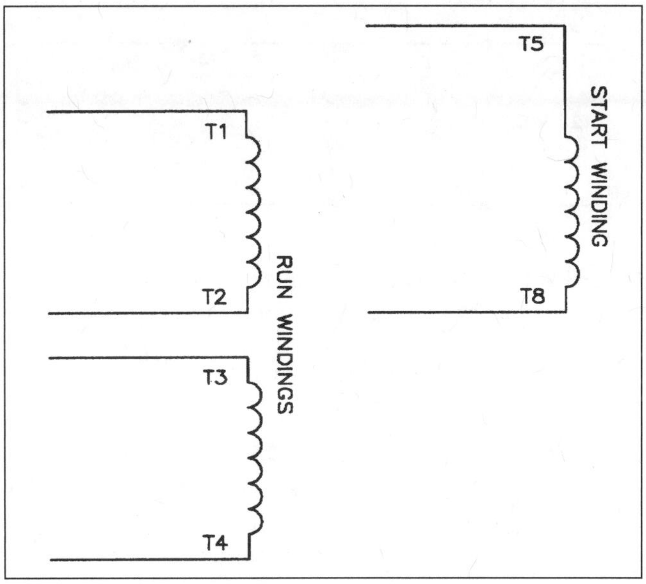

Figure 8-31 Dual-voltage motor with one start winding labelled T5 and T8.

120 V. By connecting the start winding in parallel across only one run winding, it will receive only 120 V when power is applied to the motor. If the opposite direction of rotation is desired, T5 and T8 should be changed.

If the motor is to be operated on low voltage, the windings are connected in parallel, as shown in Figure 8-33 on page 106. Since all windings are connected in parallel, each will receive 120 V when power is applied to the motor.

Determining Direction of Rotation for Single-Phase Motors

The direction of rotation of a single-phase motor can generally be determined when the motor is connected. The direction of rotation is determined by facing the back or rear of the motor. Figure 8-34 on page 106 shows a connection diagram for rotation. If clockwise rotation is desired, T5 should be connected to T1. If counterclockwise rotation is desired, T8 (or T6) should be connected to T1. It should be noted that this connection diagram assumes the motor contains two sets of run and two sets of start windings. The type of motor used example, Figure 8-32 shows the connection of a motor with two run windings and only one start winding. If this motor were to be connected for clockwise rotation, terminal T5 should be connected to T1 and terminal T8 should be connected

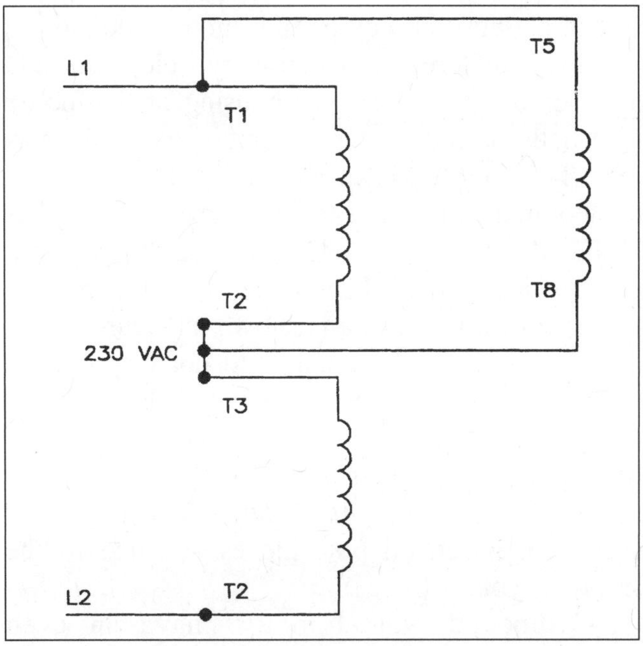

Figure 8-32 High-voltage connection with one start

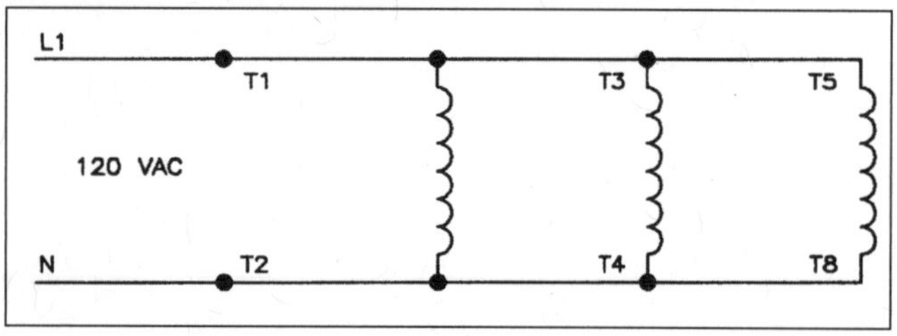

Figure 8-33 Low-voltage connection for a single-phase motor with one start winding.

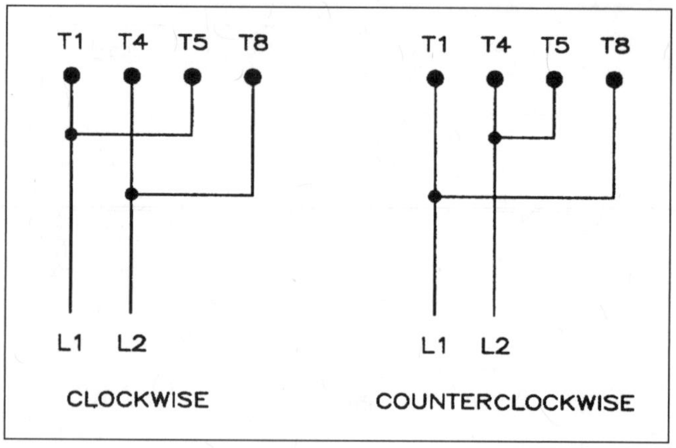

Figure 8-34 Determining direction of rotation for single-phase motors.

to T2 and T3. If counterclockwise rotation were desired, terminal T8 would be connected to T1 and terminal T5 would be connected to T2 and T3.

DIRECT-CURRENT MOTORS

Two types of machine tools in the industrial building require DC motors. Five vertical boring mills (MG) require one DC motor each and three planers (MH) require the same types of motors and controllers.

The motors used are standard compound wound DC motors and are all rated at 25 hp. The motors are not operated from regular direct-current sources, but rather are operated from 575-V AC lines through electronic controllers that rectify the current (change it from AC to DC).

Direct-current compound motors contain a rotating armature and a stationary field. The field also serves as the frame or housing of the motor. End bells or end brackets support the shaft bearings. The armature has a winding that is connected to a commutator. Brush holders and carbon brushes mounted on the front end bell contact the commutator, which rotates when the motor is running.

A typical DC motor is shown in Figure 8-35.

The compound wound field consists of two separate field windings. The shunt field is wound with relatively small wire and has thousands of turns. The series field is wound with large wire and has only a few turns. The field windings or coils are placed on pole pieces attached to the frame or yoke.

Compound wound motors have an even number of poles with the smaller motor sizes usually having two or four poles, and the larger motor sizes having a larger number of poles. The field frame of a DC motor is shown in Figure 8-36.

A part of the shunt field and a part of the series field are wound on each pole piece. The windings on alternate pole pieces are made in opposite directions, clockwise and counterclockwise. In this manner, adjacent pole pieces are alternately magnetized north and south. The ends of the shunt winding (two ends) and the series field winding (two ends) are brought out to the motor terminal box.

Commutating poles or interpoles are also provided. These very small pole pieces are placed midway between the main pole pieces. The interpoles are wound with a few turns of heavy wire. As with the main pole pieces, the interpoles are also wound in an alternate clockwise and counterclockwise manner. The pole pieces are connected permanently in series with the armature brush holders and are considered to be a part of the armature circuit. Interpoles counteract the distortion of the field magnetism caused by the rotation of the heavily magnetized armature in the field flux. As a result, sparking or arcing at the brushes is eliminated.

A DC compound motor can be connected in several ways. When the shunt field is connected across only the armature, it is known as a *short shunt connection* (Figure 8-37 on page 108). If, on the other hand, the shunt field is connected across both the armature and the series field, it is called a

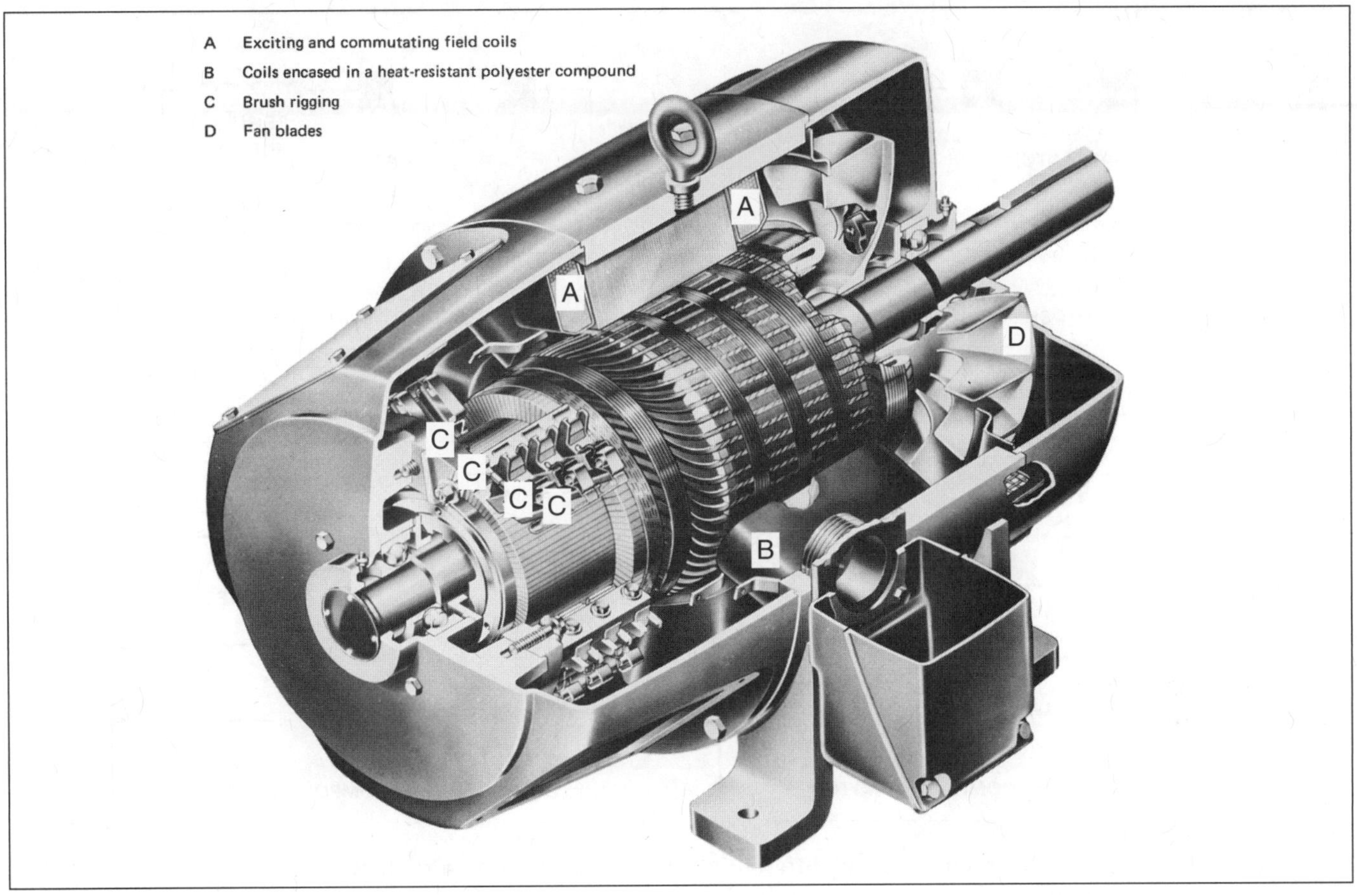

Figure 8-35 Cutaway view of DC motor.

long shunt connection. When the motor is connected short shunt, the shunt field current is added to the series field current. This generally causes a slight overcompounding of the motor, which permits it to exhibit stronger torque characteristics. When the motor is connected long shunt, it exhibits better speed regulation.

If the motor terminal connections are made so that the series field magnetism aids or strengthens the magnetism produced by the shunt field, then the motor is said to be a cumulative compound motor (Figure 8-38 on page 108). If the motor terminal connections are reversed so that the magnetism of the series field opposes or weakens the magnetism of the shunt field, the motor is called a differential compound motor (Figure 8-38).

Although the differential compound motor gives a more constant speed at all loads, the motor is somewhat unstable. For this reason, this type of motor is not used in as many applications as the cumulative compound motor.

Figure 8-36 Field frame of a DC motor.

The strength of the shunt field is constant. However, since the series field is connected in series with the armature, the strength of the series field varies with the load on the motor. When the

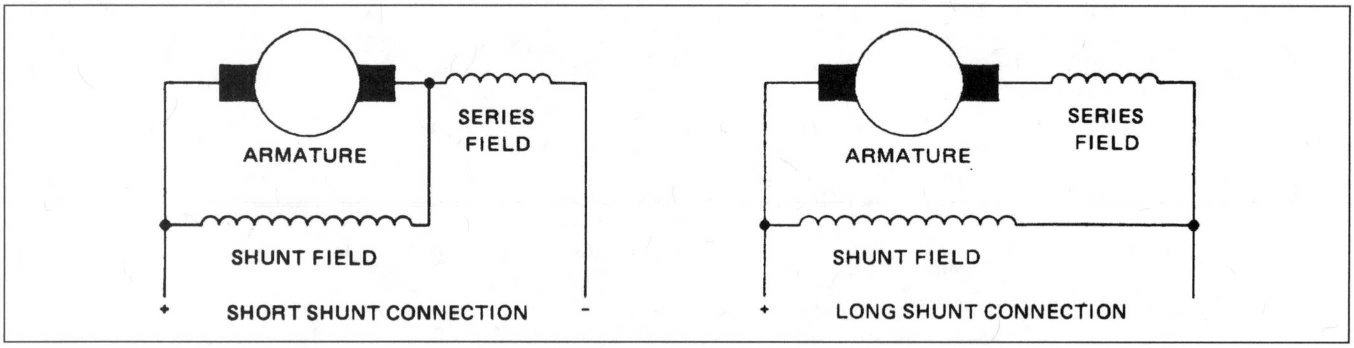

Figure 8-37 DC motor connection.

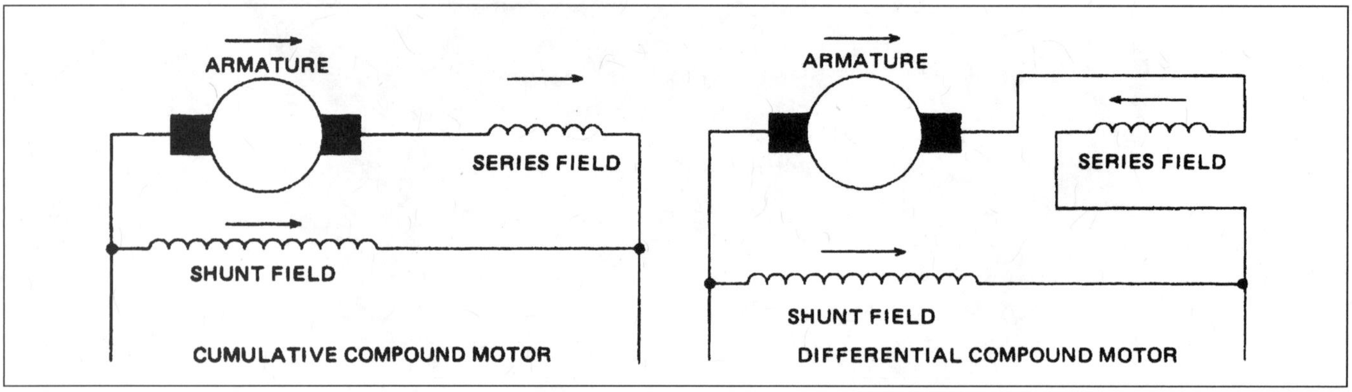

Figure 8-38 Connections for cumulative and differential compound connection motors.

motor is running at idle speed (no output), the series field contributes almost no magnetism to that of the shunt field. When the motor is loaded, the series field increases the magnetism of the shunt field to produce more torque and cause a slight drop in the motor speed.

The armature/commutator also has poles. This component of the motor is a wrought copper cylinder with segments or bars. These segments are insulated from one another and serve as a mounting to which the armature winding is connected. A two-pole armature has a coil span equal to the diameter of the armature, less a few slots. A four-pole armature has a coil span equal to one-quarter of the circumference of the armature, less a few slots. A six-pole armature has a coil span equal to one-sixth of the circumference of the armature, less one or two slots (Figure 8-39). The coil span arrangement depends entirely on the number of poles present. A four-pole armature cannot be used with a two-pole field. The two units, the armature and the field, must be wound with the same number of poles.

It was shown that for alternating-current motors, the torque and horsepower are proportional to the square of the voltage applied, and the speed of rotation depends upon the frequency and the number of poles in the motor. However, the performance of a direct-current motor depends upon entirely different factors. The speed of a DC motor increases when the voltage increases and decreases if the field strength is increased or if there is an increase in the number of poles or turns of wire wound on the armature.

For all motors, the horsepower output is:

$$\text{hp} = \frac{2\pi F \times R \times S}{33\,000} \quad or \quad \frac{T \times S}{5250}$$

where

F = force, in pounds

R = radius, in feet

S = speed, in rpm

T = torque, in pound feet

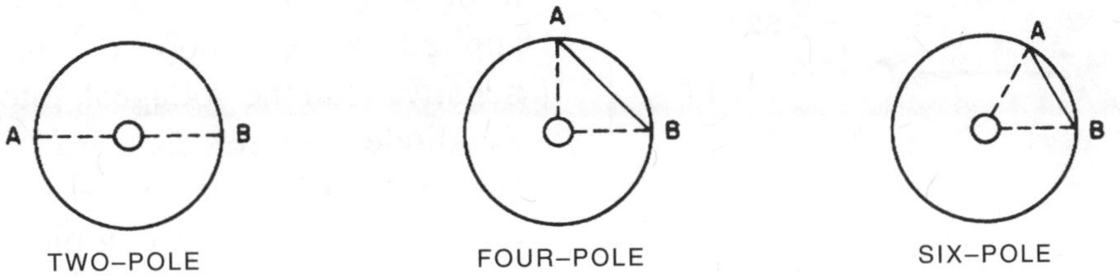

The coil span is the line A–B. With a two-pole motor, coil span is 180°. A four-pole motor has a coil span of 90°, and a six-pole motor has a coil span of 60°. In actual practice, coil span is chorded and is slightly less than the full span.

Figure 8-39 Relation of armature coil span to number of poles.

Terminal Identification for DC Motors

The terminal leads of DC machines are labelled so they can be identified when they are brought outside the motor housing to the terminal box. Figure 8-40 illustrates this standard identification. Terminals A1 and A2 are connected to the armature through the brushes. The ends of the series field are identified with S1 and S2, and the ends of the shunt field are marked F1 and F2. Some DC machines will provide access to another set of windings called the commutating field or interpoles. The ends of this winding will be labelled C1 and C2, or S3 and S4. It is common practice to provide access to the interpole winding on machines designed to be used as motors or generators.

Determining the Direction of Rotation of a DC Motor

The direction of rotation of a DC motor is determined by facing the commutator end of the motor. This is generally the back or rear of the motor. If the windings have been labelled in a standard manner, it is possible to determine the direction of rotation when the motor is connected. Figure 8-41 on page 110 illustrates the standard connections for a series motor. The standard connections for a shunt motor are illustrated in Figure 8-42 on page 110, and the standard connections for a compound motor are shown in Figure 8-43 on page 110.

The direction of rotation of a DC motor can be reversed by changing the connections of the armature leads or the field leads. It is common practice to change the connection of the armature leads. This is done to prevent changing a cumulative compound motor into a differential compound motor.

DC POWER SUPPLIES

The use of direct-current motors in industry creates a need for a supply of DC power. Since most of industry operates on AC power, the DC power needed is generally produced within the industrial

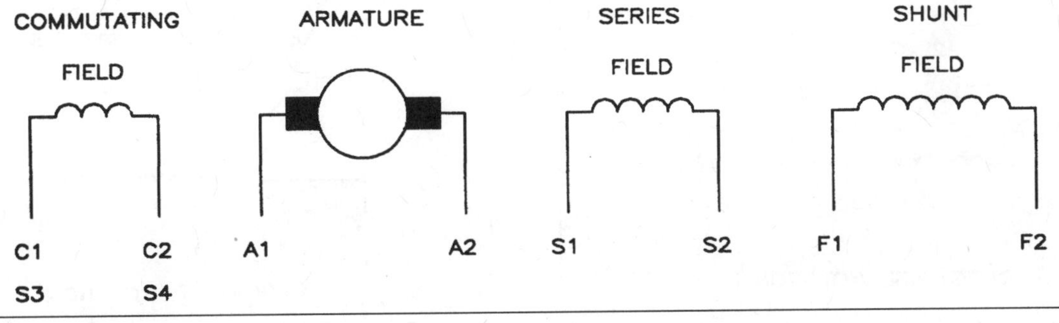

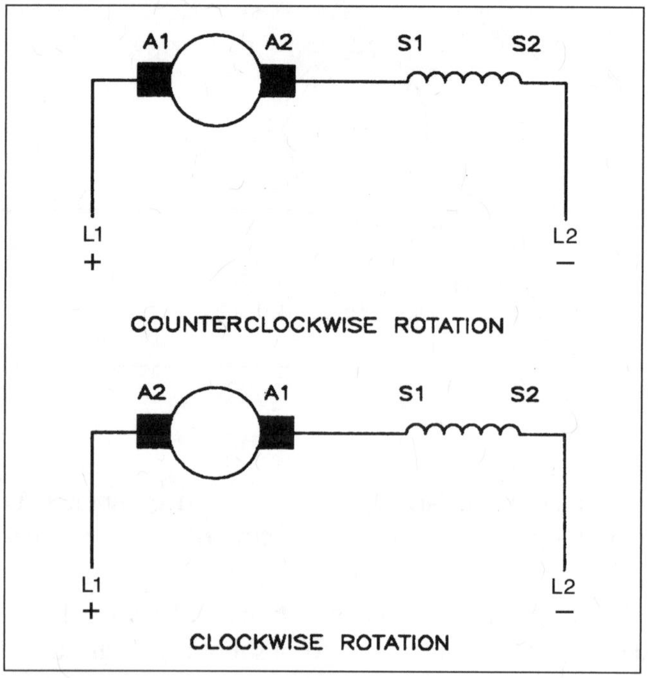

Figure 8-41 Series motor.

plant. The most common method to convert AC voltage to DC voltage is by the use of solid-state components.

A simple half-wave rectifier is shown in Figure 8-44. The diode is used to convert the AC voltage to DC voltage. The diode operates like an electric check valve; it permits the current to flow through it in only one direction. When the voltage applied to the cathode end of the diode is more negative than the voltage applied to the anode end, the diode becomes *forward biased*. This permits current to flow through the load resistor and then through the diode to complete the circuit. When the voltage applied to the cathode end of the diode becomes more positive than the voltage applied to the anode end, the diode becomes *reverse biased* and turns off. When the diode is reverse biased, no current flows in the circuit. The waveforms in Figure 8-44 illustrate this condition. The negative half of the AC input wave has been cut off to produce the DC output wave. This type of rectifier is called a half-wave because only one-half of the AC waveform is used. The output voltage is pulsating. It turns on and off, but the direction of current flow never reverses. Since the output voltage never reverses direction, it is direct current.

Single-Phase, Full-Wave Rectifiers

Full-wave rectification of single-phase AC can be obtained by using either of two circuits. Figure 8-45 shows these two types of full-wave rectifiers: the two-diode type and the bridge type. The *two-diode* rectifier requires the use of a centre-tapped transformer. It is the more efficient of the two

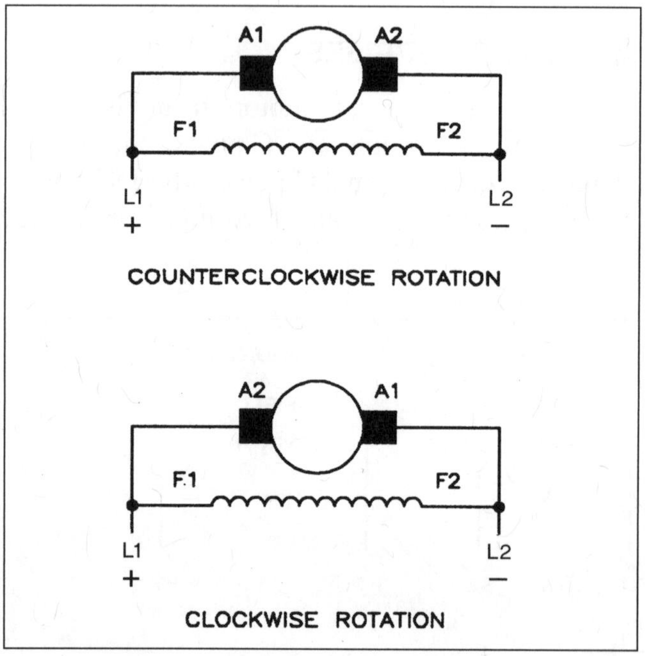

Figure 8-42 Shunt motor.

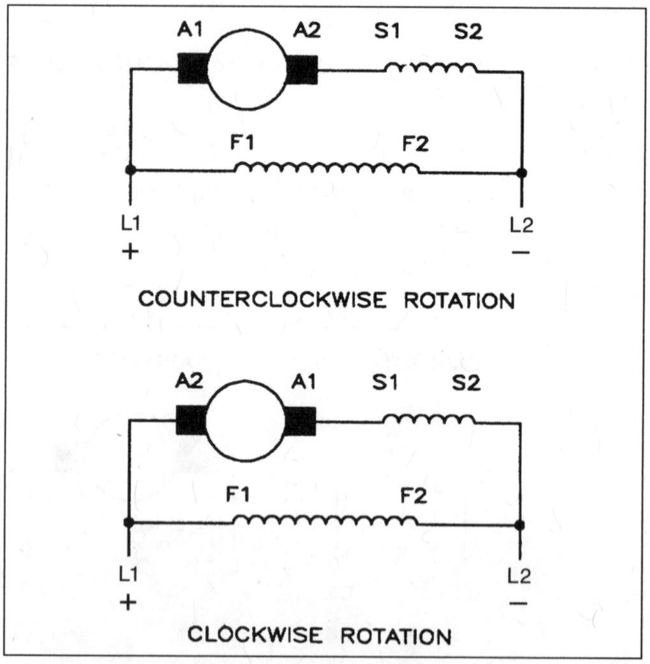

Figure 8-43 Compound motor.

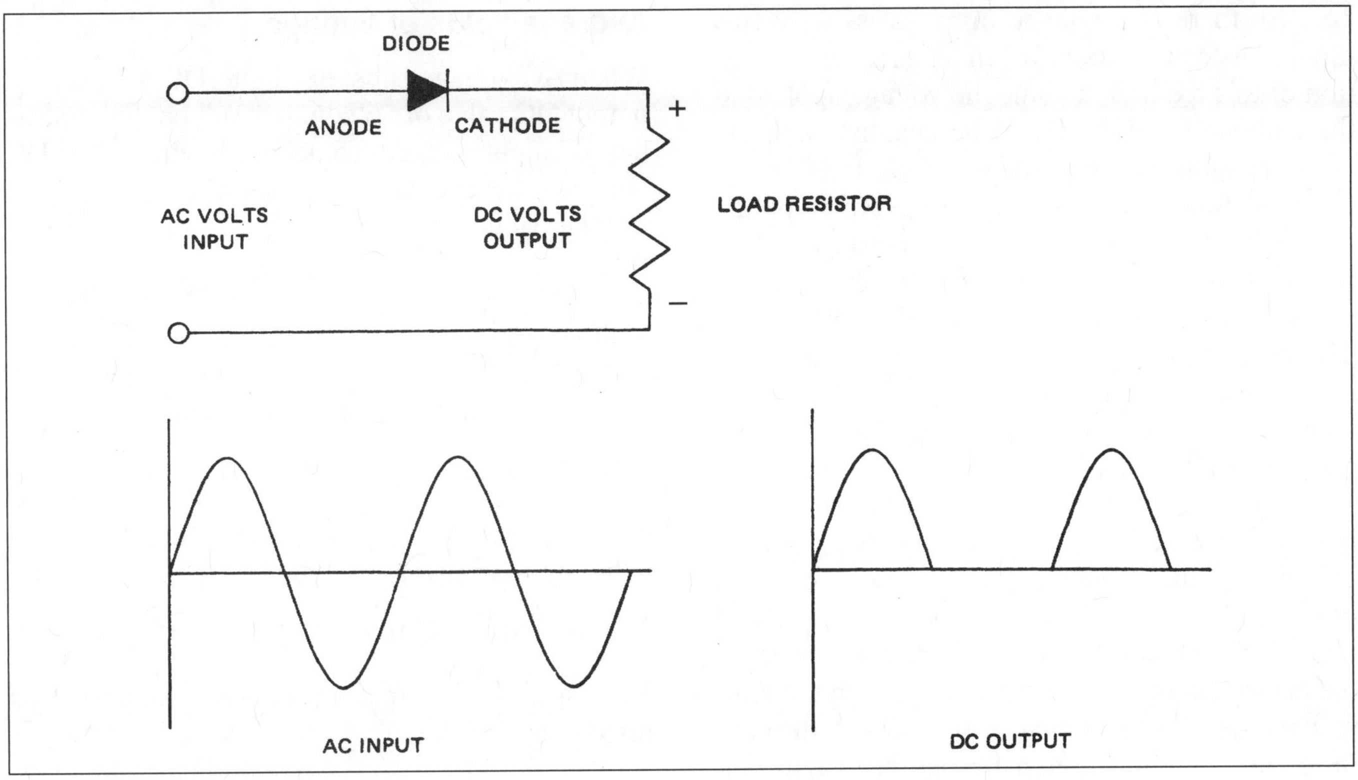

Figure 8-44 Half-wave rectifier.

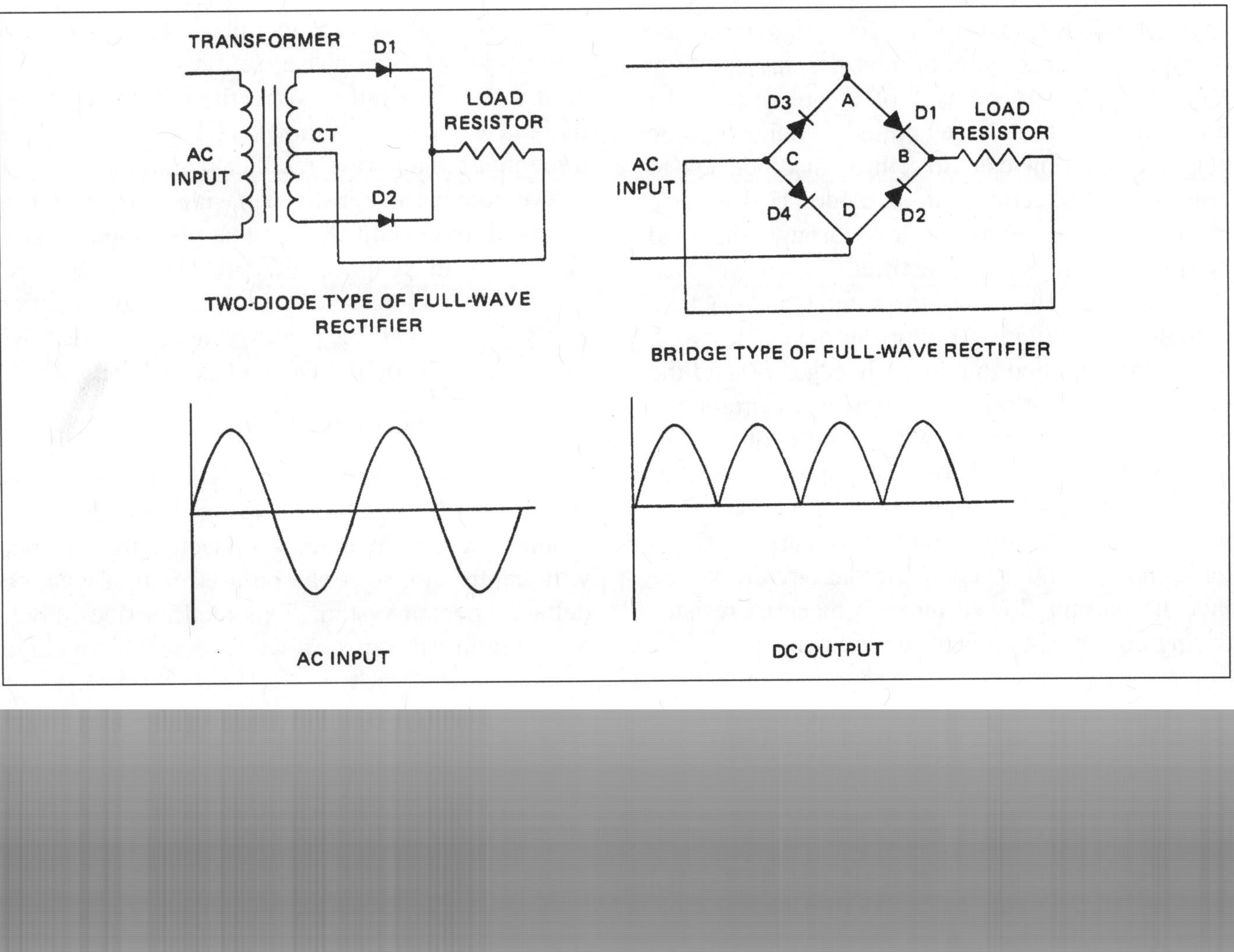

because there is a voltage drop across only two diodes instead of four. To understand the operation of this rectifier, assume the voltage applied to the cathode of diode D1 to be negative, and the voltage applied to the cathode of diode D2 to be positive. Since diode D1 has a negative voltage applied to its cathode, it is forward biased and current can flow through it. Diode D2, however, is reverse biased and no current can flow through it. The current must flow from the centre tap of the transformer, through the load resistor, and complete the circuit through diode D1 back to the transformer.

During the next half-cycle of AC voltage, a negative voltage is applied to the cathode of diode D2 and a positive voltage is applied to the cathode of diode D1. Diode D2 is now forward biased and diode D1 is reverse biased. Current can flow from the centre tap of the transformer, through the load resistor, and then complete the circuit through diode D2 back to the transformer. Notice in this rectifier that current flowed through the load resistor during both half-cycles of AC voltage. Since both cycles of AC voltage were changed into DC, it is full-wave rectification.

The *bridge-type* rectifier requires the use of four diodes, but it does not require the use of a centre-tapped transformer. To understand the operation of this type of rectifier, assume the voltage applied to point *A* of the rectifier to be positive, and the voltage applied to point *D* to be negative. Current can flow through diode D4 to point *C* of the rectifier. Since diode D3 is reverse biased, the current must flow through the load resistor to point *B* of the rectifier. The current then flows through diode D1 to point *A* and back to complete the circuit. During the next half-cycle, the voltage applied to point *A* is negative, and the voltage applied to point *D* is positive. Current can now flow through diode D3 to point *C* of the rectifier. Since diode D4 is reverse biased, the current must flow through the load resistor to point *B* of the rectifier. At this point, the current flows through diode D2 to complete the circuit. Notice that the current flowed through the load resistor during both half-cycles of AC voltage.

Average Value of Voltage

When AC voltage is changed into DC voltage, the output DC value of voltage will not be the same as the AC input voltage. To determine the output DC voltage, the average value must be found. The average value of DC voltage for a full-wave rectifier can be found by multiplying the peak AC value by 0.637. For example, assume an AC voltage has an RMS value of 120 V. To determine the value of DC voltage after rectification, change this RMS value into a peak value by multiplying by 1.414.

$120 \times 1.414 = 169.68$ V

Now change the peak value into the average value by multiplying by 0.637.

$169.68 \times 0.637 = 108$ V DC

If a half-wave rectifier is used, the answer is divided by 2.

Three-Phase Rectifiers

Most of industry operates on three-phase power instead of single phase. When it is necessary to change AC voltage to DC voltage, it is generally done with three-phase rectifiers. There are two basic types of three-phase rectifiers: the half-wave rectifier and the full-wave rectifier. A three-phase, half-wave rectifier is shown in Figure 8-46. The three-phase, half-wave rectifier requires the use of a wye-connected transformer with a centre tap to complete the circuit. Notice that only three diodes are used to make this connection. The average DC output voltage for a three-phase, half-wave rectifier is 0.827 of peak. If the peak voltage of this rectifier is 169.68 V, the output DC voltage will be:

$169.68 \times 0.827 = 140.32$ V DC

A three-phase, full-wave type of rectifier is shown in Figure 8-47. This rectifier does not require the use of a wye-connected transformer with centre tap, so it can be used with a wye- or delta-connected system. This rectifier does, however, require the use of six diodes. The average

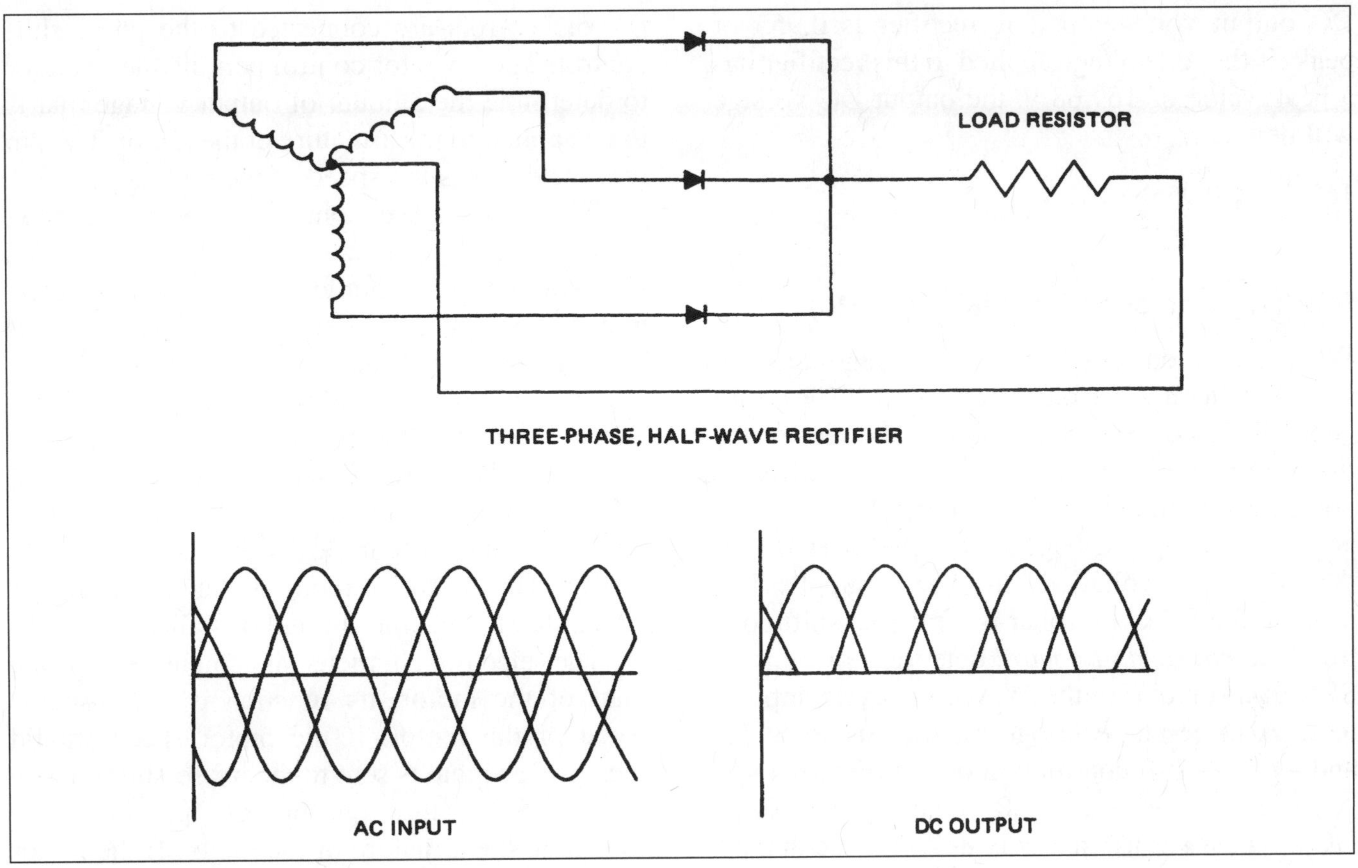

Figure 8-46 Three-phase, half-wave rectifier.

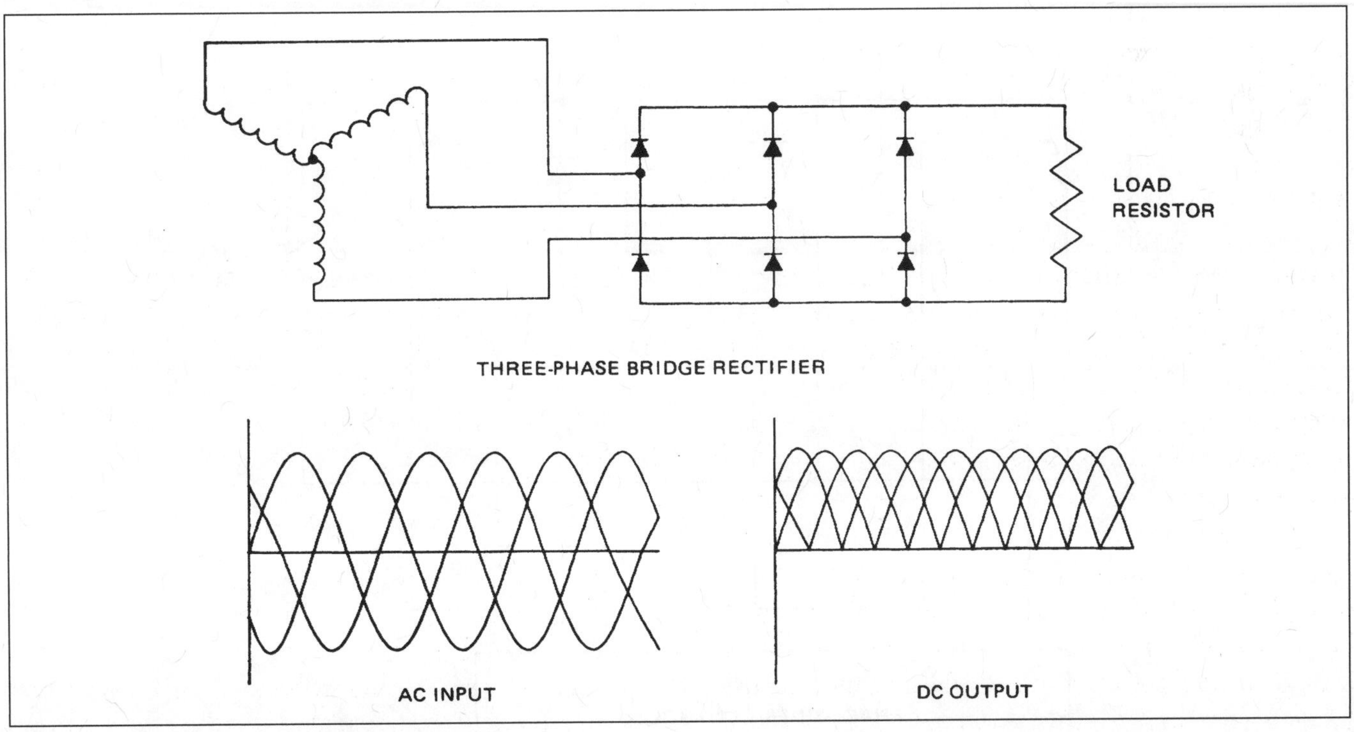

Figure 8-47 Three-phase, full-wave rectifier.

DC output voltage for this rectifier is 0.955 of peak. If the AC voltage applied to this rectifier has a peak value of 169.68 V, the output DC voltage will be:

$$169.68 \times 0.955 = 162 \text{ V DC}$$

Silicon Controlled Rectifiers (SCRs)

When the amount of DC output voltage must be varied, silicon controlled rectifiers (SCRs) are generally used instead of diodes. The reason for this is that the SCR can be turned on at different points during the AC waveform applied to it. This permits the output voltage to be varied from 0 V to the full output voltage of the power supply. The heart of the SCR controller is the phase-shift control. The *phase-shift control* determines when the SCR turns on during the AC voltage cycle applied to it. A three-phase bridge rectifier using SCRs and a phase-shift control is shown in Figure 8-48. A basic diagram of an SCR control system for a DC motor is shown in Figure 8-49. Notice that all sensor controls are connected to the phase-shift control. The operator control permits the operator to determine the amount of output voltage that is to be applied to the armature of the motor. This, in turn, determines the speed of the motor.

The field-failure control senses the current flow through the shunt field of the motor. If the shunt-field current should drop below a predetermined level, a signal is sent to the phase-shift control, which turns off the SCRs.

The current-limit control senses the input current to the controller. If a predetermined amount of current should be sensed, the phase-shift control will not permit the SCRs to turn on more and produce more current flow. This is designed to prevent damage to the motor and controller if the motor should become shorted or stalled.

The electrotachometer is connected to the shaft of the motor. Its function is to sense the speed of the motor. If the motor speed should decrease, a signal is sent to the phase-shift control and the SCRs turn on more to provide more voltage to the armature of the motor. If the motor

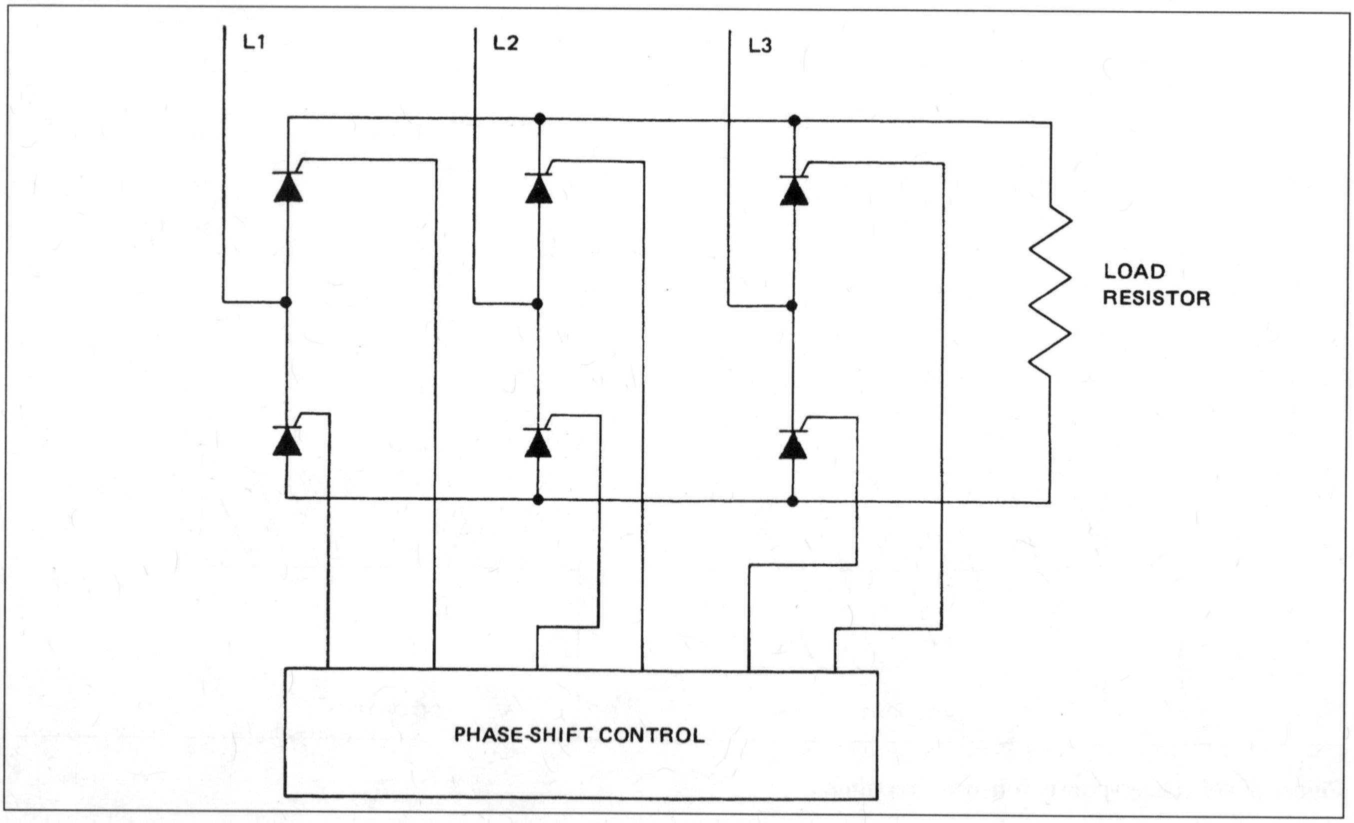

Figure 8-48 Three-phase rectifier using SCRs.

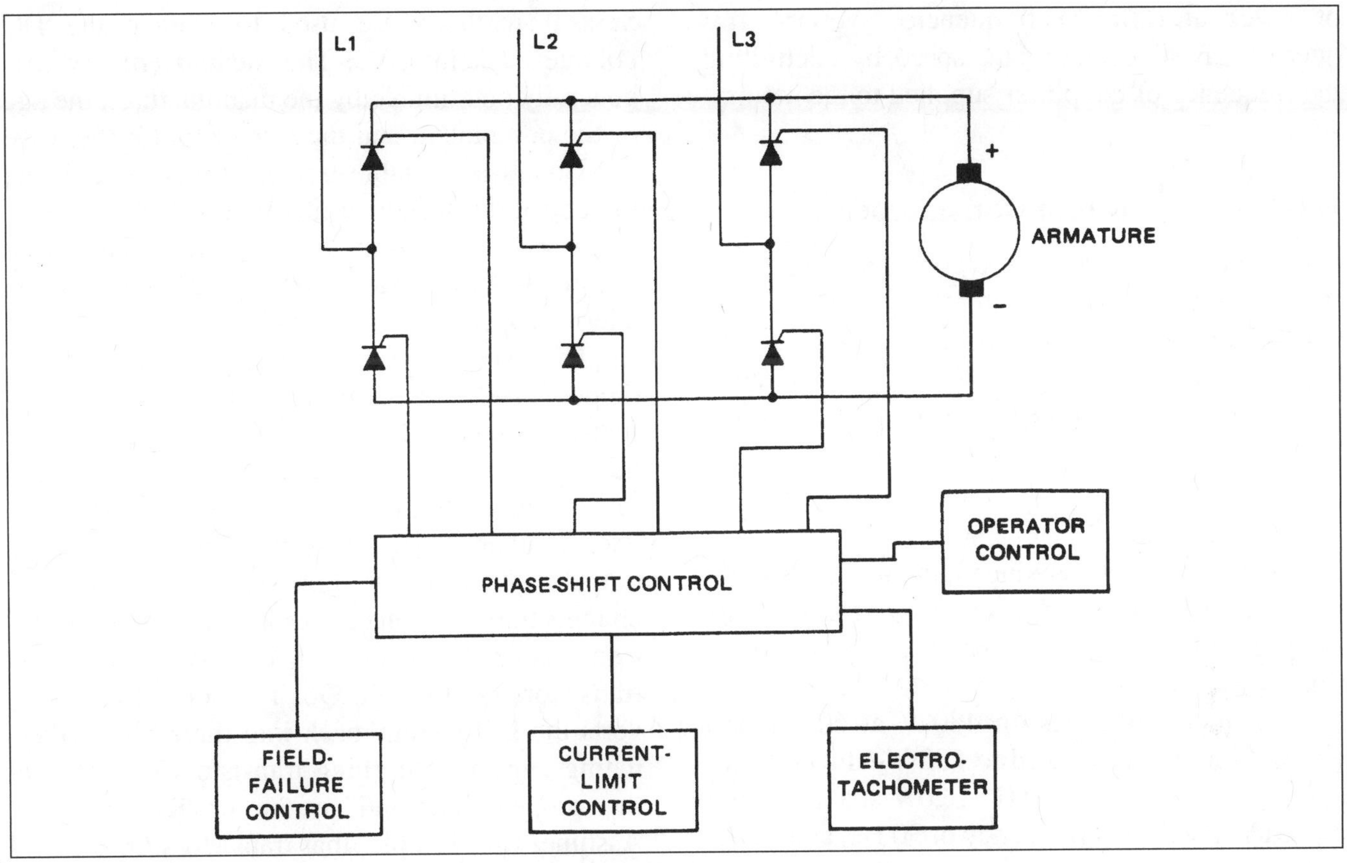

Figure 8-49 The phase-shift control unit determines the output voltage.

speed should increase, the phase-shift control will cause the SCRs to turn on less of the time; thus, the voltage applied to the armature will decrease.

Variable-Frequency Drives

Although direct-current motors are still used in many industries, they are being replaced by variable-frequency drives controlling squirrel-cage induction motors. The advantage of a direct-current motor compared to an alternating-current motor is the fact that the speed of the DC motor can be controlled. Although the wound rotor induction motor does permit some degree of speed control, it does not have the torque characteristics of a DC motor. Direct-current motors can develop maximum torque at 0 rpm. Variable-frequency drives can give these same speed control and torque characteristics to squirrel-cage induction motors. A variable-frequency drive and AC squirrel-cage motor are less expensive to purchase than a comparable DC drive and DC motor. Variable-frequency drives and squirrel-cage motors have less downtime and fewer maintenance problems than DC drives and DC motors.

Variable-Frequency Drive Operating Principles

The operating principle of all polyphase AC motors is the rotating magnetic field. The speed of the rotating field is called *synchronous* speed and is controlled by two factors: frequency of the applied voltage and the number of stator poles. Table 8-5 lists the synchronous speed for different numbers

Poles	Frequency in Hertz					
	60	50	40	30	20	10
2	3 600	3 000	2 400	1 800	1 200	600
4	1 800	1 500	1 200	900	600	300
6	1 200	1 000	800	600	400	200
8	900	750	600	450	300	150

Table 8-5 Motor revolutions per minute for different

of poles at different frequencies. Variable-frequency drives control motor speed by controlling the frequency of the power supplied to the motor.

Voltage and Current Considerations

A critical factor that must be considered when the frequency supplying a motor load is reduced is overcurrent. Motor current is limited by the inductive reactance of the stator winding, and inductive reactance is proportional to the frequency applied to the inductor.

$$X_L = 2\pi FL$$

If the frequency is reduced, the inductive reactance will be reduced also. To overcome this problem, the voltage must be reduced in proportion to the frequency.

If a motor operates on 480 V at 60 Hz, the voltage should be reduced to 400 V when the frequency is decreased to 50 Hz, 320 V at a frequency of 40 Hz, 240 V at a frequency of 30 Hz, and so on.

Basic Construction of a Variable-Frequency Drive

Most variable-frequency drives operate by first changing the AC voltage into DC and then changing it back to AC at the desired frequency. Several methods are used to change the DC voltage back into AC. The method employed is generally determined by the manufacturer, the age of the equipment, and the size of motor the drive must control. Variable-frequency drives intended to control the speeds of motors up to 500 hp generally use transistors. In the circuit shown in Figure 8-50, a single-phase bridge changes the alternating current into direct current.

The bridge rectifier uses two SCRs and two diodes. The SCRs permit the output voltage of the rectifier to be controlled. As the frequency decreases, the SCRs fire later in the cycle and lower the output voltage to the transistors. A choke coil and capacitor bank are used to filter the output voltage before transistors Q1 through Q6 change the DC voltage back into AC. An electronic control unit is connected to the bases of transistors Q1 through Q6. The control unit converts the DC voltage back into three-phase alternating current by turning transistors on or off at the proper time and in the proper sequence. Assume, for example, that transistors Q1 and Q4 are switched on at the same time. This permits stator winding T3 to be connected to a positive voltage and T2 to be connected to a negative voltage. Current can flow through Q4 to T2, through the motor stator winding and through T3 to Q1.

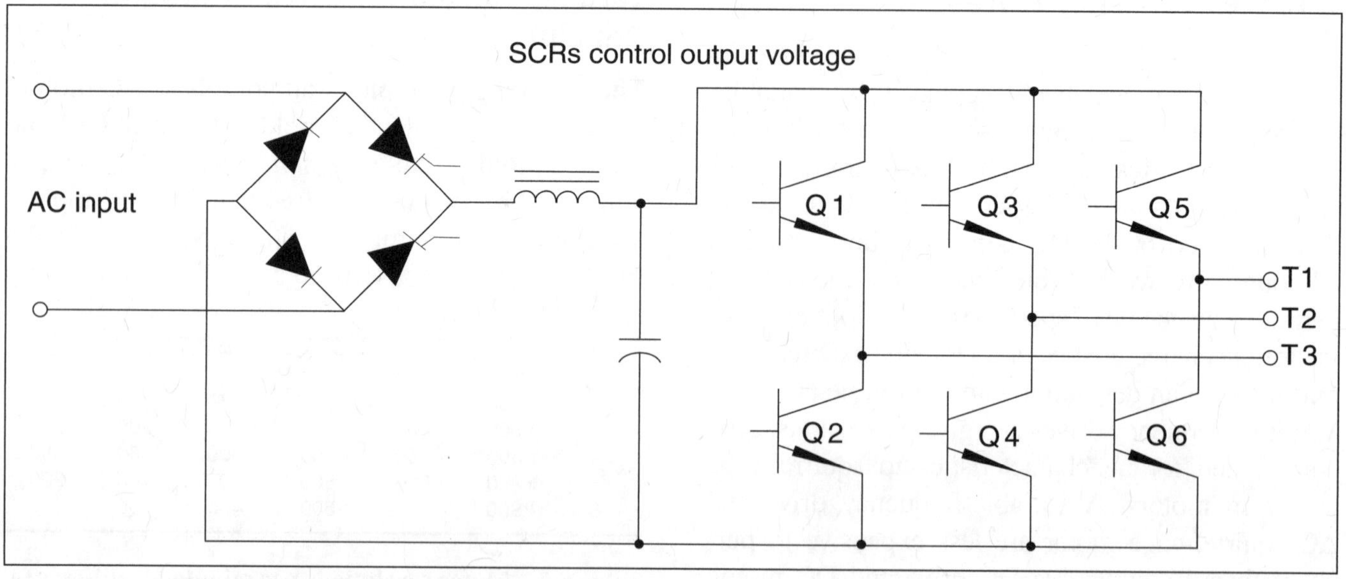

Figure 8-50 Basic schedule of a variable-speed drive.

Now assume that transistors Q1 and Q4 are switched off and transistors Q3 and Q6 are switched on. Current will now flow through Q6 to stator winding T1, through the motor to T2, and through Q3 to the positive of the power supply.

Since the transistors are turned completely on or completely off, the waveform produced is a square wave instead of a sine wave (Figure 8-51). Induction motors will operate on a square wave without a great problem. Some manufacturers design units that will produce a stepped waveform as shown in Figure 8-52. The stepped waveform is used because it more closely approximates a sine wave.

Some Related Problems

The circuit illustrated in Figure 8-50 employs the use of SCRs in the power supply and junction transistors in the output stage. SCR power supplies control the output voltage by chopping the incoming waveform. This can cause harmonics on the line that cause overheating of transformers and motors, and can cause fuses to blow and circuit breakers to trip. When bipolar junction transistors are employed as switches, they are generally driven into saturation by supplying them with an excessive amount of base-emitter current. Saturating the transistor causes the collector–emitter voltage to drop to between 0.04 V and 0.03 V. This small voltage drop allows the transistor to control large amounts of current without being destroyed. When a transistor is driven into saturation, however, it cannot recover or turn off as quickly as normal. This greatly limits the frequency response of the transistor.

IGBTs

Many transistor-controlled variable drives now employ a special type of transistor called an insulated gate bipolar transistor (IGBT). IGBTs have an insulated gate very similar to some types of field effect transistors (FETs). Since the gate is insulated, it has a very high impedance. The IGBT is a voltage-controlled device, not a current-controlled device. This gives it the ability to turn off very quickly. IGBTs can be driven into saturation to provide a very low voltage drop between emitter and collector, but they do not suffer from the slow recovery time of common junction transistors. The schematic symbol for an IGBT is shown in Figure 8-53 on page 118.

Drives using IGBTs generally use diodes to rectify the AC voltage into DC, not SCRs (Figure 8-54 on page 118). The three-phase rectifier supplies a constant DC voltage to the transistors. The output voltage to the motor is controlled by pulse-width modulation (PWM). PWM is accomplished by turning the transistor on and off several times during each half-cycle (Figure 8-55 on page 118). The output voltage is an average of the peak or maximum voltage and the amount of time the transistor is turned on or off. Assume that 480 V three-phase AC is rectified to DC and filtered. The DC voltage applied to the IGBTs is approximately 630 V. The output voltage to the motor is

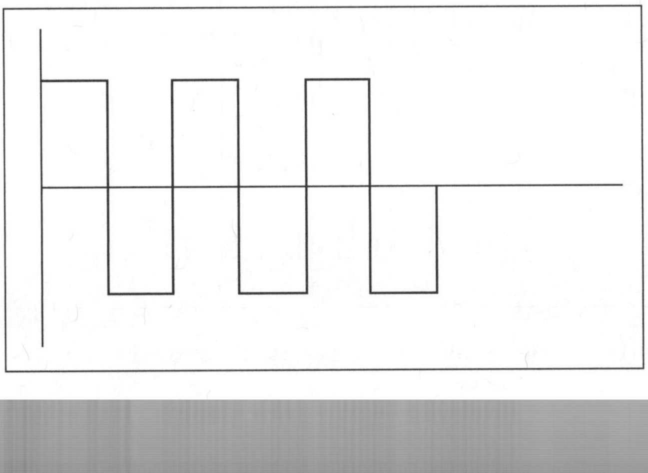

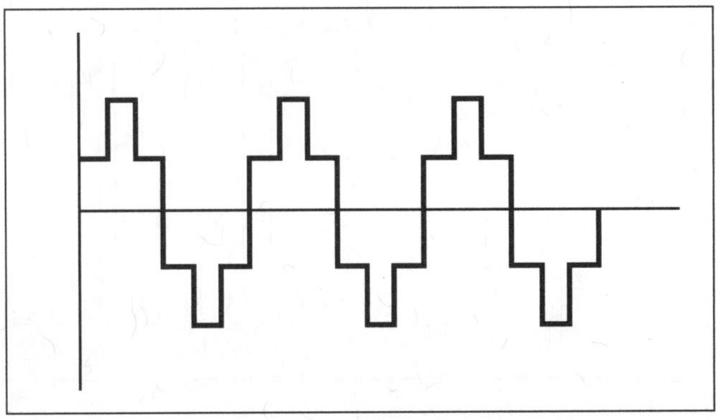

Figure 8-52 A stepped waveform approximates a sine

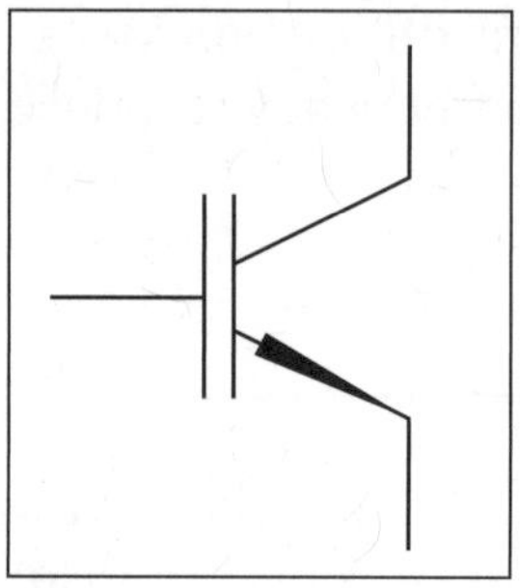

Figure 8-53 Schematic symbols for an insulated gate bipolar transistor.

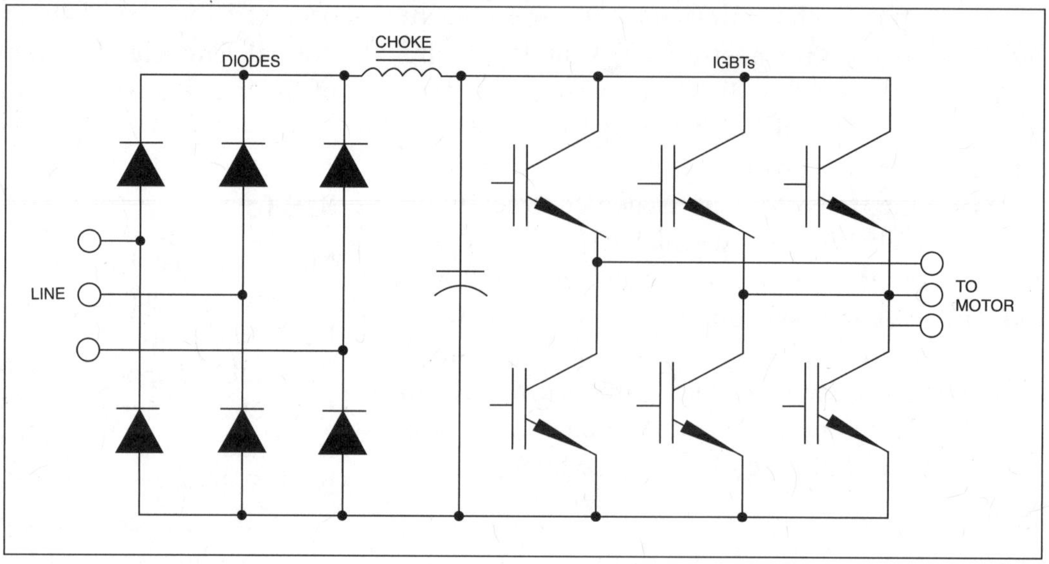

Figure 8-54 Variable-frequency drives using IGBTs with diodes in the rectifier instead of SCRs.

controlled by the switching of the transistors. Assume that the transistor is on for 10 microseconds and off for 20 microseconds. In this example, the transistor is on for one-third of the time and off for two-thirds of the time. The voltage applied to the motor would be 210 V (630 / 3).

Advantages and Disadvantages of IGBT Drives

A great advantage of drives using IGBTs is the fact that SCRs are generally not used in the power supply and this greatly reduces problems with line harmonics. The greatest disadvantage is that the

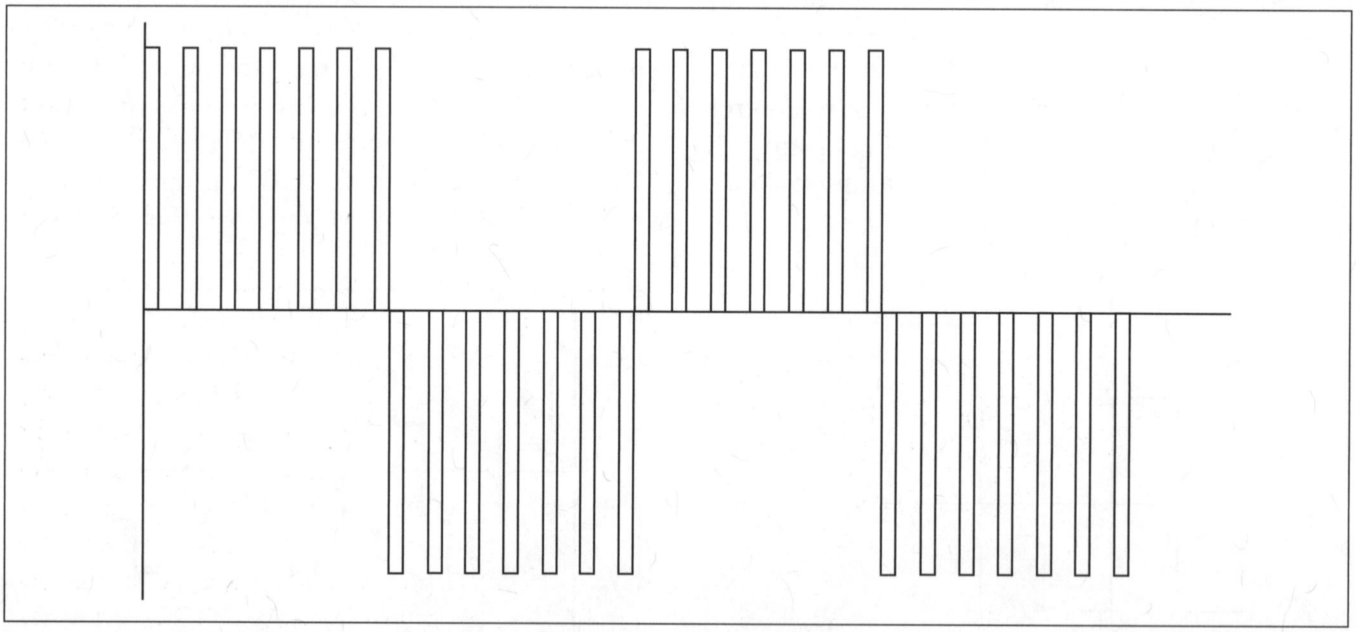

Figure 8-55 Pulse-width modulation is accomplished by turning the voltage on and off several times during each half-cycle.

fast switching rate of the transistors can cause voltage spikes in the range of 1600 V to be applied to the motor. These voltage spikes can destroy some motors. Line length from the drive to the motor is of great concern with drives using IGBTs. The shorter the line length, the better.

Inverter Rated Motors

Due to the problem of excessive voltage spikes caused by IGBT drives, some manufacturers produce a motor that is "inverter rated." These motors are specifically designed to be operated by variable-frequency drives. They differ from standard motors in several ways:

1. Many inverter rated motors contain a separate blower to provide continuous cooling for the motor regardless of the speed. Many motors use a fan connected to the motor shaft to help draw air though the motor. When the motor speed is reduced, the fan cannot maintain sufficient air flow to cool the motor.
2. Inverter rated motors generally have insulating paper between the windings and the stator core (Figure 8-56). The high-voltage spikes produce high currents that produce a high magnetic field. This increased magnetic field causes the motor windings to move. This movement can eventually cause the insulation to wear off the wire and produce a grounded motor winding.

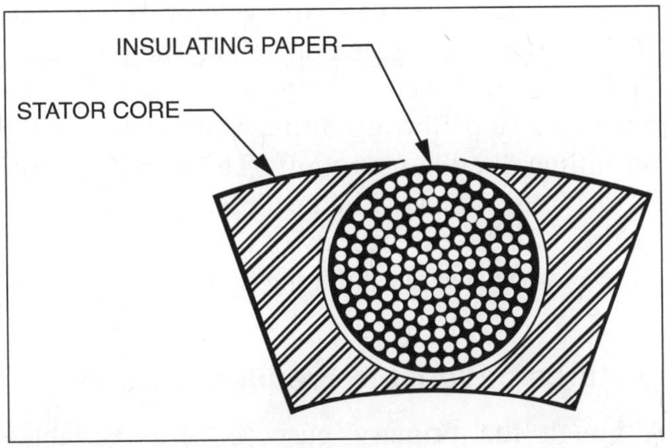

Figure 8-56 Insulated paper placed between the windings and the stator frame.

3. Inverter rated motors generally have phase paper added to the terminal leads. Phase paper is insulating paper added to the terminal leads that exit the motor. The high-voltage spikes affect the beginning lead of a coil much more than the wire inside the coil. The coil is an inductor that naturally opposes a change of current. Most of the insulation stress caused by high-voltage spikes occurs at the beginning of a winding.
4. The magnet wire used in the construction of the motor windings has a higher rated insulation than other motors.
5. The case size is larger than most three-phase motors. The case size is larger because of the added insulating paper between the windings and the stator core. Also, a larger case size helps cool the motor by providing a larger surface area for the dissipation of heat.

Variable-Frequency Drives Using SCRs and GTOs

Variable-frequency drives intended to control motors of more than 500 hp generally use SCRs or gate turnoff devices (GTOs). GTOs are similar to SCRs except that conduction through the GTO can be stopped by applying a negative voltage, negative with respect to the cathode, to the gate. SCRs and GTOs are thyristors and have the ability to handle a greater amount of current than transistors. An example of a single-phase circuit used to convert DC voltage to AC voltage with SCRs is shown in Figure 8-57 on page 120.

In this circuit, the SCRs are connected to a control unit that controls the sequence and rate at which the SCRs are gated on. The circuit is constructed so that SCRs *A* and *A′* are gated on at the same time and SCRs *B* and *B′* are gated on at the same time. Inductors L1 and L2 are used for filtering and wave shaping. Diodes D1 through D4 are clamping diodes and are used to prevent the output voltage from becoming excessive. Capacitor C1 is used to turn one set of SCRs off when the other set is gated on. This capacitor must be a true AC capacitor because it will be charged to the

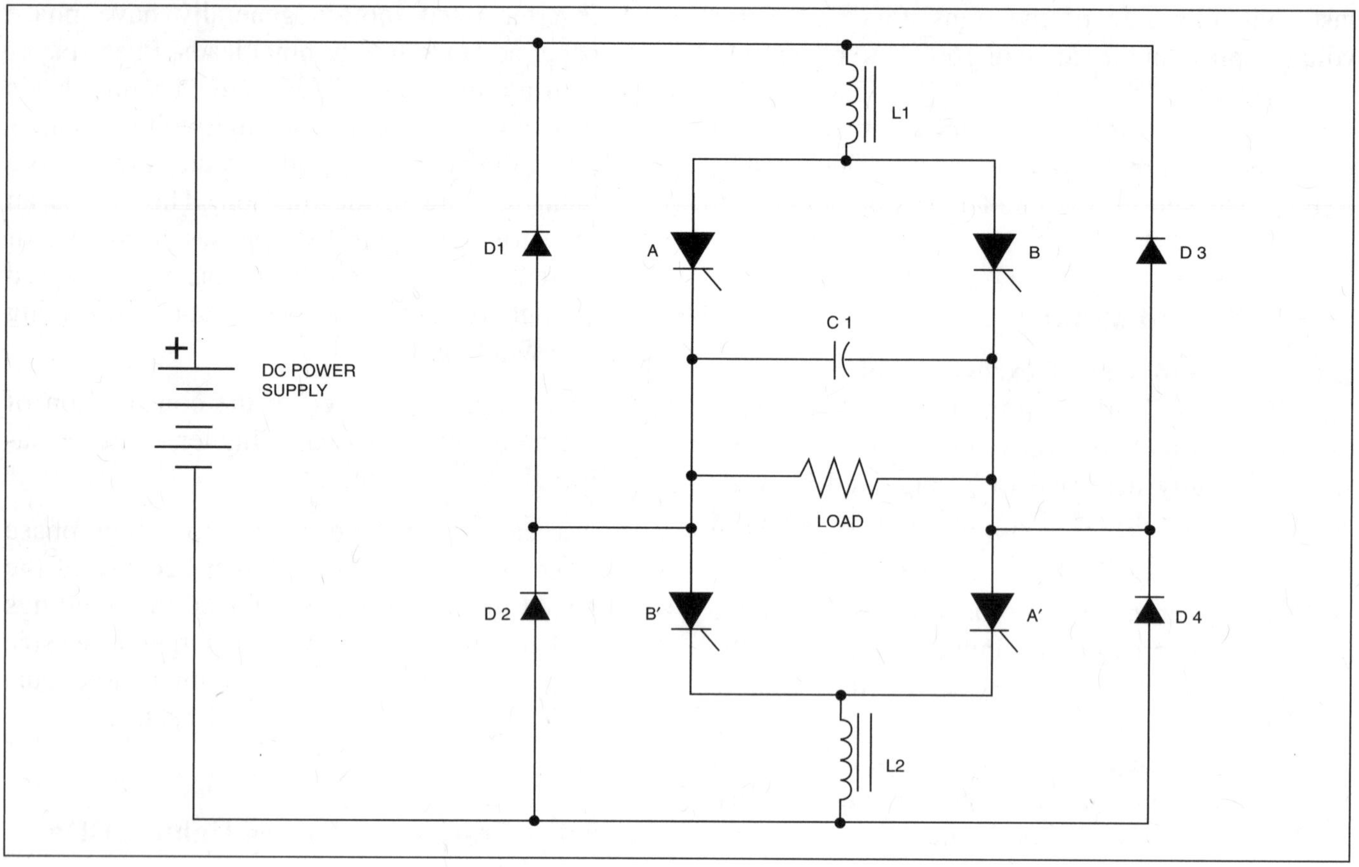

Figure 8-57 Changing DC to AC using SCRs.

alternate polarity each half-cycle. In a converter intended to handle large amounts of power, capacitor C1 will be a bank of capacitors.

To understand the operation of the circuit, assume that SCRs *A* and *A′* are gated on at the same time. Current will flow through the circuit as shown in Figure 8-58. Notice the direction of current flow through the load and that capacitor C1 has been charged to the polarity shown. When an SCR is gated on, it can be turned off only by permitting the current flow through the anode–cathode section to drop below a certain level called the holding current level. As long as the current continues to flow through the anode–cathode, the SCR will not turn off.

Now assume that SCRs *B* and *B′* are turned on. Because SCRs *A* and *A′* are still turned on, two current paths now exist through the circuit. The positive charge on capacitor C1, however, causes the negative electrons to see an easier path. The current will rush to charge the capacitor to the opposite polarity, stopping the current flowing through SCRs *A* and *A′* and permitting them to turn off. The current now flows through SCRs *B* and *B′* and charges the capacitor to the opposite polarity (Figure 8-59 on page 122). Notice that the current now flows through the load in the opposite direction, which produces alternating current across the load.

To produce the next half-cycle of AC current, SCRs *A* and *A′* are gated on again. The positively charged side of the capacitor will now cause the current to stop flowing through SCRs *B* and *B′*, permitting them to turn off. The current again flows through the load in the direction indicated in Figure 8-58. The frequency of the circuit is determined by the rate at which the SCRs are gated on.

Features of Variable-Frequency Control

Although the primary purpose of a variable-frequency drive is to provide speed control for an AC motor, most drives provide functions that other types of controls do not. Many variable-

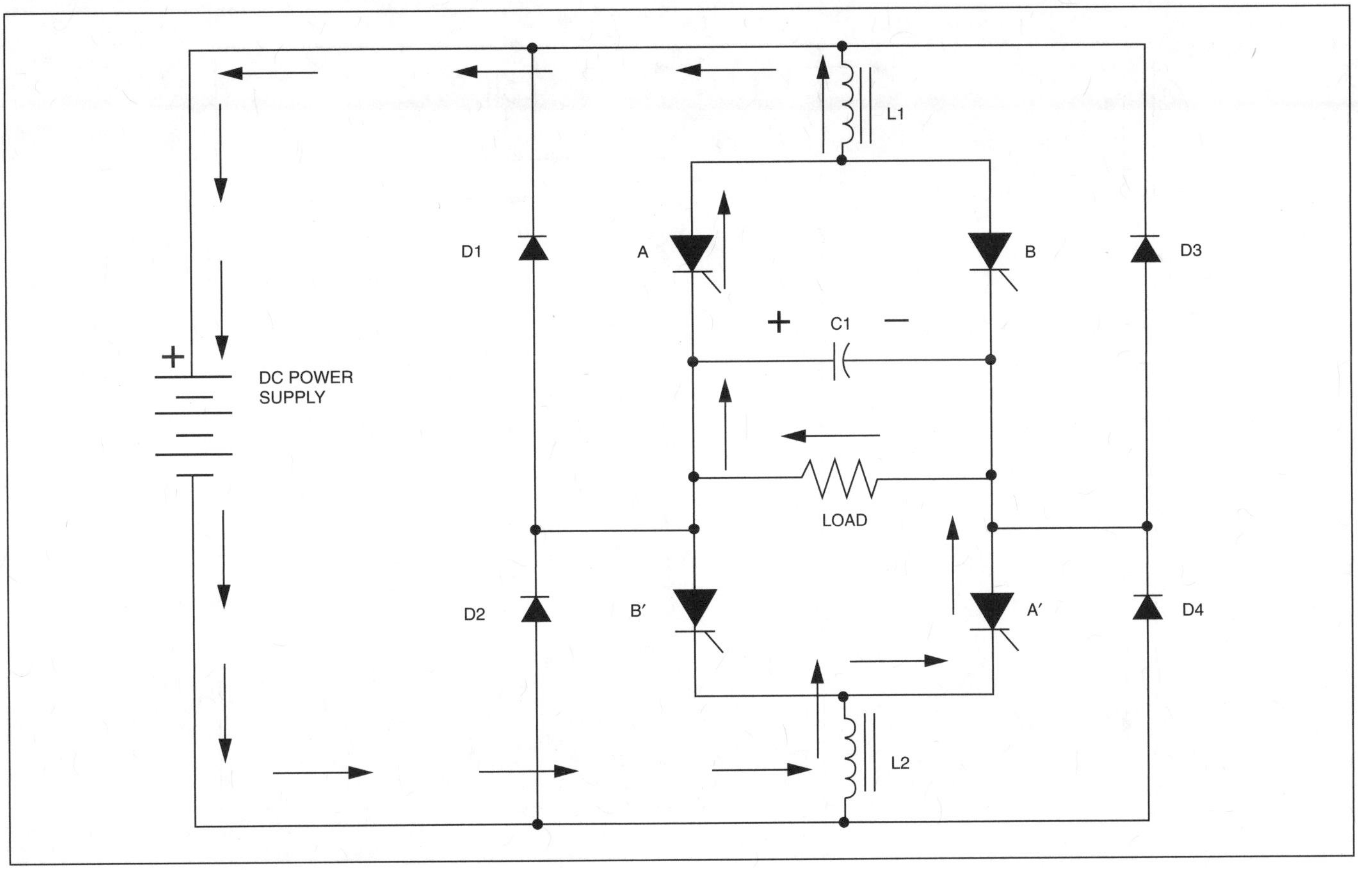

Figure 8-58 Current flows through SCRs *A* and *A′*.

frequency drives can provide the low-speed torque that is so desirable in DC motors. It is this feature that permits AC squirrel-cage motors to replace DC motors for many applications. Many variable-frequency drives also provide current limit and automatic speed regulation for the motor. Current limit is generally accomplished by connecting current transformers to the input of the drive and sensing the increase in current as load is added. Speed regulation is accomplished by sensing the speed of the motor and feeding this information back to the drive.

Another feature of variable-frequency drives is acceleration and deceleration control, sometimes called *ramping*. Ramping is used to accelerate or decelerate a motor over some period of time. Ramping permits the motor to bring the load up to speed slowly, as opposed to simply connecting the motor directly to the line. Even if the speed control is set in the maximum position when the start button is pressed, ramping permits

maximum rpm over several seconds. This feature can be a real advantage for some types of loads, especially gear drive loads. In some units the amount of acceleration and deceleration time can be adjusted by setting potentiometers on the main control board. Other units are completely digitally controlled and the acceleration and deceleration times are programmed into the computer memory.

Some other adjustments that can usually be set by changing potentiometers or programming the unit are as follows:

- ***Current Limit:*** This control sets the maximum amount of current the drive is permitted to deliver to the motor.
- ***Volts per Hertz:*** This sets the ratio by which the voltage changes as frequency increases or decreases.
- ***Maximum Hertz:*** This control sets the maximum speed of the motor. Most motors are intended to operate between 0 Hz and 60 Hz,

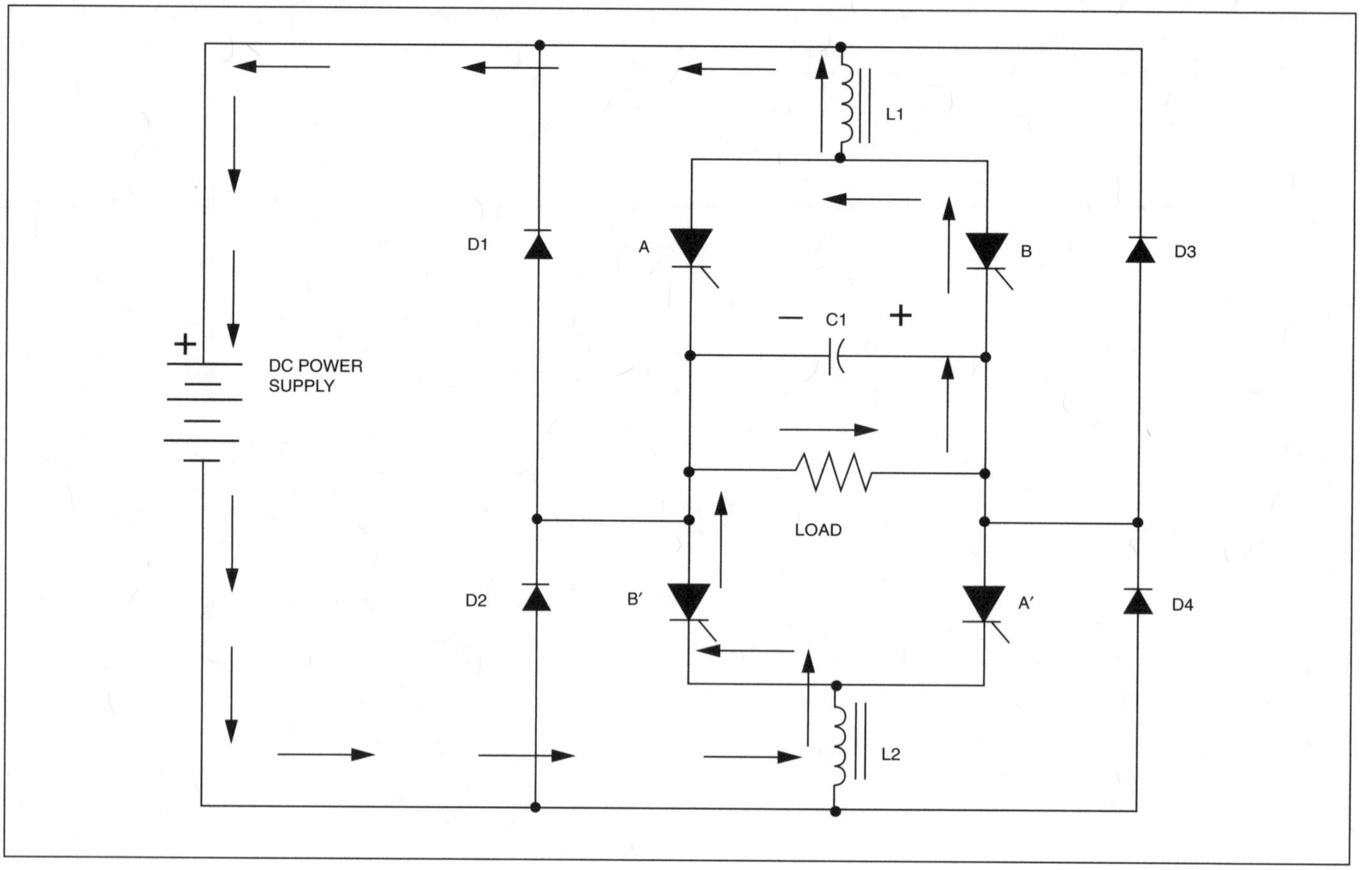

Figure 8-59 Current flows through SCRs *B* and *B′*.

be set above 60 Hz, which would permit the motor to operate at higher-than-normal speed. The maximum hertz control can also be set to limit the output frequency to a value less than 60 Hz, which would limit the motor speed to a value less than normal.

- ***Minimum Hertz:*** This sets the minimum speed at which the motor is permitted to run. Some variable-frequency drives permit adjustment of current limit, maximum and minimum speed, ramping time, and so on by adjustment of trim resistors located on the main control board. Other drives employ a microprocessor as the controller. The values of current limit, speed, ramping time, and so on, for these drives are programmed into the unit, are much easier to make, and are generally more accurate than adjusting trim resistors. A variable-frequency drive is shown in Figure 8-60.

Figure 8-60 Adjustable-speed drive.

REVIEW

All answers should be written in complete sentences, calculations should be shown in detail, and Code references should be cited when appropriate.

1. What is the source of electric power for the motor branch circuits?
2. What provides branch-circuit protection and where is it located?
3. What information is needed to select the correct size motor branch-circuit protection?
4. What would be the calculated full-load current of a 15-hp, three-phase, 480-V motor that operates with an 85% efficiency and 75% power factor?
5. What current value would be used to size the branch-circuit overcurrent protection of the motor described in the previous question?
6. Describe the construction of the squirrel-cage motor.
7. Describe the construction of the wound rotor motor.
8. Describe the construction of direct-current motors.
9. What will be the synchronous speed of a 50-Hz, eight-pole motor?
10. Describe the operation of an across-the-line starter.
11. Describe the operation of the primary resistance starter.
12. Describe the operation of the autotransformer starter.
13. The control circuit for an autotransformer starter is shown in Figure 8-10. Describe what happens when the start button is pushed.
14. A connection diagram for a bridge-type full-wave rectifier is shown in Figure 8-45. Describe the current path for both a positive and negative pulse of AC input.
15. What is the principle of operation of all polyphase induction motors?
16. What two factors determine synchronous field speed?
17. As the frequency applied to a motor is reduced, what must be done to prevent excessive current to the motor?

UNIT 9

Motor Installation

OBJECTIVES

After studying this unit, the student should be able to:

- determine the conductor size for installing a single motor
- determine the conductor size for a multimotor installation
- determine the overload ampacity for various motors
- determine the fuse or circuit-breaker ampacity for a single motor installation
- determine the fuse or circuit-breaker ampacity for a multimotor installation
- determine the ampacity of disconnect switch for motor applications

MOTOR TABLES

There are different types of motors, such as direct-current, single-phase AC, two-phase AC, and three-phase AC. Different tables are used to list the running current for different types of motors.

- *CEC* Table D2 lists the currents for direct-current motors
- *CEC* Table 45 lists the currents for single-phase AC motors
- *CEC* Table 44 lists the full-load currents for three-phase motors
- *CEC* Table D16 lists the ampacities of conductors, overload, and overcurrent devices for AC and DC motors.

The tables list the amount of current the motor is expected to require under full-load conditions. A motor will have a lower current demand if it is not under a full load.

These tables list the ampere rating of the motors according to horsepower and connected voltage. It should be noted that the notes at the bottom of *CEC* Tables 44, 45, and D1 indicate that the currents listed in these tables are to be used as a guide only. When determining conductor, fuse, and overload ampacities, the motor nameplate rating must be used.

DIRECT-CURRENT MOTORS

CEC Table D2 lists the full-load running current for direct-current motors. These are typical values based on the horsepower rating and the voltage for motors operating at a moderate speed with normal torque characteristics and a belted drive. The table shows that a 1-hp motor operating at 120 V DC has a typical full load current of 9.4 A. If the 1-hp motor is designed to be connected to 240 V DC, it will have a full-load current of 4.7 A.

SINGLE-PHASE ALTERNATING-CURRENT MOTORS

The current ratings for single-phase AC motors are given in *CEC* Table 45. These ratings are for motors that operate at normal speeds and torques. Motors especially designed for low speed and high torque, or multispeed motors, are not listed. In all cases, when determining conductor, overcurrent, and overload ampacities, the motor nameplate current must be used.

EXAMPLE A 3-hp single-phase motor is connected to a 208-V supply. To size the conductors properly, it is necessary to know the full-load current. Since the nameplate information is not available, we will use *CEC* Table 45 as a guide. The full-load current for single-phase motors is given in the table as 17 A when connected to 230 V. Note 1 at the end of the table indicates that this value must be increased by 10% when the motor is connected to a 208-V source. The full-load current for a 3-hp motor connected to a 208-V single-phase AC supply is therefore $17 \times 1.10 = 18.7$ A.

THREE-PHASE MOTORS

CEC Table 44 can be used as a guide in determining the full-load current of a three-phase motor running at usual speeds and normal torque characteristics. The full-load current of low speed–high torque and multispeed motors are not shown. Notice that the right side of the table is devoted to the full-load currents of synchronous-type motors. The currents listed are for motors that are to be operated at unity or 100% power factor. Since synchronous motors are often made to have a leading power factor by overexcitation of the rotor current, the full-load current rating must be increased when this is done. If the motor is operated at 90% power factor, the rated full-load current in the table is to be increased by 10%. If the motor is to be operated at 80% power factor, the full-load current is to be increased by 25%. (See Note 4, *CEC* Table 44.)

EXAMPLE A 150-hp, 460-V synchronous motor is to be operated at 80% power factor. What will be the full-load current rating of the motor?

$158 \times 1.25 = 197.5$ A

Determining Minimum Conductor Ampacity for a Single Motor

CEC Rule 28-106 states that the conductor size for a motor connection shall be based on the full load current rating of the motor. Although the full load current values obtained for the relevant *CEC* table (*CEC* Tables 44, 45 and D1) may be used as a guide, the nameplate full load current of the motor must be used. The rule states that the conductors supplying a single motor shall have an ampacity of not less than 125% of the motor full-load current. *CEC* Tables 1, 2, 3, or 4 are used to select the conductor size after the ampacity has been determined. The exact table employed will be determined by the wiring conditions. Probably the most frequently used table is *CEC* Table 2, which is provided in this text as Table 6-1.

Another factor that must be taken into consideration when determining the conductor size is the insulation class temperature rating of the motor. *CEC* Rule 28-104(1) indicates that the temperature rating of the motor conductors must be equal to or greater than the values specified in *CEC* Table 37 based on the type of motor enclosure and the motor insulation class rating, unless the motor is marked otherwise. This rule also states that the ampacities of the conductors shall be based on 75°C conductors regardless of the temperature rating of the conductors actually installed. The exception is that when the motor has an insulation class rating *A*, and the conductors are rated for 90°C, the ampacity may also be determined based on the 90°C columns of *CEC* Tables 1, 2, 3, and 4. When conductors rated in excess of 75°C are required, they must extend a minimum of 1.2 m from the motor connection and terminate in a location not less than 600 mm from any part of the motor. If the motor is rated 100 hp or more, the conductors must terminate in a location not less than 1.2 m from any part of the motor (*CEC* Rule 28-104(2)).

PROBLEM 1

A 30-hp, three-phase squirrel-cage induction motor of the open ventilated type is connected to a 480-V line. The nameplate indicates a full load current of 40 A and an insulation class rating *B*. The conductors shall be copper and are to be run in conduit. What size and temperature rating of conductor must be used?

The first step is to check *CEC* Table 37 to determine the temperature rating of the conductors. By referring to this table, it is determined that a conductor must have a minimum temperature rating of 75°C. This would indicate that a 75°C conductor such as RW75 could be used. However, the more common RW90 or T90 Nylon would most likely be installed. *CEC* Rule 28-106 requires that the conductor be rated at not less than 125% of the full load current of the motor. Therefore:

$$40 \times 1.25 = 50 \text{ A}$$

Referring to *CEC* Table 2 for copper conductors in raceway and using the 75°C column as required by *CEC* Rule 28-104(1), a #6 AWG conductor would be required. Remember, even though the conductors installed may have a temperature rating of 90°C, the ampacity of the conductors is determined based on the 75°C column.

OVERLOAD AMPACITY

When determining the overload ampacity for a motor, the nameplate current rating of the motor is to be used instead of the current values listed in *CEC* Tables 44, 45, and D1. The service factor (SF) of the motor is also to be used to determine the overload ampacity of a motor. *CEC* Rule 28-306 indicates that the overload ampacity is based on a percentage of the full-load current of the motor. The percentage is determined by the service factor of the motor. For motors with a marked service factor of 1.15 or greater, the overloads are sized at a maximum of 125% of the motor full load current. Where the marked service factor is less than 1.15 or the service factor is not marked, the overloads shall be sized to a maximum of 115% of the motor full load current. Manufacturers' overload rating or setting charts are usually sized based on a service factor of 1.15 or greater. Be sure to consult the notes at the end of any manufacturer's chart to be sure that overloads are selected properly.

DETERMINING LOCKED ROTOR CURRENT

In most cases, locked rotor current will be marked on the motor nameplate. When locked rotor current is not indicated, *CEC* Rule 28-010 states that it shall be calculated as six times the marked full load current or the currents listed in *CEC* Table 44 or 45.

PROBLEM 2

A 25-hp, three-phase induction motor has a nameplate rating of 32 A. The nameplate also shows a service factor of 1.15. What is the maximum overload ampacity for this motor?

CEC Rule 28-306 indicates that the overload ampacity is to be a maximum of 125% of the full-load current rating of the motor.

$$32 \times 1.25 = 40 \text{ A}$$

In some circumstances, some motors may cause the overloads to operate before the motor gets up to speed. This usually occurs with motors that are started under heavy load. If this occurs, the overload device may be shunted out of the circuit during the starting period in accordance with *CEC* Rule 28-310.

OVERCURRENT PROTECTION

The ratings of the overcurrent protective devices are set forth in Table 9-1 (*CEC* Table 29). The far left-hand column lists the type of motor that is to be protected. To the right of this are three columns that list different types of short-circuit protective devices: time-delay fuse, non-time delay fuse and time-limit type circuit breaker. Although it is permissible to use non-time-delay fuses, most motor circuits are protected by dual-element time-delay fuses or time-limit circuit breakers.

Each of these columns lists a percentage of the motor current that is to be used in determining overcurrent device ampacity. The full load current rating as listed on the motor nameplate must be used when applying the percentages as listed. Note that the ampacity of the overcurrent device calculated in this manner is a maximum value and the installed device must not exceed the calculated value. If the calculated value does not correspond to a standard rating or setting of a fuse or circuit breaker, the next smaller standard ampacity of device shall be installed. Although not intended for this purpose, *CEC* Table 13 may be used as a listing of standard ratings for overcurrent devices not exceeding 600 A.

CEC Table 29

(See Rules 28-200, 28-204, 28-208, and 28-308)

Rating or Setting of Overcurrent Devices for the Protection of Motor Branch Circuits

Type of Motor	Percent of Full Load Current		
	Maximum Fuse Rating		Maximum Setting Time-Limit Type Circuit Breaker
	Time-Delay* Fuses	Non-Time-Delay Time-Delay*	
Alternating Current			
Single-Phase all types	175	300	250
Squirrel-Cage and Synchronous:			
Full-Voltage, Resistor and Reactor Starting	175	300	250
Auto-Transformer and Star Delta Starting:			
Not more than 30 A	175	250	200
More than 30 A	175	200	200
Wound Rotor	150	150	150
Direct Current	150	150	150

*Includes time-delay "D" fuses referred to in Rule 14-200.

Notes: (1) Synchronous motors of the low-torque low-speed type (usually 450 rpm, or lower) such as are used to drive reciprocating compressors, pumps, etc., and which start up unloaded, do not require a fuse rating or circuit-breaker setting in excess of 200% of full-load current.

(2) For the use of instantaneous trip (magnetic only) circuit breakers in motor branch circuits see Rule 28-210.

Table 9-1 Rating or setting of overcurrent devices for the protection of motor branch circuits.

PROBLEM 3

A 100-hp, three-phase squirrel-cage induction motor has a full load current rating of 248 A. A dual-element time-delay fuse is to be used as the overcurrent device. What is the correct fuse rating?

CEC Table 29 indicates that a dual-element time-delay fuse is to be set at 175% of the full-load current for an AC polyphase (more than one phase) squirrel-cage motor.

$248 \times 1.75 = 434$ A

The next standard fuse rating equal to or less than this computed value as listed in *CEC* Table 13 is 400 A. A 400-A fuse will be used to protect this motor circuit.

If for some reason the overcurrent devices calculated in this manner will not permit the motor to start, *CEC* Rule 28-200(d) will allow the ampacity of the devices to be increased as follows.

For non-time-delay fuses:

- Not in excess of 400% of the motor nameplate current rating for fuses up to 600 A
- Not in excess of 300% of the motor nameplate current rating for fuses rated 601 A to 6000 A

For time delay fuses:

- Not in excess of 225% of the motor nameplate current rating
- For inverse time circuit breakers
- Not in excess of 400% of the motor nameplate current rating for breakers up to 100 A
- Not in excess of 300% of the motor nameplate current rating for breakers rated in excess of 100 A.

Determine the conductor size, maximum overload ampacity, and maximum overcurrent device ampacity of the following motors.

PROBLEM 4

A 40-hp, 240-V DC motor has a nameplate current rating of 132 A. The conductors are to be copper with T90 insulation. The overcurrent device is to be an instantaneous trip circuit breaker. Refer to Figure 9-1.

The conductor ampacity must be determined from the nameplate current and *CEC* Rule 28-106, which states that *the conductors must be oversized by a factor of 125%.*

$132 \times 1.25 = 165$ A

CEC Table 2 is used to find the conductor size. Even though the conductors have a 90°C insulation, they must be sized based on the 75°C column of the table. Using this information, it can be found that a #2/0 copper conductor is required for this motor.

The instantaneous trip circuit breaker for a DC motor is sized by *CEC* Rule 28-210. For motors of 50 hp or less, the breaker must be set to trip at not more than 250% of the motor full load current.

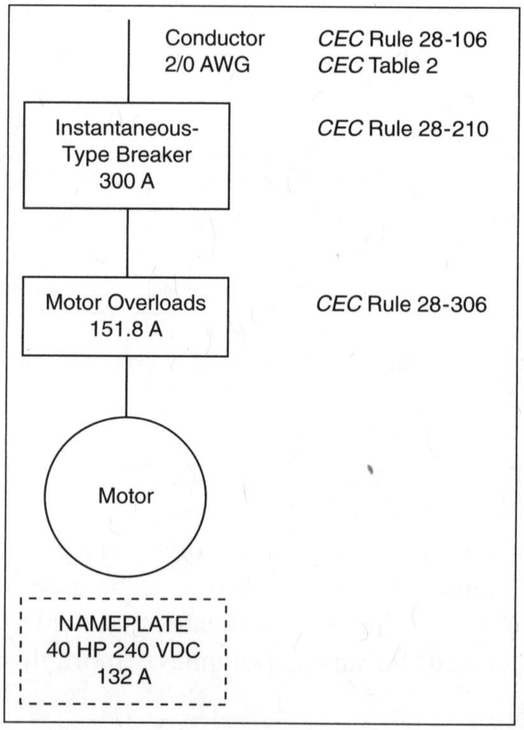

Figure 9-1 Problem 4.

$132 \times 2.50 = 330$ A

Since 330 A is not one of the standard ratings of circuit breakers listed in *CEC* Table 13, a 300-A instantaneous breaker would be used. An alternative would be to use an adjustable instantaneous trip breaker set at 330 A.

The overload ampacity is determined from *CEC* Rule 28-306. Since the service factor of the motor is not known, it is assumed to be less than 1.15. The motor nameplate current will be increased by 15%.

$132 \times 1.15 = 151.8$ A

PROBLEM 5

A 150-hp, three-phase squirrel-cage induction motor is connected to 440 V. The motor nameplate lists the following information:

Motor amps 175 SF 1.25 Insulation Class B

The conductors are to be copper with type RW90 insulation. The overcurrent device is to be an inverse-time circuit breaker. Refer to Figure 9-2.

First, by referring to *CEC* Table 37 it is determined that type RW90 conductors are suitable for a motor with a *B* insulation class. The minimum conductor ampacity is determined from the nameplate current and *CEC* Rule 28-106.

$175 \times 1.25 = 218.75$ A

CEC Table 2 is used to determine conductor size. Type RW90 insulation is located in the 90°C column. However, the ampacity of the conductors must be determined based on 75°C. The conductor size will be #4/0 AWG.

The overload ampacity is determined from the nameplate current and *CEC* Rule 28-306. Since the motor has a marked service factor of 1.25, the motor nameplate current will be increased by 25%.

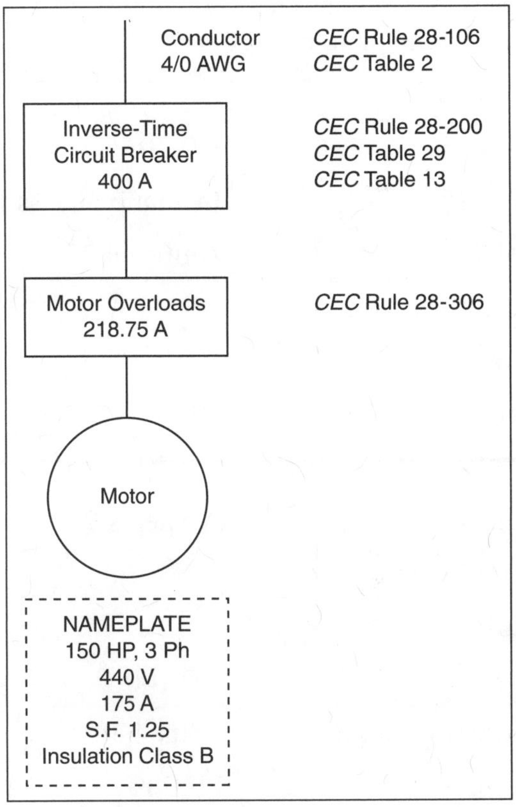

Figure 9-2 Problem 5.

$175 \times 1.25 = 218.75$ A

The percentage of full-load current listed in Table 9-1 (*CEC* Table 29) is used to determine the maximum circuit-breaker ampacity. The table indicates a factor of 250% for squirrel-cage motors.

$175 \times 2.50 = 437.5$ A

Since this is a maximum value, the overcurrent device cannot exceed 437.5 A. Referring to *CEC* Table 13, it is noted that this is not a standard rating for a breaker. Therefore, the next smaller standard size, 400 A, would be installed.

MULTIPLE MOTOR CALCULATIONS

The feeder overcurrent device and minimum conductor ampacity for a multiple motor connection are set forth in *CEC* Rules 28-204 and 28-108, respectively. When taps are taken off of a motor feeder for individual motors, *CEC* Rule 28-110(2) applies. In this example, three motors are connected to a common feeder. The feeder is 460 V, three-phase, and the conductors are to be copper with type RW90 insulation. Each motor is to be protected with a dual-element time-delay fuse and a separate overload device. The feeder is also protected by a dual-element time-delay fuse. The motor nameplate ratings are as follows:

Motor #1

Phase 3	HP 20
SF 1.25	Insulation Class B
Volts 460	Amperes 27
Type Induction	

Motor #2

Phase 3	HP 60
Insulation Class F	
Volts 460	Amperes 77
Type Induction	

Motor #3

Phase 3	HP 100
Insulation Class A	Volts 460
Amperes 106	PF 90%
Type Synchronous	

Motor #1 Calculations

The first step is to calculate the minimum conductor ampacity, maximum overload ampacity, and maximum overcurrent device ampacity for each motor. These values for motor #1 are shown in Figure 9-3. *CEC* Rule 28-106 states that the conductor must be rated for a minimum of 125% of the full load current of the motor. The minimum conductor ampacity is therefore:

$27 \times 1.25 = 33.75$ A

The conductor size is now chosen from *CEC* Table 2 for copper conductors in raceway. Although type RW90 insulation is located in the 90°C column, the conductor size will be chosen from the 75°C column, as per *CEC* Rule 28-104(1). A check of *CEC* Table 37 confirms that 90°C conductors are suitable for a motor with a *B* insulation class. And 33.75 A requires 8 AWG conductors.

The maximum overcurrent device is determined by using the motor full load current rating and the demand factor from Table 9-1 (*CEC* Table 29). The percent of full-load current for a dual-element time-delay fuse protecting a squirrel-cage motor is 175 percent. The full load current will be increased by 175 percent.

$27 \times 175\% = 47.25$ A

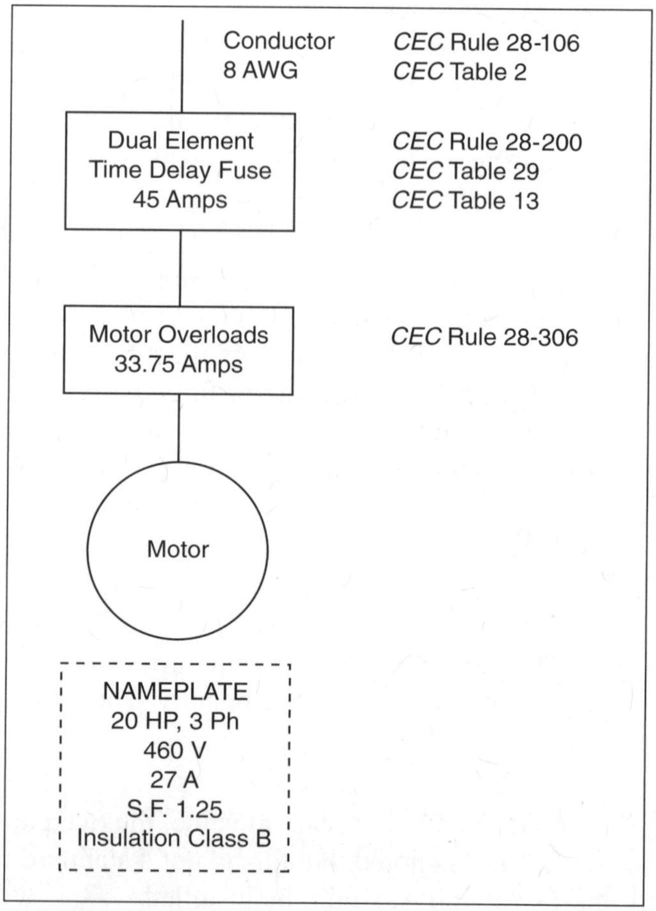

Figure 9-3 Values for motor #1.

Since this is a maximum value and it does not correspond to a standard rating of fuse as listed in *CEC* Table 13, the next smaller rating of fuse, 45 A, would be installed.

The maximum overload ampacity is computed from the nameplate current and the factors specified in *CEC* Rule 28-306. Since this motor has a marked service factor of 1.25, the overload will be sized at a maximum of 125% of the motor nameplate current.

27 × 1.25 = 33.75 A

Motor #2 Calculations

Figure 9-4 shows an example for the calculation of motor #2. The conductor size will be determined based on a minimum ampacity of 125% of the full load motor current.

77 × 1.25 = 96.25 A

Referring to the 75°C column of *CEC* Table 2, it is found that a #3 AWG conductor would be used for this motor connection. A check of *CEC* Table 37 confirms that 90°C conductors are suitable for a motor with an *F* insulation class.

The maximum overcurrent device ampacity will be determined using Table 9-1 (*CEC* Table 29). The full load current is increased to 175% for squirrel-cage motors.

77 × 1.75 = 134.75 A

This value is not a standard ampacity of fuse as determined form *CEC* Table 13. Therefore, the next smaller size, 125 A, would be installed.

The overload ampacity is determined from the full load current and *CEC* Rule 28-306. Since the service factor is not known, it is assumed to be 1.15. Therefore, the nameplate current is multiplied by a factor of 115%.

77 × 1.15 = 88.55 A

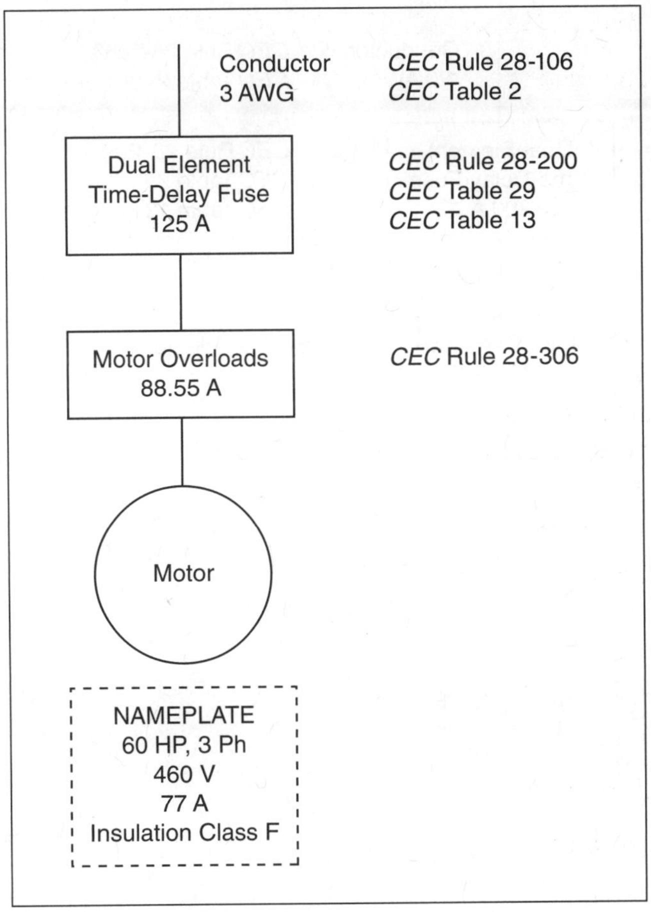

Figure 9-4 Values for motor #2.

Motor #3 Calculations

Motor #3 is a synchronous motor intended to operate with a 90% power factor. Figure 9-5 on page 132 shows an example of this calculation. The full load current of a synchronous motor is listed at unity power factor. When this motor is operating at a power factor of 90%, the full load current must be increased by 10%. (See *CEC* Table 44, Note 4.)

106 × 1.10 = 116.6 A

The minimum conductor ampacity is computed by using this current rating as calculated above and increasing it by 25%.

116.6 × 1.25 = 145.75 A

CEC Table 2 indicates that a #1/0 AWG conductor will be acceptable for this circuit. A check of *CEC* Table 37 confirms that 90°C conductors are suitable for a motor with an *A* insulation class.

The maximum fuse rating is determined using Table 9-1. The percentage of full-load current for a synchronous motor is 175%.

116.6 × 1.75 = 204.05 A

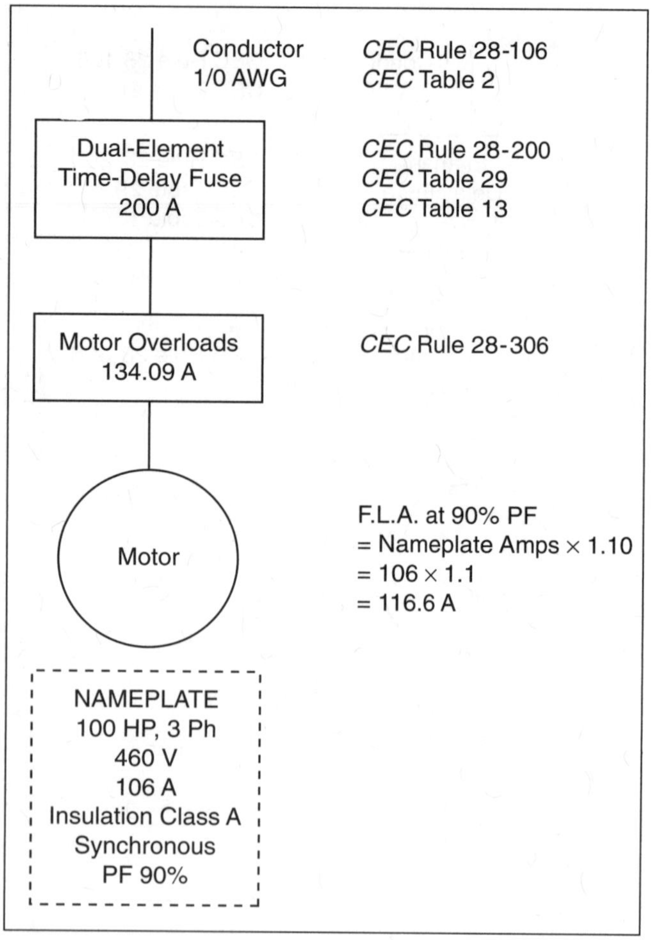

Figure 9-5 Values for motor #3.

This value is not a standard ampacity of fuse as determined form *CEC* Table 13. Therefore, the next smaller size, 200 A, would be installed.

This motor does not have a marked service factor. The maximum overload ampacity will be calculated by increasing the full load current by 15%, as indicated in *CEC* Rule 28-306.

$116.6 \times 1.15 = 134.09$ A

Main Feeder Calculation

An example of a main feeder arrangement with relevant *CEC* rules is shown in Figure 9-6, as found in *CEC* Appendix B, Section 28. This section of Appendix B also has a complete sample motor calculation for a group of three motors.

The conductor ampacity feeding a group of two or more motors is calculated in accordance with *CEC* Rule 28-108. This rule states that the feeder must be capable of carrying 125% of the full load current of the largest motor plus the sum of the remaining motor full load currents. The motor with the largest full load current is motor #3. When this full load current was adjusted for the 90% power factor, the new current became 116.6 A. Therefore:

$116.6 \times 1.25 = 145.75$ A

$145.75 + 77 + 27 = 249.75$ A

Since the feeder conductors do not terminate in a motor connection box, it is not necessary to determine the ampacity of the conductors based on the 75°C column of *CEC* Table 2. Assuming that 90°C conductors such as RW90XLPE will be used, it is determined that three 250-kcmil conductors are required as the main feeder conductors.

The maximum ampacity of overcurrent device is determined from *CEC* Rule 28-204. This rule requires that the maximum overcurrent device for the largest motor in the group be determined and then the sum of the remaining full load currents be added. The highest fuse size was that of the 100-hp synchronous motor. The fuse calculation for this motor was 204.05 A. The running currents of the other two motors will be added to this value to determine the rating of the fuse for the main feeder.

$204.05 + 77 + 27 = 308.05$ A

Since this calculated value does not correspond to a standard value of overcurrent device, the next smaller size, 300 A, would be installed.

Taps from a Motor Feeder

In most applications, a conductor feeding a group of motors will terminate in a motor control centre (MCC) or a splitter. The *CEC* refers to this device as a feeder tap box. Since the terminations in the MCC or splitter are extensions of the feeder conductors, the ampacities of these devices would have to be at least equal to the calculated minimum conductor ampacity of the feeders, in this case, 249.75 A. This value does not represent a standard ampacity of MCC or splitter; therefore, the next standard size of 400 A would be installed.

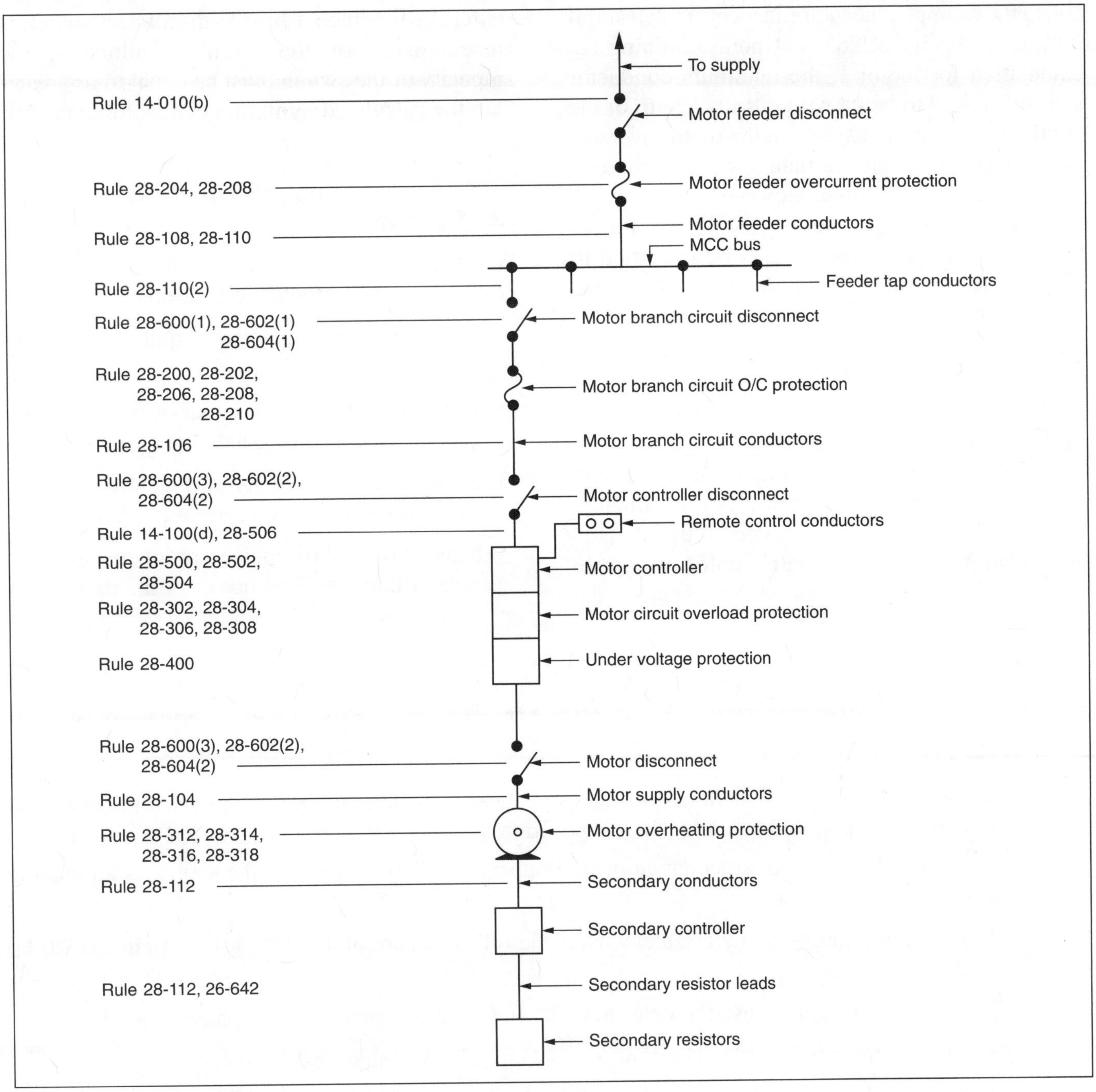

Figure 9-6 Example of feeder calculations (from *CEC* Appendix B).

The extensions from the feeder tap box must meet the requirements of *CEC* Rule 28-110(2). This rule states that the ampacity of the tap conductors must not be less than the ampacity of the feeder unless one of the following conditions exists.

1. If the length of the tap does not exceed 3 m and is enclosed in metal, the conductors can be

these conditions, the conductor would only have an ampacity sufficient to handle the connected load.

2. If the tap conductors are greater than 3 m but not more than 7.5 m in length, the conductors must have an ampacity at least equal to one-third the ampacity of the feeders.

In the example, the motor feeders are 250 kcmil with an ampacity of 265 A. Upon examining the calculation for motor 1, the minimum conductor size was found to be #8 AWG. If the length of the conductors from the tap box to the motor overcurrent devices is not greater than 3 m, these conductors would be acceptable. However, if the length of the conductors is greater than 3 m but not more than 7.5 m, their ampacity must be increased to a minimum of one-third of the ampacity of the 250-kcmil feeders.

250 kcmil rated 265 amps × 1/3 = 88.33 A

This installation would require a minimum of #3AWG conductors.

When conductors terminate in a fusible switch, additional rules apply. All conductors feeding a fusible disconnect switch must be rated at the ampacity of the switch unless adequate overcurrent protection is provided ahead of the switch. Also, since a fusible disconnect switch is an extension of the circuit conductors, the ampacity of the switch must be equal to or greater than the calculated minimum conductor ampacity.

FUSIBLE DISCONNECT SWITCH SELECTION

When selecting a disconnect switch for motor purposes, all of the following conditions must be met:

- Must have a voltage rating equal to or greater than the circuit voltage
- Must have sufficient number of poles to interrupt all unidentified conductors
- Must have an ampacity sufficient to hold the fuses selected for overcurrent protection
- Must have a horsepower rating equal to or greater than the horsepower of the motor(s)

REVIEW

All answers should be written in complete sentences, calculations should be shown in detail, and Code references should be cited when appropriate.

Unless otherwise stated, all conductors are copper type T90 Nylon, and the supply is alternating current.

1. From the appropriate *CEC* table, what is the full-load current of a 500-V, direct-current, 20-hp motor?
2. Which *CEC* table is used to determine the full-load current of a three-phase motor?
3. What is the rated full-load current of a 3/4-hp, 208-V single-phase motor?
4. What is the full-load current of a 230-V, three-phase, 125-hp synchronous motor when it is operated at an 80% power factor?
5. What is the full-load current of a 600-V, three-phase, 50-hp induction motor?
6. What is the minimum conductor ampacity and size, maximum overload ampacity, and maximum dual-element fuse rating for a circuit supplying a 575-V, three-phase, insulation class *F*, 125-hp motor with a nameplate full load current of 115 A?
7. What is the minimum conductor size, maximum overload ampacity, and maximum installed rating of inverse-time circuit-breaker for a circuit supplying a 230-V, three-phase, insulation class *A*, 75-hp synchronous motor operating at an 80% power factor with a nameplate full-load current of 185 A?

8. What size conductor would be required to supply three motors connected to a 460-V, three-phase branch circuit? Motor #1 is a 50-hp induction motor, motor #2 is a 40-hp induction motor, and motor #3 is a 10-hp induction motor.
9. What would be the installed rating of an inverse-time circuit breaker required for the branch circuit serving the three motors in the previous question? What would be the rating of a dual-element fuse?

UNIT 10

Programmable Logic Controllers

OBJECTIVES

After studying this unit, the student should be able to:

- discuss the operation of programmable logic controllers
- discuss the differences between a programmable logic controller and a home or business computer
- name the major components of a programmable logic controller
- determine installation requirements for programmable logic controllers

Programmable logic controllers (PLCs) were first used by the automobile industry in the late 1960s. Each time a change in design was made, it was necessary to change the control systems operating the machinery—this consisted of physically rewiring the control system to make it perform the new operation. Rewiring the system was, of course, extremely time-consuming and costly. What the industry needed was some type of control system that could be changed without the extensive rewiring required to change relay control systems.

PLC AND COMMON COMPUTER DIFFERENCES

All programmable logic controllers are computers, but not all computers are programmable logic controllers. There are some differences between a PLC and a home or business computer.

- The PLC is designed to be operated in an industrial environment. Any computer used in industry must be able to operate in extremes of temperature. It must be able to ignore voltage spikes and drops on the incoming power line, and to survive in an atmosphere that often contains corrosive vapours, oil, and dirt. It must also withstand shock and vibration.
- Most programmable controllers are designed to be programmed with relay schematic and ladder diagrams instead of the common computer languages such as BASIC or FORTRAN. An electrician who is familiar with relay logic diagrams generally can be trained to program a PLC in a few hours. It generally requires several months to train someone to program a standard computer.

BASIC COMPONENTS

Programmable logic controllers can be divided into four basic parts:

- the power supply
- the central processing unit (CPU)
- the program loader or terminal
- the I/O (pronounced eye-oh) track

The Power Supply

The power supply is used to lower the incoming AC voltage to the desired level, rectify it to DC, and then filter and regulate it. The internal logic circuits of programmable logic controllers operate on 5 V DC to 15 V DC, depending on the type of controller. This voltage must be free of voltage spikes and other electrical noise. It must also be regulated to within 5% of the required voltage value. Some manufacturers of PLCs use a separate power supply, and others build the power supply into the central processing unit.

The CPU

The central processing unit (CPU) is the brain of the programmable logic controller. It contains the microprocessor chip and related integrated circuits to perform all the logic functions. The microprocessor chip used in most PLCs is a common computer chip used in many home and business machines. The central processing unit generally has a key switch located on the front panelboard. This switch must be turned on before the CPU can be programmed. This is done to prevent the circuit from being changed accidentally. Plug connections mounted on the central processor are used to provide connections for the programming terminal and the I/O tracks. Most CPUs are designed so that once the program has been tested, it can be stored on tape or disk. In this way, if a central processing unit fails and has to be replaced, the new unit can be reprogrammed from the tape or disk. This eliminates the time-consuming process of reprogramming by hand.

The Programming Terminal

The programming terminal or loading terminal is used to program the CPU. Most terminals are one of two types. One type is a small hand-held device that uses a liquid crystal display to show the program (Figure 10-1). This terminal, however, will display only one line of the program at a time.

Some older models of PLCs use a proprietary terminal similar to a portable television set with a keyboard attached (Figure 10-2). It will display from four to six lines of the program at a time depending on the manufacturer. Most modern industries use a standard personal or laptop computer as the programming terminal (Figure 10-3 on page 138).

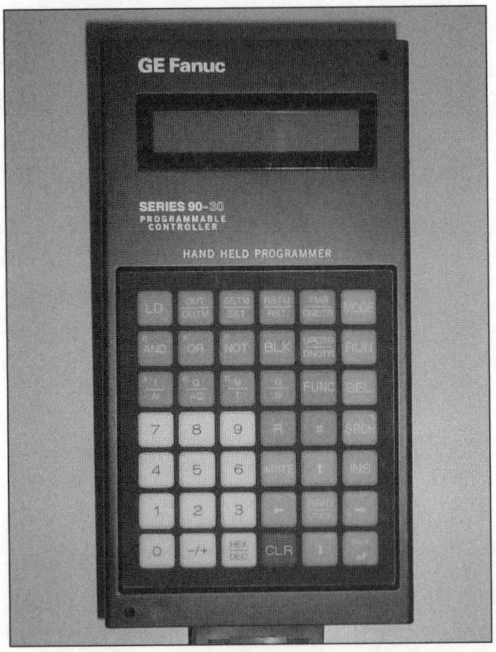

Figure 10-1 Handheld programming terminal.

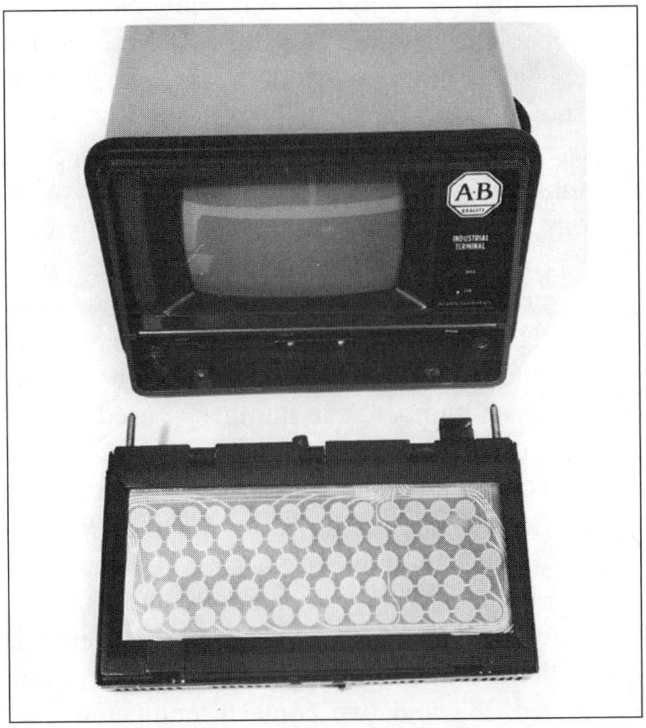

Figure 10-2 Programming terminal with keypad.

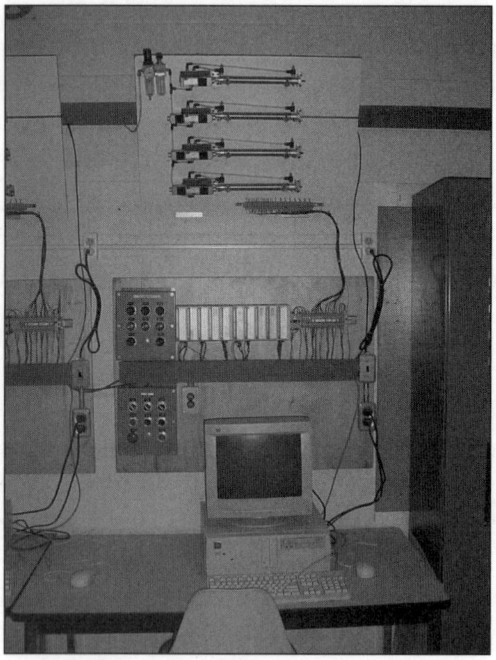

Figure 10-3 PLC training station with a personal computer as a programming terminal.

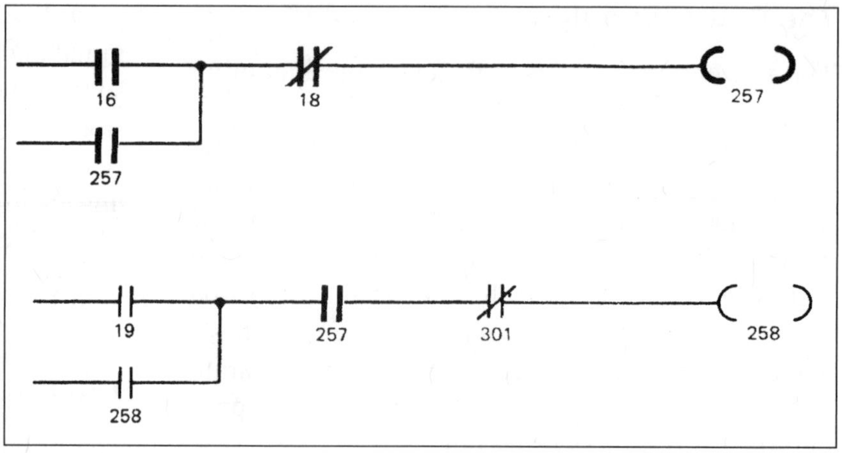

Figure 10-4 Analyzing circuit operation with the terminal.

The programming terminal is used not only to program the controller but also to troubleshoot the circuit. When the terminal is connected to the CPU, the circuit can be examined while it is in operation. Figure 10-4 illustrates a circuit typical of those that are seen on the display. Notice that this schematic diagram is a little different from a typical ladder diagram. All of the line components are shown as normally open or normally closed contacts. There are no NEMA (National Electrical Manufacturers Association) symbols for pushbuttons, float switches, limit switches, and so on. The programmable controller recognizes only open or closed contacts. It does not know whether a contact is controlled by a pushbutton, a limit switch, or a float switch. Each contact does, however, have a number. The number is used to distinguish one contact from another.

The coil symbols look like a set of parentheses instead of a circle as shown on most ladder diagrams. Each line ends with a coil, and each coil has a number. When a contact symbol has the same number as a coil, it means that the contact is controlled by that coil. Figure 10-4 shows a coil numbered 257 and two contacts numbered 257. When relay coil 257 is energized, the controller interprets both of these contacts to be closed.

Notice that the 257 contacts, contacts 16 and 18, and coil 257 are drawn with dark heavy lines. When a contact has a complete circuit through it, or a coil is energized, the terminal will illuminate that contact or coil. Contact 16 is illuminated, which means that it is closed and providing a current path. Contact 18 is closed, providing a current path to coil 257. Since 257 is energized, both 257 contacts are closed and providing current paths.

Contacts 19, 258, and 301 are not illuminated. This means that contacts 19 and 258 are de-energized and open. Contact 301, however, has been energized. This contact is shown as normally closed. Since it is not illuminated, it is open and no current path exists through it. Notice that the illumination of a contact does not mean that the contact has energized or changed position; it means that there is a complete path for current flow.

When the terminal is used to load a program into the central processing unit, contact and coil symbols on the keyboard are used. These symbol keys are used to load a ladder diagram similar to the one shown in Figure 10-4 into the CPU.

The I/O Track

The I/O track is used to connect the central processing unit to the outside world. It contains input modules that carry information to the CPU, and output modules that carry information from the CPU. An I/O track with input and output modules is shown in Figure 10-5. Most modules contain more than one input or output. Any number from two to eight is common depending on the manufacturer. This means that each input module can handle many different inputs from pilot devices such as pushbuttons, float switches, or limit switches. Each output module can control several external devices such as pilot lights, solenoids, or motor starter coils. The operating voltages can be direct current or alternating current and are generally 120 V or 24 V. The number of I/O devices that a PLC can handle is limited by the number of devices per module and the number of modules that can be installed on the I/O track.

One factor that determines the size and cost of a programmable controller is its I/O capacity. Many small units are designed to handle 16 or 32 inputs or outputs. Large units can handle several hundred. Many PLCs have a relatively short I/O track but provide some method of adding additional track for expansion.

The central processing unit of a programmable controller is extremely sensitive to voltage spikes and electrical noise. For this reason, many input I/Os use *opto-isolation* to separate the incoming signal from the CPU electrically. Another job performed by the input I/O is debouncing any switch contacts connected to it.

Figure 10-6 shows a typical circuit used for the input. The bridge rectifier changes the AC voltage into DC voltage. A resistor is used to limit current to the light-emitting diode (LED). When the LED turns on, the light is detected by the phototransistor, which signals the CPU that there is a voltage present at the input terminal.

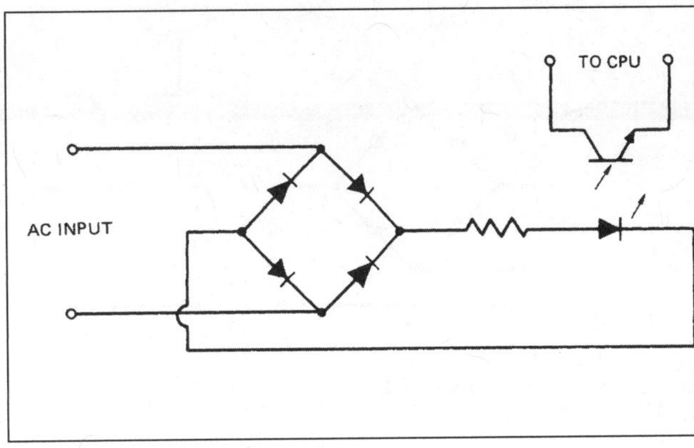

Figure 10-6 Input circuit.

When the module has more than one input, the bridge rectifiers are connected together on one side to form a common terminal. On the other side, the rectifiers are labelled 1, 2, 3, and 4. Figure 10-7 shows four bridge rectifiers connected together to form a common terminal.

Figure 10-8 on page 140 shows a limit switch connected to the input. Notice that the limit switch completes a circuit from the AC line to the bridge

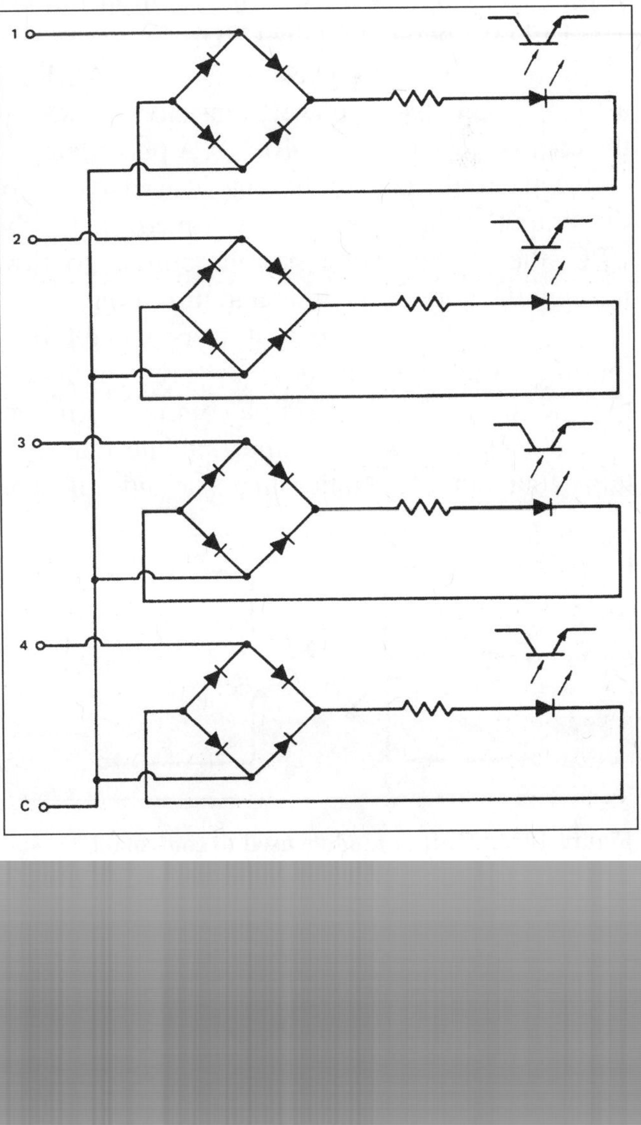

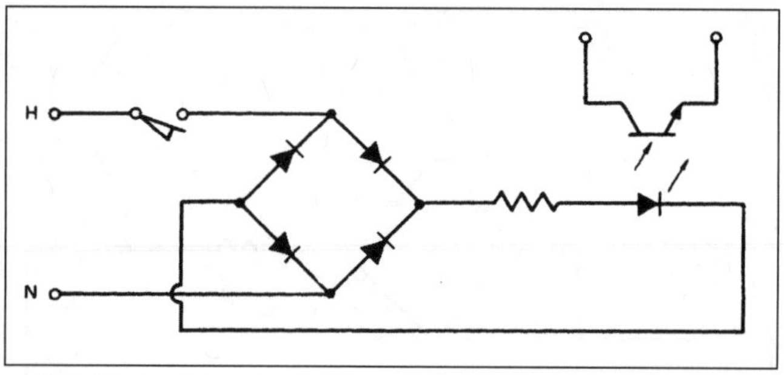

Figure 10-8 Limit switch completes circuit to rectifier.

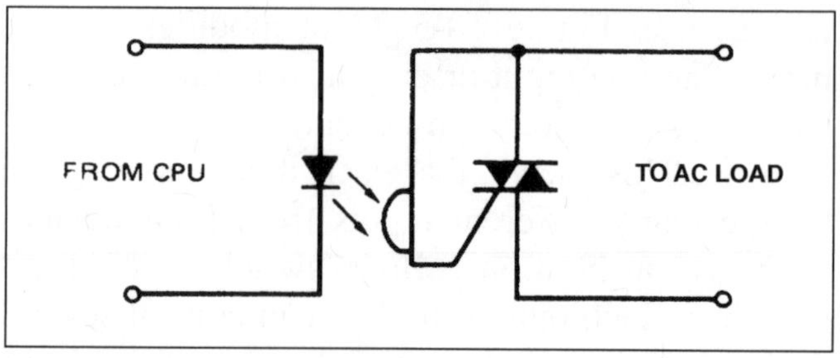

Figure 10-10 Output module used to control an AC module.

rectifier. When the limit switch closes, 120 V AC are applied to the rectifier, causing the LED to turn on.

The output module is used to connect the central processing unit to the load. The output is an opto-isolated solid-state relay. The current rating can range from 0.5 A to 3 A, depending on the manufacturer. Voltage ratings are generally 24 V or 120 V and can be AC or DC.

If the output is designed to control a DC voltage, a power transistor is used to control the load (Figure 10-9). The transistor is a phototransistor that is operated by a light-emitting diode. The LED is operated by the CPU.

If the output is designed to control an AC load, a triac, rather than a power transistor, is used as the control device (Figure 10-10). A photodetector connected to the gate of the triac is used to control the output. When the LED is turned on by the CPU, the photodetector permits current to flow through the gate of the triac and turn it on.

If more than one output is contained in a module, the control devices are connected together on one side to form a common terminal. Figure 10-11 shows an output module that contains four outputs. Notice that one side of each triac has been connected to form a common terminal. On the other side, the triacs are labelled 1, 2, 3, and 4. If power transistors are used as the control devices, the emitters or collectors can be connected to form a common terminal.

Figure 10-12 shows a solenoid coil connected to an AC output module. Notice that the triac is used as a switch to complete a circuit so that current can flow through the coil. The output module does not provide power to operate the load. The power must be provided by an external power source. The amount of current an output can control is limited. Small current loads, such as solenoid coils and pilot lights, can be controlled directly by the I/O output, but large current loads, such as motors, cannot. When a large amount of

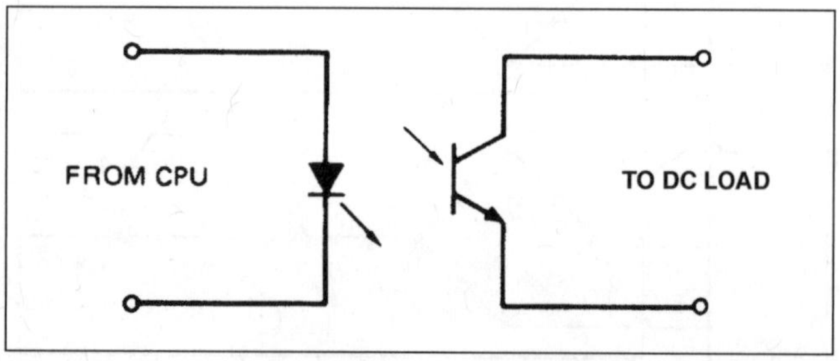

Figure 10-9 Output module used to control a DC module.

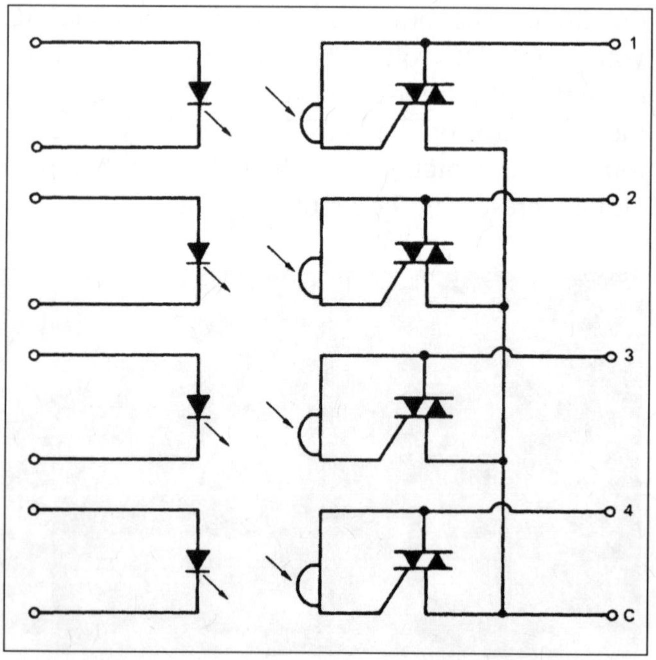

Figure 10-11 Four AC outputs in one module.

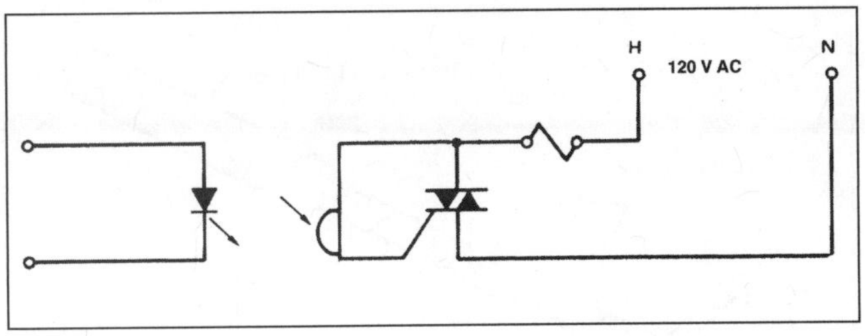

Figure 10-12 An output controls a solenoid.

current must be controlled, the output is used to operate the coil of a motor starter or contactor, which can be used to control almost anything.

INTERNAL RELAYS

The actual logic of the control circuit is performed by *internal relays*. An internal relay is an imaginary device that exists only in the logic of the computer. It can have any number of contacts, from one to several hundred. The contacts can be normally open or normally closed. The method used to program internal relays into the CPU varies from one manufacturer to another, and it is necessary to be familiar with the particular controller used. Some manufacturers program the relays by assigning a coil a number that is greater than the I/O capacity of the unit. For example, if a PLC has a maximum I/O capacity of 256, coil number 257 would be an internal relay. Other manufacturers assign a certain range of numbers to be used for internal relays, such as 1000 to 2000.

Counters and Timers

The internal relays of a programmable controller can be used as counters and timers. When timers are used, most of them are programmed in 0.1-second time intervals. For example, assume that a timer is to be used to provide a delay of 10 seconds. When the delay time is assigned to the timer, the number 00100 is used. This means the timer has been set for 100 tenths of a second, which is 10 seconds. The method used to program timers and counters into the CPU varies from one manufacturer to another just as it does with

The number of internal relays, timers, and counters contained in a programmable controller is determined by the memory capacity of the computer. As a general rule, PLCs that have large I/O capacities will have a large memory, and machines that have less I/O capacity will have less memory.

INSTALLING PROGRAMMABLE LOGIC CONTROLLERS

When installing programmable logic controllers, several general rules should be followed. These rules are basically common sense and are designed to help reduce the amount of electrical noise that can be induced into the input cables. Electrical noise is such a problem in some installations that several manufacturers are using optical cables instead of wires for connection to the I/O track.

Enclosures

Even though PLCs are of a more robust construction than a desktop computer, they must still be protected from the harsh installation environments encountered in industry. This protection is in the form of a cabinet that also will provide protection from live electrical connections.

The enclosure should be of adequate size and depth for all of the equipment to be contained. It must also provide some method of cooling, either by convection or by utilizing cooling fans. Since the cabinet will have openings for cooling, it must be located away from or protected from the entrance of foreign materials such as dust, dirt, and liquids such as water and chemicals. When selecting a location, consideration must also be given to factors such as vibration, separation from sources of electromagnetic interference, distance to the equipment to be controlled, and ease of access for servicing the equipment. The door must be able to open fully and it is recommended that the cabinet have a removable back panel.

When installing the equipment in the enclosure, it is recommended that the PLC be installed near the bottom of the cabinet with other heat-producing and surge suppressors installed at the top. This will help to protect the PLC from the heat generated within the cabinet.

Power Wiring

Power wiring for a PLC should be as short as possible after entering the enclosure and be separated as far as possible from other wiring in the cabinet. When selecting routing of conductors, be sure to separate AC and DC wiring. A separate disconnecting means should be provided at or on the enclosure.

Emergency Stops

Despite the increased flexibility and reliability of PLCs, things still go wrong. It is essential that an emergency stop circuit be installed to remove power to the inputs and outputs in the event of a PLC failure or emergency. These circuits must be hardwired using electromechanical components and should operate motor starters and other devices without being processed by the controller. Each machine controlled by a PLC must also have an independent emergency stop in an easily accessible location.

Input/Output Circuits

Try to keep the wire runs as short as possible. A long wire run has more surface area of wire to pick up stray electrical noise. Be sure to consult the manufacturer's information for conductor recommendations such as length, gauge, and any shielding that may be required.

Shielded cable is used for the installation of signal wiring. One of the most common types, shown in Figure 10-13, uses twisted wires with a Mylar foil shield. The ground wire must be grounded if the shielding is to operate properly. This type of shielded cable can provide a noise reduction ratio of about 30 000:1.

Another type of signal cable uses a twisted pair of signal wires surrounded by a braided shield. This type of cable provides a noise reduction of about 300:1.

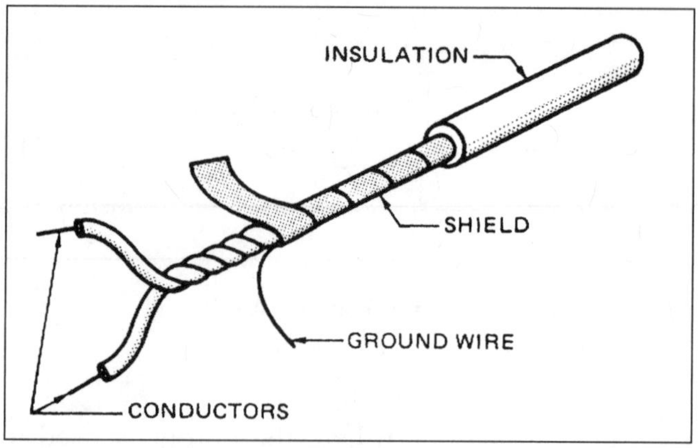

Figure 10-13 Shielded cable.

Common coaxial cable should be avoided. This cable consists of a single conductor surrounded by a braided shield. This type of cable offers very poor noise reduction.

Plan the Route of the Signal Cable

Before starting, plan how the signal cable should be installed. *Never run signal wire in the same conduit with power wiring*. Try to run signal wiring as far away from power wiring as possible. When it is necessary to cross power wiring, install the signal cable so that it crosses at a right angle, as shown in Figure 10-14.

Connection of I/O Devices

In hardwired control circuits, it is common practice to connect several input devices together in series/parallel combinations as is the case in com-

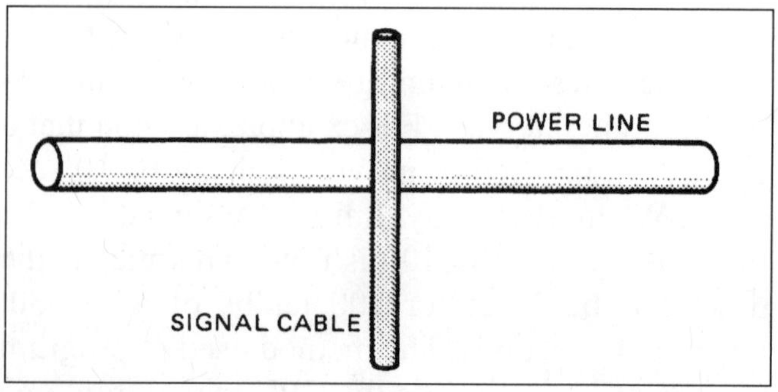

Figure 10-14 Signal cable crosses power line at a right angle.

plex motor control applications. However, when changes are required, it is often necessary to make significant changes to the wiring scheme.

PLCs are wired differently. Each input device is wired independently back to the PLC input module. Each set of terminals on the input module has an LED associated with it. When the input device is "on," the LED will be lit. Having this visual reference is a great advantage when troubleshooting an inoperative system. After the devices are wired, the program within the PLC determines the combination of "on" and "off" input devices required before the load is turned on. When changes are required, it is often only necessary to change the program. Input devices should never be wired in series/parallel arrangements. Each input device requires its own set of input terminals. If it becomes necessary to relocate an individual input device, the remainder of the wiring is left untouched.

The same rules apply to output devices. Each output device is wired independently back to the output module. As the PLC turns the output on, an LED on the output module is lit. Again, this visual reference is valuable when determining proper program operation or troubleshooting a malfunctioning system. The timing and number of outputs energized is determined by the program. Outputs must never be wired in series or parallel.

The power and current capabilities of the output modules is limited. Check the manufacturer's documentation to be sure the module specifications are not exceeded. When controlling loads with higher voltage and current requirements, it is often necessary to install a control relay. The PLC would turn on the control relay, which would then control the load.

THE DIFFERENTIAL AMPLIFIER

An electronic device that is often used to help overcome the problem of induced noise is the differential amplifier. This device, as illustrated in Figure 10-15, detects the voltage difference between the pair of signal wires and amplifies this difference. Since the induced noise level should be the same in both conductors, the amplifier will ignore the noise. For example, assume a sensor is

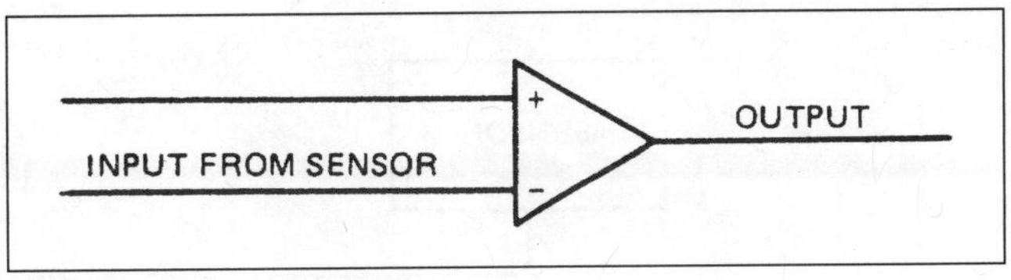

Figure 10-15 Differential amplifier detects a difference in signal level.

producing a 50-mV signal. This signal is applied to the input module, but induced noise is at a level of 5 V. In this case the noise level is 100 times greater than the signal level. The induced noise level, however, is the same for both of the input conductors. Therefore, the differential amplifier ignores the 5-V noise and amplifies only the voltage difference, which is 50 mV.

BONDING

Be sure to bond all metal, non-current-carrying equipment to ground. The power supply bonding conductor should be attached to the enclosure as close as is practical to where it enters the enclosure. If a cabinet with a backplate is used, be sure to provide an adequate bonding jumper from the backplate to the enclosure. Do not rely on the screws or bolts that fasten in the backplate.

Ground is generally thought of as being electrically neutral or zero at all points. However, this may not always be the case in practical application. It is not uncommon to find that different pieces of equipment have ground levels that are several volts apart (Figure 10-16 on page 144). To overcome this problem, large cable is sometimes used to bond two pieces of equipment together. This forces them to exist at the same potential. This method is sometimes referred to as the brute-force method.

Where the brute-force method is not practical, the shield of the signal cable is bonded at only one end. The preferred method is generally to bond the shield at the sensor.

POWER FAILURE PROTECTION

In industry, downtime is very costly. It is not practical for an industry to reprogram every PLC every time that a power failure occurs. For this reason

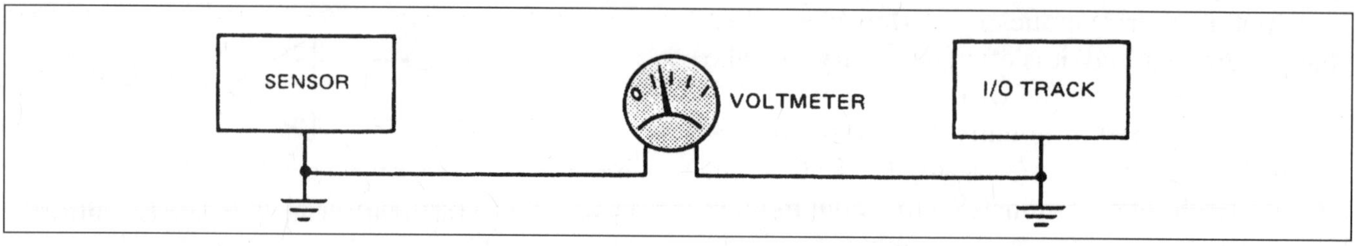

Figure 10-16 All grounds are not equal.

most industry has a system in place to make sure that the program is initialized after a power failure.

One method is to use a means to maintain power to the PLC. This could be in the form of an uninterruptible power supply (UPS). The UPS would maintain power to the PLC, thereby keeping the program in memory. However, the outputs would still not function. Many PLCs use a battery backup method. A small cell, usually a lithium cell, is used to keep power on the CPU of the PLCs. The amount of power required to keep the program in memory is minimal. Others use a capacitor that stores the electrical energy before the power failure and then releases it after the power failure to keep the program active

Some PLCs use a solid state device called an EPROM or an EEPROM. An EPROM is an Erasable Programmable Read Only Memory. Using special equipment, the PLC program is entered into the EPROM, which is placed into the PLC. Whenever the PLC is powered on, the program is loaded from the EPROM into the PLC memory. If the program is changed, the EPROM can be erased and then reprogrammed. An EPROM is erased by exposing a small clear area on the chip to ultraviolet light for a few minutes. The clear area is covered under normal conditions. An EEPROM—or Electrically Erasable Programmable Read Only Memory—is similar to an EPROM except that it can be erased by an electronic means.

Many modern electronic devices, such as digital cameras, use a flash memory card. Data can be written to these cards using a standard computer and a relatively low cost flash writer. Some PLCs are utilizing this technology as their program backup means.

The use of programmable logic controllers has steadily increased since their invention in the late 1960s. A PLC can replace hundreds of relays and occupy only a fraction of the space. The circuit logic can be changed easily and quickly without requiring extensive hand rewiring. The PLC has no moving parts or contacts to wear out, and its downtime is less than an equivalent relay circuit. A programmable logic controller used to control a DC drive unit is shown in Figure 10-17.

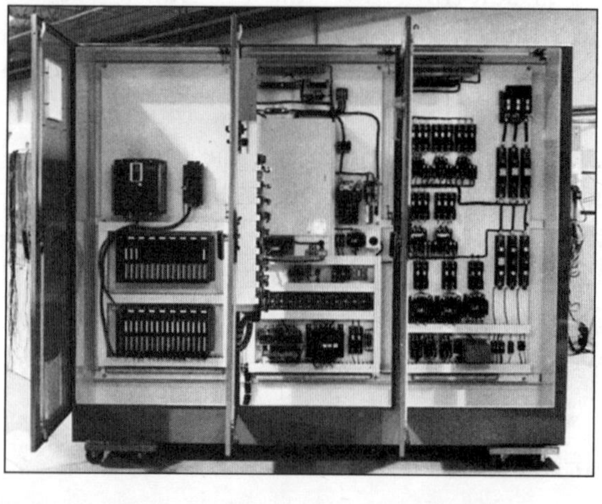

Figure 10-17 DC drive unit controlled by a programmable controller.

REVIEW

All answers should be written in complete sentences, calculations should be shown in detail, and Code references should be cited when appropriate.

1. What industry first started using programmable logic controllers?
2. Name the four basic sections of a programmable logic controller.
3. In what section of the PLC is the actual circuit logic performed?
4. What device separates the programmable logic controller from the outside circuits?
5. If an output I/O controls an AC voltage, what electronic device is used to actually control the load?
6. What is opto-isolation?
7. List the factors that must be considered when selecting a location for the PLC enclosure.
8. Why should signal wire runs be kept as short as possible?
9. Why is it necessary to install emergency stops on the PLC?
10. Why is shielded wire used for signal runs?
11. What is the brute-force method of bonding?
12. Explain the operation of a differential amplifier.

UNIT 11

Power Factor

OBJECTIVES

After studying this unit, the student should be able to:

- define and use the concept of power factor
- correct low power factor situations with a synchronous condenser
- correct low power factor situations with capacitors

LOADING ON AC CIRCUITS

Three kinds of electrical loads may be placed on the lines of AC circuits:

- a resistive load consisting solely of resistance
- an inductive load consisting of some resistance combined with a larger amount of inductance
- a capacitive load consisting almost entirely of capacitance

All three of these loads are present in varying degrees in nearly all AC lines. The resistive part of the total load is due to the fact that metal conductors do not have 100% efficiency in conducting electricity; thus, some losses will occur in the conductors. All metals used as conductors have some resistance that opposes the free flow of electrons. The resistance depends upon the kind of metal used as the conductor, the length of the conductor, the size or circular mil area of the cross section, and the temperature of the conductor.

When the load includes electromagnetic devices such as motors with windings formed from turns of wire wound on steel cores, then inductance is a factor in analyzing the total load. Inductance creates an additional opposition to the flow of current in an alternating-current system.

The amount of opposition due to inductance, called inductive reactance, depends upon the amount of inductance present and the frequency (in hertz) of the AC system. The inductive reactance is determined by the following equation:

Inductive reactance $(X_L) = 2\pi f L$

where

f = the frequency of the system, in hertz

L = the inductance, in henrys

Since two forces (resistance and reactance) are now opposing the current, it becomes necessary to combine the effect of the two forces to find the total opposition, which is called impedance. Each of these factors (resistance, reactance, and impedance) is measured in ohms.

Reactance can be either leading (capacitance) or lagging (inductance). When both are present, they cancel. In motor circuits the reactance is primarily inductive.

The inductive reactance adds to the resistance in a geometric manner, rather than in an arithmetic manner. That is, the inductive reactance is at right angles to the resistance. The impedance, as given by the following formula, is the resultant (hypotenuse of a right triangle) of these two forces.

$$\text{Impedance} = \sqrt{(\text{Resistance})^2 + (\text{Reactance})^2}$$

or

$$Z = \sqrt{R^2 + X_L^2}$$

For example, in the circuit shown in Figure 11-1, there is a 0.5-ohm resistance and a 0.6-ohm inductive reactance. Thus, the impedance is:

$$Z = \sqrt{0.5^2 + 0.6^2} = 0.781 \text{ ohms}$$

When the circuit current lags behind the voltage, an angle is formed. The tangent of this angle is the inductive reactance divided by the resistance, or

$$\tan \theta = X_L / R = 0.6 / 0.5 = 1.2$$

A table of trigonometric functions shows that the angle whose tangent is 1.2 is 50°. The vector diagram in Figure 11-1 shows the relationship among the resistance, the reactance, and the impedance.

Power Factor

The power factor is determined by the cosine of the angle between the voltage and the current. In Figure 11-1, the power factor is 0.643; this value is the cosine of 50°. Note that the angle between the

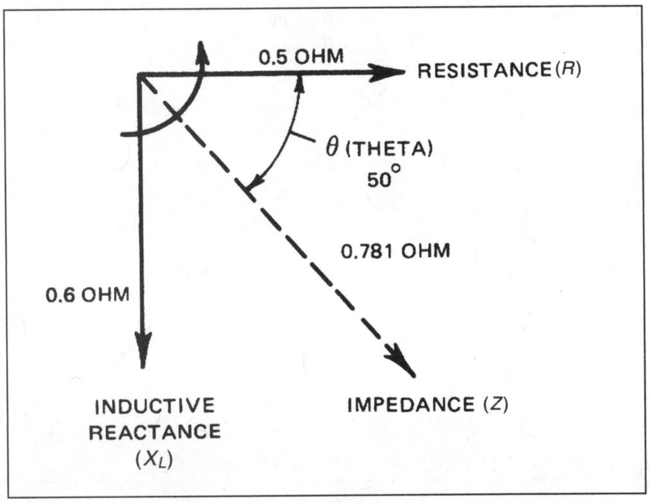

Figure 11-1 Vector diagram showing angular displacement of resistance, reactance, and impedance

resistance and the impedance in the figure is 50°. If this angle were zero, then the power factor would be 1.0. This indicates perfect conditions in that all of the current is active and useful. The power factor can also be expressed as the true power divided by the apparent power (watts/volt-amperes).

POWER FACTOR MEASUREMENT

When an industrial plant has a lagging power factor, the value of the power factor should be maintained between 0.9 and 1.0, if possible. This condition is desirable because of a number of factors, including the need to reduce the reactive current to achieve more capacity for useful current on the mains, feeders, and subfeeders; the need for better voltage regulation and stability; and the desirability of obtaining lower power rates from the power company.

As shown in the following list, there are several ways of determining the power factor of an entire plant, a single feeder, or even a branch circuit. The power factor can be determined by the use of:

1. A power factor meter
2. A kilovarmeter and kilowattmeter
3. Wattmeters or kilowattmeters in combination with voltmeters and ammeters

The last of the three methods listed is the most convenient one in terms of the connections to be made. However, the use of a permanently connected kilovarmeter is also convenient. When the power factor of the plant is 1.0 (unity), the kilovarmeter reads zero.

The instrument has a zero-centre scale. The needle indicates the number of reactive kilovolt-amperes (kilovars) by which the system is lagging or leading. The electrician can tell at a glance whether it is necessary to supply either a larger or a smaller leading component to the system.

Methods of Power Factor Correction

Power factor is corrected by connecting into the circuit a device that has a leading power factor. Both capacitors and synchronous condensers operate at a leading power factor and can be used for this purpose. The use of synchronous condensers, discussed later in this unit, was very common into the 1950s for power factor correction. With advances in the technology with respect to the construction of capacitors, synchronous condensers became far less common. However, they are making a comeback in today's modern industrial settings.

Most industrial environments now rely heavily on electronic equipment. This equipment tends to create electrical currents on the distribution system operating at multiples of the base 60 Hz frequency. These frequencies, known as harmonics, will be discussed in greater depth in Unit 19. Capacitors used for power factor correction can be adversely affected by these harmonic frequencies while synchronous condensers remain unaffected.

As the frequency of a circuit increases, we know that the capacitive reactance will decrease. This decrease in reactance will result in an increase in current flow, causing operation of the capacitor overcurrent devices or failure of the capacitor. For this reason, synchronous condensers are once again becoming popular for power factor correction. Synchronous condensers are readily available in sizes ranging from 200 KVAr to 2000 KVAr.

Power Factor Correction

Power or true power is expressed in kilowatts. The term *kilovolt-amperes*, which means volts multiplied by amperes and divided by 1000, is called the apparent power. Reactive power is not power at all, but rather is a component that is 90° out of phase with the true power. Reactive power is measured in volt-amperes reactive (VAr).

For example, let's assume that the total motor load on feeder is approximately 927 hp. This load requires nearly 1293 A per leg to supply the three-phase, 480-V, 60-Hz motors. The apparent power required for this load is found as shown by the following calculation:

$$\text{Apparent power} = 1293 \times 480 \times 1.73 / 1000$$
$$= 1074 \text{ kVA}$$

The actual value of the apparent power is obtainable only when all of the motors are running and loaded. If the motors are running at less than the full rated horsepower, the power factor will be less than the value of 0.85 used in previous examples.

For the present example, assume that the power factor is 0.74. Recall that the power factor is the cosine of the angle of lag (θ). When the value of 0.74 for the cosine is located on a table of functions, the angle θ is found to be about 42°, as in Figure 11-2. The kilovar (kVAr) reactive (useless) component in the power group is equal to the value of the apparent power (in kVA) multiplied by the sine of u:

$$\text{kVAr} = \text{kVA sine } 42°$$
$$= 1074 \times 0.67$$
$$= 720 \text{ KVA reactive}$$

Since 180° separate the leading component supplied by a synchronous condenser and the lagging component caused by the inductive characteristics of the motor load (90° lead and 90° lag, respectively), the leading kVAr value needed to cancel the lagging kVAr value would be 720. It is not necessary to reduce the reactance to zero as shown in Figure 11-3. This illustration shows that a synchronous condenser is supplying 520 kVAr of

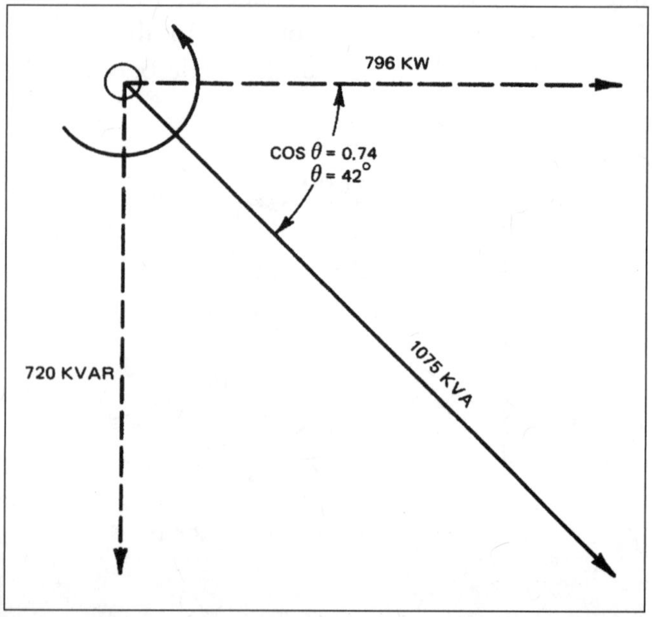

Figure 11-2 Angular displacement without synchronous condensers, power factor = 0.742.

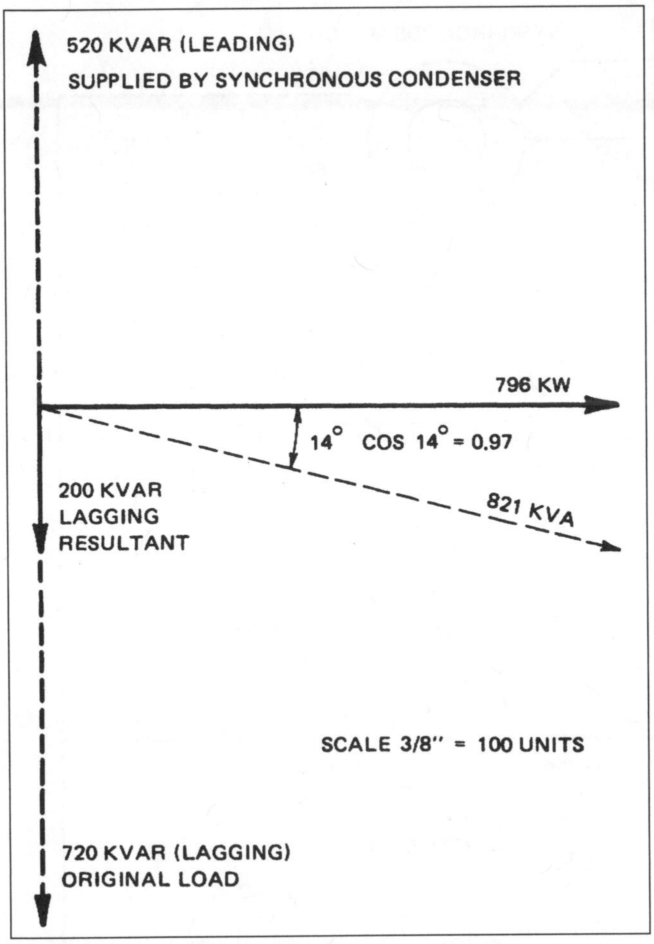

Figure 11-3 Vector diagram with synchronous condenser, power factor = 0.97.

leading reactance. This value reduces the original lagging reactance to 200 kVAr. However, the power factor is increased to 0.97 and the apparent power to 821 kVA. The kilowatt value is unchanged as it is established by the loading of the motors and the friction losses in the motor. Both of these quantities are actual loads. Generally, power factor is corrected to between 0.90 and unity.

THE SYNCHRONOUS CONDENSER

The synchronous condenser is a rotating electrical machine, as shown in Figure 11-4. It is similar to a synchronous motor or an AC generator. However, in operation, there are no electrical or mechanical loads connected to it. The only power required for the operation of a synchronous condenser is the power needed to supply its own small losses.

Figure 11-4 Synchronous condenser with directly connected exciter.

The synchronous condenser has a stationary three-phase armature winding rated at 480 V and 60 Hz. The rotating field of the condenser is excited from a source of DC, usually a small DC generator mounted on the shaft of the synchronous condenser. The schematic diagrams of the controller and the control scheme for a synchronous condenser are shown in Figure 11-5 on page 150.

The operation of the synchronous condenser is such that when the field winding is overexcited, the machine has a leading current. As the field excitation is reduced to rated value, there is no lead or lag by the condenser, and the current in the synchronous condenser branch is in phase with the voltage.

When the industrial plant is not operating at its full capacity, the excitation must be regulated to maintain a low kVAr value in the feeder. Periodic inspections and adjustments as necessary will ensure that a high power factor is maintained. The power factor is corrected or increased only from the point of attachment of the synchronous condenser back to the source of supply (Figure 11-6 on page 151).

To cancel the lagging currents in the feeder, the synchronous condenser must be overexcited. To accomplish this, the strength of the field excitation is increased by adjusting the field rheostat on the control panelboard.

When the synchronous condenser is started from the control panelboard, it performs in the same manner as any synchronous motor with the

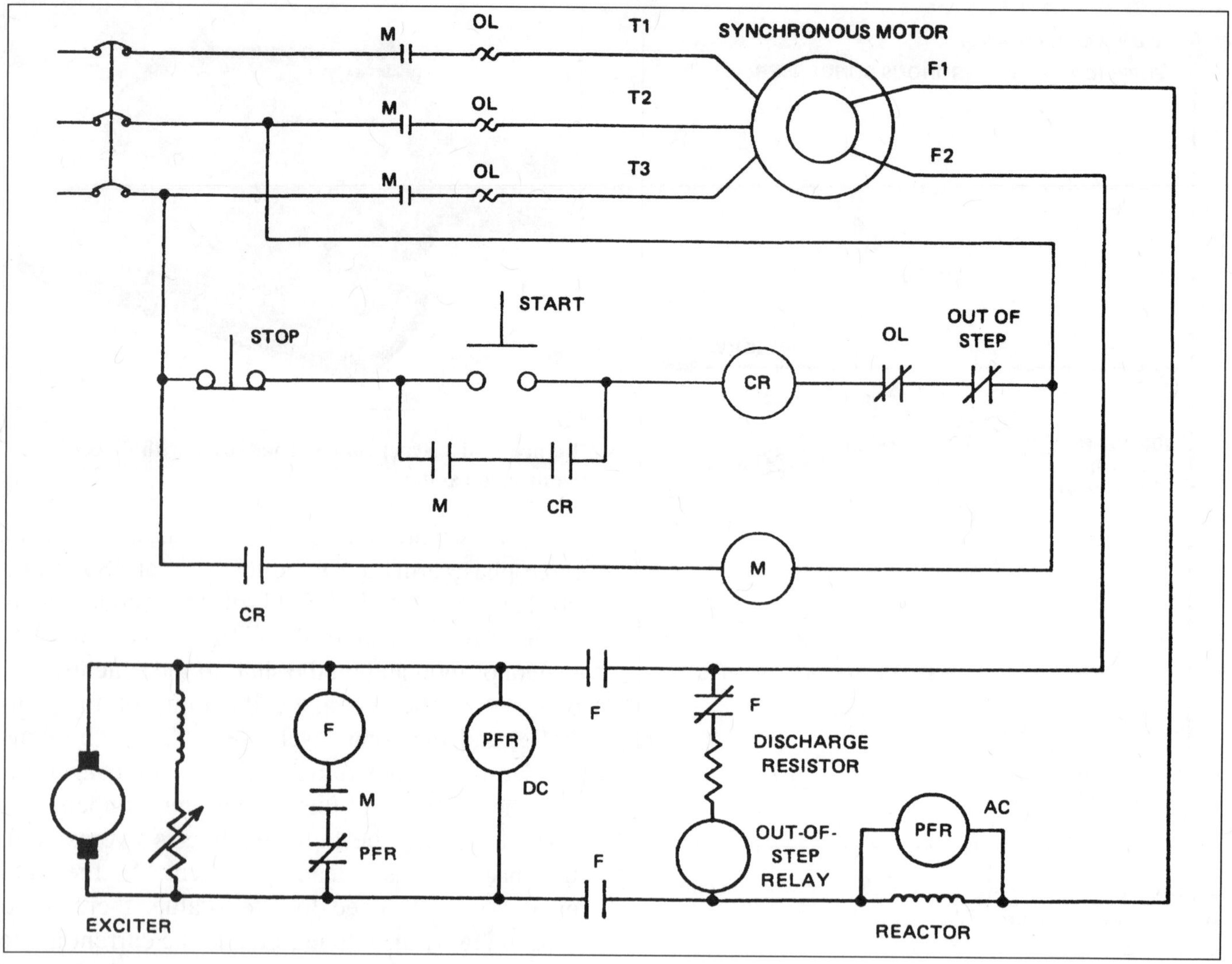

Figure 11-5 Basic synchronous motor controller circuitry.

exception that a load is not connected. Before the condenser starts, a normally closed contactor shorts out the field windings to prevent a high-voltage buildup. As soon as the machine is close to its synchronous speed, the contactor removes the short and connects the field to the exciter. As soon as the normal field excitation is achieved, the current decreases to a relatively low value. The AC ammeter on the control panelboard will rise rapidly when the field rheostat is adjusted for either underexcitation or overexcitation.

When the machine is underexcited by a lower-than-normal field current, the current lags the voltage. But when the field excitation is stronger than normal, the current leads the voltage and provides a leading kVAr value to counteract the lagging kVAr value in the feeder. This lagging value is caused by the inductive effect of the AC motor load. By using the field rheostat to regulate the field excitation, any value of leading kVAr is made available up to the rated output of the machine.

THE TIE-IN

In the existing portion of the building, the synchronous condensers are connected to the plug-in busway (Figure 11-7 on page 152). The wiring for these connections is sized according to *CEC* Rule 28-106. The conductors must have an ampacity of at least 125% of the full load current rating of the

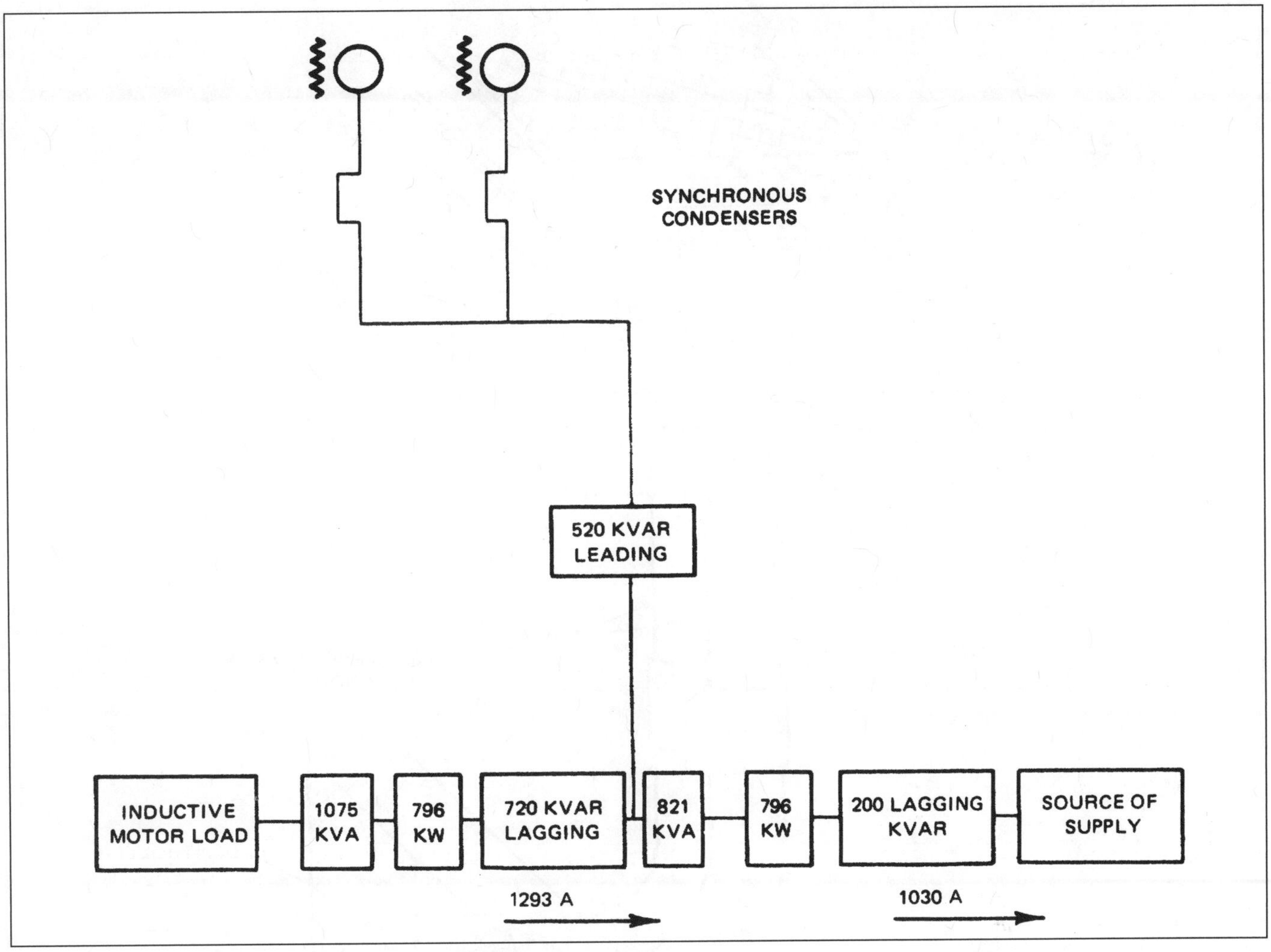

Figure 11-6 Block diagram showing how the power factor is corrected.

synchronous condenser that is supplied by the manufacturer. Using 340 A for a 200 kVAr synchronous condenser as an example, when 340 is multiplied by 1.25, the result is 425 A, the required ampacity of the conductors. To permit the use of smaller conductors and conduit, it is acceptable to parallel the feeders. Several rules must be followed when using parallel feeders (see *CEC* Rule 12-108):

- All phase conductors, and the neutral if used, as well as all equipment bonding conductors must be grouped in each raceway.
- The conductors must be 1/0 AWG or larger.
- The conductor in one grouping must be the same size, have the same type of insulation, and be terminated in the same manner as the conductors in the other grouping(s).
- The raceways containing the groups of conductors must have the same physical characteristics.

CORRECTING POWER FACTOR WITH CAPACITORS

Although this plant uses synchronous condensers for power factor correction, it is common practice in many industrial installations to use banks of capacitors, as shown in Figure 11-8 on page 153, to perform this task. A capacitor is a device that has a leading current and, therefore, a leading

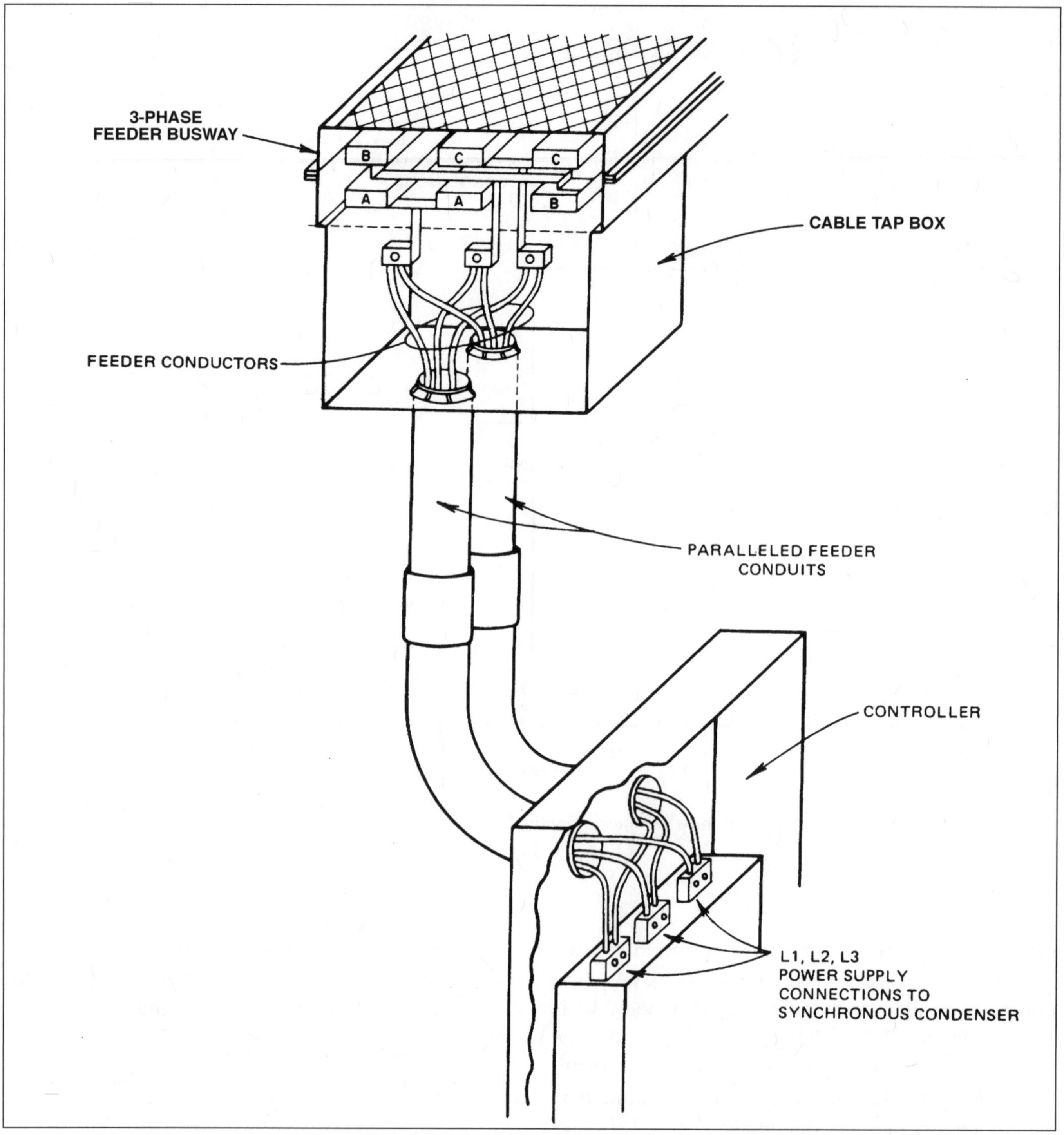

Figure 11-7 Synchronous condenser tie-in.

circuit with inductors, the leading VAr of the capacitors acts to cancel the lagging VAr of the inductors. In this way, power factor can be corrected.

To correct the power factor of a circuit or motor, the existing power factor must first be determined. In the example shown in Figure 11-9, a three-phase wattmeter, an ammeter, and a volt-

Figure 11-8 Capacitors used for power factor correction.

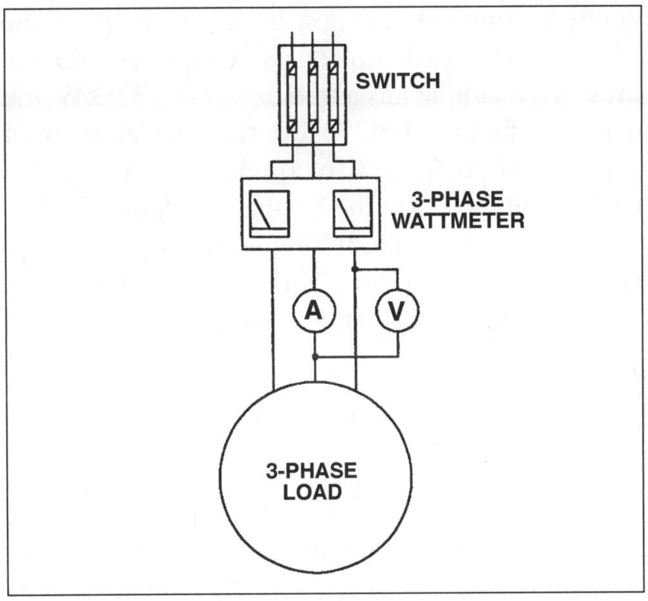

Figure 11-9 Measuring power factor.

meter have been connected to a three-phase circuit. It is assumed the meters indicate the values shown:

Wattmeter: 13.9 kW

Ammeter: 25 A

Voltmeter: 480 V

To compute the power factor, it will be necessary first to compute the apparent power. In a three-phase circuit, the apparent power can be computed using the formula:

$$VA = \sqrt{3} \times Volts \times Amps$$

$$VA = 1.732 \times 480 \times 25$$

$$VA = 20.8\ kVA$$

Now that both the apparent power and the true power of the circuit are known, the power factor can be determined by comparing the true power and apparent power.

$$PF = kW / kVA = 13.9 / 20.8 = 0.668 = 66.8\%$$

The amount of reactive power in the circuit can now be calculated using the formula:

$$kVAr = \sqrt{kVA^2 - kW^2} = \sqrt{20.8^2 - 13.9^2}$$
$$= \sqrt{432.64 - 193.21} = \sqrt{239.43}$$
$$= 15.47\ kVAr$$

To determine the capacitive kVAr needed to correct the power factor to 97%, first determine what the apparent power would be with a 97% power factor.

$$kVA = kW / PF = 13.9 / 0.97 = 14.3$$

Now determine the amount of inductive VAr necessary to produce an apparent power to 14.3 kVA.

$$kVAr = \sqrt{kVA^2 - kW^2}$$

$$kVAr = \sqrt{14.3^2 - 13.9^2}$$

$$kVAr = 3.36$$

Since the circuit presently contains 15.5 inductive kVAr, 12.14 capacitive kVAr (15.5 – 3.36) would be added to the circuit.

Another method used to determine the capacitance needed to correct the power factor is to use Table 11-1. To find the amount of capacitance needed, compute the power factor in the same manner described previously. The circuit in the previous example has a true power of 13.9 kW and a power factor of 67%. To find the amount of capacitive VAr needed to correct the power factor to 97%, find 67% in the left-hand column. Follow this row across to the 97% column. The multiplication factor is 0.857. Multiply the true power value by the multiplication factor.

$$13.9 \text{ kW} \times 0.857 = 11.9 \text{ kVAr}$$

CORRECTING MOTOR POWER FACTOR

It is often desirable to correct the power factor of a single motor. The amount of capacitance needed can be determined in the same manner as shown previously, by connecting a wattmeter, ammeter, and voltmeter in the circuit. Charts similar to the ones shown in Table 11-2 can also be used. These two charts list the horsepower and synchronous speed of both U-frame and T-frame motors. The charts assume a correction factor of 93% to 97%. The values shown are the kVAr of capacitance needed to correct the motor power factor. For motors designed to operate on 208 V, the kVAr value shown should be increased by 1.33. For motors designed to operate on 50 Hz, increase the chart values by a factor of 1.2.

INSTALLING CAPACITORS

CEC Rules 26-200 to 26-222 cover the installation and protection of capacitor circuits. Conduc-

Original Power-Factor Percentages	80	81	82	83	84	85	86	87	88	89	90	91	92	93	94	95	96	97
50	0.982	1.008	1.034	1.060	1.086	1.112	1.139	1.165	1.192	1.220	1.248	1.276	1.306	1.337	1.369	1.403	1.440	1.481
51	0.937	0.962	0.989	1.015	1.041	1.067	1.094	1.120	1.147	1.175	1.203	1.231	1.261	1.292	1.324	1.358	1.395	1.436
52	0.893	0.919	0.945	0.971	0.997	1.023	1.050	1.076	1.103	1.131	1.159	1.187	1.217	1.248	1.280	1.314	1.351	1.392
53	0.850	0.876	0.902	0.928	0.954	0.980	1.007	1.033	1.060	1.088	1.116	1.144	1.174	1.205	1.237	1.271	1.308	1.349
54	0.809	0.835	0.861	0.887	0.913	0.939	0.966	0.992	1.019	1.047	1.075	1.103	1.133	1.164	1.196	1.230	1.267	1.308
55	0.769	0.795	0.821	0.847	0.873	0.899	0.926	0.952	0.979	1.007	1.035	1.063	1.093	1.124	1.156	1.190	1.227	1.268
56	0.730	0.756	0.782	0.808	0.834	0.860	0.887	0.913	0.940	0.968	0.996	1.024	1.054	1.085	1.117	1.151	1.188	1.229
57	0.692	0.718	0.744	0.770	0.796	0.822	0.849	0.875	0.902	0.930	0.958	0.986	1.016	1.047	1.079	1.113	1.150	1.191
58	0.655	0.681	0.707	0.733	0.759	0.785	0.812	0.838	0.865	0.893	0.921	0.949	0.979	1.010	1.042	1.076	1.113	1.154
59	0.619	0.645	0.671	0.697	0.723	0.749	0.776	0.802	0.829	0.857	0.885	0.913	0.943	0.974	1.006	1.040	1.077	1.118
60	0.583	0.609	0.635	0.661	0.687	0.713	0.740	0.766	0.793	0.821	0.849	0.877	0.907	0.938	0.970	1.004	1.041	1.082
61	0.549	0.575	0.601	0.627	0.653	0.679	0.706	0.732	0.759	0.787	0.815	0.843	0.873	0.904	0.936	0.970	1.007	1.048
62	0.516	0.542	0.568	0.594	0.620	0.646	0.673	0.699	0.725	0.754	0.782	0.810	0.840	0.871	0.903	0.937	0.974	1.015
63	0.483	0.509	0.535	0.561	0.587	0.613	0.640	0.666	0.693	0.721	0.749	0.777	0.807	0.838	0.870	0.904	0.941	0.982
64	0.451	0.474	0.503	0.529	0.555	0.581	0.608	0.634	0.661	0.689	0.717	0.745	0.775	0.806	0.838	0.872	0.909	0.950
65	0.419	0.445	0.471	0.497	0.523	0.549	0.576	0.602	0.629	0.657	0.685	0.713	0.743	0.774	0.806	0.840	0.877	0.918
66	0.388	0.414	0.440	0.466	0.492	0.518	0.545	0.571	0.598	0.626	0.654	0.682	0.712	0.743	0.755	0.809	0.846	0.887
67	0.358	0.384	0.410	0.436	0.462	0.488	0.515	0.541	0.568	0.596	0.624	0.652	0.682	0.713	0.745	0.779	0.816	0.857
68	0.328	0.354	0.380	0.406	0.432	0.458	0.485	0.511	0.538	0.566	0.594	0.622	0.652	0.683	0.715	0.749	0.786	0.827
69	0.299	0.325	0.351	0.377	0.403	0.429	0.456	0.482	0.509	0.537	0.565	0.593	0.623	0.654	0.686	0.720	0.757	0.798
70	0.270	0.296	0.322	0.348	0.374	0.400	0.427	0.453	0.480	0.508	0.536	0.564	0.594	0.625	0.657	0.691	0.728	0.769
71	0.242	0.268	0.294	0.320	0.346	0.372	0.399	0.425	0.452	0.480	0.508	0.536	0.566	0.597	0.629	0.663	0.700	0.741
72	0.214	0.240	0.266	0.292	0.318	0.344	0.371	0.397	0.424	0.452	0.480	0.508	0.538	0.569	0.601	0.635	0.672	0.713
73	0.186	0.212	0.238	0.264	0.290	0.316	0.343	0.369	0.396	0.424	0.452	0.480	0.510	0.541	0.573	0.607	0.644	0.685
74	0.159	0.185	0.211	0.237	0.263	0.289	0.316	0.342	0.369	0.397	0.425	0.453	0.483	0.514	0.546	0.580	0.617	0.658
75	0.132	0.158	0.184	0.210	0.236	0.262	0.289	0.315	0.342	0.370	0.398	0.426	0.456	0.487	0.519	0.553	0.590	0.631
76	0.105	0.131	0.157	0.183	0.209	0.235	0.262	0.288	0.315	0.343	0.371	0.399	0.429	0.460	0.492	0.526	0.563	0.604
77	0.079	0.105	0.131	0.157	0.183	0.209	0.236	0.262	0.289	0.317	0.345	0.373	0.403	0.434	0.466	0.500	0.537	0.578
78	0.052	0.078	0.104	0.130	0.156	0.182	0.209	0.235	0.262	0.290	0.318	0.346	0.376	0.407	0.439	0.473	0.510	0.551
79	0.026	0.052	0.078	0.104	0.130	0.156	0.183	0.209	0.236	0.264	0.292	0.320	0.350	0.381	0.413	0.447	0.484	0.525
80	0.000	0.026	0.052	0.078	0.104	0.130	0.157	0.183	0.210	0.238	0.266	0.294	0.324	0.355	0.387	0.421	0.458	0.499
81		0.000	0.026	0.052	0.078	0.104	0.131	0.157	0.184	0.212	0.240	0.268	0.298	0.329	0.361	0.395	0.432	0.473
82			0.000	0.026	0.052	0.078	0.105	0.131	0.158	0.186	0.214	0.242	0.272	0.303	0.335	0.369	0.406	0.447
83				0.000	0.026	0.052	0.079	0.105	0.132	0.160	0.188	0.216	0.246	0.277	0.309	0.343	0.380	0.421
84					0.000	0.026	0.053	0.079	0.106	0.134	0.162	0.190	0.220	0.251	0.283	0.317	0.354	0.395
85						0.000	0.027	0.053	0.080	0.108	0.136	0.164	0.194	0.225	0.257	0.291	0.328	0.369
86							0.000	0.026	0.053	0.081	0.190	0.137	0.167	0.198	0.230	0.264	0.301	0.342
87								0.000	0.027	0.055	0.083	0.111	0.141	0.172	0.204	0.238	0.275	0.316
88									0.000	0.028	0.056	0.084	0.114	0.145	0.177	0.211	0.248	0.289
89										0.000	0.028	0.056	0.086	0.117	0.149	0.183	0.220	0.261
90											0.000	0.028	0.058	0.089	0.121	0.155	0.192	0.233

Courtesy of ARCO Electric Products Corp.

Table 11-1 Kilowatt multipliers for determining capacitor kilovars.

Kilovolt-Ampere-Reactive for U-Frame Motors
Suggested Capacitor Ratings for Approximately 93% to 97% Power Factor

HP	3600 RPM	1800 RPM	1200 RPM	900 RPM	720 RPM	600 RPM
5	2.5	2.5	2.5	3	4	4
7½	2.5	2.5	3	4	5	6
10	3	3	3	5	6	7.5
15	4	4	5	6	8	8
20	5	5	6	7.5	8	10
25	6	6	7.5	8	10	13
30	8	8	8	10	13	15
40	10	10	10	13	15	20
50	12	10	13	15	18	23
60	13	13	15	18	21	26
75	17	15	18	21	26	35
100	21	21	25	26	35	40
125	26	26	30	30	40	50
150	30	30	35	37	50	50
200	40	37	40	50	60	60
250	50	45	50	60	70	75
300	60	50	60	60	80	90
350	60	60	75	75	90	95

Kilovolt-Ampere-Reactive for T-Frame Motors
Suggested Capacitor Ratings for Approximately 94% to 97% Power Factor

HP	3600 RPM	1800 RPM	1200 RPM	900 RPM	720 RPM	600 RPM
5	2.5	2.5	3	4	4	5
7½	2.5	3	4	5	5	6
10	4	4	5	6	7.5	8
15	5	5	6	7.5	8	10
20	6	6	7.5	9	10	12
25	7.5	7.5	8	10	12	18
30	8	8	10	14	15	20.5
40	12	14	16	18	20	25
50	15	18	20	21	23	30
60	18	20	23	25	30	35
75	20	25	25	30	35	40
100	23	30	30	35	40	45
125	25	35	35	40	45	50
150	30	40	40	50	50	60
200	35	50	50	70	70	90
250	40	60	60	80	90	100
300	45	70	75	100	100	
350	50	75	90			

Abbreviated table: Courtesy of ARCO Electric Products. For maximum benefit, locate at motor. For a 208-V system, use 33% larger.

Table 11-2 Correcting the power factor of motors.

tors in capacitor circuits must be rated no less than 135% of the current rating of the capacitor. If the capacitor is used in a motor circuit, the conductors connecting the capacitor cannot be less than one-third the rating of the motor current and in no case less than 135% of the rated current

If capacitors are to be used to correct the power factor of a single motor, the manner in which the capacitors are installed can greatly influence the Code requirements. For example, *CEC* Rules 26-212 and 26-214 state that an overcurrent device must be provided for each ungrounded conductor a separate disconnecting means rated no less than 135% of the rated capacitor current. However, *CEC* Rule 26-218 states that a separate overcurrent device does not need to be provided if the capacitor bank is connected to the load side of the motor overload protective device and that a separate disconnect means is not required if the capacitor is connected to the load side of the motor disconnecting means, as shown in Figure 11-10. If the capacitor is connected ahead of the overload protective device, as shown in Figure 11-11, a separate overcurrent device is required but a disconnecting means is not. Table 11-3 provides a list of sizes of wire, fuses, and switches for different kVAr capacitor ratings on different voltages of three-phase systems.

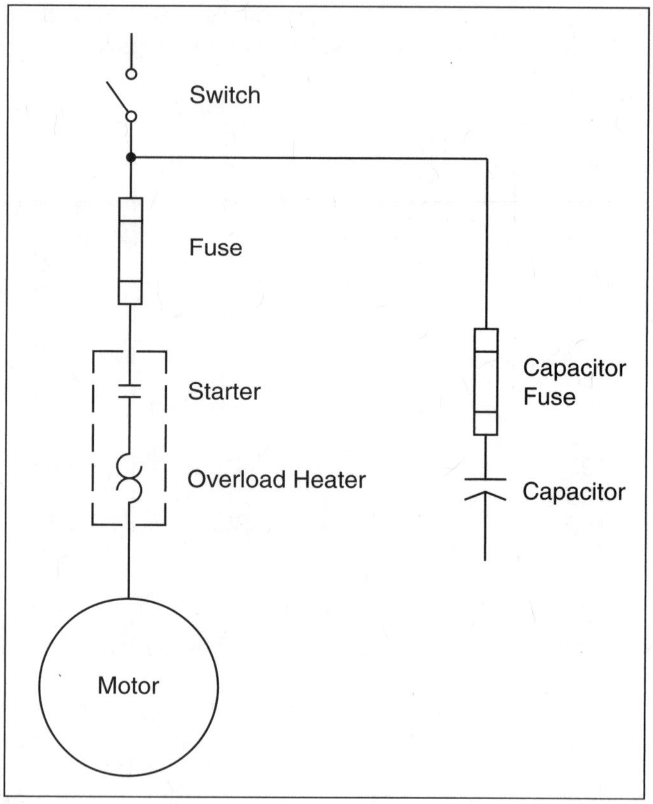

Figure 11-11 Capacitor connected ahead of overload protective device.

TESTING CAPACITORS

To understand how to test a capacitor, it is necessary first to understand what a capacitor is. Most capacitors used in industry, especially for power factor correction, are called AC or non-polarized capacitors. This simply means that the capacitor is not sensitive to which polarity of voltage is connected to which plate. These capacitors are generally constructed of two metal plates separated by an insulating material called the dielectric, as illustrated in Figure 11-12. To test a capacitor accurately, two measurements must be made. One is to measure the capacitance value of the capacitor to determine whether it is the same or approximately the same as the rate value. The other is to test the strength of the dielectric.

The first test should be made with an ohmmeter. With the power disconnected, connect the terminals of an ohmmeter directly across the capacitor terminals as shown in Figure 11-13. (It is a good practice to discharge the capacitor, by touching the leads together, before connecting to the ohmmeter.)

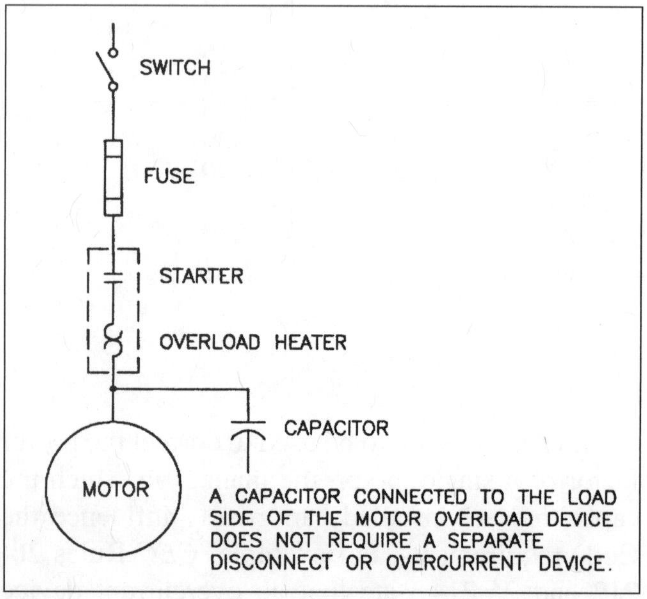

Figure 11-10 Capacitor connected to load side of motor.

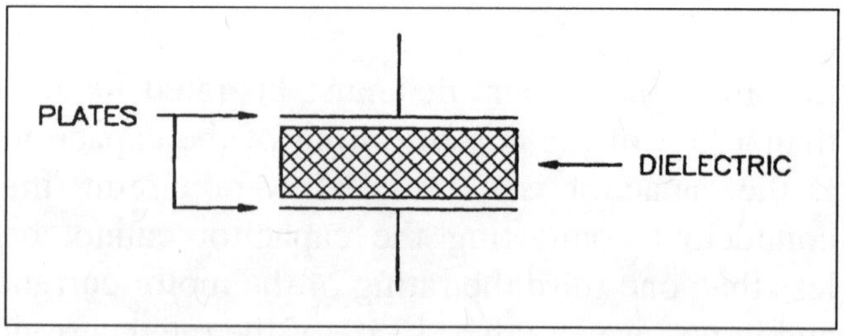

Figure 11-12 Basic capacitor.

KVAR	240 VOLTS NOM. AMPS.	240 VOLTS SIZE RW90 WIRE	240 VOLTS FUSE	240 VOLTS Switch	480 VOLTS NOM. AMPS.	480 VOLTS SIZE RW90 WIRE	480 VOLTS FUSE	480 VOLTS Switch	600 VOLTS NOM. AMPS.	600 VOLTS SIZE RW90 WIRE	600 VOLTS FUSE	600 VOLTS Switch
1	2.4	14	5	30	1.2	14	5	30				
2.5	6.0	14	10	30	3.0	14	5	30	2.4	14	5	30
3	7.2	14	15	30	3.6	14	10	30	3.0	14	5	30
4	9.6	14	20	30	4.8	14	10	30	3.8	14	10	30
5	12.0	12	20	30	6.0	14	10	30	4.8	14	10	30
6	14.4	12	25	30	7.2	14	15	30	5.7	14	10	30
7.5	18.0	10	30	30	9.0	14	20	30	7.0	14	15	30
8	19.2	10	35	60	9.6	14	20	30	7.6	14	15	30
10	24.0	8	40	60	12.0	12	25	30	9.5	14	20	30
13	31.2	6	50	60	15.6	10	30	30	12.2	12	20	30
15	36.0	6	60	60	18.0	10	30	30	14.2	12	25	30
18	43.4	4	80	100	21.7	10	35	60	17.3	10	30	30
20	48.0	4	80	100	24.0	8	40	60	19.0	10	35	60
21	50.5	4	80	100	25.2	8	40	60	20.1	10	40	60
23	55.2	3	90	100	27.6	8	50	60	22.8	10	40	60
25	60.0	2	90	100	30.0	6	60	60	23.8	8	40	60
26	62.5	2	90	100	31.2	6	60	60	24.8	8	40	60
30	72.0	2	125	200	36.0	6	60	60	28.8	8	50	60
33	79.2	1	150	200	39.6	6	80	100	31.3	6	60	60
35	84.0	1	150	200	42.0	4	80	100	33.6	6	60	60
37	88.8	1/0	150	200	44.4	4	80	100	35.1	6	60	60
40	96.0	1/0	175	200	48.0	4	80	100	38.0	6	80	100
45	108.0	2/0	200	200	54.0	3	90	100	42.7	4	80	100
50	120.0	2/0	200	200	60.0	2	90	100	47.6	4	80	100
55	132.0	3/0	225	400	66.0	2	100	100	52.4	3	90	100
60	144.0	3/0	250	400	72.0	2	125	200	57.6	3	90	100
65	156.0	3/0	250	400	78.0	1	150	200	62.4	2	90	100
70	168.0	4/0	300	400	84.0	1	150	200	66.2	2	100	100
75	180.0	250	300	400	90.0	1/0	150	200	71.0	2	125	200
80					96.0	1/0	175	200	77.0	1	150	200
85					102.0	1/0	175	200	81.0	1	150	200
90					108.0	2/0	200	200	85.5	1/0	150	200
95					114.0	2/0	200	200	90.0	1/0	150	200
100					120.0	2/0	200	200	95.0	1/0	175	200
125					150.0	3/0	250	400	119.0	2/0	200	200

Table 11-3 Three-phase wiring and fusing for capacitor installations.

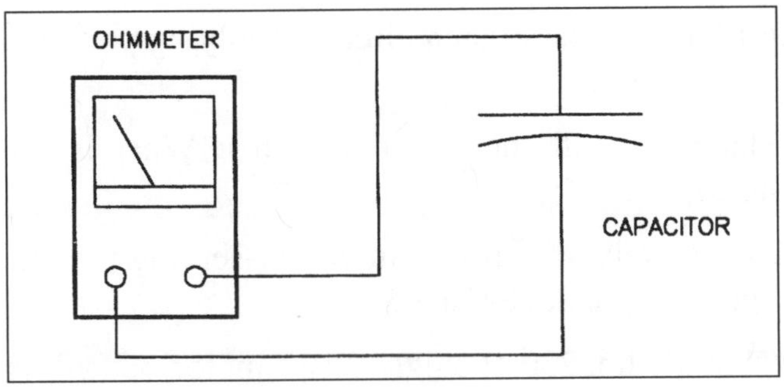

Figure 11-13 Testing a capacitor with an ohmmeter.

This test determines whether the dielectric is shorted. When the ohmmeter is connected, the needle should swing up-scale and return to infinity. The amount of needle swing is determined by the capacitance of the capacitor. Then reverse the ohmmeter connection and the needle should move twice as far up-scale and return to

If the ohmmeter test is successful, the dielectric must be tested at its rated voltage. This is called a dielectric strength test. To make this test, a dielectric test set must be used. This device is often referred to as a HIPOT because of its ability to produce a high voltage or high potential. The dielectric test set contains a variable voltage control, a voltmeter, and a microammeter. To use the HIPOT, connect its terminal leads to the capacitor terminals. Increase the output voltage until rated voltage is applied to the capacitor. The microammeter indicates any current flow between the plates and the dielectric. If the capacitor is good, the microammeter should indicate zero current.

The capacitance value must be measured to determine whether there are any open plates in the capacitor. To measure the capacitance value of the capacitor, connect, as shown in Figure 11-14 on page 158, some value of AC voltage across the plates of the capacitor. This voltage must not be

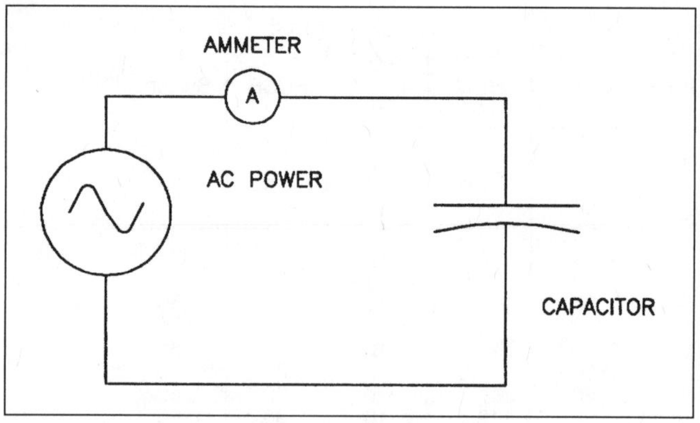

Figure 11-14 Determining the capacitance with a ammeter.

measure the amount of current in the circuit. Now that the voltage and current are known, the capacitive reactance can be computed using the formula:

$$X_C = E / I$$

After the capacitive reactance has been determined, the capacitance can be computed using the formula:

$$C = \frac{1}{2\pi f X_C}$$

REVIEW

All answers should be written in complete sentences, calculations should be shown in detail, and Code references should be cited when appropriate.

1. List the three kinds of electrical loads that are connected to an AC circuit.
2. An electrician uses a clamp-on ammeter and a voltmeter to measure the current and voltage of a motor.
   (a) If the two values are multiplied, is the product the true power or the apparent power?
   (b) What would you need to know to be able to calculate the other power value?
3. The ballast in some of the older fluorescent luminaires (fixtures) was said to have a low power factor. What device would be added to the circuit to improve the power factor?
4. What effect does the power factor of a motor have on the branch circuit supplying power to the motor?
5. Inductive reactance, resistance, and impedance are all measured in ohms. What is the common characteristic that makes this possible?
6. Inductive reactance, resistance, and impedance are always present in circuit-serving motors. Which of the three actually determines the required conductor size?
7. We are told that 1 hp is equivalent to 746 W, but a 1-hp, 230-V single-phase motor, according to *CEC* Table 45, has a current of 8 A. Explain this apparent discrepancy.
8. A 240-V, three-phase circuit has a current of 116 A. A wattmeter connected to the circuit indicates a load of 34.7 kW.
   (a) What is the power factor?
   (b) How many capacitive volt-amperes reactive (VAr) would be needed to correct the power factor to 95%?
9. When a 60-V, 60-Hz supply is connected to a capacitor, the current reads 0.6 A. What is the capacitance of the capacitor?

UNIT 12

HVAC (Heating, Ventilating, and Air Conditioning) Systems and Other Facilities

OBJECTIVES

After studying this unit, the student should be able to:

- identify the major components of a cooling system
- describe the basic refrigeration cycle
- determine the branch circuit requirements for hermetic compressors

SPECIAL TERMINOLOGY

Chiller

A packaged system incorporating a compressor, an evaporator (which is used to chill water), a condenser (which is used to reject heat), and a safety and operating control package.

Latent Heat

The heat required to cause a change in the state of a material, from a solid to a liquid or from a liquid to a gas. The latent heat of fusion is the heat required to change a solid to a liquid. The latent heat of vaporization is the heat required to change a liquid to a vapour.

Sensible Heat

The heat required to cause a change in the temperature of a substance without causing a change in state.

Ventilation

The process of supplying and removing air from a building.

Hermetic Compressor

A compressor including motor and drive that is sealed in a welded case containing the refrigerant and lubricating oil.

Maximum Continuous Current

The *maximum continuous current* is determined by the manufacturer of the hermetic refrigerant motor-compressors under specific test conditions. The maximum continuous current is needed to design the unit properly. The electrician need not know this information, and it is not placed on the nameplate.

Rated-Load Current

The *rated-load current* is determined by the manufacturer of the hermetic refrigerant motor-compressor by testing at rated refrigerant pressure, temperature conditions, and voltage. In most instances, the rated-load current is at least equal to 64.1% of the hermetic refrigerant motor-compressor's maximum continuous current.

Branch-Circuit Selection Current

Some hermetic refrigerant motor-compressors are designed to operate continuously at currents greater than 156% of the rated-load current. In such cases, the unit's nameplate is marked with branch-circuit selection current. The *branch-circuit selection current* will be no less than 64.1% of the maximum continuous current rating of the hermetic refrigerant motor-compressor.

Minimum Circuit Ampacity

The manufacturer of an air-conditioning unit is required to mark the nameplate with the *minimum circuit ampacity*. This is important information for the electrician. The manufacturer determines the minimum circuit ampacity by multiplying the rated-load current, or the branch-circuit selection current of the hermetic refrigerant motor-compressor, by 125%. The current ratings of all other concurrent loads, such as fan motors, transformers, relay coils, and so on, are then added to this value.

Maximum Overcurrent Protection Device

The manufacturer is required to mark the *maximum overcurrent protection device* on the nameplate. This value is determined by multiplying the rated-load current, or the branch-circuit selection current of the hermetic refrigerant motor-compressor, by 225%, then adding all concurrent loads such as electric heaters, motors, and so on.

THE COOLING EQUIPMENT

Heating and cooling for industrial buildings can be provided with a number of rooftop units or a central system. The cooling equipment for the industrial building consists of a central system that uses a liquid chiller and associated equipment as shown in Figure 12-1 and a number of fan coil units as shown on Sheet M2 of the plans. The water circulating pumps are located in the chiller room. Although the actual installation of the cooling equipment is the responsibility of another contractor, the electrician should be familiar with and understand the basic operation of the cooling system.

The Basic Refrigeration Cycle

Refrigeration systems remove heat from a low-temperature medium and transfer the heat to a high-temperature medium. Two types of refrigeration systems are commonly used in large buildings: compression refrigeration systems and absorption refrigeration systems. Absorption systems are more complex but are ideal where there is a lot of waste heat derived from an industrial process.

The compression refrigeration cycle operates on the principle that the boiling point of a liquid depends on the pressure of the liquid. For example, water in a kettle boils at 100°C at sea level but would boil at a much lower temperature if the kettle were at the top of Mount Everest.

A compression refrigeration system has four main components: compressor, condenser, evaporator, and metering device (Figure 12-2 on page 162).

The refrigeration cycle starts at the evaporator, which is connected to the compressor. As the compressor runs, it reduces the pressure in the evaporator (places it under a vacuum) and increases the pressure at the condenser. When the metering device permits liquid refrigerant to enter the evaporator, the refrigerant immediately absorbs heat from the evaporator and flashes into a gas because of the low pressure. The vapour travels (via the suction line) from the evaporator to the compressor, where it is compressed, raising its temperature and pressure. The high-pressure refrigerant vapour moves from the compressor to the condenser (via the high-pressure line). Heat is transferred from the high-pressure vapour to the condenser, causing the vapour to condense into a

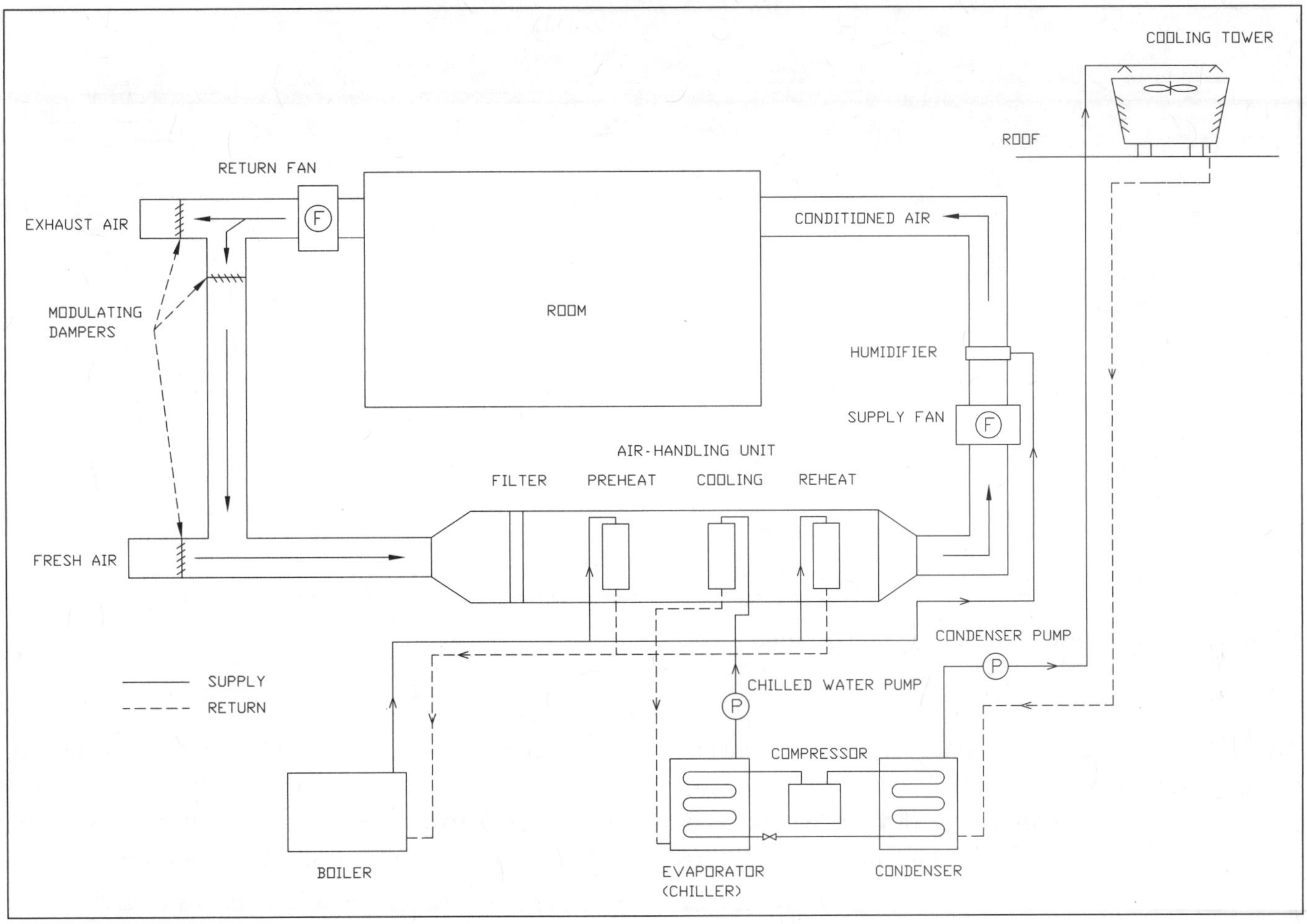

Figure 12-1 A central conditioned air system.

liquid. The liquid flows from the condenser back to the metering device where it is metered into the evaporator, starting the cycle again.

The Absorption Refrigeration Cycle

The absorption refrigeration cycle operates on the principle that the amount of refrigerant held in a solution can be changed by changing the pressure and temperature of the solution. Absorption systems use heat instead of a compressor to obtain high pressures and temperatures. The propane refrigerator is an example of an absorption refrigeration system.

The main components of the absorption system are an evaporator, vapour absorber, solution transfer pumps, generator, and condenser (Figure 12-3 on page 163).

The absorption cycle begins at the evaporator. Liquid refrigerant (in this case, water) is vaporized in the evaporator, which causes heat to be removed from the evaporator. Low-pressure refrigerant vapour moves from the evaporator to the absorber, where some of the refrigerant is absorbed by the solvent, forming a solution of refrigerant and solvent (this produces some heat, which must be removed from the process). The solution of solvent and refrigerant is pumped from the absorber to the generator. At the generator, heat is added to the solution, causing some of the refrigerant to be driven out of the solution. The refrigerant vapour moves to the condenser, while the remaining solution is returned to the absorber

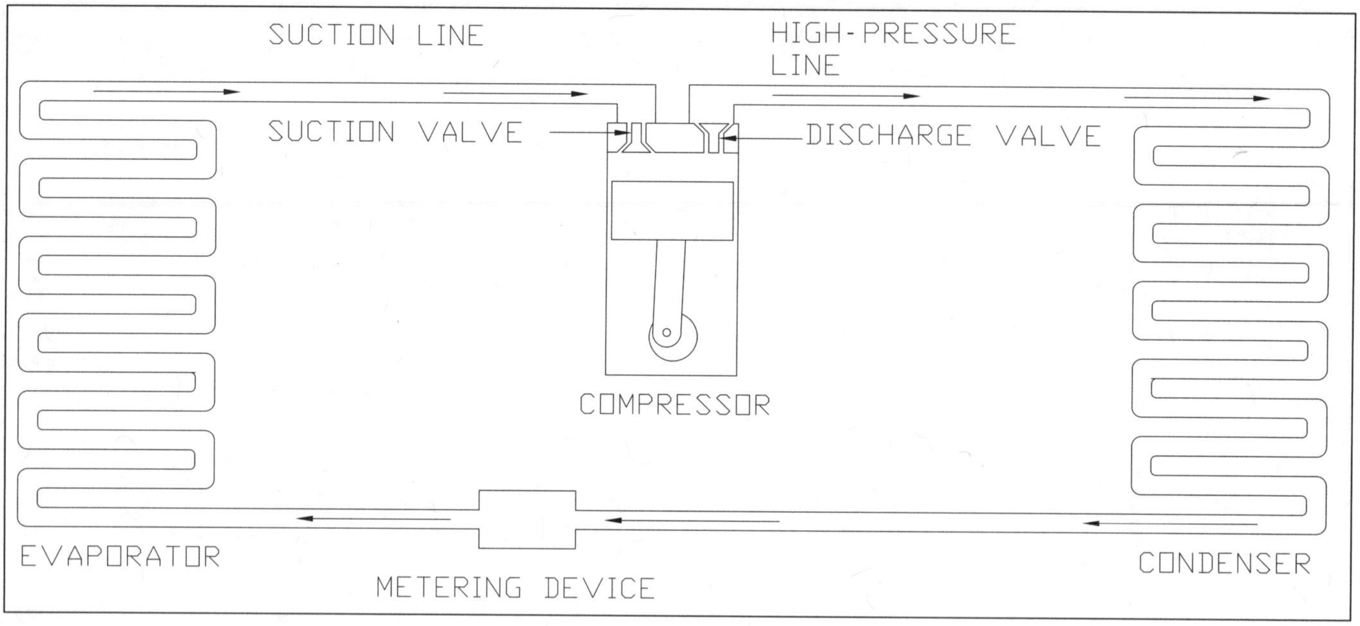

Figure 12-2 The basic compression refrigeration cycle.

The refrigerant gives up heat in the condenser, causing the vapour to condense to a liquid. The liquid returns to the metering device, where it is metered into the evaporator, causing the cycle to repeat.

Industrial absorption systems often use ammonia as the refrigerant and water as an absorbent, while institutional and commercial systems use water as the refrigerant and lithium bromide as the absorbent because of the high toxicity of ammonia. In large central systems, chilled water is used to extend the effect of the refrigeration cycle (Figure 12-1).

The chiller (Figure 12-4 on page 164) is used to circulate water through a piping system to a central air-handling unit (Figure 12-1) or to fan coil units located at various points in the industrial building (Figures 12-5A and B on page 164). Cool air is then blown from these units into the immediate area. Each serves to maintain a comfortable air temperature by lowering the temperature and removing humidity from the air.

Each fan coil unit in the existing plant is equipped with a 2-hp induction motor driving a squirrel-cage type fan. The fan moves nearly 3000 ft^3 of air per minute through a fin tube coil (Figure 12-6 on page 165). The movement of air through the coil removes the heat from the air, which is then forced through ductwork to the proper area to be cooled. Whenever the specific area is cooled to the desired temperature, a thermostat opens the control circuit to the motor controller and the air movement stops until the area again requires cooling. The controller for each fan coil unit is located adjacent to the cooling unit.

The motors of the fan coil units can be expected to run continuously for extended periods of time. Thus, these motors are considered to be continuous duty motors. Protection must be provided for the motors and is sized according to *CEC Part 1,* Section 28. See Unit 9 for details on installing motors.

When motors are installed for use with refrigeration or other equipment that requires a belt drive, the electrician may be called upon to align the motor and adjust the drive belts. The drives for the cooling units in the existing part of the building require four V-belts. It is recommended that the four belts be purchased as a set so that they all have the same length. The belts should be installed only after the motor is loosened from its base and moved closer to the fan sheave. The belts should not be pulled on over the sheaves because the belt fabric can be damaged. The motor should

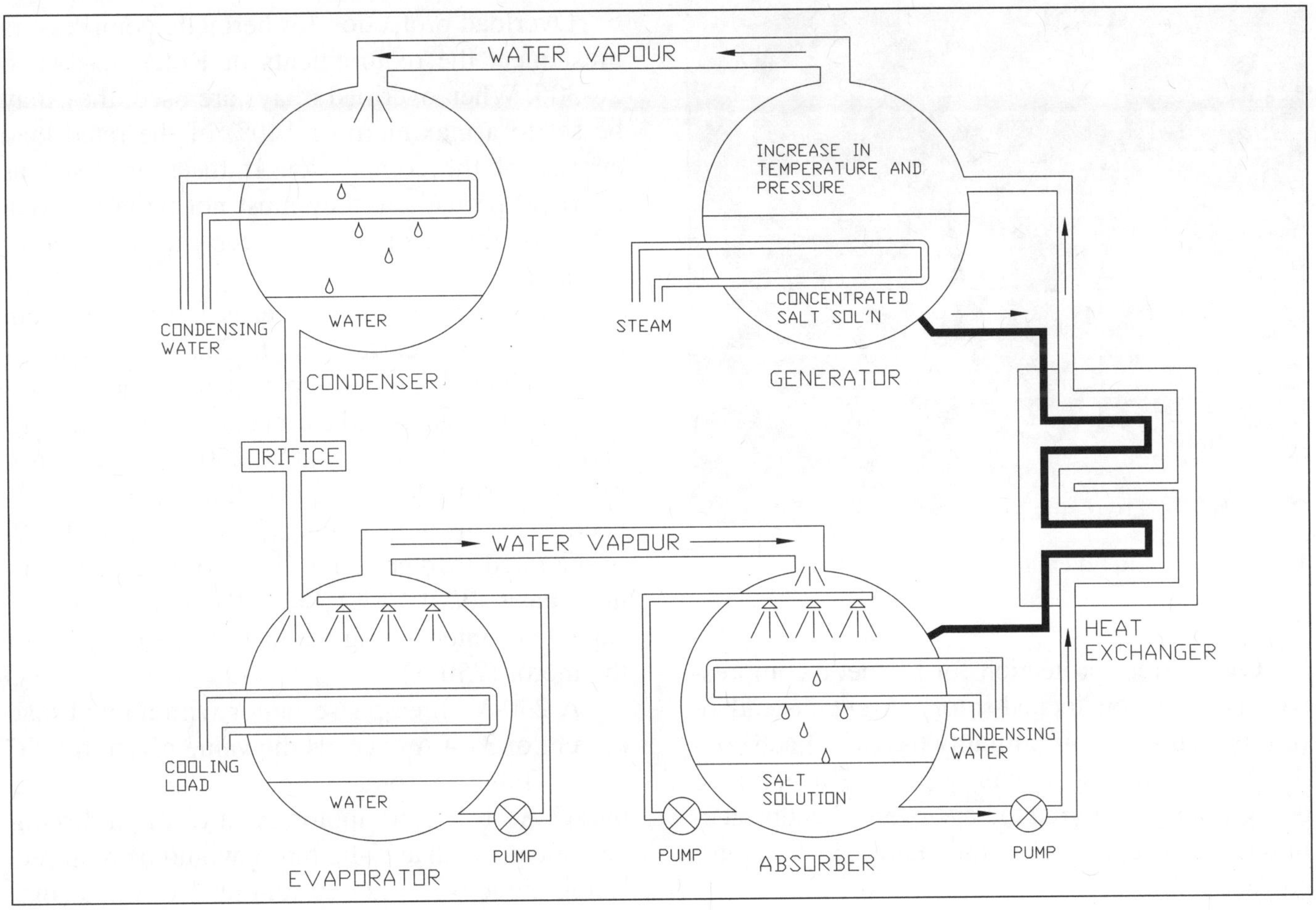

Figure 12-3 The absorption refrigeration cycle.

be placed so that the sheaves are in perfect alignment (Figure 12-7 on page 165). The motor is then moved to tighten the belts.

The correct tension for a belt can be determined from the motor manufacturer's literature. A measurement can be made to find the force that is required to deflect the belt a distance equal to 1⁄64 of the belt span (Figure 12-8 on page 165). Depending upon the class of the belt cross section, representative values of the deflection are shown in Table 12-1 on page 165.

Cooling towers (Figure 12-9 on page 165) transfer heat from the condenser water to the outside air. Water from the condenser enters the cooling tower and falls through the tower in the form of droplets. Some of the water in the droplets evaporates (absorbing heat from the remaining water in the droplet), which cools the remaining water in the droplet. The amount of heat rejected by the cooling tower is controlled by bypassing water around the tower or controlling the air flow through the tower. See Unit 8 on variable frequency drives.

HERMETIC COMPRESSORS

A hermetic compressor (Figure 12-10 on page 166) includes a motor and drive that are sealed in a welded case containing the refrigerant and lubricating oil. These motors use the refrigerant from the compressor to cool the motor. The installation of hermetically sealed compressors is covered in *CEC Part 1,* Sections 28-700 to 28-714.

Conductors supplying hermetic compressors are based on the rated-load current of the compressor and Rule 28-106, that is, 125% of the full-load current of the motor.

Figure 12-4 Liquid chiller.

Overcurrent protection for hermetic compressors is based on locked-rotor current instead of full load current as is normally the case. Each conductor of a branch circuit supplying a hermetic compressor is required to have overcurrent protection rated or set at 50% of the motor's locked rotor current.

Overload protection for hermetic compressors must meet the requirements of Rules 28-302 to 28-306. When overload relays are used, they may be set to a maximum of 140% of the rated-load current of the compressor. If fuses are used as overload protection, they must not be larger than 125% of the rated full-load current of the compressor.

When the disconnect means is selected, both the locked-rotor current and the rated-load current are considered. For example, if a hermetic compressor has a rated-load current of 37.4 A (at 230 V) and a locked-rotor current of 250 A, the requirements of Rule 28-714 apply: that is, the disconnecting means must be capable of carrying 115% of the rated-load current of the motor on a continuous basis (37.4 × 1.15 = 40.01 A) and must be capable of interrupting the locked-rotor current of the motor (250 A).

A 230-V, three-phase motor with a rated-load current of 37.4 A exceeds the value given in *CEC Part 1,* Table 45, for a 10-hp motor but is less than the 42 A of a 15-hp motor. As a result, a disconnect means with a 15-hp rating would be required. Using the locked-rotor current of 250 A and comparing that to the locked-rotor current of a 15-hp motor (42 A × 600% = 252 A), it is found that a disconnecting means rated at 15 hp is acceptable.

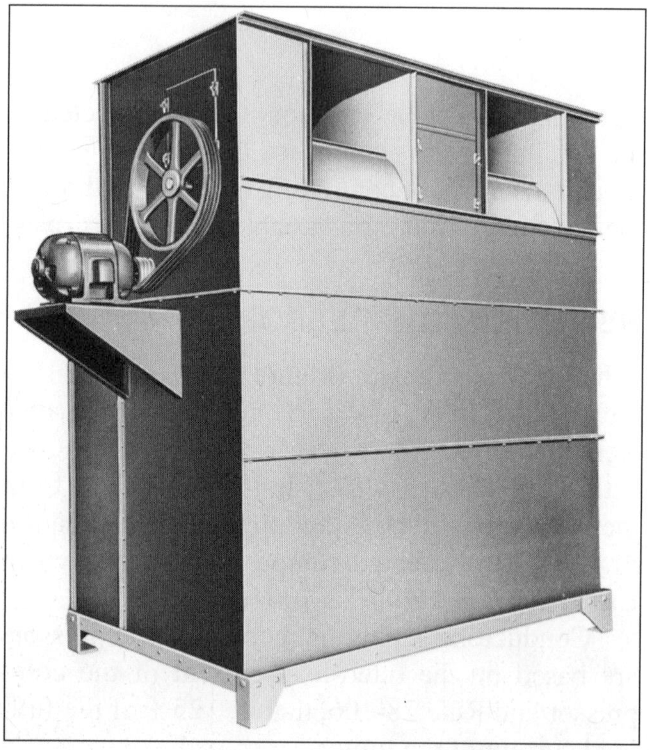

Figure 12-5A Fan coil units in the existing building.

Figure 12-5B Fan coil units in the addition.

Figure 12-6 Fin tube coil.

Belt Cross Section	Deflection Force in Pounds	
	Minimum	Maximum
A	2	3-1/2
B	2-1/2	6
C	6	12
D	13	25
E	25	36

Table 12-1 Values of belt deflections.

The Ventilator and Exhaust Systems

According to the plans and specifications, some ventilating units are to be installed and connected for operation. These units are located on the roof of the addition (see Sheet E4 of the plans). Each ventilating unit consists of a steel housing designed for mounting on a flat surface and a blower unit enclosed in the steel housing.

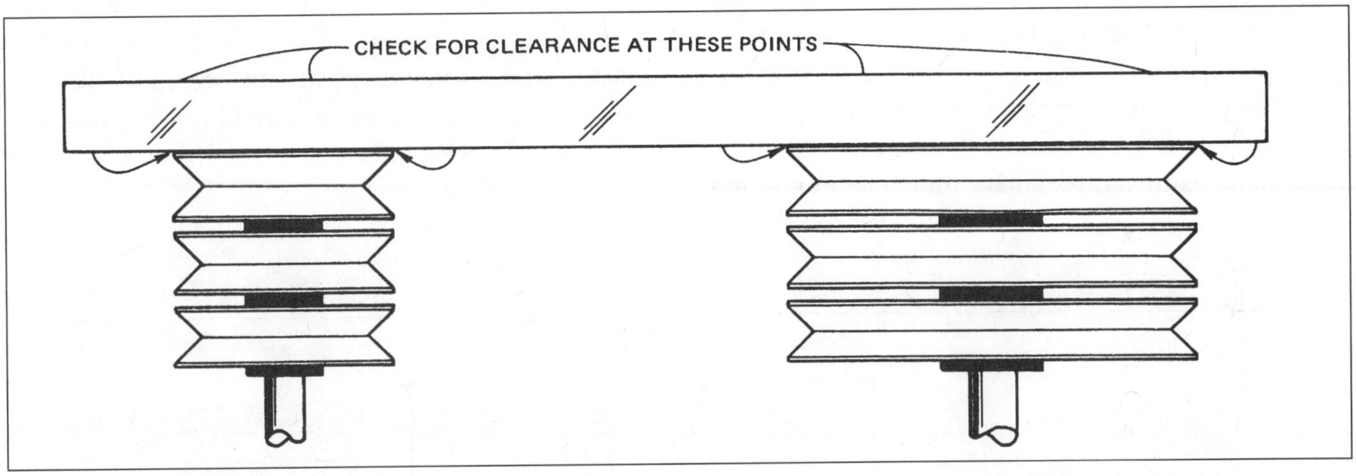

Figure 12-7 Aligning sheaves with straightedge.

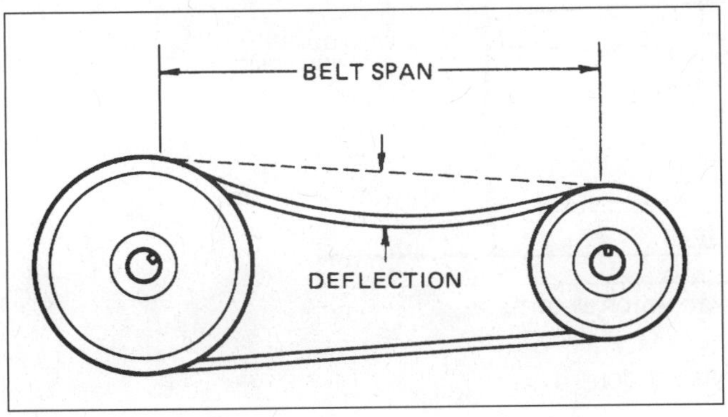

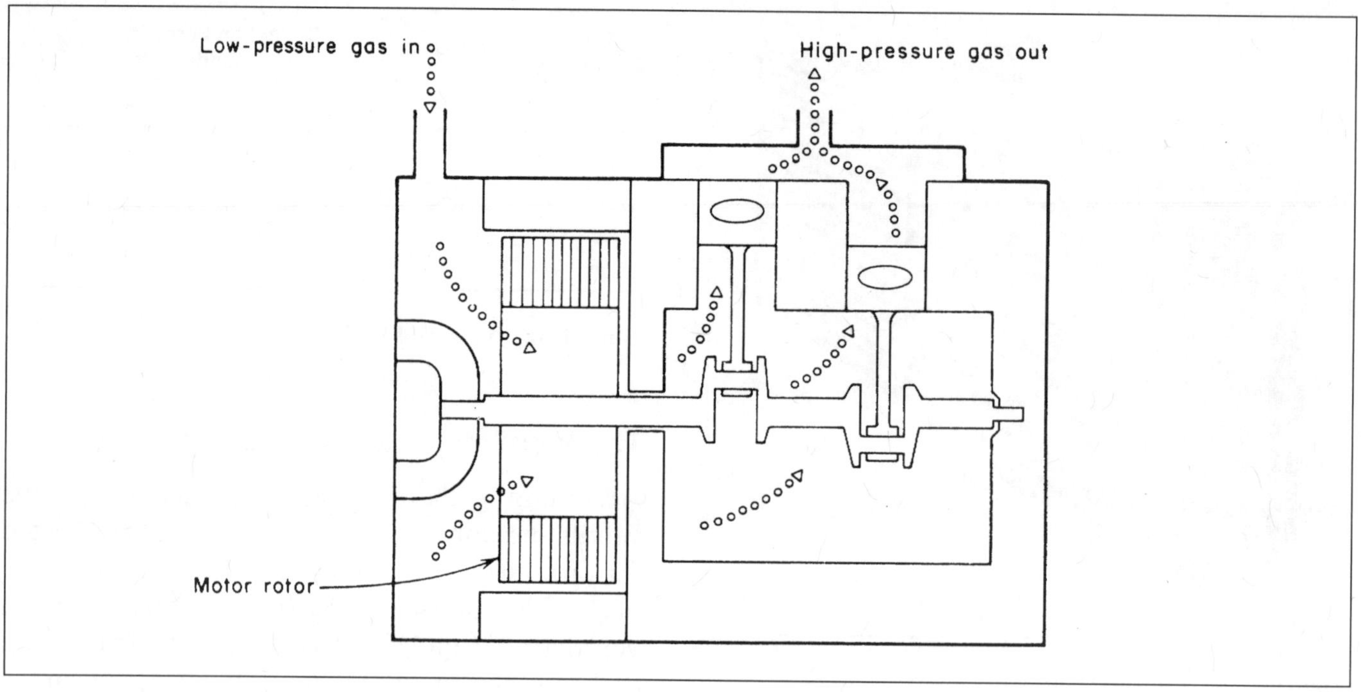

Figure 12-10 Hermetic compressor.

The typical exhaust blower unit shown in Figure 12-11 has a 3-hp motor driving a propeller-type fan through a V-belt drive This arrangement results in a quieter mode of operation than is obtainable using a direct drive unit. The motor and fan assembly are cushion-mounted to absorb vibration. As a result, the unit is almost noiseless during operation except for the sound of the rush of air. The fan rotates at a speed of 905 rpm and is rated at 17 300 ft^3 per minute (cfm) at a static air pressure of 0 in.

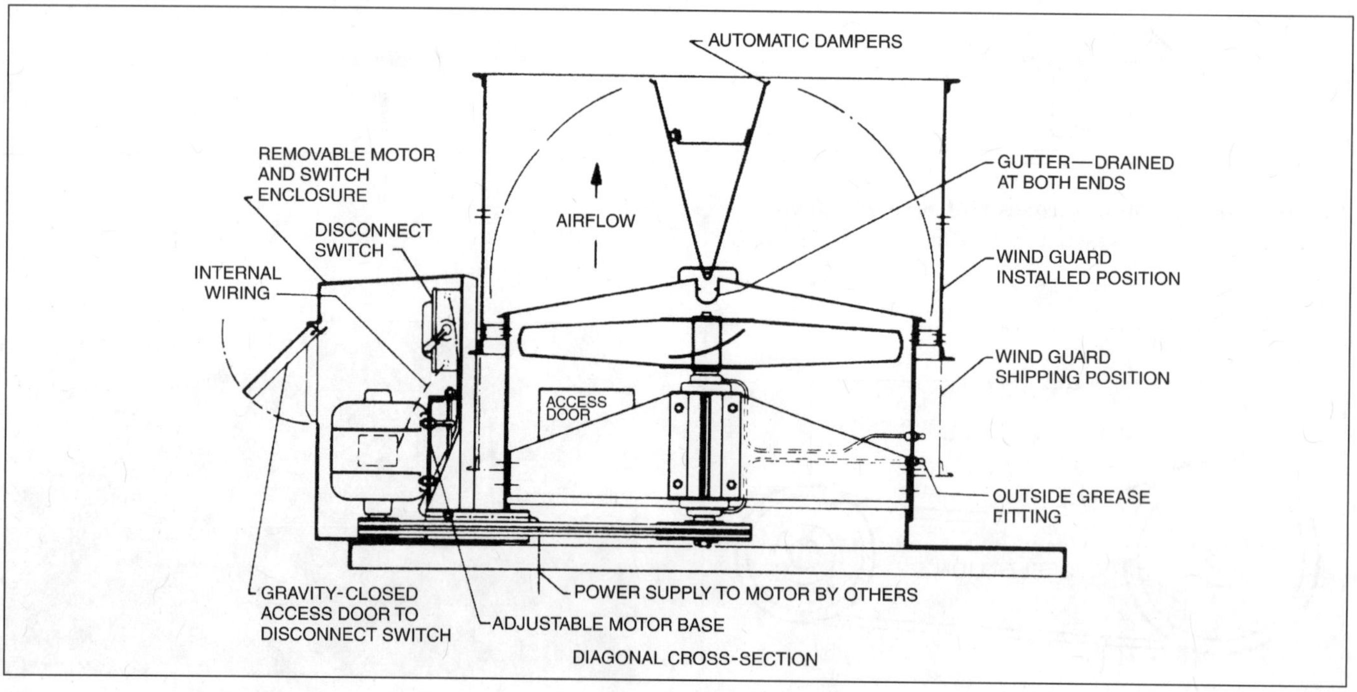

Figure 12-11 Exhaust blower.

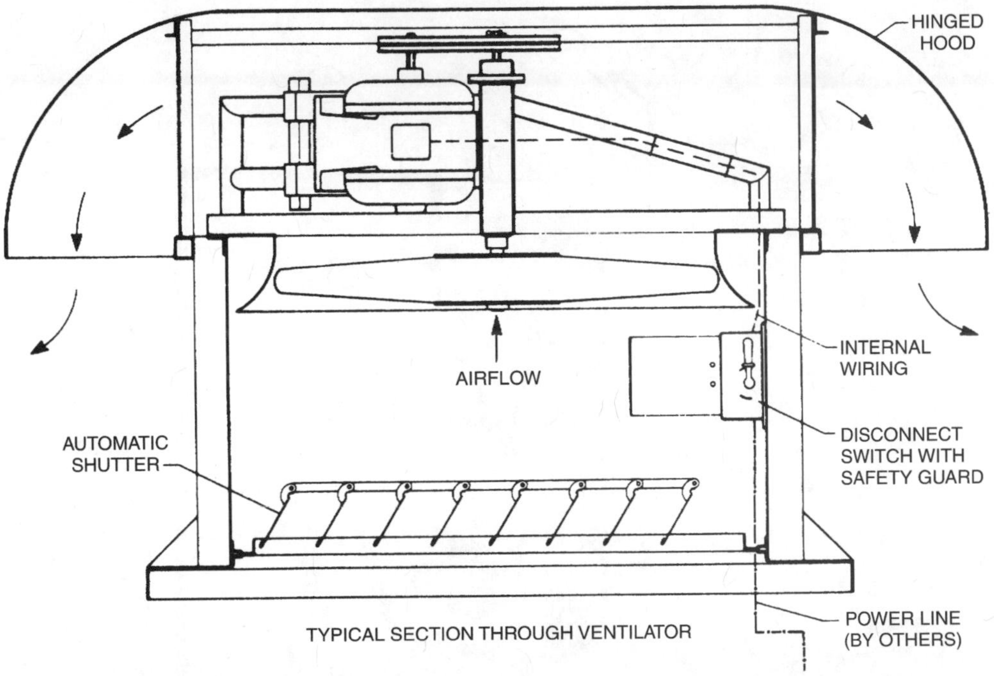

Figure 12-12 Ventilating blower.

A typical ventilating blower unit is shown in Figure 12-12. These blowers exhaust the air from the toilets and washrooms and locker room. The fan has a speed of 913 rpm and should be used with a static air pressure of less than 1 in.

The Precipitation Unit

Oil mist is present in the air of most large machine shops. The mist consists of tiny, almost microscopic, droplets of oil or coolant. High-speed machine tools such as boring mills, grinders, and turret lathes tend to pollute the surrounding air with an oil mist. A single high-speed grinder can give off nearly 38 L (10 gal) of coolant oil in the form of mist in an eight-hour period.

The oil mist in the air reduces visibility within the manufacturing area and leaves a coating or residue on any surrounding machinery and equipment. In addition, the mist may be the cause of skin and eye irritations, as well as throat and lung ailments among the workers.

One method of removing this pollutant is by the use of precipitation units such as the one shown in Figure 12-13 on page 168. These units with groups of machines or in a small package unit that can be installed at the individual machine causing the oil mist. Precipitation units can be installed directly behind, above, or beside a machine; however, a site at the rear of the machine is the most common location.

The specifications for the industrial building call for individual precipitation units to be installed at the rear of each vertical boring mill, turret lathe, and cylindrical grinder. Each precipitation unit occupies a floor area of 15 in (381 mm) by 23 in (584 mm). The unit is 55 in (1.4 m) in height and is mounted on a low, specially constructed stand. The unit has an air-handling capacity of 600 ft^3 per minute (17 m^3 per minute).

The basic operation of the precipitation unit is as follows: mounted at or near a high-speed machine tool, it draws the contaminated air from around the cutting or grinding operation, removes the oil mist and smoke as well as the odour, and returns the cleaned air to the shop space. The salvaged coolant oil is returned to the machine coolant supply reservoir and is reused.

This air-cleaning unit consists of a rugged steel cabinet, which can be installed easily. The entire

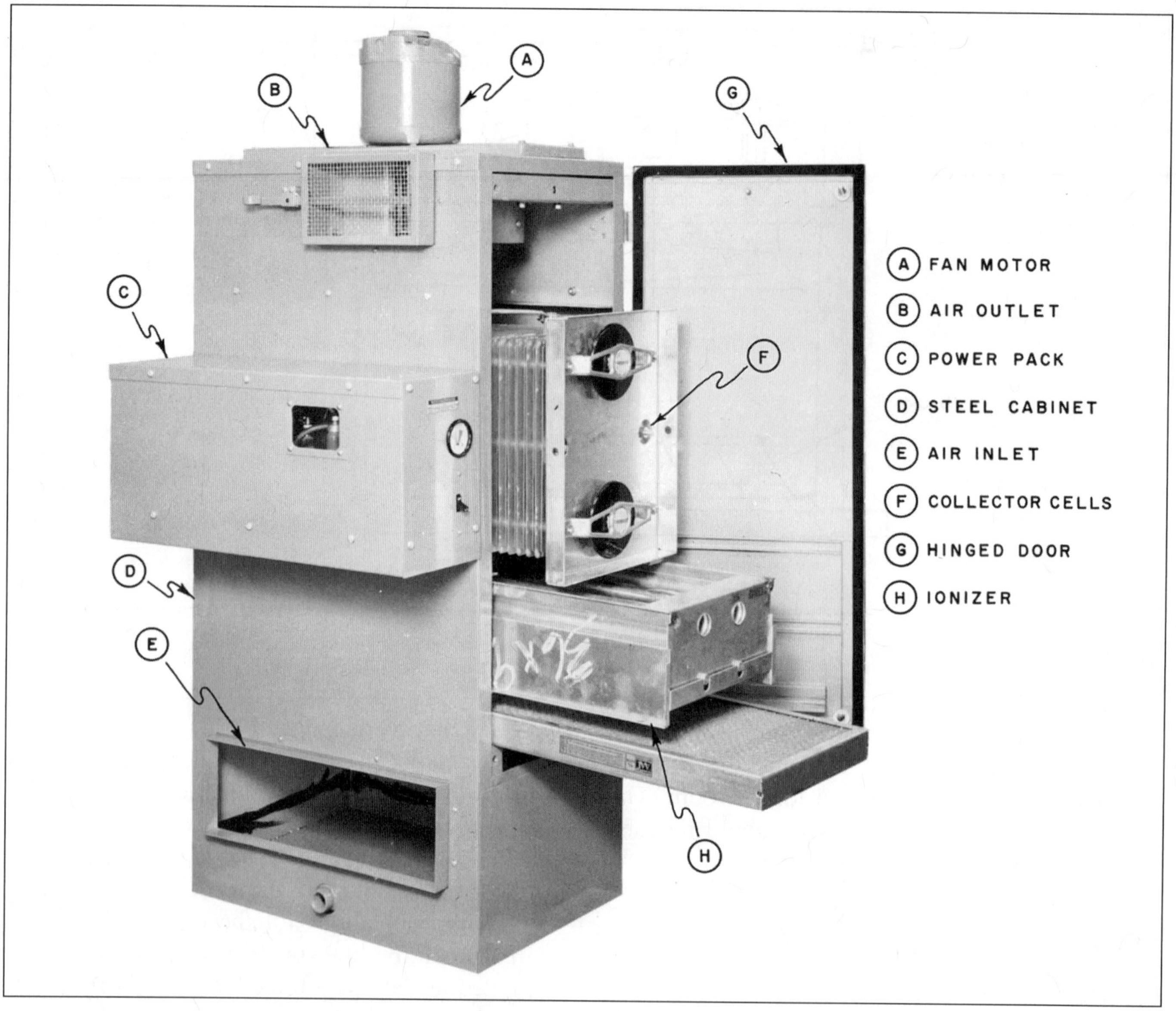

Figure 12-13 The precipitation oil mist control unit.

(with quick-acting fasteners) permits ready access to the unit. The cabinet contains collector cells, an ionizer, a power pack, and the fan assembly.

The Fan Assembly

The fan assembly consists of a single-inlet, multi-blade blower. The blower is a 1⁄4-hp 60-Hz motor connected to a 575-V, three-phase circuit (see Figure 12-14). In addition, the assembly contains a built-in volume damper to control the amount of air passing through the fan. The motor is totally enclosed and is mounted at the top of the unit in a vertical position. The motor requires no oiling.

The precipitation unit has an air inlet located near the bottom of the cabinet. This inlet is connected to the source of the oil mist or the hood of the machine. Flexible or fixed piping similar to aluminum stovepipe is used to make the connection. A connecting flange provides a means of attachment between the machine and the air inlet.

The air outlet is located near the top of the steel cabinet enclosure and is provided with a grille.

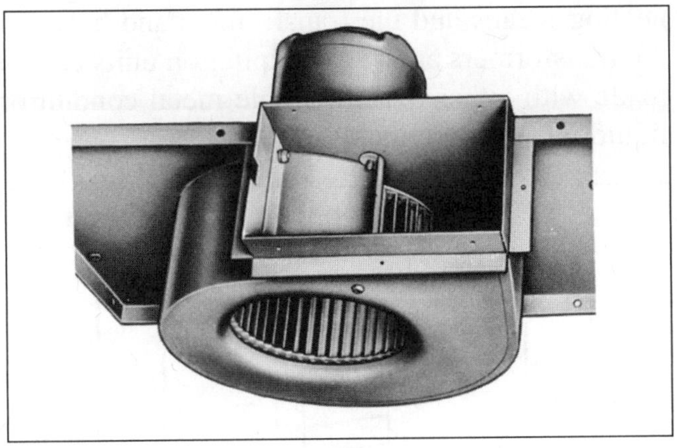

Figure 12-14 Fan assembly.

The Ionizer

The air moving into the precipitation unit passes through the ionizer (Figure 12-15). This component contains the tungsten ionizing wires and the grounded electrodes that place an electric charge on each particle of oil mist or smoke that passes through the ionizer.

The tungsten wires are held in a grid supported by large insulators. The wires are equipped with an antivibration bead that helps to prolong the life of the wire. The high-voltage DC charge on the wire is supplied by a power pack.

The Power Pack

The power pack, shown in Figure 12-16, houses the electronic components that convert the alternating current to the high-voltage DC power

Figure 12-16 The power pack.

required to activate the ionizer and the collector cells. The power pack can be installed on either side of the cabinet. Built-in safety switches provide complete protection from accidental contact with the live high-voltage parts. The power pack requires only 60 W.

The Collector Cells

The collector cells, Figure 12-17, gather the oil mist and smoke particles from the air. The cells are made of aluminum to resist corrosion. A single collector cell assembly contains both the charged and the grounded collector plates. There is more than 140 ft^2 (13 m^2) of plate surface in the precipitation unit. Each assembly can be removed from the unit for inspection or cleaning.

To reduce electrical losses and prevent leakage, each cell assembly has four large insulators, which support the high-voltage plate section and insulate it from the grounded frame. The insulators are

placed out of the way of the airstream to keep them clean and free of oil and smoke deposits. The possibility of arcing or flashover between the charged and the grounded plates is reduced because the plates are accurately spaced, held in position with precision machined spacers.

The Power Supply

The precipitation units require only a small amount of power. Thus, they can be connected to the same motor branch circuits that supply power to the machines with which they are to be used. Small, dry-type transformers serve as power packs for each machine. The single-phase transformer is rated for 0.1 kVA and 600 V to 120 V (Figure 12-18).

A transformer is attached to the back of each machine using a precipitation unit. Mounting holes for the transformer are drilled and tapped, and machine screws are used to attach the transformer. The connections between the disconnecting means and the transformers and between the transformers and the precipitation units can be made with either 0.5-in flexible metal conduit or liquidtight flexible metal conduit.

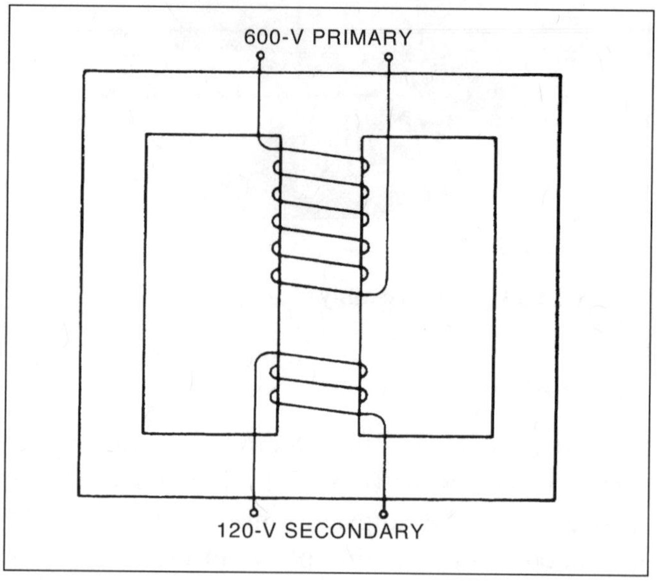

Figure 12-18 Schematic diagram of transformer.

REVIEW

All answers should be written in complete sentences, calculations should be shown in detail, and Code references should be cited when appropriate.

1. How many conductors should be installed from the motor control centre to the chilled water circulating pump CHWP-01? What size would they be?

For the following questions, the nameplate information for a hermetic refrigerant motor-compressor unit is given. In each case, the branch-circuit protection is located in an equipment room remote from the cooling unit. The conductor size and type need to be determined, along with the disconnect switch rating. Voltage drop is a critical consideration and should be kept within recommended limits.

2. The system voltage is a 208Y/120-V single-phase. The branch-circuit conductors will be 75 ft long.
   (a) Conductor size
   (b) Conductor type
   (c) Switch rating
   (d) Voltage drop

   Voltage 208 to 230 Phase 1

   Use copper conductors only.

   Minimum Circuit Ampacity 23.3 A

Compressor RLA 17.6	LRA 87
Fuse Max. Amps 40	Hz 60
Max. HACR Circuit Breaker	40-A
Fan Motor FLA 1.3	hp 1/6

3. The system voltage is a 208Y/120-V three-phase. The branch-circuit conductors will be 100 ft long.
   (a) Conductor size
   (b) Conductor type
   (c) Switch rating
   (d) Voltage drop

Voltage 208 to 230	Phase 1 Hz 60
Minimum Circuit Amps	38
Compressor RLA 29.1	LRA 141
Branch-Circuit Selection Current	29.1
Maximum Fuse	60/50 A
Maximum HACR Circuit Breaker	60/50 A
Fan Motor FLA 1.9	hp 1⁄4

4. Give the purpose and describe the function of the precipitation unit.

UNIT 13

System Protection

OBJECTIVES

After studying this unit, the student should be able to:

- identify the devices used to provide system protection
- explain the operation of circuit breakers, fuses, and ground fault protective devices
- make the proper adjustments of those devices with adjustable elements
- determine when selective coordination is achieved

SYSTEM PROTECTION

The previous units of this text described numerous devices and methods of providing system protection. This unit evaluates the complete power protective system to determine whether it complies fully with the recommendations of the *CEC*.

Ground-Fault Protection in a Coordinated System

CEC Rule 14-102 specifies that ground fault protection shall be provided on certain electrical equipment. Ground fault protection systems are *required* under the following conditions:

- For 1000 A or larger, solidly grounded circuits of more than 150 V to ground but less than 750 V phase to phase
- Ground fault protection set to operate at a maximum of 1200 A
- The maximum time delay for the ground fault device to operate must not exceed 1 second for fault levels equal to or greater than 3000 A

Ground fault protection systems are *recommended* under the following conditions:

- For feeder and branch-circuit protection
- For service of less than 1200 A where it is solidly grounded and for more than 150 V to ground not exceeding 750 V phase to phase

Of equal importance to the requirement for ground fault protection is the need to coordinate the proper selective overcurrent protection. To achieve coordination, the electrician must be knowledgeable with regard to the operating characteristics of the various types of protective devices. Thus, after the proper selection of equipment is made, the electrician must be able to check and make adjustments where necessary to achieve coordination (Figure 13-1).

Selective coordination means that when an overload or fault condition occurs, only the part of the electrical system that is in jeopardy is disconnected. For example, a fault on a branch circuit causes the branch-circuit protective device to open. At the same time, all of the other protective devices remain closed. Similarly, an overload on a

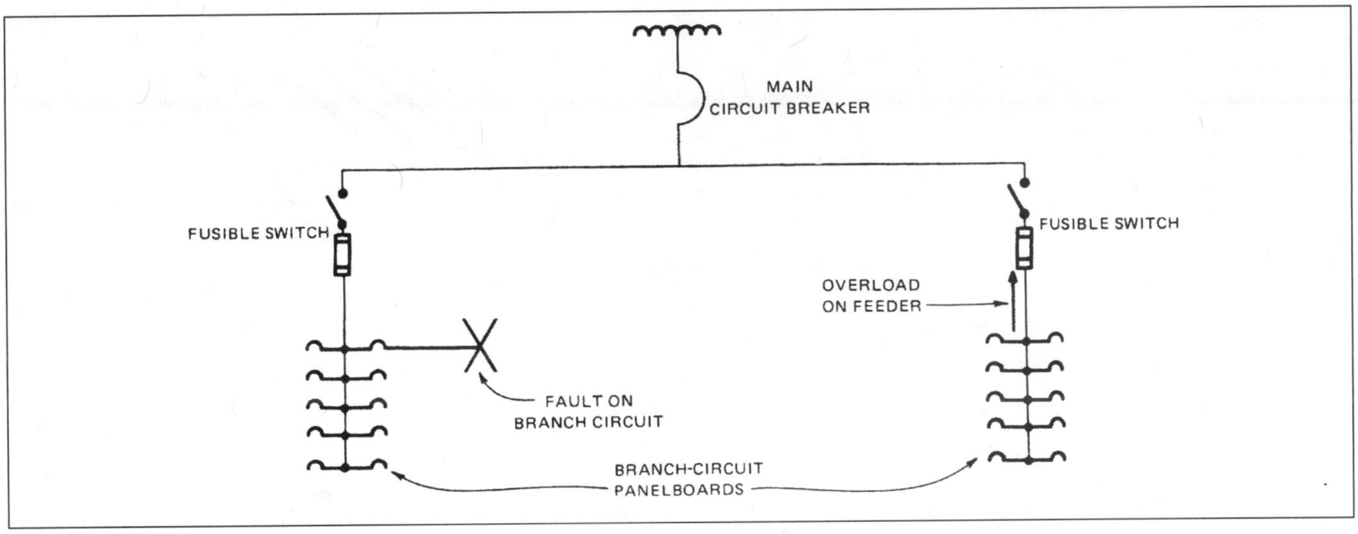

Figure 13-1 Selective overcurrent protection coordination.

feeder causes only the feeder overcurrent protective device to open.

The three basic types of devices involved in selective coordination are circuit breakers, fuses, and ground-fault protectors. Circuit breakers and fuses are installed in the ungrounded conductors of an electrical system to protect the system by monitoring the current in those conductors. These protective devices disconnect the conductors from the power source if a specified abnormal condition occurs (Figure 13-2 on page 174).

A ground fault protective device consists of a ground fault sensor (current transformer) and a relay. All of the phase conductors and the neutral of the system are installed through the centre of the sensor. As long as the current in these conductors is balanced (the normal condition), the relay is static. However, if one of the conductors makes contact with ground, the resulting current through the sensor is unbalanced.

If this fault has sufficient magnitude and lasts for a long enough period, the relay sends a signal to the circuit protective device, which then opens the circuit. The following detailed description of the operating characteristics of these devices is presented to help the student gain an understanding of the devices' operation.

CIRCUIT BREAKERS

Circuit breakers are categorized by the method guish the arc) when the contacts open. The three major types of circuit breakers are air, oil, and vacuum. Regardless of the method employed to extinguish an arc, circuit breakers sense circuit current in one of two ways. One method of sensing circuit current is through the production of heat. These breakers are often referred to as thermal circuit breakers. Thermal circuit breakers generally use some type of heating element inserted in series with the load (Figure 13-3 on page 174). The heater is located close to a bimetallic strip. The bimetallic strip is mechanically connected to the movable contacts of the circuit breaker.

When there is a current through the heater, it causes the bimetallic strip to bend or warp. If the current is higher than a predetermined limit, the bimetallic strip will warp far enough to cause the contacts to snap open.

Since the action of the circuit breaker depends on heating a bimetallic strip, there is some amount of time delay before the circuit opens. The amount of time delay depends on the amount of overcurrent. If the amount of overcurrent is small, it may take several minutes before the circuit breaker opens its contacts. A large overcurrent will cause the contacts to open much faster. A single-pole thermal circuit breaker is shown in Figure 13-4. The schematic symbol generally used to represent a thermal-type circuit breaker is shown in Figure 13-5 on page 175.

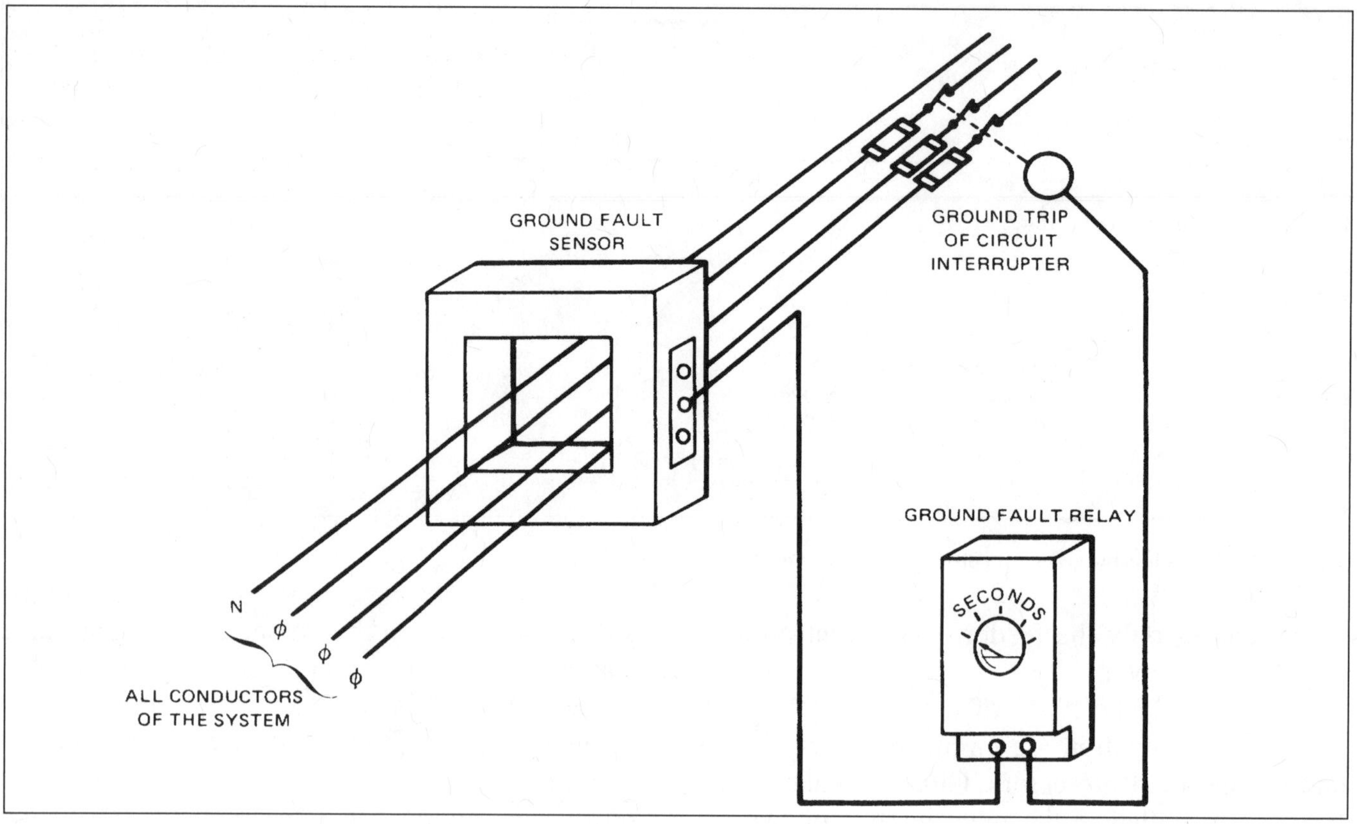

Figure 13-2 Ground fault protection for a three-phase system.

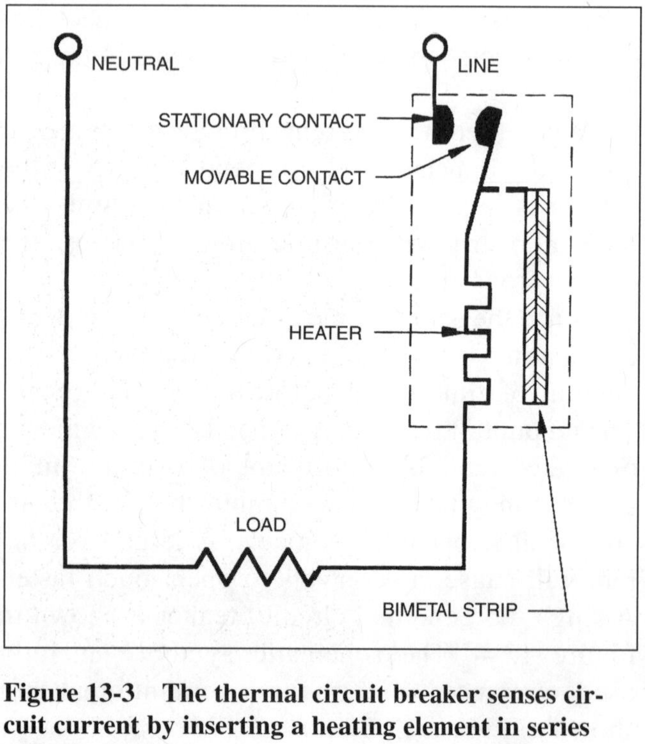

Figure 13-3 The thermal circuit breaker senses circuit current by inserting a heating element in series with the load.

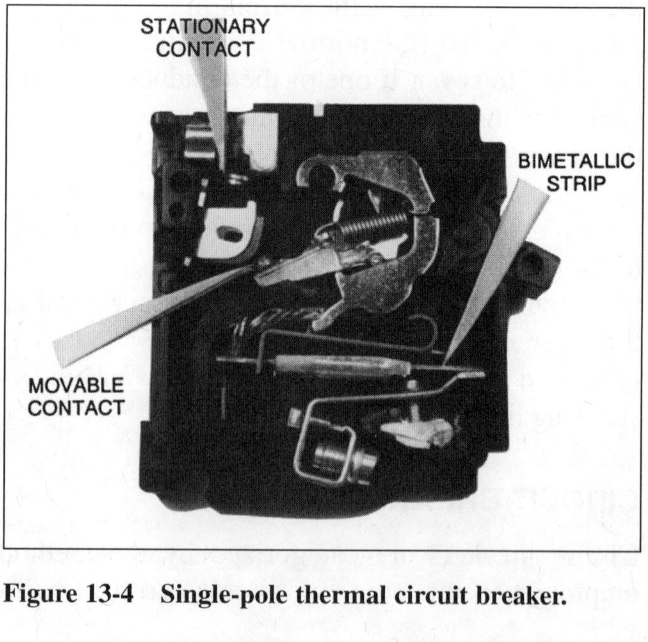

Figure 13-4 Single-pole thermal circuit breaker.

Magnetic Circuit Breakers

The second method of sensing circuit current is accomplished by connecting a coil in series with the load (Figure 13-6). As current flows through the circuit, a magnetic field is established around the coil. The magnetic field attracts the metal arm of a solenoid. If the magnetic field becomes intense enough, the metal arm mechanically opens the contacts of the circuit breaker. Circuit breakers that operate on this principle are referred to as magnetic circuit breakers. A three-pole magnetic circuit breaker is shown in Figure 13-7.

The internal construction of the magnetic circuit breaker is shown in Figure 13-8 on page 176. In Figure 13-9 on page 176, one of the solenoids has been removed. This permits the series coil to be seen. The schematic symbol generally used to represent a magnetic circuit breaker is shown in Figure 13-10 on page 176.

Since magnetic-type circuit breakers do not depend on heating a bimetallic strip, there is very little time delay in the opening of the contacts when an overload occurs. For this reason, they are often referred to as instantaneous trip circuit breakers.

There are some types of circuit breakers that employ both thermal and magnetic current sensors. These circuit breakers are known as thermomagnetic circuit breakers. The schematic symbol generally used to denote the use of a thermomagnetic breaker is shown in Figure 13-11 on page 176.

Circuit-Breaker Current Ratings

Circuit breakers actually have two different current ratings: the *trip* rating and the *interrupt* rating. The trip current rating is the amount of current that should cause the circuit breaker to open its contacts when it is exceeded. Trip current ratings range from 15 A to 6000 A.

The interrupt rating indicates the maximum amount of current a circuit breaker is intended to interrupt when its contacts open. The amount of current that will flow during a short-circuit condition is determined by two factors:

1. The circuit voltage
2. The circuit impedance

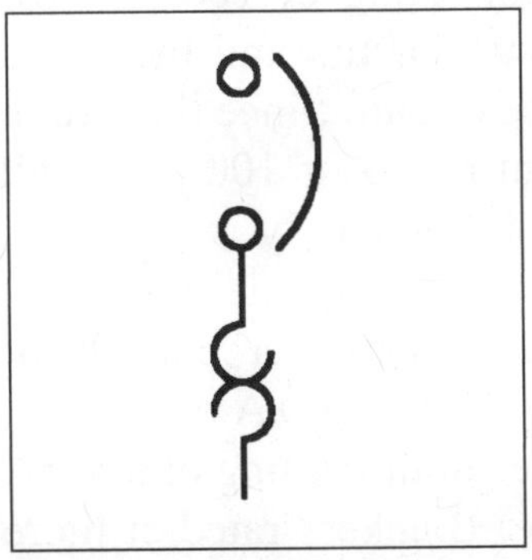

Figure 13-5 Schematic symbol used to represent a single-pole thermal circuit

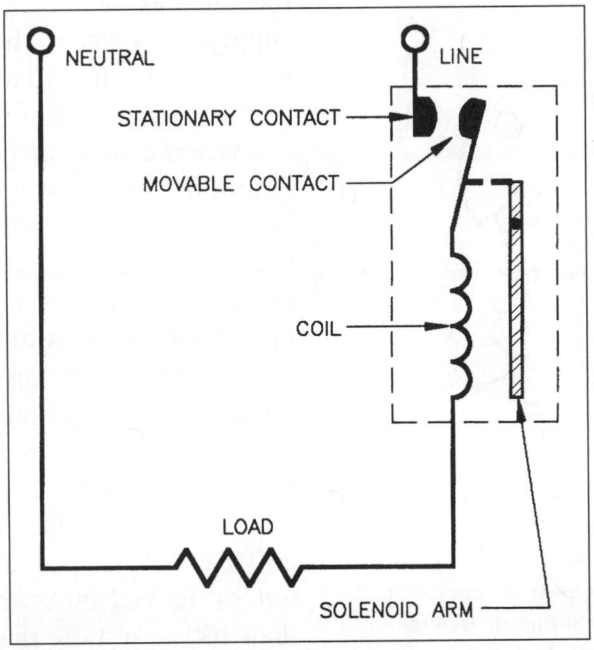

Figure 13-6 The magnetic circuit breaker senses circuit current by inserting a coil in series with

Figure 13-7 Three-pole mag-

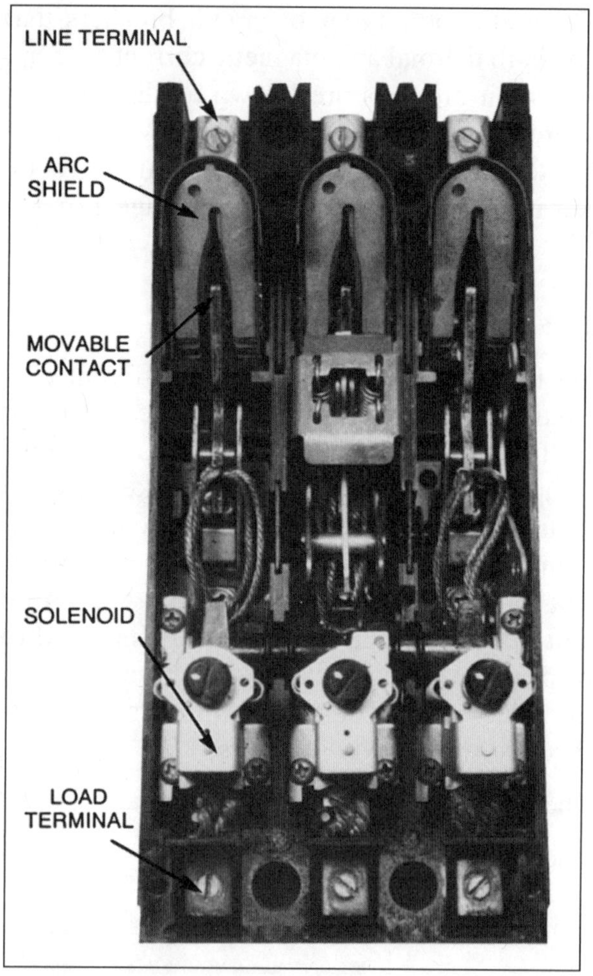

Figure 13-8 Internal construction of a three-pole magnetic circuit breaker.

Figure 13-9 Series coil of a magnetic circuit breaker.

Figure 13-10 Schematic symbol generally used to represent a magnetic circuit breaker.

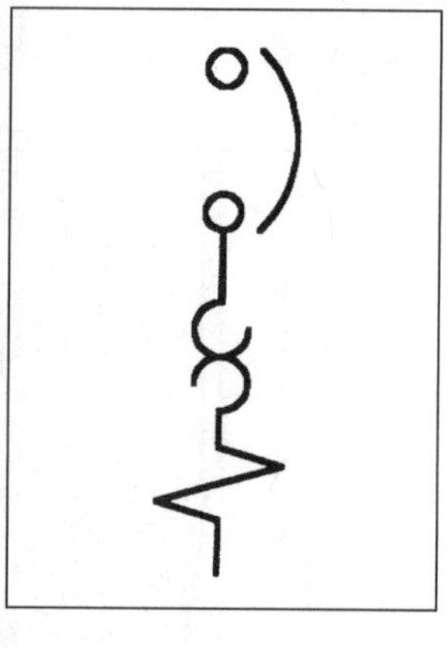

Figure 13-11 Schematic symbol generally used to represent a thermomagnetic circuit breaker.

The circuit impedance is determined by factors such as the kVA capacity of the transformers supplying power to the branch circuit, the size of wire used in the circuit, the contact resistance of connections, and so on.

When a short or grounded circuit occurs, the circuit breaker must be capable of interrupting the current. Assume, for example, that a circuit breaker has a trip current rating of 100 A. Now assume that a short circuit occurs and there is a current of 15 000 A in the circuit. Since the circuit breaker has a trip current rating of 100 A, it will open its contacts almost immediately.

For the circuit breaker to stop the current, it must be capable of interrupting a current of 15 000 A. Circuit breakers rated 100 A or less and 250 V or less have an interrupting rating of 5000 A unless marked otherwise. Breakers rated at more than 100 A or more than 250 V will have an interrupting rating of 10 000 A unless marked otherwise. In Figure 13-12, notice that the interrupting rating is specified as 10 000 A.

When it is necessary to replace a circuit breaker, always make sure of the interrupt rating. If a circuit breaker with an interrupt rating of 5000 A is used to replace a breaker with an interrupt rating of 10 000 A, a short circuit could cause a great deal of damage both to equipment and to individuals.

Shunt Trips and Auxiliary Switches

Some circuit breakers contain a small solenoid coil known as a *shunt trip*. Shunt trips are used to open the circuit breaker contacts by energizing the solenoid from an external source.

Assume, for example, that it is desirable to disconnect the power to a circuit if the temperature rises above a certain level. If the circuit breaker protecting the circuit contains a shunt trip, a thermostat can be connected in series with the solenoid. If the temperature rises above the desired level, the thermostat contact will close and energize the coil (Figure 13-13). When the coil energizes, the circuit-breaker contacts will open and disconnect power to the circuit. A three-pole circuit breaker containing a shunt trip and auxiliary switch is shown in Figure 13-14. The shunt trip connection for the circuit breaker is shown in Figure 13-15 on page 178.

Some circuit breakers contain an auxiliary switch as shown in Figure 13-14. The auxiliary switch is a small micro-limit switch whose contacts

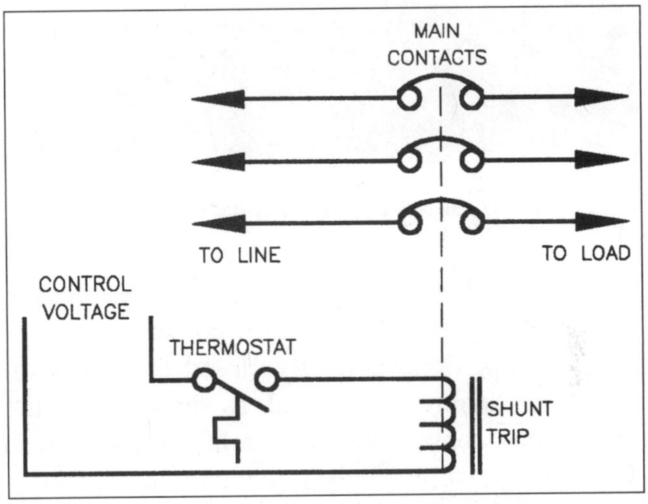

Figure 13-13 A thermostat is used to disconnect power to the circuit if the temperature rises to a certain point.

Figure 13-12 Circuit breaker interrupt rating of 10 000 A.

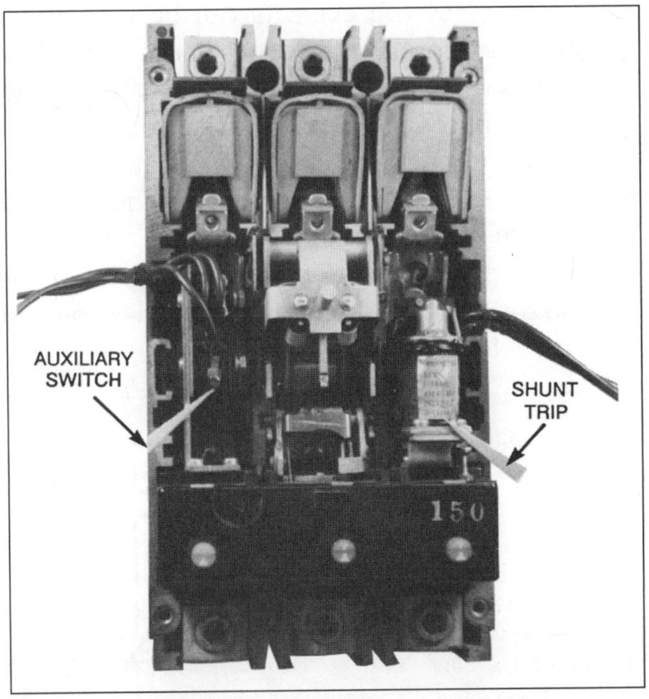

Figure 13-14 Circuit breaker with shunt trip and auxiliary switch.

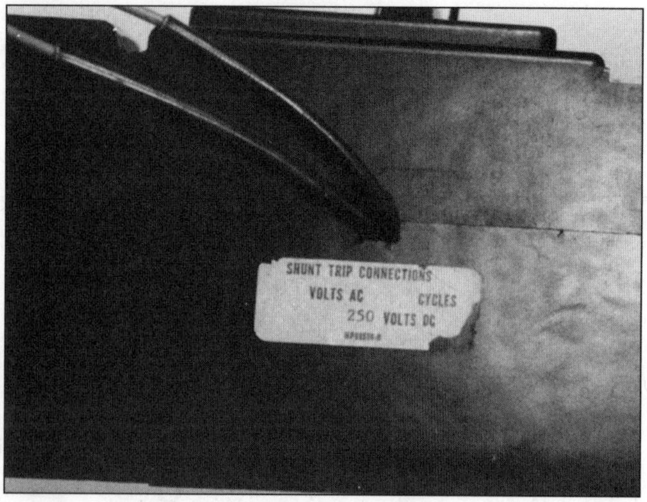

Figure 13-15 Shunt trip connection.

are controlled by the action of the circuit breaker. The auxiliary switch generally contains a set of normally open and normally closed contacts connected to a common terminal, as shown in Figure 13-16. The contacts are shown in the position in which they will be when the circuit breaker is turned off, or open. When the circuit breaker is turned on, or closed, the auxiliary switch contacts will change position. The normally closed contact will open and the normally open contact will close.

Auxiliary switch contacts can be used for a variety of purposes. In some instances, if the circuit breaker should open, it may be desirable to disconnect power to some other control device on a different circuit. In another application, if the breaker should open, the auxiliary contacts may be used to illuminate an indicator light on the operator's panelboard. The auxiliary switch connection for a three-pole circuit breaker is shown in Figure 13-17.

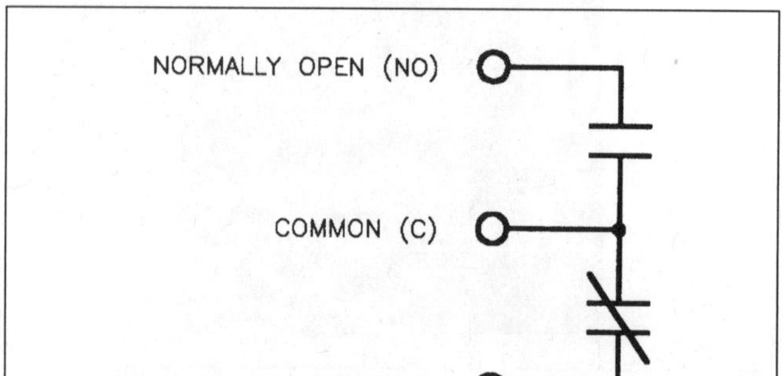

Figure 13-16 Auxiliary switch contacts.

Figure 13-17 Auxiliary switch connection.

Air Circuit Breakers

Air circuit breakers are so named because they utilize air as the insulating medium to break the arc when contacts open. They can be divided into three basic types:

1. Moulded case circuit breakers
2. Low-voltage power circuit breakers
3. Medium-voltage circuit breakers

Regardless of the type of air circuit breaker employed, all have one similar characteristic: they use air as a medium to extinguish an arc. When contacts separate to interrupt the current, an arc is produced that contains a great deal of heat. The farther apart the contacts become, the longer the arc becomes and the greater the cooling effect. Convection airflow will cause the arc to rise, Figure 13-18.

Moulded Case Circuit Breakers

Moulded case circuit breakers are used in low-voltage (600 V or less), low-current circuits. They are characterized by the use of a moulded case, which results in minimum space requirements. They are used to protect small motor, lighting, and appliance circuits.

Circuit breakers intended for lower voltage and current ratings often depend on the distance between

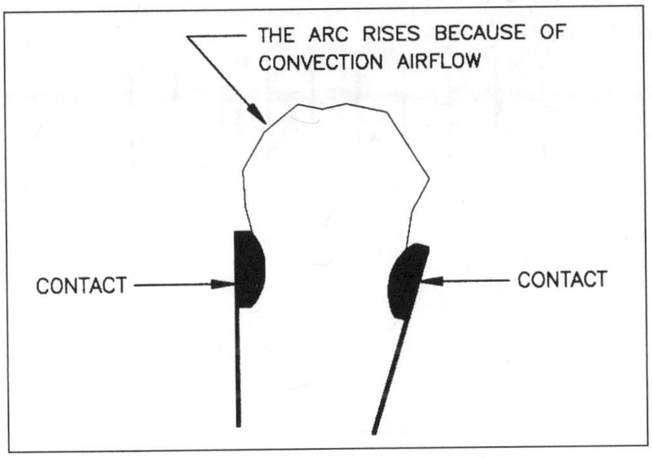

Figure 13-18 An arc is produced when contacts open.

the contacts being sufficient to stretch the arc far enough to extinguish it. Circuit breakers intended for use on higher-voltage circuits often employ other devices to help extinguish an arc. One of these devices is the *splitter*, which consists of metal or insulated plates located at the top of the contacts, Figure 13-19. Their function is to permit hot gases to escape and lengthen the path of the arc so the cooling effect is increased. The longer arc path weakens the arc to the point that it is eventually extinguished. A two-pole moulded case circuit breaker with an arc splitter is shown in Figure 13-20. The arc splitter is shown outside the circuit breaker in Figure 13-21.

Low-Voltage Power Circuit Breakers

Low-voltage power circuit breakers are generally constructed with a metal case. They can be obtained in case sizes that range from 100 A to 6000 A, and can have trip current ratings that range from 15 A to 6000 A. Since they are intended to interrupt higher currents, the contact

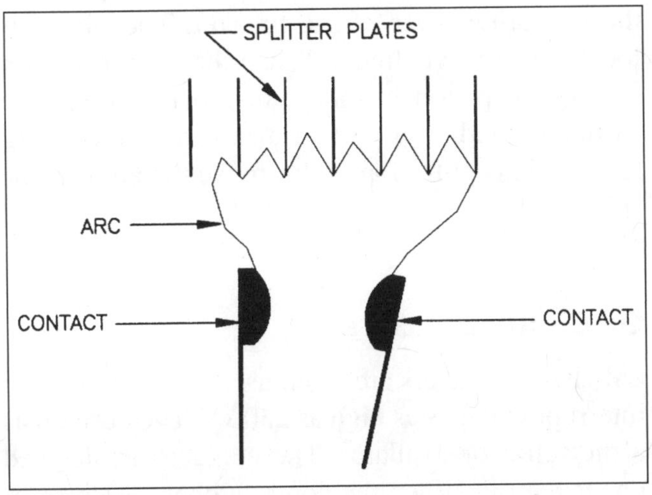

Figure 13-19 Splitter plates lengthen the arc, which

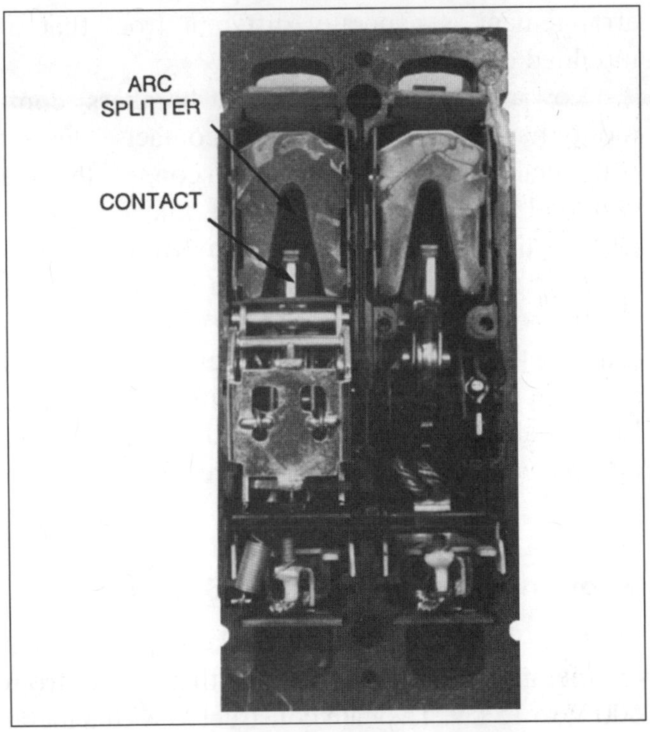

Figure 13-20 Two-pole moulded case circuit breaker with arc splitter.

Figure 13-21 The arc splitter is constructed of indi-

arrangement is generally different from that of moulded case circuit breakers.

Low-voltage power circuit breakers commonly have two separate sets of contacts. One set is the main contacts and is used to connect the line and load together. The second set, the arcing contacts, is used to direct the arc away from the main contacts (see Figure 13-22). The arcing contacts are further assisted by an *arc horn*, which aids in drawing the arc away from the arcing contacts and also helps stretch the arc. A splitter is generally located above the arc horn, which breaks the arc into pieces to extinguish it (Figure 13-23).

Medium-Voltage Air Circuit Breakers

Medium-voltage air circuit breakers are intended to operate on system voltages that range from 600 V to 15 kV. They are constructed with a metal case and generally contain *blow-out coils* and a *puffer*, as well as a splitter and an arc horn to help extinguish the arc.

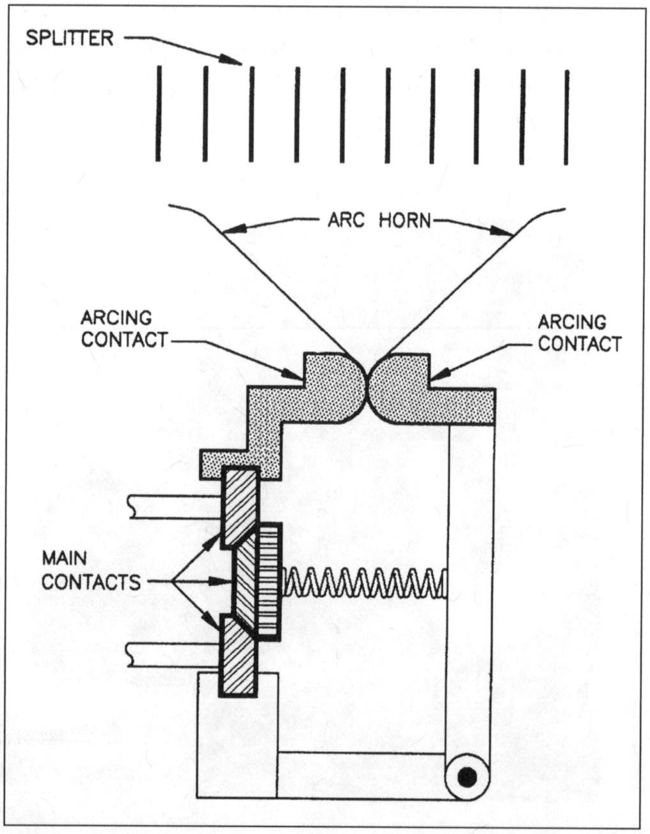

Figure 13-22 Low-voltage power circuit breakers generally contain two sets of contacts and an arc horn.

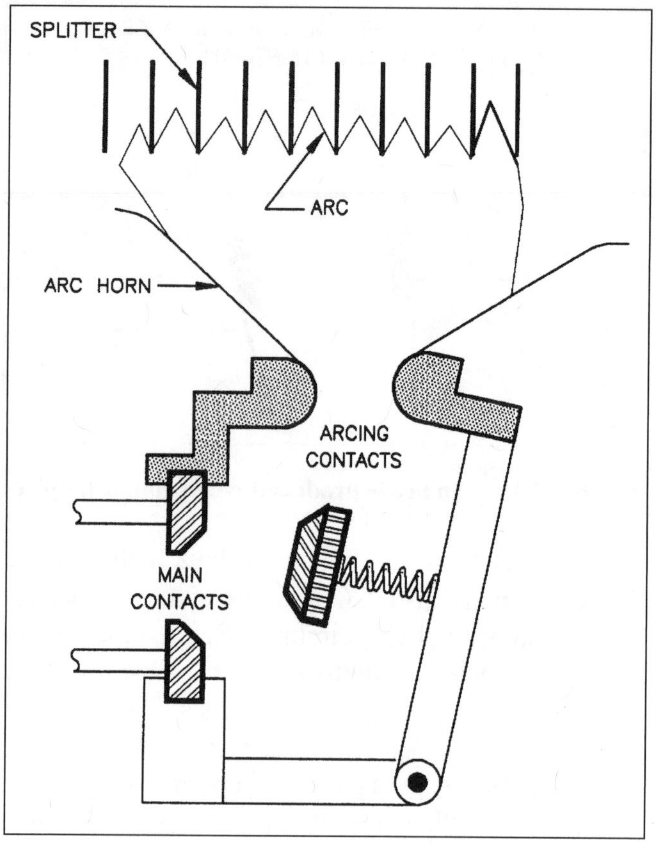

Figure 13-23 The arc horn draws the arc away from the arcing contacts.

Blow-out coils are connected in series with the arcing contacts so that current flows through them when the main contacts open. The current through the coils produces a magnetic field, which attracts the arc and helps to move it into the splitter. The puffer is constructed by attaching a small piston to the operating lever of the breaker. The piston is located inside a cylinder. When the circuit breaker opens, the piston is forced to move through the cylinder, sending a puff of air in the direction of the arc. This puff of air helps move the arc into the splitter.

Oil Circuit Breakers

Oil circuit breakers are often used in substations to interrupt voltages as high as 230 kV. They use oil as a dielectric or insulator. The contacts are located under the oil. When the contacts open, the heat of the arc causes the surrounding oil to decompose and form a gas. The gas extinguishes the arc.

There are two basic types of oil circuit breakers, the *full tank* or *dead tank* type and the *low oil* or *oil poor* type. The dead tank type is the oldest and is generally used for voltages above 13.8 kV. The construction of a typical dead tank circuit breaker is shown in Figure 13-24. The dead tank circuit breaker receives its name from the fact that the tank is at ground potential and insulated from the live parts by the dielectric oil. The circuit breaker shown is a double-break type containing of a set of main contacts and arcing contacts. The movable parts of both the main and arcing contacts are controlled by an actuator rod, which is manually operated.

Oil poor circuit breakers are manufactured in several different styles. The *plain-break* type relies on the surrounding oil and the pressure generated by the production of gas to control the arc when the contacts open (Figure 13-25). The pressure is eventually vented between the case and the movable contact. Another type of low oil circuit breaker is often referred to as a *vented* type and is designed with vents that permit the pressure produced by the formation of gas to exit the arc chamber (Figure 13-26). Another type of low oil circuit breaker

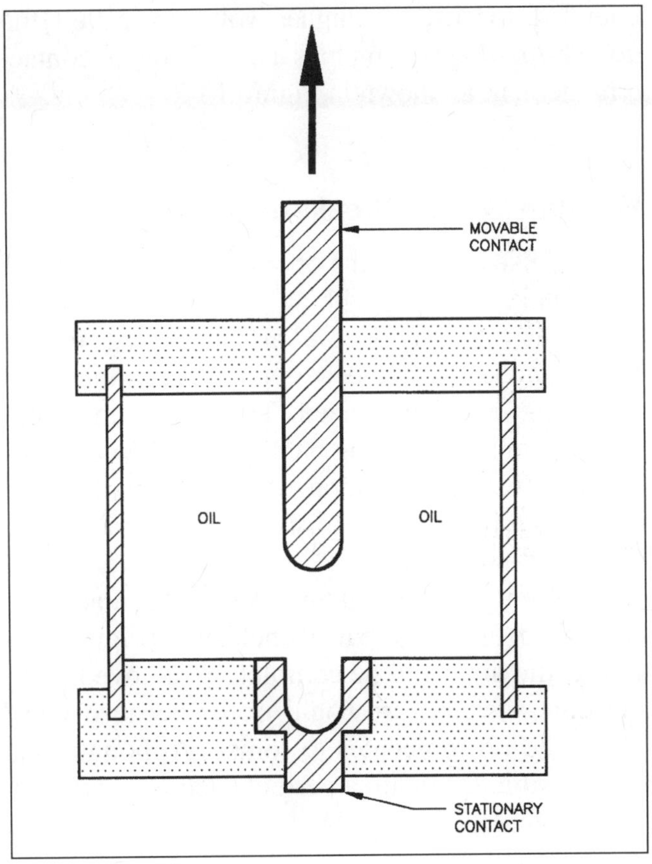

Figure 13-25 Plain-break low oil type circuit breaker.

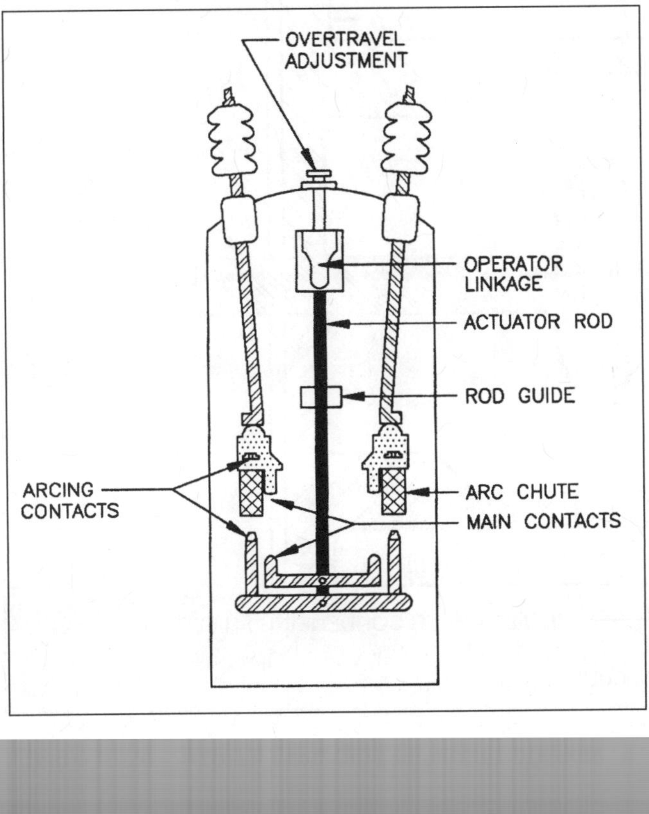

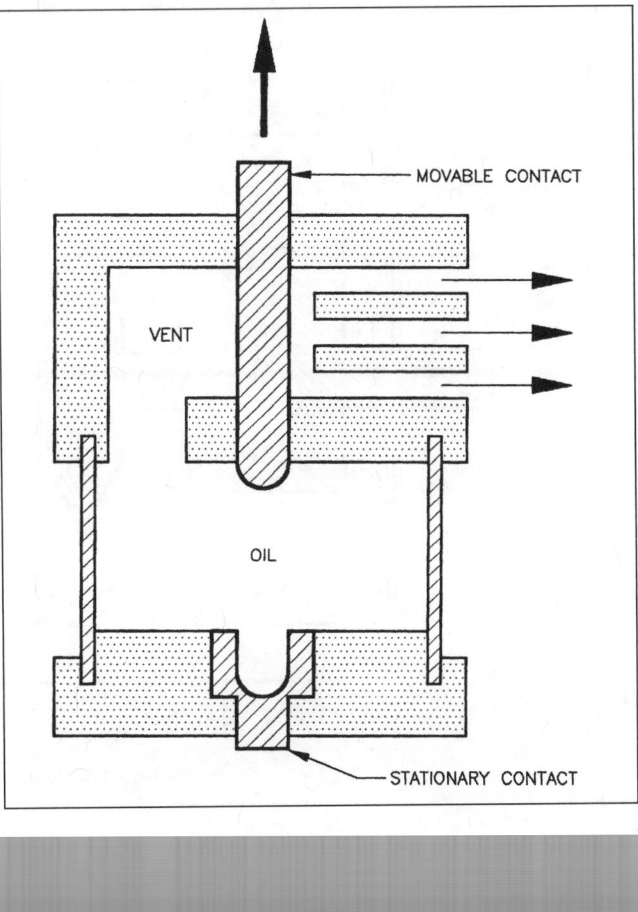

intended for use on higher voltages, called the *double-break* type, employs a double-break contact arrangement as shown in Figure 13-27.

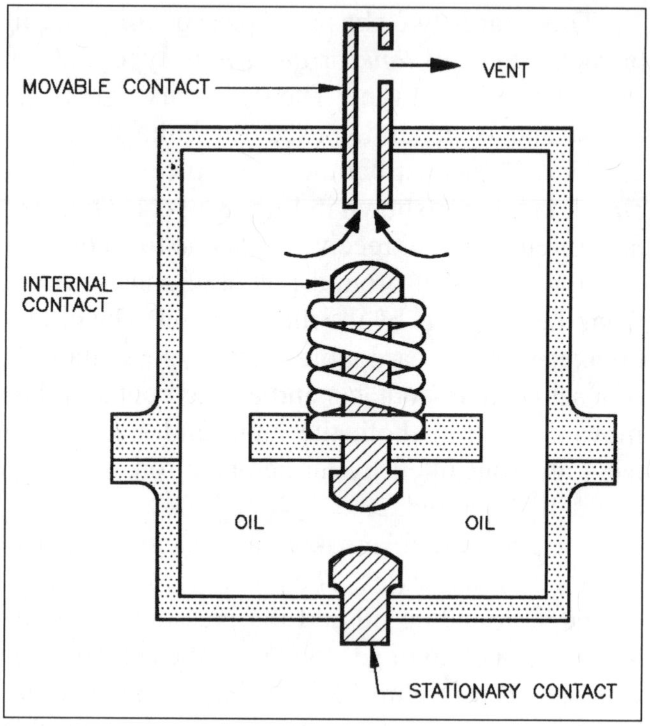

Figure 13-27 Typical double-break low oil circuit breaker.

Vacuum Circuit Breakers

An understanding of the operation of vacuum circuit breakers begins with an understanding of the mechanics of an electric arc occurring in air. When an electric arc occurs in air, gas molecules in the air become ionized. These ionized molecules form a conducting path for the flow of electrons. It is the ionization of gas molecules that makes the job of extinguishing an electric arc in air so difficult.

In the vacuum circuit breaker, the contacts are contained inside a sealed enclosure (Figure 13-28). If the air could be completely removed from the container, no arc could occur because there would be no molecules to ionize. Although it is not possible to obtain a perfect vacuum, very few

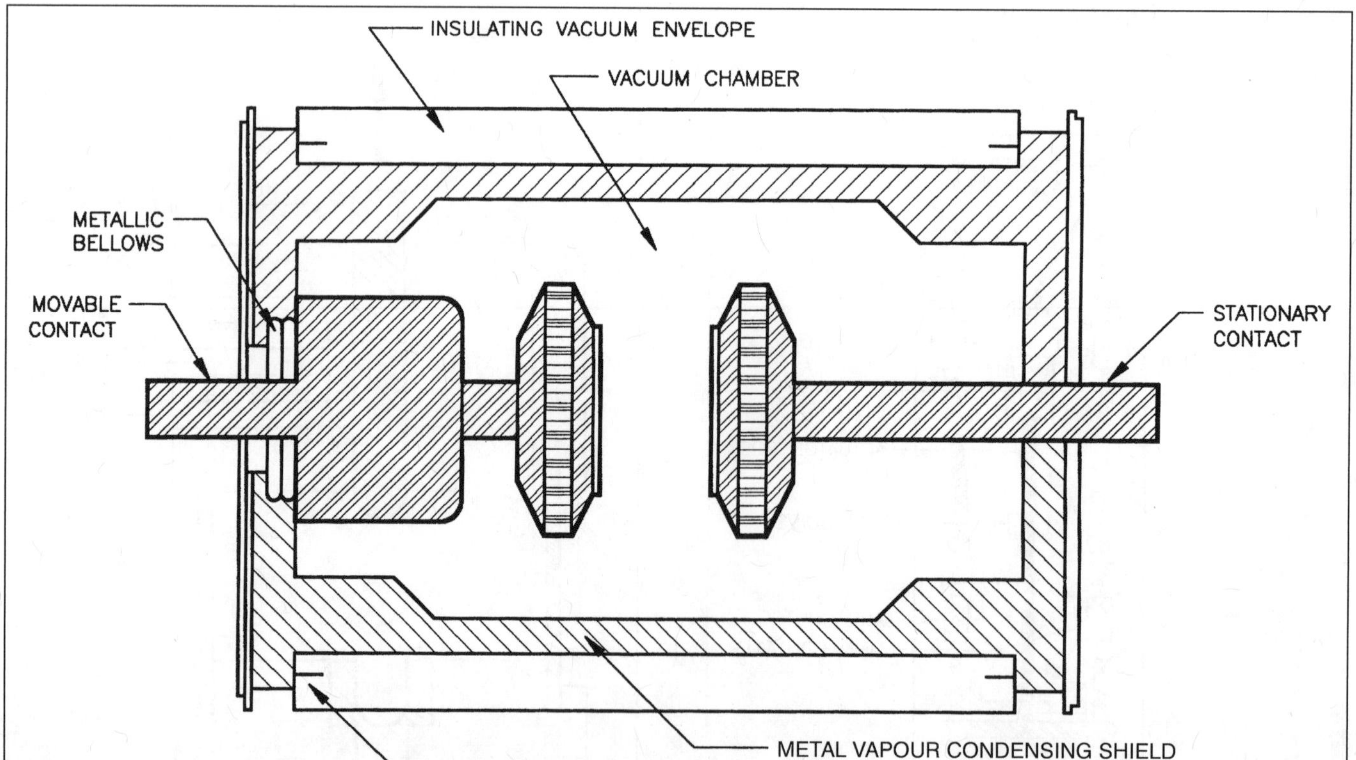

Figure 13-28 Typical vacuum circuit breaker.

air molecules are left in the chamber and any arc produced by the opening of the contacts will be extremely small. This small arc is extinguished by the distance between the contacts. Most vacuum circuit breakers require only about 0.5″ to 0.75″ clearance between the contacts to control voltages over 13.8 kV. A metallic bellows is connected to the movable contact. The bellows permits movement of the contact while maintaining the vacuum. Vacuum circuit breakers are being used to replace the older oil circuit breakers because they are smaller in size and require very little maintenance.

CIRCUIT-BREAKER TIME–CURRENT CHARACTERISTIC CHARTS

Time–current characteristic charts are published for most protective devices (Figure 13-29). A log–log grid is used for the chart with time on the vertical axis and current on the horizontal axis. In general, time is given in seconds and current is in amperes. Terms used with circuit-breaker curves are trip coil rating, frame size, long-time delay, long-time pickup, instantaneous pickup current, short-time delay, short-time pickup, unlatching time, and interrupting rating.

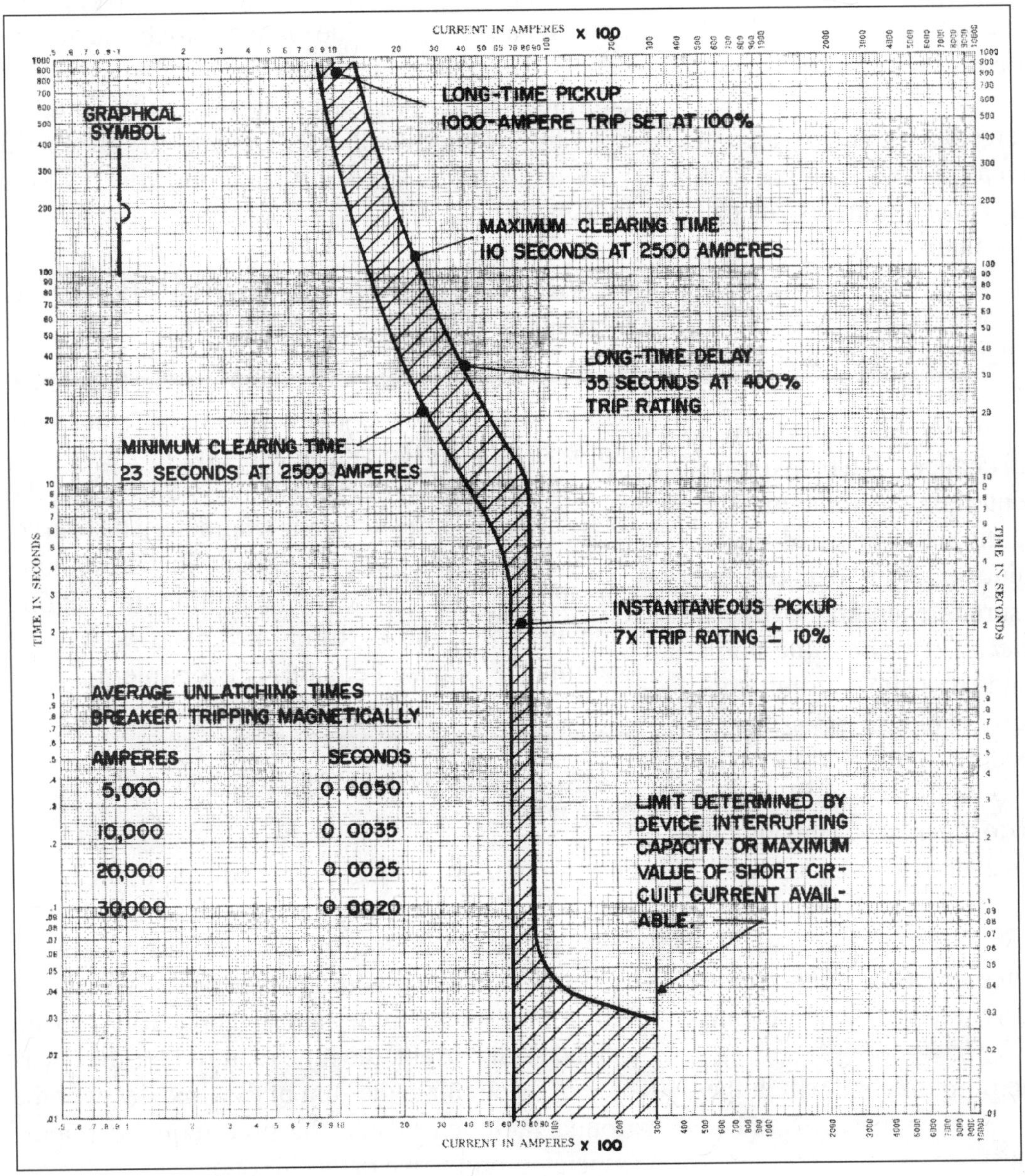

The *trip coil rating* is also known as the breaker rating. That is, a 150-A breaker is a breaker with a 150-A trip coil. This rating is not adjustable in moulded case circuit breakers. However, in some breaker models, the physical construction is such that breakers of various ratings are interchangeable. Because of this, a breaker of a different size (rating) can be installed to meet specific protective needs. Most air-type circuit breakers are adjustable. The rating can be changed from 80% to 160% of the trip coil rating. An adjustment above 100% of the trip coil rating should be made only in those installations where motors or other surge-generating loads are factors.

The value of current at which the trip coil operates is called the *long-time pickup*. A 200-A trip coil adjusted to 120% has a long-time pickup of 240 A.

The *frame size* indicates the maximum size of trip unit that a specific breaker can accommodate. Thus, a breaker with a 100-A frame size will accept a trip unit of any standard rating ranging from 15 A to 100 A.

The *long-time delay* portion of the curve indicates the operating characteristic of a breaker under overload conditions. For moulded case circuit breakers, this delay is usually controlled by a device sensitive to thermal changes. If a breaker has long-time delay adjustment, the time value may be set to a low value for lighting and resistive loads. However, a high time value setting is required for motor starting and other surge-generating loads.

The *instantaneous pickup current* is the point at which a breaker responds to a short-circuit current through a magnetically actuated trip arrangement. This value is adjustable in many breakers.

The *instantaneous opening* is the time required for the breaker to open when no intentional delay is added. However, when the trip must be delayed intentionally, a short-time delay is added (Figure 13-30). This feature is available only on more sophisticated breakers. *Short-time pickup* is that value of current at which short-time delay is initiated.

Unlatching time is the point beyond which the opening action of the breaker is irreversible (Figure 13-31 on page 186).

The characteristic curve of a circuit breaker is a band that represents the range of time or current through which the breaker can be expected to operate. The upper limit of the band indicates the maximum value; the lower band limit is the minimum value. In Figure 13-29, the curve indicates that a 250% load (2500 A) can be cleared in no less than 23 seconds or in no more than 110 seconds.

Each protective device that is designed to open a circuit under fault conditions must be able to interrupt the maximum current that can flow in that circuit (*CEC* Rule 14-012). The *interrupt rating* of a protective device indicates the maximum current that the device can interrupt. For currents above this value, an arc may be sustained across the contact gaps after they open. This arc continues to supply current to the fault and damages the protective device. Devices are available with interrupting capacities ranging from 5000 A to 200 000 A.

FUSE TIME–CURRENT CHARACTERISTIC CHARTS

A fuse has a highly predictable performance, which is usually represented on a chart by a single curve similar to the right-hand line in Figure 13-32 on page 187. A curve of this type is called the total clearing time–current characteristic curve. Another value is also significant in determining the selectivity of fuses. The minimum melting time is that value of time–current at which the opening of the fuse becomes irreversible.

GROUND FAULT PROTECTOR TIME–CURRENT CHARACTERISTIC CHARTS

Ground fault protector curves indicate the reaction of the device at a specific time-delay setting, Figure 13-33 on page 188. A ground fault sensor is always used in conjunction with another protective device that can respond to a signal. Thus, for a given ground fault current, the time required for the clearance of its circuit is the sum of the time delay of the ground fault sensor and the time required for the associated protective device to open.

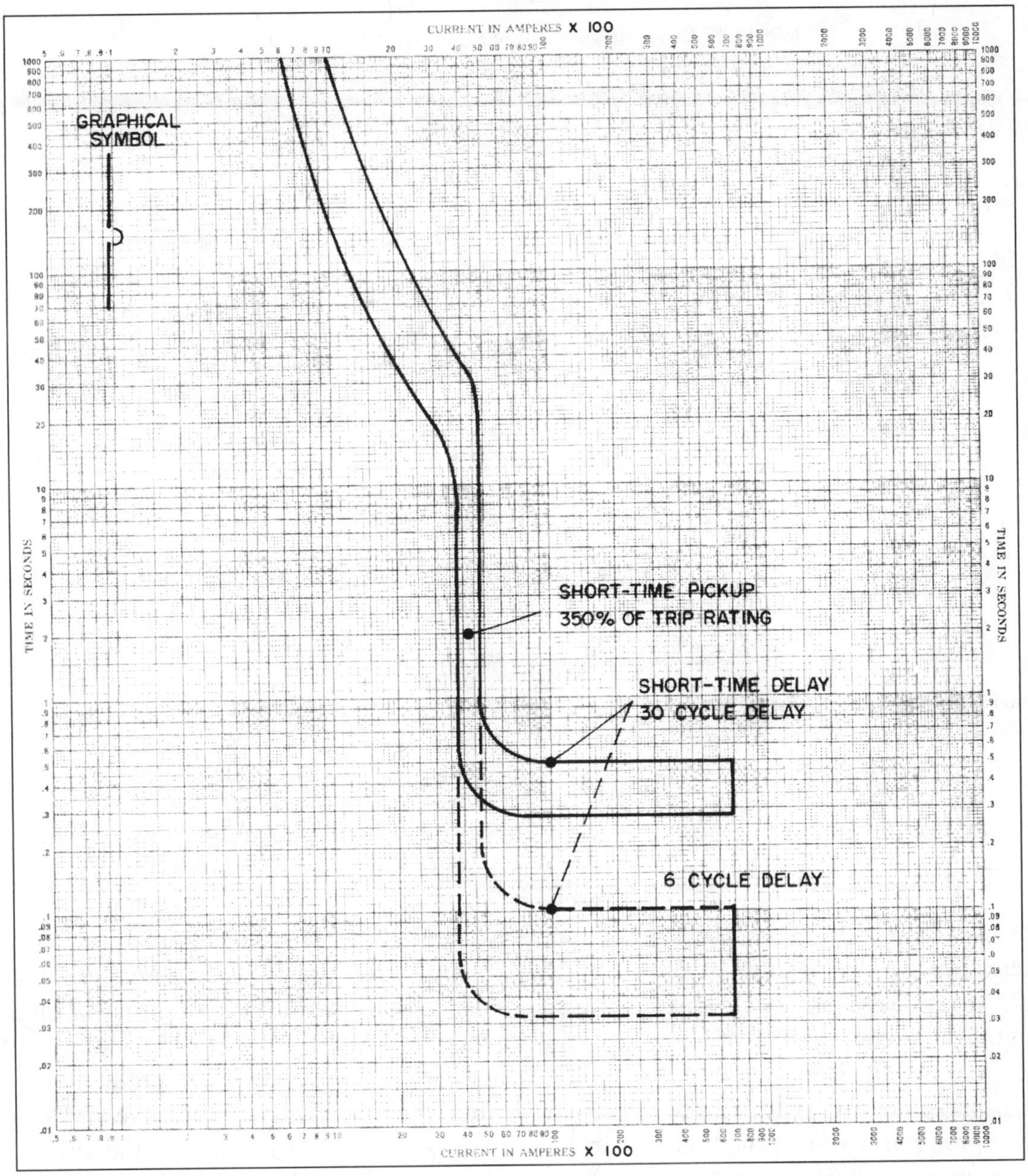

Figure 13-30 Characteristic curve for a circuit breaker with adjustable short-time delay.

COORDINATION

Each of the three types of protective devices described previously has distinct operating characteristics. The addition of these devices to a coordinated system requires that the proper selection of the rating be made. Figure 13-34 on page 189 shows the characteristic curves of two circuit breakers, a 1600-A main and an 800-A feeder. The cross-hatching in the figure indicates areas in which the breakers do not coordinate. For this situation, if a 5000-A overload continues for 20 seconds, there is a high probability that both breakers will open. Thus, instead of protecting a feeder circuit, the open breakers will cause an entire building to be without power. The same end result will occur for a short circuit of more than 18 000 A. This problem can be minimized by the proper selection, adjustment and maintenance of the protective devices. However, it must be noted that circuit breakers in general are difficult to coordinate. In particular,

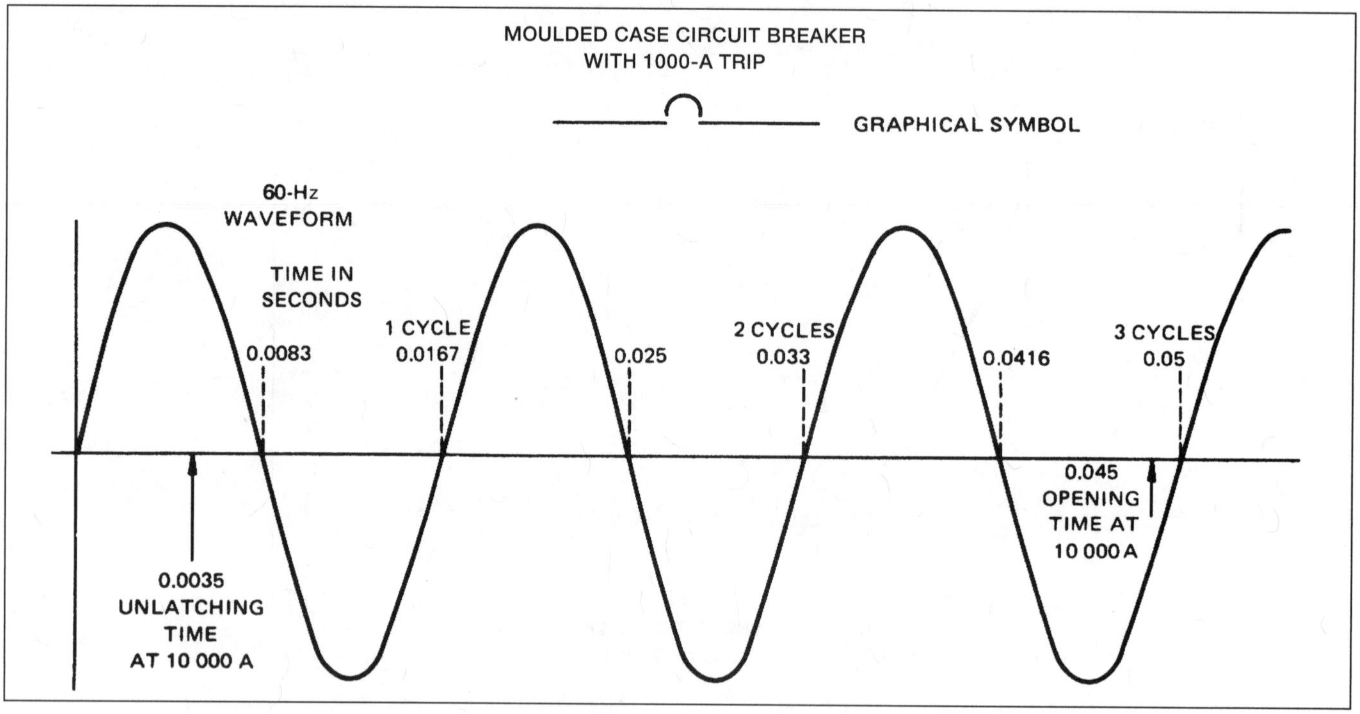

Figure 13-31 A comparison of latching and opening time for a circuit breaker tripping magnetically.

moulded case circuit breakers are almost impossible to coordinate, except at low overload current values.

All circuit breakers in a system, except the branch-circuit breakers, must have a short-time delay feature if coordination is to be achieved. The insertion of a delay in the magnetic tripping of the feeder and main devices makes it possible to achieve coordination, as indicated in Figure 13-35 on page 190. There is a problem with this method of obtaining coordination: a condition is established where a fault may not be opened for several cycles. This increases the possibility of damage that may occur as a result of the faulting condition.

Coordination can be accomplished easily, as shown in Figure 13-36 on page 191, by using fuses alone or in combination with circuit breakers. The 800-A fuse coordinates with the 1600-A circuit breaker, and coordination is achieved—with one possible exception. The unlatching time of the breaker may, under certain conditions, exceed the speed of the fuse, in which case coordination will not be obtained.

A system containing only fuses is the easiest situation to coordinate. When the fuses are selected according to the manufacturer's recommendation, complete coordination can be achieved. That is, fuses are used with a certain ratio to the upstream protective device. For example, a 1600-A current-limiting fuse used for a main will coordinate on a 2:1 basis with another current-limiting fuse or on a 4:1 basis with a time-delay fuse (such as the type used with motors). If ground fault protection is required after the overcurrent protective devices are coordinated, it should be added to the system without disrupting the coordination. If more than one ground fault protector is installed, a double problem is posed: both protectors should coordinate with the overcurrent system and with one another (Figure 13-37 on page 192).

Coordination with overcurrent devices can be achieved by selecting and adjusting the ground fault protector so that its characteristic curve is above the total clearing curve of the next downstream overcurrent protective device. Coordination with other ground fault protectors is achieved by using a lower trip setting and progressively shorter time settings on each of the downstream devices, or by making interlock connections between the devices so that the device that first senses a fault locks the upstream

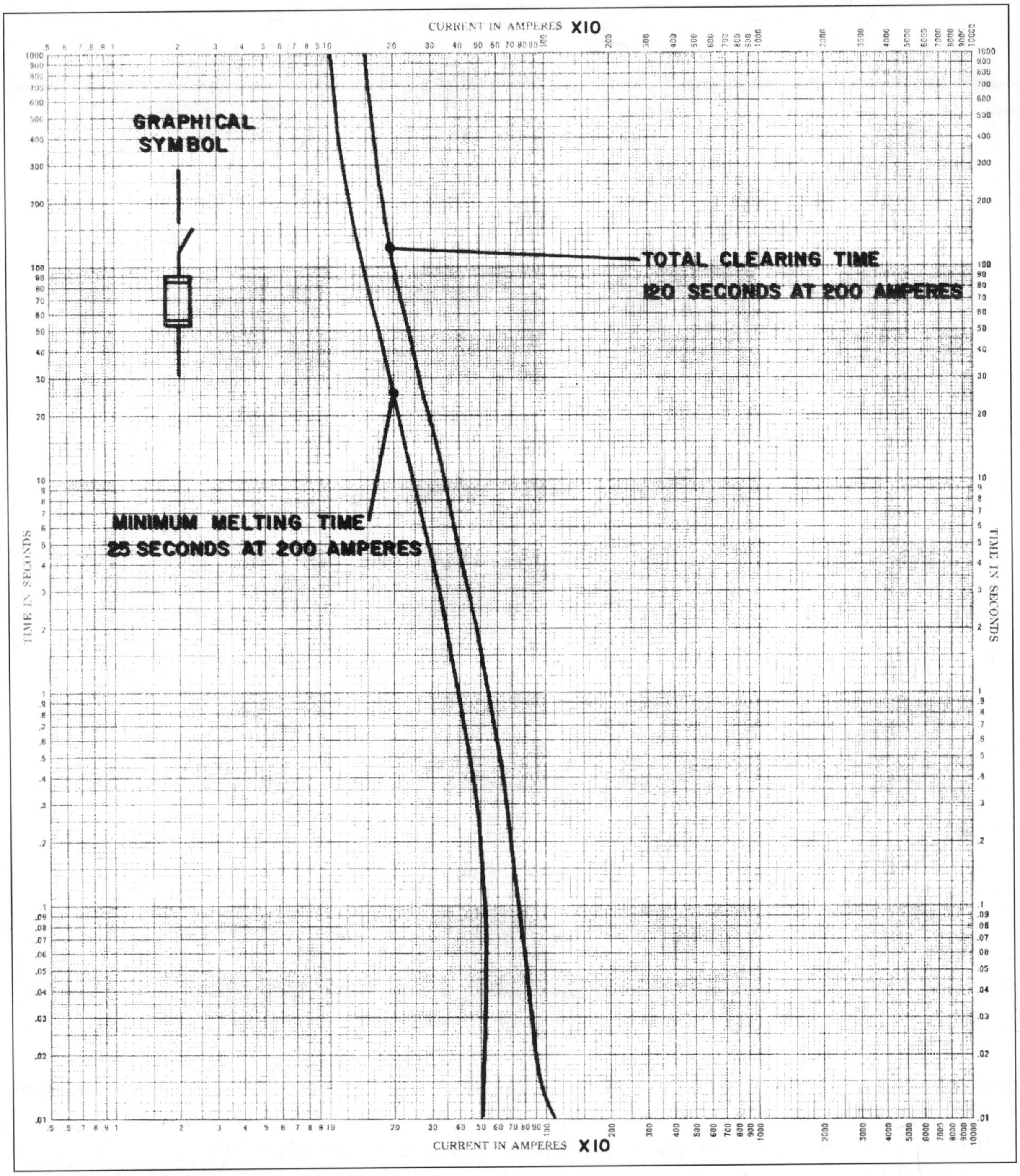

Figure 13-32 Characteristic curve for a current-limiting fuse.

device in until the time setting of the downstream device is exceeded.

Selective System Using Fuses

The proper choice among the various classes of fuses is necessary if selectivity is to be achieved. classes, time–current characteristics, and even manufacturers may cause a system to become non-selective.

To ensure selective operation under low overload conditions, it is necessary only to check and compare the time–current characteristic curves of fuses. Selectivity occurs when the curves do not

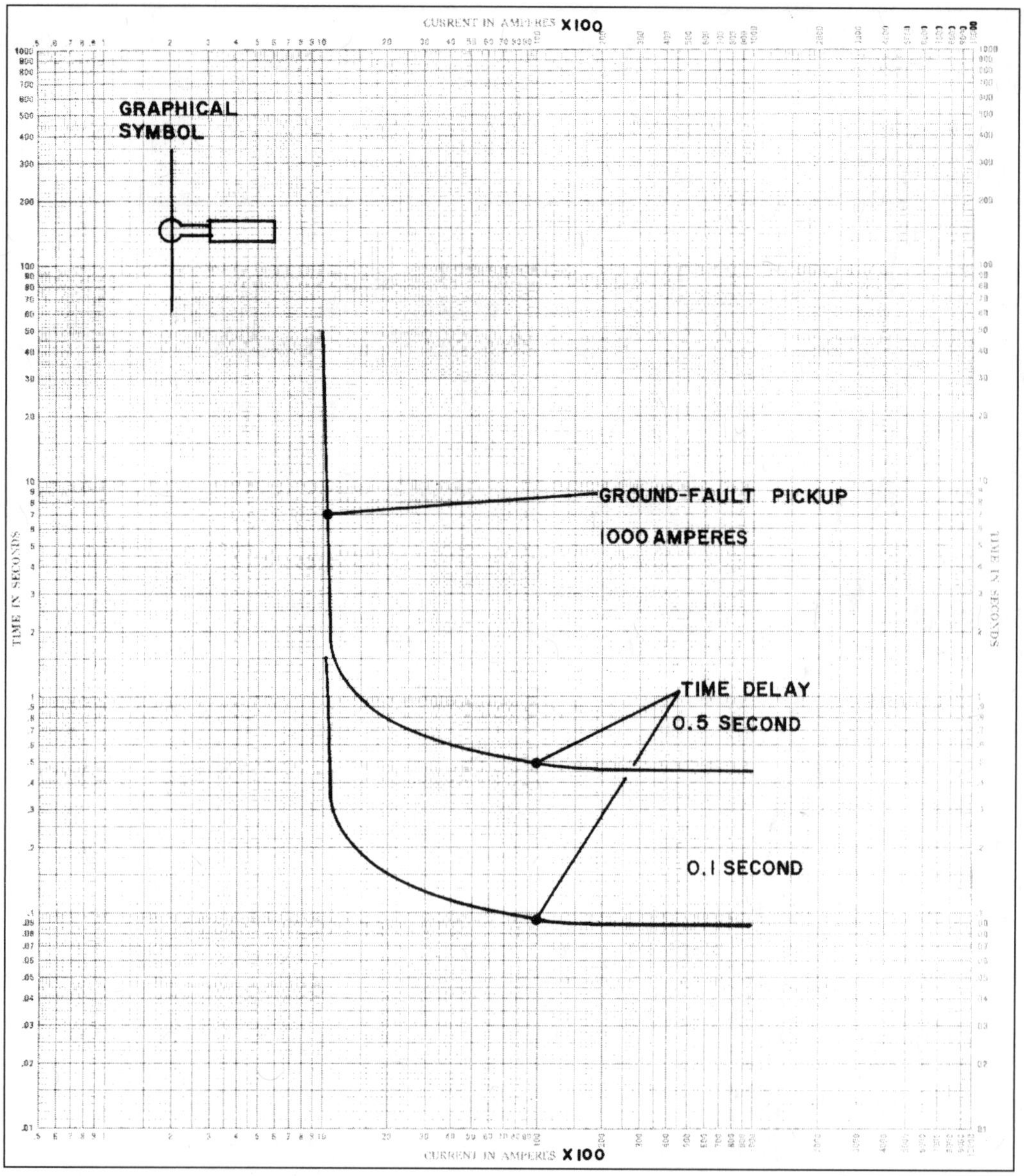

Figure 13-33 Characteristic curve for a ground fault protector with adjustable time delay.

selectivity guides, similar to the one shown in Figure 13-38 on page 193, to be used for short-circuit conditions. When using these guides, selectivity is achieved by maintaining a specific ratio between the various classes and types of fuses. A selectivity chart is based on any fault current up to the maximum interrupting ratings of the fuses listed in the chart.

To use the chart, select the type of line-side fuse in the column on the left of the chart. Next select the type of load-side fuse in the row at the top. The cell where the two intersect represents the ratio of the ampere rating of the line-side fuse to the ampere rating of the load-side fuse.

EXAMPLE A 200-A type FRN-R fuse is ahead of a 100-A type KTN fuse. Will this arrangement provide selective coordination?

Yes. From the table in Figure 13-38 on page 193, the ratio is found to be 1.5:1. That is, the line-side fuse only needs to be 1.5 times larger than the load-side fuse. Therefore, any line-side fuse of the type FRN-R of 150 A or more will provide selective coordination.

In summary, to coordinate a system, proper selection of the protective devices must be accompanied by the correct sizing of the various components followed by careful adjustment of these devices. In addition, the proper maintenance of

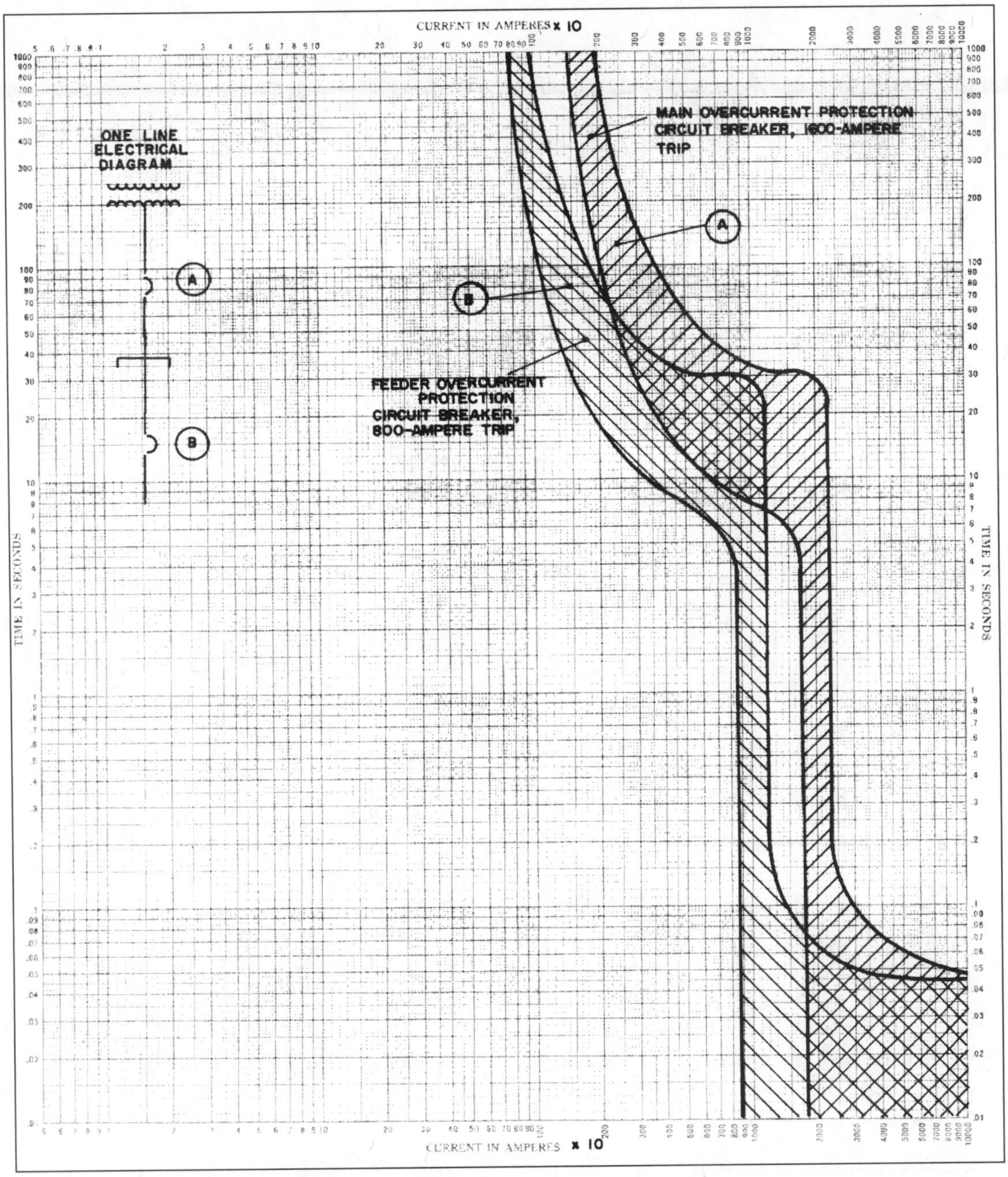

Figure 13-34 Circuit-breaker curve indicating areas where coordination is not achieved.

the devices after they are placed in operation will help to ensure that coordination, once achieved, will be maintained. Selecting circuit breakers for proper coordination should only be attempted by persons with considerable knowledge in this area. Circuit-breaker manufacturers can provide this service to the end user.

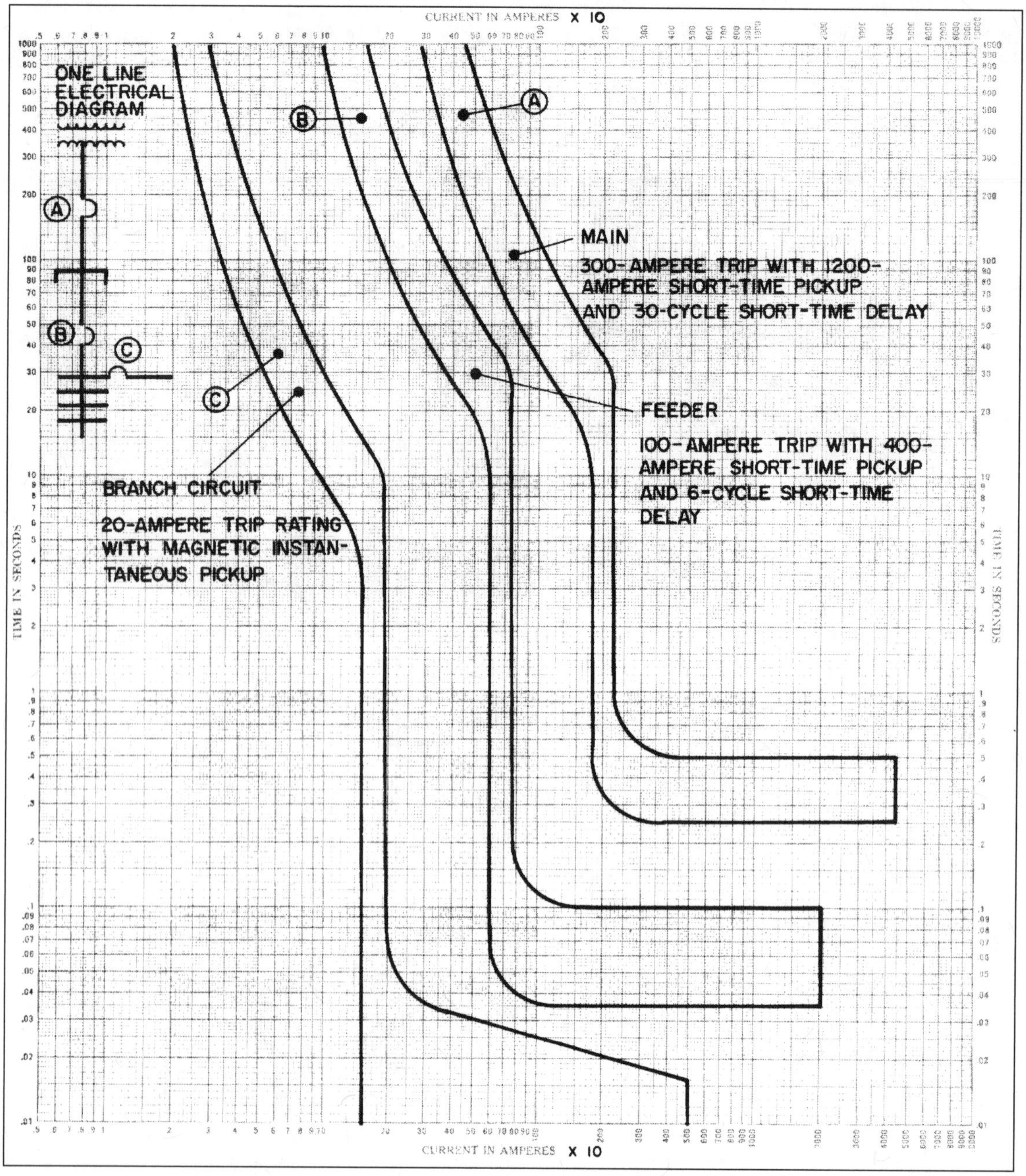

Figure 13-35 Circuit-breaker curves indicating coordination.

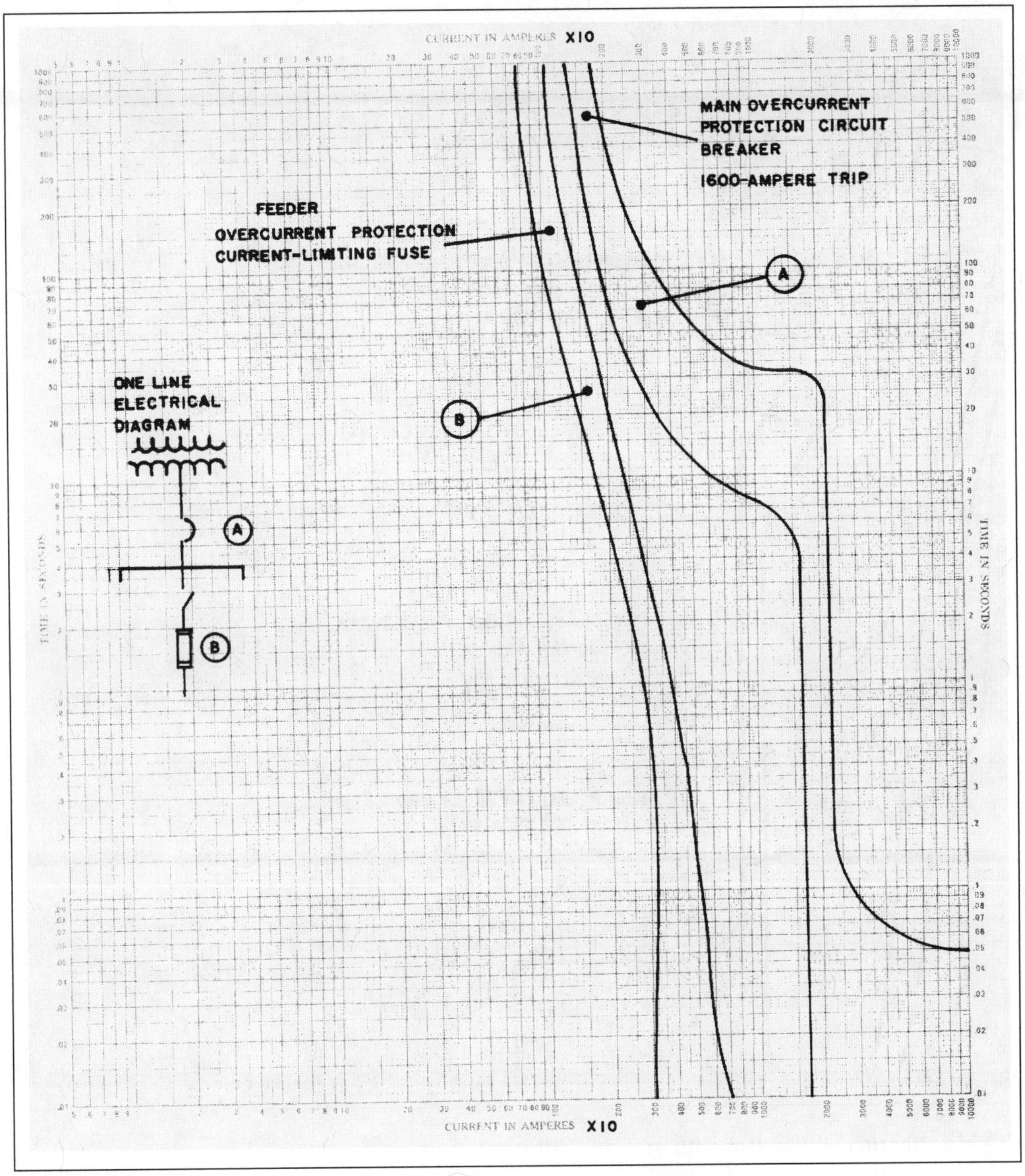

Figure 13-36 A circuit breaker and a fuse achieving coordination.

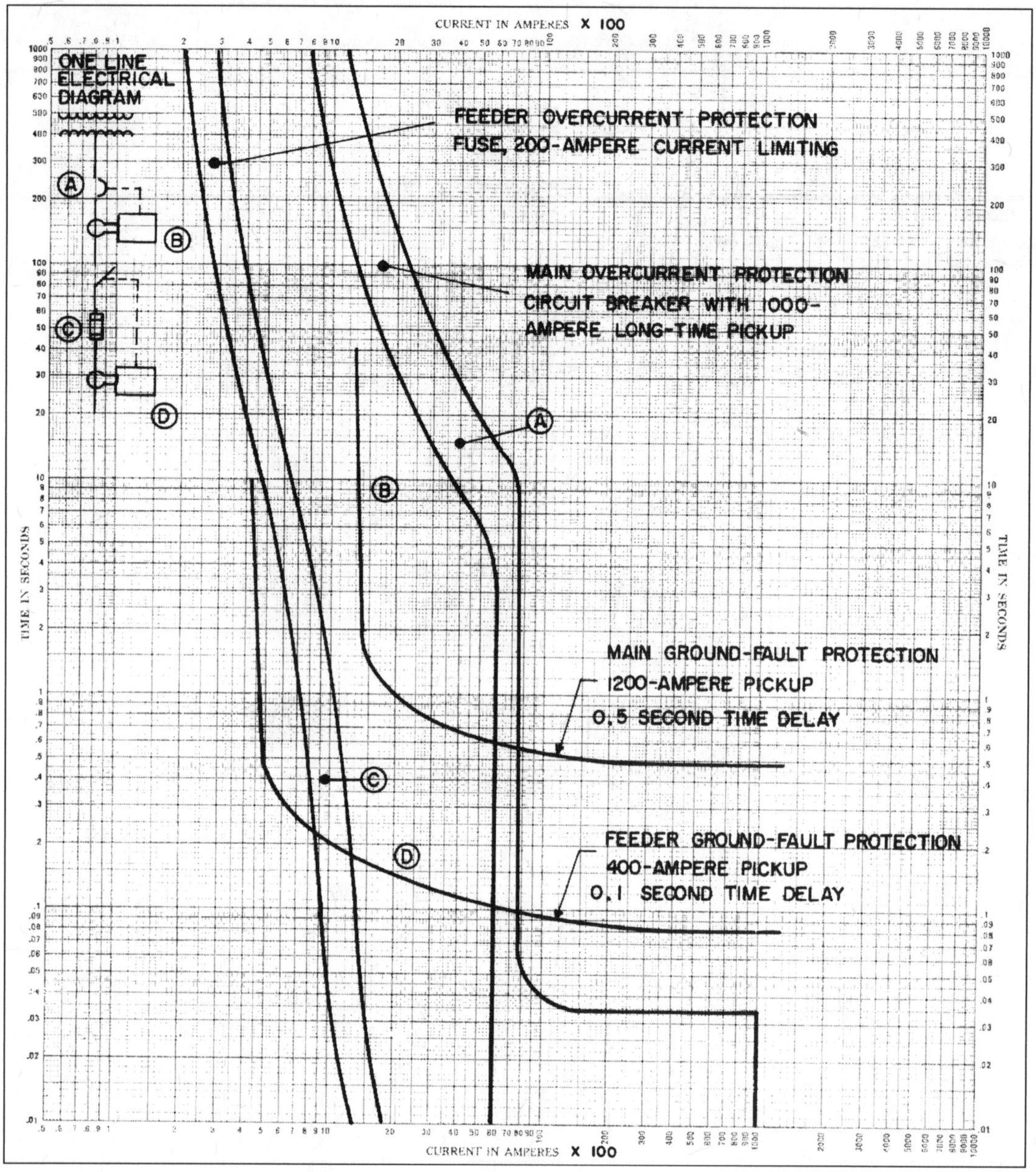

Figure 13-37 Selective coordination of a system with ground fault protection.

RATIOS FOR SELECTIVITY

LINE-SIDE FUSE	LOAD-SIDE FUSE									
	KRP-C HI-CAP time-delay Fuse 601-6000A Class L	KTU LIMITRON fast-acting Fuse 601-6000A Class L	KLU LIMITRON time-delay Fuse 601-4000A Class L	KTN-R, KTS-R LIMITRON fast-acting Fuse Class K 0-600A	JJS, JJN TRON fast-acting Fuse Class T 0-600A	JKS LIMITRON quick-acting Fuse Class J 0-600A	FRN-R, FRS-R FUSETRON dual-element Fuse Class K 0-600A	LPN-R, LPS-R LOW-PEAK dual-element Fuse Class K 0-600A	LPJ LOW-PEAK time-delay Fuse Class J 0-600A	SC Type Fuse (Class G) 0-60A
KRP-C HI-CAP time-delay Fuse 601-6000A Class L	2:1	2:1	2.5:1	2:1	2:1	2:1	4:1	2:1	2:1	••
KTU LIMITRON fast-acting Fuse 601-6000A Class L	2:1	2:1	2.5:1	2:1	2:1	2:1	6:1	2:1	2:1	••
KLU LIMITRON time-delay Fuse 601-4000A Class L	2:1	2:1	2:1	2:1	2:1	2:1	4:1	2:1	2:1	N/A
KTN-R, KTS-R LIMITRON fast-acting Fuse 0-600A Class RK1	N/A	N/A	N/A	3:1	3:1	3:1	8:1	3:1	3:1	4:1
JJN, JJS TRON fast-acting Fuse 0-600A Class T	N/A	N/A	N/A	3:1	3:1	3:1	8:1	3:1	3:1	4:1
JKS LIMITRON quick-acting Fuse 0-600A Class J	N/A	N/A	N/A	3:1	3:1	3:1	8:1	3:1	2:1	4:1
FRN-R, FRS-R, FUSETRON dual-element Fuse 0-600A Class RK5	N/A	N/A	N/A	1.5:1	1.5:1	1.5:1	2:1	1.5:1	1.5:1	1.5:1
LPN-R, LPS-R LOW-PEAK dual-element Fuse 0-600A Class RK1	N/A	N/A	N/A	3:1	3:1	3:1	8:1	2:1	2:1	4:1
LPJ Low-Peak Fuse 15-600A Class J	N/A	N/A	N/A	3:1	1.5:1	1.5:1	8:1	1.5:1	2:1	2:1
SC Type Fuse 0-60A Class G	N/A	N/A	N/A	2:1	2:1	2:1	4:1	3:1	3:1	2:1

N/A = NOT APPLICABLE

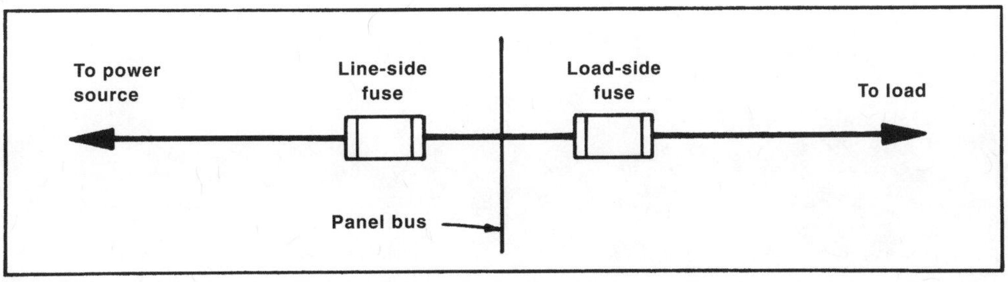

REVIEW

All answers should be written in complete sentences, calculations should be shown in detail, and Code references should be cited when appropriate.

1. Under what conditions must a service or circuit have ground fault protection?
2. List the service types that are recommended to have ground fault protection.
3. How many conductors of a three-phase, four-wire system must be installed through the sensor of a ground fault protective device?
4. What is the range of trip time for a current of 3000 A?
5. When referring to circuit breakers, what is meant by the *instantaneous opening time*?
6. When referring to circuit breakers, what is meant by the *long-time delay*?
7. What is meant by the phrase *minimum melting time*?

Questions 8 and 9 refer to Figure 13-32.

8. For a current of 300 A, the opening time of the fuse is how many seconds?
9. For a current of 300 A, the opening action of the fuse is irreversible after how many seconds?
10. What is the difference between a short-circuit fault and a ground fault?
11. Explain what is meant by *selective coordination,* and list three types of devices that are involved.
12. If a 1000-A fault were to occur on the system represented in Figure 13-34, what would probably happen?
13. What are the maximum current and time-delay settings of ground fault protection as set forth by the *CEC*?

UNIT 14

Short-Circuit Calculations

OBJECTIVES

After studying this unit, the student should be able to:

- perform short-circuit calculations using the point-to-point method
- calculate short-circuit currents using the appropriate tables and charts
- define the term *interrupting rating* and explain its significance

The student must understand the intent of Rules 14-012, 14-014, and 14-012 Appendix B. These rules ensure that the fuses and/or circuit breakers selected for an installation are capable of interrupting—at the rated voltage—the current that may flow under any condition (overload, short circuit, or ground fault) with complete safety to personnel and without damage to the panel, load centre, switch, or electrical equipment in which the protective devices are installed.

An overloaded condition resulting from a miscalculation of load currents will cause a fuse to blow or a circuit breaker to trip in a normal manner. However, a miscalculation, a guess, or ignorance of the magnitude of the available short-circuit currents may result in the installation of breakers or fuses having inadequate interrupting ratings. Such a situation can occur even though the load currents in the circuit are checked carefully. **Breakers or fuses having inadequate interrupting ratings need only be subjected to a short circuit to cause them to explode, which could injure personnel and seriously damage the electrical equipment.** *The interrupting rating of an overcurrent device is its maximum rating*

In any electrical installation, individual branch circuits are calculated as has been discussed previously in this text. After the quantity, size, and type of branch circuits are determined, these branch-circuit loads are then combined to determine the size of the feeder conductors to the respective panelboards. Most consulting engineers will specify that a certain number of spare branch-circuit breakers be installed in the panelboard, plus a quantity of spaces that can be used in the future.

The next step is to determine the interrupting rating requirements of the fuses or circuit breakers to be installed in the panel. Rule 14-012 is an all-encompassing rule that covers the interrupting rating requirements for services, mains, feeders, subfeeders, and branch-circuit overcurrent devices. For various types of equipment, normal currents can be determined by checking the equipment nameplate current, voltage, and wattage ratings. In addition, an ammeter can be used to check for normal and overloaded circuit conditions.

A number of formulas can be used to calculate short-circuit currents. Manufacturers of fuses, circuit breakers, and transformers publish numerous short-circuit current. A standard ammeter must *not* be used to read short-circuit current, because this practice will result in damage to the ammeter and possible injury to personnel.

SHORT-CIRCUIT CALCULATIONS

The following sections will cover several of the basic methods of determining available short-circuit currents. As the short-circuit values given in the various tables are compared to the calculations, it will be noted that there are slight variances in the results. These differences are due largely to (1) the rounding off of the numbers in the calculations, and (2) variations in the resistance and reactance data used to prepare the tables and charts. For example, the value of the square root of 3 (1.732) is used frequently in three-phase calculations. Depending on the accuracy required, values of 1.7, 1.73, or 1.732 can be used in the calculations.

In actual practice, the available short-circuit current at the load side of a transformer is less than the values shown in Problem 1. However, this simplified method of finding the available short-circuit currents will result in values that are conservative.

The actual impedance value on a CSA-approved 25-kVA or larger transformer can vary ±10% from the transformer's marked impedance. This will affect the available fault-current calculations.

For example, in Problem 1, the *marked* impedance is reduced by 10% to reflect the transformer's possible *actual* impedance. The calculations show this "worst-case" scenario. All short-circuit examples in this text have the marked transformer impedance values reduced by 10%.

Another factor that affects fault-current calculations is voltage. Utility companies are allowed to vary voltage to their customers within a certain range. This might be ±10% for power services and ±5% for lighting services. The higher voltage will result in a larger magnitude of fault current.

Another source of short-circuit current comes from electric motors that are running at the time the fault occurs. This is covered later in this unit.

Thus, it can be seen that no matter how much data we plug into our fault-current calculations, there are many variables that are out of our control. What we hope for is to arrive at a result that is reasonably accurate so that our electrical equipment is reasonably safe insofar as interrupting ratings and withstand ratings are concerned.

In addition to the methods of determining available short-circuit currents that are provided below, there are computer programs that do the calculations. These programs are fast, particularly where there are many points in a system to be calculated.

Determining the Short-Circuit Current at the Terminals of a Transformer Using Tables

Table 14-1 on page 198 shows the short-circuit currents for a typical transformer. Transformer manufacturers publish short-circuit tables for many sizes of transformers having various impedance values. Table 14-1 provides data for a 300-kVA, three-phase transformer with an impedance of 2%.

According to the table, the symmetrical short-circuit current is 42 090 A at the secondary terminals of a 120/208-V three-phase transformer (refer to the zero-foot row of the table). This value is on the low side because the manufacturer that developed the table did not allow for the ± impedance variation allowed by the CSA standard. Problem 1 indicates that the available short-circuit current at the secondary of the transformer is 46 334 A at 2% impedance.

Determining the Short-Circuit Current at Various Distances from a Transformer Using Table 14-1

The amount of available short-circuit current decreases as the distance from the transformer increases, as indicated in Table 14-1. See Problem 2 on page 199.

PROBLEM 1

The existing three-phase pad-mounted transformer installed by the utility company has a rating of 300 kVA at 120/208 V with an impedance of 4% (from the transformer nameplate). The available short-circuit current at the secondary terminals of the transformer must be determined. To simplify the calculation, it is also assumed that the utility can deliver unlimited short-circuit current to the primary of the transformer. In this case, the transformer primary is known as an *infinite bus* or an *infinite primary.*

The first step is to determine the normal full-load current rating of the transformer:

$$I \text{ (at the secondary)} = \frac{\text{kVA} \times 1000}{E \times 1.73} = \frac{300 \times 1000}{208 \times 1.73}$$

$$= 834 \text{ A normal full load}$$

Using the impedance value given on the nameplate of the transformer, the next step is to find a multiplier that can be used to determine the short-circuit current available at the secondary terminals of the transformer.

The factor of 0.9 shown in the calculations below reflects the fact that the transformer's actual impedance might be 10% less than that marked on the nameplate and would be a worst-case condition. In electrical circuits, the lower the impedance, the higher the current.

If the transformer is marked 4% impedance, then

$$\text{Multiplier} = \frac{100}{4 \times 0.9} = 27.778$$

and Short-circuit current = 834 × 27.778 = 23 167 A.

If the transformer is marked 2% impedance, then

$$\text{Multiplier} = \frac{100}{2 \times 0.9} = 55.556$$

and Short-circuit current = 834 × 55.556 = 46 334 A.

If the transformer is marked 1% impedance, then

$$\text{Multiplier} = \frac{100}{1 \times 0.9} = 111.111$$

and Short-circuit current = 834 × 111.111 = 92 667 A.

Determining Short-Circuit Currents at Various Distances from Transformers, Switchboards, Panelboards, and Load Centres Using the Point-to-Point Method

A simple method for determining the available short-circuit currents (also referred to as fault current) at various distances from a given location is the *point-to-point method.* Reasonable accuracy is obtained when this method is used with three-phase and single-phase systems.

The following procedure demonstrates the use of the point-to-point method:

Step 1 Determine the full-load rating of the transformer in amperes from the transformer nameplate, Table 14-2 on page 199, or the following formulas:

a. For three-phase transformers:

$$I_{FLA} = \frac{\text{kVA} \times 1000}{E_{L-L} \times 1.73}$$

Table 14-1 Symmetrical short-circuit currents at various distances from a liquid-filled transformer (300 kVA transformer, 2% impedance).

SYMMETRICAL SHORT-CIRCUIT CURRENTS AT VARIOUS DISTANCES FROM A LIQUID-FILLED TRANSFORMER (300 kVA TRANSFORMER, 2% IMPEDANCE)

	WIRE-SIZE (COPPER)																						
	DIST. (FT.)	#14	#12	#10	#8	#6	#4	#1	0	00	000	2-000	0000	250 kcmil	2-250 kcmil	3-300 kcmil	350 kcmil	2-350 kcmil	3-350 kcmil	3-400 kcmil	500 kcmil	2-500 kcmil	750 kcmil	4-750 kcmil
208 V	0	42090	42090	42090	42090	42090	42090	42090	42090	42090	42090	42090	42090	42090	42090	42090	42090	42090	42090	42090	42090	42090	42090	42090
	5	6910	10290	14730	19970	25240	29840	34690	35770	36640	37340	39610	37930	38270	40100	40870	38840	40410	40960	41030	39300	40650	39650	41460
	10	3640	5610	8460	12350	17090	22230	29030	30760	32210	33410	37340	34420	35030	38270	39710	36040	38840	39870	40010	36850	39300	37480	40840
	25	1500	2360	3670	5650	8430	12150	18930	21170	23240	25090	31710	26750	27780	33590	36560	29550	34780	36930	37230	31020	35730	32190	39090
	50	760	1200	1890	2950	4530	6810	11740	13670	15610	17510	25090	19320	20520	27780	32250	22660	29550	32850	33340	24520	31020	26050	36480
	100	380	600	960	1510	2350	3610	6610	7920	9320	10810	17510	12320	13380	20520	26010	15400	22660	26850	27530	17250	24520	18860	32190
	200	190	300	480	760	1190	1860	3510	4280	5140	6090	10810	7110	7860	13380	18660	9360	15400	19590	20370	10820	17250	12150	26050
	500	80	120	190	310	480	760	1460	1800	2180	2630	4990	3130	3500	6510	10030	4290	7820	10770	11400	5100	9120	5870	16570
	1000	40	60	100	150	240	380	740	910	1110	1350	2630	1620	1820	3500	5650	2250	4290	6140	6560	2710	5100	3160	10310
	5000	10	10	20	30	50	80	150	180	230	280	550	330	380	740	1260	470	930	1380	1490	570	1130	670	2560
240 V	0	37820	37820	37820	37820	37820	37820	37820	37820	37820	37820	37820	37820	37820	37820	37820	37820	37820	37820	37820	37820	37820	37820	37820
	5	7750	11330	15810	20720	25260	28940	32560	33340	33960	34460	36080	34870	35120	36420	36960	35520	36640	37020	37070	35840	36800	36090	37370
	10	4140	6320	9400	13430	18040	22670	28230	29560	30660	31550	34460	32290	32730	35120	36140	33470	35520	36260	36350	34060	35840	34510	36930
	25	1720	2700	4180	6360	9360	13190	19640	21620	23380	24920	30240	26260	27090	31650	33860	28480	32530	34130	34340	29610	33230	30510	35680
	50	870	1380	2160	3360	5130	7620	12730	14630	16480	18230	24920	19850	20900	27090	30610	22740	28480	31060	31430	24300	29610	25570	33780
	100	440	700	1100	1730	2680	4100	7380	8770	10220	11720	18230	13220	14240	20900	25600	16150	22740	26280	26830	17860	24300	19310	30510
	200	220	350	550	880	1370	2130	3990	4830	5770	6790	11720	7880	8650	14240	19200	10190	16150	20030	20710	11650	17860	12960	25570
	500	90	140	220	350	560	870	1670	2050	2490	2990	5610	3540	3960	7230	10890	4820	8590	11620	12250	5700	9920	6520	17200
	1000	40	70	110	180	280	440	850	1050	1280	1550	2990	1850	2080	3960	6300	2560	4820	6820	7270	3070	5700	3570	11130
	5000	10	10	20	40	60	90	170	210	260	320	630	380	430	860	1440	540	1070	1580	1710	660	1290	770	2910
480 V	0	18910	18910	18910	18910	18910	18910	18910	18910	18910	18910	18910	18910	18910	18910	18910	18910	18910	18910	18910	18910	18910	18910	18910
	5	10450	12820	14750	16150	17080	17690	18200	18310	18400	18470	18690	18520	18550	18730	18800	18610	18760	18810	18810	18650	18780	18690	18850
	10	6750	9170	11630	13780	15400	16530	17540	17740	17910	18040	18470	18150	18210	18550	18690	18320	18610	18710	18720	18400	18650	18470	18800
	25	3180	4740	6770	9150	11520	13570	15690	16160	16540	16840	17830	17100	17250	18040	18380	17490	18180	18410	18440	17690	18280	17840	18630
	50	1680	2590	3900	5680	7840	10170	13190	13960	14600	15120	16840	15560	15820	17250	17870	16260	17490	17940	18000	16610	17690	16890	18360
	100	860	1350	2090	3180	4680	6600	9820	10810	11690	12460	15120	13130	13540	15820	16930	14240	16260	17060	17170	14810	16610	15260	17840
	200	440	690	1080	1680	2560	3810	6370	7320	8240	9110	12460	9930	10450	13540	15300	11370	14240	15530	15710	12150	14810	12780	16890
	500	180	280	440	700	1080	1670	3040	3640	4290	4960	8010	5560	6140	9360	11820	7050	10320	12190	12500	7880	11150	8600	14550
	1000	90	140	220	350	550	860	1620	1970	2370	2800	4960	3270	3610	6140	8520	4300	7050	8940	9290	4960	7880	5560	11830
	5000	20	30	40	70	110	180	340	420	510	620	1210	750	840	1610	2600	1040	1980	2820	3020	1250	2350	1450	4730
600 V	0	15130	15130	15130	15130	15130	15130	15130	15130	15130	15130	15130	15130	15130	15130	15130	15130	15130	15130	15130	15130	15130	15130	15130
	5	10210	11790	12920	13690	14180	14500	14770	14820	14870	14900	15010	14930	14940	15040	15070	14970	15050	15080	15080	15000	15060	15010	15100
	10	7270	9270	11010	12350	13280	13890	14410	14520	14610	14680	14900	14730	14770	14940	15020	14820	14970	15020	15030	14870	15000	14900	15070
	25	3740	5370	7280	9230	10920	12200	13410	13670	13870	14040	14570	14170	14250	14680	14850	14380	14750	14870	14890	14490	14800	14570	14980
	50	2040	3080	4500	6270	8170	9950	11940	12400	12770	13060	14040	13310	13460	14250	14590	13700	14380	14620	14650	13900	14490	14050	14840
	100	1060	1650	2510	3730	5290	7080	9650	10350	10930	11420	13060	11840	12090	13460	14080	12510	13700	14150	14210	12850	13900	13120	14570
	200	540	850	1330	2040	3040	4390	6840	7640	8390	9050	11420	9640	10010	12090	13160	10640	12510	13290	13390	11160	12850	11580	14050
	500	220	350	550	860	1330	2010	3550	4180	4830	5480	8180	6110	6530	9210	10960	7310	9900	11210	11400	7990	10470	8560	12700
	1000	110	170	280	440	680	1050	1950	2360	2800	3270	5480	3760	4110	6530	8540	4780	7310	8860	9120	5410	7990	5970	10940
	5000	20	40	60	90	140	220	420	520	640	770	1470	910	1030	1930	3030	1260	2340	3270	3480	1510	2750	1740	5180

where E_{L-L} = Line-to-line voltage

b. For single-phase transformers:

$$I_{FLA} = \frac{\text{kVA} \times 1000}{E_{L-L}}$$

Step 2 Find the percent impedance (Z) on the nameplate of the transformer.

Step 3 Find the transformer multiplier M_1:

$$M_1 = \frac{100}{\text{Transformer \% impedance} \times 0.9}$$

Note: Because the marked transformer impedance can vary ±10% per the CSA standard, the 0.9 factor above takes this into consideration to show "worst-case" conditions.

Step 4 Determine the transformer let-through short-circuit current at the secondary terminals of transformer. Use tables or the following formula:

a. For three-phase transformers (*L–L–L*):

$$I_{SCA} = \text{Transformer FLA} \times M_1$$

b. For single-phase transformers (*L–L*):

$$I_{SCA} = \text{Transformer FLA} \times M_1$$

c. For single-phase transformers (*L–N*):

$$I_{SCA} = \text{Transformer FLA} \times M_1 \times 1.5$$

At the secondary terminals of a single-phase centre-tapped transformer, the *L–N* fault current is higher than the *L–L* fault current. At some distance from the terminals, depending on the wire size and type, the *L–N* fault current is lower than the *L–L* fault current. The *L–N* fault current can vary from 1.33 to 1.67 times the *L–L* fault current. These figures are based on the different turns ratios between the primary and the secondary, infinite source current, zero distance from the terminals of the transformer, and 1.2 × % reactance (*X*) and 1.5 × % resistance (*R*) for the *L–N* versus *L–L* resistance and reactance values. For simplicity, in Step 4c. we used an approximate multiplier of 1.5. See Figure 14-1 (page 203) for example.

Voltage+ and Phase	KVA	Full Load Amps	% Impedance†† (Name plate)	†Short-Circuit Amps
120/240 1 ph.*	25	104	1.6	11 431
	37.5	156	1.6	16 961
	50	209	1.7	21 065
	75	313	1.6	32 789
	100	417	1.6	42 779
	167	695	1.8	60 038
120/208 3 ph.	150	417	2.0	23 166
	225	625	2.0	34 722
	300	834	2.0	46 333
	300	834	4.0	23 166
	500	1 388	2.0	77 111
	750	2 080	5.0	66 036
	1 000	2 776	5.0	88 127
	1 500	4 164	5.0	132 180
	2 000	5 552	5.0	123 377
	2 500	6 950	5.0	154 444
277/480 3 ph.	112.5	135	1.0	15 000
	150	181	1.2	16 759
	225	271	1.2	25 062
	300	361	1.2	33 426
	500	601	1.3	51 368
	750	902	5.0	28 410
	1 000	1 203	5.0	36 180
	1 500	1 804	5.0	57 261
	2 000	2 406	5.0	53 461
	2 500	3 007	5.0	66 822

† Three-phase short-circuit currents based on "infinite" primary.

* Single-phase values are *L–N* values at transformer terminals. These figures are based on change in turns ratio between primary and secondary, 100 000 KVA primary, zero feet from terminals of transformer, 1.2 (%X) and 1.5 (%R) for *L–N* vs. *L–L* reactance and resistance values, and transformer X/R ratio =3.

†† UL listed transformers 25KVA or greater have a ± 10% impedance tolerance. "Short Circuit Amps" reflect a worst case scenario.

\+ Fluctuations in system voltage will affect the available short-circuit current. For example, a 10% increase in system voltage will result in a 10% increase in the available short-circuit currents shown in the table.

Notes: The interrupting rating for an overcurrent protective device is the device's *maximum* rating under standard test conditions. This interrupting rating must not be exceeded.

Three-phase line-to-ground (neutral) can vary from 25% to 125% of the *L–L–L* bolted fault-current value. Use 100% as typical.

For single-phase, centre-tapped transformers, it is common practice to multiply the *L–L* bolted fault current value by 1.5 to determine the approximate *L–G* (*L–N*) fault current value. Maximum short-circuit current will occur across the 120-volt transformer terminals.

Table 14-2 Short-Circuit Currents Available from Various Size Transformers.

PROBLEM 2

For a 300-kVA transformer with a secondary voltage of 208 V and 2% impedance, find the available short-circuit current at a main switch that is located 7.6 m (25 ft) from the transformer. The main switch is supplied by four 750-kcmil copper conductors per phase in steel conduit.

Refer to Table 14-1 and read the value of 39 090 A in the column on the right-hand side of the table for a distance of 25 ft.

AWG or kcmil	Copper Conductors Three Single Conductors						Copper Conductors Three Conductor Cable					
	Steel Conduit			Nonmagnetic Conduit			Steel Conduit			Nonmagnetic Conduit		
	600 V	5 KV	15 KV	600 V	5 KV	15 KV	600 V	5 KV	15 KV	600 V	5 KV	15 KV
14	389	—	—	389	—	—	389	—	—	389	—	—
12	617	—	—	617	—	—	617	—	—	617	—	—
10	981	—	—	981	—	—	981	—	—	981	—	—
8	1557	1551	1557	1556	1555	1558	1559	1557	1559	1559	1558	1559
6	2425	2406	2389	2430	2417	2406	2431	2424	2414	2433	2428	2420
4	3806	3750	3695	3825	3789	3752	3830	3811	3778	3837	3823	3798
3	4760	4760	4760	4802	4802	4802	4760	4790	4760	4802	4802	4802
2	5906	5736	5574	6044	5926	5809	5989	5929	5827	6087	6022	5957
1	7292	7029	6758	7493	7306	7108	7454	7364	7188	7579	7507	7364
1/0	8924	8543	7973	9317	9033	8590	9209	9086	8707	9472	9372	9052
2/0	10755	10061	9389	11423	10877	10318	11244	11045	10500	11703	11528	11052
3/0	12843	11804	11021	13923	13048	12360	13656	13333	12613	14410	14118	13461
4/0	15082	13605	12542	16673	15351	14347	16391	15890	14813	17482	17019	16012
250	16483	14924	13643	18593	17120	15865	18310	17850	16465	19779	19352	18001
300	18176	16292	14768	20867	18975	17408	20617	20051	18318	22524	21938	20163
350	19703	17385	15678	22736	20526	18672	19557	21914	19821	22736	24126	21982
400	20565	18235	16365	24296	21786	19731	24253	23371	21042	26915	26044	23517
500	22185	19172	17492	26706	23277	21329	26980	25449	23125	30028	28712	25916
600	22965	20567	17962	28033	25203	22097	28752	27974	24896	32236	31258	27766
750	24136	21386	18888	28303	25430	22690	31050	30024	26932	32404	31338	28303
1000	25278	22539	19923	31490	28083	24887	33864	32688	29320	37197	35748	31959

AWG or kcmil	Aluminum Conductors Three Single Conductors						Aluminum Conductors Three Conductor Cable					
	Steel Conduit			Nonmagnetic Conduit			Steel Conduit			Nonmagnetic Conduit		
	600 V	5 KV	15 KV	600 V	5 KV	15 KV	600 V	5 KV	15 KV	600 V	5 KV	15 KV
14	236	—	—	236	—	—	236	—	—	236	—	—
12	375	—	—	375	—	—	375	—	—	375	—	—
10	598	—	—	598	—	—	598	—	—	598	—	—
8	951	950	951	951	950	951	951	951	951	951	951	951
6	1480	1476	1472	1481	1478	1476	1481	1480	1478	1482	1481	1479
4	2345	2332	2319	2350	2341	2333	2351	2347	2339	2353	2349	2344
3	2948	2948	2948	2958	2958	2958	2948	2956	2948	2958	2958	2958
2	3713	3669	3626	3729	3701	3672	3733	3719	3693	3739	3724	3709
1	4645	4574	4497	4678	4631	4580	4686	4663	4617	4699	4681	4646
1/0	5777	5669	5493	5838	5766	5645	5852	5820	5717	5875	5851	5771
2/0	7186	6968	6733	7301	7152	6986	7327	7271	7109	7372	7328	7201
3/0	8826	8466	8163	9110	8851	8627	9077	8980	8750	9242	9164	8977
4/0	10740	10167	9700	11174	10749	10386	11184	11021	10642	11408	11277	10968
250	12122	11460	10848	12862	12343	11847	12796	12636	12115	13236	13105	12661
300	13909	13009	12192	14922	14182	13491	14916	14698	13973	15494	15299	14658
350	15484	14280	13288	16812	15857	14954	15413	15490	15540	16812	17351	16500
400	16670	15355	14188	18505	17321	16233	18461	18063	16921	19587	19243	18154
500	18755	16827	15657	21390	19503	18314	21394	20606	19314	22987	22381	20978
600	20093	18427	16484	23451	21718	19635	23633	23195	21348	25750	25243	23294
750	21766	19685	17686	23491	21769	19976	26431	25789	23750	25682	25141	23491
1000	23477	21235	19005	28778	26109	23482	29864	29049	26608	32938	31919	29135

Ampacity	Plug-In Busway		Feeder Busway		High Imped. Busway
	Copper	Aluminum	Copper	Aluminum	Copper
225	28700	23000	18700	12000	—
400	38900	34700	23900	21300	—
600	41000	38300	36500	31300	—
800	46100	57500	49300	44100	—
1000	69400	89300	62900	56200	15600
1200	94300	97100	76900	69900	16100
1350	119000	104200	90100	84000	17500
1600	129900	120500	101000	90900	19200
2000	142900	135100	134200	125000	20400
2500	143800	156300	180500	166700	21700
3000	144900	175400	204100	188700	23800
4000	—	—	277800	256400	—

Table 14-3 Table of *C* values.

Step 5 Determine the *f* factor:

a. For three-phase faults:

$$f = \frac{1.73 \times L \times I_{SCA}}{N \times C \times E_{L\text{–}L}}$$

b. For single-phase, line-to-line (*L–L*) faults on single-phase, centre-tapped transformers:

$$f = \frac{2 \times L \times I_{SCA}}{N \times C \times E_{L\text{–}L}}$$

c. For single-phase, line-to-neutral (*L–N*) faults on single-phase, centre-tapped transformers:

$$f = \frac{2 \times L \times I_{SCA}}{N \times C \times E_{L\text{–}N}}$$

where

L = the length of the circuit to the fault, in feet

C = the constant derived from Table 14-3 for the specific type of conductors and wiring method

$E_{L\text{–}L}$ = the line-to-line voltage

$E_{L\text{–}N}$ = the line-to-neutral voltage

N = the number of conductors in parallel

Step 6 After finding the *f* factor, refer to Table 14-4 and locate the corresponding value of the multiplier M_2, or, calculate it as follows:

$$M_2 = \frac{1}{1+f}$$

Step 7 Multiply the available fault current at the beginning of the circuit by the multiplier M_2 to determine the available symmetrical fault current at the fault.

$$I_{SCA} \text{ at fault} = I_{SCA} \text{ at beginning of circuit} \times M_2$$

Motor Contribution All motors running at the instant a short-circuit occurs contribute to the short-circuit current. The amount of current from the motors is equal approximately to the starting (locked rotor) current for each motor. This current value depends upon the type of motor and its characteristics. It is a common practice to multiply the full-load ampere rating of the motor by 4 or 5 to obtain a close approximation of the locked rotor current and provide a margin of safety. For energy-efficient motors, multiply the motor's full-load current rating by six to eight times for a reasonable approximation of the fault-current contribution. The current contributed by running motors at the instant a short circuit occurs is added to the value of the short-circuit current at the main switchboard prior to the start of the point-to-point calculations for the rest of the system. To simplify the following problems, motor contributions have not been added to the short-circuit currents.

Chart for M_2 Multiplier

f	M_2	f	M_2
0.01	0.99	1.20	0.45
0.02	0.98	1.50	0.40
0.03	0.97	2.00	0.33
0.04	0.96	3.00	0.25
0.05	0.95	4.00	0.20
0.06	0.94	5.00	0.17
0.07	0.93	6.00	0.14
0.08	0.93	7.00	0.13
0.09	0.92	8.00	0.11
0.10	0.91	9.00	0.10
0.15	0.87	10.00	0.09
0.20	0.83	15.00	0.06
0.30	0.77	20.00	0.05
0.40	0.71	30.00	0.03
0.50	0.67	40.00	0.02
0.60	0.63	50.00	0.02
0.70	0.59	60.00	0.02
0.80	0.55	70.00	0.01
0.90	0.53	80.00	0.01
1.00	0.50	90.00	0.01
		100.00	0.01

$$M_2 = \frac{1}{1+f}$$

Table 14-4 Simple chart to convert *f* values to M_2 multiplier when using the point-to-point method.

SHORT-CIRCUIT CURRENT VARIABLES

Phase-to-Phase-to-Phase Fault

The three-phase fault current determined in Step 7 is the *approximate* current that will flow if the three "hot" phase conductors of a three-phase system are shorted together, in what is commonly referred to as a "bolted fault." This is the worst-case condition.

Phase-to-Phase Fault

To obtain the *approximate* short-circuit current values when two "hot" conductors of a three-phase system are shorted together, use 87% of the three-phase current value. In other words, if the three-phase current value is 20 000 A when the three "hot" lines are shorted together (*L–L–L* value), then the short-circuit current to two "hot" lines shorted together (*L–L*) is approximately:

$20\,000 \times 0.87 = 17\,400$ A

Phase-to-Neutral (Ground)

For solidly grounded three-phase systems, such as a 347/600-V system that supplies the industrial building, the phase-to-neutral (ground) bolted short-circuit current can vary from 25% to 125% of the *L–L–L* bolted short-circuit current. Therefore, it is common practice to consider the *L–N* or *L–G* short-circuit current value to be the same as the *L–L–L* short-circuit current value.

EXAMPLE If the three-phase *L–L–L* fault current has been calculated to be 20 000 A, then the *L–N* fault current is approximately:

$20\,000 \times 1.00 = 20\,000$ A

In summary:

L–L bolted short-circuit current = 87% *L–L–L*
L–N bolted short-circuit current = 100% *L–L–L*

The main concern is to provide the proper interrupting rating for the overcurrent protective devices and the adequate withstand rating for the equipment. Therefore, for most three-phase electrical systems, the line–line–line bolted fault-current value will provide the desired level of safety.

As shown in Problem 3, the fuses or circuit breakers located in the main switchboard of the building must have an interrupting capacity of at least 15 007 RMS symmetrical amperes. It is good practice to install protective devices having interrupting ratings at least 25% greater than the actual calculated available fault current. This practice

PROBLEM 3

It is desired to find the available short-circuit current at the main switchboard of the commercial building. The building is fed from a 1000 KVA 600/RW347V 30 transformer with a 7% impedance. The conductors will be four parallel runs of 500 kcmil RW90XLPE copper, 50 ft long, in PVC. Once this value is known, the electrician can provide overcurrent devices with adequate interrupting ratings and the proper bus bar bracing within the switchboard (Rules 14-012, 14-014, and Appendix B). As each of the following steps in the point-to-point method is examined, refer to the entries given in Tables 14-3 and 14-4 to determine the necessary values of C, f, and M_2.

Step 1: $I_{FLA} = \dfrac{\text{KVA} \times 1000}{E_{L\text{-}L} \times 1.73} = \dfrac{1000 \times 1000}{600 \times 1.73} = 963\text{ A}$

Step 2: Multiplier, $M_1 = \dfrac{100}{\text{Transformer \% impedance} \times 0.9} = \dfrac{100}{7 \times 0.9} = 15.87$

Step 3: $I_{SCA} = 963 \times 15.87 = 15\,282.8$

Step 4: $f = \dfrac{1.73 \times L \times I}{4 \times C \times E_{L\text{-}L}} = \dfrac{1.73 \times 50 \times 15\,282.8}{4 \times 26\,706 \times 600} = 0.0206$

Step 5: $M_2 = \dfrac{1}{1 + f} = \dfrac{1}{1 + 0.0206} = 0.9798$

Step 6: The short-circuit current available at the line-side lugs on the main switchboard is: $15\,282.8 \times 0.9798 = 14\,974$ RMS symmetrical amperes.

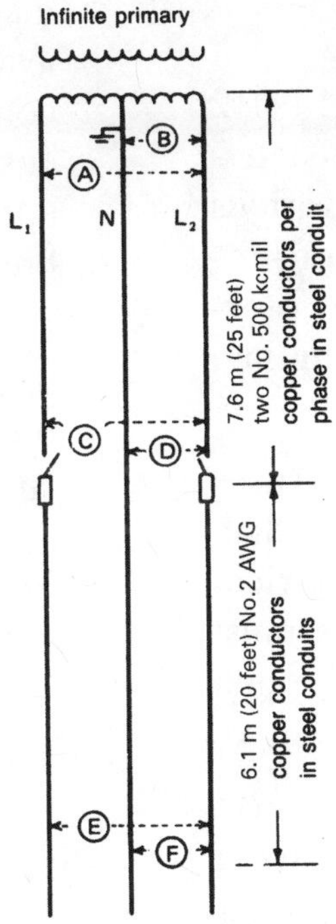

Transformer:
167 kVA, 120/240 volts, single-phase
2% impedance, 696 FLA

Fault $A_{L\text{-}L}$

Transformer FLA = 696 amperes

$$M_1 = \frac{100}{2 \times 0.9} = 55.556$$

$$I_{SCA} = 696 \times 55.556 = 38\,667 \text{ amperes}$$

Fault $C_{L\text{-}L}$

$$f = \frac{2 \times L \times I}{N \times C \times E_{L-L}}$$

$$= \frac{2 \times 25 \times 38\,667}{2 \times 22\,185 \times 240} = 0.18$$

$$M_2 = \frac{1}{1+f} = \frac{1}{1+0.18} = 0.85$$

$$I_{SCA} = 38\,667 \times 0.85 = 32\,867 \text{ amperes}$$

Fault $E_{L\text{-}L}$

$$f = \frac{2 \times L \times I}{N \times C \times E_{L-L}}$$

$$= \frac{2 \times 20 \times 32\,867}{1 \times 5906 \times 240} = 0.93$$

$$M_2 = \frac{1}{1+f} = \frac{1}{1+0.93} = 0.52$$

$$I_{SCA} = 32\,867 \times 0.52 = 17\,091 \text{ amperes}$$

Fault $B_{L\text{-}N}$

Transformer FLA = 696 amperes

$$M_1 = \frac{100}{2 \times 0.9} = 55.556$$

$$I_{SCA} = 696 \times 55.556 \times 1.5 = 58\,000 \text{ amperes}$$

Fault $D_{L\text{-}N}$

$$f = \frac{2 \times L \times I}{N \times C \times E_{L-N}}$$

$$= \frac{2 \times 25 \times 58\,000}{2 \times 22\,185 \times 120} = 0.54$$

$$M_2 = \frac{1}{1+f} = \frac{1}{1+0.54} = 0.65$$

$$I_{SCA} = 58\,000 \times 0.65 = 37\,700 \text{ amperes}$$

Fault $_{L\text{-}N}$

$$f = \frac{2 \times L \times I}{N \times C \times E_{L-N}}$$

$$= \frac{2 \times 20 \times 37.700}{1 \times 5906 \times 120} = 2.13$$

$$M_2 = \frac{1}{1+f} = \frac{1}{1+2.13} = 0.32$$

$$I_{SCA} = 37\,700 \times 0.32 = 12\,064 \text{ amperes}$$

Figure 14-1 Point-to-point calculation for single-phase, centre-tapped transformer. Calculations show *L–L* and *L–N* values.

generally provides a margin of safety to permit the rounding off of numbers, as well as compensating for a reasonable amount of short-circuit contribution from any electrical motors that may be running at the instant the fault occurs.

The fuses specified for the industrial building have an interrupting rating of 200 000 A (see the Specifications). In addition, the switchboard bracing is specified to be 50 000 A.

If current-limiting fuses are installed in the main switchboard feeders protecting the various panelboards, breakers having an interrupting rating of 10 000 A may be adequate for the panelboards. The manufacturer's series tested combination charts must be consulted to be sure the installation meets the requirements of *CEC* Rules 14-012 and 14-014.

If non-current-limiting overcurrent devices (standard moulded case circuit breakers) are to be installed in the main switchboard, breakers having adequate interrupting ratings must be installed in the panelboards. A short-circuit study must be made for each panelboard location to determine the value of the available short-circuit current.

The cost of circuit breakers increases as the interrupting rating of the breakers increases. The most economical protection system generally results when current-limiting fuses are installed in the main switchboard to protect the breakers in the panelboards or series rated breaker combinations are used. In this case, the breakers in the panelboards will have the standard 10 000-A interrupting rating.

PROBLEM 4 Single-Phase Transformer

This problem is illustrated in Figure 14-1. The point-to-point method is used to determine the currents for both line-to-line and line-to-neutral faults for a 167-kVA, 2% impedance transformer on a 240/120-V, single-phase system. Note that the impedance has been reduced by 10%.

Summary

1. To meet the requirements of Rules 14-012 and 14-014, it is absolutely necessary to determine the available fault currents at various points on the electrical system. If a short-circuit study is not done, the selection of overcurrent devices may be in error, resulting in a hazard to life and property.

2. For an installation using fuses only, the fuses must have an interrupting rating *not less* than the available fault current. The electrical equipment to be protected by the fuses must be capable of withstanding the let-through current of the fuse.

3. For an installation using fuses to protect panels that contain circuit breakers having inadequate interrupting ratings (less than the available fault current), use the series tested combinations tables from manufacturers to ensure the proper selection of fuses that will adequately protect the downstream circuit breakers.

4. For an installation using standard circuit breakers only, the breakers must have an interrupting rating *not less* than the available fault current at the point of application. It is recommended that the breakers used have interrupting ratings at *least 25% greater* than the available fault current.

To use current-limiting circuit breakers, refer to the manufacturer's application data.

REVIEW

All answers should be written in complete sentences, calculations should be shown in detail, and code references should be cited when appropriate.

Note: Refer to the *CEC, Part I* or the plans as necessary.

1. Using Table 14-1, determine the available short-circuit currents on a 208-V system for the following:
   (a) 15.24 m (50 ft) of No. 1 conductor __________ A
   (b) 7.62 m (25 ft) of No. 3/0 conductor __________ A
   (c) 15.24 m (50 ft) of 500-kcmil conductor __________ A
   (d) 15.24 m (50 ft) of two No. 3/0 conductors per phase __________ A
   (e) 30.48 m (100 ft) of No. 4/0 conductor __________ A
2. (a) Define *selectivity.*
   (b) Define *nonselectivity.*
3. A series-connected panel contains a 1200-A main breaker with many branch-circuit breakers rated at 100 A and 225 A. The branch-circuit breakers have an individual interrupting rating of 10 000 A. The main circuit breaker has an individual interrupting rating of 42 000 A. In combination the panel is CSA listed as suitable for use at fault currents not to exceed 65 000 A.
   (a) For a fault current above 10 000 A on the load side of one of the 225-A breakers, the main breakers (will trip) (will not trip). Circle the correct answer.
   (b) For a fault current of 4000 A on the load side of one of the 100-A breakers, the main breaker (will trip) (will not trip). Circle the correct answer.

4. Refer to Figure 14-2 and calculate the available short-circuit current at Panel "A." This panel is supplied by a 7.6 m (25 ft) run of No. 3/0 copper conductors in steel conduit. Use the point-to-point method and show all calculations.

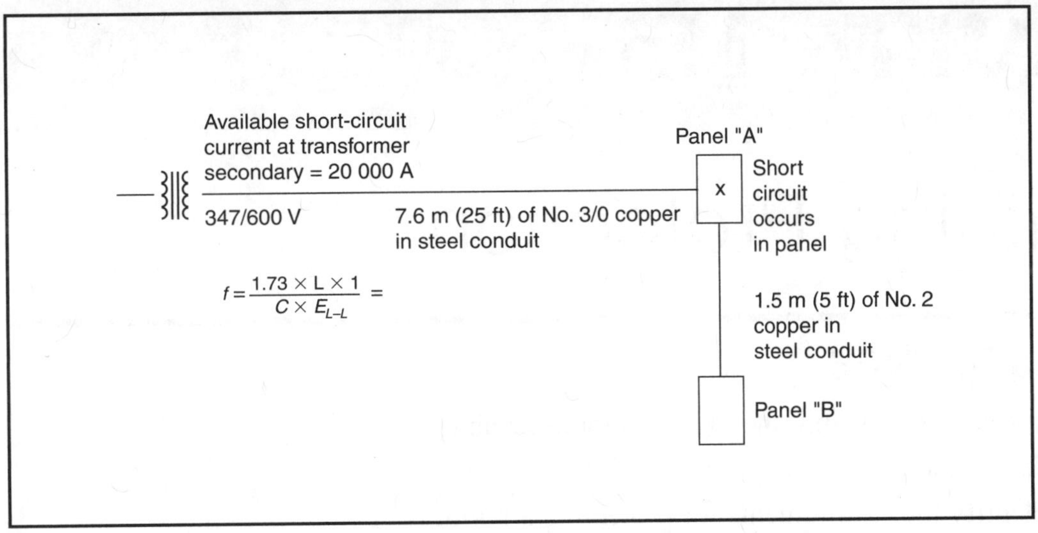

Figure 14-2

5. Calculate the available fault current if a short circuit occurs in Panel "B" in Figure 14-2. Use the point-to-point method and show all calculations.

6. A three-phase, *L–L–L* bolted short-circuit current has been calculated to be 40 000 RMS symmetrical amperes. What is the approximate value of:

   (a) a line-to-line fault? __________

   (b) a line-to-ground fault? __________

UNIT 15

Lightning Protection

OBJECTIVES

After studying this unit, the student should be able to:

- describe the lightning process
- identify the requirements for protecting a building
- list lightning safety rules

THE LIGHTNING PROCESS

Lightning is simultaneously a fascinating, awesome, and mysterious phenomenon. It is beautiful to witness but destructive and potentially fatal to experience. Yet, it is a natural, necessary occurrence. Lightning is electricity on exhibit; and, as with the electrical power in our homes, businesses, and factories, specific precautions are to be taken or we must expect to suffer the consequences.

To understand the intricacies of lightning protection, it is necessary also to understand, or at least to be aware of, the rudiments of atomic structure and what occurs within that structure. For that reason, this study of lightning protection begins with a brief presentation of the theory of atomic structure.

ATOMIC STRUCTURE

All matter is made up of *atoms*. For example, a single drop of water contains about 100 billion atoms. Each atom has at its centre a *nucleus* that comprises of *protons* and *neutrons*. The nucleus is considered to have a positive charge equal to the number of protons. Under normal conditions, the nucleus is surrounded by a number of *electrons*, each having a negative charge, equal to the number of protons in the nucleus.

The exact numbers of protons or electrons are different for each element and are stated as the atomic number of that element. Hydrogen has an atomic number of 1, copper 29, lead 82, and so on.

If a force is exerted on an atom to the extent that an electron is dislodged or added, the atom is said to become an *ion*. The atom that loses an electron has a net positive charge and, thus, is called a *positive ion*; the atom that gains an electron is a *negative ion*. This phenomenon of being able to remove electrons from atoms, or *ionizing* them, makes it possible to store electrical energy and to transfer that energy from place to place.

Electrons at Work

For the purpose of further explanation, assume a hypothetical situation in which a large number of positive ions are collected at Point *A*. At another point (call it Point *B*), located in space, are the collected electrons that have been dislodged from the atoms at Point *A*. If 6 250 000 000 000 000 000

(6.25×10^{18}) electrons are transferred from Point *A* to Point *B*, the quantity of charge is referred to as a *coulomb*.

For a moment, digress from the hypothetical situation and turn your attention to the basic nature of charges. It is a fundamental law that charged bodies of unlike charges attract each other, and charged bodies of like charges repel each other. The force of attraction or repulsion between charges is directly proportional to the square of the distance between these charges. This brings us to another definition of the coulomb. A coulomb (C) is that quantity of charge that, when placed one metre (m) from a like charge, repels it with a force of 9 000 000 000 (9×10^9) newtons (N). It follows that it takes work (force multiplied by distance) to collect charges at a point, for, as one coulomb of charge is formed, a force of 9 000 000 000 (9×10^9) newtons must be exerted over a distance of one metre. The work done (energy released) by a force of one newton, acting over a distance of one metre, is expressed as one joule (J).

Going back to Points *A* and *B*, it should now be apparent that, as electrons are forced from Point *A* to Point *B*, work is done and an energy differential is established. In electrical studies, this is called a *potential difference*, which is measured in volts (V). A *volt* is that potential energy a charge gains when one joule of work is done on one coulomb of charge.

$$1\,V = \frac{1\,J}{1\,C}$$

The Ionosphere

We now expand on the hypothetical example by giving locations to Points *A* and *B*. Since the subject is lightning, it is reasonable to locate Point *B* on Earth and Point *A* in a region called the ionosphere. The *ionosphere* is located at altitudes of 64 km or so above the Earth, where the atmosphere contains more ions than neutral atoms (Figure 15-1).

The Earth has a surplus of electrons and is about 300 000 (3×10^5) V negative with respect to the ionosphere. This means that a person of average height, while standing, is covered from foot to head by a potential gradient of about 260 V, (Figure 15-2). The typical reaction to this statement is, "Why doesn't the person feel a shock?" Electrical shock is measured in terms of current, and the current in this case is infinitesimal. (The air–Earth current is calculated to be between 1400 A and 1800 A or about one microampere per three square kilometres.) But the total current from Earth is sufficient to upset nature's balance, and lightning is thought to be a natural way of restoring the balance. It is estimated that, on the average, the Earth is struck by lightning 100 times per second, and in about 90% of these times electrons flow to the Earth. However, there is not full agreement on how this comes about.

HOW LIGHTNING IS GENERATED

Lightning is generated by the ominous cumulonimbus cloud or thundercloud. Here the action is so violent that charges may be formed on the lower portion of the cloud. Most of these charges are neg-

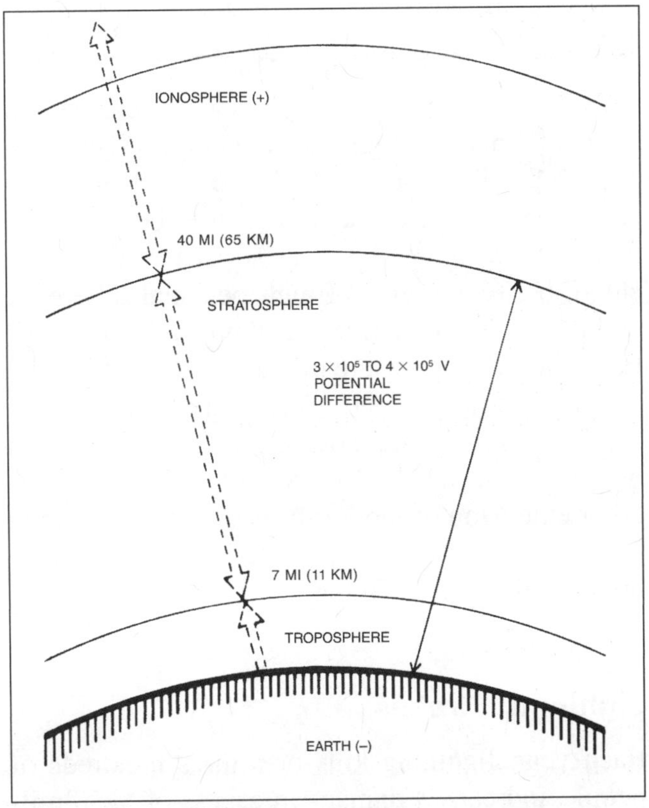

Figure 15-1 Location of the ionosphere in relation to the Earth

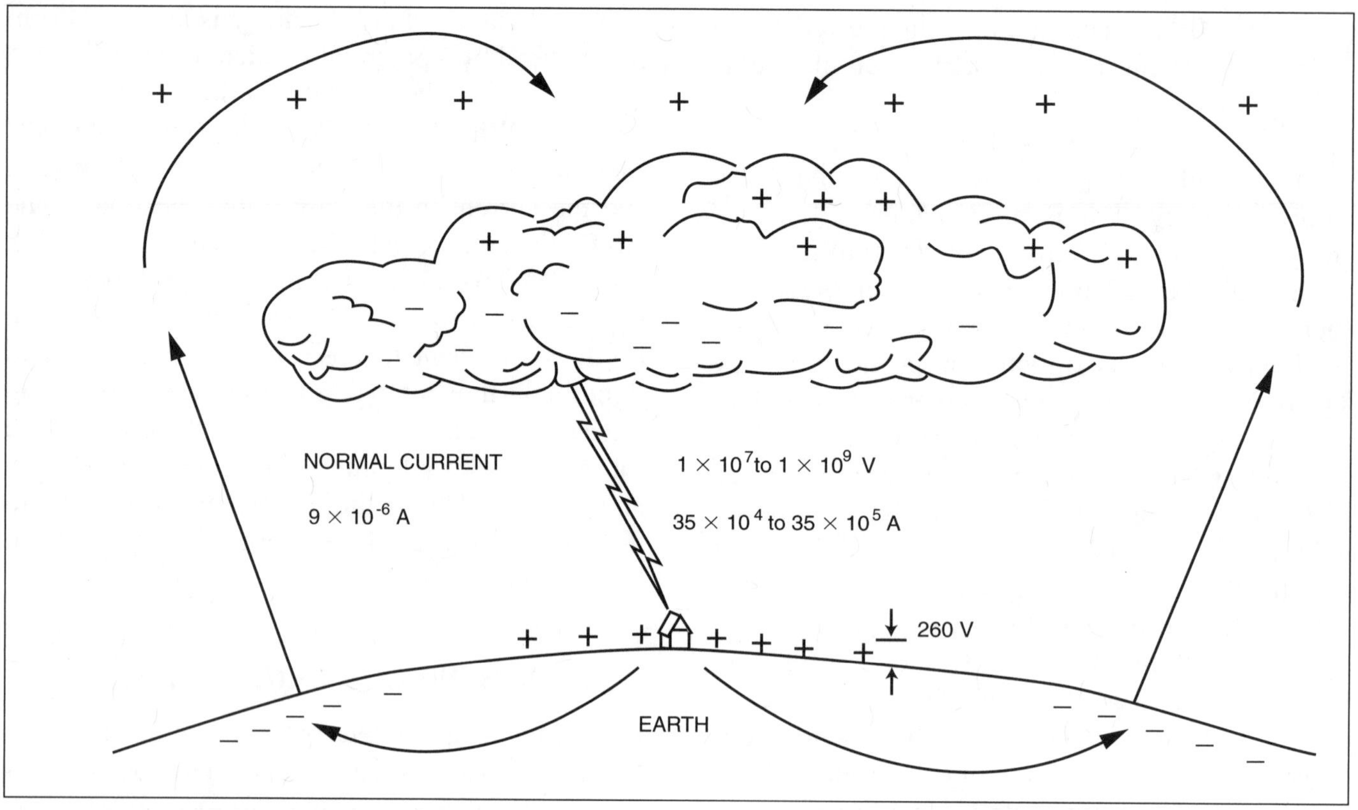

Figure 15-2 Person standing on Earth is surrounded by a potential gradient of about 260 V.

ative with respect to the upper portion of the cloud and to the Earth below the cloud. Now, we essentially have a Point *B* at a high negative charge and several Points *A* at high positive charges. What happens depends upon how high the potential differences become and the impedance between the points. There may be lightning strokes from cloud to cloud, between points of high potential difference within a cloud, or between the thundercloud and the Earth. We, of course, are primarily interested in the cloud-to-Earth strokes (Figure 15-3 on page 209).

These strokes are most likely to occur at a high point; that is, where a tree, a tall building, or some other extension of the Earth rises upward, thereby reducing the distance and, thus, the impedance between the charge on Earth and the cloud charge.

Lightning Strokes

Each year, lightning kills or injures hundreds of people and causes damage in excess of $250 million. These disasters are all caused by the enormous energy transfer that takes place during a cloud-to-Earth stroke. The current may rise to as high as 200 000 A (200 kA), and the potential difference may be as much as 100 megavolts. Yet, the stroke lasts only a fraction of a second. Our goal in lightning protection is to provide a low-impedance path from the high point, where the stroke makes contact with the Earth, so that the energy may be dissipated over a large area.

STANDARD FOR LIGHTNING PROTECTION SYSTEMS

All installations of lightning protection systems are governed by *CAN/CSA-B72-M87 Installation Code for Lightning Protection Systems.* This standard identifies five classes of installations based upon the height, type, and location of the building and the types of materials in the building. Most industrial buildings would fall within Class I or II. The intent of this unit of study is to provide basic information regarding the concepts and installation of lightning protection systems. For more detailed information, please refer to the aforementioned standard.

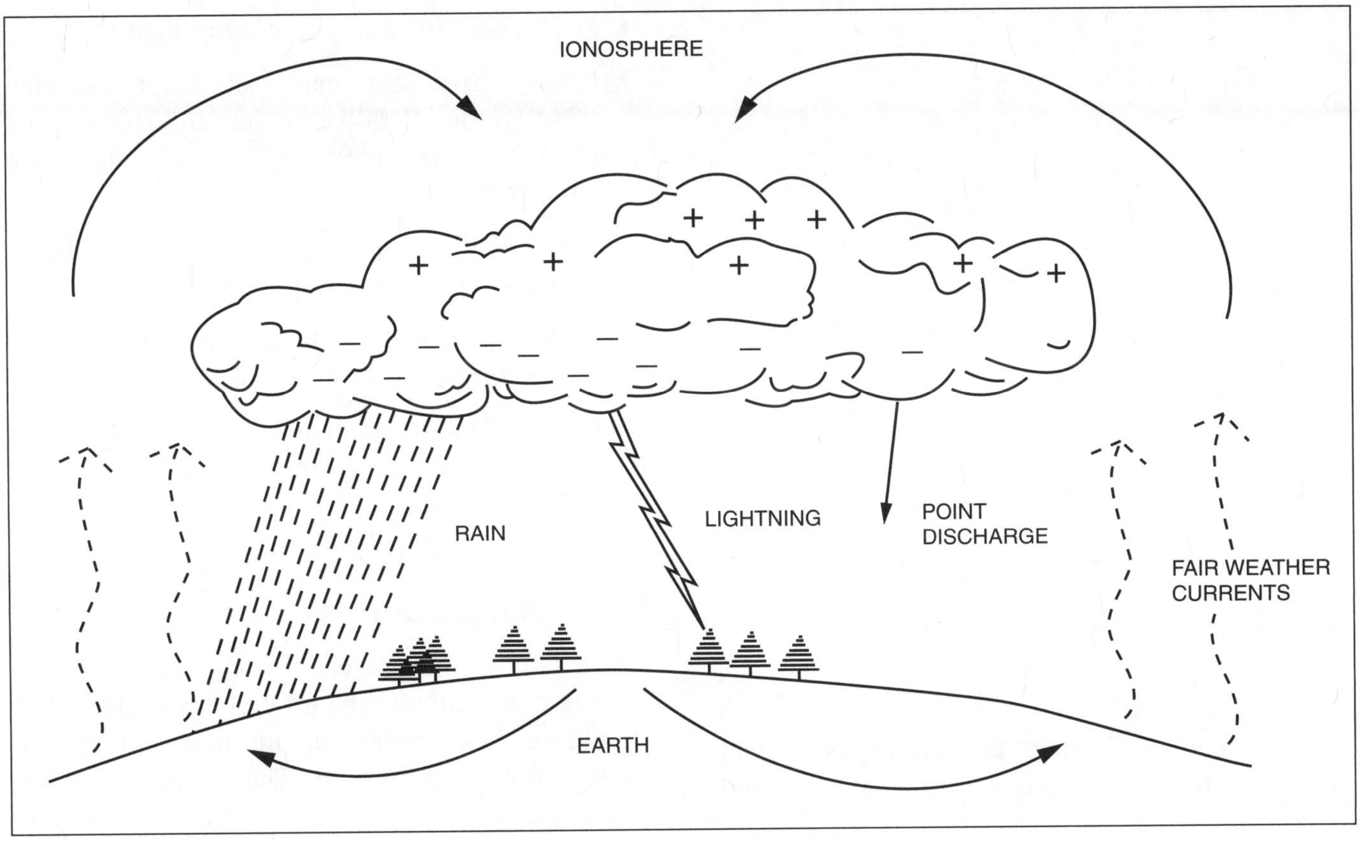

Figure 15-3 Lightning strokes are generated between the thundercloud and the Earth.

The installation of lightning protection systems for buildings, trees, and other structures must be guided by the requirements of *CAN/CSA-B72-M87*. The systems required by this standard are based upon the basic principle of providing a low-impedance path for the stroke to follow to Earth while minimizing the possibility of damage, fire, and personal injury or death as the stroke follows that path.

BUILDING PROTECTION

Lightning protection systems have four basic components: air terminals, intercepting conductors, down conductors, and ground electrodes.

Air Terminal (Lightning Rod)

The air terminal, or lightning rod, is the highest element of a lightning protection system. It is a solid or tubular rod made of copper or aluminum. Usually sharply pointed, it is available with a safety point, as shown in Figure 15-4 on page 210. Safety point air terminals are installed where a sharp point would create a hazard to personnel, such as on a flat roof.

The terminal attracts lightning but does not prevent lightning, as originally supposed by Benjamin Franklin. The lightning stroke is attracted to the terminal because it is a part of the path that offers the least impedance to ground. In general, air terminals should:

- extend above the object to be protected not less than 50 mm
- be placed on ridges of gable, gambrel, and hip roofs within 0.5 m of the ends and at intervals not exceeding 8 m
- be placed on the perimeter of flat roofs at intervals not exceeding 8 m, within 0.5 m of the edge, and not more than 0.5 m from a corner
- be placed in the centre of a roof area at intervals not exceeding 15 m

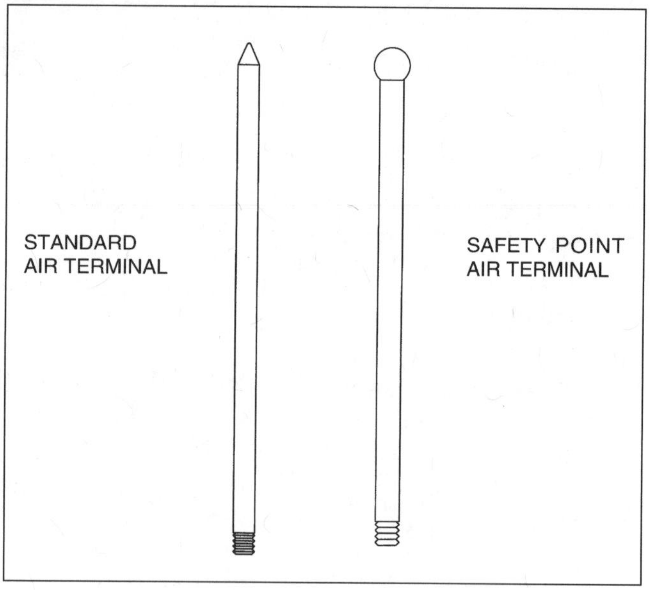

Figure 15-4 Air terminals.

- be placed on dormers and chimneys, except when these projections are protected by other terminals

Intercepting Conductors

The purpose of an intercepting conductor is the same as an air terminal: to attract lightning. If a conductor can be placed around the perimeter of a building on the highest point, the air terminals can be, but are often not, eliminated. Additional intercepting conductors, connected at both ends and at intervals not exceeding 50 m, must be installed inside this perimeter loop such that no part of the roof is more than 10 m from an intercepting conductor. If the intercepting conductor is covered with any type of roofing material, air terminals must be installed at intervals not exceeding 15 m. The intercepting conductors may be of copper or aluminum but the conductor type must be selected so that galvanic action is minimized. This would indicate that copper conductors cannot be used when in contact with aluminum roof flashings and aluminum conductors cannot be used when in contact with copper flashings. In general, intercepting conductors should:

- not be bent to a radius of less than 200 mm
- not be bent to an angle of more than 90°
- have a cross-sectional area of not less than #2AWG or 59 000 circular mils for copper or 1/0 AWG or 98 500 circular mils for aluminum
- connect all metallic bodies, such as exhaust fans and roof vents, to the protection system
- be securely fastened to the air terminals, the down conductors, and the structure
- not be concealed in metallic conduit, unless the conductor is securely bonded to the conduit at both ends

Down Conductors

Down conductors are used to connect the intercepting conductors to the ground electrodes. They should be the same size as the intercepting conductors for the type used. The number of down conductors installed will be equal to one for every 30 m or portion thereof of building perimeter but in no case shall be less than two. If only two down conductors are installed, they must be placed at opposite corners of the building. If more than two are required, they must be distributed around the perimeter at distances not exceeding 35 m. If the down conductors are made of aluminum, they must not terminate at the ground electrodes below grade. The ground rods may extend from the ground a maximum of 300 mm or the aluminum conductor may connect to a copper conductor above grade using an approved connector. The copper tail may then be connected to the ground electrode below grade level. In general, a down conductor should follow a downward direction and be as straight as possible.

Ground Electrodes

The grounds are a minimum of 3 m long and 12 mm in diameter if made of copper or copper-clad steel. Galvanized steel rods 15 mm in diameter may also be used. However, where the topsoil is very shallow, groundplates may be used. In general, grounding connections should be:

- made with rods driven into the Earth, at least 600 mm from the protected object
- made to underground metallic water pipes or well casings within 7.5 m of the protected building
- interconnected with driven ground electrodes for the electric or telephone system

PROTECTION OF ELECTRICAL SYSTEMS

It is important to provide separation of the lightning protection system and the building electrical system. *CEC* Rule 12-016 states that whenever practical, a separation of at least two metres be maintained between the lightning rod conductors and any electrical wiring. If this separation is not possible, the ground electrodes of the two systems must be connected together at or below ground level with a conductor equal in size to that of the electrical system grounding conductor (*CEC* Rule 10-706). The grounding system for the lightning rods must not be used to ground any other system or equipment, as indicated in *CEC* Rule 10-710.

SAFETY RULES

Following these specific requirements will result in a structure that is free from the hazards of lightning. But, inasmuch as humans are also vulnerable to lightning, we should be aware of various safety rules that will help us avoid the shocking experience of a lightning stroke. The following safety rules for human protection when lightning threatens should be observed:

- Stay indoors and do not venture outside unless absolutely necessary.
- Stay away from open doors and windows, fireplaces, radiators, stoves, metal pipes, sinks, and plug-in electrical appliances.
- Do not use plug-in electrical equipment such as hair dryers, electric toothbrushes, or electric razors during the storm.
- Do not use the telephone during the storm—lightning may strike telephone lines outside.
- Do not take laundry off the clothesline.
- Do not work on fences, telephone or power lines, pipelines, or structural steel fabrication.
- Do not use metal objects such as fishing rods and golf clubs. Golfers wearing cleated shoes are particularly good lightning rods.
- Do not handle flammable materials in open containers.
- Stop tractor work and dismount, especially when the tractor is pulling metal equipment. Tractors and other implements in metallic contact with the ground are often struck by lightning.
- Get out of the water and off small boats.
- Stay in your automobile if you are driving. Automobiles offer lightning protection.
- Seek shelter in a building. If a building is unavailable, seek protection in a cave, a ditch, a canyon, or under head-high clumps of trees in open forest glades.
- When there is no shelter, avoid the highest object in the area. If only isolated trees are nearby, the best protection is to crouch in the open, keeping twice as far away from isolated trees as the trees are high.
- Avoid hilltops, open spaces, wire fences, metal clotheslines, exposed sheds, and any electrically conductive elevated objects.
- Should you feel the electrical charge—if your hair stands on end or your skin tingles—lightning may be about to strike you. Drop to the ground immediately.

Persons struck by lightning suffer a severe electrical shock and may be burned, but they carry no electrical charge and can be handled safely. A person thought to be killed by lightning can often be revived by prompt mouth-to-mouth resuscitation, cardiac massage, and prolonged artificial respiration. In a group struck by lightning, the apparently dead should be treated first. Those who show vital signs will probably recover spontaneously, although burns and other injuries may require treatment. Recovery from lightning strokes is usually complete, except for possible impairment or loss of sight or hearing.

If you are ever present when a person is struck by lightning, immediately begin cardiopulmonary resuscitation. If you do not know how to apply this basic life-support technique, contact your local Red Cross, ambulance service, employer, or Health and Safety office regarding the availability of training courses. Encourage your friends to learn, too; for, if lightning ever strikes you, it may save your life to have friends who are able to come to your aid.

REVIEW

All answers should be written in complete sentences, calculations should be shown in detail, and Code references should be cited when appropriate.

1. In your own words, write two definitions of a coulomb.
2. In your own words, explain what causes lightning.
3. List the general rules for placement of lightning air terminals.
4. List the general rules for ground electrodes and the connections to them.
5. If you were asked to evaluate a lightning protection installation, what would you look for?
6. If you were attending a Little League baseball game when nearby lightning was observed, what actions would you advise others to take?
7. State the minimum separation between the conductors of the lightning protection system and the building electrical system.
8. Can a television satellite dish be grounded to the lightning protection system grounding electrode?

UNIT 16

Lighting

OBJECTIVES

After studying this unit, the student should be able to:

- list the important considerations in lamp selection for lighting systems
- select illuminance values for site lighting
- compute the power limit and power demand for site lighting
- locate luminaires (fixtures) for site lighting
- list control options for lighting systems

LAMP SELECTION

When choosing an appropriate lamp for a lighting system, at least three factors should be considered: (1) the amount of power the lamp requires to provide the needed light, (2) the colour the lamp creates, and (3) the maintenance requirements of the lamp.

At first thought, the study of site lighting could be perceived as a limited subject. However, a few experiences will reveal an array of options that can be applied in the lighting of a large area site. To examine these options, it is useful to divide the system into three parts: power control, light sources, and light distribution.

Power Control

A toggle switch may be adequate if the load is small and the control requirements minimal. As the load increases, it is common to install a contactor that will, on signal, turn on (or off) a large number of light sources. A contactor is similar to a motor starter in that completing the control circuit will energize a coil that closes a set of contacts. The circuit controlled may connect directly to the light sources, or it may energize a panelboard where many circuits are connected to an array of light sources. The operation of the system may be manual, such as the toggle switch, or it may be fully automated. The advantage to using a toggle switch is initial cost; the disadvantage is that a person must perform the operation, which can be costly and likely unreliable. The automated system has a high initial cost but only a minimal maintenance cost, and it is reliable. For site lighting, it would need to be sensitive to the day and night cycle. The simplest option is an astronomical time clock. These clocks would be set for the time and the date, then they would automatically adjust the on period for the seasonal changes in nighttime hours. A control device with greater reliability would be a photocell that could be adjusted to a precise intensity of light for on and off control. On a cloudy day, it would probably energize the lighting earlier than the time clock

Light Sources

Light sources (lamps) can be placed in three categories: incandescent, fluorescent, and high intensity discharge. It is recommended that the person selecting or installing the light source have at hand a lamp specification and application guide (this is available from most electrical distribution centres or can be requested from any of the major lamp manufacturers) for there are hundreds of lamp types available and all with different characteristics. Following are abbreviated descriptions of several types of lamps.

Incandescent There are two styles of incandescent lamps: the Edison type and the tungsten halogen lamp. The *Edison* type lamp uses a wire filament enclosed in a glass bulb to produce the light. The bulb may be vacuumed or filled with an inert gas. The filament is a coil of wire that emits light when heated. The light output varies from 100 lm (lumen) to 10 000 lm and the lamp wattage varies from 3 W to 1500 W. Both the light output and the lamp life are sensitive to the voltage applied. A small increase in voltage above the rated value will result in a higher intensity of light and a much shorter lamp life. In practice, where lamp life is an important factor, lamps rated for 130 V are installed on 120-V systems, which will almost double the lamp life. The *halogen* type lamp uses a tightly wound tungsten filament coil in a small quartz tube. The light is produced at a higher temperature, and thus it has superior colour-rendering properties when compared to the Edison lamps. The lamp is costly but life is longer than, sometimes double that of, the Edison lamp. The luminaires (fixtures) are smaller and could provide superior control of the light distribution.

Due to their low efficiency and high maintenance costs, incandescent lamps have limited application in industrial applications.

Fluorescent The fluorescent lamp is a tubular type of lamp with a filament at both ends of the tube. The tube size and length vary greatly from a few inches (millimetres) to 8 ft (2.5 m) in length and from 5/8 in to 12/8 in (15.87 to 38 mm) in diameter. Light output varies from slightly over 400 lm to nearly 6000 lm. The light is produced by electrons bombarding phosphors, thus the colour-rendition properties of the light can be varied by the selection of phosphors. They have a long life and a fair tolerance for voltage swings. Their application in outdoor lighting has been limited because the lamp light output drops with the ambient temperature and because of the length, the luminaires (fixtures) must be strongly supported if there is the possibility of high-velocity winds.

High Intensity Discharge (HID) There are four styles of HID lamps: mercury, metal halide, high-pressure sodium, and low-pressure sodium. The vast majority of these lamps have a single screw type base. The *mercury* lamp is the oldest style but is now in diminished use. It is usually available with power ratings of 100 W to 1000 W with a light output of 2850 lm to 63 000 lm. Light depreciation over the lamp's life is high and the colour rendition poor.

The *metal halide lamp* is available in power ratings from 39 W to 1000 W with the light output varying from 2300 lm to 125 000 lm and lamp life from 10 000 to 24 000 hours. The lamps vary in length from 4 to 15 in (100 to 375 mm). They are preferred over the mercury lamp, which is considered obsolete.

Pulse start metal halide lamps are a recent improvement to higher wattage metal halide lamps (175 W to 1000 W). Pulse start luminaries use a new family of metal halide lamps, a separate pulse start igniter (instead of a starting electrode in the lamp), and reduced crest factor ballasts. This results in a system that has higher lamp efficacy, improved lumen maintenance, longer lamp life, and faster start-up and restrike time.

Pulse start lamps are not interchangeable with standard metal halide lamps. They will not start on a standard metal halide ballast. Standard metal halide lamps may explode if used in pulse start luminaires.

The arc tube of a metal halide lamp operates at high temperatures and pressures. There is a small risk of the arc tube rupturing when the lamps reach their end of life or if they are operated beyond their rated life. This can cause the release of hot particles from the lamp.

To minimize the risk, certain precautions should be taken with metal halide lamps:

- When replacing lamps in open fixtures, be sure the replacement lamp is suitable for use in open fixtures. E-type lamps must be used in enclosed fixtures. S-type (when operated in the vertical position) and O-type lamps may be used in open fixtures.
- Always group re-lamp metal halide lamps as recommended by the manufacturer.
- If metal halide lamps are operated on a continuous basis (24 hours a day, seven days per week), they must be turned off for a minimum of 15 minutes per week.
- Ballasts used on metal halide lamps must match the characteristics of the lamp.

The *high-pressure sodium* lamp is available with power ratings from 35 W to 1000 W with the light output varying from 1250 lm to 140 000 lm. Lamp life varies from 10 000 to 24 000 hours. Colour rendition is poor, but colour discrimination is possible.

The *low-pressure sodium* lamp has a power rating that varies from 18 W to 180 W and light output from 1800 lm to 33 000 lm. Lamp life ranges from 14 000 to 18 000 hours. The light output and the life are excellent, but colour discrimination is void, with everything appearing the same colour: yellow. People parking in a lot could not identify their automobiles by colour.

Table 16-1 provides a comparison of lamps that might be selected for illuminating the industrial building. The operational data for the listed lamps is provided in columns two through six. In the last column, a comparison is made by choosing a quantity of light to be produced, then calculating the number of lamps and the electrical power required. As can be seen in the table, the low-pressure sodium will be the least expensive to operate, but this does not indicate that it will be the lamp of choice. When all other factors such as colour discrimination, lamp life, and number of poles required are considered, the metal halide will be a strong contender.

Light Distribution

The distribution of the light after it has been created in the lamp is affected by three factors: the lamp, the reflectors, and the lenses. Many halogen and all the fluorescent lamps are tubular in shape, thus emitting light in 360° the entire length of the tube. In most cases, a reflector is installed to redirect 50% or more of the light. When light is reflected by a surface, there is absorption dependent on the reflectivity of the surface. When selecting a reflector, keep in mind that white has the highest reflectivity. This surface should be cleaned before installation and every time the lamps are replaced. Although the distribution from the other types of lamps is more directed, most likely there will be a reflector to redirect the light in a specific pattern. Lenses are made of clear glass or plastic and are designed to redirect the light. They should be cleaned regularly and replaced if they begin to yellow, as is the tendency

Lamp Type	Watts Rating	Lumen Rating	Total Watts	Lamp Life	Lamp Length	(Lamps) Load*
Incandescent	1 000	17 700	1 000	1 000	13 in	(17) 17 kW
Halogen	1 000	21 000	1 000	3 000	10 in	(14) 14 kW
Fluorescent (800 ma)	60	4 050	100	12 000	48 in	(74) 7.4 kW
Fluorescent F96T8/HO	86	7 100	92.5	18 000	96 in	(44) 4.1 kW
Mercury	250	12 100	285	24 000	8.5 in	(25) 7.1 kW
Metal halide (std)	400	23 500	454	20 000	11.5 in	(12) 5.5 kW
Metal halide Pulse Start	350	27 500	400	20 000	11.5 in	(11) 4.4 kW
High-pressure sodium	250	28 500	310	28 500	10 in	(11) 3.4 kW
Low-pressure sodium	135	22 500	180	18 000	20 in	(13) 2.3 kW

* The approximate number of lamps and the resultant load required to produce 300 000 lm. All values are generic approximations; manufacturer's data should be consulted for specific information.

of some plastics. With most luminaires (fixtures), charts are available to detail the light distribution. These should be studied to determine whether the luminaire (fixture) has the proper distribution pattern for the application. For example, a luminaire (fixture) designed for illuminating bookshelves would be a poor choice for an assembly room.

Lamp Efficacy

To be fair in comparing the power requirements of lamps, it is assumed that the light output of the lamps is the same. Since this is rarely the case, a technique has been developed that compares the light output of a lamp (lumen) with the power requirement (watt). By dividing the lumen rating of a lamp by the watts rating, a value called the *efficacy* of the lamp is determined. A high efficacy means that the lamp produces a great amount of light for each watt of power. When evaluating lamps that use ballasts, the watts rating of the ballast should also be included.

Typical lamp types and their efficacies are shown in Table 16-1. A review of Table 16-1 would indicate that the low-pressure sodium lamp is preferred, when considering *power only*; the high-pressure sodium lamp is second; and the standard metal halide lamp and the high-output fluorescent lamp are tied for third.

Lamp Colour Characteristics

The colours that a person perceives when viewing a building and its surrounding area can be very important. The image of the structure, the automobiles in the parking lot, the materials in the storage yard, and the people entering the building will all have a different appearance when illuminated by light with different colour content.

The perceived colour of any of these objects is affected by the colour of the object itself and the colour of the light used to illuminate the object. A common example of this is often observed in parking lots, where automobiles take on an entirely different look at nighttime when the parking lot lighting is turned on.

When it is important that good colour discrimination be possible, then lamps must be selected to make this possible. If exact colour discrimination is required, the objects to be seen should be viewed under the lamps before the lamps are selected for installation. However, for general usage, the listing in Table 16-2 can be used as a guide.

A comparison of the characteristics in Table 16-2, along with the performance information in Table 16-1, would indicate the low-pressure sodium lamp to be the best lamp if colour discrimination is unimportant. The low-pressure sodium lamp would be acceptable for the majority of exterior uses, and the others would be used in cases where colour was more important.

Lamp Maintenance

The maintenance of any lighting system is strongly sensitive to how often the lamp can be expected to fail and how difficult it is to replace. Looking back at Table 16-1, it can be noticed that the incandescent lamp has, by far, the shortest life expectancy. Fluorescent and metal halide lamp life varies widely. Consult manufacturers' data sheets before making a selection. High-pressure sodium lamps have the longest life expectancy.

For the industrial building, the high-pressure sodium lamp will be used as the light source for all the outdoor site areas.

Lamp Type	Discussion
Incandescent	Is accepted by many as the colour standard; is considered a warm light; blues will appear somewhat grey
Mercury deluxe	Has a cool, greenish light; reds and oranges will appear somewhat grey
Fluorescent	A wide variety of lamp colour types makes any degree of colour rendering possible
Metal halide	Similar to mercury; whitest light of HID sources
High-pressure sodium	Has an orange-yellow light; permits good colour discrimination, except with some reds and blues
Low-pressure sodium	A yellow monochromatic light that permits no colour discrimination, except with yellow objects

Table 16-2 Lamp colour characteristics.

INDOOR LUMINAIRES

The indoor lighting requires a white light source. This limits the choice to fluorescent or metal halide lighting systems. The existing factory floor has HO fluorescent luminaries. The addition will use pulse start metal halide luminaries. The systems are comparable in terms of energy efficiency. The final decision will rest on colour rendering (fluorescent is better), installation and maintenance costs (metal halide is lower), and shadowing (fluorescent is better due to size of fixture and larger number of fixtures).

Exterior lighting systems are usually HPS or metal halide.

Illuminance Selections

The amount of light, or illuminance, needed for exterior areas is dependent upon the type of activity that is to take place in a specific area. The Illuminating Engineering Society of North America (IES) has published recommendations for various activity areas. Unless otherwise specified, the illuminance value given is the footcandle that can be measured on the horizontal surface of the area, on the pavement in a parking lot or roadway, or on the sidewalk where people walk.

For the areas on the industrial building site, the recommended illuminances are as shown in Table 16-3. Note that the storage area is recommended to have a considerably higher lighting level than the other areas. This is because it is considered a work area, as compared with the other areas where only walking or driving take place.

Site Activity	Illuminance (footcandles)	Lux
Parking	0.5	5
Roadway	0.6	6
Storage	20	200
Pedestrian	0.9	9
Building Activity		
Assembly—medium	50	500
Machine shop—med.	50	500
Machine shop—fine	200	2 000
Shipping/receiving	30	300
Cafeteria	50	500
Offices	50	500
Storage	15	150
Packaging, labelling	30	300

POWER LIMITATION

During the design of a building, consideration is given to the amount of power dedicated to lighting. Several procedures are common, but the one adopted by the majority of the construction industry is "ASHRAE/IES Standard 90, Energy Conservation in New Building Construction."

For the areas on the industrial building site, the power allowances are shown in Table 16-4. The procedure dictates that the power values determined for each of the areas be totalled and only the total value be considered the power limit.

For the industrial building site, the power limits are shown in Table 16-5. The actual connected load is shown in Table 16-6 on page 218. Since the total connected load is not significantly greater than the power limit, this installation complies with the typical energy code.

Luminaire Placement

The location and selection of luminaires (fixtures) and the sizing of the lamps are facilitated by drawings similar to that shown in Figure 16-1 on page 218. This type of drawing, which is provided

Site Area	Power Allowance (watts)
Parking	30 watts per space
Roadway	2 W/ft (6.5 W/m)
Storage	0.4 W/ft^2 (4.3 W/m^2)
Pedestrian	30 W/ft (100 W/m)

Table 16-4 Power allowances.

Site Activity		Power Allowance	Area Watts
Parking	90 spaces	18 m 30 watts per space	2 700
Roadway	425 ft	2 watts per linear foot	850
	130 m	6.5 watts per metre	3 160
Storage	7900 sq ft	0.4 watts per square foot	
	735 sq m	43 watts per square metre	1 800
Pedestrian	60 ft	30 watts per linear foot	
	18 m	10 watts per metre	
Power limit (watts)			8 510

Table 16-5 Industrial lighting power limit.

Site Activity	Number of Luminaires	Watts per Luminaire	Total Watts
Parking1	12	310	3 720
Roadway	6	125	750
Storage	6	480	2 880
Pedestrian	18	65	1 170
Total watts			8 520

Table 16-6 Site-lighting power requirements.

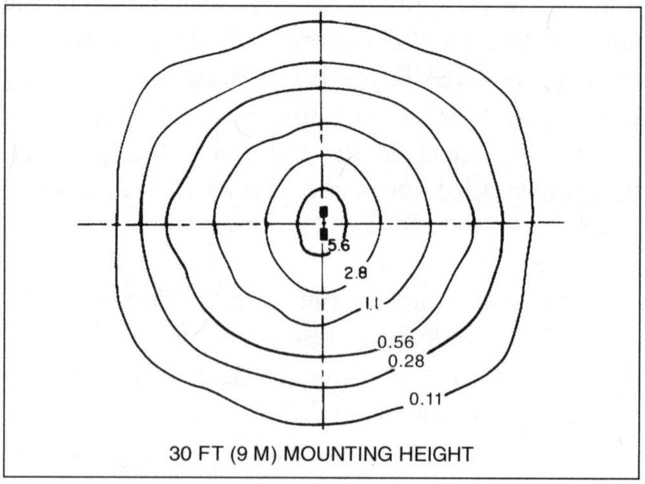

Figure 16-1 Isofootcandle curves.

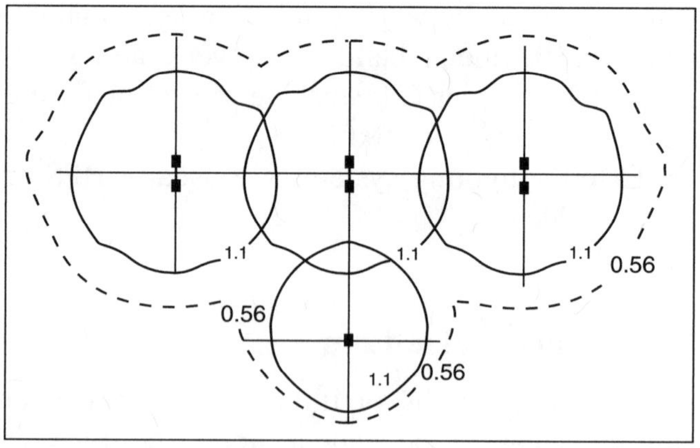

Figure 16-2 Determining footcandle values.

by the luminaire manufacturers, is called isoilluminance curves or, in this specific instance, isofootcandle curves. Each curve represents a line, if drawn on the horizontal surface being illuminated, where the illuminance is at the designated value. In Figure 16-1, the egg-shaped curve next to the centre symbol shows that 5.6 footcandles are present along that line. The centre symbol designates that this is for a twin luminaire. The labelling also indicates that it is for a 250-W, high-pressure sodium lamp in each luminaire, and that the luminaires are mounted 30 ft (9 m) above the surface being illuminated.

Parking Lighting

In practice, this curve is combined with other similar and dissimilar curves to form a pattern such as that shown in Figure 16-2. This is the layout for an industrial parking lot, showing three of the pole-mounted twin luminaires (fixtures) and a single luminaire installed next to the street. The values assigned to the curves are additive, thus this layout indicates that there will be a little more than 2.2 footcandles where the light patterns overlap. Since the recommendation was for 2 footcandles, this value is acceptable. This same technique was used to locate the remaining luminaires.

Pedestrian Lighting

The lighting of the sidewalks and the entryway was placed so that it is close to the walk surface. The luminaires (fixtures) are located using the same technique described earlier but are designed into the landscaping to be as discreet as possible. The outer sidewalk, shown in Figure 16-3 is designed for use with a 50-W high-pressure sodium lamp at a 36 in (900 mm) mounting height. The centre entry walk, shown in Figure 16-4 is designed with 50-W high-pressure sodium lamps at less than 24 in (600 mm) mounting height built into the planter.

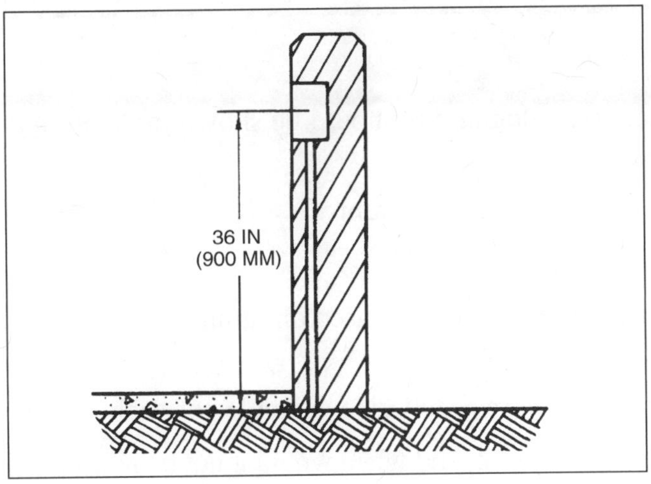

Figure 16-3 Sidewalk illumination.

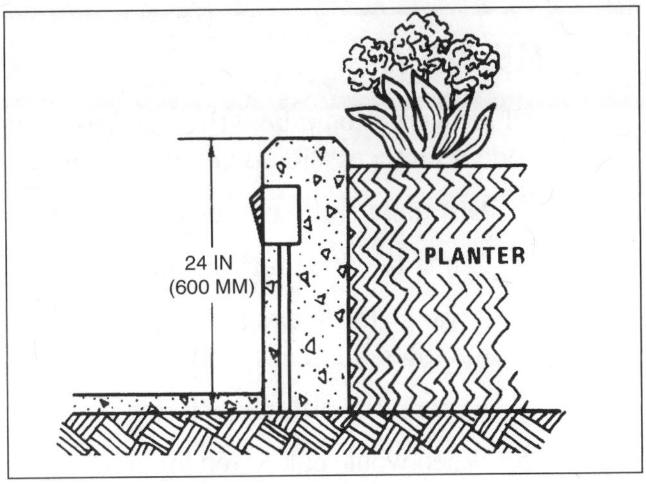

Figure 16-4 Centre entry walk illumination.

ELECTRICAL INSTALLATION

Direct-burial conductors, type RWU90, are used to service the lighting installation.

Two very important considerations dictated the selection of conductor size and the circuit arrangement. First, the conductors were sized to ensure a low voltage drop. This is particularly important because of the long distances that the conductors must run. The second important consideration was to be able to have selective control of the lighting in the various activity areas.

Lighting Control

Because of the high energy cost, the use of advanced electric lighting control for site lighting is cost-effective in many instances.

Photocell control is essentially a must for all site lighting. It can be installed on individual lighting units or at master control points. The photocell is used to ensure that the site lighting is turned off during the daylight hours.

Time clocks are often used in conjunction with photocells to deactivate the lighting when there is no longer a use for it. The industrial building uses a photocell to activate the pedestrian lighting at twilight, then a time clock is used to deactivate that lighting after the last worker has left.

Dimmers for site lighting are rapidly gaining in popularity. Dimming has the advantage, over other control systems, of being able to lower the lighting and the energy use while maintaining uniform lighting throughout the area. Energy use can be reduced by 20% or more of the original value. A dimming system is to be installed on the storage area and the parking lot. A photocell will signal when to turn the lights on; then, a time clock will initiate the dimmers when the high level of lighting is no longer needed. Override switches will be located in convenient places if there is a need to have full lighting at any time.

REVIEW

All answers should be written in complete sentences, calculations should be shown in detail, and Code references should be cited when appropriate.

1. List three common devices used to control for illumination systems.
2. Name the three major light source types.
3. Arrange the lamps listed in Table 16-1 in order of their efficacy based on ratings, starting with the lowest efficacy, and indicating the calculated efficacy.
4. Explain the difference in the terms *efficacy* and *efficiency* and give examples of each.
5. When would colour rendition be important in a parking lot, and when would it not be important?
6. Explain why a storage area might require a higher level of lighting than a parking area.
7. List the factors that should be considered when selecting a lamp type for a parking lot.
8. Explain an isofootcandle curve.
9. List some devices that can be used with area lighting to reduce energy usage.

UNIT 17

Data Infrastructure

OBJECTIVES

After studying this unit, the student should be able to:

- discuss advantages and disadvantages of copper and fibre optic cabling systems
- discuss the construction of copper and fibre optic cable
- discuss factors that adversely affect copper cabling systems
- discuss refraction
- explain how light is transmitted through fibre optic cable
- discuss fibre optic transmitters
- discuss fibre optic receivers
- list different types of fibre optical cable connectors
- discuss concerns when making fibre optic connections

Modern industrial environments rely heavily on data acquisition and automation controls. These systems require that the individual pieces of equipment communicate with each other and with computers collecting the data and controlling the systems.

For many years, the physical network connecting this equipment was mostly proprietary. Each manufacturer used a different physical network structure and a communication language that was specific to the equipment. Some manufacturers even used several different network structures based upon the model of equipment. Although these proprietary systems were very effective, they created considerable problems when it came time to update the equipment, often requiring the installation of a completely new

STANDARDS FOR THE INSTALLATION OF DATA COMMUNICATION SYSTEMS

In 1990, the IEEE and TIA introduced a "standard" that was to change the telecommunications industry forever. The purpose of the standard was to establish a set of guidelines for the design and installation of copper ethernet networks and equipment that would ensure proper operation of equipment regardless of the manufacturer. This standard has been continually updated and improved to reflect advances in technology and performance requirements. Almost all installations in residential and commercial environments follow this standard.

However, industry is considerably more demanding on the network infrastructure than is the typical commercial customer. The average industrial installation is subjected to dirt, dust, oil, vibration, EMI (electromagnetic interference), RFI (radio frequency interference), and fluctuating temperatures. Copper ethernet also has length restrictions requiring the installation of telecommunications closets to house the equipment necessary to extend the length. Because of the physical size of many industrial buildings, several telecommunications closets may be necessary if copper cabling is to be used. This is often not convenient or practical.

A NEW STANDARD FOR INDUSTRY

Industry is moving to a variation of the standard ethernet network used in residential and commercial buildings. This variation is known as EtherNet/IP with a new standard being developed to address the issues specific to the industrial environments. Many of the conditions encountered in industry are unavoidable. The EtherNet/IP network must find ways to reduce the impact of the harsh industrial environment.

Cable

The cable used most often for copper networks is usually a four-pair 22- to 24-gauge unshielded twisted pair (UTP) cable. This cable consists of four groups of two conductors twisted together. The four pairs are then twisted together and covered with a jacket. The twist rates of the individual conductors and the pairs cannot be altered without affecting the performance of the cable. When the cable is terminated, care must be taken not to change the twist rate or untwist any more conductor than is absolutely necessary to complete the termination. The purpose of the twists is to greatly reduce the "crosstalk" between conductors. Shielded twisted pair cable is also available but is not as widely used.

Temperature

In industry, one of the most common problems that affects the copper network system is the high temperatures encountered within the plant. The cabling is often installed close to the ceiling in the factory, where the temperature is considerably higher than at floor level. As temperature increases, the attenuation or signal loss increases. If the temperature is high enough, the attenuation is sufficient to reduce the signal to a level where the system will not operate reliably. To overcome this problem, a higher quality cable with lower losses may be required. This is rarely the case in commercial environments. To reduce the attenuation losses, the length of cable must also be considered as losses increase with length. To decrease the losses caused by the cable length, routes and pathways may need to be altered or equipment relocated.

Electromagnetic Interference

Industry typically will have more circuits operating at higher currents than commercial environments. We know that the magnetic field created around a conductor is proportional to the amount of current flowing in the conductor. These alternating magnetic fields will cause a voltage to be induced in any electrical conductors close by, including the copper data cabling. The amount of voltage induced is proportional to the strength and frequency of the magnetic field. Many industries use variable frequency drives operating at greater than 60 Hz. This higher frequency will cause larger induced voltages.

A certain level of protection from EMI can be provided by shielding the data cables, either by using a metallic raceway or a shielded cable. However, when coupled with the other problems encountered in industry, these methods are seldom enough. When the data cable is installed close to electrical cables, the magnetic field will cause a voltage to be induced in the shielding. Because the shielding is bonded to ground, a current will flow in the shielding, causing another magnetic field to be created, this time around the data cable. Although the overall magnetic field is reduced, it is not eliminated. The only way to reduce the effects of EMI effectively is to provide adequate separation between power and data cables. Although minimum separations for commercial installations have been established, separations for industrial applications have yet to be determined. In general, the distances between power and data cables should be as great as is reasonably possible. When providing shielding for data systems, care must be taken to prevent ground loops as they can create a greater problem than if the shielding were not present.

The consequences of EMI are not limited to the physical wiring. Network Interface Cards, or NICs, are also affected by EMI. NICs designed for industrial applications are constructed to higher standards and are more resistant to EMI than those intended for home or commercial applications.

Connectors

Although temperature and EMI have a direct effect on the cabling system, other industrial factors such as dust, dirt, oil, solvents, corrosives, and vibration affect the connecting devices. Enclosures can be constructed to protect the connectivity from all of these factors except for vibration. It is estimated that a few minutes of vibration on a commercial grade connector can wear down the contact surfaces as much as a normal lifetime of use. Therefore, industrial connectors must be constructed to a much higher standard than commercial connectors.

Length of Cable Run

The Ethernet standard, which forms the basis for the EtherNet/IP protocol, limits the length of cable runs to 90 m. Due to the affects of EMI, it is often difficult to install cable runs of this length without the performance dropping below acceptable levels. Many industrial plants are so large that it is impossible to limit the lengths of runs to less than 90 m.

FIBRE OPTICS

Fibre optic cable is becoming increasing popular for data transmission in industrial environments. Fibre optic cable has several advantages over copper wire for transmission of data. Copper wire is very susceptible to electromagnetic interference caused by electrical devices that draw large amounts of current, such as motors, transformers, and variable frequency drives. Fibre optic cable is totally immune to electromagnetic interference.

Also, the data transmission rate for fibre optic cable is much higher than for copper. In industry, twisted-pair copper cable is generally limited to a data transmission rate of about 100 mbps (million bits per second). Although copper ethernet networks are capable of speeds up to 1000 mbps or 1 gigabit per second (Gbps), these speeds are rarely obtainable in an industrial setting, due mostly to the harsh installation environment. Coaxial cable can carry about 10 mbps. Some special coaxial cable can handle 400 mbps. Fibre optic cable can typically handle 8000 mbps, and laboratory tests have shown that rates as high as 200 000 mbps are possible.

Due to the high frequency of light, fibre optic cable has a very wide bandwidth as compared to copper wire. The bandwidth of fibre optic cable is about a million times that of copper wire. Fibre optic cables are much smaller and lighter in weight than copper cables. A single fibre is approximately 0.001 in (1 micron) in diameter and can carry five times more information than a telephone cable containing 900 pairs of 22 AWG twisted conductors. Single and duplex fibre optic cables are shown in Figure 17-1 on page 224.

Cable Construction

Fibre optic cable comprises three sections: the core, the cladding, and the sheath (Figure 17-2 on page 224). The core comprises either glass or plastic. Glass has a higher bit rate of transmission or bandwidth than plastic, and it has less line loss than plastic. Glass fibres are also able to withstand higher temperatures and are less affected by corrosive atmospheres and environments. Plastic core fibres are more flexible and can be bent to a tighter radius than glass. Plastic fibres are stronger and can be cut, spliced, and terminated with less difficulty than glass.

The cladding or clad surrounds the core and is made of glass or plastic also. The clad serves two basic functions: it protects the core from the

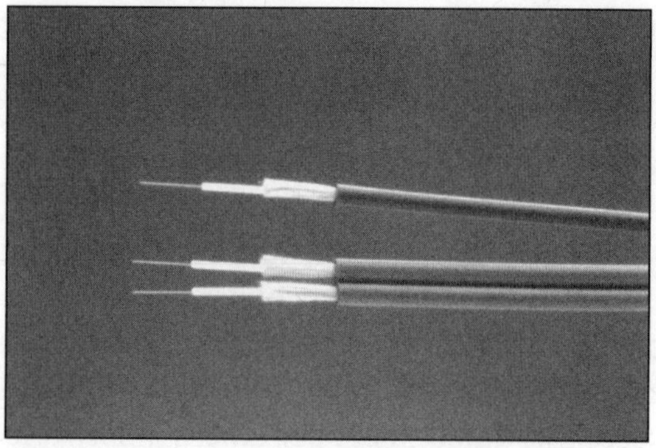

Figure 17-1 Single and duplex fibre optic cables.

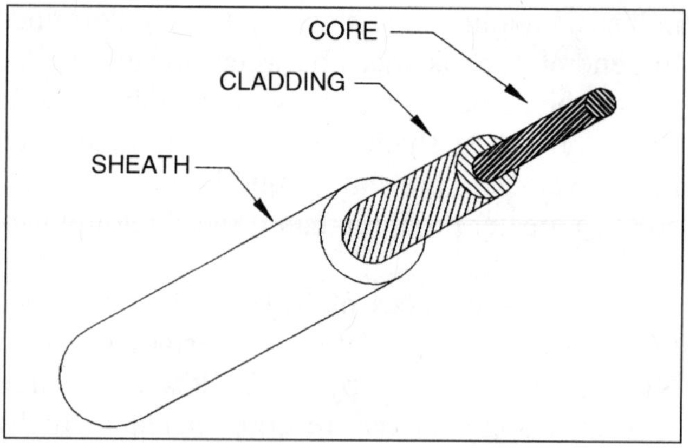

Figure 17-2 Fibre optic cable.

surrounding environment, and it increases the size and strength of the cable itself. Increasing the size of the cable makes it easier to handle. The core and cladding are considered the fibre optic.

The sheath is a polyurethane jacket that surrounds the cable. The sheath protects the fibre optics from the environment. Fibre optic cables may be packaged as a single fibre, fibre pairs, or several thousand fibres.

How Fibre Optic Cable Works

Light travels in a straight line. Fibre optic cable, however, makes it possible to bend light around corners and conduct it to any desired location (Figure 17-3).

The reason that light can travel through an optical fibre is because of refraction. Imagine that you are standing on the shore of a clear mountain lake on a calm, windless day. If you looked out over the surface of the lake, you would probably see the sun, clouds, and trees reflected on the surface of the water. If you looked directly at the water at your feet, you would no longer see reflections of the clouds or trees, but you would see down into the water. This is an example of refraction instead of reflection. The angle at which you stopped seeing the reflection of clouds and trees and started seeing down into the water is called the critical angle or acceptance angle. The critical angle occurs because air and water have a different optical property. The optical property is the speed at which light can travel through a material. Optical property is generally expressed as a term called index of refraction (IR or η). The index of refraction is the speed at which light travels through a material. It is determined by comparing the speed of light travelling through vacuum to the speed of light travelling through a particular material.

$$\eta = \frac{\text{Speed of light in vacuum}}{\text{Speed of light in material}}$$

In glass optical fibres, the index of refraction is approximately 1.46 to 1.51.

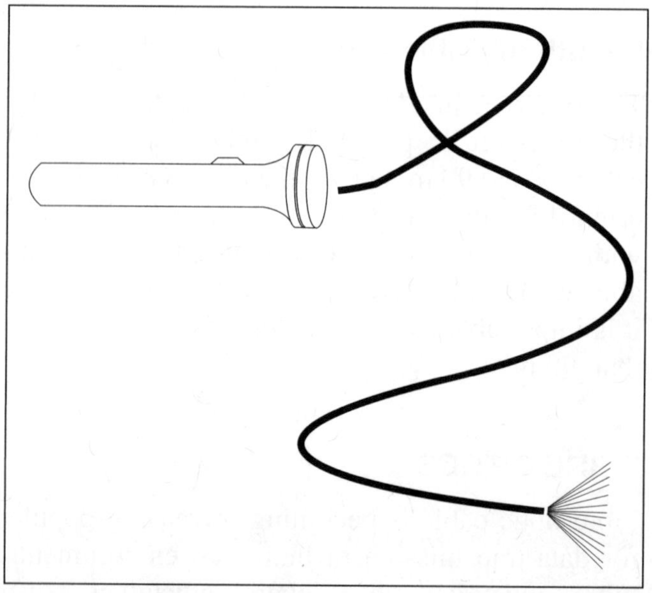

Figure 17-3 Fibre optic cable permits light to be bent.

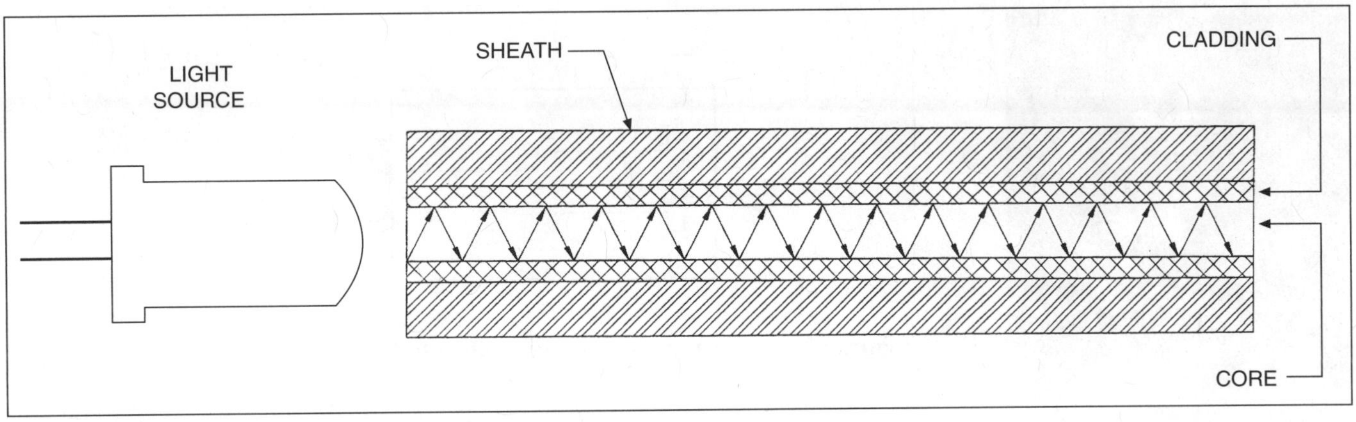

Figure 17-4 Light propagates through the core because of refraction.

When an optical fibre cable is connected to a light source (Figure 17-4), light strikes the cable at many different angles. Some photons strike at an angle that cannot be refracted and are lost through the cladding and absorbed by the sheath. Photons that can be refracted bounce down the core to the receiving device. This bouncing action of the photons causes a condition known as modal dispersion. Since photons enter the cable at different angles, some bounce more times than others before they reach the end of the cable, causing them to arrive later than photons that bounce fewer times. This causes a variance in the phase of the light reaching the source. Modal dispersion can be greatly reduced by using fibre cables called single-mode cables. Single-mode cables have a diameter of 1 to 2 microns. The cladding also affects modal dispersion. If the cladding thickness is kept to within three times the wavelength of the light, modal dispersion is eliminated.

Another type of cable that is much larger than single-mode cable is multimode cable. Multimode cable ranges in thickness from about 5 microns to 1000 microns. Multimode cable can cause severe modal dispersion in long lengths of several thousand feet. For short runs, however, it is generally preferred because it is larger in size and easier to work with than single-mode cable. Multimode cable is also less expensive than single-mode cable, and for short runs the modal dispersion generally is negligible.

Another type of multimode cable called graded cable has a core made of concentric rings. The rings on the outside have a lower density than the rings beneath. This produces a sharper angle of refraction for the outer rings. This arrangement helps to eliminate modal dispersion.

Cable Losses

Fibre optic cables do suffer some losses or attenuation. No fibre optic cable is perfect, and some amount of light does escape through the cladding and is absorbed by the sheath. The greatest losses generally occur when cable is terminated or spliced. The ends of fibre optic cable must be clean and free of scratches, nicks, or uneven strands. It is generally recommended that the ends of fibre optic cable be polished when they are terminated. A special hot knife cutting tool is available for cutting fibre optic cable. A cable with multiple fibre optic cables is shown in Figure 17-5 on page 226.

Transmitters

Several factors should be considered when selecting a transmitter or light source for a fibre optic system. One is the *wavelength* of the light source. Many fibre optic cables specify a range of wavelengths for best performance. The wavelength can be measured by the colour of the emitted light.

Another consideration is the *spectral width*. Spectral width is a measure of the range of colours that are emitted by the light source. The spectral width affects the colour distortion that occurs in the optic fibre.

Figure 17-5 Multiple fibre optic cables.

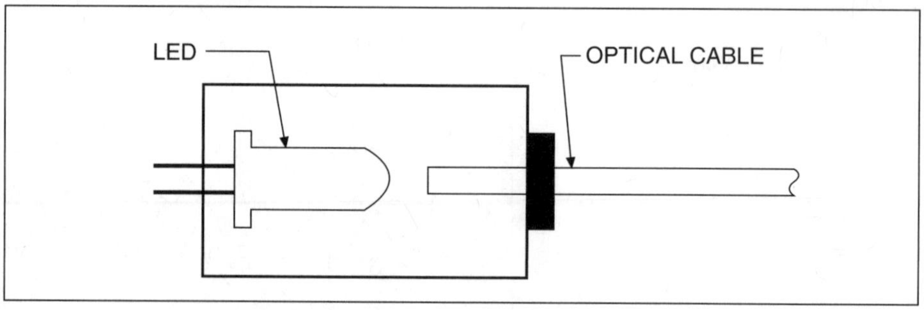

Figure 17-6 A transmitter is generally a light-emitting diode or a laser diode.

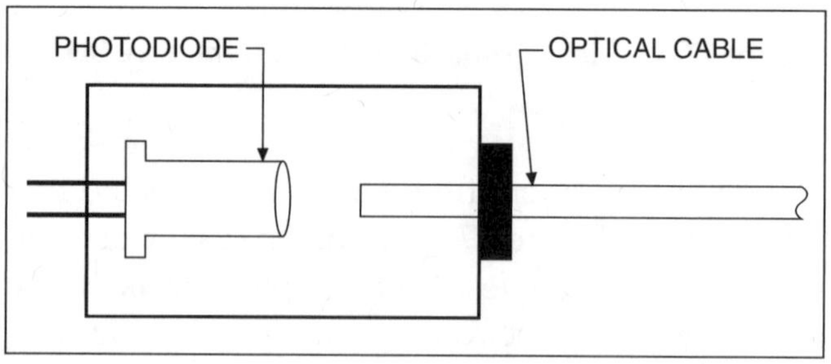

Figure 17-7 The receiver receives light from the optical cable.

The numerical aperture (NA) is a measure of the angle at which light is emitted from the source. If the NA of the source is too wide, it can overfill the NA of the optical fibre. If the NA of the source is too small, it will underfill the fibre. A low-NA light source helps reduce losses both in the optical fibre and at connection points.

Transmitter light sources are generally light-emitting diode (LED) or laser (Figure 17-6). Light-emitting diodes are relatively inexpensive, operate with low power, and have a wide spectral width. They are generally used for short distances of about 7 km or 4.3 mi. Light-emitting diodes have relatively low bandwidths of about 200 MHz or less. They can be used for data bit transmission rates of about 200 mbps or less. Light-emitting diodes have wavelengths that range from about 850 nm to 1300 nm.

Laser diodes are expensive, require a large amount of operating power, and have a narrow spectral width. They can be used for extremely long distance transmission and can handle very high rates of data transmission. Laser diodes are generally used for telephone and cable television applications. Laser diodes operate at a wavelength of about 1300 nm.

Receivers

Receivers convert the light input signal into an electrical signal that can be used by the programmable controller or other devices. Receiver units generally consist of a photodiode (Figure 17-7). Photodiodes are preferred over other types of photodetection devices because of their speed of operation.

Transceivers

Transceivers house both a transmitter and receiver in the same package. Transceivers are often used as photodetection devices. Assume that half of the fibre optic fibres in a cable are connected to the transmitter and the other half are connected to the receiver. If a shiny object, such as a can on an assembly line, should pass in front of the cable, the light supplied by the transmitter would be reflected off the can back to the receiver (Figure 17-8). The output of the receiver could be connected to the input of a programmable controller that causes a counter to step each time a can is detected.

Another device that contains both a transmitter and a receiver is called a *repeater*. A repeater is used to boost the signal when fibre optic cable is run long distances. Repeaters not

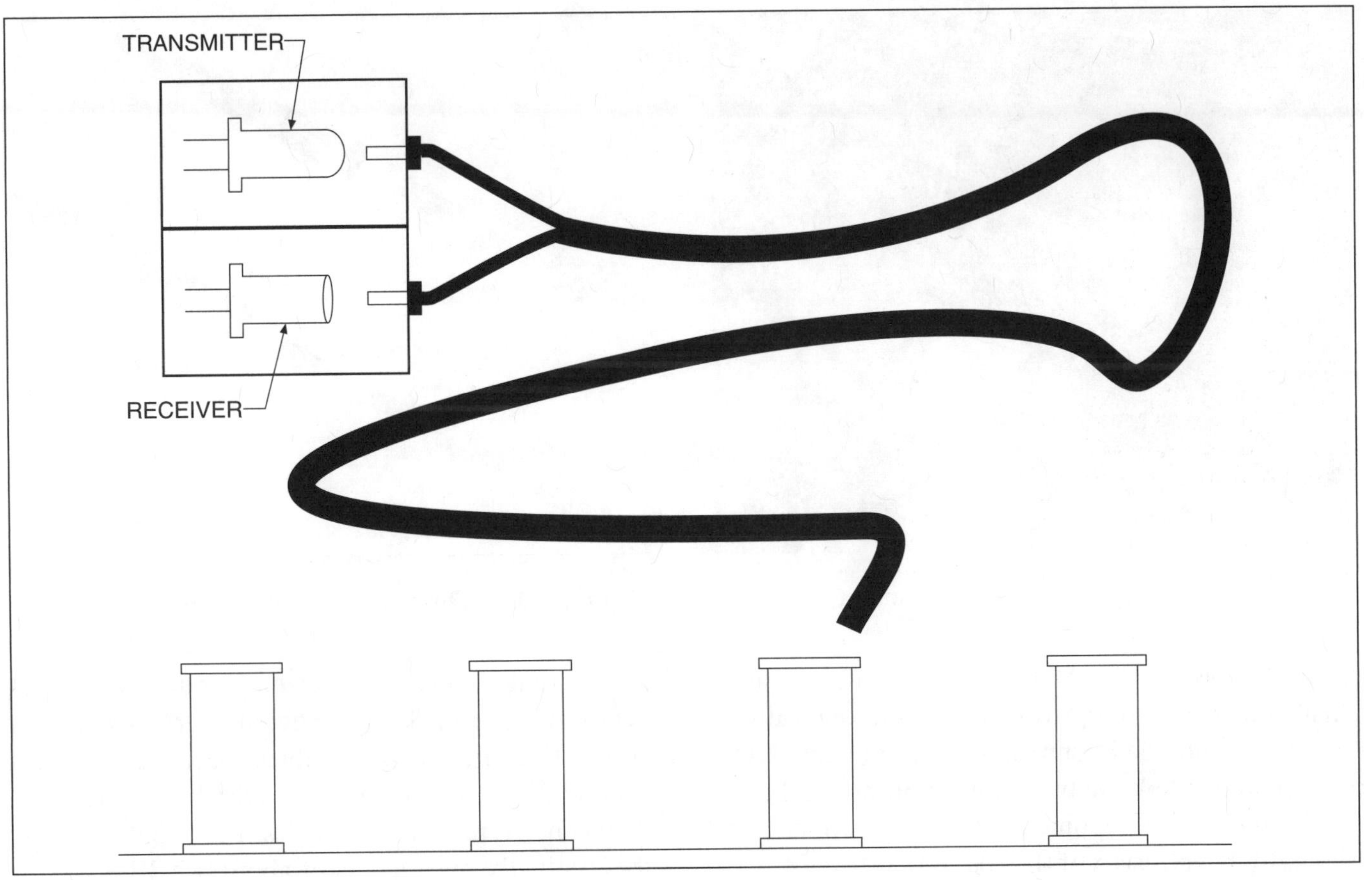

Figure 17-8 A transceiver contains both a transmitter and a receiver.

only amplify the signal but also can reshape digital signals back to their original form. This ability of the repeater to reshape a digital signal back to its original form is one of the great advantages of digital-type signals over analog. The repeater "knows" what the original digital signal looked like, but it does not "know" what an original analog signal looked like. A great disadvantage of analog-type signals is that any distortion of the original signal or noise is amplified.

FIBRE OPTIC CONNECTORS

One of the greatest problems with fibre optic systems is poor connections. There are two conditions that generally account for poor connections: bad alignment between cables or devices and air gaps between cables or devices. An air gap changes the index of refraction, causing fresnel reflection at the point of connection. An air gap can produce an

This resonant cavity causes light to be reflected back to the transmitter where it is bounced back again, to be reflected back to the receiver.

If the fibre optic cable is not aligned correctly, part of the light signal will not be transmitted between the two cables and the device to which it is connected. Losses due to poor connection can be substantial. Losses are measured in decibels (dB).

$$\text{dB} = 10 \log_{10} \frac{\text{Power out}}{\text{Power in}}$$

Coupling Devices

There are three basic types of fibre optic connectors: the threaded, the bayonet, and the push–pull, as illustrated in Figure 17-9 on page 228. The threaded type, shown in Figure 17-10 on page 228, was one of the earliest to be introduced. The use of threaded connectors has decreased because of poor

Figure 17-9 Different types of optic connectors.

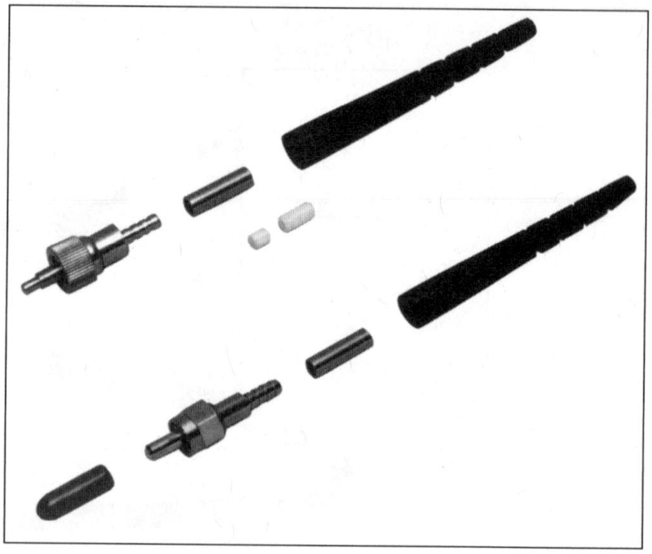

Figure 17-10 Threaded optic connectors.

connector is how tight to make the connection. Also, there is nothing to control rotational alignment. If a threaded connector is disconnected and then reconnected, the two cables will probably not be in the same alignment. Threaded connectors typically have losses of 0.6 dB to 0.8 dB.

In the mid-1980s, the bayonet connector, shown in Figure 17-11, was introduced. This connector solved some of the basic problems of the threaded connector. The twist-lock action provides uniform tightness each time the connector is used, and rotational alignment is more constant. This connector typically has a loss of about 0.5 dB. Bayonet connectors are still widely used throughout industry. The push–pull type connector, Figure 17-12, has become very popular for connecting fibre optic cables because it offers excellent alignment and has less back reflection than other types of connectors. Push–pull connectors typically have a loss of about 0.2 dB.

Electrical connection devices, such as extension cords, generally have a male connector on one end and a female on the other. Fibre optic cables generally employ male connectors on both ends. Devices that they connect to have a female connection. When two fibre optic cables are to be joined together, a coupler with two female ends is employed as illustrated in Figure 17-13.

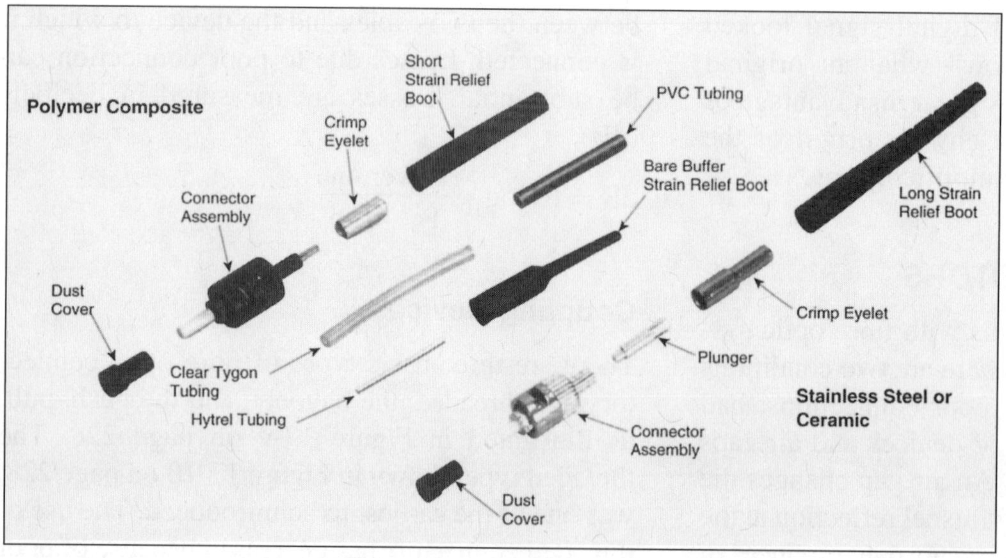

Figure 17-11 Bayonet-type optic connectors.

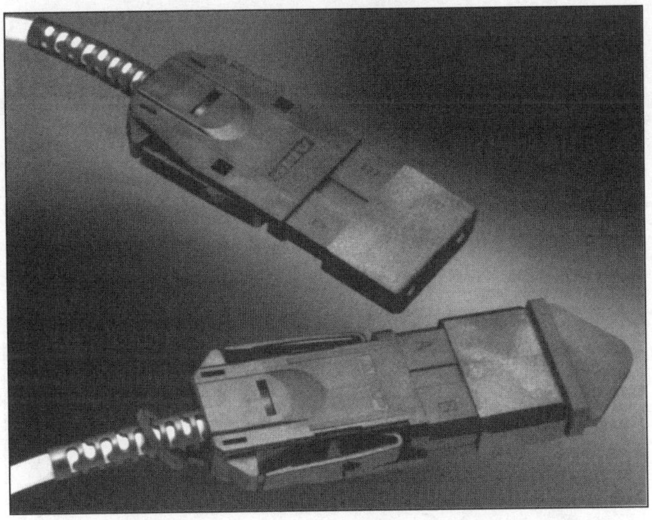

Figure 17-12 Push–pull type fibre optic connectors.

Figure 17-13 Adapter for connecting two push–pull optic connectors.

Making Fibre Optic Connections

Attaching a connector to a fibre optic cable is different from connecting a male plug to an electrical extension cord. Fibre optic connections must be precise. The connections are epoxied and polished. Special crimp tools and dies are employed depending on the size of the cable. A microscope is generally used to examine the connection for possible problems. A kit containing the tools necessary for making fibre optic connections is shown in Figure 17-14. This kit contains a crimp tool and crimping dies, polishing bushings, polishing film, cable and fibre strippers, microscope

Figure 17-14 Toolkit for making fibre optic connections.

FIBRE OPTIC LIGHTING

Fibre optic lighting has several advantages over conventional lighting.

- It can be employed in swimming pools and fountains without the shock hazard and electrical requirements of waterproof luminaires (fixtures).
- It can be located in outdoor areas for accent lighting of buildings and walkways.
- It is supplied by a single light source; thus, the luminaires (fixtures) produce no heat, have no electrical connections, and never need replacement.
- It is ideal for applications in museums to accent valuable works of art because it does not produce heat or ultraviolet radiation, which is a major cause of colour fading.
- The individual light sources do not produce an electromagnetic field that could interfere with sensitive electrical equipment. The only electrical connection is at the illuminator; thus, individual light sources do not produce an electromagnetic field.

Fibre optic lighting has a significant limitation: it cannot provide the amount of illumination that can be obtained with conventional light sources.

in the near future it is likely that fibre optic cables will deliver the quantity of light necessary to compete with the common luminaire (fixture). Fibre optic cables could then be employed to provide illumination in hazardous locations without expensive explosionproof luminaires (fixtures).

Fibre optic lighting systems comprise three primary sections: the illuminator, the cable, and the end fixtures (Figure 17-15). The illuminator is the only part of the system requiring electrical connections, permitting it to be located where it is convenient for maintenance and lamp (bulb) replacement.

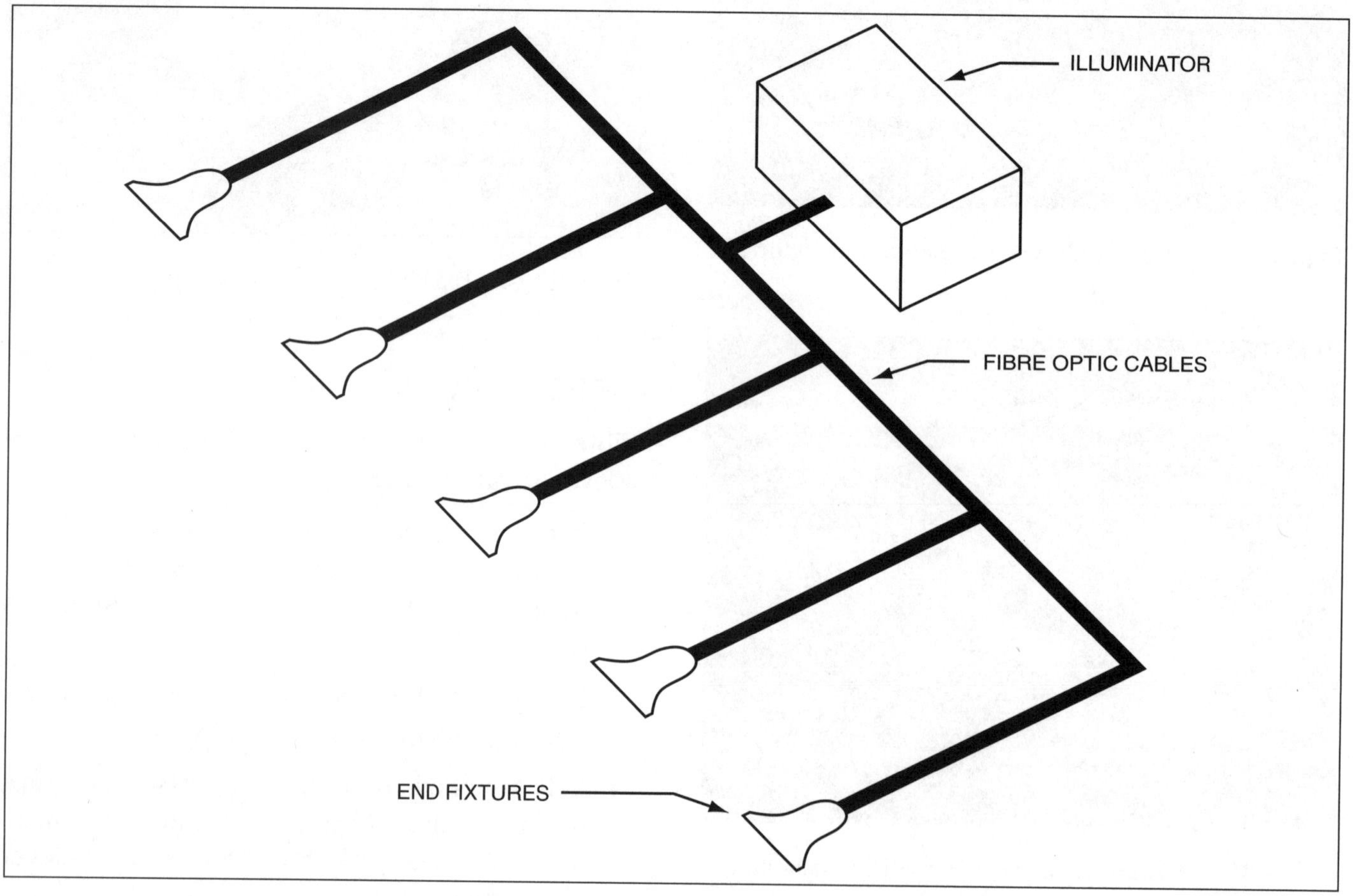

Figure 17-15 Fibre optic lighting system.

REVIEW

All answers should be written in complete sentences, calculations should be shown in detail, and Code references should be cited when appropriate.

1. List the conditions found in industry that have a negative effect on copper data cables.
2. What is the maximum length of run for a copper data cable?
3. What precautions must be taken when terminating a UTP cable?
4. Name at least two advantages of fibre optic cable over copper wires.
5. Which type of fibre optic cable has a higher bit rate of transmission: glass or plastic?
6. Which type of fibre optic cable is more flexible and can be bent to a tighter radius: glass or plastic?
7. What is the index of refraction?
8. Name two devices that are generally used to transmit light in a fibre.
9. Name three types of coupling devices used to connect fibre optic cables.
10. Which fibre optic connector exhibits the least amount of loss?
11. Does fibre optic lighting transmit UV radiation?
12. What is the main disadvantage of fibre optic lighting systems?
13. What are the three sections in a fibre optic lighting system?

UNIT 18

Hazardous Locations

OBJECTIVES

After studying this unit, the student should be able to:

- discuss the different classes, divisions, and groups of hazardous locations
- describe intrinsically safe circuits
- discuss vertical and horizontal seals
- describe the difference between explosionproof and enclosed and gasketed luminaires (fixtures)
- discuss the installation requirements of pendant luminaires (fixtures)
- list the conditions for the use of flexible cord in a hazardous location

Caution! Some provinces and territories may require special licensing to perform electrical work within hazardous environments associated with the delivery of fuels such as natural gas, propane, gasoline, or diesel fuel. Check with the branch of government responsible for fuel safety *before* beginning any installation or repair of any equipment within a hazardous area, as specified later in this chapter, used for the delivery of fuels.

Hazardous locations are areas that exhibit a high risk of fire or explosion due to elements in the surrounding atmosphere or vicinity. The *CEC* Section 18 divides hazardous locations into three classes. Class I locations are areas in which there are or may be high concentrations of flammable or explosive gases or vapours, Class II locations contain flammable or explosive dusts, and Class III locations are areas that contain combustible fibres.

Prior to 1998, the *CEC* further divided Class I environments into Divisions 1 and 2, a system that is still used in the United States. In order to harmonize the requirements of hazardous locations with the European community, the division system was retained for Class II and III locations while changing to a three-zone system for Class I locations. In recognizing that there may be a need to add to or modify a Class I system installed prior to 1998 under the division system, the *CEC* will allow the old system to be used for such modifications. The rules applying to the Class I division system can be found in Appendix J of the *CEC*. All new installations must follow the zone system. Class I locations are further divided into three zones based upon the type and degree of hazard as follows:

Zone 0

- Environments in which explosive gases exist continuously or for long periods of time

Zone 1

- Under normal operations, explosive gases are likely to occur

- Explosive gases may exist often due to leakage or maintenance operations
- The area is next to a Class1 Zone 0 environment

Zone 2

- Explosive gases are not likely to occur under normal operation and, if they occur, will exist for a short duration
- Flammable liquids, gases, or vapours are handled or processed within closed containers or systems and will only leak upon breakdown of equipment or accidental rupture of the system or containers
- Explosive environments are prevented due to adequate ventilation; failure or improper operation of the ventilation system may allow the buildup of explosive gases
- The area is next to a Class I Zone 1 environment from which gases could be transported

For example, an area in which gasoline is manufactured would be considered Class I Zone 1. An area in which maintenance is done on trucks that transport the gasoline would be Class I Zone 2.

Classes I and II are subdivided into several groups, each of which contains hazardous materials having similar properties and characteristics. The chart in Table 18-1 on page 234 lists groups and typical atmospheres or hazards in each. The chart also indicates the typical ignition temperature of these hazardous materials and both the North American and IEC gas groups.

Class II and III hazardous locations are divided into two divisions that depend on the likelihood of the hazard being present. Division 1 locations are areas considered to be hazardous at any or all times during normal operations. Division 2 locations are areas that could become hazardous through a foreseeable accident. For example, the production area of a flour mill where the flour dust is in high enough concentration to ignite would be a Class II Division 1 area. Areas where the concentration of dust is not high enough to ignite but where significant amounts may settle on equipment and ignite due to heat or spark

EQUIPMENT APPROVAL

CEC Rule 18-050 states that equipment shall be approved not only for the class location but also for the specific type of atmosphere that will be present. In addition, equipment located in a Class I location cannot have an exposed surface that operates at a temperature greater than the ignition temperature of the surrounding gas or vapour (*CEC* Rule 18-052(4)). Equipment located in a Class II location must be marked with the group or specific dust for which it is approved.

- **Group A** is an atmosphere that contains acetylene.
- **Group B** contains flammable gas or flammable liquid-produced vapour having either a maximum experimental safe gap (MESG) value less than or equal to 0.45 mm or a minimum ignition current ratio (MIC) less than or equal to 0.40 mm.
- **Group C** contains flammable gas or flammable liquid-produced vapour having either a maximum experimental safe gap value greater than 0.45 mm and less than or equal to 0.75 mm, or a minimum ignition current ratio greater than 0.40 mm and less than or equal to 0.80 mm.
- **Group D** contains flammable gas or flammable liquid-produced vapour having either a maximum experimental safe gap value greater than 0.75 mm or a minimum current ratio greater than 0.80 mm. Typical materials and atmosphere ignition temperatures are shown in Table 18-1 for different groups.
- **Group E** contains combustible metal dusts, including aluminum, magnesium, and their commercial alloys, or other combustible dusts whose particle size, abrasives, and conductivity present similar hazards in the use of electrical equipment.
- **Group F** contains combustible carbonaceous dusts that have more than 8% total entrapped volatiles or that have been sensitized by other materials so that they present an explosion

Atmosphere	Minimum Ignition Temperature Limit, °C	Gas Group (North American)	Gas Group (IEC)
acetylene	305	A	IIC
butadiene	420	B	IIB
hydrogen	429	B	IIC
manufactured gases containing more than 30% hydrogen (by volume)	500	B	
propylene oxide	499	C	IIB
acetaldehyde	175	C	IIA
cyclopropane	498	C	IIA
diethyl ether	160	C	IIB
ethylene	450	C	IIB
hydrogen sulphide	260	C	IIB
unsymmetrical dimethyl hydrazine (UDMH 1, 1-dimethyl hydrazine)	249	C	IIB
acetone	465	D	IIA
acrylonitrile	481	D	IIB
alcohol (see ethyl alcohol)			
ammonia	651	D	IIA
benzene	498	D	IIA
benzine (see petroleum naphtha)			
benzol (see benzene)			
butane	287	D	IIA
1-butanol (butyl alcohol)	343	D	IIA
2-butanol (secondary butyl alcohol)	405	D	IIA
butyl acetate	425	D	IIA
isobutyl acetate	421	D	IIA
ethane	472	D	IIA
ethanol (ethyl alcohol)	363	D	IIA
ethyl acetate	426	D	IIA
ethylene dichloride	413	D	IIA
gasoline	280	D	IIA
heptanes	204	D	IIA
hexanes	223	D	IIA
isoprene	395	D	IIA
methane	537	D	IIA
methanol (methyl alcohol)	385	D	IIA
3-methyl-1-butanol (isoamyl alcohol)	350	D	IIA
methyl ethyl ketone	404	D	IIB
methol isobutyl ketone	448	D	IIA
2-methyl-1-propanol (isobutyl alcohol)	415	D	IIA
2-methyl-2-propanol (tertiary butyl alcohol)	478	D	IIA
naphtha (see petroleum naphtha)			
natural gas	482	D	IIA
petroleum naphtha	288	D	IIA
octanes	206	D	IIA
pentanes	260	D	IIA
1-pentanol (amyl alcohol)	300	D	IIA
propane	432	D	IIA
1-propanol (propyl alcohol)	412	D	IIA
2-propanol (isopropyl alcohol)	399	D	IIA
propylene	455	D	IIA
styrene	490	D	IIA
toluene	480	D	IIA
vinyl acetate	402	D	IIA
vinyl chloride	472	D	IIA
xylenes	463	D	IIA

Note: Ignition temperatures of other gases and vapours may be found in the British Standard Code of Practice BS 60079-14:1997.

Table 18-1 Temperature and Gas Groups.

- **Group G** contains combustible dusts not included in Groups E or F, including flour, grain, wood, plastic, and chemicals.

INTRINSICALLY SAFE CIRCUITS AND EQUIPMENT

The *CEC* Section 18 indicates that equipment and associated apparatus that has been identified as intrinsically safe is permitted in any hazardous location. The equipment must be approved for the type of atmosphere in which it is to be used. Intrinsically safe equipment and circuits operate at low power levels. These circuits and equipment operate at a low enough power that, even under overload or fault conditions, they do not contain enough electrical or thermal energy to cause ignition of the surrounding atmosphere. Abnormal conditions are considered to be accidental damage to field wiring, failure of equipment, accidental application of overvoltage, and misadjustment of equipment. Intrinsically safe circuits must be physically separated from all other circuits that are not so considered. Seals must be used to prevent the passage of gas or vapour as they are in higher-voltage systems. Installation of intrinsically safe systems is covered on Appendix F of the *CEC.* Intrinsically safe circuits and wiring are the only acceptable means for installations in Class I Zone 0 environments.

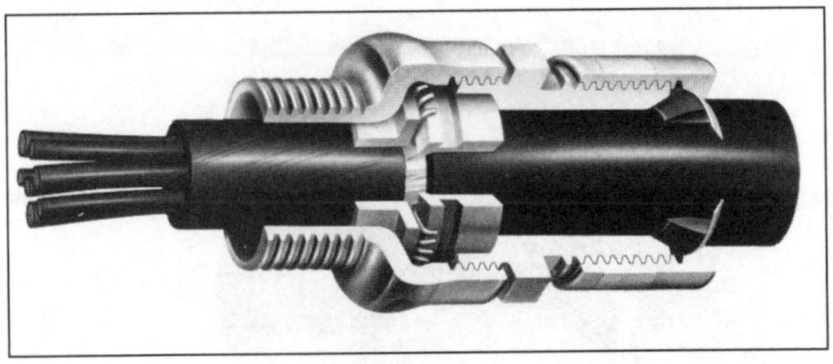

Figure 18-1 A cable with approved termination fitting.
(Courtesy of Crouse-Hinds ECM)

EQUIPMENT

CEC Rule 18-050 states that the equipment used in a hazardous location must be approved not only for that location but also for the particular type of atmosphere in which the equipment is used. Threaded rigid metal conduit, or cables approved for hazardous locations with approved termination fittings, are acceptable wiring methods in all classes and zones/divisions except Class I Zone 0. Other methods may be acceptable depending on the class and division of the installation. A cable with an approved termination fitting is shown in Figure 18-1.

Next to Class I Zone 0, Class I Zone 1 locations are considered to be the most hazardous. Equipment used in a Class I Zone 1 location must be marked with the symbols **Ex** or **EEx**, which indicate the protection method, temperature rating of the heat-producing type, and the gas group. Equipment utilizing the class and division system must be marked, indicating the class and division as well as the gas group or specific gas. This equipment is commonly referred to as "explosionproof." Explosionproof equipment is designed to withstand an internal explosion without permitting hot gases or vapours to escape to the outside atmosphere. This is accomplished by forcing the escaping gas to travel across large, flat surfaces or through screw threads before it exits to the outside atmosphere (Figure 18-2). This cools the hot gas or vapour below the ignition point of the surrounding atmosphere.

As a general rule, equipment installed in a Class II location must be dust-ignitionproof. A dust-tight enclosure is constructed so that dust cannot enter the enclosure. Manufacturers of equipment intended for use in hazardous locations

often design the equipment so that it can be used in more than one area. In Figure 18-3, several outlet boxes are shown.

SEALS

CEC Section 18 requires the use of conduit seals. Seals are used to minimize the passage of gas and to prevent the passage of flame through the conduit. In general, they are required within 450 mm (18 in) of an explosionproof enclosure containing arc-producing equipment and in any conduit that exits from a more hazardous location to a less hazardous location (Figure 18-4). Seals are available in standard conduit sizes and can be installed vertically or horizontally. Seals designed to be installed in a vertical position are shown in Figure 18-5. Those designed to be installed in a horizontal position are shown in Figure 18-6 on page 238.

When seals are installed, the conductors must be pulled through the seal and the system tested for shorts or grounds before the sealing compound is added. A cutaway view of a vertical seal is shown in Figure 18-7 on page 238. To add the sealing compound, the large plug is removed. A

Figure 18-3 Explosionproof outlet boxes.

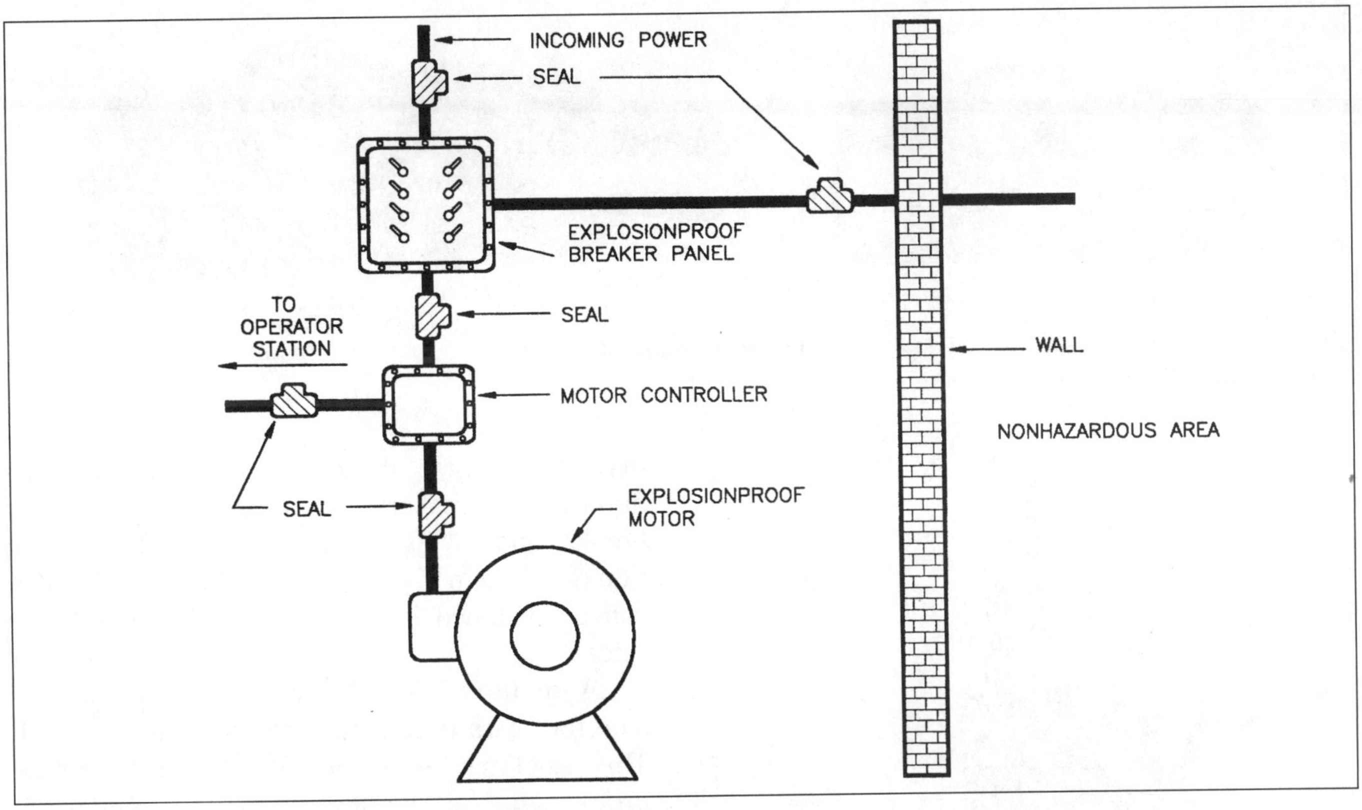

Figure 18-4 Seals are required in explosionproof installations.

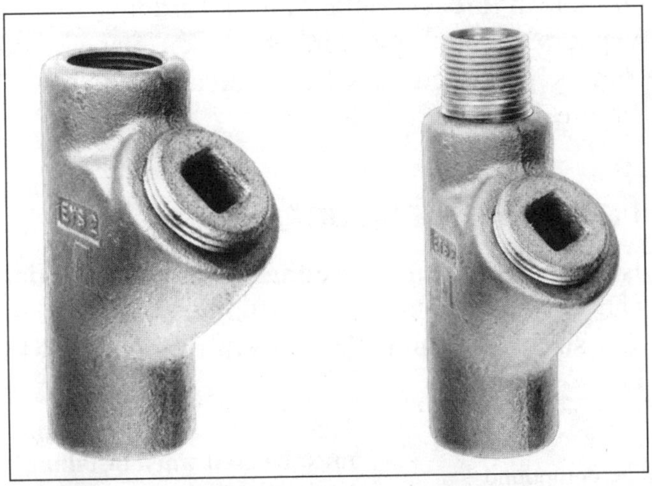

Figure 18-5 Seals designed to be installed in the vertical position.
(Courtesy of Crouse-Hinds ECM)

fibre material is then packed around the inside bottom of the seal to form a dam. The dam prevents the sealing compound, before it becomes hard, from flowing down the conduit.

When horizontal seals are installed, two separate fibre dams must be used, as shown in plugs, a large one and a small one. When the seal is installed, the large plug is removed first to permit the installation of the fibre material. Once this has been accomplished, the plug is replaced and the liquid sealing compound is poured in through the opening provided by the smaller plug.

Condensation is sometimes a problem because it causes moisture to collect inside the conduit. To help prevent this problem, some vertical seals are designed with drain plugs (Figure 18-9 on page 239). These seals are installed in low areas where long horizontal runs of conduit turn down. The seals are designed so that a hollow shaft extends through the sealing compound. The plugs can be removed periodically to drain moisture from the system. Some drain seal fittings contain *weep* holes to permit continuous draining.

CIRCUIT-BREAKER PANELBOARDS

When circuit breakers are installed in hazardous locations, they must be approved for the purpose. The type of enclosure used is determined by the

Figure 18-6 Seals designed to be installed in the horizontal position.
(Courtesy of Crouse-Hinds ECM)

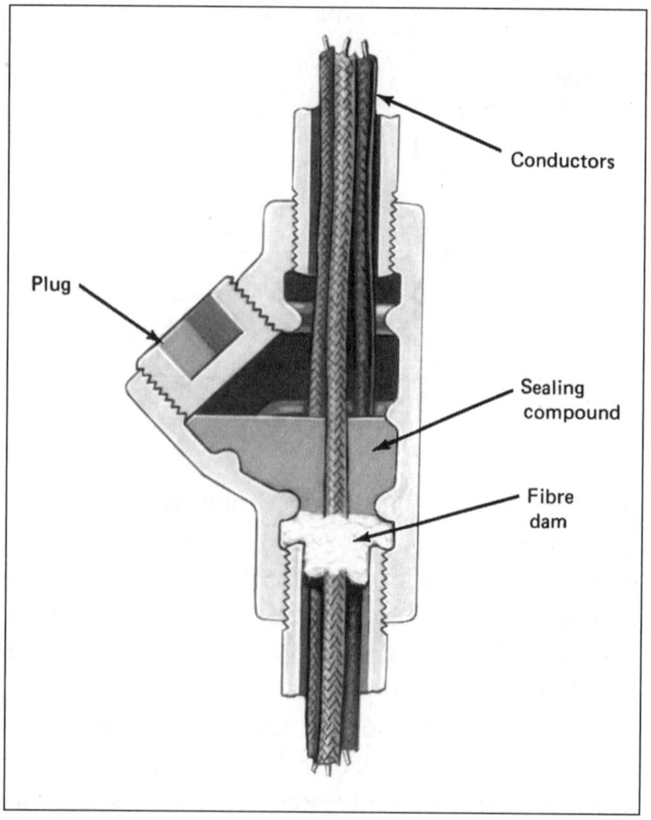

Figure 18-7 Cutaway view of a vertical seal.

installed, the size of the breaker needed, and the number of breakers required. A single circuit breaker and enclosure suitable for a Class I location is shown in Figure 18-10. This type of breaker can be obtained in 50-, 100-, and 225-A frame sizes.

A multiple circuit-breaker panelboard, suitable for Class II areas, is shown in Figure 18-11. This panelboard is considered to be dust-ignition-proof and can contain up to 24 single-pole breakers, 12 double-pole breakers, or 8 three-pole breakers. This panelboard, however, is not permitted in areas containing hazardous gas or vapours. A multiple circuit-breaker panelboard that is permitted in Class I areas is shown in Figure 18-12.

LUMINAIRES (FIXTURES)

Luminaires (fixtures) used in hazardous locations can be obtained in many different types, styles, and sizes. The luminaires shown in Figure 18-13

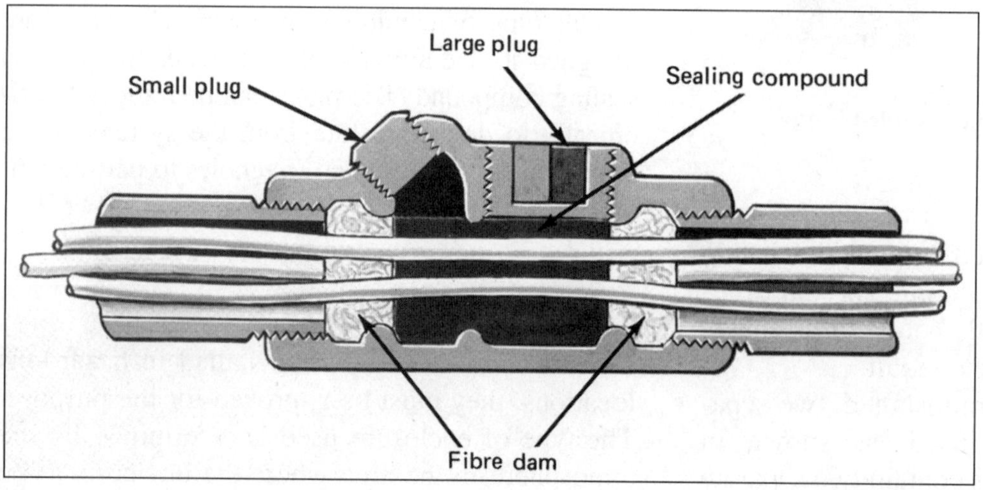

Figure 18-8 Two fibre dams must be used when installing horizontal seals.
(Courtesy of Crouse-Hinds ECM)

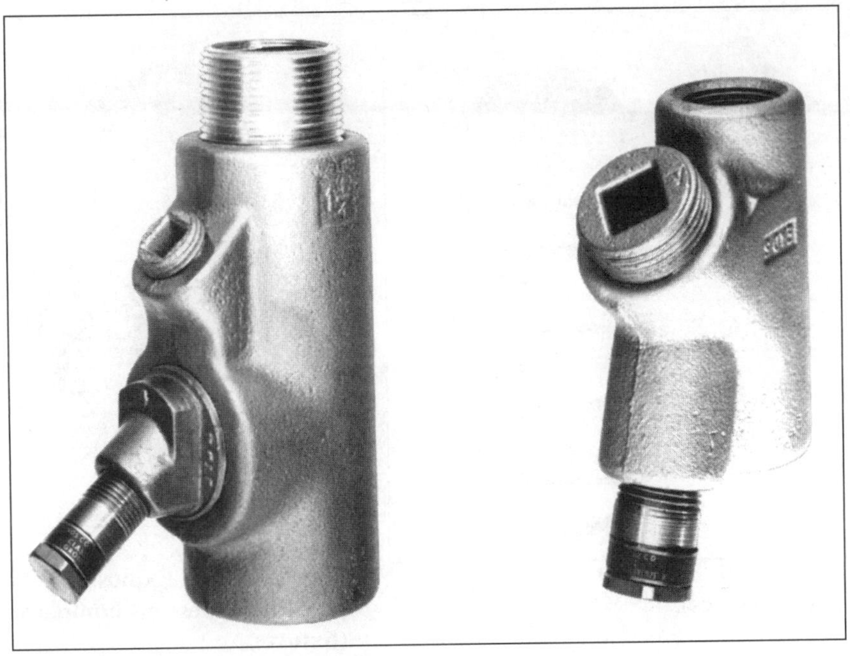

Figure 18-9 Vertical seals with drain plugs.
(Courtesy of Crouse-Hinds ECM)

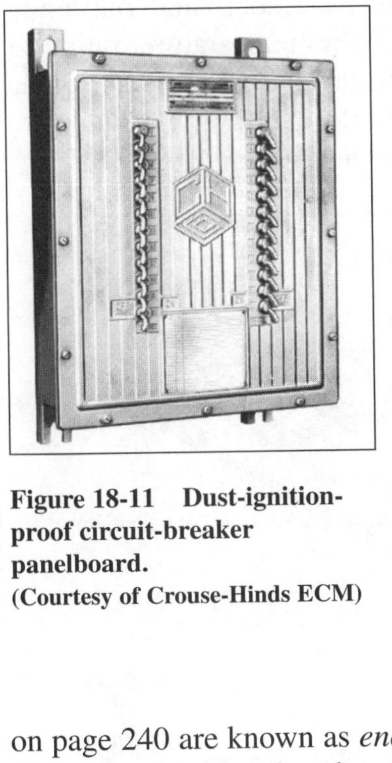

Figure 18-11 Dust-ignition-proof circuit-breaker panelboard.
(Courtesy of Crouse-Hinds ECM)

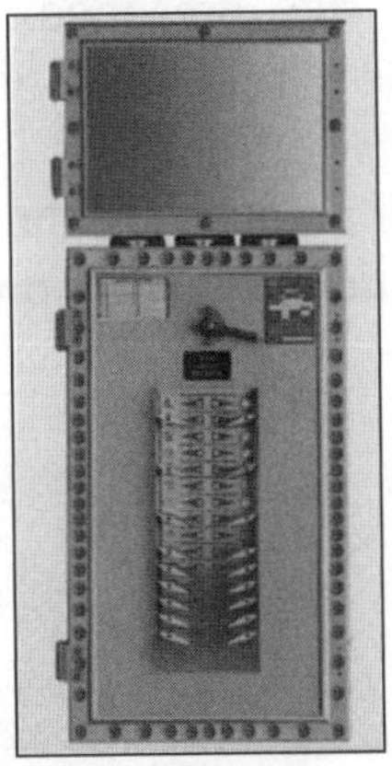

Figure 18-12 Explosionproof circuit-breaker panelboard.
(Courtesy of Crouse-Hinds ECM)

on page 240 are known as *enclosed* and *gasketed*. They are considered to be vapourtight, but they are not explosionproof. The glass globe that covers the lamp is not designed to contain an internal explosion. For this reason, these luminaires are not permitted in a Class I Zone 1 location. However, they may be used in a Class I

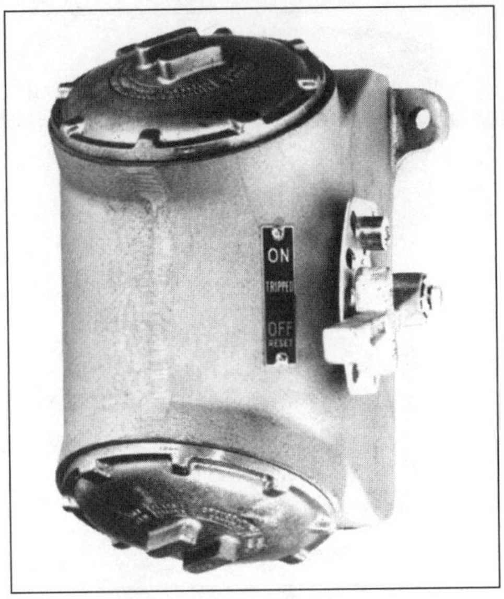

Figure 18-10 Single circuit breaker in an explosionproof enclosure.
(Courtesy of Crouse-Hinds ECM)

An explosionproof luminaire is shown in Figure 18-14 on page 240. This luminaire can be used in a Class I Zone1 location. The glass globe is made of tempered glass, which can withstand an internal explosion. This type of luminaire can also be equipped with an inner globe of coloured glass if desired. A cutaway view of this type of luminaire is shown in Figure 18-15 on page 240.

Fluorescent-type luminaires can also be obtained for use in hazardous locations. The luminaire shown in Figure 18-16 on page 240 can be used in Class I and Class II locations. These luminaires are also permitted in paint-spray areas and wet locations. They use heavy-duty glass tubes to cover the fluorescent lamps. The ballast is contained in an explosionproof enclosure.

T Ratings of Luminaires

Luminaires intended for use in hazardous locations have a temperature or "T" rating. The T rating indicates the maximum operating temperature of the luminaire. The operating temperature must be kept below the ignition temperature of the surrounding atmosphere. The chart in Table 18-2 on page 241 lists the temperature code and the

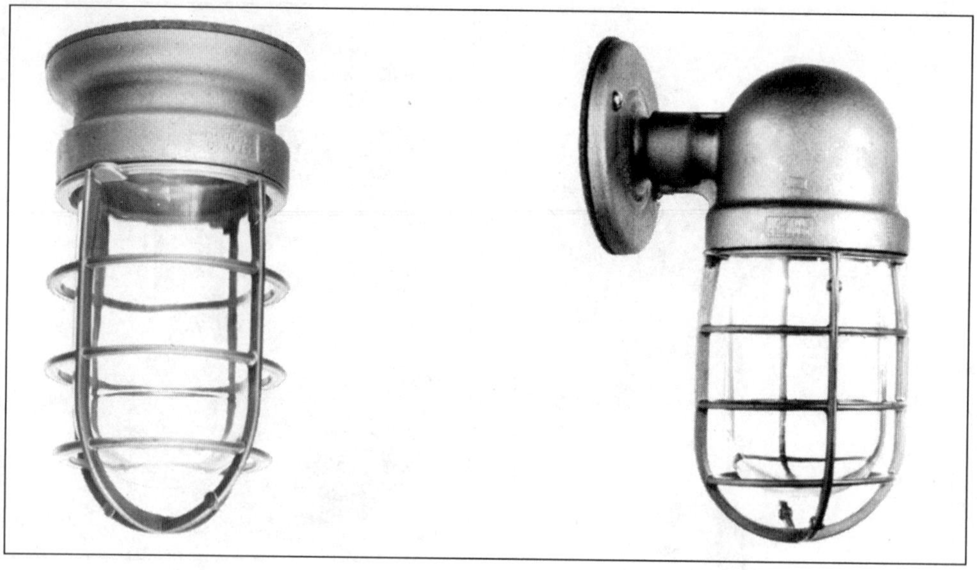

Figure 18-13 Enclosed and gasketed luminaires (fixtures).
(Courtesy of Crouse-Hinds ECM)

Figure 18-14 Explosion-proof incandescent luminaire (fixture).
(Courtesy of Crouse-Hinds ECM)

with that number. Luminaires listed for use in Zone 1 locations are expected to be installed in areas where hazardous material is present at all times. For this reason, the temperature rating is established by measuring the temperature on the outer surface of the luminaire. Luminaires listed for use in Zone 2 locations are not expected to be in the presence of hazardous material under normal conditions. The temperature rating of these luminaires is established by measuring the temperature at the hottest spot on the luminaire, which is the lamp itself.

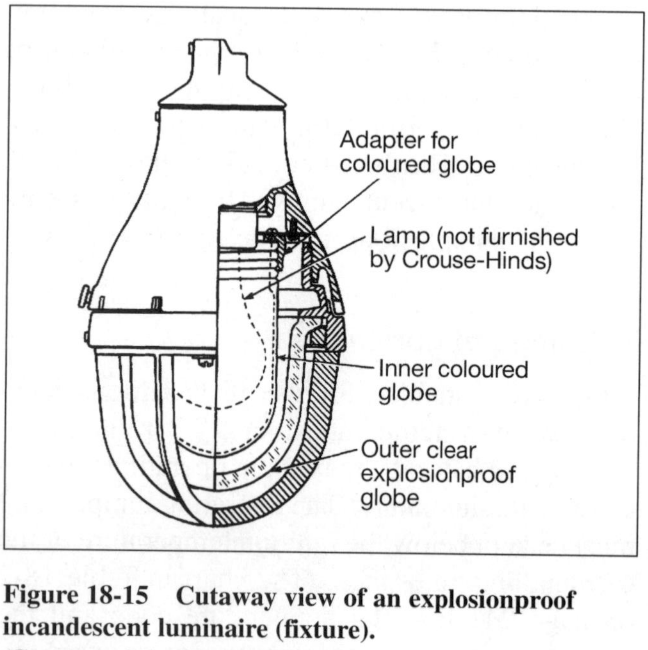

Figure 18-15 Cutaway view of an explosionproof incandescent luminaire (fixture).
(Courtesy of Crouse-Hinds ECM)

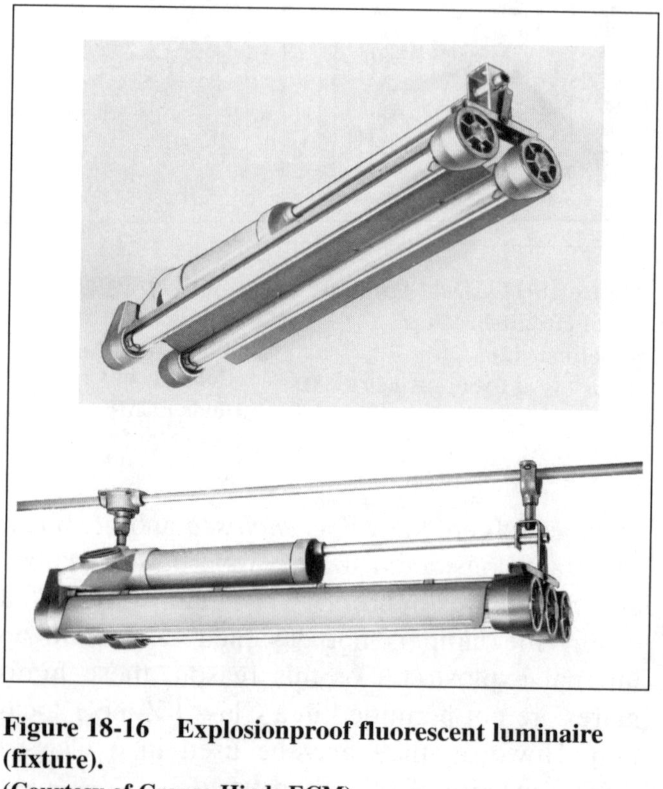

Figure 18-16 Explosionproof fluorescent luminaire (fixture).
(Courtesy of Crouse-Hinds ECM)

Temperature Code Number	Maximum Surface Temperature °C
T1	450
T2	300
T2A	280
T2B	260
T2C	230
T2D	215
T3	200
T3A	180
T3B	165
T3C	160
T4	135
T4A	120
T5	100
T6	85

Table 18-2 Temperature codes and corresponding temperatures.

Installation of Luminaires

CEC Rules 18-118(4), 18-172(2), 18-216(4), and 18-266(2) describe the method for installing pendant (hanging) luminaires in hazardous locations. In general, power is supplied through threaded rigid metal conduit. If the stem is 300 mm (12 in) long or less, no extra bracing is required. If the stem is longer than 300 mm (12 in), however, lateral braces must be placed within 300 mm (12 in) of the luminaire, or an explosionproof flexible coupling must be used within 300 mm (12 in) of the junction box (Figure 18-17). An explosionproof flexible coupling used for this purpose is shown in Figure 18-18 on page 242.

MOTOR CONTROLS

The *CEC* states that switches, circuit breakers, and make-and-break contacts of pushbuttons, relays, alarms, and so on must be in enclosures approved for the hazardous environment in which they are installed. There is an exception, however, if the contacts are immersed in oil, hermetically sealed, or if the circuit does not contain sufficient energy to ignite the surrounding atmosphere. Explosionproof manual motor starters are shown in Figure 18-19 on page 242. These starters can be used to control AC or DC motors. They contain heaters to provide running-overcurrent protection for the motor. A single manual motor starter is shown in Figure 18-20 on page 242. This particular starter can be used in atmospheres that contain hydrogen.

When using explosionproof starters, it is often necessary to adjust the rating of the overload heater size. This is because the heater must be

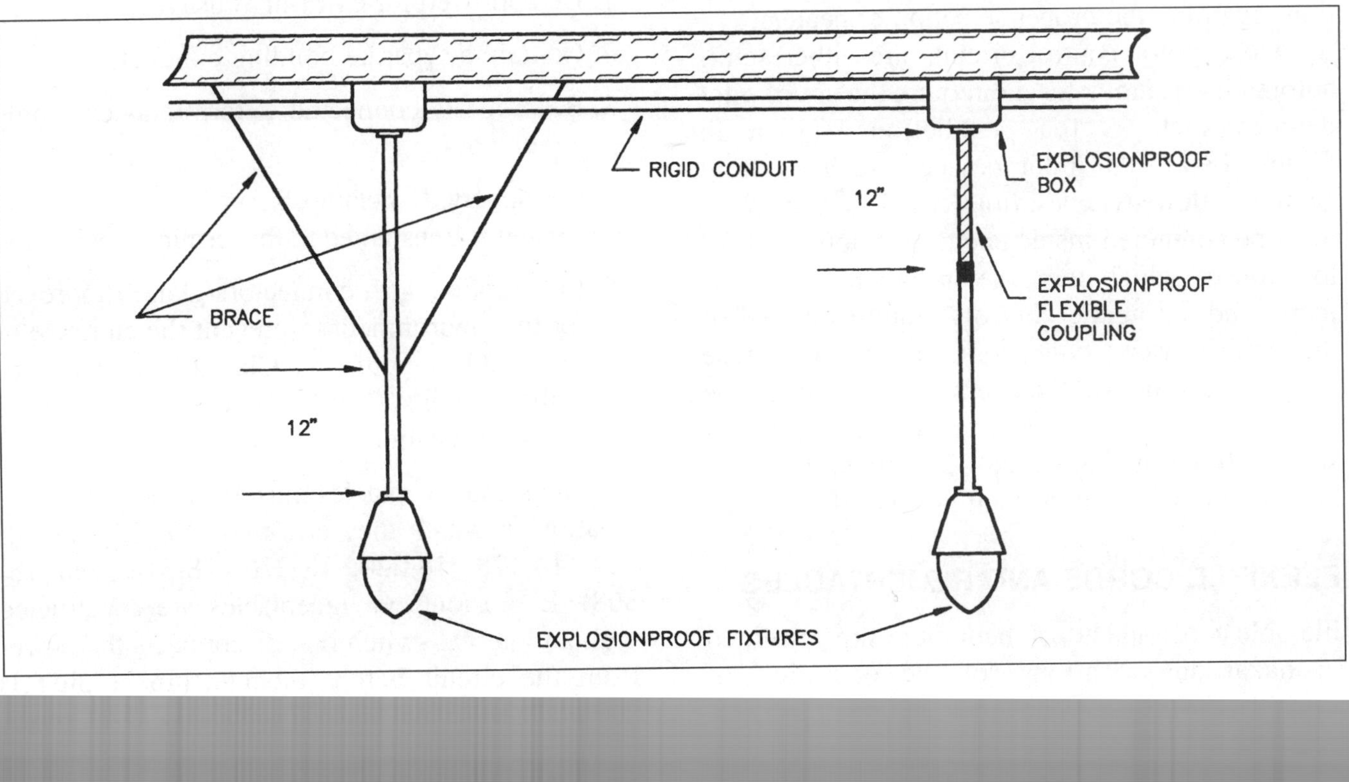

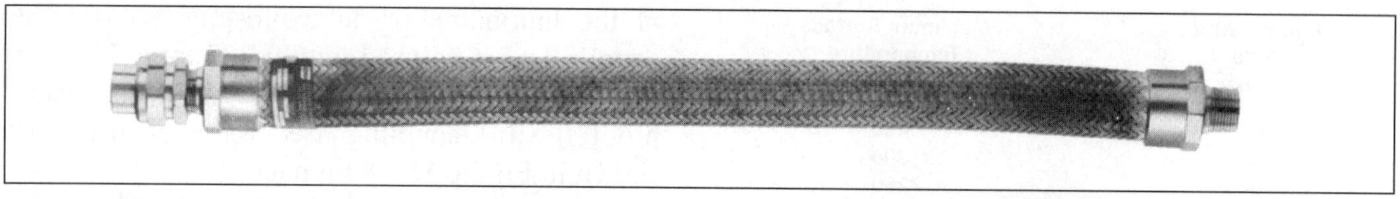

Figure 18-18 Explosionproof flexible coupling.
(Courtesy of Crouse-Hinds ECM)

Figure 18-19 Dual manual motor starter used in hazardous locations.
(Courtesy of Crouse-Hinds ECM)

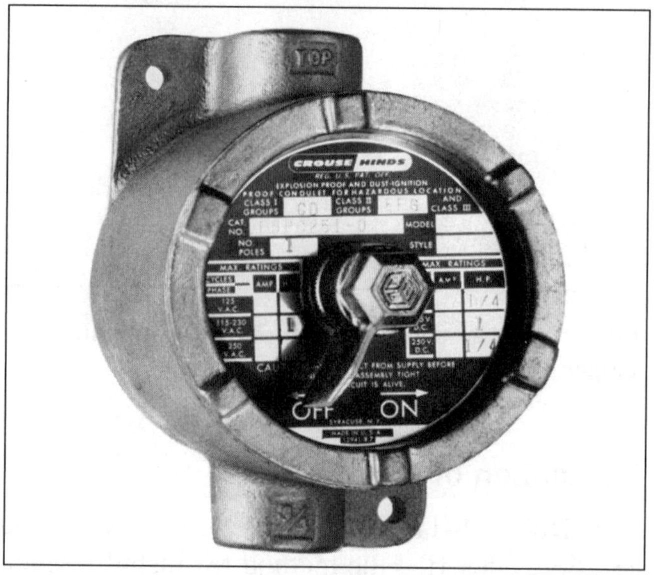

Figure 18-20 Single manual motor starter used in hazardous location.
(Courtesy of Crouse-Hinds ECM)

contained inside the explosionproof enclosure, which makes heat dissipation difficult. Refer to the manufacturers' literature for further information regarding the proper selection of heaters.

Most motor control circuits are either semiautomatic or automatic and require the use of pilot devices such as the pushbuttons shown in Figure 18-21. All pilot devices, such as limit switches, flow switches, float switches, and so on, must be contained inside enclosures approved for location in which they are installed. Semiautomatic and automatic controls require the use of magnetic starters, contactors, and relays. These contactors and/or starters also must be contained inside suitable enclosures. The motor starter shown in Figure 18-22 contains a circuit breaker and motor starter with overload relay.

FLEXIBLE CORDS AND RECEPTACLES

Flexible cords and attachment plugs are permitted in hazardous locations for the operation of portable lights or equipment (Figure 18-23 on page 244). When they are used, they must comply with the following conditions:

1. Be approved for extra-hard usage
2. Contain a separate bonding conductor
3. Be properly connected to terminals or supply conductors
4. Be supported by clamps in such a manner that no tension is transmitted to the terminal connection
5. Be supplied with connectors/glands approved for the environment to prevent the entrance of flammable vapours in a Class I location, flammable dust in a Class II location, or fibres in a Class III location

Plugs and receptacles must be approved for the location in which they are used (*CEC* Rules 18-124, 18-178, 18-220, 18-270, 18-318, and 18-368). Explosionproof receptacles are constructed with an internal switch that disconnects the power from the circuit before the attachment plug is removed. A cutaway view of this type of receptacle

Figure 18-21 Pushbuttons used in hazardous location.
(Courtesy of Crouse-Hinds ECM)

is shown in Figure 18-24 on page 244. This plug and receptacle are constructed in such a manner that the attachment plug can be inserted into or removed from the receptacle only when the disconnect switch is in the off position. This is done to prevent the possibility of an arc being produced outside of the explosionproof enclosure when the plug is connected or disconnected. Once the plug has been inserted into the receptacle, the switch is turned on by twisting the plug in a clockwise direction. An explosionproof receptacle and attachment plug are shown in Figure 18-25 on page 244.

HAZARDOUS AREAS

Commercial Garages

Locations where motor vehicles are serviced or repaired are considered to be hazardous environments. These vehicles include automobiles, trucks, buses, and tractors. In general, the floor area of a garage, up to a level of 50 mm (2 in) above the floor, is considered to be a Class I Zone 2 location (Figure 18-26 on page 245). The only exception to this is if a mechanical ventilation system provides sufficient airflow to produce at least four changes of air per hour. A pit area below the floor is considered to be a Class I Zone 2 location regardless of presence of a mechanical ventilation system. Any adjacent areas—such as office or storage space that is separated by a curb or ramp of 50 mm or more—is not considered to be a hazardous environment.

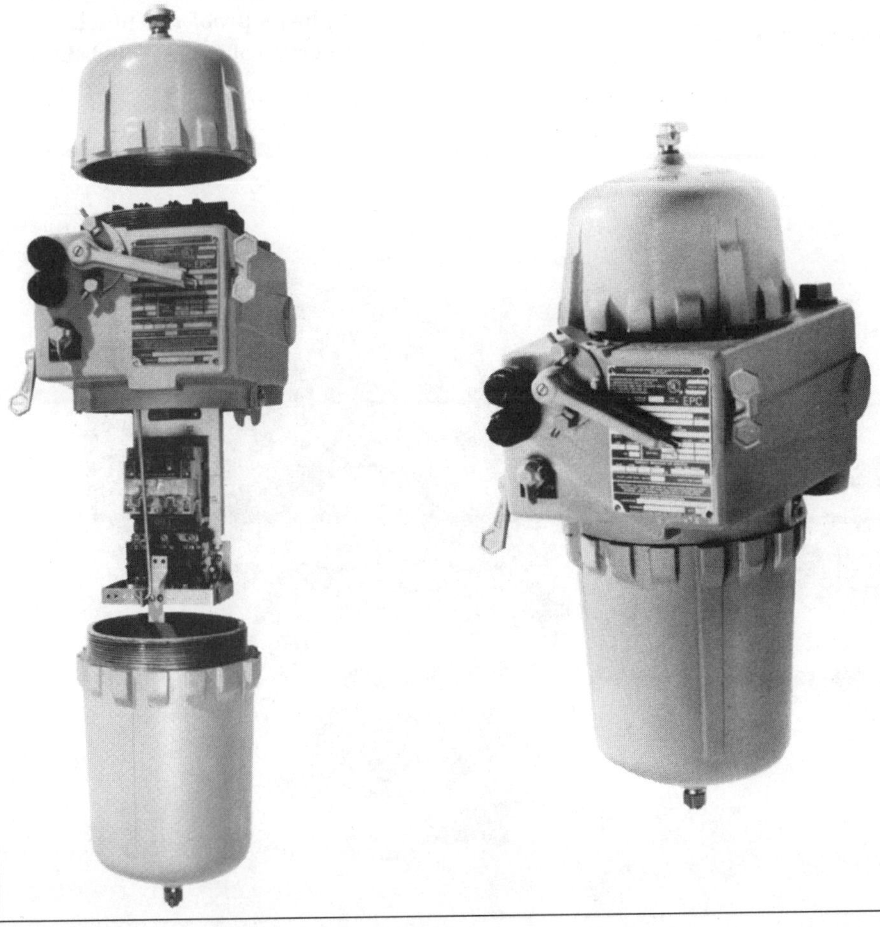

Figure 18-22 Explosionproof motor starter with circuit breaker.

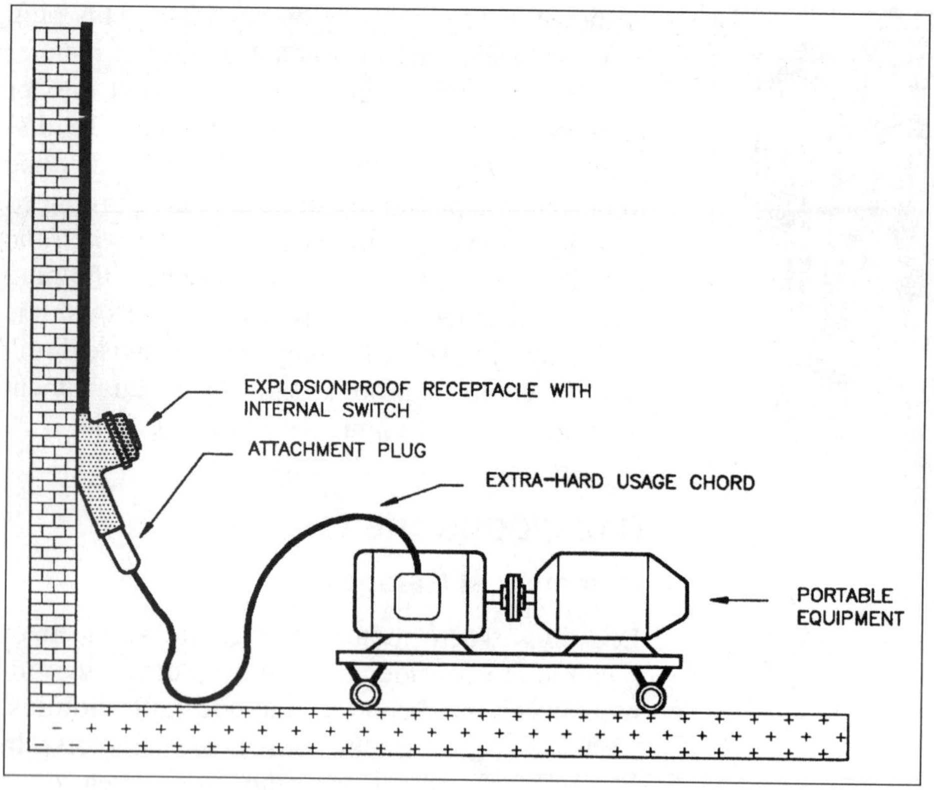

Figure 18-23 Portable equipment connected by a cord.

Figure 18-24 Cutaway view of explosionproof receptacle.
(Courtesy of Crouse-Hinds ECM)

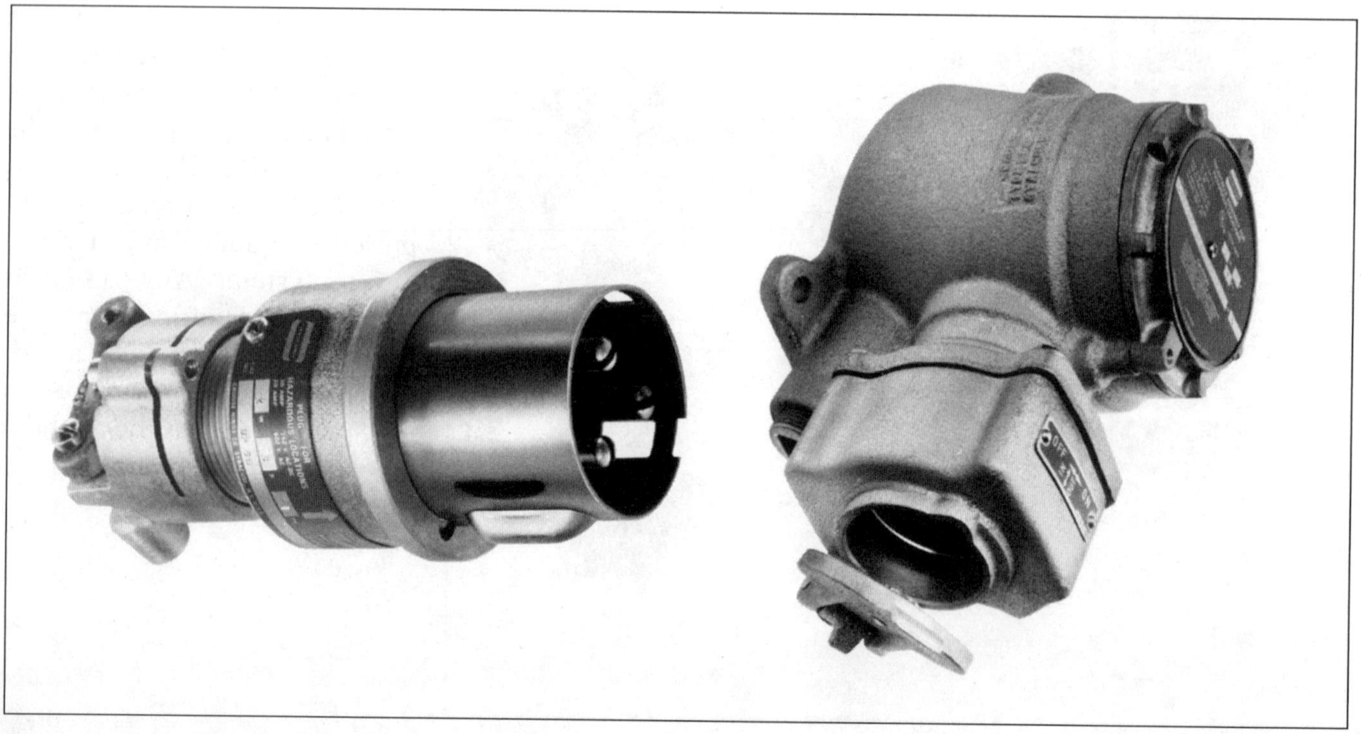

Figure 18-25 Explosionproof attachment plug and receptacle.
(Courtesy of Crouse-Hinds ECM)

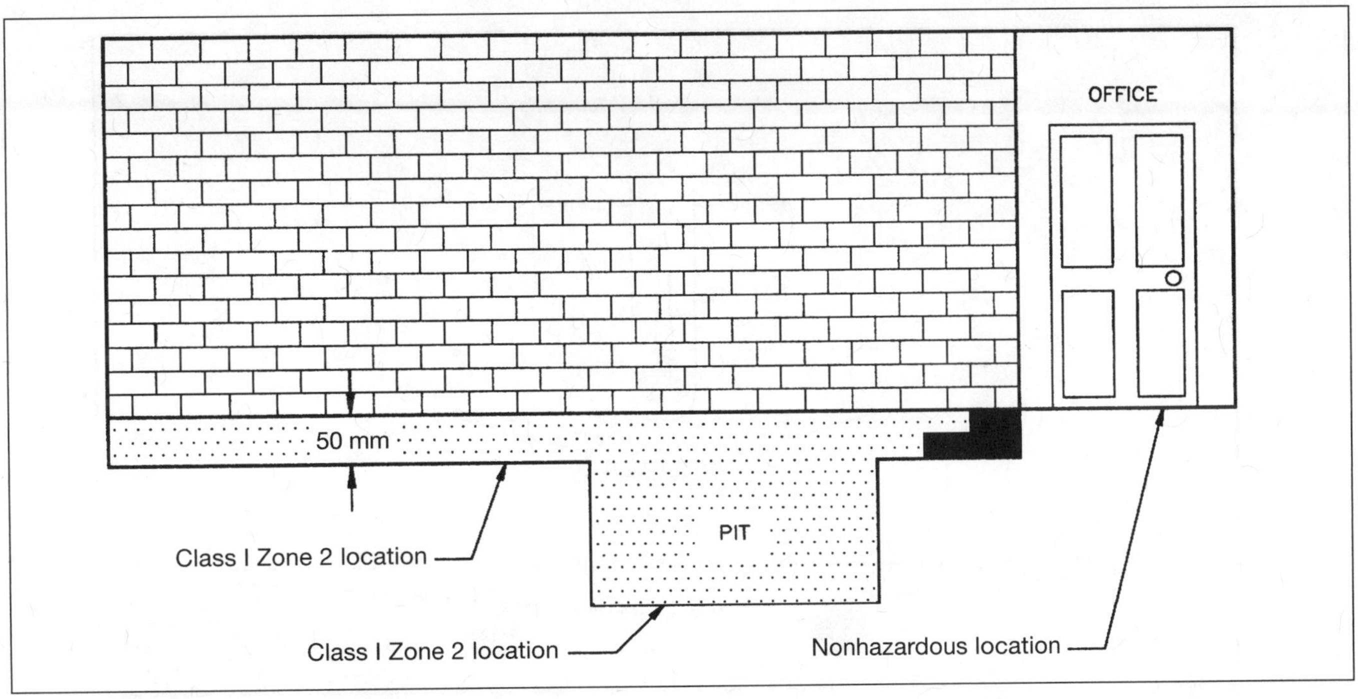

Figure 18-26 Commercial garage.

Aircraft Hangars

An aircraft hangar is a location used to store or service aircraft that contains gasoline, jet fuel, or other flammable vapours. Areas used to store aircraft that have never contained flammable fuel or that have been drained and purged are not included in this definition.

In general, any pit located below floor level is considered to be a Class I Zone 1 location (Figure 18-27 on page 246). Any area up to a level of 450 mm (18 in), any area within 1.5 m (5 ft) of the engine or engines, any area within 1.5 m (5 ft) of fuel tanks, and any area extending 1.5 m (5 ft) above the surface of the wings or engines is considered to be a Class I Zone 2 location.

Gasoline Dispensing and Service Stations

CEC Rule 20-004 describes the classes and zones for different areas where gasoline is stored or dispensed. In general, any space below grade level, within 3 m (10 ft) of an underground tank fill pipe (Figure 18-28 to 450 mm (18 in) above grade level. Any area within a 900 mm (3 ft) spherical radius of a gasoline tank vent is considered to be Class I Zone 1. Any space between 900 mm and 1.5 m (3 ft and 5 ft), extending in all directions, of a gasoline tank vent is considered to be a Class I Zone 2 location. If the tank vent does not open upward, the cylindrical area below the aforementioned Zone 1 and Zone 2 areas is considered to be Class I Zone 2.

Any space within 6 m of the exterior of an outside gasoline-dispensing pump is considered to be Class I Zone 2 up to a height of 450 mm above the driveway of ground level. Any space inside the pump enclosure, up to a height of 1.2 m above the base, any space below the dispenser, and any space within 450 mm of the dispenser is considered to be Class I Zone 1 (Figure 18-29 on page 247). Class I Zone 2 locations are as follows:

1. Any area 450 mm above grade level, within 6 m, of an outside dispensing pump

2. Any space, within the interior of the pump enclosure, isolated by a solid vapour tight

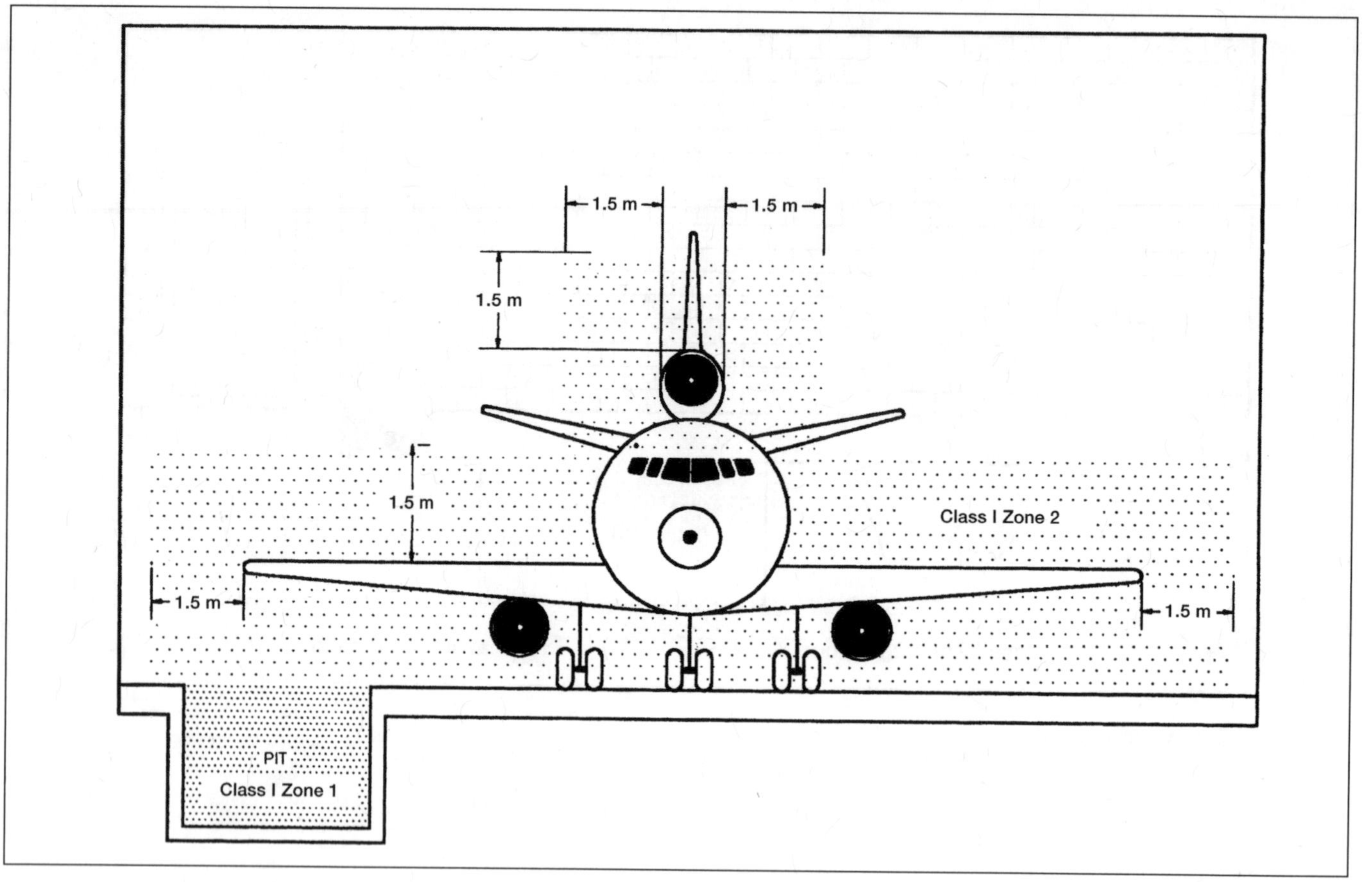

Figure 18-27 Aircraft hangar.

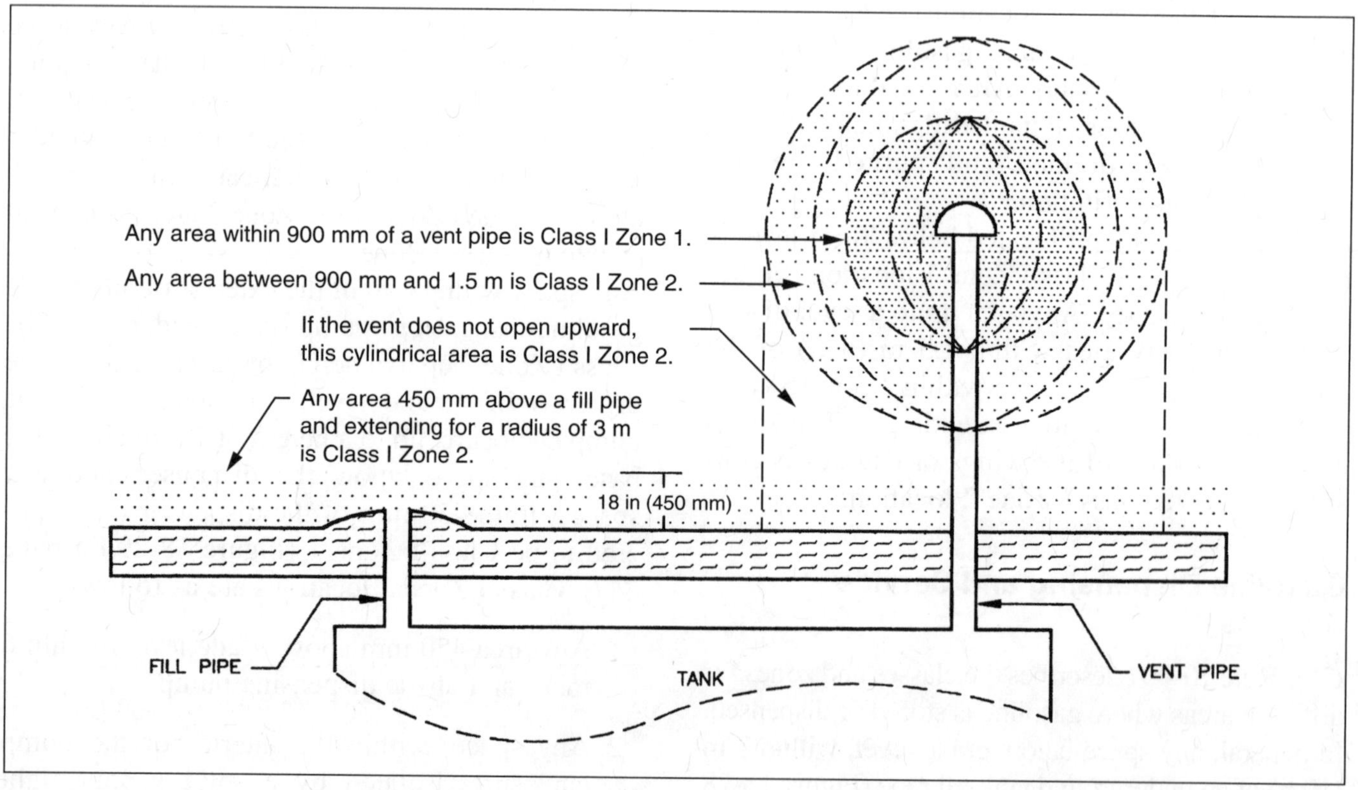

Figure 18-28 Underground gasoline tank.

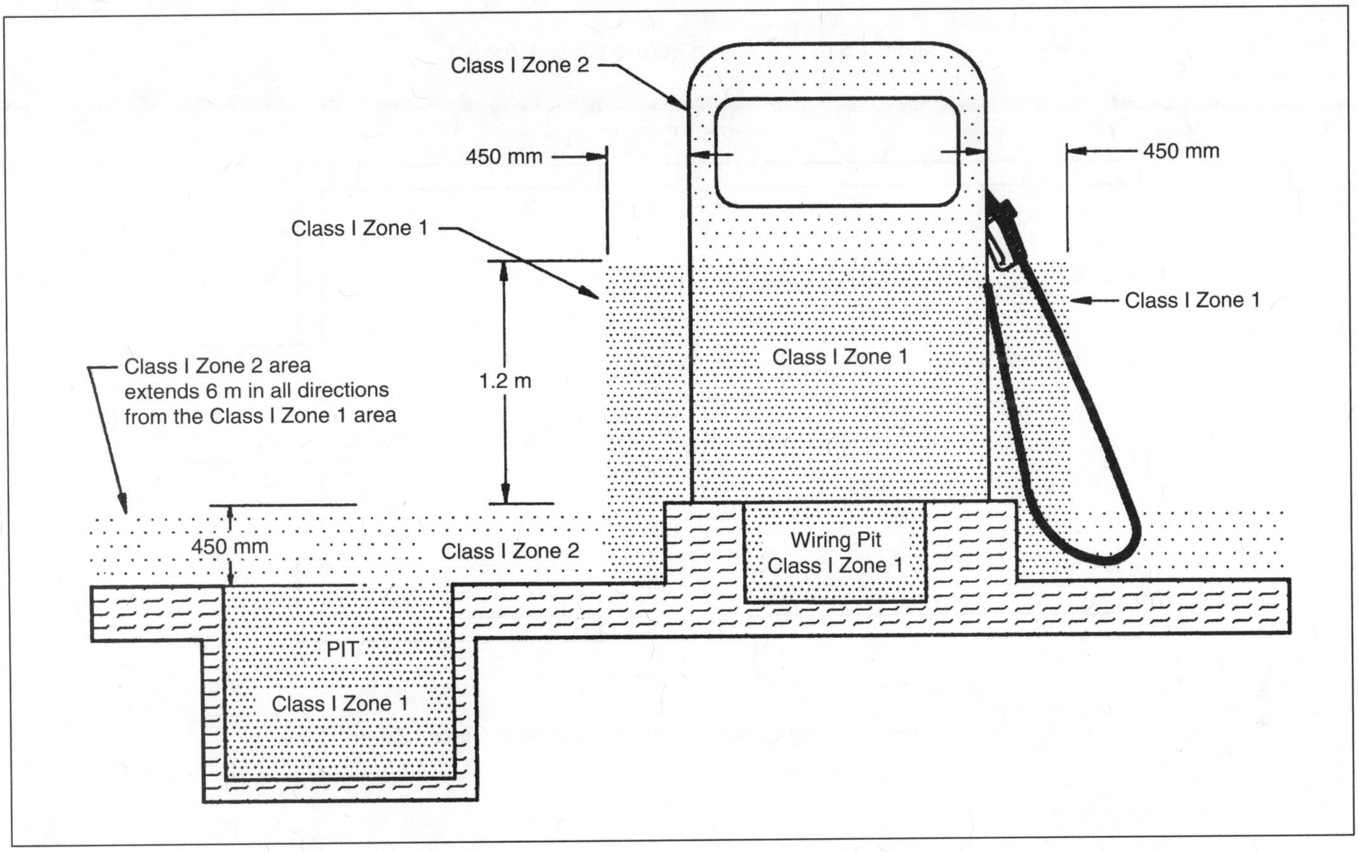

Figure 18-29 Gasoline-dispensing pump.

Spray Processes

CEC Rule 20-404 requires that all spray booths shall be ventilated and that the spray equipment be inoperable unless the ventilation system is turned on and providing air flow. *CEC* Rule 20-402 gives the location classification for areas that contain hazardous concentrations of flammable vapour or dusts produced by spraying.

Class I Zone 1 locations are as follows:

1. The interior of spray booths or rooms (Figure 18-30 on page 248)
2. The interior of exhaust ducts
3. For spraying not in a spray booth, any area within 6 m in any direction and 1 m above the item to be painted

Class I Zone 2 locations are as follows:

1. For open spraying, any space outside the Class I Zone1 area within the room (Figure 18-31 on
2. For open-front spray booths with a closed top and closed sides, any space within 1.5 m of the front opening extending 1 m above the top of the booth or the area ceiling, whichever is less
3. Any area within 1 m in any direction of any opening in a completely enclosed spray booth is considered to be Class I Zone 2

EXPLOSIONPROOF EQUIPMENT

Great care must be exercised when installing or maintaining explosionproof equipment. The improper installation or maintenance of this equipment can completely negate the system's integrity. The mating surfaces of explosionproof boxes are ground flat to provide a very close fit. A screwdriver gouge or deep scratch can provide the exit point for hot gases to escape and ignite the surrounding atmosphere (Figure 18-32 on

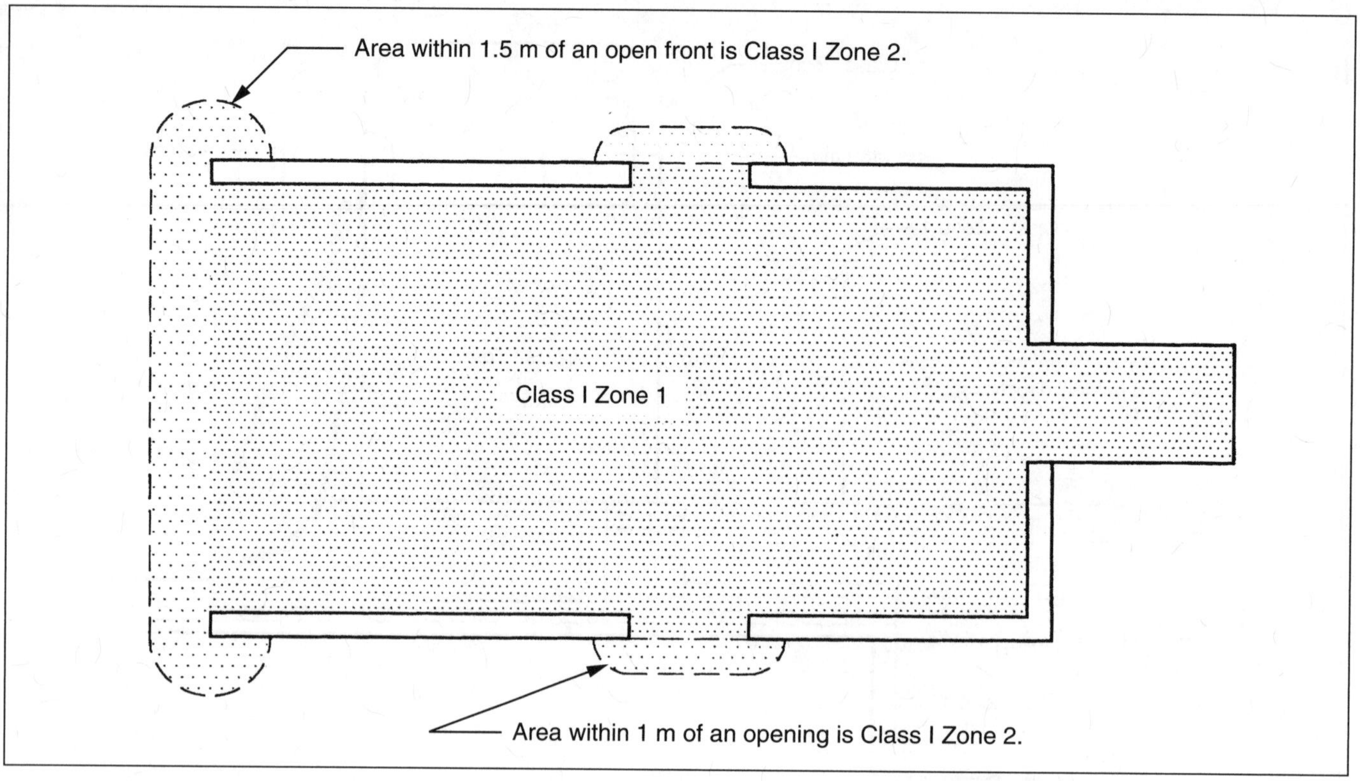

Figure 18-30 Spray booth.

The ground surfaces of explosionproof enclosures should be cleaned with solvent to remove dirt particles before the parts are bolted together. If it is necessary to remove a substance that cannot be cleaned with solvent, use fine steel wool, never sandpaper or a sharp scraping instrument such as a putty knife. All bolts must be in place and tight. If one bolt is missing, the enclosure may not be able to prevent ignition of the surrounding atmosphere in the event of an internal explosion.

Seals must be installed between explosionproof enclosures to prevent a condition known as pressure piling. Pressure piling occurs when the hot gases produced by an internal explosion travel through a conduit to an adjacent enclosure (Figure 18-33 on page 250).

These hot gases add to the volume of gas already present in the second enclosure. If the gases in the second enclosure are ignited by the hot gas produced by the explosion in the first enclosure, the pressure produced in the second enclosure can be as great as three times what would be normally expected. A properly installed seal, however, prevents the passage of hot gas from one enclosure to the other (Figure 18-34 on page 250).

Seals are especially important when the conduit leaves a hazardous location and enters a nonhazardous location, Figure 18-4. The equipment and enclosures in a nonhazardous location are not designed to withstand any type of internal explosion and would be completely destroyed.

Some types of explosionproof enclosures are designed to be drilled and tapped in the field. When this is done, at least five full threads should be engaged between the conduit and the enclosure Figure 18-35 on page 251).

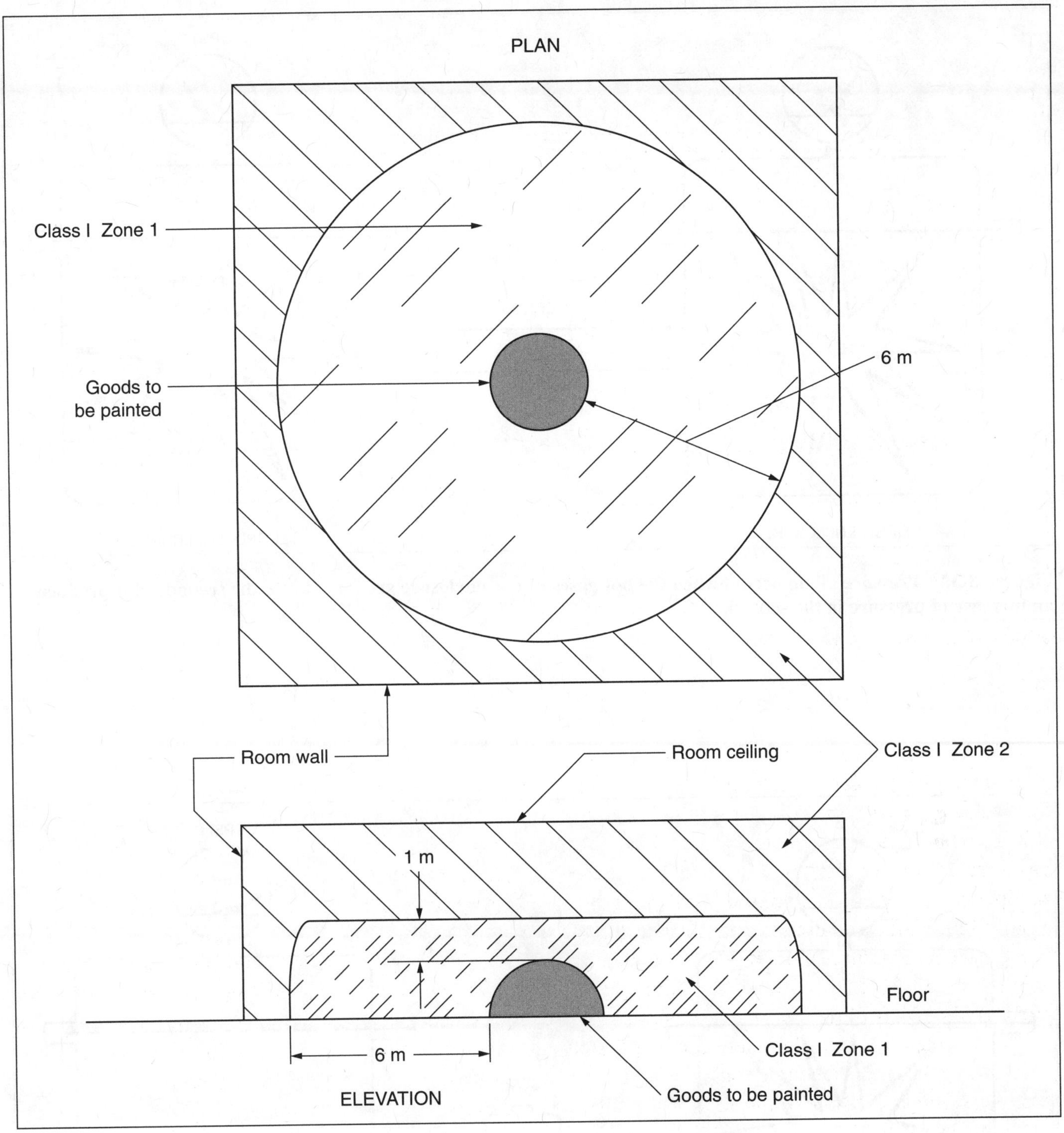

Figure 18-31 Open area spraying operations.

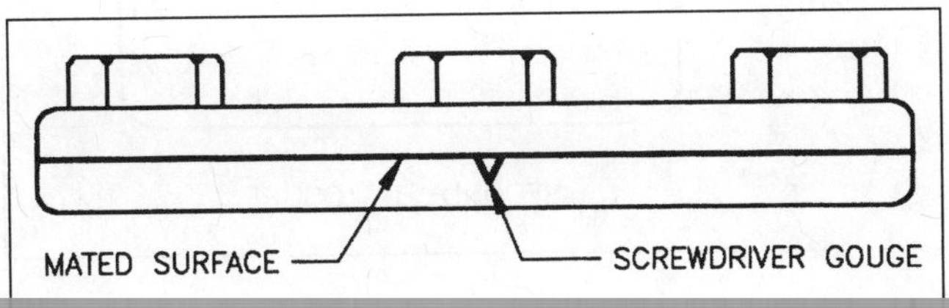

Figure 18-32 A screwdriver gouge or scratch can destroy the integrity of the enclosure by providing an exit point for hot gas.

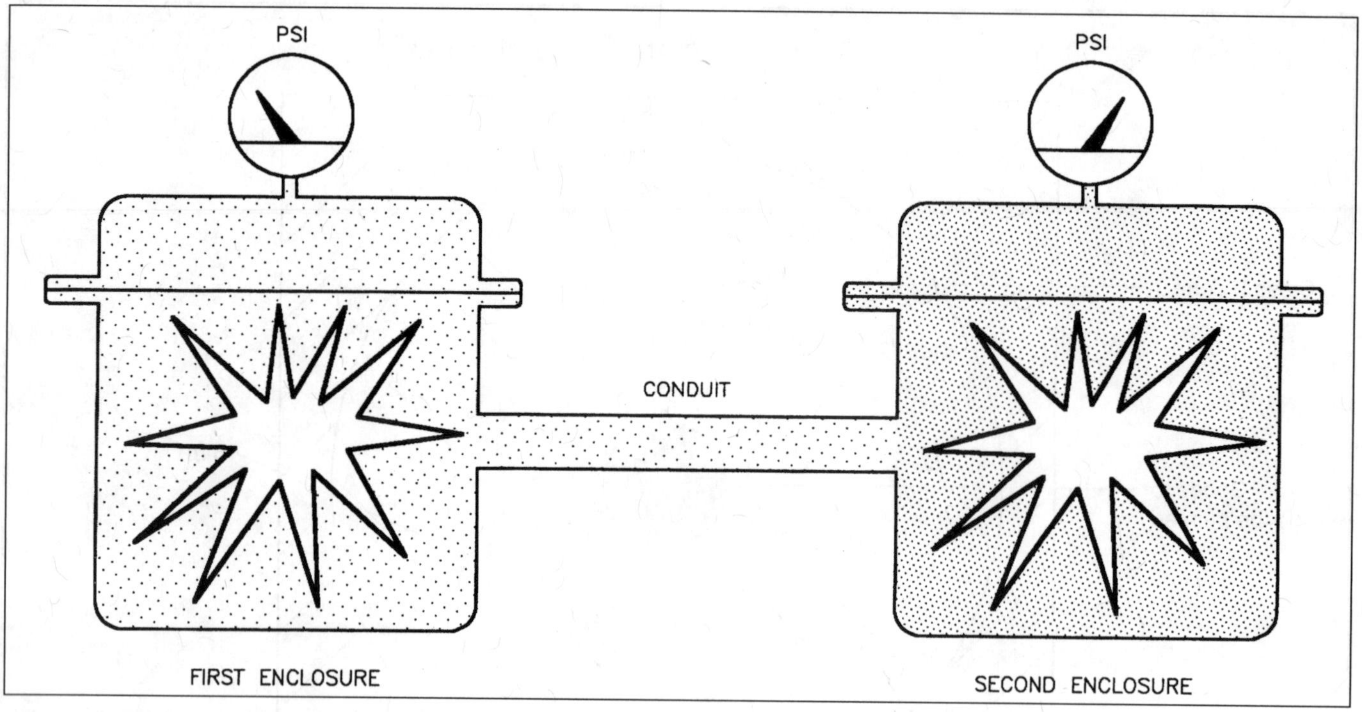

Figure 18-33 Pressure piling occurs when the hot gases of one enclosure are forced into the second. This produces an increase of pressure in the second.

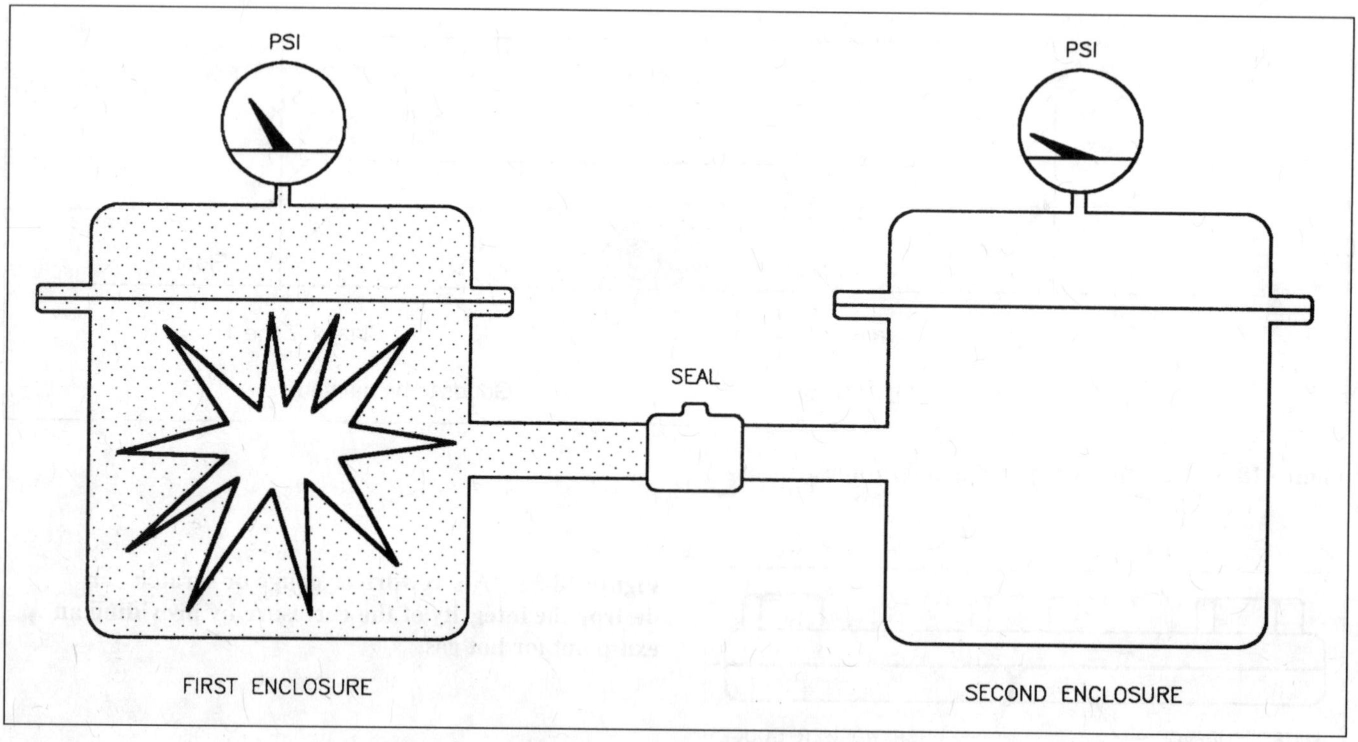

Figure 18-34 A seal prevents the passage of hot gas from one enclosure to the other.

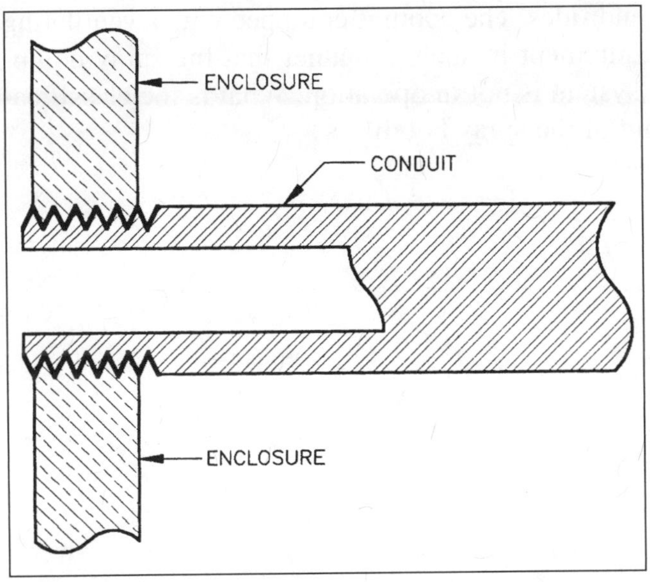

Figure 18-35 At least five full threads should be made between the enclosure and the conduit.

REVIEW

All answers should be written in complete sentences, calculations should be shown in detail, and Code references should be cited when appropriate.

1. What would be the class, zone/division, and group of an area in which acetylene gas was manufactured?
2. What would be the class, zone/division, and group of an area in which gasoline was manufactured?
3. What would be the class, zone/division, and group of an area in which flour was manufactured?
4. What would be the class, zone/division, and group of an area in which coal was stored?
5. What class is used for areas in which combustible fibres are woven into cloth?
6. What are intrinsically safe circuits?
7. What is the maximum length of a stem used for pendant lighting before bracing is required?
8. Why are seals used in explosionproof wiring systems?
9. Are "enclosed and gasketed" luminaires (fixtures) permitted in a Class II Division 1 location?
10. Name five conditions that must be met before flexible cords can be used in a hazardous location.
11. In a commercial garage, what is the classification of any area less than 450 mm above the floor (other than a pit)?
12. To what height above an aircraft wing does a Class I Zone 2 location extend?
13. The interior of a gasoline-dispensing pump enclosure is considered to be Class I Zone 1 up to

14. An open-front spray booth has a closed top and sides. The booth is equipped with a ventilating system that is interlocked with the spray equipment in such a manner that the spray equipment will not operate when the ventilation system is not in operation. What is the classification of the area 2.5 m in front of the opening of the spray booth?

UNIT 19

Harmonics

OBJECTIVES

After studying this unit, the student should be able to:

- describe a harmonic
- discuss the problems concerning harmonics
- identify the characteristics of different harmonics
- perform a test to determine whether harmonic problems exist
- discuss methods of dealing with harmonic problems

HARMONICS

Harmonics are voltages or currents that operate at a frequency that is a multiple of the fundamental power frequency. If the fundamental power frequency is 60 Hz, for example, the second harmonic would be 120 Hz, the third harmonic would be 180 Hz, and so on. Harmonics are produced by nonlinear loads that draw current in pulses rather than in a continuous manner. Harmonics on single-phase power lines are generally caused by devices such as computer power supplies, electronic ballasts in fluorescent lights, triac light dimmers, and so on. Three-phase harmonics are generally produced by variable-frequency drives for AC motors and electronic drives for DC motors. A good example of a pulsating load is one that converts AC current into DC and then regulates the DC voltage by pulse-width modulation, Figure 19-1 on page 254. Many regulated power supplies operate in this manner. The bridge rectifier in Figure 19-1 changes the alternating current into pulsating direct current. A filter capacitor is used to smooth the pulsations. The transistor turns on and off to supply power to the load. The amount of time the transistor is turned on as compared to the time it is turned off determines the output DC voltage. Each time the transistor turns on, it causes the capacitor to begin discharging. When the transistor turns off, the capacitor will begin to charge again. Current is drawn from the AC line each time the capacitor charges. These pulsations of current produced by the charging capacitor can cause the AC sine wave to become distorted. These distorted current and voltage waveforms flow back into the other parts of the power system, Figure 19-2 on page 254.

HARMONIC EFFECTS

Harmonics can have very detrimental effects on electrical equipment. Some common symptoms of harmonics are overheated conductors and transformers and circuit breakers that seem to trip when they should not. Harmonics are classified by name, frequency, and sequence. The name refers to whether the harmonic is the second, third, fourth,

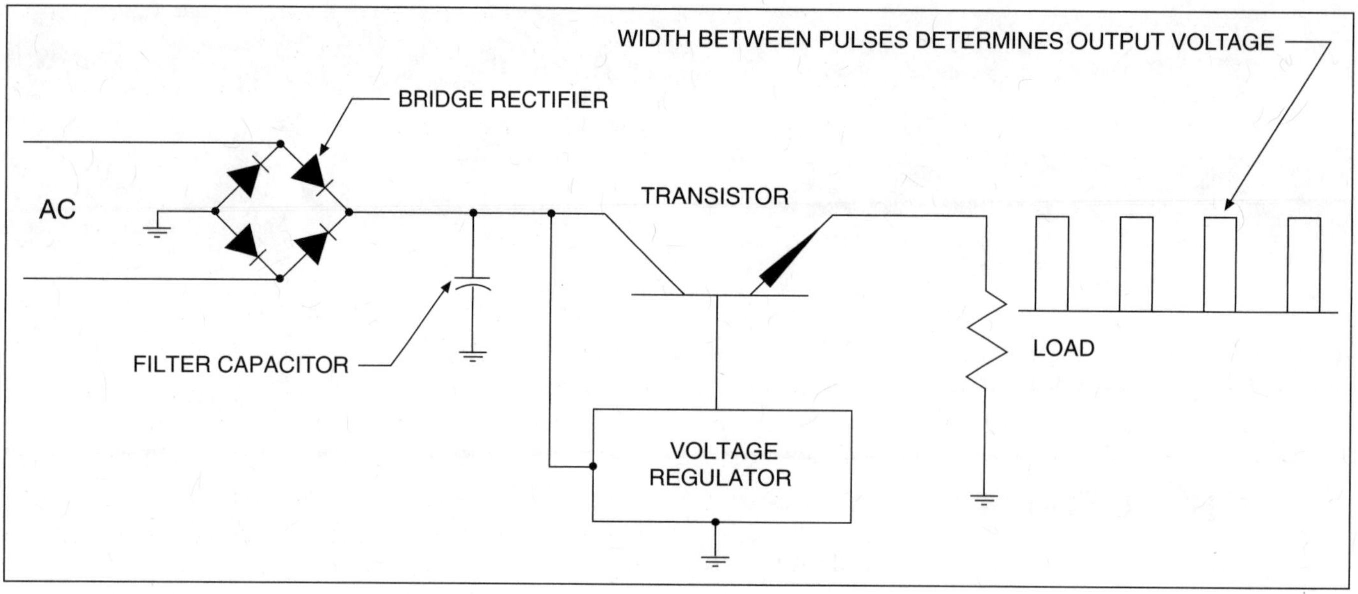

Figure 19-1 Pulse-width modulation regulates the output voltage by varying the time the transistor conducts as compared to the time it is off.

and so on, of the fundamental frequency. The frequency refers to the operating frequency of the harmonic. The second harmonic operates at 120 Hz, the third at 180 Hz, the fourth at 240 Hz, and so on. The sequence refers to the phasor rotation with respect to the fundamental waveform. In an induction motor, a positive sequence harmonic would rotate in the same direction as the fundamental frequency. A negative sequence harmonic would rotate in the opposite direction of the funda-

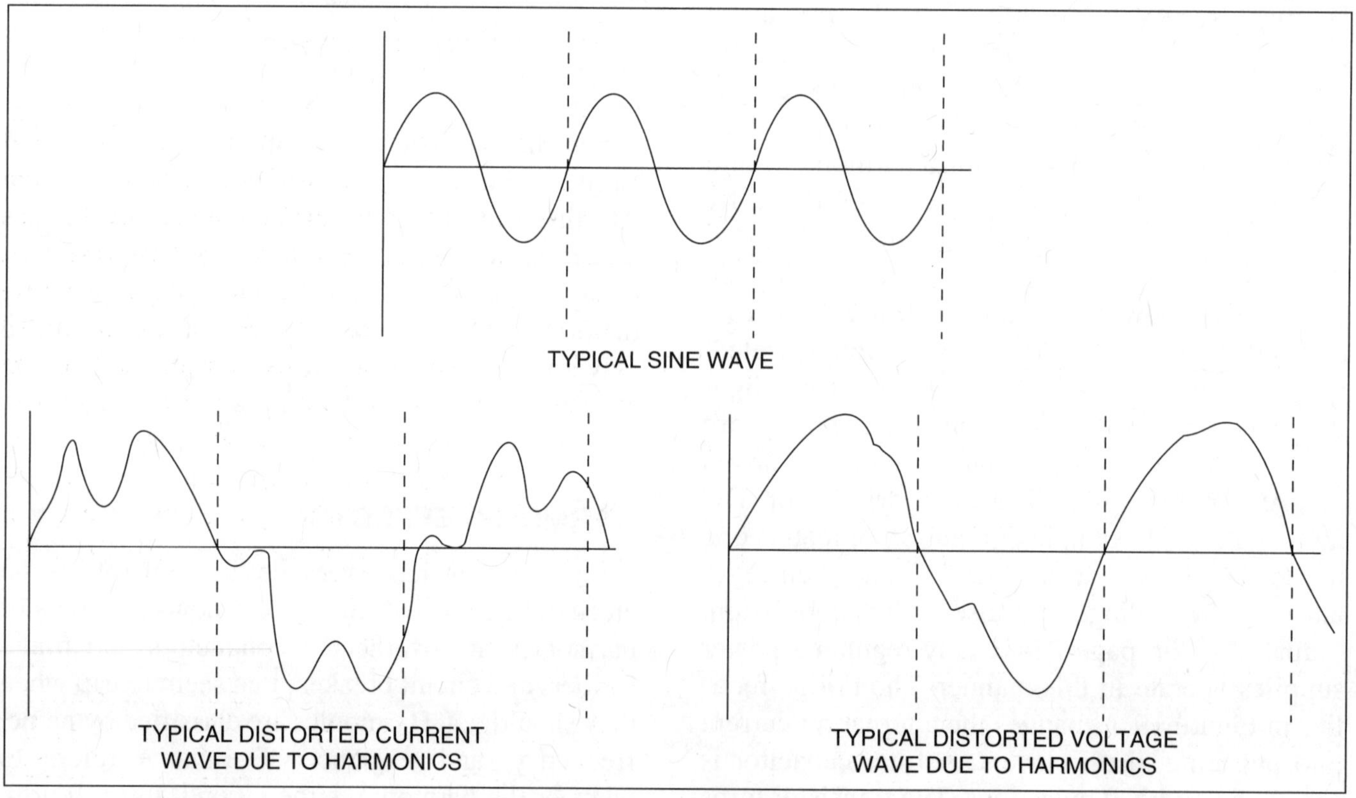

Figure 19-2 Harmonics cause an AC sine wave to become distorted.

mental frequency. Harmonics called *triplens* have a zero sequence. Triplens are the odd multiples of the third harmonic (3rd, 9th, 15th, 21st, and so on). A chart showing the sequence of the first nine harmonics is shown in Table 19-1.

Harmonics with a positive sequence generally cause overheating of conductors, transformers, and circuit breakers. Negative sequence harmonics can cause the same heating problems as positive harmonics plus additional problems with motors. Since the phasor rotation of a negative harmonic is opposite that of the fundamental frequency, it will tend to weaken the rotating magnetic field of an induction motor, causing it to produce less torque. The reduction of torque causes the motor to operate below normal speed. The reduction in speed results in excessive motor current and overheating.

Although triplens do not have a phasor rotation, they can cause a great deal of trouble in a three-phase, four-wire system, such as a 208/120-V or 480/277-V system. In a common 208/120-V wye-connected system, the primary is generally connected in delta and the secondary is connected in wye (Figure 19-3 on page 256).

Single-phase loads that operate on 120 V are connected between any phase conductor and the neutral conductor. The neutral current will be the vector sum of the phase currents. In a balanced three-phase circuit (all phases having equal current), the neutral current will be zero. Although single-phase loads tend to cause an unbalanced condition, the vector sum of the currents will generally cause the neutral conductor to carry less current than any of the phase conductors. This is true for loads that are linear and draw a continuous sine wave current. When pulsating (nonlinear) currents are connected to a three-phase, four-wire system, triplen harmonic frequencies disrupt the normal phasor relationship of the phase currents and can cause the phase currents to add in the neutral conductor instead of cancel. Since the neutral conductor is not protected by a fuse or circuit breaker, there is real danger of excessive heating in the neutral conductor.

Harmonic currents are also reflected in the delta primary winding where they circulate and cause overheating. Other heating problems are caused by eddy current and hysteresis losses. Transformers are typically designed for 60-Hz operation. Higher harmonic frequencies produce greater core losses than the transformer is designed to handle. Transformers that are connected to circuits that produce harmonics must sometimes be derated or replaced with transformers that are specially designed to operate with harmonic frequencies.

Transformers are not the only electrical component to be affected by harmonic currents. Emergency and standby generators can be affected in the same way as transformers. This is especially true for standby generators used to power data processing equipment in the event of a power failure. Some harmonic frequencies can even distort the zero crossing of the waveform produced by the generator.

CIRCUIT-BREAKER PROBLEMS

Thermomagnetic circuit breakers use a bimetallic trip mechanism that is sensitive to the heat produced by the circuit current. These circuit breakers are designed to respond to the heating effect of the true RMS current value. If the current becomes too great, the bimetallic mechanism trips the breaker open. Harmonic currents cause a distortion of the RMS value, which can cause the breaker to trip when it should not, or not to trip when it should. Thermomagnetic circuit breakers, however, are generally better protection against harmonic currents than electronic circuit breakers. Electronic breakers sense the peak value of current. The peaks

Name	Fund.	2nd	3rd	4th	5th	6th	7th	8th	9th
Frequency	60	120	180	240	300	360	420	480	540
Sequence	+	–	0	+	–	0	+	–	0

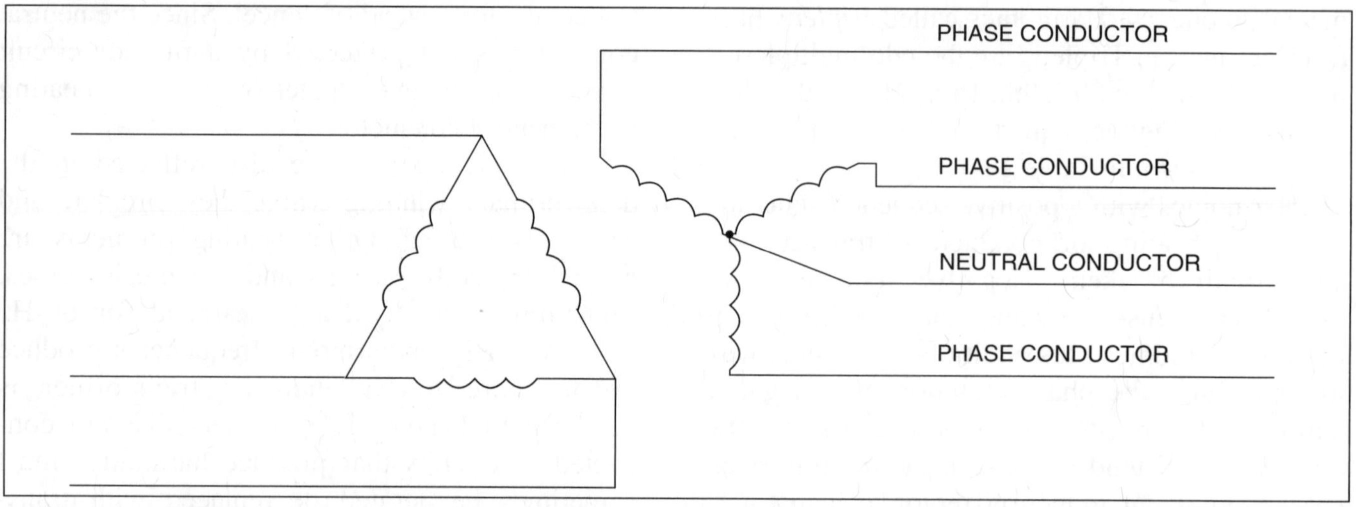

Figure 19-3 In a three-phase, four-wire connected system, the centre of the wye-connection secondary is tapped to form a neutral conductor.

of harmonic currents are generally higher than the fundamental sine wave (Figure 19-4). Although the peaks of harmonic currents are generally higher than the fundamental frequency, they can be lower. In some cases, electronic breakers may trip at low currents, and in other cases they may not trip at all.

BUS DUCTS AND PANELBOARD PROBLEMS

Triplen harmonic currents can also cause problems with neutral bus ducts and connecting lugs. A neutral bus is sized to carry the rated phase current. Since triplen harmonics can cause the neutral current to be higher than the phase current, it is possible for the neutral bus to become overloaded.

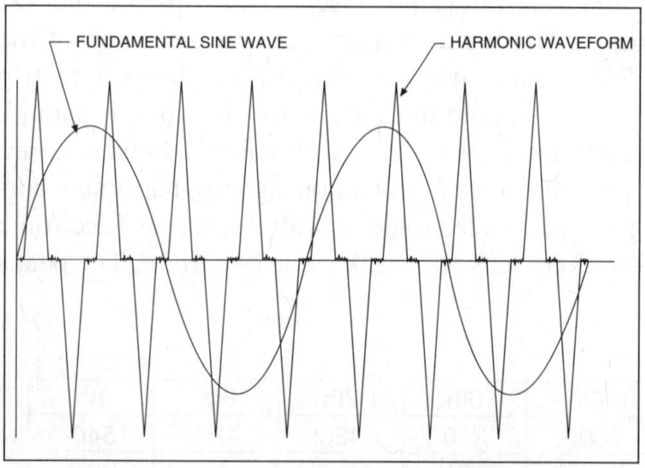

Figure 19-4 Harmonic waveforms generally have higher peak values than the fundamental waveforms.

Electrical panelboards and bus ducts are designed to carry currents that operate at 60 Hz. Harmonic currents produce magnetic fields that operate at higher frequencies. If these fields should become mechanically resonant with the panelboard or bus duct enclosures, the panelboards and bus ducts can vibrate and produce buzzing sounds at the harmonic frequency.

Telecommunications equipment is often affected by harmonic currents. Telecommunication cable is often run close to power lines. To minimize interference, communications cables are run as far from phase conductors as possible and as close to the neutral conductor as possible. Harmonic currents in the neutral conductor induce high-frequency currents into the communications cable. These high-frequency currents can be heard as a high-pitched buzzing sound on telephone lines.

DETERMINING HARMONIC PROBLEMS ON SINGLE-PHASE SYSTEMS

Several steps can be followed in determining whether there is a problem with harmonics. One step is to do a survey of the equipment. This is especially important in determining whether there is a problem with harmonics in a single-phase system.

1. Make an equipment check. Personal computers, printers, and fluorescent lights with electronic ballast are known to produce harmonics. Any piece of equipment that draws current in pulses can produce harmonics.
2. Review maintenance records to see whether there have been problems with circuit breakers tripping for no apparent reason.
3. Check transformers for overheating. If the cooling vents are unobstructed and the transformer is operating excessively hot, harmonics could be the problem. Check transformer currents with an ammeter capable of indicating a true RMS current value. Make sure that the voltage and current ratings of the transformer have not been exceeded.

It is necessary to use an ammeter that responds to true RMS current when making this check. Some ammeters respond to the average value, not the RMS value. Meters that respond to the true RMS value generally state this on the meter. Meters that respond to the average value are generally less expensive and do not state that they are RMS meters. A clamp-on type ammeter that responds to a true RMS current is shown in Figure 19-5.

Meters that respond to the average value use a rectifier to convert the alternating current into direct current. This value must be increased by a factor of 1.111 to change the average reading into the RMS value for a sine wave current. True RMS responding meters calculate the heating effect of the current. The chart in Figure 19-6 on page 258 shows some of the differences between average indicating meters and true RMS meters. In a distorted waveform, the true RMS value of current will no longer be the average value multiplied by 1.111, Figure 19-7 on page 258. The distorted waveform generally causes the average value to be as much as 50% less than the RMS value.

Another method of determining whether a harmonic problem exists in a single-phase system is to make two separate current checks. One check is made using an ammeter that indicates the true RMS value and the other is made using a meter that indicates the average value (Figure 19-8 on page 259). In this example, it is assumed that the true RMS ammeter indicates a value of 36.8 A and the average ammeter indicates a value of 24.8 A. Determine the ratio of the two measurements by dividing the average value by the true RMS value.

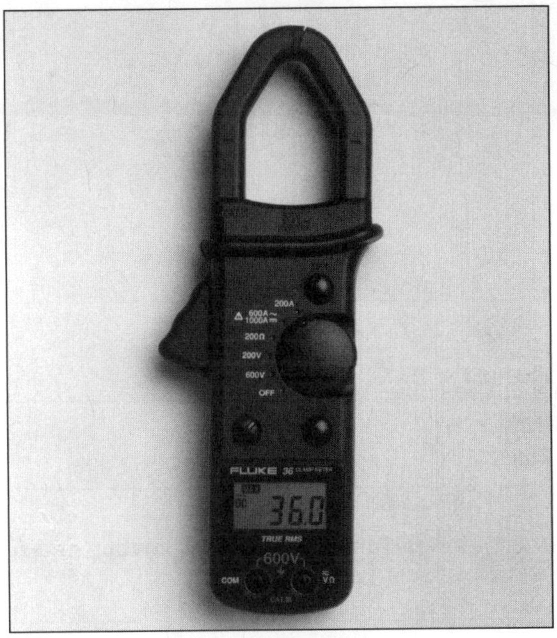

Figure 19-5 True RMS ammeter.

$$\text{Ratio} = \frac{\text{Average}}{\text{RMS}}$$

$$= \frac{24.8}{36.8}$$

$$= 0.674$$

A ratio of 1 would indicate no harmonic distortion. A ratio of 0.5 would indicate extreme harmonic distortion. This method does not reveal the name or sequence of the harmonic distortion, but it does give an indication that there is a problem with harmonics.

The most accurate method for determining whether there is a harmonics problem is to use a harmonic analyzer. The harmonic analyzer will determine the name, sequence, and amount of harmonic distortion present in the system. A harmonic analyzer is shown in Figure 19-9 on page 259.

Ammeter Type	Sine Wave Response	Square Wave Response	Distorted Wave Response
Average Responding	Correct	Approx. 10% High	As much as 50% low
True RMS Responding	Correct	Correct	Correct

Figure 19-6 Comparison of average responding and true RMS responding ammeters.

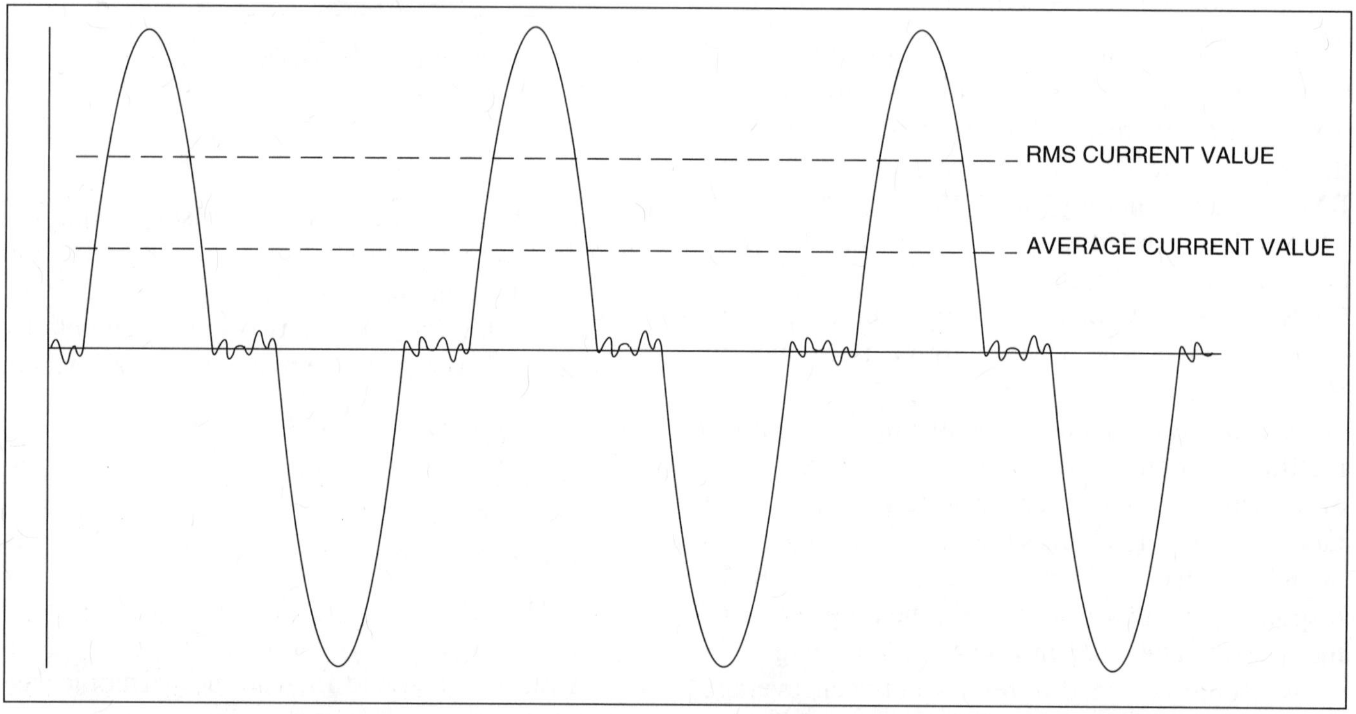

Figure 19-7 Average current values are generally greater than the true RMS value in a distorted waveform.

DETERMINING HARMONIC PROBLEMS ON THREE-PHASE SYSTEMS

Determining whether a problem with harmonics exists in a three-phase system is similar to determining the problem in a single-phase system. Since harmonic problems in a three-phase system generally occur in a wye-connected four-wire system, this example will assume a delta-connected primary and wye-connected secondary with a centre-tapped neutral as shown in Figure 19-3. To test for harmonic distortion in a three-phase, four-wire system, measure all phase currents and the neutral current with both a true RMS indicating ammeter and an average indicating ammeter. It will be assumed that the three-phase system being tested is supplied by a 200-kVA

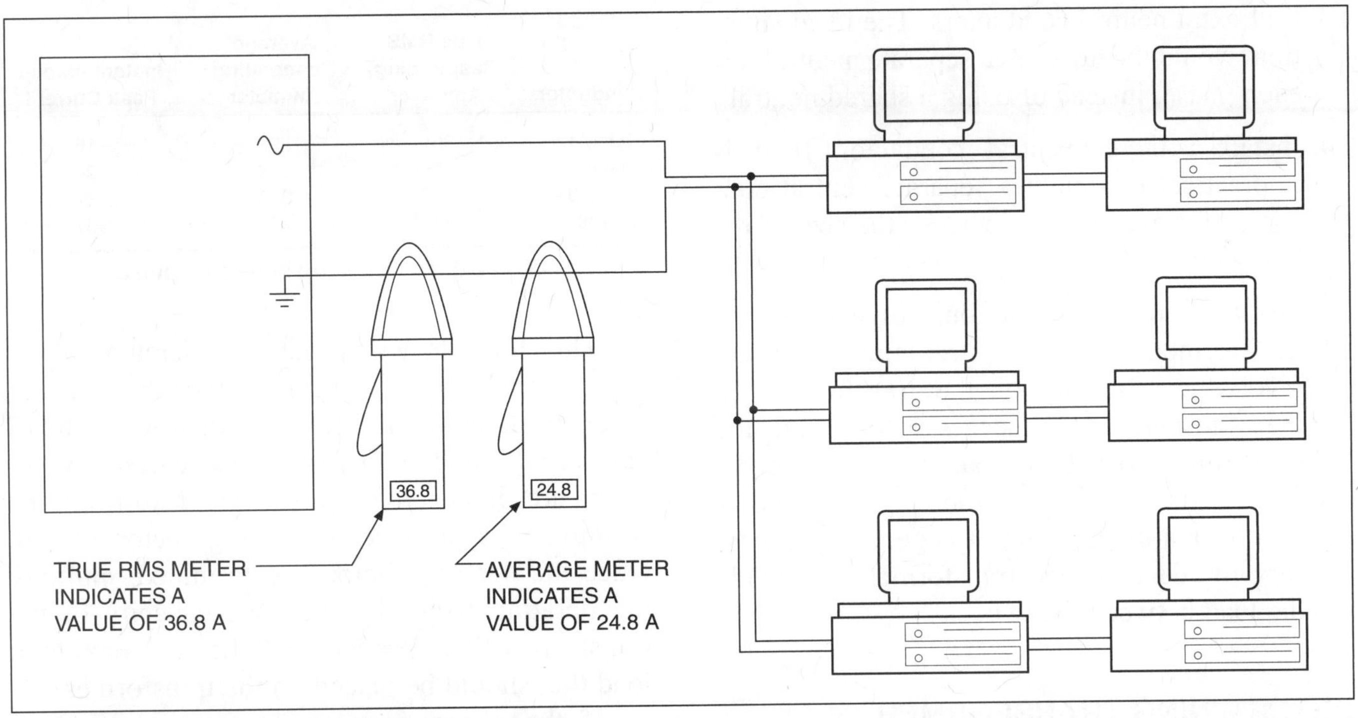

Figure 19-8 Determining the harmonic problems using two ammeters.

transformer, and that the current values shown in Table 19-2 are recorded. The current values indicate that a problem with harmonics does exist in the system. Note the higher current measurements made with the true RMS indicating ammeter, and also the fact that the neutral current is higher than any phase current.

Conductor	True RMS Repsonding Ammeter	Average Responding Ammeter
Phase 1	365	292
Phase 2	396	308
Phase 3	387	316
Neutral	488	478

Table 19-2 Measuring phase and neutral currents in a three-phase, four-wire wye-connected system.

DEALING WITH HARMONIC PROBLEMS

After it has been determined that harmonic problems exist, something must be done to deal with the problems. It is generally not practical to remove the equipment causing the harmonic distortion, so other methods must be employed. It is a good idea to consult a power quality expert to determine the exact nature and amount of harmonic distortion present. Some general procedures for dealing with harmonics are as follows:

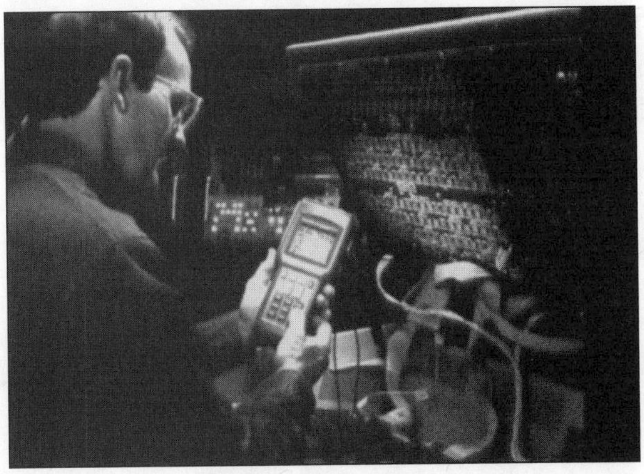

1. In a three-phase, four-wire system, reduce the 60-Hz part of the neutral current by balancing the current on the phase conductors. If all phases have equal current, the neutral current would be zero.
2. If triplen harmonics are present on the neutral conductor, add harmonic filters at the load. These filters can help reduce the amount of

3. Pull extra neutral conductors. The ideal situation would be to use a separate neutral for each phase, instead of using a shared neutral.
4. Install a larger neutral conductor. If it is impractical to supply a separate neutral conductor for each phase, increase the size of the common neutral.
5. Derate or reduce the amount of load on the transformer. Harmonic problems generally involve overheating of the transformer. In many instances it is necessary to derate the transformer to a point that it can handle the extra current caused by the harmonic distortion. When this is done, it is generally necessary to add a second transformer and divide the load between the two.

DETERMINING TRANSFORMER HARMONIC DERATING FACTOR

Probably the most practical and straightforward method for determining the derating factor for a transformer is recommended by the Computer & Business Equipment Manufacturers Association. To use this method, two ampere measurements must be made. One is the true RMS current of the phases and the second is the instantaneous peak phase current. The instantaneous peak current can be determined with an oscilloscope connected to a current probe or with an ammeter capable of measuring the peak value. Many of the digital clamp-on ammeters are capable of measuring the average, true RMS, and peak values of current. For this example, it will be assumed that peak current values are measured for the 200-kVA transformer discussed previously. These values are added to the previous data obtained with the true RMS and average indicating ammeters, Table 19-3.

The formula for determining the transformer harmonic derating factor is:

THDF = (1.414) (RMS phase current) / Instantaneous peak phase current

Conductor	True RMS Responding Ammeter	Average Responding Ammeter	Instantaneous Peak Current
Phase 1	365	292	716
Phase 2	396	308	794
Phase 3	387	316	737
Neutral	488	478	957

Table 19-3 Peak currents are added to chart.

This formula will produce a derating factor somewhere between 0 and 1.0. Since the instantaneous peak value of current is equal to the RMS value multiplied by 1.414, if the current waveforms are sinusoidal (no harmonic distortion), the formula will produce a derating factor of 1.0. Once the derating factor is determined, multiply the derating factor by the kVA capacity of the transformer. The product will be the maximum load that should be placed on the transformer.

If the phase currents are unequal, find an average value by adding the currents together and dividing by 3.

Phase (RMS) = (365 + 396 + 387) / 3

Phase (RMS) = 382.7

Phase (Peak) = (716 + 794 + 737) / 3

Phase (Peak) = 749

THDF = (1.414) (382.7) / 749

THDF = 0.722

The 200-kVA transformer in this example should be derated to 144.4 kVA (200 kVA multiplied by 0.722).

REVIEW

All answers should be written in complete sentences, calculations should be shown in detail, and Code references should be cited when appropriate.

1. What is the frequency of the second harmonic?
2. Which of the following are considered triplen harmonics: 3rd, 6th, 9th, 12th, 15th, and 18th?
3. Would a positive rotating harmonic or a negative rotating harmonic be more harmful to an induction motor? Explain your answer.
4. What instrument should be used to determine what harmonics are present in a power system?
5. A 22.5-kVA single-phase transformer is tested with a true RMS ammeter and an ammeter that indicates the peak value. The true RMS reading is 94 A. The peak reading is 204 A. Should this transformer be derated, and if so by how much?

APPENDIX

For educational purposes only; not for construction.

Division 15 Mechanical Specifications

Portions of Division 15 specifications relating to the work of Division 16.

SECTION 15500 HEATING AND COOLING

Chiller

The unit shall be completely factory assembled. Water-cooled centrifugal chiller shall operate on HFC-134a refrigerant. Unit shall be ULC listed.

The unit shall meet the capacities detailed in the equipment schedule at the voltage and current shown in the schedule.

The unit shall be shipped with a full operating charge of refrigerant and oil.

Motor to be refrigerant cooled, high efficiency type. Thermistors shall be provided in each winding to stop the compressor if excessive temperature is sensed. Provide factory-installed surge capacitors.

Control panel to be factory wired DDC control system. The system to have all necessary pressure and temperature sensors factory mounted and wired. The control system shall employ PID control algorithms to control water temperature without hunting, drooping or overshooting the setpoint.

Provide all necessary control wiring as recommended by the manufacturer.

Controller to incorporate surge-guard protection. In the event of a surge the controller shall shut down and announce an alarm.

The controller shall be provided with output contacts to control the chilled water and condensing water pumps.

Provide a unit-mounted CSA wye-delta closed transition in a NEMA 1 enclosure. Provide starter with the following accessories:

- Unfused disconnect
- Voltmeter with transfer switch
- Watthour meter with PTs and CTs suitable for monitoring through EMCS
- Power factor correction capacitors to correct full load power factor to not less than 0.95

Unit-mounted starters shall be factory mounted and wired.

Cooling Tower

The mechanical contractor install cooling towers as shown in the drawings or herein specified or both, in accordance with the manufacturer's recommendations.

Fan motor and drive as indicated in the mechanical equipment schedule. Motor to be located in an enclosure on an adjustable motor base. V belt to be designed for 150% of nameplate power.

Provide 8 KW pan heater.

Control panel to be unit mounted, weatherproof, complete with suitable starters and contactor for a two-speed fan motor and pan heater.

Panel to be factory mounted and connected to the motor and heater.

Cooling Tower Chemical Treatment

Division 16 to provide dedicated 15 A power receptacles as required.

SECTION 15700 HYDRONIC EQUIPMENT

Centrifugal Pumps

Motor: High efficiency, EEMAC Class B, squirrel cage induction, continuous duty, drip proof, ball bearing, 40°C temperature rise. Size as indicated.

All wiring under Division 16.

Vertical In-line Pumps

Motor: Resilient mounting, drip proof, sleeve bearing. Size as indicated.

All wiring under Division 16.

Fan Coil Units

Fan coil units to be exposed four-pipe units consisting of heating coil, cooling coil, drain pan and centrifugal fan. Units shall be provided complete with filter racks, starter and speed controller.
Motors to be three-speed and include internal thermal overload protection. 10% utilization range. Size as indicated in mechanical equipment schedule.

All wiring under Division 16.

SECTION 15800 AIR DISTRIBUTION

Air-Handling Units

Air-handling units to be CSA and ULC approved ARI rated, suitable for indoor installation.

All wiring to be number tagged to match electrical diagrams. All units to be supplied c/w service switch, and 120 V service receptacle. Units to be fully tested prior to shipment.

The unit shall have a single point of connection. Division 16 to provide unfused disconnect on unit as required. All power wiring by Division 16.

All power and control wiring to be run in EMT.

Provide DDC control system to operate unit.

Testing to conform to Section 16050.

Fans

All fans supplied under this contract to be CSA approved with AMCA seal.

Roof-mounted exhaust fans shall be complete with backdraft damper, bird screen and built in disconnect.

All power wiring by Division 16.

SECTION 15900 CONTROLS AND INSTRUMENTATION

All electrical work relating to the installation of thermostats and automatic controls shall be supplied under this section.

The provision of power to DDC panels shall be supplied under this section.

Item	Designation	Description	Location	Volt	Amp	Ph/Hz	Control		Remarks
							Type	Location	
1	CH-01	Water Chiller 105 kW	Chiller room	575	101 A	3ph 60 Hz	Disconnect Starter (RVNR) Controls	On unit On unit Div 15	Line voltage wiring to unit and fuses by Division 16.
2	CH-02	Water Chiller 105 kW	Chiller room	575	101 A	3ph 60 Hz	Disconnect Starter (RVNR) Controls	On unit On unit Div 15	Line voltage wiring to unit and fuses by Division 16.
3	CHCP-01	Chiller Condenser Pump 20 hp	Chiller room	575	22 A	3ph 60 Hz	Disconnect (Unfused) Com. Starter (VFD) Controls	At unit In MCC 1A Div 15	H-O-A switch and red pilot in starter cover. Hand position to bypass control circuit.
4	CHCP-02	Chiller Condenser Pump 20 hp	Chiller room	575	22 A	3ph 60 Hz	Disconnect (unfused) Com. Starter (VFD) Controls	At unit In MCC 1A Div 15	H-O-A switch and red pilot in starter cover. Hand position to bypass control circuit.
5	CWCP-01	Chilled Water Circulating Pump 25 hp	Chiller room	575	27 A	3ph 60 Hz	Disconnect (Unfused) Com. Starter (FVNR) Controls	At unit In MCC 1A DIV 15	H-O-A switch and red pilot in starter cover. Hand position to bypass control circuit.
6	CWCP-02	Chilled Water Circulating Pump 25 hp	Chiller room	575	27 A	3ph 60 Hz	Disconnect (Unfused) Com. Starter (FVNR) Controls	At unit In MCC 1A DIV 15	H-O-A switch and red pilot in starter cover. Hand position to bypass control circuit.
7	CT-01	Cooling Tower 25 hp Fan (two-speed) 10 kW Heater	Penthouse	575	27 A	3ph 60 Hz	Disconnect Starter 2 Speed	Included in control panel Included in control panel	Line voltage wiring to unit by Division 16.
8	CT-02	Cooling Tower 25 hp Fan (two-speed) 10 kW Heater	Penthouse	575	27 A	3ph 60 Hz	Disconnect Starter 2 speed	Included in control panel Included in control panel	Line voltage wiring to unit by Division 16.

Table A-1 Mechanical equipment schedule. (For educational reference purposes only; not for construction.)

Item	Designation	Description	Location	Volt	Amp	Ph/Hz	Control		Remarks
							Type	Location	
9	SF-01	Air Handling Unit Supply Fan (VFD) 15 hp	Penthouse	575	17 A	3ph 60 Hz	Disconnect VFD Controls	Included in control panel Included in control panel Div 15	Line voltage wiring to unit by Division 16.
	EXF-01	Exhaust Fan (VFD) 10 hp			11 A		Disconnect VFD	Included in control panel Included in control panel	
10	EXF-02	Chiller Room Exhaust Fan 1.5 hp	Chiller room	575	2.1 A	3ph 60 Hz	Disconnect (unfused) Comb. Starter	At unit Chiller rm.	Wiring by Division 16 H-O-A switch and red pilot in starter cover. Hand position to bypass control circuit.
11	EXF-03	Penthouse Exhaust Fan 1.5 hp	Penthouse	575	2.1 A	3ph 60 Hz	Disconnect (unfused) Comb. Starter	At unit Penthouse	Wiring by Division 16 H-O-A switch and red pilot in starter cover. Hand position to bypass control circuit.
12	SF-02	Penthouse Supply 2.0 hp	Penthouse	575	2.9 A	3ph 60 Hz	Disconnect (unfused) Comb. Starter	At unit Penthouse	Wiring by Division 16 H-O-A switch and red pilot in starter cover. Hand position to bypass control circuit.
13	EXF-04	Electrical Room Exhaust Fan 1/2 hp	Electrical room	575	0.8 A	3ph 60 Hz	Disconnect (unfused) Comb. Starter	At unit Electrical room	Wiring by Division 16 H-O-A switch and red pilot in starter cover. Hand position to bypass control circuit.
14		Fan Coil Unit 3/4 hp /1/60 FC-01 FC-02 FC-03 FC-04 FC-05 FC-06	Factory	208	7.61 A	3ph 60 Hz	Manual motor starter	At unit	Wiring by Division 16.
15	CNC-1	CNC Milling Machine Main Motor 10 hp Secondary motor 1 hp	Factory floor	575	11 A 1.4 A	3ph 60 Hz	Bus Plug 1	Busway 101	Wiring by Division 16. Provide flexible cord drop and connector based on nameplate ratings.
	CNC-2						Bus Plug 2	Busway 101	

Table A-1 Mechanical equipment schedule. (For educational reference purposes only; not for construction.) (continued)

Item	Designation	Description	Location	Volt	Amp	Ph/Hz	Control		Remarks
							Type	Location	
16	CNC-3	CNC Lathe Main Motor 10 hp Secondary motor 1 hp	Factory floor	575	11 A 1.4 A	3ph 60 Hz	Bus Plug 3	Busway 101	Wiring by Division 16. Provide flexible cord drop and connector based on nameplate ratings.
	CNC-4						Bus Plug 4		
17	PUNCH PRESS	Punch Press 5 hp	Factory floor	575	6.1 A	3ph 60 Hz	Bus Plug 9	Busway 101	Wiring by Division 16. Provide flexible cord drop and connector based on nameplate ratings.
18	W-1	Welder 30 kVA	Factory floor	575	28.8 A	3ph 60 Hz	Bus Plug 11	Busway 101	Wiring by Division 16. Provide receptacle based on nameplate ratings.
19	Radial drill 1	Radial Arm Drill 5 hp	Factory floor	575	6.1 A	3ph	Bus Plug 7	Busway 101	Wiring by Division 16. Provide flexible cord drop and connector based on nameplate ratings.
	Radial drill 2					60 Hz	Bus Plug 8	Busway 101	
20	CNC-5	CNC Lathe Main Motor 10 hp Secondary motor 1 hp	Factory floor	575	3ph 11 A 1.4 A	60 Hz	Bus Plug 5	Busway 101	Wiring by Division 16. Provide flexible cord drop and connector based on nameplate ratings.
	CNC-6						Bus Plug 6	Busway 101	Provide additional 15 A 120 V flexible cord drop and connector.
21	RB-1	Robot	Factory floor	208	23.6 A	3ph 60 Hz	Breaker	PP- 102	Wiring by Division 16. Provide receptacle based on nameplate ratings.
22	SURFG-1	Surface Grinder 5 hp 1 hp	Factory floor	208	18 A 3.22 A	3ph 60 Hz	Breaker	PP-102	Wiring by Division 16.
23	CYLG-1	Cylinder Grinder 5 hp 1 hp	Factory floor	208	18 A 3.22 A	3ph 60 Hz	Breaker	PP-102	Wiring by Division 16.
24	VAC-1	Vacuum System 5 hp	Factory floor	208	18 A	3ph 60 Hz	Breaker	PP-102	Wiring by Division 16.
25	EDM-1	EDM Machine	Factory	208	20 A	3ph 60 Hz	Breaker	PP-101	Wiring by Division 16.
26	DL-1	Dock Leveller	Loading dock 1	575	1.72 A	3ph 60 Hz	Breaker	PP-101	Wiring by Division 16.
27	OHD-1	Overhead Door	Loading dock 1	575	1.72 A	3ph 60 Hz	Breaker	PP-101	Wiring by Division 16.

Table A-1 Mechanical equipment schedule. (For educational reference purposes only; not for construction.)

Division 16 Electrical Specifications

SECTION 16010 ELECTRICAL GENERAL REQUIREMENTS

General

Comply with Division 1—General Requirements.

The specifications for this division are an integral part of the contract documents and shall be read accordingly.

Electrical drawings indicate only the general location of equipment and outlets. The contactor shall be responsible for the detail layout of equipment, outlets, raceways and wiring.

Outlets shown on architectural room elevations take precedence over positions or mounting heights on electrical drawings.

The owner reserves the right to move the location outlets 3 m without additional charge, providing the contractor is advised prior to installation.

Refer to architectural and structural drawings for accurate building dimensions.

Scope

The electrical contractor shall furnish all labour, tools, equipment and material to install, test and put into operation the electrical systems shown in the drawings or herein specified or both.

The electrical contractor will provide all disconnect switches, motor starters, power wiring, conduit and connections for motorized equipment supplied under Division 15 unless otherwise indicated. For control wiring responsibility, see mechanical equipment schedule.

The electrical contractor shall arrange, pay for, and carry out all excavation and backfilling relating to electrical and telephone systems and services and including wiring to outdoor lighting in accordance with Division 2.

The electrical contractor shall provide concrete covering or encasement of electrical and telephone raceways as indicated, concrete bases for outdoor lighting standards and concrete pads for outdoor transformers in accordance with Division 3.

Definitions

The following abbreviations shall apply in referring to the source of specifications.

ANSI	American National Standards Association
ASTM	The American Society for Testing Materials
CEC	Canadian Electrical Code
ESA	Electrical Safety Authority
EEMAC	Electrical and Electronic Manufactures Association
IEC	International Electro-Technical Commission
IESNA	Illumination Engineering Society North America
NEMA	National Electrical Manufactures Association
CSA	Canadian Standards Association
ULC	Underwriters Laboratories' of Canada

Submittals

Immediately after this contract is awarded the contractor shall submit a list of equipment, fixtures and materials to be incorporated into the work including:

- Manufacturer's name
- Equipment numbers
- Catalogue numbers

- Approval agencies
- Equipment description including accurate dimensions, capacities and performance
- Method of support
- Delivery date

The list must have the approval of the engineer before work is commenced.

Shop Drawings

Prepare and submit drawings necessary for approvals to any authority having jurisdiction. Supply three copies of approved drawings to the consulting engineer prior to commencing work on the project.

Certify as correct and submit for approval eight copies of shop drawings, catalogue cuts, data sheets and descriptive literature of all major pieces of equipment installed as part of this contract.

Review of shop drawings by the consulting engineer does not in any way relieve the contractor or manufacturer of equipment of the responsibility for the satisfactory performance and adequacy of design of equipment supplied under this contract.

Prepare and submit three copies of sleeving drawings that show the location, elevation and size of all sleeving required by this division.

Provide record drawings showing:

- The locations of buried raceways and cables dimensioned to the centre line of building columns. Show elevations with respect to finished grade or finished floor.
- All access panels for junction boxes, pull boxes and terminal cabinets.
- All changes in the location and size of equipment, outlets, wiring and such other changes as may occur during the work.

Submit record drawing of the project in AutoCAD 2000 or a later version. Satisfactory record drawings must be filed with the architect before a final certificate of acceptance will be issued.

Submit three copies of an Operation and Maintenance manual that will include:

- the names, addresses and phone numbers of equipment suppliers, contractors and consultants, as well as the names and emergency telephone numbers of service representatives to be contacted during the warranty period
- copies of commissioning reports and certificates
- shop drawings, schematic and wiring diagrams, parts lists, data sheets, and descriptive literature for each piece of equipment
- complete operating instructions for each piece of equipment or system
- complete maintenance instructions for each piece of equipment or system

Request for Shut-Down: Obtain permission in writing from the owner for systems shut-down or service interruption prior to disrupting service to any system or piece of equipment.

Request for Start-Up: Obtain permission in writing from the owner prior to starting or returning to service any piece of equipment.

Approvals

Equipment manufacturers shall obtain all necessary approvals and design equipment in accordance with applicable standards of NEMA, CSA, ANSI and ESA.

Permits, Inspection Certificates and Fees

Deliver to the owner final certificates of inspection and approval by the inspection authority having jurisdiction when all work has been completed, tested and placed in operation.

Notify inspection authorities in sufficient time to inspect work.

Pay all fees and costs.

Delivery, Handling and Storage

The contractor shall assume full responsibility to receive, handle, store and protect equipment, fixtures and materials covered under this contract.

Relations with Other Trades

The work of the electrical trade shall be carried out in co-operation with other trades in such a manner as to avoid unnecessary delays and ensure the work of all trades is installed to the best advantage. The contractor shall assume full responsibility for laying out the work and for any damage to the owner or other trades caused by improper layout.

Workmanship

All work shall be in accordance with the *Canadian Electrical Code,* Provincial and Local Codes. Workmanship shall be of a uniformly high quality in regards to durability, efficiency, safety and neatness of detail. Inferior work shall be replaced without cost when so ordered by the owner or owner's representative.

Cutting and Patching

The contractor shall bear all costs of cutting and patching resulting from the work of this division. Cutting and patching of new and existing work will be done by the general contractor unless otherwise indicated. Layout such work for approval before commencing.

Neatly cut out or drill holes in existing construction to accommodate cable, cable tray, conduit, piping, raceways or ductwork.

Layout cutting of structural elements and obtain approval before starting work.

Cleaning

The contractor shall clean up all refuse caused by the work at the end of the day and remove waste on a weekly basis. On completion of the work the contractor shall remove all surplus materials and waste.

Excavating and Backfilling

The contractor shall bear all costs of excavating and backfilling resulting from the work of this division.

Excavate and backfill as required. This type of work shall be performed by a recognized civil installation contractor experienced in underground electrical installations.

Obtain from the engineer a list of acceptable contractors.

Carefully avoid and prevent from being damaged existing underground services.

Grade bottom of excavation for conduits and ducts.

Keep excavations dry at all times by bailing, pumping or other means.

Carefully cut and trim banks and shore as required to prevent caving in.

Support conduits, ducts and raceways that pass through the foundation walls of the building.

Do not commence backfilling before approval has been obtained.

Backfill with thoroughly tamped sand in 6″ layers to a height of 600 mm above cables, conduits or duct-banks. Fill remainder of trench with approved excavated material that is free from stones or water.

When backfilling under roads and paved areas, consult with engineer.

Supports and Hangers

Provide all necessary supports, hangers, inserts and sleeves necessary to properly execute the work.

Testing

Test and check electrical and communication systems for correct operation in the presence of the engineer.

Conduct an insulation resistance test using a "megger" (500 V instrument on circuits up to 350 V) on all lighting and power circuits prior to connecting devices and equipment. Record all test results and submit to engineer for reference. Remove and replace at no cost any cable that fails to meet test criteria. Repair or replace at no cost all circuits that do not meet the minimum requirements of the inspection authority.

In co-operation with mechanical trades take and record clamp-on ammeter readings of mechanical equipment motors while the equipment is operating under load. Check the operation of motor starters, overload relays, contactors and control stations.

Ensure the correct operation of all control circuits installed under this contract.

Check the operation and adjustment of all safety devices supplied under this contract.

Check electrical system voltages after the facility has been in operation for 60 days. Adjust tap settings as required.

Identification

Each piece of equipment shall be identified with a nameplate or label.

Obtain from consulting engineer a nameplate schedule.

Nameplates to be engraved lamacoid, with white face and black core c/w provision for attachment with self-tapping screws. Nameplates shall be provided for the following equipment: distribution, power and lighting panels, transformers, disconnect switches, contactors, motor starters, telephone panels, miscellaneous systems panels, automatic transfer switches.

Labels shall be printed on 50 mm × 150 mm plastic coated tape or approved equal. Labels to have a yellow background and black lettering. Labels shall be provided for all feeder conduits, cables, pull boxes and runs of busway.

SECTION 16050 BASIC MATERIALS AND METHODS

Products

Prior to the submission of a bid, the contractor shall obtain from the consulting engineer a list of acceptable equipment manufactures. All other manufactures may bid as alternate only.

All material shall be new and bear the label of the Canadian Standards Association or other approval agency recognized by the inspection authority having jurisdiction.

Unless otherwise indicated, factory finish all equipment with ANSI/ASA #61 grey paint.

SECTION 16106 INSTALLATION OF CABLES IN TRENCHES AND DUCTS

Install underground cables as shown on the drawings.

Comply with the requirements of Section 16120.

Install direct buried cables in sifted sand free of rock, stone and other sharp objects with a 3″ layer above and below.

Where direct buried cables pass under a roadway or area subject to vehicular traffic, install in suitable concrete encased ducts.

Provide 150 mm wide polyethylene underground warning tape at 300 mm below grade centred lengthwise on all buried ducts and cables. Use red-coloured "BURIED ELECTRICAL LINE" or orange-coloured "TELEPHONE LINE" as applicable.

After installation of cables, seal duct ends with approved sealing compound.

Section 16110 Raceways

All raceways shall be approved for intended use.

Except for flexible conduit, conduits shall be not smaller than 19 mm.

Provide a separate bonding conductor in all non-metallic raceways and all runs of EMT.

Install exposed conduits symmetrical to the building construction. Route conduits to avoid beams columns and other obstructions. Conduits to cause minimum interference in spaces through which they pass.

Group conduits together whenever possible. Securely attach exposed conduits in place at intervals not exceeding the requirements of the *CEC*.

Use beam clamps to secure conduits to exposed steel.

Feeders shall be installed in either rigid metal conduit or rigid non-metallic conduit.

Where conduits cross expansion joints, provide an expansion joint in each run of conduit.

Do not locate conduits running parallel to a steam line closer than 75 mm from the steam line and not closer than 50 mm where conduits cross stem lines.

When conduits are installed in slabs, protect the conduits from damage where they exit the slab. Install conduits in centre 1/3 of slab.

Do not place conduit in slabs with a thickness of less than four times the diameter of the conduit unless approval has been obtained from the structural engineer.

Use rigid PVC conduit outside the building up to 53 mm in size.

Label all conduits, cables and bus ducts at each point of termination and every 15 m along the run. Labels must be visible from the floor or adjacent platform.

Section 16114 Cabletroughs

The electrical contractor shall install cabletroughs as shown in the drawings or herein specified or both, in accordance with *CEC* and the inspection authority having jurisdiction and the manufacturer's recommendations.

Provide elbows, tees, wyes, drop-outs, vertical risers and drops, expansion joints, reducers and end plates as required. Minimum radius of fittings to be 600 mm.

Include all supports and hangers. Support cabletroughs on both sides. Supports and hanger rods to be galvanized.

Maintain effective bonding continuity.

Install cabletroughs parallel to the lines of the building.

Cabletrough
Cabletrough to be ladder ventilated type, Class C1 to CSA 22.2 M1991. Size as indicated.

Communications Cable Tray
Communications cable tray to be centre hung, bottom rung, open style cable tray suitable for use with plenum cable. Class 1 to CSA 22.2 M1991.

Construction to be solid aluminium main support channel with 12 mm diameter. Rods on 150 mm centres. Size as indicated.

Maintain 300 mm clearance above tray to permit the installation of cables.

Maintain a separation between communications cable tray and sources of electromagnetic interference. Minimum spacing requirements—from motors: 1200 mm; from transformers: 1200 mm; from cables and conduits operating at less than 1KV: 300 mm. For other pieces of equipment, consult engineer.

Section 16115 Busway

The electrical contractor shall install busways as shown in the drawings or herein specified or both, in accordance with *CEC* and the inspection authority having jurisdiction and the manufacturer's recommendations.

Busways shall have CSA approval for the current ratings indicated and for the manner and location in which it is mounted.

Busways shall have a minimum interrupting rating of 100 000 A symmetrical.

When a neutral is required it shall be full capacity.

Provide elbows, tees, offsets, expansion joints, flanges, cable tap boxes, reducers and end closures as required.

Include all supports and hangers. Hanger rods to be galvanized.

Maintain effective bonding continuity.

Install busways parallel to the lines of the building.

Plug in busway to have 1 plug-in opening every 300 mm.

Provide fusible bus plugs c/w fuses complying with Section 16478.

Torque connection bolts to manufacturer's recommendations.

Enclose ventilated busways with a heavy plastic cover immediately after installation. This cover is to remain in place until the building is clean and dry and the busway is to be put into service.

Remove and relocate existing 100 A trolley busways as shown on the drawings. Install trolley at 2.5 m A.F.F. Provide one trolley for every 3 m of installed trolley duct. Turn over to the owner any unused trolleys.

Section 16120 Conductors and Cables

Provide wires of the number and size shown in the drawings or described herein with spare conductors as indicated for the complete electrical system.

Limit pulling tensions and minimum bending radii to manufacturer's recommendations.

Utilize cable lubricant when pulling cables through conduits and ducts.

Ensure conduits are free of obstructions and debris before pulling in conductors or cables.

Conductors shall have a 90°C rating, types RW90XLPE or T90 Nylon unless specified otherwise. All conductors shall be copper.

The minimum size conductors will be No. 12 AWG copper.

The neutral conductor of any feeder circuit shall not be smaller than the other circuit conductors.

Do not connect more than three lighting circuits from a three-phase panel or two circuits from a single-phase panel to a common neutral.

When supplying receptacles for computer equipment, each circuit shall have its own neutral.

Do not exceed the *CEC* requirements for voltage drop on any branch circuit or feeder.

Install multiple cables in ducts simultaneously.

Colour code feeder circuits, maintaining phase and colour sequence throughout.

Section 16123 Voice and Data Cables

All data and voice cables shall be CMP or FT6 flamespread rated.

All voice cables shall be minimum 4 pair Category 3 rated.

All data cables shall be minimum 4 pair UTP Category 5e rated.

All voice and data cable installations shall conform to EIA/TIA standards 568-B, 569-B, 606, and 607.

All termination jacks shall be of a modular style, from a manufacturer approved by the engineer.

A minimum of 10% spare termination jacks will be supplied to the owner by the voice/data contractor.

All data runs shall be tested and passed by an independent third party contractor, approved by both the owner and the voice/data contractor, at the expense of the voice/data contractor. Test results for all runs shall be presented to the owner in both paper and electronic format. Any data runs failing the test will be repaired and retested at the expense of the voice/data contractor.

Section 16130 Boxes

Provide access panels in ceilings where pull or junction boxes are not readily accessible.

Neatly make cut-outs for outlet boxes recessed in walls and ceilings.

Support boxes independently of conduit and raceways.

Identify branch circuit outlet boxes, pull boxes and junction boxes by applying a small dab of paint to the inside cover using the following colour code:

Colour	System	Colour	System
None	Lighting and power	Black	Computer systems
Red	Fire alarm and emergency voice	Brown	Security systems
Dark blue	Telephone	Orange	TV systems
Grey	Clock	Green	Intercom and public address

Table A-2 Colour codes for box identification.

Section 16140 Wiring Devices

Switches shall be AC general-use, specification grade, 20 A, 120-277 or 347 V, either single-pole, three-way, or four-way, as shown on the plans.

When two or more switches are required at the same location, they shall share a common wall plate unless otherwise noted.

The electrical contractor shall furnish and install, as indicated in blueprint E1 (Electrical Symbols), receptacles meeting CSA standards and approved by the CSA. No more than two 5-15R receptacles to be on one two-wire circuit.

Wall plates for switches and receptacles shall be stainless steel unless otherwise noted on the drawings. Install wall plates after the painting of room surfaces has been completed.

Do not use wall plates on surface mounted device boxes.

Push-in connections will not be accepted. Use terminal screws or lugs to terminate conductors on all wiring devices.

Mount receptacles vertically 300 mm A.F.F. unless otherwise noted. Receptacles in factories, fan rooms, electrical rooms and mechanical rooms to be mounted at 900 mm unless otherwise noted. Receptacles above counters or benches to be 200 mm above work surface.

Section 16400 Low-Voltage Electrical Distribution

The work to be done under this contract shall include supply, testing, delivery, installation, commissioning and guarantee of electrical distribution equipment.

Site work by the equipment supplier to include the services of a competent supervisor to witness unloading, lifting, placement, connection, testing and commissioning of equipment supplied under this contract.

Commissioning work at the site by the manufacturer shall include on-site testing, calibration, adjustment and verification of equipment to assure proper functioning and system integrity.

Submit co-ordination curves for review.

Section 16402 Underground Service

Co-ordinate with and meet the requirements of the supply authority.

The supply authority will install transformers and all primary service. The electrical contractor will provide a concrete pad and conduit rough in as required by the supply authority.

Provide in the base bid price an amount of $150 000.00 as a cash allowance for payment of supply authority charges.

The electrical contractor will furnish and install a service lateral as shown on the drawings. Conductors will be RW90XLPE (600 V) copper.

Allow sufficient conductor length to make terminations.

Install raceways and cables in accordance with their respective sections.

Supply and install meter socket and conduit.

Section 16421 Service Entrance Board

The electrical contractor will furnish and install service entrance equipment, as shown in the plans and detailed herein.

Switchboard shall be of a type, rating and arrangement shown. Construction to be indoor, weatherproof, free standing, rigid, dead front conforming to CSA standard C22.2 special purpose enclosures. Busbars and main connections to be of copper.

Equipment to be wall mounted on a concrete pad.

Short circuit rating 42 000 A RMS symmetrical. Breaker and fuse ratings to match switchboard.

Provision to be made for Supply Authority metering.

Submit co-ordination curves for review.

Engraved plastic nameplates shall be provided for all cubicles. Submit nameplate samples and designations for approval.

For fuses, refer to Section 16478.

For moulded case circuit breakers, refer to Section 16477.

A full copper ground bus of adequate cross sectional area shall be provided that will extend the full length of the switchboard assembly and securely bolted to the structural members of the enclosure. The ground bus shall be fully accessible. Lugs shall be provided for grounding cable, size as indicated.

Section 16428 Digital Metering System/Circuit Monitor

Supply and install as indicated a Digital Metering/Circuit Monitoring System.

The circuit monitor shall display and provide access to the following metered quantities as well as the minimum/maximum values of each instantaneous quantity since the last minimum/maximum reset:

- Current, per phase RMS, phase to neutral, and three phase average

- Voltage, phase to phase, phase to neutral, and three phase average
- Real power
- Reactive power
- Apparent power
- Power factor
- Frequency
- Demand current
- Demand real power
- Demand apparent power
- Accumulated energy
- Total Harmonic Distortion, current and voltage per phase
- K-factor, current, per phase
- Temperature

The circuit monitor shall communicate via RS-232, RS-485, and Ethernet.

The following demand readings shall be reported:

- Average demand current per phase
- Peak demand current per phase
- Average demand for real, reactive and apparent power
- Predicted demand for real, reactive and apparent power
- Peak demand for real, reactive and apparent power

All circuit monitors shall include current and waveform capture capability.

Each circuit monitor shall be able to log data, alarms and events. The following classes of events shall be available as alarm events:

- Over/under current
- Over/under voltage
- Current imbalance
- Phase loss, current
- Phase loss, voltage
- Voltage imbalance
- Over KVA
- Over KW or KVAR into/out of load
- Over/under frequency
- Under power factor true or displacement
- Over THD
- Over K factor
- Over demand
- Reverse power
- Phase reversal
- Status input change
- Over/under analog inputs
- Current sags/swells
- Voltage sags/swells

Connect all wiring.

Program the system as directed by the owner. Provide complete manuals and training to operate the system.

Section 16440 Disconnect Switches

Supply and install fusible disconnects complete with fuses.

Disconnect switches to be of the quick-make quick-break type.

Provide provision for locking in on-off positions.

Fuse holders to suitable for use without adaptors for the size of fuse indicated.

Provide size 4 nameplates indicating the load controlled.

Section 16450 Bonding and Grounding

The electrical contractor will install and test a complete, permanent and continuous bonding and grounding system as shown in the drawings or herein specified or both, in accordance with section 10 of the *CEC* and the inspection authority having jurisdiction.

Bond transformers, panelboards, metal enclosures, exposed building steel and metallic piping to the main ground bus. Provide ground connections to building steel with thermit welds or 9 mm silicon bronze alloy bolts. Peen ends of bolts after installation.

Clean grounding metal contact points of paint, rust and other contaminates.

Protect exposed grounding conductors from mechanical damage with rigid PVC conduit.

Test ground continuity and resistance prior to energizing electrical circuits. Test the grounding system efficiency for compliance with the *Canadian Electrical Code.* Verify ohmic resistance in the presence of the inspection authority.

Supply two copies of the test report to the consulting engineer.

Provide grounding of each switchboard to perimeter ground bus with two separate runs of 4/0 green insulated copper conductors.

Section 16461 Dry Type Transformers (750 V or Less)

The electrical contractor will furnish and install dry-type transformers as shown in the plans and detailed herein.

Dry-type transformers shall conform to CSA standards for energy efficient transformers.

Low-voltage transformers 15 kVA and larger shall be ventilated, incorporating a 220°C insulation system. Two 2.5% taps shall be provided on the primary side of the transformer for above normal operation and two for below normal operation.

Transformers shall incorporate an electrostatic shield for the attenuation of voltage spikes, line noise and transients.

All 600-V class transformers shall have a BIL of 10 kV.

Three phase transformers shall have delta connected primary and 120/208 V wye connected secondary unless otherwise noted. KVA rating as indicated.

Transformers must be floor mounted if 30 kVA or larger.

Typical transformer data must be submitted for approval. Transformer data must contain is not limited to:

- Efficiencies at 25%, 50%, 75% and 100% load
- Regulation at 80% power factor
- Insulation class and rated temperature rise
- Impedance
- IR, IX, IZ percentages
- No-load losses
- Full-load losses
- Polarity and phase rotation
- Sound level
- Weights and dimensions
- Applied potential tests
- Induced potential tests
- Excitation current

Mount transformers with adequate clearance for ventilation.

If transformer is provided with isolation pads, loosen bolts until no compression is visible.

When practicable, energize transformers immediately after the installation is complete.

Section 16471 Panelboards Breaker Type

The electrical contractor shall furnish panelboards as shown on the plans and detailed in the panelboard schedules.

Panelboards shall be approved by the CSA and suitable for bolt- on breakers.

All 250 V and 600 V panelboard bus shall be rated for 25 KA RMS symmetrical.

Number of circuit positions and number and size of branch circuit breakers as indicated.

Provide minimum 25% spare breakers and 25% breaker spaces in each panel.

All interiors will have main bus as indicated with lugs, rated at 75°C, for incoming conductors. Boxes will be of galvanized sheet steel and will provide wiring gutters, as required by the *CEC, Part I* (2002). Fronts will be suitable for either flush or surface installation and shall be equipped with a keyed lock and a directory card holder.

A typewritten directory identifying each breaker shall be provided in each panelboard.

Panelboards shall have an equipment grounding bus bonded to the cabinet.

Panelboards located in sprinklered rooms to have sprinkler shields.

All panelboards are to be keyed alike and supplied c/w two keys for each panelboard.

All surface-mounted panelboards to be mounted on 19-mm primed and painted plywood backboards. Group panelboards on a common backboard where practicable.

Top of panelboards to be 1900 mm.

Section 16477 Moulded Case Circuit Breakers

Moulded case circuit breakers shall be installed in branch circuit panelboards as indicated on the panelboard schedules.

Each breaker shall provide inverse time delay under overload conditions and magnetic tripping for short circuits. The breaker operating mechanism shall be trip-free and multipole units will open all poles if one pole trips.

Breakers shall have sufficient interrupting rating to interrupt a minimum 22 000 A at 240 V and 18 000 A at 600 V. Minimum interrupting rating to be not less than the interrupting rating of the panelboard or switchboard in which they are installed.

Section 16478 Fuses

Fuses 601 A and larger shall have an interrupting rating of 200 000 RMS symmetrical amperes. They shall provide a time delay of not less than 4 seconds at 500% of their ampere rating. They shall be current limiting Class L.

Fuses 600 A and less shall have an interrupting rating of 200 000 RMS symmetrical amperes. They shall provide a time delay of not less than 10 seconds at 500% of their ampere rating. They shall be current limiting Class J.

All fuses shall be selected to assure selective co-ordination.

Spare fuses shall be provided in the amount of 20% of each size and type installed, but in no case shall fewer than three spare fuses be supplied. These spare fuses shall be delivered to the owner at the time of acceptance of the project and shall be placed in a spare fuse cabinet mounted on the wall adjacent to or located in the switchboard.

Fuse identification labels, showing the size and type of fuses installed, shall be placed inside the cover of each switch.

SECTION 16500 LIGHTING SYSTEMS

Luminaires

The electrical contractor will furnish and install luminaries, as described in the schedule shown in the plans. Luminaries shall be complete with all necessary supports, hangers, diffusers and lamps.

For alternative luminaries, submit complete photometric data for review by consulting engineer. Photometric data to include input wattage, candlepower summary, candela distribution curves, luminaire efficiency, CIE type, coefficient of utilization, lamp type and lumen rating in accordance with IESNA testing procedures.

Luminaires other than those specified shall only be used with the written approval of the engineer.

Fluorescent lamps to be warm white, 3500°K, rapid start T-8, CRI 85, 20 000 hr rated lamp life wattage as indicated.

Compact fluorescent lamps to be 3500°K, twin or quad tube, CRI 83, 10 000 hr rated lamp life, wattage as indicated.

Fluorescent ballasts shall be rapid start, high power factor, solid state, suitable for use with T-8 32-W fluorescent lamps.

Provide 20% spare lamps.

HID lamps to be coated, wattage and types as indicated.

HID ballasts to be integral to the fixture unless otherwise noted. 90% power factor, crest factor 1.8, minimum starting temperature –30°C, input voltage +/–13% nominal voltage. Voltage and wattage as indicated.

Luminaries shall be adequately supported. Luminaires installed in or on ceilings shall be supported independently of the ceiling by means of chains. Fluorescent luminaires shall be supported by two chains, each supporting two corners of the fixture.

Metal strut may be used to mount luminaires in electrical rooms.

Section 16519 Exit Lights

The electrical contractor will furnish and install exit lights, as described in the schedule shown in the plans. Exit lights shall be complete with all necessary supports, hangers, diffusers and lamps.

Exit lights shall provide a minimum 50 000 hours hour of operation between re-lamping.

Letters to be 150 mm high and 19 mm wide,

Recessed, wall, end or ceiling as indicated. Single or double faced as indicated. Arrow as indicated. Provide necessary canopy mounting plate.

SECTION 16700 COMMUNICATION SYSTEMS

Time Clock

A time clock shall be installed to control the outdoor security lighting. The clock will be connected to existing Panel EM circuit No. 22.The clock will be 120 V, one circuit, with astronomic control and a spring-wound carry-over mechanism.

Section 16721 Fire Alarm Systems

Supply and install a complete fire alarm system including fire alarm equipment, conduit, wire, boxes and fittings as indicated on the drawings or described herein.

Comply with section 16010.

Install the fire alarm system in conformance with the latest edition of *ULC/CAN S524 Standard for the Installation of Fire Alarm Systems,* Section 32 of the *CEC,* Provincial and Local Codes, and Manufacturer's recommendations.

All components to have CSA and/or ULC approval.

The manufacturer shall provide on company letterhead confirmation that the system including all equipment and devices will be supported for a period of ten years. Verify the fire alarm system in conformance with the latest edition of ULC/CANS537 Standard for Verification of Fire Alarm Systems.

The location of end of line resistors and isolation modules to be recorded on as-built drawings.

Install all wiring in EMT.

Testing of the fire alarm system is to be done in the presence of the Owner and Consulting engineer. Live smoke or open sources of heat are not to be used for testing.

The manufacturer shall supply technical assistance to the contractor as required to complete the installation and verify the system.

Upon completion of the installation the manufacturer will issue to the Owner a Certificate of Verification along with a verification report and warranty certificates for batteries, ancillary devices, etc.

The manufacturer to provide the name, address and telephone number of service representatives to be contacted during the warranty period.

All costs of inspection and verification to be included in the tender price.

Locate heat and smoke detectors away from bulkheads. Maintain a minimum distance of 1 m from supply and exhaust registers.

Include all monies to program the new system.

Section 16741 Telephone Systems

Supply and install a complete system of empty conduits, terminal cabinets, pull boxes and outlets for the telephone wiring as shown on the drawings or described herein. Minimum size conduit shall be 3/4". Conduit runs shall have not more than 3 quarter bends and bending radius shall not be less than ten times the conduit diameter.

Supply a pull string in all conduits.

SECTION 16800 – MOTORS

All motors to meet CSA standards for energy efficient motors.

Section 16801 Fractional Horsepower Motors

All fractional HP motors up to 1/2" hp shall be drip proof unless otherwise noted. Motors shall have Class B insulation a minimum service factor of 1.15. Totally enclosed motors to have a service factor to 1.0.

Section 16802 Motors up to 200 HP

Motors shall be drip proof, unless otherwise noted. Motors shall have Class B insulation a minimum service factor of 1.15. Totally enclosed motors to have a service factor to 1.0.

Section 16811 Motor Starters

All motor starters to be CSA certified EEMAC rated, in EEMAC 12 enclosures unless otherwise noted. IEC starters and contactors will not be accepted.

Manual motor starter shall be of a size and type as shown on the drawings. Manual motor starters to have an overload heater in each ungrounded conductor, manual reset and trip indicating handle.

Magnetic motor starters shall be of a size and type indicated on the drawings c/w minimum 100 VA fused control transformer. Control voltage to be 120 VAC. Magnetic motor starters to have 1 N.C. and 2 N.O. auxiliary contacts. Overload relays to have 1 N.C. and 1 N.O. contact. Magnetic starters to have thermal magnetic overloads with an overload element in each ungrounded conductor and manual reset. Overloads relay heaters to be sized according to the manufactures recommendations.

Provide combination starters where practicable.

Section 16820 Motor Control Centre (MCC)

The electrical contractor will furnish and install MCCs as shown in the plans and detailed herein.

MCCs to be CSA approved Class II, type B, sectional, free standing, floor mounted, front mount.

Provide sprinkler shield in areas that are sprinklered.

Minimum horizontal bus 600 A, tin plated aluminium, bus bracing 42 000 A symmetrical.

Minimum vertical bus 300 A, tin plated aluminium, bus bracing 42 000 A symmetrical.

Neutral bus 1/2 neutral, Ground bus 6 × 100 mm tin plated aluminium.

Draw out units fusible disconnect, stab ratings 60 A, 150 A, 300 A, 400 A. Minimum Interrupting rating 22 000 A symmetrical.

Motor starters as per Section 16811.

Provide a motor running indicating light on each unit.

Provide a nameplate for each unit.

	LUMINAIRE						LAMPS	
STYLE	DESCRIPTION	MFG.	CAT. No.	V	VA	MOUNTING	No.	TYPE
A	Fluorescent industrial luminaire c/w electronic ballast, baked white enamel finish	Day-Brite	IAC32347	120	61	Chain	2	F32T8
B	Tandem unit identical to style A	Day-Brite	TIAC232347	120	122	Chain	4	F32T8
C	Fluorescent industrial high bay c/w specular aluminium deep parabolic reflectors	Day-Brite	FTV480HO M43474/1CUL	347	358	Pendant	4	F80T5HO
D	HID industrial luminaire c/w adjustable prismatic borosilicate glass reflector, safety glass bottom and triple tap ballast	LUMARK	MHSGSGB	347	395	Pendant	1	350 W Pulse Start Metal Halide
E	Wall cube HID weatherproof die-cast aluminium, dark bronze finish			120	120	Wall	1	100 W HPS lamp
F	Trapezoid full cut-off weatherproof wall luminaire, dark bronze finish	LUMARK		120	91	Wall	1	70 W HPS
G1	Single pole-mounted area luminaire c/w 250 mm arm (cutoff style to reduce light pollution) and 6 m steel pole	LUMARK	PFH125H20		300	Pole	1	250W HPS
G2	As above, double unit	LUMARK	PFH225H20		600	Pole	2	
H	150 mm × 900 mm Bollard	Magraw Edison		120	82	Concrete base	1	70 W HPS
I	Fluorescent enclosed gasketed one-piece fibreglass luminaire c/w electronic ballast, acrylic lens		IAC32347	120	61	Chain	2	
X	LED exit sign c/w die cast aluminium body and faceplate, oyster finish			120	5	Universal bracket		

Table A-3 Luminaire schedule. (For educational reference purposes only; not for construction.)

RACEWAY AND CABLE SCHEDULE

For educational reference purposes only; not for construction

ITEM	USE	FROM	TO	RACEWAY / CABLE		NO. RUNS	WIRE			
				TYPE	SIZE		NO.	SIZE	CU/AL	INSUL.
1	SERVICE A	TRANSFORMER T-101	SERVICE A	PVC		4	4	500 kcmil	CU	RW90XLPE
2	SERVICE B	TRANSFORMER T-102	SERVICE B	PVC		4	4	500 kcmil	CU	RW90XLPE
3	FEEDER	MAIN SWITCHBOARD	TRANS. T104 EL. RM. 1	RA90		4	1	500 kcmil	CU	RW90XLPE
	FEEDER	TRANS. T-104	DIST. PANEL DP-102	EMT		3	4	500 kcmil	CU	RW90XLPE
4	FEEDER	MAIN SWITCHBOARD	POWER PANEL PP-201	EMT		2	3	350 kcmil	CU	RW90XLPE
5	BUSWAY 101	MAIN SWITCHBOARD	400 A BUSWAY			1	4			
6	FEEDER	MAIN SWITCHBOARD	DIST. PANEL DP-001	EMT		2	3	350 kcmil	CU	RW90XLPE
7	FEEDER	POWER PANEL PP-201	CHILLER CH-01	EMT		1	3	1 AWG	CU	RW90XLPE
8	FEEDER	POWER PANEL PP-201	CHILLER CH-02	EMT		1	3	1 AWG	CU	RW90XLPE
9	FEEDER	POWER PANEL PP-201	COOLING TOWER 1	EMT		1	3	8 AWG	CU	RW90XLPE
10	FEEDER	POWER PANEL PP-201	COOLING TOWER 2	EMT		1	3	8 AWG	CU	RW90XLPE
11	FEEDER	POWER PANEL PP-201	MCC-101	EMT		1	3	1 AWG	CU	RW90XLPE
12	FEEDER	POWER PANEL PP-201	POWER PANEL PP-202	EMT		1	3	3 AWG	CU	RW90XLPE
13	FEEDER	MCC-101	CHCP-01	EMT		1	3	10 AWG	CU	RW90XLPE
14	FEEDER	MCC-101	CHCP-02	EMT		1	3	10 AWG	CU	RW90XLPE
15	FEEDER	MCC-101	CWCP-01	EMT		1	3	8 AWG	CU	RW90XLPE
16	FEEDER	MCC-101	CWCP-02	EMT		1	3	8 AWG	CU	RW90XLPE
17	FEEDER	DIST. PANEL DP-001	POWER PANEL PP-101	EMT		1	3	3 AWG	CU	RW90XLPE
18	FEEDER	DIST. PANEL DP-001	LIGHTING PANEL LP-D	EMT		1	4	3 AWG	CU	RW90XLPE
19	FEEDER	DIST. PANEL DP-001	TRANS. T-103	EMT		1	3	3/0	CU	RW90XLPE
20	FEEDER	TRANS. T-103	T-103 SPLITTER	EMT		2	4	250 kcmil	CU	RW90XLPE
22	FEEDER	TRANS. T-103 SPLITTER	DISCONNECT 1	EMT		1	4	3 AWG	CU	RW90XLPE
23	FEEDER	TRANS. T-103 SPLITTER	DISCONNECT 2	EMT		1	4	3/0	CU	RW90XLPE
24	FEEDER	TRANS. T-103 SPLITTER	DISCONNECT3	EMT		1	4	3/0	CU	RW90XLPE
25	FEEDER	TRANS. T-103 SPLITTER	LIGHTING PANEL LP-E	EMT		1	4	1/0	CU	RW90XLPE
26	FEEDER	DISCONNECT 1	LIGHTING PANEL LP-F	EMT		1	4	3 AWG	CU	RW90XLPE
27	FEEDER	DISCONNECT2	POWER PANEL PP-102	EMT		1	4	3/0	CU	RW90XLPE
28										

Table A-4 Raceway and cable schedule.

RACEWAY AND CABLE SCHEDULE

For educational reference purposes only; not for construction

ITEM	USE	FROM	TO	RACEWAY / CABLE	NO. RUNS	WIRE			
						NO.	SIZE	CU/AL	INSUL.
29	BR. CIRCUIT	BUSWAY 101 BP-1	CNC-1	EMT	1	3	12 AWG	CU	RW90XLPE
30	BR. CIRCUIT	BUSWAY 101 BP-2	CNC-2	EMT	1	3	12 AWG	CU	RW90XLPE
31	BR. CIRCUIT	BUSWAY 101 BP-3	CNC-3	EMT	1	3	12 AWG	CU	RW90XLPE
32	BR. CIRCUIT	BUSWAY 101 BP-4	CNC-4	EMT	1	3	12 AWG	CU	RW90XLPE
33	BR. CIRCUIT	BUSWAY 101 BP-5	CNC-5	EMT	1	3	12 AWG	CU	RW90XLPE
34	BR. CIRCUIT	BUSWAY 101 BP-6	CNC-6	EMT	1	3	12 AWG	CU	RW90XLPE
35	BR. CIRCUIT	BUSWAY 101 BP-7	RADIAL DRILL 1	EMT	1	3	12 AWG	CU	RW90XLPE
36	BR. CIRCUIT	BUSWAY 101 BP-8	RADIAL DRILL 2	EMT	1	3	12 AWG	CU	RW90XLPE
37	BR. CIRCUIT	BUSWAY 101 BP-9	PUNCH PRESS	EMT	1	3	12 AWG	CU	RW90XLPE
38	BR. CIRCUIT								
39	BR. CIRCUIT	BUSWAY 101 BP-11	WELDER	EMT	1	3	10 AWG	CU	RW90XLPE
40	BR. CIRCUIT	POWER PANEL PP-201	POWER PANEL PP-202	EMT	1	3	3 AWG	CU	RW90XLPE
41	BR. CIRCUIT	POWER PANEL PP-201	CHILLER CH-01	EMT	1	3	1 AWG	CU	RW90XLPE
42	BR. CIRCUIT	POWER PANEL PP-201	CHILLER CH-02	EMT	1	3	1 AWG	CU	RW90XLPE
43	BR. CIRCUIT	POWER PANEL PP-201	COOLING TOWER 1	EMT	1	3	8 AWG	CU	RW90XLPE
44	BR. CIRCUIT	POWER PANEL PP-201	COOLING TOWER 2	EMT	1	3	8 AWG	CU	RW90XLPE
45	BR. CIRCUIT								
46	BR. CIRCUIT	POWER PANEL PP-102	CUT-OFF SAW	EMT	1	3	10 AWG	CU	RW90XLPE

Table A-4 Raceway and cable schedule. (continued)

LIGHTING PANEL LP-D

VOLTS 347/600 PHASE 3 WIRE 4
TYPE ______ MAINS 225 A MOUNTING SURFACE

BRANCH CIRCUIT PANELBOARD

A B C M/B 100 A

M - MOTOR R - RECEPTACLE L - LIGHTING

VA	LOAD DESCRIPTION	BREAKER POLES	BREAKER AMPS	CCT	CCT	BREAKER AMPS	BREAKER POLES	LOAD DESCRIPTION	VA
3160	(L) FACTORY ROW 1 NORTH END	1	20	1	2	15	1		
3160	(L) FACTORY ROW 2	1	20	3	4	15	1		
3160	(L) FACTORY ROW 3	1	20	5	6	15	1		
3160	(L) FACTORY ROW 4	1	20	7	8				
3160	(L) FACTORY ROW 5	1	20	9	10				
4500	(L) PARKING LOT, FRONT AND WEST	1	20	11	12				
				13	14				
				15	16				
				17	18				
				19	20				
				21	22				
				23	24				

REVISIONS

NO.	DESCRIPTION	DATE

NOTES:

LIGHTING PANEL LP-E

VOLTS 120/208 PHASE 3 WIRE 4
TYPE NBLP MAINS 225 A MOUNTING SURFACE

BRANCH CIRCUIT PANELBOARD

A B C M/B 150 A

M - MOTOR R - RECEPTACLE L - LIGHTING

VA	LOAD DESCRIPTION	BREAKER POLES	BREAKER AMPS	CCT	CCT	BREAKER AMPS	BREAKER POLES	LOAD DESCRIPTION	VA
720	(R) MAIN ELECTRICAL RM	1	15	1	2	20	1	(L) EL. RM, MET., TOOL RM, CHILLER RM.	1830
720	(R) CHILLER RM	1	15	3	4	15	1	(L) DOCK LIGHT	150
720	(R) COLUMN E13, E14	1	15	5	6	15	1		
720	(R) COLUMN E11, E12	1	15	7	8	15	1		
720	(R) COLUMN D11, D12	1	15	9	10				
720	(R) COLUMN D13, D14	1	15	11	12				
720	(R) COLUMN C12	1	15	13	14				
720	(R) COLUMN C13, C14	1	15	15	16				
720	(R) COLUMN C15, TOOL RM	1	15	17	18				
720	(R) COLUMN B11, B12	1	15	19	20				
720	(R) COLUMN B13, B14	1	15	21	22				
720	(R) COLUMN A11, A12	1	15	23	24				
720	(R) COLUMN A13, A14	1	15	25	26				
1080	(R) INSPECTION TABLE, COMPUTERS	1	15	27	28				
1080	(R) TOOL RM	1	15	29	30				
1080	(R) METALURGY	1	15	31	32				
				33	34				
				35	36				
				37	38				
				39	40				
				41	42				

REVISIONS

NO.	DESCRIPTION	DATE

NOTES:

Table A-5 Lighting panels.

LIGHTING PANEL LP-F

VOLTS 120/208 PHASE 3 WIRE 4
TYPE ______ MAINS 100 A MOUNTING SURFACE

BRANCH CIRCUIT PANELBOARD

A B C — M/B 100 A

M - MOTOR R - RECEPTACLE L - LIGHTING

VA	LOAD DESCRIPTION	BREAKER POLES	BREAKER AMPS	CCT	CCT	BREAKER AMPS	BREAKER POLES	LOAD DESCRIPTION	VA
3160	(L) PENTHOUSE LIGHTING	1	20	1	2	20	1	(R) PENTHOUSE EAST END	
	SPARE	1	20	3	4	20	1	(R) PENTHOUSE WEST END	
	SPARE	1	20	5	6	20	1	SPARE	
	SPARE	1	20	7	8	20	1	SPARE	
	SPARE	1	20	9	10	20	1	SPARE	
	SPARE	1	20	11	12				
				13	14				
				15	16				
				17	18				
				19	20				
				21	22				
				23	24				

REVISIONS

NO.	DESCRIPTION	DATE

NOTES:

Table A-5 Lighting panels. (continued)

POWER PANEL PP-101

VOLTS 347/600 PHASE 3 WIRE 4
TYPE NHDP MAINS 225 A MOUNTING SURFACE

BRANCH CIRCUIT PANELBOARD

A B C — M/B 100 A

M - MOTOR R - RECEPTACLE L - LIGHTING

VA	LOAD DESCRIPTION	BREAKER POLES	BREAKER AMPS	CCT	CCT	BREAKER AMPS	BREAKER POLES	LOAD DESCRIPTION	VA
266			15	1	2	15	1		597
266	(M) ELECTRICAL RM EXHAUST FAN	3	15	3	4	15	1	(M) DOCK LEVELLER	597
266			15	5	6	15	1		597
597			15	7	8				
597	(M) OVERHEAD DOOR	3	15	9	10				
597			15	11	12				
3000			15	13	14				
3000	(R1) BATTERY CHARGER WEST WALL	3	15	15	16				
3000			15	17	18				
3000			15	19	20				
3000	(R2) BATTERY CHARGER WEST WALL	3	15	21	22				
3000			15	23	24				
3000			15	25	26				
3000	(R3) BATTERY CHARGER WEST WALL	3	15	27	28				
3000			15	29	30				
3817			30	31	32				
3817	(R) OUTDOOR WEST WALL	3	30	33	34				
3817			30	35	36				
				37	38				
				39	40				
				41	42				

REVISIONS

NO.	DESCRIPTION	DATE

NOTES:

POWER PANEL PP-102

VOLTS 120/208 PHASE 3 WIRE 4
TYPE NBLP MAINS 225 A MOUNTING FLUSH

BRANCH CIRCUIT PANELBOARD

A B C — M/B 200 A

M - MOTOR R - RECEPTACLE L - LIGHTING

VA	LOAD DESCRIPTION	BREAKER POLES	BREAKER AMPS	CCT	CCT	BREAKER AMPS	BREAKER POLES	LOAD DESCRIPTION	VA
2545				1	2	15	2	FAN COIL UNIT	790
2545	(M) SURFACE GRINDER	3	40	3	4	15			790
2545				5	6	15	2	FAN COIL UNIT	790
2545				7	8	15			790
2545	(M) SURFACE GRINDER	3	40	9	10	15	2	FAN COIL UNIT	790
2545				11	12	15			790
2159				13	14	15	2	FAN COIL UNIT	790
2159	(M) VACUUM SYSTEM	3	40	15	16	15			790
2159				17	18	15	2	FAN COIL UNIT	790
2833				19	20	15			790
2833	(M) ROBOT	3	30	21	22	15	2	FAN COIL UNIT	790
2833				23	24	15			790
2833				25	26	15			
2833	EDM MACHINE	3	30	27	28	15	3		
2833				29	30	15			
720				31	32				
720	(R) CUT OFF SAW	3	15	33	34				
720				35	36				
2400				37	38				
2400	(R) METALURGY	3	30	39	40				
2400				41	42				

REVISIONS

NO.	DESCRIPTION	DATE

NOTES:

POWER PANEL PP-201

VOLTS 347/600 PHASE 3 WIRE 4
TYPE MAINS 225 A MOUNTING SURFACE

BRANCH CIRCUIT PANELBOARD

A B C — M/B 100 A

M - MOTOR R - RECEPTACLE L - LIGHTING

VA	LOAD DESCRIPTION	BREAKER POLES	BREAKER AMPS	CCT	CCT	BREAKER AMPS	BREAKER POLES	LOAD DESCRIPTION	VA
5637			50	1	2	15			
5637	(M) AIR HANDLING UNIT SUPPLY FAN	3	50	3	4	15	3	SPARE	
5637			50	5	6	15			
962			15	7	8				
962	PENTHOUSE SUPPLY FAN	3	15	9	10				
962			15	11	12				
697			15	13	14				
697	PENTHOUSE EXHAUST FAN	3	15	15	16				
697			15	17	18				
697			15	19	20				
697	CHILLER ROOM EXHAUST FAN	3	15	21	22				
697			15	23	24				

REVISIONS

NO.	DESCRIPTION	DATE

NOTES:

Table A-6 Panel schedules. (continued)

INDEX

G

H

I

J

O

P

Q

R

S

T

U

V